PICHARDO'S TREATISE ON THE LIMITS OF LOUISIANA AND TEXAS

VOLUME IV

PICHARDO'S TREATISE ON THE LIMITS OF LOUISIANA AND TEXAS

AN ARGUMENTATIVE HISTORICAL TREATISE WITH REFERENCE TO
THE VERIFICATION OF THE TRUE LIMITS OF THE PROVINCES
OF LOUISIANA AND TEXAS: WRITTEN BY FATHER JOSE
ANTONIO PICHARDO, OF THE CONGREGATION OF THE
ORATORY OF SAN FELIPE NERI, TO DISPROVE THE
CLAIM OF THE UNITED STATES THAT TEXAS
WAS INCLUDED IN THE LOUISIANA PUR-
CHASE OF 1803

PUBLISHED FOR THE FIRST TIME FROM A TRANSCRIPT OF THE ORIGINAL MANU-
SCRIPT IN THE MEXICAN ARCHIVES; TRANSLATED INTO ENGLISH BY
CHARLES WILSON HACKETT, PH.D., AND CHARMION
CLAIR SHELBY, PH.D., AND ANNOTATED BY

CHARLES WILSON HACKETT

VOLUME IV

(Part III, Paragraphs 1047–1613, Inclusive,
and Part IV, Paragraphs 1-505, Inclusive)

BOOKS FOR LIBRARIES PRESS

FREEPORT, NEW YORK

Originally published 1946 by the University of Texas Press

Reprinted 1971 by arrangement

F 372
P53213
V. 4

INTERNATIONAL STANDARD BOOK NUMBER:
0-8369-5800-4

LIBRARY OF CONGRESS CATALOG CARD NUMBER:
72-157340

PRINTED IN THE UNITED STATES OF AMERICA

Dedicated to

Jean Hunter Hackett

PREFACE

With this volume, at long last, is completed the publication of the English translation (begun in 1931), with introductions and annotations by the editor, of Father José Antonio Pichardo's treatise with reference to the verification of the true limits of the provinces of Louisiana and Texas. As regards organization, in this volume is concluded that portion of Father Pichardo's treatise which he himself designated as Part III, the English translation of which began on page 111 of Volume III of the English translation of the treatise; this Part terminates on page 249 of the present volume. On page 251 of this volume begins the author's Part IV.

That portion of Part III which was published in Volume III was divided by the editor into thirteen chapters. Hence the first chapter in this volume as divided by the editor is Chapter XIV. Three additional chapters—likewise divided by the editor—conclude Part III.

Part IV, constituting as it does the final portion of Pichardo's work as divided by him, is published in its entirety in this volume; it also terminates the entire work of the erudite investigator of the historic boundaries between Texas and Louisiana. Part IV has been divided by the editor into two chapters.

Editorial methods which were followed in the first three volumes of this publication have been continued in this, the final volume.

The tentative draft of the English translation of the Spanish text of that part of Pichardo's treatise which is published in this volume was made by Dr. Charmion Clair Shelby. As in the case of the first three volumes, however, the editor personally has approved or revised Dr. Shelby's tentative translation; therefore, upon him rests full responsibility for the final published English translation. To Dr. Shelby the editor is deeply indebted for her careful and accurate translation of this final section of Pichardo's work. Also, the editor expresses his appreciation to Miss Florence Escott for painstaking assistance in reading the proof of this volume.

The editor gratefully acknowledges his indebtedness to the Bureau of Research in the Social Sciences and to the administration of The University of Texas for financial aid which has made possible the translation and publication of this volume.

CHARLES WILSON HACKETT.

The University of Texas.

CONTENTS

EDITOR'S INTRODUCTION

As indicated in the introduction of Volume III,[1] the purpose of Father Pichardo in the first twelve chapters of his Part III that were published in the last-mentioned volume was to justify—on the basis of French exploration and occupation of the territory north of Natchitoches and west of the Mississippi River—the boundary line between Texas and Louisiana that had been proposed by the celebrated French geographer, Jean Baptiste Bourguignon d'Anville. In the thirteenth chapter of the author's Part III—as published in Volume III—the author, in developing the boundary between Texas and Louisiana to the west and north of Natchitoches, devoted a lengthy discussion to the case of the crown against Governor Sandoval of Texas for alleged neglect with reference to French aggressions westward from Natchitoches,[2] beginning in 1735.

With the conclusion of Chapter XIII of the author's Part III as published in Volume III, the author in Chapter XIV (as divided by the editor, and the first chapter published in this volume) quotes at length from documents relating to the tumultuous disputes over provincial boundaries between Louisiana and Texas in the middle of the eighteenth century.[3] Following his presentation of much documentary evidence, Pichardo drew his conclusions, based on this evidence, concerning these boundary disputes. These conclusions have been incorporated by the editor as Chapter XV of the present volume.[4] They, like all earlier conclusions of Father Pichardo, are argumentative in character and are supported by generous inclusions of excerpts from documents—both old ones and others that were current to him.

Pichardo's conclusions, in a nutshell, are that, despite "the injustice with which the French appropriated for themselves all the lands of Louisiana," they, "in consequence of the [act of] possession of Monsieur de la Salle which extended to all of the Mississippi

---

[1] "Editor's Introduction," in Vol. III, p. xxi.
[2] *Ibid.*, p. xxii.
[3] Pp. 1–118, *infra.*
[4] Pp. 119–186, *infra.*

and to all of the rivers that flow into it, directly or indirectly, with the lands which they drain," were justified in moving, in 1735, "their presidio of Nachitoches from the island on which they founded it to the other side of the river on the site where they had erected houses, gardens, and corrals. . . ."[5] This conclusion Father Pichardo justified on the ground that the territory in question "was drained by the Red River or, so to speak, was protected by the shield of its current."[6] In view of the fact that the French believed that "this protection did not extend over a small area of land, but over a more or less large quantity, according to the way the land lay," they were justified, according to Father Pichardo, in extending their territory in that region to La Gran Montaña and the Arroyo Hondo,[7] both of which lay about midway between the westernmost French outpost of Natchitoches and the easternmost Spanish outpost of Los Adaes, seven leagues to the west of Natchitoches.

Chapter XVI, as divided by the editor,[8] relates to the reorganization undertaken by Spain as a result of the cession of French Louisiana to Spain in 1762. This cession, as pointed out by Father Pichardo, nullified the usefulness to Spain of the presidio of Los Adaes, "since the French, now being vassals of Spain, could no longer commit any hostility or damage whatever against the province of Texas."[9] In reaching this conclusion, Father Pichardo relied heavily upon the well-known recommendations of the Marquis of Rubí, which recommendations were incorporated in a pamphlet issued in Madrid by order of the king in 1772 under the translated title of *Regulation and Instruction for the Presidios that are to be established on the frontier line of New Spain. . . .*[10] The remainder of Chapter XVI is devoted to a presentation of documents, with generous comments by the author on the reorganization that was undertaken in line with the above-mentioned *reglamento.*

Having previously shown "what the French appropriated for themselves north of their presidio of Nachitoches and west of the Mississippi"[11] (editor's Chapter XII in Volume III), Father

---

5P. 119, *infra.*
6*Ibid.*
7*Ibid.*
8Pp. 187–213, *infra.*
9P. 187, *infra.*
10P. 193, *infra.*
11P. 214, *infra.*

Pichardo, in the editor's Chapter XVII, as printed in this volume,[12] points out what the French "took from this same presidio toward the south, or rather toward the south-southeast, as far as where the Río Chafalaya entered the sea by way of the bay which the Spaniards have always called La Ascensión."[13] The events in this chapter relate mainly to the aggressions of the French in the region to the south-southeast of Natchitoches that were initiated during the administration of Don Angel Martos y Navarrete, who was governor of Texas from about 1759 to 1766. It was in the latter year that the Spaniards formally took over Louisiana from the French and began to administer it as a Spanish province under Don Juan Antonio de Ulloa.

Part IV,[14] which is the shortest sub-division of Pichardo's treatise (divided thus by the author, and sub-divided by the editor into two chapters) is devoted almost exclusively to indirect reiterations of his many earlier endorsements of the boundary between Louisiana and Texas as proposed by the celebrated French geographer, Jean Baptiste Bourguignon d'Anville. This line is indicated on the map published in a folder following the index of Volume II. D'Anville's line is described on this map as the "Linea Divisoria Propuesta Por M. d'Anville Y Confirmado Por El Padre Don José Pichardo."

In brief, the thesis of Part IV is indicated by Father Pichardo in the following words: "In Part IV the objections are refuted which have been raised against accepting the limits proposed by D'Anville's line. [This is the case] alike on the part of the Anglo-Americans, as well as on the part of those Spaniards who consider them illegal and claim that they should be contracted, or who, because of not knowing them, wish to withdraw them on the one hand or to extend them on the other, in contravention of the agreement between the two powers whereby Spain retrocedes precisely that which was ceded to her, without any addition or diminution."[15]

Chapter I (as divided by the editor)[16] of Part IV is, in fact, devoted almost exclusively, not to objections on the part of Anglo-Americans in general, but, instead, to a refutation of an article, paragraph by paragraph, which was published "in the *Mississippi*

[12]Pp. 214–249, *infra.*
[13]P. 214, *infra.*
[14]Pp. 251–476, *infra.*
[15]P. 253, *infra.*
[16]Pp. 253–396, *infra.*

Messenger, number 121 of volume three, dated December 23, 1806, the title of which is 'Limits and Extent of Louisiana: A Treatise taken from some Manuscript Notes on Louisiana, made by a Military Gentleman who has Resided in Mississippi since the Spring of the year 1803.' "[17] By refuting the statements of one anonymous American, Father Pichardo, by inference, assumes that the conclusions of the Military Gentleman were universally held by all Americans.

A chief object of Father Pichardo's ire in Chapter II[18] of Part IV was none other than the Spanish governor of Texas, Don Angel Martos y Navarrete, whose administration extended from about 1759 to 1766. Father Pichardo begins this final section of his work by charging that Governor Martos y Navarrete "either ignorant of D'Anville's line or disregarding it, boldly intervened on his own authority and without having any commission for it, to establish a dividing line between the French lands of Louisiana and the Spanish lands of Texas."[19] Rejecting the line as proposed by Governor Martos y Navarrete, Father Pichardo sarcastically asked: "Can there be a more absurd line than this one?"[20] He adds: "By ending his line at the Misuri, Señor Martos indicated that this great river should be the dividing line on the north of the lands that remained to Spain. Thus Spain could not possess any land north of the Misuri. And would Spain consent to the loss of a country as extensive as is that from the other side of the Misuri to the [North] pole?"[21]

Evidently suspecting Martos y Navarrete of being pro-French, Father Pichardo condemns him by charging that "at his caprice" Martos y Navarrete formed "a line by which at the same time he gave to and took from Spain and France their lands, by which act he harmed both nations so that neither of them could consent to it."[22]

In his introduction to Volume I, the editor generalized upon the historical method followed by Father Pichardo and paid tribute to him as a scholar and a scientific historian.[23] With the following paragraphs it is appropriate to terminate this introduction, since

---

[17]Pp. 253–254, *infra.*
[18]Pp. 397–476, *infra.*
[19]P. 397, *infra.*
[20]P. 399, *infra.*
[21]Pp. 399–400, *infra.*
[22]P. 401, *infra.*
[23]"Editor's Introduction," in Vol. I, pp. xviii–xx.

the paragraphs in question give some insight into Pichardo's own estimate of his technique and his motive. They follow:

> . . . I have assembled seventy-three documents, taken from the said papers of the secretariat of your Excellency and from the ministry of the superior government, and from many other manuscripts and published materials which my diligence, stimulated by zeal for the service of God, of the king, our lord, and of our country, has furnished me; and from almost the whole of four books, very rare, although printed, one in Italian, two in French, and the other in English, which I have translated from their own languages into Spanish. To all this I have added fifteen maps (after the date of this report others were added). . . .
>
> This work is none other than the notes prescribed by the royal order and taken from the documents that I have collected and concerning which I have had the honor of reporting to your Excellency in my official letter of last January 27. These notes are divided into three parts. In the first I show with most forcible arguments that Spain was the legitimate, sole, and absolute owner of all the land on which the French founded Louisiana, and that consequently the latter acted with great injustice and iniquity in settling it when they discovered it. In the second I showed what the French took and what the piety of the Catholic King, in order to avoid wars and the effusion of human blood, permitted them (although with grief in his heart) to keep, and consequently the limits of the lands usurped and left to France by permission of the king of Spain were established. In the third the objections are removed which are raised against accepting these limits, alike on the part of the United States as well as on that of those Spaniards who consider them illegal and claim that they should be contracted, or who, because of not knowing them, wish to withdraw them on the one hand or extend them on the other, in contravention of the agreement between the two powers whereby Spain retrocedes precisely what was ceded her, without any addition or diminution.
>
> (I had divided my work in this manner when I wrote this *consulta*, but later, considering it most necessary to give a description of those lands, and noting that each one of these parts was becoming very long, I changed the division of them in the way that is seen in the work as a whole.) [24]

---

[24] Pp. 441–442, *infra.*

CHAPTER XIV

DOCUMENTS RELATING TO TUMULTUOUS DISPUTES OVER BOUNDARIES BETWEEN LOUISIANA AND TEXAS IN THE MIDDLE OF THE EIGHTEENTH CENTURY

1047. The case against Señor Sandoval, governor of the province of Texas, was terminated in the manner that we have just seen. But the limits between that province and Louisiana did not cease to be discussed because of this fact, as we shall see presently. The lines which this new discussion followed begin to be apparent in document 37, from number 1 on. These lines were pursued until this very important and serious matter was terminated by France's cession of Louisiana to Spain. Let us hear what is said in the document mentioned, which is as follows:

Don Juan Francisco de Güemes y Horcasitas, Count of Revilla Gigedo,[1] lord of the bedchamber of his Majesty with familiar access, lieutenant general of the royal armies, viceroy, governor, and captain-general of this New Spain, and president of its royal audiencia, etc. A *consulta* of the following tenor has been presented to me:

"*Most excellent señor. Señor:* Moved by the obligation placed upon me by the honor which I owe to the king's charity in having put in my charge the government and captaincy-general of the province of Texas, and being informed that the capital of the said province is the royal presidio of Los Adaes, whose garrison consists of sixty men, including among them the lieutenant, the *alférez*, and the sergeant, and that of these, seventeen mounted men are detached to garrison the new presidio of San Xavier,[2] which has been established by your Excellency's order, I feel it my duty to present for your Excellency's high consideration the purpose for which the said sixty men are intended. Their principal object is to maintain the honor of the king's arms on his frontiers in the presence of a nation which attempts to be dominant, and is proud in proportion to the great authority which it arrogates to itself.

---

[1] Juan Francisco Güemes y Horcasitas, the Count of Revilla Gigedo, was viceroy of New Spain from 1746 to 1755.

[2] Reference is to the presidio of San Xavier, which was founded in 1751 on the present San Gabriel River, near modern Rockdale. For details see Bolton, *Texas* . . . , pp. 241–250. As early as July 27, 1747, however, a viceregal order had "required sent to San Xavier thirteen soldiers from La Bahía and seventeen from Los Adaes . . . . In the following March . . . Lieutenant Juan Galván was sent to San Xavier with the garrison of thirty soldiers borrowed from La Bahía and Los Adaes, as ordered by the viceroy. . . ."—Bolton, *ibid.*, pp. 47–48.

1049. "Although at present friendly relations exist between our forces, unexpected occurrences at the [respective] courts can disturb them, and the French forces can receive notice of it ahead of us, by way of El Guarico,[3] where ships are so numerous that they would arrive [with the news] far in advance, as cannot be hidden from your Excellency, with your deep penetration. If this contingency arises, the French arms can avail themselves of the opportunity offered them by the deplorable state of a presidio which at times is left with fewer than three men, helpless in the midst [of a wilderness] of more than 200 leagues, in which there is neither a town, nor any troops to support them.

1050. "In order that your Excellency may see the serious consideration that motivates me, I shall inform you of the routine and necessary service assigned to the troops of Los Adaes by order of the superior government. This service consists of [supplying] fifteen men for guarding the horses, seven for guard duty and protection of the reverend missionary fathers, and fifteen who must always be considered detached for the convoy of the supplies and horses of that presidio; they have to go as far as Saltillo to take charge of these effects. Their march going and returning is more than nine hundred leagues, and this hardship is indispensable, necessary, and of annual occurrence for the subsistence of that presidio. In the performance of these tasks, besides other incidental ones that may arise, fifty-four men, including the seventeen at San Xavier, are detached continually away from the presidio. Their duties, consequently, are fixed and they cannot be moved about. Six men remain for the service of the presidio.

1051. "Your Excellency will understand, in view of the foregoing, how exact and justified is this representation, made to the end that I need not expose my reputation to the risks of the many casualties that may befall us, either through the arms of France if a break comes, or through the Indians who, knowing of the defenseless state of the royal presidio of Los Adaes, can attack it, the reputation of the king's arms thereby being lost, and consequently my own, since I have the honor of being at their head. I have verbal orders from the Señor Marquis of La Ensenada[4] and Señor Don José de Caravajal[5] to indicate whatever may be necessary to place that presidio and the others under my charge in a state of the strongest defense, as well as to erect others if this should be necessary in order to restrain the arms of France within their limits, since the province which is in my care is the safeguard of New Spain. The two most excellent señores expressed themselves

---

[3]Guarico was a port on the French-owned part of the island of Española, or modern Haiti.

[4]A notable financial reformer of Spain "was Somodevilla, a Castillian of very humble birth who became the Marquis of Ensenada, by which name he is more generally known. The period of his power was from 1743 to 1754 . . . ." He is famous for his financial reforms and his measures to develop commerce and improve the army and navy. He "was especially remarkable in his endeavors on behalf of the Spanish Navy."—Chapman, *A History of Spain*, pp. 434–435.

[5]Caravajal evidently was an associate of the Marquis of Ensenada in Spain.

in these terms when they gave me this order, along with another to make a separate memorandum immediately for each of them of whatever was necessary for the said purpose.

1052. "If the foregoing arguments seem valid to your Excellency, and if it be your pleasure, you will kindly order that the seventeen men of San Xavier be withdrawn so as to place that presidio [Los Adaes] under protection. Without doubt the ministry considers this post important, because of the orders mentioned above. Your Excellency with your unerring foresight will resolve upon that which seems to you most fitting, justifying in your operations the confidence shown by the king in recognizing your Excellency's high merits by conferring upon you the distinguished position which you occupy in these kingdoms. I comply, most excellent señor, with what I feel is my duty. Your Excellency will do whatever may seem best to you. Mexico, December 31, 1750. Don Jacinto de Barrios y Jáuregui."[6]

1053. In view of the above document, and bearing in mind that which was requested by the señor *fiscal* of his Majesty in a reply of the first of the current month, I requested an opinion from the señor *auditor general de la guerra* and, agreeing to everything it contained, I thought it well to conform with both in the present decree, dated today. Accordingly, in view of the fact that the measure adopted by this captaincy-general in detaching from the presidio of Los Adaes the seventeen men mentioned, to guard the new missions founded on the banks of the Río de San Xavier of the province of Texas, was taken during the time in which judicial proceedings were in progress concerning the establishment of a presidio in that place; and, in as much as these proceedings were terminated and decided by me in a decree, likewise of even date, in view of which a *junta de guerra y hacienda* will determine what is to be done in the matter; and, since, in consideration of the arguments advanced in the enclosed *consulta*, it becomes necessary to apply effective measures to avert the damage and fatal consequences which may be justly feared,

1054. I have resolved to issue the present [order], by which I command that the seventeen soldiers who have been detached from the presidio of Los Adaes for the protection of the said missions of San Xavier be restored to that presidio immediately. I therefore command the said governor to replace their number at that post [San Xavier][7] in such manner as he may find most convenient, in view of the present circumstances, so that the number of forty-eight considered necessary there may be complete. [He may do this] either by detaching the seventeen men from the other presidios, if their condition will permit it, or by enlisting the same number from among those residents if there are that many, or by taking suitable measures for raising them from the nearby provinces pending the meeting of the junta already mentioned, which will make the final decision.

[6]Jacinto de Barrios y Jáuregui succeeded Pedro del Barrio Junco y Espriella as governor of Texas in 1751, and served until 1759.

[7]". . . when, in June, 1751, Barrios reached San Xavier, on his way to eastern Texas, he immediately fulfilled part of his orders requiring him to restore the seventeen soldiers to Los Adaes."—Bolton, *Texas . . .* , p. 243.

1055. Furthermore, Don Juan de Yarza y Ascona, captain-commandant of the Island of Santa Rosa, Punta de Sigüenza,[8] in a *consulta* (this *consulta* of Señor Yarza is not found in the *autos* which we are copying, nor in our document 35, in number 41 of which, copied by us in paragraph 477, is found a reference to it, nor have we seen it; therefore we do not make a transcript of it) of June 30 of last year has informed me, among other things, that four men-of-war have arrived at the French colony laden with people (besides thirty-six merchant vessels which are in the Mississippi River and are bringing clothing and other things)—with soldiers, settlers, women, and children for the settlement of the many lands which they possess today. They are constantly penetrating farther inland, and are fortifying themselves with several forts in different places, having already formed a cavalry corps, which they have not had hitherto. The said commandant adds that the French adjacent to that presidio, in the annual entry that they make, introduce their clothing in exchange for meat, silver, and other things, and that the soldiers of the Spanish presidios, as well as the citizens, transport all these goods together on rafts, along with the saddles for their horses, which they drive by land to New Orleans. Thus on the return journey they can transport their clothing and themselves back to the Spanish settlements from which they come. He says that a similar trade has been carried on by the Frenchmen themselves on the Island of Santa Rosa.

1056. [He also states] that in the year 1749, some soldiers and sailors having been despatched with their officers in search of food, they saw more than forty men of the said [Spanish] soldiers and residents in the villa of New Orleans. It must be noted—as has already been pointed out by the señor *auditor general de la guerra* in his opinion of September 1, 1745, in the *autos* concerning the disputes between the residents of the villa of San Fernando, capital of the presidio of San Antonio de Béxar, and the missionary fathers[9]— that the extensive province of Texas is on the frontier of the hostile Apaches and of other barbarian Indians, and is as well a barrier against the French nation which, having gone eighty leagues beyond the Mississippi River, which should serve it as a boundary, can enter more easily into the adjoining provinces of New Mexico, Coahuila, Nueva Vizcaya, and the New Kingdom of León, availing itself of their rich minerals, and introducing its illicit trade, as the said captain-commandant charges and as Don Antonio de Mederos[10]

---

[8]The western extremity of Santa Rosa island near Ft. Pickens.—Leonard, *Spanish Approach to Pensacola, 1689–1693*, p. 187, n. 6.

[9]"In 1744, during the perennial quarrel between the Canary Island settlers and the other inhabitants of San Antonio, it was suggested that one of the parties should move to the San Xavier, but the proposal was not acted upon."— Bolton, *Texas . . .* , pp. 141–142.

[10]One Don Antonio Mederes is mentioned in a document published in *Pichardo's Treatise . . .* , Vol. III, p. 345. In that document he is referred to as the senior *regidor* of the villa of San Fernando and as the author of a *consulta* of July 19, 1749. Mederos is probably the correct spelling for this proper name. There is a discrepancy of one month in the dates of the two *consultas* mentioned.

did previously in a *consulta* of June 19, 1749. The latter states that it has been secretly rumored that the governor who is completing his term, Don Pedro del Barrio,[11] was trading in the French colony, putting goods into his store through the hands of the *teniente reformado*, González, and the *teniente actual*, Losoya, and Marcos Ruiz, and that in view of this fact the application of effective measures is necessary to avert the dangers and fatal consequences which it justly must be feared will result from this illicit trade between the French and Spanish soldiers and settlers.

1057. In order that this condition may be corrected, remedied, and checked, I direct the said new governor,[12] without losing an instant of time and with the careful vigilance and activity that is expected from the zeal which he manifests for the royal service, to proceed to make an investigation of those accused of the said illicit commerce, and to apprehend those found guilty of it and confiscate all their goods. Having secured their goods (and persons), he will inform me in order that I may render whatever decision is consonant with justice, the said governor adopting for the accomplishment of these ends the most efficacious and just measures, for the purpose of destroying such illicit commerce.

1058. And in as much as the said commandant likewise has informed me in his cited *consulta* that the French of New Orleans are each day penetrating inland toward the presidio of Los Adaes, so that they have gone eighty leagues beyond the Mississippi River, which should serve as a boundary to restrain them (from the investigations of the year 1753, copied below in paragraph 1165, and from many other documents which we have cited, it is clear that the French had restricted themselves to the boundaries that were prescribed for them from the beginning, and thus this report proceeded from an error), and that they will easily be able to pass on and enter the provinces adjacent to that of Texas, it appears that a matter of such importance should not be overlooked and even that an examination of it should not be delayed, but that it ought to be attended to at once.

1059. In order that it may so be, I likewise direct the said new governor that, exercising the degree of diligence and zeal that such a lofty matter demands, he make the corresponding investigations with regard to this particular. To this end he will keep in mind the statements of the said commandant and that which the señor *auditor* explains in his opinion of September 1, 1745, in the *autos* concerning disputes which have been referred to—and which are delivered to him in 252 folios in conformance with that provided by me in the decree dated today, issued in reply to the señor *fiscal* and the opinion of the señor *auditor*, with which I agreed—in order that he may apply himself to composing, adjusting, and terminating extrajudicially and to the satisfaction of all interested parties the differences under discussion. [There will be delivered to him] as well any previous documents that may

---

[11]Pedro del Barrio Junco y Espriella was governor of Texas from 1748 to 1750.

[12]See note 6, *supra*.

exist concerning the matter, and those setting forth the fact that the Mississippi River ought to serve as the boundary line with the French nation.

1060. The said governor will give me an account of these proceedings so
that I may report them to his Majesty on the first occasion that offers, and
at the same time adopt such measures as are needful in the service of both
Majesties. Mexico, February 10, 1751. The Count of Revilla Gigedo. By
order of his Excellency. José de Gorráez.

1061. In compliance with his Excellency's order the governor
restored the soldiers to Los Adaes,[13] as is shown by the same document 21, and then he proceeded to make an investigation, which is
found beginning with number 23 of the said document 37, to ascertain whether the preceding governor, Don Pedro del Barrio Junco
y Espriella, had carried on illicit commerce with the French of
Louisiana. In this inquiry he discovered that the said governor
was absolutely innocent of such a crime, whereupon the sycophants
who had tried to defile his honor with such a black and false
accusation were left confounded. This investigation having been
made, he proceeded to make another with regard to the boundaries between the Spanish and French territories, which begins as
follows:

1062. (Number 89 of the said document 37.) In the royal presidio of
Nuestra Señora del Pilar de los Adaes, on the first day of the month of
October, 1751, I, Don Jacinto de Barrios y Jáuregui, lieutenant colonel of
cavalry of the royal armies of his Majesty, governor and captain-general of
this province of the Texas and Nuevas Filipinas, its presidios, conversions,
and frontiers, and military commandant of those of Coahuila and Pensacola,

1063. Having examined these *autos* and seeing that for the complete fulfillment of that which I am ordered in the superior dispatch which has been
mentioned, there remains only to proceed with the investigation as to whether
the French have penetrated toward this presidio of Los Adaes, I should and
do command the corresponding information to be received, an interrogatory
of questions being drawn up for greater clarity, so that by means of them
the witnesses called may be examined. They shall be the most trustworthy
persons available, alike intelligent and experienced, so that they may give
clear and exact answers to the questions which may be asked them. I thus
decreed, commanded, and signed, before myself and the assisting witnesses,
as is stated and to which I certify. Don Jacinto de Barrios. Witness, Manuel
Ybarbo. Assisting witness, Manuel Antonio de Soto Bermúdez.

1064. In the said royal presidio on the said day, month, and year, I, the
said governor, in conformance with that ordered by me in the preceding *auto*,

---

[13]See note 7, *supra.*

should and do command the following interrogatory to be made. First, let the witnesses be examined as to whether the French have penetrated inland in the direction of this presidio of Los Adaes, going beyond the Mississippi River, which should serve as a boundary to restrain them within their limits; so let them state, etc.

1065. [In reply] to the second question, let them state whether they have known or seen that many troops and families from Europe have arrived at New Orleans; let them say when and how many, etc.

1066. [In reply] to the third question, let them declare whether they have heard the destination for which so many people have come, and where they are maintained, how, and for what purpose; so let them state, etc.

1067. [In reply] to the fourth question let them state whether they have known that the commandant of Nachitos [Natchitoches] has received any special orders since the arrival here of the said people; so let them state, etc.

1068. [In reply] to the fourth [fifth] question let them state whether they have known that the paymaster of the royal warehouse at Nachitos has orders to supply the *alférez*, Don Luis de St. Denis, with some goods, since when, and for what purpose; so let them state, etc.

1069. [In reply] to the sixth question let them say whether this officer, Don Luis de St. Denis,[14] is exceedingly beloved by all the Texas, Nacodoches [Nacogdoches], and other Indians, and whether, by availing himself of this influence, the said official has committed any excesses in this province. Let them state in what manner and when, etc. Dated in this royal presidio in the said month and year, before me and the assisting witnesses as has been stated, to which I certify. Don Jacinto de Barrios. Assisting witness, Manuel de Soto Bermúdez. Witness, Manuel Ybarbo.

1070. In number 92 of the said document 37 there is added:

In the said royal presidio, on the day, month, and year stated above, I, the said governor, for the purpose of the investigation which I have ordered made, caused to appear before me the present lieutenant, Don Manuel Antonio Losoya, a Spaniard, whom I affirm that I know, from whom I received the oath which he made in due legal form before God, our Lord, and with a sign of His holy cross, under charge of which he promised to tell the truth

---

[14]"For twenty years after the Aguayo expedition, the Frenchman St. Denis, or 'Big Legs,' as the natives fondly called him, ruled the border tribes with paternal sway from his post at Natchitoches on the Red River. The relations of French and Spaniards on this border were generally amicable. Intermarriages and a mutual love of gayety made friendship a pleasanter and more natural condition for the Latin neighbors than strife. Indeed, when in June, 1744, the long career of the redoubtable St. Denis came to a close, prominent among those assembled at Natchitoches to assist in the funeral honors were Governor Boneo and Father Vallejo, from Los Adaes, across the international boundary line. And yet, when, a few days later, Boneo reported the event to his Viceroy in Mexico, he did so in terms which meant, 'St. Denis is dead; thank God; now we can breathe more easily.' "—Bolton, *The Spanish Borderlands*, pp. 229–230. A son, Don Luis, succeeded St. Denis.

in regard to everything he might know and might be asked. Being questioned in accordance with the preceding interrogatory, he said:

1071. To the first question he replied that he knows as squad corporal, which rank he held when he entered with the Señor Marquis of San Miguel de Aguayo[15] to settle this presidio, that the French have penetrated in the direction of this presidio, settling and fortifying themselves on this side of the Río Colorado [Red River] during the time of the governorship of Don Manuel de Sandoval,[16] who could not prevent it, because he was on his general visit and also because the men whom he had in this presidio were not sufficient to restrain the French pride; and that before this aggression, the said Frenchmen were settled on the other side of the aforesaid Río Colorado on the island in the center of it, the said river serving at that time as boundary between the French and the Spanish. Thus he replies.

(Note that above in paragraph 1025 the Señor Marquis of Altamira,[17] summarizing an investigation made in Mexico concerning these limits, states that the witnesses declared that Monsieur de St. Denis, although he had moved his presidio to the west bank of the Red River, had not placed it on lands of Spain but on land which the French had taken for themselves from the beginning, for the dividing lines were at La Gran Montaña or Arroyo Hondo.[18] See the remark which we made above in paragraph 1043 concerning this witness and the following ones, in a note which we added to the report of the said Señor Marquis of Altamira.)

1072. To the second question he replied that he knows, because he has heard it from different Frenchmen of greater or lesser rank, that in the past year of 1750 many ships have arrived at the port of New Orleans, from which many regular troops and a large number of families have disembarked, and that during the present year of 1751, aside from those mentioned above, about four hundred regular troops have arrived at the said New Orleans, and that many more are expected. Thus he replies.

1073. To the third question he replied that according to what he had heard, these troops and families have come to extend and fortify the settlements of Caudachos [Cadodachos], Puente Cupé, Cirinue (that is, Ylinoes), and Nachitos, which they plan to do as soon as the crops have been harvested

---

[15]In 1721, the Marquis of San Miguel de Aguayo "re-established the six abandoned missions and the presidio of Dolores, and added a presidio at Los Adaes facing Natchitoches."—Bolton, *The Spanish Borderlands*, p. 228.

[16]See "The Sandoval Case" in *Pichardo's Treatise* . . . , Vol. III, pp. 475–553.

[17]The Marquis of Altamira was *auditor de guerra* in Mexico City near the middle of the eighteenth century.—See *Pichardo's Treatise* . . . , Vol. III, p. 543.

[18]Consult the index of *Pichardo's Treatise* . . . , Vol. III, and particularly p. 481, n. 15.

and the water of the said Río Colorado [Red River] is abundant; at the present time it is known to be very low. For that reason the said people are being kept in New Orleans. Thus he replies.

1074. To the fourth question he replied that he knows in the same manner stated in the first question that the commandant of Nachitos has, among the many orders with which he finds himself since the arrival of the aforesaid people, of whom nothing has been learned, one order not to impede or obstruct the trade and communication which the *alférez*, Don Luis de St. Denis, son of the deceased commandant, Don Luis de St. Denis, has with all the Nacodoches, Texas, and other Indians, and that although the said commandant has always had the said order, at the present time he has been given it anew, to fulfil with special care. Thus he replies.

1075. To the fifth question he replied that he knows from the same source that the paymaster of the royal warehouse of Nachitos, by special order, always keeps the warehouse open for the said officer, Don Luis de St. Denis, who has supplied himself of late more than ever before with muskets, powder, shot, flannel, breech-clouts, vermilion, and other effects which he distributes liberally as presents to the Indians already mentioned. In this manner he has made himself so beloved by them and they idolize him to such a degree that the declarant believes they would suffer a thousand martyrdoms if it were necessary to please him, for they respect only this officer, and they obey as the great captain, as they call him, the son of him who was so revered by them. Thus he replies.

1076. To the sixth and last question he replied that he knows, because it was public knowledge, that the said officer, Don Luis de St. Denis, during the past year of 1750, arrived at this presidio to ask for permission from the señor governor to go and trade with the Indians. It was denied him and, irritated, the said Don Luis embarked in a canoe and went by way of the river which they call Los Adaes to the pueblo of Yátasi,[19] from whence he passed to that of Nasones [Nazones],[20] and he continued inland to the other nations with a large supply of the goods which have been mentioned in the preceding question. In these pueblos he has aroused the Indians to such a degree that the captain of the pueblo of Nacodoches took up his arms and went in search of the father missionary, Fray José Calahorra,[21] whom he would have killed with his musket if the abject submission and humility with which the said father received him had not restrained him. The father told him [the deponent] later of having listened to countless insults and abuses, [the Indians] even declaring that he and all the Spaniards must leave their lands, where they did not want them because they prevented the

---

[19]The Yatasi Indians were located "some fifty miles northwest of Natchitoches."—See *Pichardo's Treatise* . . . , Vol. III, pp. 430–443.

[20]For the location of the pueblo of the Nazones, see *Pichardo's Treatise* . . . , Vol. III, p. 293, n. 67.

[21]Father Calahorra was a "veteran missionary at Nacogdoches," who "made efforts to restore peace in the northern tribes and to establish them in missions, even if it involved war with the Apaches."—Bolton, *Texas* . . . , p. 91.

French from trading with them; and that just at that time their captain, Don Luis, had arrived very furious against them because they [the Spaniards] had denied him passage. They did not want Don Luis angered. [The witness declared] that this is the truth with regard to what he has been asked, in accordance with the oath administered, under which he affirmed and ratified it. He said he was fifty-one years of age, and he signed with me, the said governor, and the assisting witnesses, as has been stated and to which I certify. Don Jacinto de Barrios. Manuel Antonio Losoya. Witness, Manuel Ybarbo. Assisting witness, Manuel Antonio de Soto Bermúdez.

1077. (Number 93 of the cited document.) Second declaration, namely that by Lieutenant Don José González, fifty-five years of age. In the said royal presidio on the said day, month, and year, I, the said governor, for the purpose of the investigation which is in progress, caused to appear before me Lieutenant Don José González, resident of the royal presidio, whom I certify that I know, from whom I received the oath which he made before God, our Lord, and a sign of His holy cross, under charge of which he promised to tell the truth in so far as he knew it and might be asked, and having been questioned in accordance with the interrogatory which has been mentioned, he said:

1078. To the first question he replied that he knows, because he has seen it, that the French have gone beyond their boundaries, trespassing on our lands, settling and fortifying themselves in them on the banks of the Río Colorado [Red River], which should serve them as boundary in accordance with what the declarant has seen since he entered this province with the troops. For it was said that the land on this side of the river belonged to Spain and that on the other side of the river to the French, where they were settled. Their encroachment occurred during the governorship of General Don Manuel de Sandoval at the time when he was on his general visit, and I remained as his lieutenant. I was unable to prevent it because I had too few men to withstand such arrogant determination. Thus he replies.

1079. To the second question he replied that he knows, because he has heard it said by so many people that it is now almost public knowledge, that during the present year and the past year of 1750 various ships have arrived from Europe at New Orleans and in them many troops and a large number of families, and that they are waiting in the said port for more people, for still not all who are expected have arrived. Thus he replies.

1080. To the third question he replied that he heard that the purpose for which so many had come was to settle and fortify the presidios of Caudachos, Puente Cupé, Cirinue [Illinois], and Nachitos. They will do this as soon as the Río Colorado [Red River] permits it, this being impossible at present because of the great scarcity of water and the lack of supplies, all this being the reason why they are still staying in the said Orleans. Thus he replies.

1081. To the fourth question he replied that he knows because of having heard it from persons of good character among those who are in Nachitos, that the commandant of this presidio is frequently notified that in no manner shall he disturb the trade that the *alférez*, Don Luis de St. Denis, carries on with the Texas, Nacodoches, and other Indians, and that although the said commandant has always had the aforesaid order, recently they have reiterated it here with special emphasis. Thus he replies.

1082. To the fifth question he replied that he knows for the reason already stated in the preceding question that the paymaster of the royal warehouse which is in Nachitos always kept the said warehouse at the disposal of the aforesaid *alférez*, Don Luis de St. Denis, by a superior order which was given him to that effect, but that he [St. Denis] has never used the warehouse so freely as at present. He takes from it at his pleasure muskets, powder, shot, breech-clouts, and other things valued by the Indians, among whom he distributes them, thereby causing himself to be so revered and obeyed by them that the declarant is persuaded that the Indians would not refuse to give their lives for him in any emergency. Thus he replies.

1083. To the sixth question he replied that he can say with regard to what is asked, since he has heard it publicly stated, that during the past year of 1750, in the month of August, the said *alférez*, Don Luis de St. Denis, irritated because the señor governor had denied him the permission he had asked to go and trade with the Indians, embarked on the Río de los Adaes in a canoe and went to the pueblo of Yatasi, whence he passed on to that of Nasones, and thus he craftily continued inland to the rest [of the pueblos]. In them he reduced the Indians to his will, so that the chief of the Nacodoches went with his musket in his hand to find the father missionary of the said pueblo, whom, after having insulted him a thousand times, he wanted to kill, because he and the Spaniards were the cause of their captain, Don Luis, becoming irritated with them. (See in confirmation of this occurrence the certification which Father Fray Pedro Ramírez[22] made with regard to it, copied below in paragraph 1092.) [The chief said] that all the pueblos were prepared to take up arms against the Spaniards, whom they did not want in their lands, preferring rather the French because they received from the latter everything they needed, which was not true with regard to the Spaniards. And [the witness stated] that what he has said and declared is the truth under the oath that he has taken, which he affirmed and ratified. He said that he was fifty-five years of age, and he signed it with me, the said governor, and the assisting witnesses, as has been stated and to which I certify. Don Jacinto de Barrios. José González. Witness, Manuel Ybarbo. Assisting witness, Manuel Antonio de Soto Bermúdez.

1084.   The remaining witnesses, down to the eighth one, declared entirely uniformly with these, as appears from the same document, beginning with number 94. Therefore we shall transcribe only their replies to the first question.

---

[22]According to Bolton, *Texas . . .*, pp. 419–420, Fr. Pedro Ramírez de Arrellano was president of the Texas missions.

1085. (Number 94.) Don Juan Antonio Morín, more than sixty years of age, . . . said: That it is true that the French penetrated in the direction of this presidio, which he knows to be the case because of having seen it when the troops entered, with whom he came as sergeant of a company. At that time he saw that the Río Colorado [Red River] served as boundary for the Spaniards and the French, the former being on this side and the latter on the opposite side, where they were settled and fortified, and that today they are on this side, to which place they moved their settlement and fortress. Thus he replies.

1086. (Number 95.) Don Felipe Muñoz de Mora, sixty-six years of age, . . . replied to the first question: That he knows for a certainty that the French have penetrated in the direction of this presidio, settling on this side of the Río Colorado, which lands belong to Spain, because when the troops entered the declarant heard it said that the territory on this side of the said river belonged to Spain and that on the other side of the river to France. The French used to be settled on the opposite bank of the river, on the island which they say is in midstream, the said river serving as boundary for both parties. This does not admit of any doubt whatsoever, for before this removal of the French, all the deserters from that side who came to this side of the river were free from all risk and the same thing was true of those from this side who went across the said river. (The truth regarding this matter seems to be that which St. Denis writes to Señor Sandoval above in paragraph 927.) This is not true today for the reason which the declarant has stated. It does not surprise him that the French should have expanded when they have such great influence among the Indians, for the latter would respond immediately to the least sign [from the French], to the evident danger of this province. Thus he replies.

1087. (Number 96.) Don Pedro de Sierra (if I am not mistaken, this Don Pedro Sierra is the same one who, in the opinion submitted by the Señor Marquis of Altamira, copied above in paragraph 1043, is called Felipe de Sierra, and perhaps the changing of this name was due to an error of the clerk), fifty-three years of age, . . . said: That it is clear to him, because he has seen it, that the French have gone beyond their limits, penetrating into the possessions of Spain where they are found today, settled and fortified, for when the declarant came to this province, which was when the Marquis[23] entered with the troops in which he came as corporal, he saw that the said Frenchmen were settled on the other side of the Río Colorado [Red River] on the island in the center of it. It was said that the land on this side of the river belonged to Spain, the said river serving as boundary line at that time for both parties, as was literally true before the French moved to this side of the river, for whenever any of them deserted, they did not follow him farther than to the river, and the same happened to those deserting from this side. This does not hold true today. Thus he replies.

1088. (Number 97.) Domingo del Río, more than thirty years of age, . . . said: That he knows that the French have penetrated in the direction of

[23]See note 15, *supra.*

this presidio, crossing to this side of the Río Colorado, on the banks of which they are settled today. This river ought to serve them for a boundary as it did when the troops entered this province, which was in the year 1720. In that year the witness saw that the French had their settlement and forts on the other side of the river, on the island in the center, to which point their possessions extended. The possessions of Spain extended from the banks of the said river in this direction. Thus he replies.

(When did this witness see that to which he testifies? If we subtract the year 1720 from 1751, thirty-one years remain, which proves either that this witness was one year old or very little more when the Marquis of San Miguel de Aguayo entered the Los Adaes—and in this case he could not observe with full understanding that to which he testifies—or that he learned of it later after he was already of adult age, a fact which he should have added in his declaration.)

1089. (Number 98.) Juan de Lara, twenty-six years of age, . . . said: That since he has been of an age to understand, he has always heard it said that the French have advanced in the direction of this presidio, settling on this side of the Río Colorado, and that formerly, when the troops entered this province, they had their settlement on the other side of the river from which their lands began, the said river serving as boundary for both parties. Thus he replies.

1090. (Number 99.) Felipe Sánchez, sixty years of age, . . . said: That the French have gone beyond the boundary which divided the two nations, France and Spain, a fact which the witness knows because when he entered this province with the troops, which was in the year 1720, he saw that the French were settled on the other side of the Río Colorado [Red River], on the island in the center of it, and today we see them fortified on this side, the property of Spain, for in the aforesaid time the witness always heard it said that the land on this side of the river belonged to Spain and that on the other side of the river to France. Proof of this truth is found in the fact that at that time they pursued the deserters of that nation to the said river, and now they pursue them much farther in this direction. Because of these conditions it happened that in the time of Señor Don Manuel de Sandoval, who was then governing this province, the French succeeded in penetrating into it while his lordship was making his general visit, although the witness feels certain he could not have stopped their designs, since the French had the Indians on their side, they being very numerous and exceedingly skilful in the use of firearms. Thus he replies.

1091. If these declarations are compared with those that the witnesses who were examined in Mexico made, and with those which the same ones who are now testifying made in the year 1740 and again in the year 1753, in the said presidio of Los Adaes—copied below, beginning with paragraph 1165—it will be found that the present declarations are incomplete, because they fail to state that the French, before the removal of their presidio, already had some huts, gardens, and corrals built on the west side of the Red River. See above, paragraphs 1028 and 1043, in the report and opinion of the Señor Marquis of Altamira. The depositions are also defective because they state simply that Spanish deserters were considered free only when they had crossed the Red River and had entered French lands, and likewise that the French [deserters] ceased to be pursued by their chiefs as soon as they had crossed the same Red River, because then they found themselves in lands of the crown of Spain. As a matter of fact, the Spanish deserters were safe when they succeeded in crossing the Arroyo Hondo and approaching the houses, gardens, and corrals of the French dwelling on the west bank of the said river, and the French when they arrived at the same Arroyo Hondo. These details should be added in order that the declarations may not be defective, for with them they would be complete. St. Denis, in fact, makes a statement to this effect above in paragraph 927.

1092. As a proof of the sacrilegious offense of the Indian governor of Nacogdoches and of other acts which these witnesses mention, we have the following certification obtained from the judicial proceedings conducted by Señor Don Jacinto de Barrios, which is found copied in the same document 37, in number 115:

In the mission of San Miguel de Aguayo on the said day, month, and year, I, Father Fray Pedro Ramírez, apostolic religious *de propaganda fide* of María Santísma de Guadalupe de Zacatecas, minister of this mission by order of the very reverend father, Fray Francisco Ballejo [Vallejo][24] president of these missions of Texas, certify in so far as I can and should, that in the year just passed of 1750, on the 20th day of the month of August, the Indian captain of this pueblo, called in his language Chacayauchia, and in ours Sánchez, arrived at the mission of Nacodoches. With excessive boldness, great defiance, and inexpressible pride, and with a musket in his hand, new and of a superior quality, one of those which the French customarily carry, [he came] seeking the very reverend father, Fray José Calahorra, because of the fact that the señor governor of this province was forbidding the passage of the French to these nations, as a result of which they were exceedingly angry. [He stated] that now the son of Captain Big-legs—the former commandant, Don Luis de St. Denis, called thus by all these peoples,

---

[24]Consult index in *Pichardo's Treatise* . . . , Vol. III.

and whom they loved so much—told him that he did not want to come with them or to give them muskets, powder, and shot, which he was bringing for this purpose, mistrusting that it would be resented by the Spaniards, and that therefore the said Indians, as well as all the other pueblos, were furious and ready to raise their arms against the Spaniards and in favor of the French in revenge for this affront. They would attempt by force to drive us out of their lands, in which they preferred the French to the Spaniards. [The chief uttered] many other insults, to the point of attempting to do harm with his musket to the said Father Calahorra, which the said Indian would have done on account of the irritated state in which he was, if the humility and submission with which the said father prostrated himself at his feet, begging him to calm himself, had not restrained him, whereupon he became quiet. I know this from a letter of the said Father Calahorra, and from the statements of the courier who brought the letter and of others who were present. The aforesaid official [St. Denis] made his trip to the said pueblos in spite of the señor governor having denied him permission. This is clear to me because I have heard it from the said señor governor as well as from various trustworthy persons of Nachitos, where I used to go from time to time, when I found myself alone after the death of my companion, for the purpose of having frequent recourse to the holy sacraments. [I know] that during the past year of 1750 about twenty-five companies arrived from Europe at New Orleans and with them two hundred families, for the purpose of fortifying and augmenting the three presidios of Caudachos, Puente Cupé, and Nachitos; and in the present year of 1751, four hundred regular troops arrived at the said Orleans, concerning whose destination I have not heard a single thing said. I do know that the commandant of Nachitos has special orders not to disturb or obstruct in any way the trade and communication which the said official, Don Luis de St. Denis, carries on with the Nacodoches and Texas Indians, by whom he is exceedingly beloved, not only because he is the son of Monsieur de St. Denis whom they idolized, but also because he supplies them with muskets, powder, shot, and other goods esteemed by this barbarous nation. I have been assured that for all these things he has recourse with entire freedom to the king's warehouse, whose paymaster has liberal orders sent out for this purpose. I thus certify, as I have stated. For the purposes that they may serve, I give these presents, signed by my hand as I am accustomed to do in this mission, on the said day, month, and year. Fray Pedro Ramírez de Arellano.

1093. The governor sent a report to this Excellency, along with this complete *expediente,* as is seen in what follows, which is found in number 117 of the cited document.

"*Most excellent señor. Señor:* My arrival at this presidio was on the 13th of July, last, since I had been detained in that of San Antonio for twenty-eight days in order to transact the business which your Excellency entrusted to me; but it being practically impossible to complete all of it, I finished that which seemed to me most conducive to the tranquillity of that villa and citizenry. I reserved for my visit the decision with regard to the remaining matters, because I was called to this presidio by the restlessness of the province incident to the coming of troops into the French territory. In order that your Excellency may inform yourself on the basis of the facts, the enclosed judicial proceedings will instruct your Excellency better than I could in the foundation of those rumors. Despite your Excellency's unmistakable disposition, I regard it as indispensable that as many as twenty soldiers be stationed on the Río de San Pedro[25] with an experienced, zealous officer, to observe the moves of the French and the increase that they are going to make in their post of Caudachos and other settlements. The principal care of this officer would be to reduce and attract those Indians with cunning and skill. They are the ones who rule the other nations in that whole province, and the passion that they have for the French is so blind that they would lose their lives to please them. This is proven by their action in the year just past, [an account of] which is contained in the said judicial proceedings.

1094. If this presidio or another of those under my command were capable of supplying this detachment, it would already be established by provisional order, but, since all of them together are not sufficient for their essential duties, there remains for me only the pain of knowing the evil without being able to apply the remedy.

1095. It is certain, señor, that the French have all the Indians of this province devoted to them, due to the presents which they make them of powder, vermilion, muskets, beads, and other things valued by the Indians, for which the *real hacienda* of France pays. They have in addition other goods with which to carry on their traffic, which we lack. And though we might have it [the trade] for the initial cost [of the goods] and that of transportation, it would not be profitable to the Spaniards. They [the French] regard the Indians so highly that civilized persons marry the Indian women without incurring blame, for the French find their greatest glory in that which is most profitable to them. If the Indians go to dance before the commandant of Nachitos, he gives them, at the expense of the *real hacienda*, all those things that this barbarous nation longs for. As a result, no Caudachos, Nacodoches, San Pedro, or Texas Indian is to be seen who does not wear his mirror, belt of fringes, epaulets, and breechclout—all French goods. And now, for the winter, they are giving them blankets, breechclouts, powder, and shot. Hence these nations say: "The Spaniards offer fair words; the French, fair words and presents." They give the captains belts with galloons, coats of red cloth with the same, and ruffled shirts. Thus they came to see me at the mission of Nacodoches, saying to me: "Frenchman this," and "Frenchman that." I submit all this for the high consideration of your Excellency and I assure you, as an honorable officer, that that set forth is true. An

---

[25]For the location of this river, either near or identical with the Neches River, consult the index of *Pichardo's Treatise* . . . , Vol. III, under "San Pedro, Río de."

unmistakable evidence of the prodigality of the French appears to me in the very considerable increase of troops and settlers, and the commandant of Nachitos assures me that he expects a much greater number. When I asked him what purpose the court of France could have in so greatly strengthening this province, he and the other officials told me that they were all perplexed and ignorant of the purpose which their court could have in sending so many people at such great expense, as were coming from Europe.

1096. In fulfilment of my duty I inform your Excellency of everything which I have already stated. I hope that that which my limited capacity has done by virtue of your superior decrees, which I humbly obey, will be to your Excellency's liking. At your feet I offer my regard, and desire that God may keep your Excellency many years. Royal presidio of Los Adaes, November 8, 1751. Most excellent señor. Señor, at your Excellency's feet. Jacinto de Barrios y Jáuregui. To the most excellent señor, the Count of Revilla Gigedo.

1097. This letter with the accompanying *expediente* reached his Excellency's hands around December 20 of the same year of 1751, for on this date he ordered it sent to the señor *auditor general de la guerra* so that he might render his opinion on it. But a month earlier, that is to say, around the preceding November 22, he received the royal cedula which follows. This is shown by the date on which he ordered it delivered to the same señor *auditor*, and for this reason the señores *fiscal* and *auditor de guerra* speak of it in the reports and opinions which they rendered on this *expediente* from the governor of Texas. The said royal cedula is expressed in these words, and is found in our document 39, number 244. See what Señor Valcárcel says about this below, in paragraph 1268.

1098. While the Duke of La Conquista[26] was viceroy of this kingdom of New Spain, he stated in a letter of October 8, 1740, that Don Luis de St. Denis, governor of New Orleans, had extended the dominion of that colony into territories of our king (owing to the negligence of the governor of the Texas, Don Manuel de Sandoval) as was shown by the map which he enclosed.

1099. Upon examining this map, it is found that the French had advanced from their presidio of Nachitos to construct a second one with the same name,[27] for the purpose of disguising by this means the fact that it had been built on territory of the government of Texas. And, as is shown on

---

[26]Pedro de Castro Figueroa y Salazar, the Duke of La Conquista and the Marquis of Gracia Real was viceroy of New Spain from 1740 to 1741.

[27]See *Pichardo's Treatise* . . . , Vol. III, p. 481, n. 15.

the said map, it is a short .distance from the presidio of Los Adays and on a site very important in consequence of its proximity to the mountains which, it is said, contain rich veins of silver (see the note that we have placed at the end of this royal order, in paragraph 1106, concerning these mines). By this move the French have advanced far beyond the limits of the first presidio of Nachitos and even beyond the island containing cultivated fields.

1100. As soon as the said letter and map were received, his Majesty (may he rest in saintly glory) ordered the said Duke of La Conquista, by a letter of March 23 of the following year of 1741 that, reflecting seriously upon the great harm that could result from the encroachments of the French of New Orleans, he should try to be alert to prevent it, and that to this end, and in order that the French might withdraw from what they had occupied, he should take all the measures which he might think most fitting and prudent in view of the existing conditions, since his royal will was not to allow for any reason or pretext whatever those lands to be abandoned or exposed with pernicious toleration to the schemes and designs of the said nation established in those parts.

1101. No report has been received of the results of this order, and its receipt is inferred only unofficially from the account in some documents presented by Don Carlos Franquis,[28] former governor of Texas. Although from the first notice alone the king might assume that this important matter had received attention, being aware that the existing state of affairs gives more opportunity for reflection and for applying measures conducive to the restoration of that which has been usurped or illegally occupied—for the cares of a long war and other important matters have not permitted the consideration of this with the seriousness that it deserves—

1102. His Majesty has decided that as soon as your Excellency receives this you shall instruct yourself in detail with regard to the places and the territory in which the French of New Orleans may have augmented their strength, and that you shall exchange with the commandant-general of that colony the most persuasive and efficacious dispatches and requisitions, in order that, in view of the harmonious relations and the alliance which exist between the two crowns, the subjects of France not only be not permitted to penetrate into his Majesty's dominions, but also that they be made to withdraw immediately to their old fort or presidio of Nachitos, demolishing the new one and whatever else may have been erected in his Majesty's domains.

1103. In case these dispatches and requirements should not be sufficient to dislodge promptly the French of La Movila and New Orleans from the usurped territory, the king commands that your Excellency at the same time shall issue all the orders and directions calculated to force them to leave, sending for that purpose the corresponding orders to the officials and commandants of the presidios of Texas, and especially to the governor of that province, under whose charge your Excellency may place the operation, in view of his distinguished conduct, merit, and military experience. You

---

[28]Carlos Benites Franquis de Lugo was governor of Texas in 1736.

may send him (if it seems well to your Excellency to do so) one of the engineers who are in that kingdom, so that he may assist and aid him in bringing about the restoration of the usurped territory, and so that the rule and law may be established that will result in preventing hereafter the occupation of that or any other land that may be within his Majesty's domains. In this important matter he charges your Excellency most especially, expecting its complete fulfilment from your distinguished zeal and love for the royal service. God keep your Excellency many years. Aranjuez, June 20, 1751. The Marquis of La Ensenada. To the Señor Count of Revilla Gigedo.

1104. Mexico, November 22, 1751. In order that a suitable resolution may be taken on the matter with which the foregoing royal order is concerned, let it be sent to the señor *auditor* with the *autos* on the matter, so that, having acquainted himself with its gravity and importance, and in the light of some other information which he has besides that contained in the said *autos*, he may state to me his opinion, in view of which a decision may be reached with forethought and the best advice. The Count of Revilla Gigedo.

1105. *Most excellent señor:* Because of the fact that the most excellent señor, the Duke of La Conquista, informed his Majesty that the French of New Orleans, expanding and going beyond their limits, had advanced their colony and presidio of Nachitos toward the south, penetrating into the territories of the province of the Texas, perpetrating a usurpation and fraud upon the eminent, commendable, and important domains of the Spanish monarchy, establishing themselves at a short distance from our presidio of Los. . . .

The original ends here. On page 146 of volume 71, which is found in the secretariat of this viceroyalty, where are copied the cedulas and royal orders that came during the government of the most excellent señor, the Count of Revilla Gigedo, is found this royal order, and following it, the beginning of the opinion of the señor *auditor de la guerra*, but it is not complete, for it appears that the opening lines of the said opinion were copied through a mistake of the clerk, and that therefore he suspended the copying, for the purpose of that volume is only to record the cedulas and royal orders. The said opinion will be filed with the original of the said cedula but, since it has not come into our hands, we do not copy it, regretting meanwhile that we do not know what the señor *auditor* suggested with regard to the said royal order. But we have reason to believe that it would conform with the opinions which we have mentioned.

1106. In this cedula there is noted the account which governor Franquis gave of some silver mines which existed in La Gran Montaña, where the witnesses of the aforecited declarations, and

D'Anville, locate the boundary line. The letter of Señor Franquis
is no longer among the *autos,* but Señor Oliván, *auditor de la
guerra,* makes an extract of it in his opinion dated July 4, 1737,
in these words (see document 31, number 16) :

It is not known for certain what reason moved Franquis to the decision
of imprisoning Sandoval and the lieutenant, Ibiricú,[29] of which imprisonment
the fathers speak in their letters—whether it was perhaps due to a desire
for personal revenge because of not having been provided with an escort
upon his entrance into that government; or whether it was because of the
disagreement which they had with regard to the contract which Ibiricú says
they had made concerning the supplies and merchandise (the governors
are forbidden to make such a contract by a military- ordinance of the
reglamento) ; or whether it was because of the fact that *Sandoval had permitted the [French] commandant, Monsieur de St. Denis, to build a presidio
on* lands of the presidio of Los Adays of this New Spain, [an incident] of
which Franquis wrote with such zeal to your Excellency in his letter of
September 30, 1736, in folio 34 of the next *cuaderno.* Thus the place has
been fortified, so that it will now be difficult or practically impossible to
dislodge them from it, because of its being so near the large lagoon of
Los Adays (the bank of which is two leagues from this presidio), where
our soldiers had taken specimens from the mineral veins they had found,
and had made assays of their silver ores. This probably fired the desire of
the French to occupy that country and to defend it with arms, as the
commandant threatens in his letters. If this were Franquis' reason, he would
consider it sufficient for securing Sandoval's person in prison and for keeping him in the guardroom, although at the petition of the father president,
Ballejo, he relieved him somewhat of this rigorous treatment.

But in as much as there is no confirmation whatever of this fact,
it seems that the information which was given to Señor Franquis
proved to be false, and that consequently he made a mistake in
sending this report to his most illustrious Excellency, for it was
untrue. In the same cedula a map is mentioned, according to which
it was apparent that the French presidio had been moved a short
distance from that of Los Adays and on land of much importance
and consequence because of its proximity to the mountains which,
it is said, contains rich veins of silver. If this map were very small
and reduced in scale, the new presidio of Nachitoches would certainly be shown very near Los Adaes, since according to the most
usual estimate there were seven leagues between the French and

---

[29]For references to Sandoval and Ibiricú, consult the index in *Pichardo's
Treatise* . . . , Vol. III.

Spanish presidios. Therefore the eye could be deceived, particularly if the degrees of longitude and latitude were not well designated, and the French presidio would seem to be very near the Spanish one. The French, then, simply moved their presidio to a place that belonged to them, and which was at the said distance from that of Los Adaes, nor did they aspire to possess themselves of La Gran Montaña where the supposed mines and the boundary line were located.

1107. Returning now to the *expediente* of Señor Barrios, his Excellency ordered it reviewed by the señores *fiscal* and *auditor de guerra,* and they replied, among other things, that which is seen in the following sentences (number 131 of the said document 37):

Most excellent señor: The judicial proceedings which the governor of the province of the Texas, Don Jacinto de Barrios y Jáuregui, remits, are in observance of the dispatch which is at their beginning and are concerned with the matter of the seventeen soldiers who had been detached from the presidio of Los Adays for that of San Xavier; with the illicit trade that was attributed to the preceding governor, Don Pedro del Barrio; and with the report contained in the *consulta* of the commandant, Don Juan de Yarza y Ascona, dated June 30 of the year '50, to the effect that four warships laden with people (aside from thirty-six merchant ships that were in the Mississippi River) had come to the French colony. Their purpose is to settle the many lands which they possess, penetrating farther each time and fortifying themselves with various forts in different places. The report contained also other information on this matter.

1108. Assuming that Governor Don Jacinto del Barrio submits a complete report concerning the first two points—that of the soldiers who had been detached from Los Adays and that of the illicit trade—in conformity with what he had been ordered in the cited · dispatch, for the present there is nothing further to be done, either with regard to the matter of illicit commerce—for as a result of the investigation not a single thing has been produced against Don Pedro del Barrio—or with regard to his *residencia,* as the *fiscal* reports today.

1109. As for the matter of the French, bearing in mind its special seriousness, and also having due regard for the judicial proceedings relative thereto that begin on folio 36, and for what the two *consultas* of the said governor contain concerning the same and other matters, the *fiscal* has postponed placing the whole matter before your Excellency's highness and recommending what should be done. So that he may do so, he believes it desirable that you be pleased to order that there be added to these *autos* the original *consulta* of the said commandant, Don Juan de Yarza, and also the *autos* which exist in this superior government concerning four Frenchmen who were sent from New Mexico (it seems that he is alluding here to the

Frenchmen who are discussed in document 35) and likewise any order from his Majesty on this matter, if there be such, together with all the rest that may be pertinent and helpful to the *fiscal* in making fitting recommendations.

1110. Since it is apparent from the judicial proceedings that the Mississippi River should serve as a boundary to keep the French within their limits, your Excellency will be pleased to direct likewise that the *autos* or instruments be sought which make it clear that the said river is and ought to constitute the boundary line referred to, and that it be ascertained also whether there may be any orders from his Majesty or other documents on the subject which might confirm it. Mexico, January 29, 1752. Dr. Andreu.

Mexico, January 31, 1752. To the señor *auditor*. Signed with his Excellency's rubric.

1111. *Most excellent señor:* If it be your pleasure, your Excellency will command that the *autos* and orders which the señor *fiscal* refers to be added to these, and that everything be returned to him. With regard to the Mississippi River being the boundary line between our dominions and those of Louisiana and the other French colonies, the *auditor* does not know whether there are any specific *autos* or orders. Therefore, in an opinion of June 20, 1744—concerning the difficulties between the governors of Texas, Don Manuel de Sandoval and his successor, Colonel Don Carlos de Franquis—occasioned by a report being requested by a royal cedula of July 15, 1740, and by another of December 1, 1741, the *auditor* after stating, beginning with number 10 of the cited opinion, what those lands comprised, said in number 16 that the matter had already been brought to his Majesty's attention in the *consultas* of September 15, 1715, and July 28, 1717, and that because of its importance and significance he believes that the memoranda which have been made will not prove burdensome. Above all, your Excellency will order what you may think best. Mexico, February 28, 1752. The Marquis of Altamira.

The *consultas* of which the señor *auditor* speaks here have not reached my hands, but I have seen what Señor Oliván says in document 22, number 24, under date of January 27, 1724, namely:

In a letter which the *auditor* wrote by order of the *junta general* held on August 22, 1715, presided over by the most excellent señor, the Duke of Linares,[30] and signed by his hand for his Majesty, there was brought to the royal attention, in detail, everything that had occurred concerning the ingress of the French into Louisiana and its vicinity, from [the time of] Monsieur de la Salle, who discovered it. It was stated that it would be fitting for the Mississippi River to form the boundary between New France and New Spain, and that his Majesty [should] establish this [in agreement] with his Most Christian Majesty, as a permanent boundary which the French

---

[30]Fernando de Alencastre Noroña y Silva, the Duke of Linares and the Marquis of Valdefuentes, was viceroy of New Spain from 1711 to 1716.

were not to trespass, in order that the places of Nachitos, Cadodachos, and others in the valley of the Mississippi might remain in this New Spain, included in this dominion. His Excellency sent it [the report] to his Majesty, who was pleased to examine it and to order a reply sent commending the viceroy's zeal and saying that he would make a decision on its contents. This the señor duke referred to the *auditor*.

I know further that the Señor Marquis of San Miguel de Aguayo in the year 1724 wrote to the most excellent señor viceroy, the Marquis of Casafuerte,[31] the following words that are found in the said document 22, number 13:

And thus if it seems desirable to your Excellency, it will be well that your Excellency write to Captain Luis de St. Denis, commandant on the Texas frontier, who lives in Nachitos, and has the captain of Caudodachos under his orders, and is himself under the governor of Mobile, in order to make them understand at least that the bad faith with which they apparently observe the alliance which obtains between France and Spain has come to your Excellency's notice, or your Excellency will resolve upon whatever seems best to you. Foreseeing all this, when I entered Texas by the most direct road, I represented to the king the importance of his Majesty's acquiring Nachitos and Caudachos, either by war or by peaceful capitulation. But the French are unwilling to agree to it for these reasons, and because, if the alliance should be broken, they hold in this way the most direct point of entry into New Spain.

This his Excellency endorsed as follows:

Mexico, March 1, 1752. As the señor *auditor* recommends. Signed with his Excellency's rubric.

1112. (Number 138 of the said document 37; the señor *fiscal*, Andreu, is again speaking.) *Most excellent señor:* Among various matters included in the *consultas* of June 30, 1750, and December 31 of the same year, drawn up by the commandant of the presidio of Santa Rosa, Punta de Sigüenza, Don Juan de Yarza y Ascona, and by Don Jacinto de Barrios y Jáuregui, one in the *consulta* of the said commandant related to the lively concern caused by the arrival at the French colony of four war vessels laden with people (aside from thirty-six merchant ships that were in the Mississippi River and were bringing clothing and other things)—with soldiers, settlers, women, and children for the settlement of the lands which they possess today, constantly penetrating farther inland and fortifying themselves with various forts in different places. There was also other information which the *fiscal* has already repeated in his reply to the said *consultas*, dated February 1, 1751.

---

[31]Juan de Acuña, the Marquis of Casafuerte, was viceroy of New Spain from 1722 to 1734.

1113. Besides these, the señor *auditor general de la guerra* in an opinion of September 1, 1745, in the *autos* concerning disputes between the residents of the villa of San Fernando, capital of the presidio of the villa of San Antonio de Béjar, and the missionary fathers, noted that the vast province of Texas is on the frontier of the hostile Apaches and other barbarous Indians and is also a barrier against the French nation, which, having already advanced eighty leagues beyond the Mississippi River, which should serve it as a boundary, could penetrate more easily into the adjacent provinces of New Mexico, Coahuila, Nueva Vizcaya, and the New Kingdom of León, availing itself of their rich minerals and introducing its illicit commerce.

1114. The *fiscal* having taken into consideration all that has been stated, requested in his cited reply of February 1 that your Excellency be pleased to order that the said governor, with the same diligence, activity, and zeal which a matter of such importance demands, should make the necessary investigation of it, bearing in mind what the señor *auditor* and the commandant stated, and likewise any previous documents that might exist relative to the affair, and those which may prove that the Mississippi River should serve as boundary for the French nation. The governor should make a report at once, along with the judicial proceedings, in order that your Excellency may send it to his Majesty, and adopt such other measures as may be required.

1115. So it is that the governor, having carried to completion other matters entrusted to him by the same dispatch in which he was told to make the investigation mentioned, with regard to the French having advanced beyond their boundaries and the rest that has been stated, examined for that purpose eight witnesses pursuant to the interrogatory that he drew up, in folio 36. In substance, it inquired whether the French had penetrated in the direction of the presidio of Los Adaes, going beyond the Mississippi River which should serve as a boundary to restrain them within their limits; whether many troops and families had come to New Orleans from Europe; what purpose might have brought so many people, where they are maintained, how, and why; whether the commandant of Nachitos has received any special orders since the arrival of the said people; whether the paymaster of the royal warehouse at Nachitos has orders to supply the *alférez*, Don Luis de St. Denis, with any goods, since when, and what purpose; whether this official, Don Luis de St. Denis, is exceedingly beloved by all the Texas, Nacodoches, and other Indians; and whether, availing himself of this influence, the said official had committed any excesses in the province.

1116. The result of this investigation is, first, by confirmatory statements of the eight witnesses,[32] most of them eyewitnesses with positive knowledge and experience, that the French have gone beyond the Río Colorado [Red River] which served them as boundary before 1720, penetrating since that time as far as the presidio of Los Adays. Some witnesses advanced as evidence of what they stated [the fact that] when the French were confined by the said boundary they did not follow their deserters beyond the river.

---

[32]See paragraphs 1062–1090, *supra*.

nor were the Spanish deserters followed [beyond that point], which is not true at present with regard to the Frenchmen. [The witnesses stated also] that this aggression began in the time of Governor Sandoval, through no fault of his, for he could not have remedied it because of his small force and of the strength that the Frenchman had in union with the Indians. Finally, the fourth witness says that the French have the Indians so much on their side that they would respond immediately to the slightest call, to the evident danger of the province.

1117. The *fiscal* continued to make extracts from these declarations and from the letters of Señor Barrios to his Excellency, and then he adds (number 151):

All that has been stated is included in the said judicial proceedings and *consultas*. The *fiscal* has acquainted himself likewise with the opinion of the señor *auditor* on the preceding reply that he gave in these same *autos*, dated January 29, because the said señor *auditor* now states, with regard to the Mississippi River being the dividing line between our dominions and Louisiana and the other French colonies, that he does not know whether there are any specific *autos* or orders. Therefore, in an opinion of June 20, 1744—concerning the difficulties between the governors of Texas, Don Manuel de Sandoval and his successor, Don Carlos de Franquis—occasioned by a report being requested by a royal cedula of July 15, 1740, and by another of December 1, 1741, the *auditor* after stating, beginning with number 10 of the cited opinion, what those lands comprised, said in number 16 that the matter had already been brought to his Majesty's attention in *consultas* of September 15, 1715, and July 28, 1717, and that because of its importance and significance he believes that the memoranda which have been made will not prove burdensome.

1118. The *fiscal*, bearing in mind the said opinion of the señor *auditor*, included in *cuaderno* 16— which is the one that has been formed on the difficulties of the two above-named governors—has acquainted himself also with another *cuaderno* which has been brought to him by virtue of his previous request, the said *cuaderno* consisting of a written order signed by the most excellent señor, the Marquis of La Ensenada, under date of June 20, 1751, and of the opinion of the señor *auditor*, which follows, rendered on November 27 of the same year. This *expediente* was being formed in this superior government at the time that the penetration of the French into our dominions had already been discussed in it, and the judicial proceedings had been executed which the *fiscal* and the señor *auditor* had required with regard to the *consulta* of Commandant Yarza y Ascona, so that the *fiscal's* reply and the opinion of the señor *auditor* were dated on February 1 and 8, 1751, the respective decree of conformance and dispatch on the first of the same month, and the *consultas* of the governor with the judicial proceedings on November 8 of the same year.

1119. The *fiscal*, therefore, has taken into consideration all the foregoing, and also the contents of the said written order and the resulting opinion of the señor *auditor*. This opinion is the one that the most excellent señor, the Duke of La Conquista, sent to his Majesty while he was viceroy of this kingdom, in a letter of October 8, 1740, with regard to the fact that Don Luis de St. Denis, governor of New Orleans, had extended the dominion of that colony into territories of his Majesty (owing to the negligence of the governor of Texas, Don Manuel de Sandoval), as was shown by the map which he enclosed.

1120. Upon examining this map, it was found that the French had advanced from their presidio of Nachitos to construct a second one with the same name, for the purpose of disguising by this means the fact that it had been built on territory of the government of Texas; and as was shown on the said map, it was a short distance from the presidio of Los Adaes and on a site very important in consequence of its proximity to the mountains which, it is said, contain rich veins of silver, [the French by this move] having advanced far beyond the limits of the first presidio of Nachitos and even beyond the island containing cultivated fields.

1121. As soon as the said letter and map were received, his Majesty (may he rest in saintly glory) ordered the said most excellent señor, the Duke of La Conquista, by a letter of March 23 of the following year of 1741, that, reflecting very seriously upon the great harm that could result from the encroachments of the French of New Orleans, he should endeavor to be on the alert to prevent it, and that to this end, and in order that the French might withdraw from what they had occupied, he should take all the measures which he might consider most fitting and prudent in view of the existing conditions, since his royal will was not to allow for any reason or pretext whatever those lands to be abandoned or exposed with pernicious toleration to the schemes and designs of the said nation established in those parts.

1122. Since no reports had been received of the results of this order, its receipt was inferred only unofficially from the account of some documents presented by Don Carlos Franquis, former governor of Texas. Although from the first notice alone the king might assume that this important matter had received attention, being aware that the existing state of affairs gave more opportunity for reflection and for applying measures conducive to the restoration of that which had been usurped or illegally occupied—for the cares of a long war and other important matters had not permitted the consideration of this with the seriousness that it deserves—his Majesty was pleased to decide that your Excellency, as soon as you received this, should instruct yourself in detail with regard to the places and the territory in which the French of New Orleans might have augmented their strength, and that you should exchange with the commandant-general of that colony the most persuasive and efficacious dispatches and requisitions, in order that, in view of the harmonious relations and the alliance that exist between the two crowns, the subjects of France not only be not permitted to penetrate into his Majesty's dominions, but also that they be made to withdraw immediately to their old fort or presidio of Nachitos, demolishing the new one and whatever else may have been built on his Majesty's domains.

1123. In case these dispatches and requirements should not be sufficient to dislodge promptly the French of La Movila and New Orleans from the usurped territory, the king commands that your Excellency at the same time shall issue all the orders and directions calculated to force them to leave, sending for that purpose the corresponding orders to the officials and commandants of the presidios of Texas, and especially to the governor of that province, under whose charge your Excellency may place the operation, in view of his distinguished conduct, merit, and military experience. You may send him (if it seems well to your Excellency to do so) one of the engineers who are in this kingdom, so that he may assist and aid him in bringing about the restoration of the usurped territory, and so that the rule and law may be established that will result in preventing hereafter the occupation of that or any other land that may be within his Majesty's domains. In this important matter he charges your Excellency most especially, expecting its complete fulfilment from your distinguished zeal and love for the royal service.

1124. Whereupon the señor *auditor,* having repeated the above context, explains that the information which the documents of Governor Don Carlos Franquis may have furnished is fully examined in the *autos* of the inquiry and *residencia* of Captain Manuel de Sandoval, predecessor of the said Franquis in that government, because one of the points expressly included in the investigation was the charge that the said Sandoval had dissimulated or consented to the penetration of the French, through the natural indolence or grasping opportunism of which he was accused; and that although the señor *fiscal,* Don Pedro Vedoya y Osorio, upon the first notice of the accusation or judicial inquiry [contained in] those *autos,* had given an account to his Majesty with unofficial copies, which led to the issuing of a royal cedula directed to Don Justo Boneo,[33] successor to Franquis, dated July 15 of the year 1740, ordering that he investigate, take measures, and make a report, the royal cedula was received after the investigation of the charges, of which Sandoval was absolved following a hearing by the same señor *fiscal,* Don Pedro Vedoya, who recognized how unfounded were the first unofficial notices that produced his report; all of which appears in those *autos.*

1125. The señor *auditor* took no official cognizance of these documents until, after they had already been passed upon, they were sent to him in the year '44 by virtue of the cited royal cedula addressed to Governor Boneo, and the report which the latter made to the most excellent señor, the Count of Fuenclara,[34] for his information. Having examined them at that time, the *auditor* rendered thereon the two opinions of March 6 and June 20 of the same year, in which he made a lengthy abstract or resumé not only of the thirty voluminous *cuadernos* of *autos* drawn up on the matter, but also of more than forty others relative to the previous expeditions into Texas—its location, boundaries, and resources; its discovery, progress, and present state; and the expenses incurred in its pacification, conservation, and in the mainte-

[33]Justo Boneo y Morales was governor of Texas from 1742 to 1744.
[34]Pedro Cebrián y Agustín, the Count of Fuenclara, was viceroy of New Spain from 1741 to 1746.

nance of the missionaries and presidials. He presented also a memorandum or sketch of this North America, and of Louisiana and other possessions bordering on it, pointing out the little or no result and the equally negligible experience gained in the development and advancement of these regions, or in the curtailment of expenditures therein, because of the reductions not having been based upon the one stable, solid, and essential footing—namely, towns or settlers. He also gave many other details in the two opinions. In that of June 20, in number 16, the señor *auditor* recalled that in the *consultas* of September 15 and July 8, 1717, his Majesty had been informed how important it would be for the security of these possessions to establish as boundary between the two crowns the bank of the famous Mississippi River on this side, its mighty current putting an end to all occasion for difficulties and disturbances, and that in a matter so worthy of consideration a reminder would not be tedious, nor would the repetition of this information be bothersome.

1126. In the same opinion, in numbers 41 and following, the *auditor* stated that the new presidio of Nachitos, according to information furnished by the judicial records, was at the distance of a musket shot from the old one, in the same district and on a site occupied by the French from the beginning of their settlement, where they had always had houses, gardens, and property. The dividing line was the place called La Gran Montaña, midway of the seven leagues which are between the presidio of Nachitos and ours of Los Adaes, and since the French had not gone beyond this point and since there was no new occurrence that might require action to be taken, an account should be given to his Majesty with complete certified copies of the *autos.* In as much as they have not been transcribed, the information with a certified copy of the chief and last *cuaderno,* which contained the two aforecited opinions, should be sent beforehand for his Majesty. It was so ordered for the time being, and there is a note to the effect that the certified copies were made and sent to the secretariat of the most excellent señor, the Count of Fuenclara, on July 27 of the said year.

1127. Nothing new has happened subsequently to alter the aspect of this business for, although by the agency of the governor of New Mexico some Frenchmen (see document 35, already cited) were sent [to Mexico],[35] they having come to this kingdom from New Orleans with the intention and desire of seeing if they could establish a trade in that region, the activity and zeal with which the said governor confiscated the baubles which were the only things that they brought in their baggage, is shown in the same *autos.* The Frenchmen having been conducted under guard from one point to another to this court, they were examined by the señor *auditor* by order of your Excellency. The searching and detailed inquiry did not produce a strong indication of any foreign designs beyond those usual to the [French] nation, and showed only that this had been a special, private scheme on the part of those travellers for their personal interest, *although [they acted] with the knowledge and to some extent under the patronage of the governor of New Orleans.*

---

[35]Consult *Pichardo's Treatise* . . . , Vol. III, Chap. 8.

Therefore it is ordered that a report be made to his Majesty, along with these *autos*. The one and the other will make clear to his royal mind that there has been no unusual occurrence, nor has there ever been with regard to the usurpation, extension, or penetration of the French. [They will make clear also] how a watch has been kept upon their movements in order to check any illegitimate idea of theirs that might in some manner bring about a disturbance of the present mutual accord, harmony, and alliance between the two crowns, to the regret of both, because of the transgressions of those individual commandants. Thus the señor *auditor's* advice was that your Excellency should order certified copies made of this *cuaderno* so that it might be transmitted on the first occasion; to it should be added subsequently copies of all the *autos* in case they have not already been sent for some other purpose. He recommended that at the same time your Excellency order the governor to apply himself with the utmost care and zeal to checking any scheme of the French, however insignificant, reporting everything that he might observe and note that is worthy of your Excellency's attention. He should also request orders on this matter, for which purpose a letter should be written to him, enclosing a certified copy of this opinion.

1128. This opinion was carried into effect by means of the decree issued in conformance with it on December 13, 1751, and notations placed at the end of the official letter [indicate] that on January 18 and February 19 of the current year, complete certified copies were made of the *cuaderno* in question, with other related matter, in order to give an account to his Majesty. But notwithstanding the above provisions, and that which the señor *auditor* explained in recommending them, what is the origin of the judicial proceedings referred to here, which the governor has remitted? For although he does not state fully and precisely what he has been informed and what the cited royal order expresses, nevertheless it appears from confirmatory testimony of the declarants, most of whom were eyewitnesses with personal knowledge and experience, that [individuals] of the French nation from New Orleans have passed beyond their territory and crossed the Río Colorado, which used to serve them as boundary before the year 1720, and have penetrated since that time toward the presidio of Los Adays. In proof of this the witnesses cite the action of the deserters.

(Let me be permitted to interrupt the señor *fiscal* here with the following reflections. These witnesses whom the señor *fiscal* regards so highly should not be trusted at all because their declarations are false; for we have seen above, beginning with number 37, that from the first the French appropriated the Mississippi together with all the rivers that flow into it and the lands which they drain. In as much as they considered that the land lying between the Red River and La Gran Montaña, or Arroyo Hondo, was drained by this river, they took it for their own. Therefore they placed on the west side of it, as on their own land, those houses, gardens, and corrals of which the witnesses examined in Mexico speak. We have seen that these same witnesses, so credited by the señor *fiscal*, in the declarations they made in Los Adaes in the year '40—as we have noted in paragraph 1043—made incomplete statements with regard to the matter of deserters. See also the declarations that these same ones made in February of 1753, which we have already mentioned and which we copy below, beginning with paragraph 1165.)

To this are added the movements observed in the sending of French troops and families, together with the rest that the *fiscal* has repeated. There is included also by way of information on these matters the reports made by the commandant, Yarza y Ascona, and by the present governor on the same subjects of the activity in the province incident to the sending of French troops and families; the fact that others are expected, according to the statements of the French officials themselves; the confusion and ignorance of the latter with regard to the schemes, intentions, and designs of the court of France is so greatly strengthening that province; and also the statement which the present governor makes, assuring your Excellency as an honorable officer that everything he has stated is true, and that the extravagance of the French in increasing their troops and settlers is a conspicuous confirmation of this. (It developed ultimately that the French did not intend by this move to go beyond D'Anville's line, but to populate well the lands already appropriated.)

1120. Such pressing circumstances, then, demand that that province and its presidio receive a different sort of attention from that which they have had hitherto, and especially since the reports regarding the French having gone beyond their possessions (we have seen that they have not trespassed but have remained within the limits that were determined from the beginning) into ours corresponds to reports made to his Majesty since the time of the government of the most excellent señor, the Duke of La Conquista. Even without the new information which the present judicial proceedings furnish and with only that which his Majesty had received from the said most excellent señor duke, he had ordered him that, reflecting very seriously on the great harm that could result from the encroachments of the French of New Orleans, he should endeavor to be on the alert to prevent it, and that to this end, and in order that the French might withdraw from what they had occupied, he should take all the measures which he might consider most fitting and prudent in view of the existing conditions, since his royal will was not to allow for any reason or pretext whatsoever those lands to be abandoned or exposed with pernicious toleration to the schemes and designs of the said nation established in those parts.

1130. At this juncture and under these conditions, his Majesty not having had news of the results of this order, and being aware that the existing state of affairs gave more opportunity for reflection and for applying measures conducive to the restoration of that which had been usurped or illegally occupied, his Majesty has resolved that as soon as you receive this order, your Excellency shall instruct yourself in detail with regard to the places and territory in which the French of New Orleans may have augmented their strength, and that you shall present to the commandant-general of that colony the most persuasive and efficacious dispatches and requisitions, in order that in view of the harmonious relations and the alliance which exist between the two crowns, the subjects of France not only be not permitted to penetrate into his Majesty's dominions, but also that they shall be made to withdraw immediately to their old fort or presidio of Nachitos, demolishing the new one and whatever else may have been built on his Majesty's possessions. Further orders were given to be followed in case the dislodgement of the French were not quickly attained.

1131. And his Majesty has ordered likewise that because of his distinguished conduct, merit, and military experience, your Excellency may place the operation under the charge of the present governor,[36] sending him (if it seems well to your Excellency to do so) one of the engineers who are in this kingdom, so that he may assist and aid him in bringing about the restoration of the usurped territory, and so that the rule and precedent may be established that will result in preventing hereafter the occupation of that or any other land that may be within his Majesty's domains. In this important matter he charges your Excellency most especially, expecting its complete fulfilment from your distinguished zeal and love for the royal service.

1132. So that your Excellency may succeed in carrying out [the above orders], thus justifying the royal confidence, remedying and guarding opportunely against what already has been observed and may be feared in the future concerning the penetration of the French into his Majesty's possessions—assuming the choice and approval already expressed of the present governor, assuming also that the señor *auditor* in his opinion, which the *fiscal* has repeated, advised that your Excellency order the governor to devote himself most diligently and zealously to restraining the least irregular action of the French, giving reports of everything that he may observe and note in this matter which is worthy of your Excellency's attention and which may require some action to be taken, and assuming, finally, that according to the same opinion and the annotation made on the dispatch, the governor was sent only the certified copy of the said opinion with a letter from your Excellency— superior justice will best be served by ordering that he be sent a certified copy of the royal decree with a letter from your Excellency, so that, being informed of what his Majesty orders, he may acquaint himself more minutely with the places and territory that the French of New Orleans may have strengthened. While from the judicial proceedings it is clear that they have gone beyond the Río Colorado [Red River], it is not specified with complete detail which and how much of his Majesty's lands may be occupied and

---

[36]Reference is to Jacinto de Barrios y Jáuregui who was governor of Texas at the time of the writing of this document.

usurped, nor are the greater dangers mentioned that could befall the province, dangers which would not result, or at least not so easily, if the French would remain within their limits. [The governor should be ordered also] that in accordance with what may result he shall present, in the name of your Excellency, to the commandant-general of that colony the most persuasive and efficacious dispatches and demands, in order that, in view of the harmonious relations and the alliance that exist between the two crowns, not only shall he not permit the subjects of that of France to penetrate into the possessions of his Majesty, but also he shall make them withdraw immediately to their old fort or presidio of Nachitos, destroying the new one and anything else that may have been constructed in his Majesty's domains. And for the purposes referred to, since it is not known what else the new proceedings may produce, since the province is so far away, and since in awaiting their results the affair may be delayed, your Excellency, if it be your pleasure, may order that in the letter to be written to the governor of Texas another be enclosed from your Excellency for the governor of New Orleans, so that the governor of Texas, in accordance with what may develop, can cause it to be delivered into his hands, in compliance with the aforecited royal order.

1133. Likewise, if it seems fitting to your Excellency, you will be pleased to send the said governor one of the engineers who are in this kingdom so that he may assist and aid him in bringing about the restoration of the usurped territory, and so that the rule and precedent may be established that will result in preventing hereafter the occupation of that or any other land that may be found within his Majesty's domains. It is understood that the above is to be done without attempting at this time to oblige the French by force to withdraw from the land occupied, as his Majesty directs in the second part of his royal order, the governor making use for the present of the requisitions, methods, measures, and prudent expedients which his Majesty prescribes in the first part, until, the results being seen, whatever may be necessary may be ordered by your Excellency.

The señor *fiscal* thus suggested with great prudence that the French should not be dislodged by force of arms, but that only demands be made of them. For, in truth, as was found out later, there was nothing on which these could be based, because the French had not gone beyond D'Anville's line. See what the señor *auditor de guerra*, Don Domingo Valcárcel, suggested with regard to this in paragraph 1281, below, and what was decided on in the *junta de guerra*, below in paragraph 1335.

1134. Although his Majesty orders that, in case the dislodging of the French of Mobile and New Orleans from the usurped territory may not be attained promptly by means of the dispatches and demands, your Excellency shall at the same time give all the orders and directions that may result in obliging them to leave by force, sending for this purpose proper orders to the officials and commandants of the presidios of Texas and especially to the governor of that province, this seems impossible to accomplish at present, in view of the latest news received relative to the measures taken by France and of the new forces which she has [in Louisiana]. There exists also the difficulty of being unable to assemble enough people in that province [of Texas] and the also fact that the *fiscal* thinks that the officers and soldiers of its presidios, besides being necessary to restrain the Indians, are not adapted to the kind and manner of warfare that it would be necessary to carry on with French troops sent from Europe. [This is true] because the presidial officers and soldiers were established for a different type of occupation and defense, and they receive a very different training from that which will be essential in case of having to use force in dislodging the French. Also the preparations which will be required in such a case, since it will not be possible to carry them out in the province of Texas, will demand more time. Thus it becomes necessary to await what may result from the demands and dispatches that may be issued by the governor of Texas, in order that in view of them proper measures may be applied by your Excellency.

1135. With regard to the matter which the governor brings up—stating that he considers it indispensable that as many as twenty soldiers with an experienced and zealous officer should be established on the Río de San Pedro in order to observe the schemes of the French and the increase that they are going to make in their pueblo of Caudachos and other settlements, and that the principal care of this officer should be to win over and attract those Indians with cunning and skill—if it be your Excellency's superior pleasure, you will concur in this measure which the governor suggests. You will give the corresponding orders and commands for its prompt execution, making certain that the officer and soldiers who are selected shall have the qualifications and training that are required. (Here also is seen the prudence of the señor *fiscal*, in recommending that a new presidio be built on the Río de San Pedro as Señor Barrios had suggested—see above, paragraph 1093— for, in truth, it was very fitting, and it is even today, as I shall explain presently.)

1136. In as much as this province of Texas and its presidio, as the *fiscal* suggests, now becomes another sphere, and has a status different from that which it has had formerly—because if heretofore its presidio and soldiers were mainly for the defense of the province against Indian enemies and were established on this basis and for this precise purpose, today they must be also alert and watchful of what is happening and may happen with regard to the French; and since, for this second purpose, the soldiers of its garrisons are not adequate or suitable either in number or in the rules, system, defense, and methods that they have observed for protecting the province against Indian enemies, not being disciplined and trained to meet emergencies that may arise with the French; and since we must now take care, for the reasons stated, not only of defense against the Indians but also and simultaneously of whatever may arise with the French—it therefore seemed proper to the *fiscal* that it should be suggested to his Majesty that the garrison of this presidio should be like that of the port of Vera Cruz. For this purpose adequate troops should be raised, established, and trained, and also those which may be considered essential for such protection against and pursuit of the Indians as may be necessary. Thus, these troops assisting the presidio in its defense against the French, they will be equally prepared and prompt in any eventuality and movement against the Indians. On this matter, if it be your Excellency's pleasure, the governor of Texas can report the result of his operations.

1137. In number 173 of the said document 37, the *fiscal* continues:

In view of what his Majesty has stated with regard to the report which the most excellent señor, the Duke of La Conquista, made to him and with regard to the map which he sent him, it being very natural that they should be preceded by some kind of instructions, and also that a simple or certified copy of the said report and map should remain in this superior government, your Excellency will be pleased to command that, in order to be informed in a matter of such importance with all the documents that may belong to it, the said papers be sought carefully, as well as all the rest that there may be on the matter, among the dispatches of this superior government and also in your Excellency's secretariat, and that, after they have been found, they be filed, placing with them those which the señor *auditor* cites, such as the royal cedula of December 1, 1741, and the documents relative to that which was done on this same matter in the time of the most excellent señor, the Count of Fuenclara.

1138. Notwithstanding what the señor *auditor* stated about there not being any *autos* on the matter of the Mississippi River being the boundary between the lands of New Orleans and of his Majesty, and since the witnesses said that the Río Colorado was the boundary, there being no proof for either the one or the other, your Excellency will be pleased to order that all the documents which may exist relative to the said boundary line—whether it be the Río Colorado or the Mississippi—be sought with special care. If some order or command of his Majesty on this matter be found, it will be borne in mind in order to avert the danger of the possible contravention of some treaty that may have existed between the two crowns. If these documents or others conducive to the same end are found, the governor should be informed accordingly, for his guidance in the affair, and if none is found, a statement shall be made to that effect. Finally, your Excellency will be pleased to order that for the measures which the *fiscal* has requested and the others that may be necessary, a *junta del real hacienda y guerra* be called as soon as possible, and an account given to his Majesty, with *autos*. Mexico, August 23, 1752. Dr. Andreu.

1139. His Excellency having seen this opinion, he ordered the *expediente* sent to the señor *auditor* who gave his opinion in the following words (number 176 of the said document 37):

Most excellent señor: In view of the fact that the present governor[37] of
the province of the Texas has made the inquiry which was ordered by the
superior dispatch of your Excellency of February 10 of the past year of '51,
as to whether the French of New Orleans had gone beyond their boundary,
advancing into our lands, penetrating farther every day and establishing themselves with various forts in different places; and as to what their purpose
might be in bringing families from Europe, soldiers ·as well as settlers—a
report to that effect being made by the commandant of the presidio of
Santa Rosa, Punta de Sigüenza, and confirmed by the information and proceedings that the said present governor of Texas received and executed,
according to which he has reported that the French have gone beyond the
Río Colorado which used to serve them as boundary before the year 1720,
that they have secured a close and friendly intercourse with the Indians of
that kingdom, that the arrival of ships with many troops is certain, and
that they clearly intend to fortify and extend the settlements of Caudodachos,
Puente Cupé, Cirinue (that is, Ylinois), and Nachitos—together with other
points which the señor *fiscal* has considered minutely in his reply, [the
auditor is of the opinion that] this matter has changed its aspect from that
which it formerly had when the royal order, dated in Aranjuez on June 20
of last year, was received.

1140. In it his Majesty ordered that your Excellency, as soon as you
should receive it, having acquainted yourself minutely with the places and
territory that the French of New Orleans might have strengthened, should
present the most persuasive and efficacious dispatches and demands to the
commandant-general of that province, so that in view of the good relations
and alliance [between Spain and France], he would not only not permit the
subjects of the colony of France to penetrate the dominions of his Catholic
Majesty, but would make them withdraw immediately to their old fort or
presidio of Nachitos, destroying the new one and whatever else may have
been built within his Majesty's possessions. And [the king ordered] that
if by means of the said dispatches and demands the said dislodgment of the
French from the usurped territory be not promptly attained, your Excellency
should take measures to force them to leave, sending for that purpose the
proper orders to the officials and commandants of the presidios of Texas and
especially to the governor of that province, putting him in charge of these
operations because of his distinguished conduct, experience, and merit, and
sending him one of the engineers who are in this kingdom so that he may
assist and help him in promoting this enterprise.

1141. The *auditor* took this royal order into consideration, along with
the official memorandum of the opinions which he rendered on March 6
and June 20 of the year '44, after examining and considering the *autos* of
the inquiry and *residencia* of Captain Don Manuel de Sandoval, governor
of that kingdom, together with more than forty other *cuadernos* on the
previous expeditions into Texas—its location, boundaries, and the quality

---

[37]*Ibid.*

of its land, its discovery, pacification, progress, and present state. These he managed to review or summarize in the said opinions, giving in them a notice, brief description, or sketch of this entire North America; and upon remitting the said opinions and *autos* on the matter, of which an account had already been given to his Majesty, he stated that there had been no subsequent new occurrence which would require taking measures with regard to the subject treated in the royal order of June 20 of the year just passed, nor any change, up to that time, that might alter the aspect of the business with regard to French encroachment. The *auditor* concluded, therefore, by recommending that a report be made again to his Majesty, accompanied by certified copies of the corresponding *cuaderno*, which should be sent on the first occasion, to be followed by copies of all the *autos*, including those which were drawn up relative to the entrance of some Frenchmen into New Mexico, who by order of the governor were sent under arrest to this court. [The *auditor* said] that at the same time the governor of Texas should be ordered to devote all his attention to checking the least irregular move that he might notice on the part of the French, reporting to your Excellency everything that might be worthy of your superior notice and that might give rise to the adoption of some decision or measure.

1142. It was so determined by the superior decree of December 13 of the said year just passed, and there is a notice that the certified copy was made and that the letter was written to the governor of Texas. Subsequently, however, further information on this matter was disclosed, as a result of the new proceedings sent by the said governor, which the señor *fiscal* has considered in his preceding reply, to number 28, inclusive. It is therefore proper that your Excellency send the governor of Texas a certified copy of the cited royal order as the señor *fiscal* suggests and requests in number 29, together with a letter in which he will be directed that—having informed himself of his Majesty's orders and acquainted himself exactly with the places and territories which the French may have occupied from the Río Colorado to the outposts of that kingdom, and having comprehended the damage that may result from this encroachment—he shall direct the most persuasive and efficacious dispatches to the commandant-general of that colony, to the end that, in view of the good relations, alliance, and perfect friendship that exist between the two crowns, the subjects of France may be restrained and may withdraw to their old fort, destroying the new one and whatever else may have been built within his Majesty's possessions. For this purpose, if it be your Excellency's superior pleasure, there may be enclosed in the letter written to the governor of Texas another in your Excellency's name for the commandant-general of that colony [Louisiana] or the governor of New Orleans, in conformance with the cited royal order, for whatever influence and weight the superior, respectable, and personal recommendation of your Excellency may have in this affair.

1143. It will also be very well to direct and advise the governor of Texas to send only diplomatic, courteous dispatches, without having recourse to measures that may necessitate compulsion or force, until the results of these first circumspect expedients and measures are seen. Your Excellency, being much better informed, may then make fitting dispositions, for since it is necessary to adapt the plan to the forces [available], and since those of the province of Texas are so limited and so in demand, being sufficient only to restrain the Indians, in some respects it would not be advisable to oppose them and risk them against the forces of New France, which are superior, especially today with the reinforcement of people who have come to it from Europe. Furthermore, it will always be advisable to examine the matter with attention to the fact that it demands all the consideration and authority of the two crowns, and that it may be that the crown of France is not aware of the aggressions of its subjects, and that, informed by his Catholic Majesty, it may be expected to adopt measures for applying a remedy and giving the corresponding satisfaction.

1144. Similarly, it may be conducive to the end sought and desired if, with your Excellency's approval, the said governor of Texas be sent one of the engineers who are in this kingdom, as the señor *fiscal* proposes in number 30, in order that he may assist the governor in everything that occurs, establishing the necessary rules for impeding the occupation of that territory in the future. Its demarcation would be very useful, as would the making of an exact and comprehensive map of that entire kingdom and its frontiers touching New France, showing all the intervening places, particularly those that the French have occupied, and to what point [they have reached]. The judicial proceedings state only that they have gone beyond the Río Colorado [Red River]; and although the *auditor* in his aforecited opinions points out all the ascertained facts of which he has knowledge—proven from the *autos* to which he refers with regard to what the French occupy up to their presidio of Nachitos, giving an account of the seven leagues that separate it from the frontier of Los Adaes in the said Texas, and of that which is called Gran Montaña, not because it is a large mountain but because it rises in level land which lacks other elevations—in spite of all this, a distinct map which would furnish the further information that is needed and desired would be very useful.

1145. The governor in his *consulta* also proposes as indispensable, necessary, and proper the measure providing that as many as twenty soldiers be stationed on the Río de San Pedro with an experienced and zealous officer who would observe the schemes and movements of the French and attempt to attract and win the friendship of the Indians. The señor *fiscal* consents to this in number 32, because of the arguments and reasons that the governor advances concerning the insufficiency of the soldiers of Los Adaes and the fact that its garrison could not furnish this small detachment. The señor *fiscal* adds in number 33 that since they are not disciplined or trained as they should be in order to oppose the well-trained French troops, in as much as those soldiers of Los Adaes in former times have served a very different and distinct purpose, being used only to restrain the Indians, whose [mode of] warfare is so different, it would be very expedient to suggest to his Majesty that the garrison of this presidio should be like that of the port of Vera Cruz, with trained troops in sufficient numbers not only to check the Indians, but also as a precaution against or in order to restrain the French, and that the governor of Texas shall report in regard to this matter. The *auditor* subscribes to these recommendations. Your Excellency will be pleased to send the said governor orders to this effect in the letter that is to be written to him; and with regard to the establishment of the twenty soldiers and an officer on the Río de San Pedro, and whatever else may seem proper, a *junta de real hacienda y guerra* shall be called as quickly as possible and an account given to his Majesty, with certified copies of the *autos*. With this the señor *fiscal* concludes the last part of his reply. . . . Mexico, September 13, 1752. The Marquis of Altamira.

1146. The *junta de guerra* which the señores *fiscal* and *auditor* requested was, in fact, convoked, and [its report] is found copied in the same document 37, beginning with number 186. We have taken the following from it:

In the *junta de guerra y hacienda* which the most excellent señor, Don Juan Francisco de Güemes y Horcasitas, etc., ordered convened and held today, September 25, 1752, with the attendance of the señores *oidores*, the *subdecano*, Don Domingo Balcacer [Valcarcel?] y Formento, etc.; a report was given of the *autos* drawn up at the order of this captaincy-general for the purpose of inquiring whether the French who are in the presidio of Nachitos have gone beyond their boundary, removing it [the presidio] into lands of our sovereign under the same name, in order to dissimulate it and to come closer to our presidio of Los Adaes in the province of Texas. These *autos* were begun while the most excellent señor, the Count of Fuenclara was governing this New Spain, in consequence of the royal cedula dated in Buenretiro on July 15, 1740, in which his Majesty (may he rest in saintly glory), recounting what Señor Don Pedro de Vedoya y Osorio reported to him while he was *fiscal* of this royal *audiencia* with regard to the complaints which the missionary religious of the province of Zacatecas presented to this captaincy-general against Colonel Don Carlos De Franquis Benites de Lugo while he was governor of it, and to the charges that the latter made against Captain Don Manuel de Sandoval, accusing him of having allowed the French to move their presidio of Nachitos, as a result of his natural indolence or his covetous watchfulness in furthering his own interests. . . .

1147. In number 188 the following is added:

From the opinions of the señor *auditor general de la guerra* of March 6 and June 20, 1744, which he rendered after an examination of the *autos* and the criminal case formed by the said Colonel Don Carlos de Franquis against Don Manuel de Sandoval, supposing that he had permitted the French to move their presidio of Nachitos. . . .

1148. (Number 189.) An account was also given of the royal order issued in Aranjuez (this cedula is found copied above in paragraph 1098) on June 20, 1751, in which—because the most excellent señor, the Duke of La Conquista, had informed his Majesty that the French of New Orleans, spreading out and going beyond their boundaries, had advanced their colony and presidio of Nachitos toward the south, penetrating into the territories of the province of the Texas in usurpation and fraud against the eminent, commendable, and important possessions of the Spanish monarchy, locating themselves at a short distance from our presidio of Los Adaes—[his Majesty] orders the present most excellent señor viceroy that, reflecting most seriously on the matter, he shall be on the alert to check the advances of that power in that region, opposing the schemes and designs of the French nation, without leaving our territories exposed to the pernicious results of tolerating [them]. . . .

1149. (Number 194.) An account was also given of the reply rendered on this matter by the señor *fiscal* of his Majesty on February 1, 1751, and of the opinion of the señor *auditor*, dated on the 8th of the same month, by which, your Excellency approving, the present governor was ordered that, with the activity and zeal that a matter of such importance demands, he should proceed to make the necessary investigations with regard to the subject treated in the *consulta* of the said commandant, and as to whether the Mississippi River should serve as boundary for the French nation, in order, in view of his report, to make suitable decisions.

1150. An account was also given of the *consulta* with which the said governor remits the judicial proceedings executed by him for this purpose, in which it is seen from the declarations of the witnesses examined pursuant thereto, first, that the French have gone beyond the Río Colorado [Red River] which used to serve them as boundary before the year 1720, penetrating since then toward the presidio of Los Adaes. Some [of the witnesses] stated in confirmation of this that when the French remained within the said boundary, they did not pursue their deserters beyond the river, and neither were the Spanish deserters followed [across the river]; and that this does not hold true today with regard to the French, for during the time of Governor Sandoval and through no fault of his, they came in. Nevertheless, even if he had wanted to resist them he would not have succeeded in doing so because of his small forces, and because of the many that the Frenchman has through his alliance with the Indians. . . .

1151. (Number 202.) Finally, an account was given of the superior decree of his Excellency dated on the 13th of the current month, in which he ordered that a *junta de guerra y hacienda* be called, so that the following points might be decided in it:

1152. First, as to whether a guard of twenty soldiers with an officer of experience and zeal should be stationed on the Río de San Pedro in order to observe the plans of the French and the motives they have had for increasing their settlements, the principal care of this officer being to win over and attract those Indians who rule the entire province and the rest of the nations in it.

1153. Whether one of the engineers who are in this kingdom should be sent in order to assist the governor and help him in bringing about the restoration of the usurped territory, establishing rules and preventing the occupation of any other in the future.

1154. Whether the French should be obliged for the present to leave the usurped land, without having recourse to force of arms, as his Majesty directs in the first part of his royal order, but rather making use for the moment of more circumspect measures until, the results being seen, fitting dispositions may be made; and whether in case of not attaining our ends by means of politic demands, they should be compelled by force and the requisite orders given to the governor and presidials of the province of Texas. . . .

1155. (Number 209.) Whether, in order that [the junta] may be fully informed on a matter of such importance as the present one, all the papers relative thereto should be sought and added to these *autos;* and whether all the documents should be sought with special care that have a bearing on the question of whether the boundary or dividing line between the dominions of France and Spain is the Río Colorado [Red River] or the Mississippi, inquiring if there is any order or command of his Majesty with regard to this point so that, bearing it in mind, the danger of a conflict with any treaty which may have been made between the two crowns may be avoided.

1156. Finally, whether the execution of that decided upon should be entrusted to the governor of the said province. The junta having examined all the points stated with the care, reflection, and attention that their contents demand, it was resolved unanimously that there is no occasion for the establishment which the governor of the province of Texas requests shall be made on the Río de San Pedro with a guard of twenty soldiers and an experienced and zealous officer, to observe the plans of the French and the reasons they have had for increasing their settlements. [There is even] less [occasion] for sending the engineer who has been mentioned, since, although from the proceedings drawn up by the present governor of the province of Texas it seems that the French have gone beyond their territory, beginning with the time when Don Manuel de Sandoval was governor of that province, it is not clear from these proceedings what the boundary between New Orleans and his Majesty's possessions should be—whether the Río Colorado [Red River], Gran Montaña, or some other place. Heretofore, from proceedings previously executed, *it appears that the line should be at the place of La Gran Montaña, or Arroyo Hondo,* halfway between the French presidio of Nachitos and that of Los Adaes, capital of the province of Texas, and therefore it is not known to what [places the French] should be restricted, nor the amount, extent and location of the lands they have occupied. In order to obtain a complete understanding of these lands—their extent, location, and landmarks, and of whether the Río Colorado or some other stream is the dividing line of the two territories—the present governor is ordered to take immediately all the necessary measures to obtain full information as to what is the line that divides the lands of the two monarchies, receiving for this purpose the necessary declarations and executing all the requisite judicial proceedings condusive to this end, as well as to that of clearing up the matter of what year the said French began to penetrate the lands of our sovereign, what amount they occupy, its territories and boundaries, what settlements, forts, and presidio they have built, their names and garrisons, and their present conditions and circumstances. If it results from the governor's execution of these measures that the Río Colorado, or one of the other places cited is the boundary between the two territories, and that the French have passed beyond it with settlements and fortifications, he shall require the governor, or commandant, of the presidio of Nachitos, in the name of his Catholic Majesty, to abandon and to leave free and unobstructed all the land that he may have occupied and to withdraw and restrict himself to his own possessions. For this purpose he [the governor of Texas] shall point out to him [the French commandant] that the lands into which he has penetrated belong to our sovereign, as shown by the proceedings that he may execute.

1157. [The governor is ordered] that this measure shall be repeated as many as three times, presenting to the [French] commandant all the courteous demands which his zeal may dictate in order to induce him to withdraw, and that if by reason of these representations the commandant of Nachitos should be prevailed upon to withdraw and restrict himself to his own possessions, the governor in this case shall go and destroy all the fortifications, trenches, and other strong places that he may have constructed, leaving permanent landmarks on the dividing line between the two territories, so that in the future a similar dispute may be avoided. In case the courteous demands which have been mentioned do not have any effect, the governor shall send to this captaincy-general all the proceedings that he may have executed in order that—the refusal of that commandant to return the land which he has occupied to the detriment of his Majesty being made clear to his Excellency, and the fact that neither demonstrating to him his Majesty's dominion and ownership, nor the diplomatic requirements made to him, have moved him or sufficed to make him retire—his Excellency may adopt such measures as he considers most opportune for the exact fulfillment of the royal order of June 20, 1751. A letter shall be written to the said governor [and sent] with a certified copy of [the proceedings of] this junta, informing him that when the Señor Marquis of San Miguel de Aguayo went by order of this captaincy-general to dislodge the French who had invaded those dominions, he took possession of all of them in the name of his Majesty. Among them were included the lands which they occupy today and on which they have settled and fortified themselves, for [Spain] had acquired dominion over and rights to them since the year 1690, and they began their settlement on our land subsequent to the possession taken by the said Señor Marquis of San Miguel de Aguayo, while Don Manuel de Sandoval was governor of the province of Texas.

1158. And [the governor is ordered] not to make use of arms in either case, but to avail himself only of courteous requirements which are to be sent to the commandant, bearing in mind that he must present them in the most polite and diplomatic manner, in view of the good relations existing between the two crowns and in consideration of [the maintenance of] the close alliance that may be involved therein. . . . Thus they resolved, and affixed their rubrics. Señores, his Excellency, Valcárcel, etc.

1159. The governor of Texas, having received these orders, proceeded to execute them, as he himself says in the following (number 248 of the aforecited document):

In the royal presidio of Nuestra Señora del Pilar de los Adaes on the 17th day of the month of February of this present year of 1753, I, Don Jacinto de Barrios y Jáuregui, etc., having seen the preceding decree, issued in conformance with what had been resolved in the *junta de guerra y hacienda* by the most excellent señor, Don Juan Francisco de Güemes y Horcasitas, the Count of Revilla Gigedo, etc., say that I obey it wholly and absolutely, as an order of my superior, and so that my prompt compliance with the superior mandate may be evident, and everything contained in it may be put into due operation, I hereby order, as is my obligation, that the investigation be begun as directed therein. For the attainment of this end, let reliable persons be summoned, including some of those who entered with the Señor Marquis of San Miguel de Aguayo, so that with more clarity and precision they may give individual accounts of everything upon which it is expedient to question them, for which purpose let the corresponding interrogatory be drawn up. I so provided, ordered, and signed, etc.

1160. In the abovesaid presidio on the said day, month, and year, I, the said governor, in conformance with that which I ordered in the preceding *auto*, drew up the following interrogatory:

1161. First, let the witnesses be examined as to what is the boundary line that divides the two monarchies, the Spanish and the French, in the area that lies between the royal presidio of Los Adaes and the place on which formerly stood that of San Juan Bautista de Nachitos; since when [it has been so regarded], how, and in what manner. Thus let them state, etc.

1162. [In reply] to the second question let them state in what year the French penetrated into the dominions of our sovereign in that region.

1163. [In reply] to the third question, let them state how much territory the French have usurped with the removal of their presidio to the lands of his Catholic Majesty.

1164. [In reply] to the fourth and last question, let them state what forts, settlements, or presidios they [the French] have built. On the said day, month, and year, before me and the assisting witnesses, as has been stated, and to which I attest. Don Jacinto de Barrios y Jáuregui.

1165. This interrogatory having been completed, the inquiry was begun in the following manner:

Declaration of Don Juan Antonio Amorín[38] (sixty-eight years of age, more or less), given on February 17, 1753. To the first question he replied that he

---

[38]This name is spelled "Morín" in paragraph 1085, *supra*.

knows, because he heard it said when the troops entered this presidio, that the dividing line between the two monarchies used to be the Río Colorado, for which reason he has always considered as the part belonging to our Catholic King the land on this side of the said river; and thus he replies. To the second question he replied that in conformity with what was stated in the preceding question the French moved to this side of the Río Colorado in the year '35 or '36, while Don Manuel de Sandoval was governing this province, he being at the time on his general visit of inspection; but that also a long time before this removal some Frenchmen had crossed to this side, at which place the declarant also saw that three houses remained without giving rise to any discussion. These houses were found there when the officers of the Señor Marquis of San Miguel de Aguayo went at his orders to reconnoiter the banks of the said river. Thus he replies. To the third question he replied that the territory which he considers usurped may be about the breadth of a stone's throw, which is the distance from the bank of the said Río Colorado, where they have their presidio today, to the place where it used to be on the other side of the said river. Thus he replies. To the fourth question he replied that he does not know nor has he heard it said that the French have built more forts or presidios in the dominions of our sovereign than the one which has been mentioned, etc.

1166. Declaration of Don José González, fifty-three years of age, more or less. To the first question he replied that since the time of the arrival of the troops at this royal presidio, he has always heard it said that the boundary line that divides the two monarchies is the Río Colorado, which the French call Rus (that is, Rouge) and the Spaniards Rojo [Red River]. For this reason he considers the land on this side of the river as belonging to our Catholic King, and that on the other side as belonging to the Most Christian King. He saw that the French were settled at the latter place when the Señor Marquis of San Miguel de Aguayo entered, and he saw also three little houses on this side, which were kept there without any question for a long time thereafter; thus it seems to him that the dividing line between the two crowns is the said river. He is further persuaded of this because of what happened about twenty-four years ago, more or less, when, after the very reverend father president of these missions, Fray Francisco Ballejo, at the urgent request of the commandant of Nachitos, Don Luis de St. Denis, had gone to baptize a child of his, with the permission of the curate of that place, and the latter having repented of his action, the said commandant, angered, told the said reverend father president that they would cross to this side of the said river where, since they would be on lands that belong to the Catholic King, he could baptize the child. This was not done; and thus he replies. (See the note placed at the end of this declaration with regard to this action.) To the second question, he replied that during the year '35 or '36, while Don Manuel de Sandoval was governor of this province, the French moved to this side of the river where they are settled today. But the declarant also remembers that already, a long time before this happened, some settlers had moved there, for three little houses

remain on this side of the river which were in the same place at the time
of the entrance of the said señor marquis; and thus he replies. To the third
question he replied that it seems to him that the land the French have occupied
is about the extent of a musket-shot; and thus he replies. To the fourth
question he replied that neither before nor after the French moved to this
side of the river have they built or fortified other presidios or forts in the
dominions of our sovereign than the one of Nachitos, nor have they done
so on their own lands aside from those which they had when the Spanish
troops came into this province, etc.

1167. And which were those forts that they had previously?
Most assuredly one of them was that of Cadodachos, because St.
Denis took it in very bad part that Los Adaes should be settled
by the Marquis of San Miguel de Aguayo, in as much as with this
settlement the easy and convenient passage to the said Cadodachos
(see number 88 of document 21, copied above in paragraph 333)
and to the pueblo of the Arcansas would be closed to him, as we
have proven in paragraph 64, above. Consequently, along with the
lands of the Cadodachos and Arcansas, they appropriated those
which are drained by the rivers which bear these names and by
those that flow into them, but with the limitation that we have
noted in paragraph 352. We have seen concerning the Panis,[39]
beginning with paragraph 158, that they were already known to
the French and that the latter even had a settlement among them.
See above, paragraph 361, where we mention other forts that the
French had already constructed for themselves when these declarations were made. The story told here concerning the baptism
mentioned proves nothing against the French because, taking the
child to be baptized on the other side of the river would necessitate the baptism taking place in [one of] the houses that the French
had there, or in the open, or in the church of Los Adays. [It could
not be done in] the houses, first, because it is forbidden to administer baptisms in private homes unless in case of necessity.
The holy Council of Vienne[40] so orders, from the text of which

[39]"In fact, on D'Anville's map . . . the Panis are on the banks of the Río
Panis at about 40° 52' of latitude and 78° 58' of the same longitude. There
are other Panis who are found in 42° 34' of latitude and about 80° of longitude. . . . On Bellin's map . . . the first Panis are found a little above the
41st parallel of latitude and 100° 20' of longitude west of the meridian of
Paris."—*Pichardo's Treatise* . . . , Vol. III, p. 187

[40]"Pope Clement V, by the Bull 'Regnans in coelis' of 12 Aug., 1308, called
a general council to meet on 1 Oct., 1310, at Vienne in France for the purpose
'of making provision in regard to the Order of Knights Templar, . . . and in

was drawn up the only Clementine [canon] on baptism;[41] and the *Roman Ritual*,[42] published by order of his Holiness, Paul V, in title 9, [numbers] 2 and 3, states in conformance with this canon that

although in case of urgent necessity there is no prohibition against baptizing in any place whatsoever, nevertheless the proper place for administering baptism is in the church in which there is a baptismal font, or in a baptistry adjoining the church. Aside from a case of necessity, therefore, no one shall be baptized in private homes unless it be children of kings or of great princes, and they ask that it be done thus. In such cases let baptism be administered in their oratories or chapels with baptismal water solemnly blessed.

In the second place, [the child could not be baptized in one of the houses] because these houses, as property of the French, it seems would belong to the parish of Natchitoches, and thus baptism could not be administered there against the will of the said priest. Nor could the baptism have been administered in the open, this also being forbidden because, aside from many other rules, the same one holds true which exists for not administering it in [private] houses. Then the child should have been brought to Los Adays where there was a church with all the parochial privileges. Thus, in case St. Denis might have proposed the plan described, it should be understood that he was speaking of the church of Los Adays. Why? Are we to assume that he was so ignorant that he did not know this very obvious point of the ecclesiastical discipline? Aside from this he would be charged with the further

---

regard to other things in reference to the Catholic Faith, the Holy Land, and the improvement of the Church and of ecclesiastical persons.' "—*The Catholic Encyclopedia*, Vol. XV, pp. 423–424.

[41] "The Acts of the council [of Vienne—see preceding note] have disappeared . . . consequently there is no positive certainty as to the course of the synod. . . . As already mentioned, the bishops were directed before the meeting to bring with them written suggestions as to the reform of the Church. . . . All that is certain is that a number of decrees on these subjects were proclaimed. These were issued later on 25 October, 1317, by John XXII, together with other decrees of Clement V, which the latter had been prevented by death from promulgating. John published them as the collection of the laws of the Church, the Clementines, 'Corpus Juris Canonici.' "—*The Catholic Encyclopedia*, Vol. XV, p. 424.

[42] "The Ritual *(Rituale Romanum)* is one of the official books of the Roman Rite. It contains all the services performed by a priest that are not in the Misal and Breviary and has also, for convenience, some that are in those books . . . . In 1614 Paul V published the first edition of the official ritual by the Constitution 'Apostolicae Sedis' of 17 June."—*The Catholic Encyclopedia*, Vol. XIII, pp. 88–89.

ignorance of desiring that his child be baptized by a parish priest different from his own. St. Denis knew the Latin language; he was a Catholic Christian; and it is known from all his writings and actions that he was very well informed.

1168. In view of all this I believe that the incident occurred in another way, or that if he did burst forth with the words mentioned, it was because of an outbreak of the anger which perturbs man on occasion to the point that he says that which in calmer moments he would not dare to say. Nor were the houses of the sort that this declarant and those who follow here represent them to be, for from the description that they give of them it is inferred that they were small houses, let us say, in the form of miserable huts; but they really were not such. Let us hear the following statement of the señor *auditor de guerra*, Don Domingo Valcárcel, taken from his opinion copied below, which is found in paragraph 1264:

> Some (witnesses) were on the expedition which the Marquis of San Miguel de Aguayo led during the year 1721, and they saw that they [the French] had some houses and cattle on this side of the river, to which the presidio has been moved, and the said Marquis left them in undisturbed possession there. Testimony to this effect is given by the fifth witness, who is Dr. Don José Codallos y Rabal, a canon of the holy Metropolitan Church of Mexico, an individual of extraordinary energy and intelligence, who entered with the Marquis and examined all those countries and took a leading part in the expedition, having twice lodged in a house with good accommodations which Monsieur Pierre had on this side of the Río Colorado, where he had established an hacienda. He [Dr. Codallos], replying with the other witnesses on various matters, declares openly that the transferred presidio is in territory belonging to the French, this admitting of no doubt, and that on that occasion, by agreement with the French, La Montaña Grande, which is midway between the two points, was designated by the clause "for the present" as the boundary between the presidios of Nachitos and Los Adays. The others unanimously agree with this.

1169. Is the house which Señor Codallos describes here the one which these witnesses picture? And what shall we say about these last words of Señor Codallos? To wit: that the transferred presidio was on territory belonging to the French, this admitting of no doubt, and that at that time by an agreement with them La Montaña Grande, which is midway between the two [posts] was designated by the clause "for the present" (a present which never ended) as the boundary between the presidios of Nachitos and Los Adays. Then, even though Monsieur de St. Denis might have thought through ignorance that it would be legal for him to take his son to the other side of the river in order that he might receive holy baptism, he would speak with the idea that he would have to go as far as Los Adays. All these considerations are valuable also in so far as they militate against [the testimony of] the following witnesses.

1170. Declaration of Don Felipe Muñoz de Mora, about sixty-six years of age. To the first question he replied that the dividing line between the two crowns is the Río Colorado [Red River], under which supposition he considers as the possessions of our Catholic King the lands on this side of the said river. He says this because on the Río de Nechas, when the troops entered,[43] he heard that Don Luis de St. Denis said to the Señor Marquis of San Miguel de Aguayo that he could establish his presidio on the bank of the Río Colorado on this side, for which purpose he would take away his ranch house which was there, together with two other houses.

(If this anecdote were true in all its parts, Bachiller Peña would not have been ignorant of it and consequently he would have written it down in his diary of the expedition of the Marquis of San Miguel de Aguayo, but he says not a word about this. See numbers 89 and 118 of document 21, in which he treats of the meeting that Monsieur de St. Denis had with the said Marquis, of everything that took place at it, of the contents of a letter written by Monsieur de Rerenou [Rerenau][44] and, finally, of that which oc-

_____

[43]When the Marquis of San Miguel de Aguayo in the summer of 1721 approached the Neches River en route to east Texas to re-establish the Spanish settlements there, a Frenchman arrived at the Spanish camp who had been sent by Captain Louis de St. Denis from the mission of La Concepción to request of the Marquis the safe conduct for coming and discussing matters of interest to the two crowns. The Marquis granted this safe conduct because St. Denis was represented as "commandant of French forces in Natchitoches and on the entire frontier of all that the French possessed." The Marquis advanced to meet St. Denis, but on account of the high water in the Neches River, he was delayed eight days in crossing it and, in order to do so, it was finally necessary to construct a bridge thirty-two varas long and four varas wide. There with all his captains the Marquis received St. Denis.— The Marquis of San Miguel de Aguayo to the viceroy, Nuestra Señora de Guadalupe, August 19, 1721.

[44]In a letter written by the Marquis of San Miguel de Aguayo to the king, dated Coahuila, June 13, 1722, the Marquis says: "And I continued my journey to Los Adaes, where I arrived on August 29 [1721]. Forthwith the commandant at Natchitoches, Monsieur Rerenau, endeavored by innuendos to embarras me in the occupation of that place, saying that he did not have permission from Mobile to allow me to fortify and take possession of that

curred between this captain of Natchitoches and Don Fernando
Pérez de Almazán[45] and Don Gabriel Costales.)[46]

This report was also enlarged upon later, after, by order of the said marquis,
his captains went with Doctor Codallos to examine the banks of the said
river; to them Monsieur Vrno (that is, Rerenou), at that time commandant
of Nachitos, said the same thing that the said Don Luis stated on the Nechas.
Thus he replied. To the second question he replied that in the year '34 or
'35 the French moved their presidio to this side of the Río Colorado, during
the time that Don Manuel de Sandoval was governing this province, but that
already before this occurrence some Frenchmen had crossed to this side
of the said river; and thus he replies. To the third question he replied that the
land which the French have occupied in our possessions is probably the area
covered by a stone's throw; and thus he replies. To the fourth question he
said that the French have not constructed additional forts or presidios since
they moved to this side of the river, other than that of Nachitos, nor is
he aware that they have established in their dominions other than those
they had when the troops entered, etc.

1171. Declaration of Don Manuel Antonio Losoya, fifty-three years of age,
more or less. To the first question he replied that he always considered the
Río Colorado [Red River] as the dividing line between [the possessions of]
the two Majesties, because he has heard it said ever since the Señor Marquis
of San Miguel de Aguayo entered that everything on this side of the river
belonged to our Catholic King, and everything on the other side of the said
river to the Most Christian King. The French were settled in that place at
the time of the *entrada* of the said señor marquis, with the exception of
some three houses which were on this side of the river. Although he heard
it said at that time that they would have to move to the other side, the
declarant saw that they continued in the same place in which they were; and
thus he replies. To the second question he replied that the French moved
their presidio to this side of the river, on the very bank of it where they
are settled today, in the year '34 or '35, while Don Manuel de Sandoval was
governor of this province, he being at that time in San Antonio, but that
already before this some Frenchmen had moved to this side of the said river;
and thus he replies. To the third question he replied that the land which
he judges was occupied by the French is probably the breadth of a stone's
throw, which is the distance from the bank of the said river to the place
where they are settled; and thus he replies. To the fourth question he replied that he has not seen nor has he understood that the French have built

---

district, and therefore that I ought to desist from so doing. But, having
answered him that I was carrying contrary instructions and that I was obliged
to do so in order to carry out fully the truce terms, he gave up his design,
agreeing, as did the commandant, St. Denis, that we were obliged to observe
the truce."

[45]Fernando Pérez de Almazán was governor of Texas from 1722 to 1726.
[46]Captain Gabriel Costales is mentioned by Bolton (*Texas . . .* , p. 23) as
presidio commander at La Bahía in 1740.

or fortified any other post or presidio, aside from that of Nachitos, either in the dominions of our sovereign or in their own, etc.

1172. Declaration of Don Pedro de Sierra, about fifty-one years of age. To the first question he replied that he has always considered as lands of our sovereign everything on this side of the Río Colorado [Red River], because of having heard it said ever since the time the troops entered that the Río Colorado served as the dividing line between the two crowns. This is proven by the fact that before moving to this side of the river the French did not pursue their deserters farther than to the bank on the other side of the said river, and today they follow them as far as the Arroyo Hondo; and [he stated] also that if the said site had not been considered as belonging to our sovereign, the three demands made in the name of Don Manuel de Sandoval to the commandant of Nachitos when he was moving to this side of the river, to prevent his doing it, would not have been made; and thus he replies. To the second question he replied that in the year '34 or '35 the French moved to this side of the Río Colorado, but that the deponent also remembers that before this happened some had already moved, there being previously three houses on this side of the said river, which were in the same place when the troops entered; and thus he replies. To the third question he replied that the land which the French had occupied is probably a stone's throw in breadth, more or less; and thus he replies. To the fourth question he replied that he has not seen or understood that the French have constructed or fortified additional posts or presidios in the possessions of our sovereign, other than that of Nachitos, or any others on the lands of their monarch, aside from those they had when the troops entered, etc.

1173. Declaration of Marcos Ruiz, about fifty-two years of age. To the first question he replied that since the entrance of the troops he has always heard it said that the boundary which divides the two monarchies is the Río Colorado [Red River], the land on this side of which he has always considered as belonging to Spain and that on the other side to France. This is confirmed by what he heard Don Luis de St. Denis, who used to be the commandant of Nachitos, say when at his request the very reverend father president of these missions, Fray Francisco Ballejo, went to baptize his child. When the priest on that side had declined to permit it after first having given his consent, the said commandant returned to the said father president and told him that they would all cross to this side of the river where, since they would be in the possessions of the Catholic King, he could baptize him, which was not done. The declarant, however, is not aware of any legal proof that the said Río Colorado is the only dividing line, nor yet that La Gran Montaña or Arroyo Hondo, which he also heard was the boundary between the two crowns, is such; and thus he replies. To the second question he replied that in the year '35 or '36, while Don Manuel de Sandoval was governor of this province, the French moved to this side of the river, but that some Frenchmen had already done so; and also that three houses remained on the said site which were there when the troops entered. Thus

he replies. To the third question he replied that the land which the French
have appropriated by their removal to this side of the river is probably a
stone's throw in breadth; and thus he replied. To the fourth question he
replied that from the time the troops entered until the present he has not
seen or known that the French have constructed or fortified other posts or
presidios than that of Nachitos in the possessions of our sovereign, nor does
he know that they have done so in their own possessions during the said
time . . .; and that all he has said and declared is the truth, etc.

1174. Declaration of Corporal Felipe de Sierra, about fifty-three years
of age. To the first question he replied that he has always recognized as
possessions of our Catholic King the lands on which today is established
the presidios of Nachitos, because he has heard it said since the time that
the troops entered, that the Río Colorado [Red River] was the dividing line
between the two crowns, a fact which is verified by the three demands which
were made by the señor governor, Sandoval, to the commandant of Nachitos
at the time that he was moving to this side of the said river. It is inferred
from this that if this place had not belonged to our sovereign, they would
not have made these demands to the said commandant. But the declarant is
not aware of any legal proof that the said river is the dividing line, nor
that La Gran Montaña or Arroyo Hondo would be such; he has also heard
it said, although only as a current rumor (it was not only a rumor, for the
Marquis of San Miguel de Aguayo had made an agreement with St. Denis
to this effect—see paragraph 1169), that [this place] was the boundary between the two crowns. Thus he replies. To the second question he replied
that the French moved to this side of the river in the year '34 or '35, but
that some of them had crossed a long time before this event. He also mentioned the fact that three small houses which were on this side when the
troops entered had not been moved to the other side of the river. Thus he
replies. To the third question he replied that the land which the French
appropriated for themselves when they moved to this side of the river, where
they are settled today, is about the breadth of a stone's throw; and thus
he replies. To the fourth question he replied that the French have neither
constructed nor fortified in the possessions of our sovereign any additional
forts or presidios aside from that of Nachitos, nor have they constructed any
in their own possessions other than those which they had when the troops
entered, etc.

1175. Declaration of Lázaro Ybáñez, about fifty-two years of age. To the
first question he replied that since the time that the troops entered he has
always heard it said that the Río Colorado [Red River] used to serve as the
boundary line between the two crowns. Under this supposition he has always
considered that everything on this side of the said river belonged to our
sovereign and everything on the other side of the same river belonged to
the King of France. This is corroborated by what he also heard at that
time, to the effect that three houses which were on this side of the said
river would have to be moved to the other, but they remained in the same
place without any change. The declarant has always understood that the

said river was the boundary in spite of the fact that it has also been re-ported that it was La Gran Montaña, or the Arroyo Hondo; and thus he replies. To the second question he replied that the French moved to this side of the Río Colorado in the year '34 or '35, but that already before this occurrence some others had done so; and thus he replies. To the third question he replied that the territory which the French have occupied in the lands of our sovereign is about the breadth of a stone's throw; and thus he replies. To the fourth question he replied that the French have neither constructed nor fortified in the dominions of our sovereign any additional posts or presidios aside from that of Nachitos; and that every-thing he has said is the truth, etc.

1176. Declaration of José Antonio Rosales, about fifty-five years of age. To the first question he replied that he does not know exactly what may be the boundary line that divides the two monarchies, for, although when the troops entered he heard it said that it was the Río Colorado—on this side of which everything belonged to our Catholic King, and all on the other side to the Most Christian King—he also heard it said that the boundary line between the two Majesties was La Gran Montaña or the Arroyo Hondo. However, if he were asked on the basis of what he has stated to judge which of the two places should be the boundary, the declarant would be inclined to believe that it is the said Río Colorado, not only because when the French moved their presidio to this side of the river the commandant was notified three times not to do it, but also because at the time that the Señor Marquis of San Miguel de Aguayo entered he heard it said that the commandant who was then at Nachitos had told the Spaniards, when they went to examine the banks of the said river, that they could place their presidio where the said presidio of Nachitos is today, for which purpose they [the French] would move to the other side of the said river three houses which were on this side at that time. Notwithstanding what has been stated, the de-clarant noticed that [the houses] remained where they were; and thus he replies. To the second question he replied that in the year '34 or '35 the French moved to this side of the said river, but that some of them had done so previously; and thus he replies. To the third question he replied that the territory which the French have occupied, in case the said river is the boundary line, is about a stone's throw in breadth; and thus he replies. To the fourth question he replied that the French have neither constructed nor fortified in the dominions of our sovereign any presidio whatsoever aside from that of Nachitos, etc.

1177. Declaration of Cayetano Games, about fifty-three years of age. To the first question he replied that he does not know positively what the dividing line between the two monarchies may be, for up to the present there has not come to his notice any legal instrument that would determine it, but, from reports he has heard of what happened when the officers of the Señor Marquis of San Miguel de Aguayo went at his order to examine the banks of the said Río Colorado [Red River] they told the [French] commandant, who at that time was Monsieur Vrnó (that is, Rerenou), that they were coming in the name of the Catholic King to found a presidio there. The said commandant agreed to this, saying that they could locate it on the bank of the said river on this side, for which purpose three houses which were at that time on this side would be moved to the other. The declarant judges the said Río Colorado to be the boundary that used to divide the two monarchies. The truth of this supposition is confirmed by the statement which the declarant heard the said commandant had made on that occasion, advising the aforesaid Spaniards to go upstream above Caudachos, everything they might reconnoiter on this side to belong to Spain, and everything on the other to France. This reconnaissance did not take place, nor were the said houses removed to the other side; and thus he replies. To the second question he replied that the French had moved to this side of the Río Colorado, where they are settled today, in the year '34 or '35, but that some had also done so previously; and thus he replies. To the third question he replied that the territory occupied by the French in the possessions of our monarch is about a stone's throw in breadth; and thus he replies. To the fourth question he replied that he does not know nor has he heard it said that the French have built other posts or presidios in the possessions of our sovereign aside from that of Nachitos; and that everything he has said is the truth, etc.

1178. Declaration of Cristóbal de Santiago, about fifty-three years of age. To the first question he replied that what he knows with regard to what the boundary may be between the two crowns is that the Señor Marquis of San Miguel de Aguayo, a few days after his arrival at the place where this presidio is established today, sent his captains to examine the banks of the Río Colorado on this side, and that when the commandant who was then in Nachitos received them, they told him that they were coming in the name of our Catholic King to establish a presidio there. The said commandant agreed to this, saying that they could place it on the bank of the said river and that this river would serve as the boundary that would divide the two monarchies. For this purpose three houses which were on this side would be removed to the other side of the said river. The declarant saw that the houses remained in the same place, and he stated that what he has said he knows from having heard it at that time. He heard also that La Gran Montaña or the Arroyo Hondo was the boundary that divided Nachitos and Los Adaes. Thus he replies. To the second question he replied that in the year '34 or '35 the French crossed to this side of the Río Colorado, but that also a long time before some others had already done so; and thus he replies. To the third question he replied that the territory that the French have occupied in the domains of our sovereign is about a stone's throw in breadth; and thus he replies. To the fourth question he replied that from the time the troops entered down to the present, the French have not constructed or fortified any additional forts or presidios in the possessions of our Catholic King, aside from that of Nachitos; and that everything he has said is the truth, etc.

1179. Declaration of Manuel Salvador de Pozos, about sixty years of age. He replied to the first question that because of the long time that has elapsed from the entry of the troops into this province down to the present, he cannot give a detailed account with regard to the content of this question, but that by recalling to memory some of the events that came to his attention at that time, the declarant presumes that the dividing line between the two monarchies is the Río Colorado [Red River]. His reason for saying this is based on the fact that when the Spaniards went to reconnoiter the banks of the said river, it was generally believed that everything on this side of it belonged to Spain, and all on the other to France. From this rumor also originated the report which the declarant heard to the effect that three houses which were on this side would have to be moved to the other. Since, however, the houses remain where they were, the declarant infers that from this toleration and dissimulation arises the fact that the boundary line between the two majesties is in doubt. The matter was made even more uncertain by the rumor, current at that same time, that the boundary which divided the two presidios was La Gran Montaña or the Arroyo Hondo. Thus he replies. To the second question he replied that the French moved their presidio to this side of the said river, on which bank they are settled today, in the year '34 or '35, but the declarant also remembers that even before the said occurrence some Frenchmen had crossed to the same place; and thus he replies. To the third question he replied that the territory usurped by the French from our Catholic King is about a stone's throw in breadth, this being true in case the said river is the dividing line. Thus he replies. To the fourth question he replied that assuming what he has stated in the preceding question to be true, the French from the time of the entrance of our troops to the present have neither constructed nor fortified any presidios in the possessions of our monarch aside from that of Nachitos; and that everything he has stated is the truth, etc.

As a consequence of these judicial inquiries, Señor Barrios proceeded with others, as we shall see.

1180. (Number 268.) In the royal presidio of Nuestra Señora del Pilar de los Adays, on the 28th day of the month of February of this year 1753, I, Don Jacinto de Barrios y Jáuregui, governor and captain-general of this province of Texas, Nuevas Filipinas, having seen with due attention and reflection these proceedings executed by me by virtue of the preceding superior decree of September 26 of the past year of '52, issued by the most excellent señor viceroy in conformance with what had been resolved in the *junta de real hacienda y guerra* of the 25th of the same month—since the result of these proceedings which I was ordered in the said decree to execute does not, in my opinion, demonstrate with that certainty which is required what the dividing line should be between this aforecited presidio and the place at which formerly stood that of San Juan Baptista de Nachitos, because of the variations of the witnesses in their depositions—it has seemed appropriate to me, in order to proceed with the certainty and circumspection that

a matter so serious as the present one demands, first of all, to give an account
of these proceedings to the said most excellent señor in order that his Excellency in view of it may be pleased to command me as to what I ought to
do in the matter. And so that the aforesaid may be promptly executed, I
order that complete certified copies of these proceedings be made, so that
while the copies remain in this archive, as a precaution against the accidents that may occur, the originals may be sent to the said most excellent
señor viceroy. I thus provided, ordered, and affixed my signature, together
with those of my witnesses, as stated and to which I attest. Jacinto de
Barrios y Jáuregui, etc.

Having made the report to his Excellency, he [Barrios] continued with the following proceedings which we have also cited
previously, in Part I, paragraph 400.

1181. Don Jacinto de Barrios y Jáuregui, etc. In as much as it has come
to my notice that the French trade and traffic with the Texas, San Pedro,
Nacodoches, Nasones, and Nadotes Indians, [who are] included in this province under my jurisdiction, providing them with shirts, blankets, breechclouts,
muskets, powder, shot, beads, vermilion, and other articles valued by these
nations, at the same time winning the good will of those principal Indians,
leaders in the said pueblos, distinguishing them from the others with gifts
of braided hats, military coats, and other things esteemed among them; and
bearing in mind that, the aforesaid being true, it is indispensable that
effectual measures be applied to repair the damages that might follow,
which may be justly suspected now more than ever before in view of the
great attachment that these Indians have always manifested for the French,
as experience has shown; and likewise because of the continual defensive
measures which they [the French] have taken at their forts contiguous to
this province, which they are strengthening with families, settlers, and
munitions of war;

1182. And in order to take the opportune measures, and to employ a
person of the greatest dependability, so that, proceeding to investigate all
the foregoing, he may inform me of all that seems to him worthy of attention, I have decided to entrust and hereby do entrust this expedition to
Don Manuel Antonio de Soto Bermúdez, lieutenant general of the governor
of this said province, having entire confidence in him. By virtue of the above
and in order that what I have stated may be promptly and fully executed,
I command the said Don Manuel Antonio de Soto Bermúdez to go immediately and as quickly as possible to the aforecited pueblos. Upon reaching
them he is to investigate with sagacity, skill, and energy, and by such means
as seem to him most expedient, into the truth of all the aforesaid, examining
the place or places through which the French make their entrances and
exits. In the same manner he is to inquire into the number of Indians under
arms that there may be in the said district, and, in short, he is to execute
everything as one who has the matter well in mind. Finally, having formed

a reasoned opinion of all that he may have done in this business, he shall report to me so that in view of everything I may order whatever may be most fitting. I so provided, ordered, and affixed my signature, before myself and the assisting witnesses with whom I am acting for lack of a public or royal notary, there being none here in the sense prescribed by the law, and on this common paper because there is no official paper. It is dated in this royal presidio of Nuestra Señora del Pilar de los Adaes on the 30th day of the month of October of this present year of 1752. Jacinto de Barrios, etc.

1183. In the said royal presidio on the said day, month, and year, I, Don Jacinto de Barrios y Jáuregui, governor and captain-general of this province of Texas, Nuevas Filipinas, state: That in as much as my lieutenant general, Don Manuel Antonio de Soto Bermúdez, is ready to carry out the order which he has been given by me in the preceding *auto*, and since it is expedient that for its successful execution a person should accompany him who understands perfectly the language of the said Indians, and Don Antonio Barrera being entirely competent for this because of having lived for a long time among them and because he knows their natures and customs as well as their language, I named and hereby do name him as interpreter of the said language, in order that, knowing what the said Indians may reply in the presence of my said lieutenant in answer to what it may be appropriate to ask them, he may translate it without adding or taking away or changing the meaning [of the words] to any other sense than that commonly accepted. Let him be notified so that he may accept his appointment and be aware of what has been stated and keep it confidential. I thus provided, ordered, and affixed my signature, before myself and the assisting witnesses, as has been stated and to which I attest. Jacinto de Barrios y Jáuregui, etc.

1184. The commissioner, Bermúdez, began the execution of his charge in the following manner:

In the pueblo of Nacodoches, which is about three leagues distant from the mission of this name and fifty-three from the royal presidio of Los Adaes, on the 12th day of the month of November of the year 1752, I, Don Manuel Antonio de Soto Bermúdez, lieutenant general of the governor of this province of Texas, Nuevas Filipinas, in the name of the señor governor thereof, Don Jacinto de Barrios y Jáuregui, being in the dwelling of the captain of the said pueblo—who was given this position by Señor Don Pedro del Barrio Junco y Espriella, former governor and captain-general of this aforesaid province—and there being present the said captain, two *tamas*, officials of his, Antonio Barrera, my appointed interpreter, and my assisting witnesses;

1185. Feeling that it would be conducive to the success of that which is stated in the *auto* of the 30th of the past month, which stands at the head of these proceedings, to give presents to the said captain and officials, I presented him with various articles esteemed among them, which I carried along from the said governor for this purpose, and after having made proportionate gifts to the officials, I ordered the said interpreter to tell the aforesaid captain that I was making him that present in the name of the señor governor, who was sending it to him as a demonstration of the great love that he had for him, for which purpose I had come there; and also [I had come] to see his pueblo, in which, if it were large and pleased me, I would settle with other Spaniards.

1186. The presents having been received with demonstrations of pleasure, the interpreter said that having informed the captain of everything which he had been ordered to tell him, as he indicated, he replied that he was very grateful to the señor governor for the gift he was making him and that he would be very happy for me to settle in his pueblo with the Spaniards of whom I spoke; that in this way they would have trade and everything that they might need for their subsistence and they would not be forced to go for it among the French, nor would they allow them in their pueblo, and that necessity itself forced them to trade with them. In case the Spaniards settled among them, however, it ought not to be there, because the place was not convenient, but rather in a place which they call Nevantini because it has abundant water and pasturage. Their ancestors had lived in that place, and they themselves would all move to it and would help the Spaniards work.

1187. Asked through the interpreter of how many rancherias his pueblo was composed and how many adult Indians were in it—because in order for the Spaniards to be able to settle there it would be necessary for the pueblo to be large and the Indians numerous—according to the interpreter, who had acquainted him with everything that he had been ordered, as he showed, the captain replied: That in his pueblo are eleven large rancherias and in them fifty-two Indians bearing arms, and that in addition to these there were many young men almost capable of handling muskets.

1188. Asked through the interpreter from which direction the French come there when they enter to trade, and what articles they bring, the interpreter said, having asked him the question, as he indicated, that he replied that when the French come to their pueblo they come by way of the pueblo of Yatasi, which is on this side of the river that they call Los Adaes; that they bring deerskins, buckskins, muskets, shirts, breechclouts, powder, shot, vermilion, beads, combs, razors, large and small knives, mirrors, worms for firelocks, and flintlocks to sell; that at other times, when the river is flooded, they come in canoes and disembark at the said Yatasi or at Nadotes, and from there they advance to the other pueblos with their merchandise; that when they do not wish to enter these places, they summon from one of the two the *tamas* of the pueblos and deliver the goods to them so that they may distribute them among the Indians, who deliver to the French the skins which they carry back to Nachitos; and that at other times the French summon the Indians from here and deal with them in the manner which has been described.

(Father Fray Felix de Espinosa in his *Chrónica*,[47] book 5, chapter 9, page 420, defines as follows the office of the *tamas* of the

[47]For the full title of this work consult the bibliography in *Pichardo's Treatise* . . . , Vol. I, p. 550.

Texas: "The owners of the house, when they are ready to remodel it, advise the captains, whom they call in their language *caddi*, and the day being designated, they order the proctors, whom they call *tammas*, to go to all the houses and give notice to the people so that they may come to the building." In document 14, number 11, Father Casañas also explains this word. His statement is copied in Part II, paragraph 743.) [48]

1189. Asked through the interpreter how many rancherias and adult Indians were in the pueblos of Yatasi and Nadotes, the interpreter said that having asked him the question, as he showed, he replies that in the pueblo of Yatasi there are eight rancherias and thirty Indians bearing arms, and in that of Nadotes there are five rancherias and twenty Indians with muskets.

1190. Asked through the interpreter by whom the captains of the two said pueblos are named, the interpreter said that, having asked him the question, as he showed, he replies that the captains of the pueblos which he has been questioned about are named by the French; that the pueblo of Nadotes is under the charge of the official Don Luis de St. Denis; and that no one trades there except the said official. I, the said lieutenant general, certify that everything has taken place in the manner stated, and in order that it may be recorded, I sign it with my assisting witnesses, for lack of a notary, to which I attest. Manuel Antonio de Soto Bermúdez.

1191. In the pueblo of Nasones which is about eight leagues distant from that of Nacodoches, on the 14th day of the month of November of this present year of 1752, I, the said lieutenant general, in conformity with that which is ordered in the *auto* which is at the head of these proceedings, being in the dwelling of the *tama* of this pueblo, in the presence of the abovesaid appointed interpreter and my assisting witnesses, and having presented the said *tama* with various things which I brought for that purpose, I ordered the interpreter to ask him about the captain of the said pueblo and to give him to understand that I had come there at the order of the señor governor for the purpose of finding out whether the Indians lacked anything that they need; for, since they do not come to see the said señor governor, he does not know what they may lack. The interpreter having informed him of everything, as he showed, the *tama* said that the captain was in the pueblo of Nadotes, where he lived most of the time because of having moved his house to it, and that they did not go to Los Adaes because here they received everything they needed from the French.

1192. Asked through the interpreter from what direction the French come here, the interpreter said that, having asked him the question as he was ordered, he replies that sometimes they come by way of El Yatasi and at others by way of Nadotes, and that when they do not want to come to their pueblo, the captain receives everything the Indians need in Nadotes and distributes it among them.

[48]See *Pichardo's Treatise* . . . , Vol. II, p. 146.

1193. Asked through the interpreter by whom the captain of Nadotes is named, the interpreter said that having asked the question, as he showed, he replies that he was named by the official Don Luis de St. Denis, who had sent him a coat, a baton, and a hat; that he was also captain of Nasones; that the said pueblo of Nadotes is under the charge of the said official; and that no other merchandise except his enters it. Asked by the interpreter how many rancherias there are in the pueblos of Nasones and Nadotes and the number of adult Indians in them, the interpreter said that, having asked him the question, as he showed, he replies that in the pueblo of Nasones there are twenty-four rancherias and forty adult Indians bearing arms, and that in the pueblo of Nadotes there are five rancherias and twenty adult Indians.

1194. Asked through the interpreter what nations of Indians there are from that place toward the north, the interpreter said that having asked him the question, as he showed, he replies that twenty leagues from there are the Teguacanas, an exceedingly numerous nation, which at present is much larger because the Pelones have joined it; and that the Tebancanas [Teguacanas] are followed by the Tancaguies [Tancagues], the Yujanes, the Chicais, the Aguaxani, the Aguaxo, the Tancames, the Asinays, the Guaxes, the Huesos, the Tusas, the Enanos, and many other nations which he has not seen, but that all of them are friendly to the Texas.

1195. Asked through the interpreter whether Frenchmen go to those nations to trade, the interpreter said that, having asked him the question, he replies that some are accustomed to go to the Teguacanas, although he has no information that they go to the other nations; but that these nations are supplied with muskets, powder, shot, and everything else they need from themselves [the Indians of the captain's nation] and from the Teguacanas.

1196. Asked through the interpreter what means I should use in order to see the captain of Nasones, for I had to talk to him, the interpreter said that, having asked him the question, as he showed, he replies that I would see him soon since he was expecting him. He had sent for him [the captain of the Nasones] because of having received the day before yesterday a message from Captain Sánchez, who is the chief of the pueblo of Texas by appointment of Señor Don Pedro del Barrio Junco y Espriella, in which he notified him that he had learned that many Spaniards had left Los Adaes to arrest any Frenchmen whom they might find trading, and this he would by no means permit, since they supplied themselves from the French with everything they needed, which was not true with regard to the Spaniards. I, the said lieutenant general, certify that everything has taken place in the manner described, and in order that this may be recorded I put it into this judicial proceeding which I signed with my assisting witnesses, as has been stated and to which I attest. Manuel Antonio de Soto Bermúdez.

1197. In the said pueblo of Nasones on the 16th day of the month of November, 1752, I, the said lieutenant general of the governor, being on the point of going to the pueblo of Nadotes with its captain and those who are accompanying me, the captain of the said pueblo of Nadotes called the interpreter and spoke to him in his language. When I asked the said interpreter what it was that the said captain had told him, he replied that he had told him to tell me not to proceed farther, because if I tried to it would go badly with me. Being so informed, I ordered the said interpreter to ask the captain for what reason or motive he did not now want me to go to see his pueblo when he had already decided to accompany me, and especially when he knew that I was not going to it for any other purpose except to see it and to trade with the Indians there, as I had done in the other pueblos. The interpreter having so stated, as he showed, the captain replied that I must on no account go on, because he did not permit it, and that what I could do was to return. I, the said lieutenant—seeing him seemingly irritated and accompanied by many Indians, most of whom had come to receive goods from the Frenchman named La Flor, which he had sent there for this purpose by Indians on the afternoon of the preceding day—ordered the said interpreter to tell the captain to calm himself, for I had already decided to return, which I would do as soon as my beasts arrived. This having been done by the said interpreter, as he showed, the said captain, from the appearance of his face, quieted down.

1198. This occurrence having stirred in me an unusual curiosity, I asked the said interpreter what he thought was the cause of such a strange decision on the part of the said Indian captain, especially when on the day before he had consented to my going to his pueblo. To this the said interpreter replied that it seemed to him that it was all due to the said Frenchman, because he had found the two talking together at an unusual time of the night, and they stopped talking when he was present. And I, the said lieutenant general, having executed what I have explained in the manner in which I have stated, certify to it, and in order that it may be recorded I put it into this judicial proceeding which I signed with my assisting witnesses, as has been stated, and to which I attest. Manuel Antonio de Soto Bermúdez.

1199. In the said pueblo on the said day, month, and year, I, the said lieutenant general of the governor—having seen these proceedings and it being impossible, in view of what has happened, to continue with what I am ordered therein to do, since the few men who accompany me, who consist of the four soldiers and the interpreter, do not suffice—decided to return to the presidio of Los Adays in order that the señor governor, in view of what has been done and what has happened, may make such a decision as pleases him. Thus I decided, and affixed my signature with my assisting witnesses, as has been stated and to which I attest. Manuel Antonio de Soto Bermúdez.

1200. Don Jacinto de Barrios y Jáuregui, etc., to the very reverend father, Fray Francisco Ballejo, ex-*guardián* of the apostolic college of María Santísima de Guadalupe de Zacatecas, and president of these missions of Texas. I make known [to you] that, because of reports which I have had that the French were entering the pueblos of Nacodoches, Texas, San Pedro, Nasones, and Nadotes to trade with the Indians in them, and in view of the fatal results which this unusual trade may bring about, I ordered Don Manuel Antonio de Soto Bermúdez to go to the said pueblos, and in them, by whatever

means he might consider most effective, to ascertain the truth about all the
abovesaid, and make a reconnaissance of the place or places through which the
French were making their entrances and exits. This measure did not produce
results because the captain of Nadotes blocked the way in Nasones. This
action has been followed, according to a report that has reached me, by
innumerable Indians of the aforesaid pueblos assembling in the pueblo of
Nadotes to plot the destruction of this presidio. I am informed that the very
reverend father, Fray José Calahorra, minister of the mission of Nacodoches,
knows specifically of this because the captain of Nacodoches who also attended
the said meeting has given him the information.

1201. Since it is well that I should be fully informed of everything that the
Indians discussed in that junta, in order that I may adopt the most opportune
measures to check the fatal consequences that may follow from what has
happened, I give these presents, by which in the name of his Majesty (whom
may God keep) I exhort and demand, and in my name I beg and ask, that
your reverence order the said Reverend Father Calahorra to certify to everything that he may have learned from the said captain as to what took place in
the aforesaid assembly; and that having done so, in continuation of the present
document, he return the original to me, for the purposes that have been stated.
I offer [to supply] a copy whenever I shall receive those [documents] from your
reverence. Given in this royal presidio of Nuestra Señora del Pilar de los
Adaes on the 16th day of the month of February of this year 1753. Before me
and my assisting witnesses with whom I act for lack of a public and royal
notary, there being none in the sense prescribed by law, and on this common
paper because there is none of the proper kind, to all of which I attest. Jacinto
de Barrios y Jáuregui.

1202. In the mission of San Miguel de Aguayo on the 17th day of the month
of February of this year of 1753, the very reverend father, Fray Francisco
Ballejo, president of these missions of Texas, having seen the present exhortation issued by Señor Don Jacinto de Barrios y Jáuregui, governor and captain-
general of this province, and being informed of its contents, his reverence said
that although he had a letter of obedience from his prelate in which he and
all his subordinates are forbidden to give any judicial certification that might
be presented in any tribunal whatsoever, yet his reverence knowing that the
said order would be directed at other matters, and being aware that in the
present affair his lordship is simply carrying out his chief obligation in the
prevention of any untoward incidents that may happen in the future with
regard to the matter under examination; and it being evident and understood
that he does not fail in any way in due obedience, since [this act] leaves, as it
does leave, the said order in full force and vigor for [other] cases and things
that may occur, by these presents his reverence has commanded and does
command that the Reverend Father Fray José Calahorra, minister of the mission
of Nacodoches, shall certify at the end of this auto in accordance with his
ability and obligation, everything that he may have learned from the captain
of his pueblo regarding what happened in the assembly which the Indians held
in the pueblo of Nadotes after Don Manuel de Soto Bermúdez returned to this

presidio; and it having been done in the manner in which he is ordered, he shall submit it to me for the purpose [stated]. His reverence so provided, and ordered, and affixed his signature before me, the present notary, to which I attest. Fray Francisco Ballejo. Fray Pedro Ramírez.

1203. In the abovesaid mission of San Miguel de Aguayo on the 23d day of the month of February of this year of 1753, I, the Reverend Father Fray José Calahorra, apostolic religious of [the college of] *propaganda fide* of María Santísima de Guadalupe de Zacatecas, minister of the mission of Nacodoches, by virtue of the order of the very reverend father, Fray Francisco Ballejo, president of these missions, certify in accordance with my ability and obligation that a few days after Don Manuel Antonio de Soto Bermúdez reached the presidio of Los Adays on his return from Nasones, the captain of my pueblo, which is that of Nacodoches, came to my mission and told me that he had just been with him in a junta which was convoked in the pueblo of Nadotes, which the Texas, Navidachos, Nasones, and Teguacanas had attended, all of whom together would number about five hundred Indians. In the meeting they suggested to the official, Don Luis de St. Denis, who was summoned by them for this purpose, that in view of the fact that the Spaniards did not want the French to enter and trade in their pueblos, which they so greatly desired, he should avail himself of the opportunity of becoming lord of these lands, for which purpose they were ready to kill all the Spaniards found in them. This they would do by beginning with my mission, and they would end with the presidio of Los Adays.

1204. This decision doubtless would have been carried out, in view of the Indians being so irritated against the Spaniards, if the said official had not restrained them, telling them that he would be very angry with them if they did such a thing, because, since these lands belonged to the Spaniards, they ought to know that without the latter's consent the French could not enter to trade with them. The Spaniards, moreover, having as they did a close alliance with the French, the latter could not in such an event fail to take up arms in their defense. From this action it resulted that the Indians, seeing their captain angered (for they respect him as such), became quiet. Those from *Nasones concluded* [*however*], *by saying that they would give their lives before allowing the Spaniards to place a presidio in their pueblo,* because they had abandoned them when they took away the mission which was there,[49] which act was a clear sign of their lack of love for them. When I asked my said captain what rôle he had played in the aforesaid assembly, he replied that he had attempted there to defend my mission, pointing out for that purpose my affectionate treatment of the children of his pueblo and the continual benefits

---

[49]As a result of the extinction in 1729 of the presidio of Nuestra Señora de los Dolores de los Tejas, some ten or fifteen leagues north of present Nacogdoches, the three Querétaran missions in east Texas—Concepción, San Francisco de los Neches, and San José de los Nazones—were transferred to new sites on the San Antonio River at short distances below the mission of San Antonio de Valero. "By May 4, 1731, the three missions had been established on the spots chosen."—Castañeda, *Our Catholic Heritage in Texas, 1519–1936,* Vol. II, p. 240.

which they were receiving from me; the said captain assured me that my mission would be in no danger. Thus I certify, as I have stated, and in order that it may have the proper effect I give these presents in the said mission on the said day, month, and year. Fray José de Calahorra y Sáenz.

1205. In the royal presidio of Nuestra Señora del Pilar de los Adaes on the 24th day of the month of February of this year of 1753, I, Don Jacinto de Barrios y Jáuregui, governor and captain-general in the name of his Majesty of this province of Texas—having seen the preceding certification and that everything stated therein is related to the proceedings which Don Manuel Antonio de Soto Bermúdez carried out by virtue of my order of October 30 of last year, which he placed in my hands on the 19th of November of the same year—order that it be filed with them, and when complete certified copies of everything that may be in this archive have been made, because of the accidents which may occur, that the original be sent to the most excellent señor viceroy so that his Excellency in view of it may decide upon whatever may be his superior pleasure. Thus I decided, ordered and affixed my signature, before myself and my assisting witnesses, as has been stated and to which I attest. Jacinto de Barrios y Jáuregui.

1206. Señor Barrios must have made public his plan, suggested to his Excellency above in paragraph 1093, to place a presidio on the Río de San Pedro, and it became so public that it reached the ears of the Indians and of the French; of the Indians because it appears from the certification of Father Calahorra, paragraph 1204, that they said they "would give their lives before they allowed the Spaniards to place a presidio in their pueblo"; of the French because this is made clear from the following letter of Monsieur Cesario de Blanc.[50] (The original of this letter is found in the *autos*, from which we have copied it word for word, without changing even a single syllable. Only the signature is in his hand and it is so badly written that none of our Spaniards could read it when they had to record it in the *autos* for some reason, since Señor Barrios read Cesario de Blan, others Ceser de Blanc, others Cesario de Blans, and others Cesar de Blans. The correct spelling, if I am not mistaken, ought to be Cesario [Cesaire] de Blanc. His saint thus would be San Cesario, and therefore the name should be translated Cesario de Blanc; see number 296 of the said document.)

---

[50]Cesaire de Blanc de Neuveville succeeded Louis Juchereau de St. Denis as commander of the French post at Natchitoches upon the latter's death in 1744.—Bolton, *Athanase de Mézières* . . . , Vol. I, p. 84.

Señor Don Jacinto Barrios y Jáuregui. My dear señor: The Marquis of Baudrevil [Vaudreuil][51] learned in the month of October of the past year of the decision which your lordship had made, and, as a consequence, of your having sent a dispatch to his Excellency, my señor viceroy of Mexico, for the purpose of placing a presidio at Nadote, among the Panis, and among the Apaches, for no other reason than to check the intercourse which we have with the Indians friendly to his Most Christian Majesty and to cut us off entirely from means of seeing them.

1207. I am greatly astonished that your lordship does not know that Nadotes has been in territory under our control since the founding of the presidio which your lordship now commands. The boundaries will show us the truth of this.

1208. I am also astonished at the little solicitude that your lordship shows for the Indians. In this matter I can do no less than advise your lordship for the good of your country and on behalf of my master, that you are doing an irremediable wrong, and I do not believe that his Excellency, my señor viceroy, can grant your lordship this request on his own authority, without permission from his Catholic Majesty and the concurrence of the king, my sovereign lord.

1209. In accordance, therefore, with the order that I received on December 21, 1752, from the Marquis of Baudrevil [Vaudreuil], governor of this province, to request your lordship in the name of the king, my master, to take no action pending the decision of the two crowns by which the limits will be designated, for the benefit and concord of the two nations, Monsieur de Grand Maison, lieutenant and commandant of the presidio and of the Señor Don Luis, will deliver this letter to your lordship, for which you will kindly do me the favor of giving him a receipt, signed by yourself. I hope that your lordship is enjoying perfect health, for which I am praying in this letter. May God keep your lordship many years. Nachitoos, February 22, 1753. Cesaire de Blanc.

1210. Señor Barrios answered this letter as follows:

Señor Don Cesario de Blan. My dear señor: I have not answered promptly your honor's letter of February 22, last, which I received by the hand of Monsieur Grand Maison, because of desiring to inform myself completely regarding its contents. Having done so, I must tell your honor that the Indians of Nadotes and Nasones are immediate subjects of the Catholic King, my lord, and that until the year '31 the mission of San José de Nasones was maintained at that place. In the said year it was withdrawn from that place[52] for purposes considered convenient by his Catholic Majesty. Our ancient [*antiquada*] possession therefore dates back to its founding in the year 1716.

1211. Concerning the Panis Indians whom your honor mentions to me in your letter already cited, there is no one in this presidio who has information about them. The Apaches are in the center of this province and, consequently, it is very unlikely that the Most Christian King will be able to claim dominion over them. As for the establishment of new presidios, the Catholic King,

---

[51]See *Pichardo's Treatise* . . . , Vol. III, p. 303, n. 17.
[52]See note 49, *supra.*

as sovereign, can build as many as he may consider proper in his possessions. As for the powers of the most excellent señor viceroy of this New Spain, neither can the Señor Marquis of Baudrevil [Vaudreuil] know them nor have I the right to inquire into them. I must only obey his orders blindly, as those of my sovereign, whose authority his most excellent person [the viceroy] exercises in these vast dominions. I wish your honor the most perfect health and hope that God, our Lord, may preserve your life many years, as I desire. Royal presidio of Los Adays, March 15, 1753.

1212. Señor Barrios gave an account of all these proceedings in the following manner:

Most excellent señor. Señor: I am replying to your letter of October 5 with the most profound respect, returning the certified copy with the proceedings which I have understood I was ordered in it [to draw up], so that in view of them your Excellency may order me whatever may be your superior pleasure.

1213. I also enclose for your Excellency the proceedings which Don Manuel Antonio de Soto Bermúdez drew up at my order in the nations of the Nacaxes, Nadotes, and Nasones Indians, and the results that have been obtained from them. Your Excellency will note from the statements of the Reverend Father Fray José Calahorra, minister of the mission of Nacogdoches and a man who may be believed implicitly, that we find ourselves subject to the will of the French, and that any time a break might occur between the two crowns, your Excellency may be assured that we will be sacrificed by the Indians at only a word from the French. The apprehension that this arouses in me, señor, is that malice might give rise to suspicions [of acts] foreign to an honorable officer who looks with love upon the interests of his sovereign, the glory of his arms, and the lives of so many who are exposed to becoming the victims of these brutes, for the fact that they did not finish us we owe entirely to the moderation of the French *alférez*, Don Luis de St. Denis.

1214. I am enclosing also for your Excellency the letter that I received from the commandant of Nachitoos, Don Cesar de Blans, so that you may be informed of the free hand that they wish to enjoy in our operations, as well as a copy of my reply to him, in which I shall hope that I have succeeded in pleasing your Excellency and in looking after the interests of our sovereign. Señor, the Indians are not to be controlled unless they are given presents, and the things that we have do not appeal to them. They want only powder, shot, muskets, cloth, blankets, razors, and knives from the French. In the critical state in which we find ourselves, in order to attract them your Excellency should permit freedom in buying these articles, which can be obtained without expenditure of money, for the French want deerskins more than gold or silver, since this trade affords them a huge profit. The Spaniards would pay in this specie for the goods permitted, and would not in acquiring them sacrifice saddles, horses, and other articles desired by the French, to the serious detriment of the maintenance of those troops and citizens, as I have represented to your Excellency in [my letter of] November 8, 1751.

1215. The presidio of Nachitos has been strengthened with three additional officers, who are Monsieur de Gran Mont [Grand Maison], lieutenant, and two *alféreces*, and with seven soldiers and a paymaster. Monsieur de Querleret [Kelérec][53] *capitán á alto bordo*, has arrived as governor at New Orleans. The Marquis of Baudrevil [Vaudreuil], who has been made chief-of-squadron and Cordon Bleu [Knight of the Order of Saint-Esprit], and commandant general of Canada, is going to Paris.

1216. I am also enclosing for your Excellency the letter which I received from Don Felipe Rábago (this letter of Rábago is found in number 294 of this same document 37, which we are copying) in which he informed me of having received the two Apache Indian women whom I ransomed at my own expense from the Indians of San Pedro in order to pacify the province, for when some other Indians fell upon the Apaches in the neighborhood of San Xavier, and when of the twelve Apaches none remained alive except the two ransomed Indian women whom they spared for their pleasures, the Apaches were aroused. Believing that the Spaniards were the aggressors in this crime, they began to unite and to proclaim war because of this [supposed] bad faith. The captain of San Xavier notified me of this and of the fact that he had rounded up his horses in order to be on the alert and in a state of defense. Having learned of the whereabouts of these two Indian women, I sent to ransom them, gave them clothing, and returned them. This has brought about a better union and peace with these barbarians who were convinced that it was the Spaniards [who had broken the truce]. There was no other means of satisfying them aside from the one already mentioned. My greatest satisfaction will consist in its winning your Excellency's approval.

1217. I again call your Excellency's attention to everything that I have reported to you in my preceding representations, and I add, señor, [a notice of] the very strong position in which the French are placing themselves. At present there are in New Orleans thirty-six companies of fifty men and one of Hussars, or Swiss, of a hundred men. With this governor there have arrived many ships carrying food and war supplies—even bombs and hand grenades— and a large number of families. There is not even a small pueblo that does not have interpreters paid by the king. It is our good fortune, señor, that the French are not prepared to undertake conquests in these places because of the lack of food supplies, because of the floods in the rivers, and principally because of the scarcity of horses and the fact that these provinces are inaccessible without cavalry.

1218. It is my duty, señor, to bring to your Excellency's attention [for your information] in case a break should occur, the fact that the officials and inhabitants of Nachitoos depend for their subsistence on their multitude of slaves, for there is one official who has forty-four and the relatively poorer ones have two or three each. If they [the French] intend to commit some act of hostility against us it will have to be with the favor and protection of the

---

[53]For frequent references to Chevalier de Kerlérec, Governor of Louisiana in the middle of the eighteenth century, see the index of Bolton, *Athanase de Mézières* . . . , Vol. II, p. 366.

Indians, by whom, as I have mentioned to your Excellency, they are loved in a superlative degree. In this case, señor, although it is against military practice, as your Excellency knows, I would like for you to allow me to issue a proclamation to the effect that all slaves who might come here would enjoy their freedom and the protection of the king, for since these miserable slaves are so weary of the many punishments which are inflicted upon them, with inhuman cruelty, we could promise ourselves that all or most of them would come. The French would remain exceedingly unprotected and [the slaves] would not be the least of their enemies. But I cannot do this on my own authority, although I realize that it would not be improper in case they [the French] were to avail themselves of the Indians. Your Excellency, with your mature judgment, will be pleased to order me what to do. And your Excellency may believe that negroes, and not a few of them, would come from as far as New Orleans, for their owners do not provide for these wretched ones in any way and give them only Sundays for themselves. With the work they do on this day [Sunday] they have to clothe and feed themselves for the entire week. The punishment [inflicted] is to tie them naked to a ladder and to lash them with a whip until not a part remains on their bodies which is not bloody. Later the cure is as cruel as the punishment. It consists of washing all their wounds with *chile* and vinegar. It horrifies one, señor, to consider what the spectacle would be. On two occasions the slaves have attempted to rise in rebellion in New Orleans and they subdued them with terrible punishments. But this is due to the fact that they have no one to take their part.

1219. It has seemed proper to me, in order that your Excellency may understand more fully the reason why the Indians love the French more than the Spaniards, to send you [examples of] all the different kinds of goods that have come to my notice, with which they carry on their trade, such as a musket, a red breechclout, another blue one, a blanket, blue, white, and red glass beads, a mirror, a shirt, and a little powder, in order that your Excellency may see their quality. The French give them these articles at prices for which we could not pay the freight. Besides, they would not want our muskets or cloth because the latter lacks the white edge which so pleases their vanity. The powder is of a quicker action, and the beads are of a better color and of different shapes.

1220. Your Excellency will pardon my detailed statements, which I judge necessary in view of the few occasions which present themselves [for making a report], and since I know that your Excellency should be minutely informed in order that in view of everything you may decide upon what you consider most advantageous to the royal service.

1221. I do not withdraw, señor, what I represented with regard to the establishment of the detachment of San Pedro. I consider it today even more necessary because of what has happened, in view of the fact that this is a nation that dominates by its fierce spirit, and that by controlling it we could promise ourselves the peace of the province. All persons of experience are of this opinion, for it is a nation respected even by the proud Apaches. I would be failing in my duty if I did not represent my opinion concerning it, so that I may on no occasion be accused of being dilatory in the discharge of my duty, and so that whatever may occur, charges shall not be brought against me. For even with the adoption of that measure, many fears and evident dangers still remain with regard to our neighbors [the French], because of their strength and the love that the Indians have for them, arising from the advantages of their trade, from the presents they give them, and from the fact that they never talk to them about religion, which is what the French think of least, living while they are among the Indians in the same libertinage as they. The Reverend Father Calahorra has assured me that it is the greatest vanity of the principal Indians to offer their women for the incontinent appetite of the French; to such a point reaches their unbridled passion for the French. The latter dress themselves in breechclouts and paint their entire bodies like these Indians, by means of which their predeliction for them is more firmly established. May God keep your Excellency's most excellent person many years. Royal presidio of Los Adaes, April 17, 1753. Most excellent señor. Señor, at your Excellency's feet. Jacinto de Barrios y Jáuregui. To the most excellent señor, the Count of Revilla Gigedo.

1222. The señor *fiscal* advised as follows concerning the above:

Most excellent senor: There having been specified and discussed in the *junta de guerra y hacienda* held on September 25, 1752, all the points which gave rise to it—the occasion being that which occurred with regard to the French nation of New Orleans, and that which was ordered by his Majesty on the matter in his royal decree issued at Aranjuez on June 20, 1751 (this is the cedula copied above in paragraph 1098), countersigned by the most excellent señor, the Marquis of La Ensenada—the decision [of the junta] was that there was no occasion for the establishment of a guard of twenty soldiers with an experienced and zealous officer on the Río de San Pedro, which the governor of the province of Texas requested be made in order to observe the plans of the French and the reasons they might have had for increasing their settlements. Nor [was there occasion] for sending the engineer, since, although from the proceedings executed. by the said governor it seemed that the French had advanced beyond their territory from the time that Don Manuel de Sandoval was governor of the same province, these proceedings did not show what the boundary between New Orleans and [the lands of] his Majesty ought to be— whether it should be the Río Colorado [Red River], Gran Montaña, or some other place. Before this, from the proceedings previously drawn up, it seemed that it ought to be the place of La Gran Montaña or Arroyo Hondo, which is half-way between the French presidio of Nachitos and that of Los Adaes, capital of the province of Texas. It is not known, therefore, to what place they [the French] should be confined, what amount of territory they have occupied, or its extent or limits. In order that there might be ascertained fully the amount, extent, and limits of these territories, and their landmarks, and whether the Río Colorado or some other river was the boundary line between the two lands, the present governor was ordered to draw up immediately all the necessary judicial proceedings, so that a complete knowledge might be obtained as to what is the boundary that divides the territories of the two monarchies, he receiving for this purpose the necessary depositions and executing all the proceedings leading to this end. [They were to be directed] also to clearing up the question as to the year in which the French began to penetrate the lands of our sovereign; the extent of land they occupy; its boundaries and limits; the settlements, forts, and presidios they have constructed; their names, garrisons, and the state and condition in which they are at present. If it should result from the proceedings that may be drawn up that the Río Colorado or some other place of those cited is the boundary between the two territories, and that they [the French] have passed beyond it with settlements and fortifications, he was to require the governor or commandant of the presidio of Nachitos, in the name of his Catholic Majesty, to abandon and leave free and unobstructed all the lands that he might have occupied and to withdraw and remain within his possessions. [The governor of Texas] was to point out to him for this purpose that the lands into which they had penetrated belong to our sovereign, as demonstrated by the result of the proceedings which he was to execute. He was to repeat this demand as many as three times, addressing to the French governor all the courteous requisitions that his zeal might dictate. [The above was communicated to the governor of Texas] together with the rest that was decided upon in the junta under this same order, and that which your Excellency was pleased to provide in the corresponding decree of the 26th of the same month of September.

1223. Certified copies of these orders having been sent to the present governor, Don Jacinto de Barrios y Jáuregui, in pursuance thereof he examined twelve witnesses, the first eight of whom consistently support each other in saying that the dividing line between the territories of the two crowns is the Río Colorado [Red River], though some of these make their declarations from hearsay. But they say that they have always heard it [so stated] since the time the troops entered that presidio of Los Adaes. Most of the witnesses, that is, the second, third, fifth, sixth, and seventh, give different reasons by way of proof of their statements. It is shown likewise that the ninth, tenth, eleventh, and twelfth witnesses do not testify in conformity with the preceding ones with regard to the Río Colorado being the boundary of the lands of the two crowns, in as much as the ninth one says that he is not certain about it, because, although he heard it so stated when the troops entered, he also heard that the dividing line was La Gran Montaña or Arroyo Hondo. He declares, nevertheless, that if he must give an opinion as to which of the two places ought to be the boundary, he inclines toward the Río Colorado, not only because at the time the French moved their presidio to this side of the said river the commandant was warned three times not to do so (this fact influenced some of the preceding witnesses, who state that Don Manuel de Sandoval was the one who presented these demands), but also because he heard it said when the Señor Marquis of San Miguel de Aguayo entered that the commandant who was then in Nachitoos told the Spaniards, when they went to examine the banks of the said river, that they might establish their presidio where that of Nachitos is at present.

1224. The tenth witness, although he does not know positively what the boundary may be, for he says he has never seen any legal instrument fixing it, nevertheless relates from hearsay what exchanges took place with the French commandant when at the order of the said Señor Marquis of San Miguel de Aguayo they [the Spaniards] went to reconnoiter the banks of the Río Colorado, [from which] he judges the boundary to be the same river, and the rest of his declaration is given as proof of the truth of this statement. Then follows the eleventh witness who also relates from hearsay what happened on the said occasion with the French commandant. This eleventh witness states that when the commandant of Nachitos learned that a presidio was going to be established there in the name of our king, the said commandant agreed to it, saying that they could place it on the bank of the said river and that the river would serve as the dividing line between the two monarchies. This incident is recounted in the same manner by the tenth witness also, and the twelfth, from the same information and from details which he remembered of what happened then, judges the boundary to be the said river. He adds that he has heard also that three houses belonging to the French which were on this side of the river (the other witnesses likewise recount this incident) were to be moved to the other side, and that since they remained there without being moved, he believes that this toleration and dissimulation gave rise to the fact that the boundary line between the two Majesties is in doubt (see concerning these witnesses the note which we placed in the declaration of Don José González, in paragraph 1167), the matter being further confused by the rumor which was also spread to the effect that the boundary which separated the two presidios was La Gran Montaña or Arroyo Hondo. The eleventh, eighth, seventh, and sixth witnesses also said they had heard this last statement [made].

1225. To the above is added the fact that all the witnesses consistently declare that the year '34, '35, or '36, at which time Don Manuel de Sandoval was governing, the French moved to this side of the river where they are today settled and have their presidio; that the land which they have occupied is about a stone's throw in breadth; and that they have neither constructed nor fortified any forts or presidios in the dominions of our sovereign aside from the presidio of Nachitoos; some of the witnesses add that even in their own possessions the French have not built any others than those they had when the [Spanish] troops entered.

1226. All of this [testimony] having been examined by the governor, he judged that what had been brought out in the said proceedings which he had been ordered to execute by the junta and your Excellency's superior decree, did not demonstrate with sufficient certainty what the boundary between the presidio of Los Adaes and the place on which formerly stood that of San Juan Bautista de Nachitoos ought to be. Because of the differences of the witnesses in their depositions, it seemed best to him, in order to proceed with that certainty and circumspection which a matter so important as the present one demands, to report first of all to your Excellency, [sending a copy of] the proceedings, so that in view of them you might be pleased to order him what he ought to do with regard to this matter. . . .

1227. Aside from what has been mentioned here, other proceedings have been examined, beginning with folio 27 of this *cuaderno*. It appears from these proceedings: that the governor has stated that, in as much as he had received notice that the French are trading and trafficking with the Indians of Texas, Nacodoches, Nasones, and Nadotes—included in that province under his charge—supplying them with shirts, blankets, breechclouts, muskets, powder, shot, beads, vermilion, and other articles esteemed by those nations, winning at the same time the good will of the principal Indians who govern the said pueblos by distinguishing them from the rest with gifts of laced hats, military coats, and other things valued among them; that, bearing in mind that if what has been stated is true, it would be indispensable to apply effective measures to check the harm that could result from it, which today more than ever should be justly feared in consideration not only of the great affection that these Indians have always manifested toward the French, as experience had shown, but also of the repeated measures that the French were taking with regard to their forts adjacent to that province, which they keep increasing with families, regular troops, and munitions of war; and that, deciding, in order to adopt opportune measures, to avail himself of a person in whom he had entire confidence, so that after examining everything mentioned above he might inform the governor of all that he might think worthy of attention, the governor accordingly gave a commission for the said purpose to his lieutenant general, Don Manuel Antonio de Soto Bermúdez, ordering him to go to each one of the said pueblos and instructing him with regard to everything he was to execute in them.

1228. The result of this measure, after the appointed lieutenant general had gone to the pueblo of Nacodoches (about three leagues distant from the mission of this name and fifty-three from the royal presidio of Los Adays) was that the captain of this pueblo—who was placed there by Governor Don Pedro del Barrio Junco y Espriella—in the presence of the two *tamas*, officials of the said captain, and of the assisting witnesses—he and his officials having been presented with various things which they valued and which the present governor had furnished, and the commissioner having told him of his desire to settle in their pueblo with other Spaniards—indicated that he was gratified and replied through the interpreter that he would be very happy to have him and all the other Spaniards join their pueblo; that in this way they would have trade and everything they might need for their subsistence, they would not be forced to go for supplies to the French, and would not allow them in their pueblo; that necessity itself forced them to trade with the French; but that in case the Spaniards settled among them it should not be at that place, which was not convenient, but in a place which they call Nevantini, since it is abundant in water and pasturage. Their ancestors had lived in this place, and they would all move to it and would help the Spaniards work. [The captain stated] that in his pueblo there were eleven large rancherias and in them fifty-two armed Indians, and that aside from these there were many young men almost capable of handling muskets; that the French come to their pueblo by way of that of Yatasi which is on this side of the river which they call Los Adaes; that they [the Indians] bring deerskins and buckskins to sell, the same as the governor has mentioned; that at other times when the river is flooded they disembark from a canoe at the said Yatasi or at Nadotes, and from there they spread to the other pueblos with their goods, and when they do not wish to enter these places, they summon the *tamas* from one of the two pueblos and deliver the goods to them, so that they may distribute them among the Indians, who give them the hides which are then taken to Nachitos; that at other times they [the French] summon the Indians from here and proceed in the same way with them as has been related; that in the pueblo of Yatasi there are eight rancherias and thirty armed Indians, and in that of Nadotes five rancherias and twenty Indians with muskets; that the chiefs of the two said pueblos have been named by the French; and that the pueblo of Nadotes is in charge of the [French] official Don Luis de St. Denis, and no one except the said official trades there.

1229. In the pueblo of Nasones, about eight leagues from that of Nacodoches, the lieutenant general conducted with the *tama* of the same pueblo of Nasones the same proceeding as in the foregoing pueblo, introducing it in a different manner. The *tama* declared, also through the interpreter, that the captain was in the pueblo of Nadotes where he lived most of the time because of having moved his house there, and that they did not go to Los Adaes because there [in the pueblo] they had everything they needed from the French. With regard to the trade of the French and the places through which they came to the pueblos, he replied the same as the captain of Nacodoches; [he said] also that the captain of Nadotes is named by the official, Don Luis de St. Denis, who had sent him a coat, a baton, and a hat, as was true also of the captain of Nasones; that the said pueblo of Nadotes was in charge of the said official and no other goods entered it except his; and that in the pueblo of Nasones there were twenty-four rancherias and forty adult Indians bearing arms, and in that of Nadotes there were five rancherias and twenty Indian men. Asked what Indian nations there were to the north of there, he replied that twenty leagues away were the Tebancanas, a very extensive nation, now much larger with the Pelones who had joined it, that following the Tebancanas were the Tancagueyes, the Yujuanes, the Chicaez, the Aguajuani, the Aguajo, the Tancames, the Asinays, the Guaxis, the Guesos, the Tusas, the Enanos, and many other nations that he has not seen, but that all are friendly to the Texas; that some Frenchmen are accustomed to go to the Tebancanas, and although they have no information that they go to the other nations, they do know that these other nations are supplied by themselves [the Nasones] and by the Tebancanas with muskets, powder, shot, and other things that they need. The lieutenant general would soon see the captain of Nasones, since he [the speaker] was awaiting him, for he had had him summoned because of the fact that he had received a message from Captain Sánchez, who is chief of the pueblo of Texas—so named by Governor Don Pedro del Barrio Junco y Espriella—in which he notified him that he had learned that many Spaniards had left Los Adaes to arrest any Frenchmen whom they might find trading, a thing to which he would by no means consent, because they supplied themselves with everything they needed from the French, which was not the case with regard to the Spaniards.

1230. Besides this, according to the proceedings on folio 31, it so happened that when the lieutenant general was on the point of going to the pueblo of Nadores [Nadotes?] with its captain and the persons who were accompanying the lieutenant general, the said captain called the interpreter and told him to tell the lieutenant general not to proceed, because if he tried to do so, it would go very badly with him; and in answer to the reply that was made to him the captain said that he [the Spaniard] should in nowise go on, because he would not permit it, and that what he could do was to return. When the lieutenant general saw him seemingly angered and in the midst of a large concourse of Indians, most of whom had come to receive from the Frenchman called La Flor' the goods that he had brought there for this purpose by Indian carriers on the afternoon of the preceding day, the lieutenant general had to agree to return, whereupon it was apparent that the Indian captain became calm. The captain's resolution having astonished the lieutenant general, especially since on the day before he had consented to his going to his pueblo, the interpreter [being questioned], replied to him that he was of the opinion that it was all due to the said Frenchman, because at an unusual hour of the night he had found the two talking, which they did not continue to do while he was present. As a result of these events the lieutenant general returned to the presidio of Los Adaes to report to the governor.

1231. There follows a certification made on February 23 of this current year of '53 by the Reverend Father Fray José Calahorra, apostolic religious of [the college of] *propaganda fide* of María Santísma de Guadalupe de Zacatecas, minister of the mission of Nacodoches, upon order of his president at the request or demand of the governor, with regard to the information that he had concerning the matter under discussion. This certification shows that a few days after Don Manuel de Soto Bermúdez reached the presidio of Los Adays on his return from Nasones, the captain of the pueblo of the said reverend father (which is that of Nacodoches) came to the mission and told him that he had just been with him in an assembly which was convoked in the pueblo of Nadotes, in which the Texas, Nabidachos, Nasones, and Teguacanas had assembled. All together they must have numbered some five hundred Indians, and in this assembly they suggested to the official, Don Luis de St. Denis, who was summoned by them for this purpose, that in view of the fact that the Spaniards did not wish the French to enter their pueblos to trade, they greatly desired that he would take advantage of this occasion to become master of these lands, for which purpose they were ready to kill all the Spaniards who might be in them. This they would do by beginning with the mission of the said reverend father, and would end with the presidio of Los Adays. Their resolution doubtless would have been carried out, in view of the Indians' extreme irritation against the Spaniards, if the said official had not restrained them, saying to them that he would become very angry with them if they did such a thing, for since these lands belonged to the Spaniards, they ought to know that without their permission the French could not enter there to trade; furthermore, the Spaniards having as they did a close alliance with the French, the latter in such an event would be obliged to take up arms in their behalf. As a result of this occurrence the Indians, seeing their captain angered (for they respect him as such) calmed themselves. Those of Nasones, however, concluded by saying that they would give their lives before they allowed the Spaniards to establish a presidio in their pueblo because of the latter having abandoned them when they withdrew the mission which was there, which action was a clear sign of their lack of love for them. The said father having questioned the Indian captain as to which side he had taken in the said junta, he replied to him that he had attempted there to defend the mission, calling to mind the affection with which the father treated the children of his pueblo and the continual benefits that they were receiving from him, the said captain assuring him that his mission would not be in any danger.

1232. Besides all this, on folio 36 there is a letter signed by Don Cesar de Blans who, according to the governor, is the commandant of Nachitos. In this letter, in substance, he writes Don Jacinto de Barrios y Jáuregui, remonstrating with him because of the fact that the Marquis of Baudrevil [Vaudreuil], governor of New Orleans, had received a notice that the Spaniards intended to place a presidio at Nadotes, among the Panis, and among the Apaches, for the sole purpose of closing the communication which the said Cesar states the French have with the Indians friendly to his Most Christian Majesty, and of cutting them off entirely from the means of seeing them. He states that he is greatly astonished that he [the Spanish governor] does not know that Nadotes has been on lands under French control since the founding of the presidio which the governor today commands, saying to him also that the boundaries will demonstrate the truth of this.

1233. The French commandant states that he is equally astonished at the lack of solicitude which the governor shows for the Indians in this pueblo; that he is warning him on behalf of his master, for the good of his country [i.e., Spain], that he is doing irremediable harm; that he does not think your Excellency can on your own authority accede to this request of the governor without the permission of his Catholic Majesty, [given] by agreement with the King of France; and that therefore, in accordance with the order of December 21, 1752, which he received from the Marquis of Baudrevil [Vaudreuil], governor of that province, he must notify Governor Don Jacinto del Barrio, in the name of the King of France, not to take action pending the decision of the two crowns in which the boundaries will be marked for the good and union of the two nations. This is the substantial content of the letter dated February 22 of this current year of '53.

1234. According to the copy of the letter which follows, the governor replied that the Indians of Nadotes and Nasones are immediate subjects of the Catholic King and that until the year '31 the mission of Señor San José de Nasones was maintained in that place. In the said year it was removed for purposes that his Catholic Majesty considered convenient. Because of this fact and because of its establishment as far back as the year 1716, our ancient [antiquada] possession is confirmed. [He also stated] that there is no one in that presidio who had any information about the Panis Indians of whom the commandant speaks in his letter; that the Apaches are in the center of the province, and consequently it is very unlikely that the Most Christian King would be able to claim dominion over them; that with regard to the establishment of new presidios the Catholic King, as sovereign, can build as many as he may consider proper in his possessions; and that with regard to your Excellency's powers, neither can the Señor Marquis of Baudrevil [Vaudreuil] know them nor can governor Barrios inquire into them. He can only obey your orders blindly, as those of our sovereign, whose will your Excellency expresses in these vast dominions.

1235. Along with all these proceedings the governor himself gives a report to your Excellency, so that you may be pleased to decide whatever may be your superior will. After citing the proceedings which Don Manuel Antonio de Soto [Bermúdez] executed and the certification of the Reverend Father Calahorra, who may be believed implicitly, he says that we are subject to the will of the French, and at any time that a break might occur between the two crowns your Excellency may rest assured that we would be sacrificed by the Indians at only a word from the French. He is apprehensive that malice might give rise to suspicions [of acts] foreign to an honorable officer who looks with love upon the interests of his sovereign, the glory of his arms, and the lives of so many who are exposed to becoming victims of these brutes, for the fact that they had not finished them [the Spaniards] is due entirely to the moderation of the French *alférez*, Don Luis de St. Denis.

1236. Governor Barrios encloses the said letter of the commandant, Don Cesar, in order that your Excellency may also be informed of the free hand that the French wish to enjoy in our operations; and [he sends] a copy of his own reply, with which he hopes he has succeeded in pleasing your Excellency and in looking after the interests of our sovereign.

1237. He says that the Indians are not to be controlled unless they are given presents, and that the things we have do not appeal to them, for they want only powder, shot, muskets, and other articles which he names from the French; that in the critical condition in which we find ourselves your Excellency should permit freedom in buying these articles, which can be obtained without expenditure of money, for the French want deerskins more than gold and silver, since this trade affords them a huge profit; and that the Spaniards would pay in this specie for the goods permitted and would not in acquiring them sacrifice saddles, horses, and other articles desired by the French, to the serious detriment of those troops and citizens, as he has pointed out to your Excellency in the letter which he cites.

1238. He reports that the presidio of Nachitos has been strengthened with three additional officers, seven soldiers, and a paymaster, and that Monsieur Querleret [Kelérec], *capitán á alto bordo*, has arrived as governor at New Orleans, and the Marquis of Baudrevil [Vaudreuil] is going to Paris as holder of the offices which he names.

1239. He encloses a letter (which is the one on folio 34) in which Don Felipe Rábago reports to him that he has received two Apache Indian women whom the governor says he ransomed at his own expense from the Indians of San Pedro in order to pacify the province, for when some other Indians fell upon the Apaches in the vicinity of San Xavier, and when none of the twelve Apaches remained alive except the two ransomed Indian women, whom they spared for their pleasures, the Apaches were aroused. Convinced that the Spaniards were the aggressors in this crime, they began to unite and to declare war because of this [supposed] bad faith. He continues his report [with an account of] these Indians having become quiet after the ransom of the two women, and of the other matters that he mentions.

1240. He repeats his preceding representations and he adds [a notice of] the very strong position in which the French are placing themselves at present, stating that thirty-six companies of fifty men and one of Hussars, or Swiss, of a hundred men, are in New Orleans; that there have arrived with the present governor many vessels carrying food and war supplies—even bombs and hand grenades—and a large number of families; and that there is not even a small pueblo that does not have interpreters paid by the king, it being our good fortune that the French are not prepared to undertake conquests in those places because of the lack of food supplies, because of the floods in the rivers, and principally because of the scarcity of horses and the fact that those provinces are inaccessible without cavalry.

1241. [He states] that it is his duty to inform your Excellency [for consideration] in case a break should occur, that the officials and inhabitants of Nachitos depend for their subsistence on their multitude of slaves, for there is one official who has forty-four, and the relatively poorer ones have two or three each. If they [the French] intend to commit some act of hostility against us it will have to be with the favor and protection of the Indians, by whom, as he has mentioned to your Excellency, they are loved in a superlative degree. In this case, although it is against military practice, the governor would like to be allowed to issue a proclamation to the effect that all slaves who might come there would enjoy their freedom and the protection of the king, for, since these miserable slaves are so weary of the many punishments which they inflict upon them, with inhuman cruelty, we could promise ourselves that all or most of them would come, and that the French would remain exceedingly unprotected and [the slaves] would not be the least of their enemies. The governor cannot do this, however, on his own authority, although he knows that it would not be improper in case [the French] were to avail themselves of the Indians. [He asks] that your Excellency, with your mature judgment, will be pleased to order what he shall do, and that you may believe that negroes, and not a few of them, would come from as far as New Orleans, for their owners do not provide for these wretched ones in any way and give them only Sundays for themselves, and with the work they do on this day they have to clothe and feed themselves for the entire week. The punishment [inflicted] is to tie them naked to a ladder and to lash them with a whip until not a part remains on their bodies which is not bloody. Later the cure is as cruel as the punishment. It consists of washing all their wounds with *chile* and vinegar. And [he states] that on two occasions the slaves have attempted to rise in rebellion in New Orleans and they subdued them with terrible punishments. But this is due to the fact that they have no one to take their part.

1242. In order that your Excellency may better understand the reason why the Indians love the French more than the Spaniards, he says that he is sending your Excellency examples of all the articles with which he is informed they conduct their trade, so that you may note their quality and may see why the French give them at prices for which we could not pay the freight. Aside from this they do not want our muskets or cloth, since the latter lacks the white edge which so pleases their vanity, the [French] powder is of a quicker action, and the beads are of a better color and of different shapes.

1243. [He states] that he is making such detailed statements in view of the few occasions that present themselves to him, and because he knows that your Excellency should be minutely informed in order that in view of everything you may decide upon what you consider most advantageous to the royal service.

1244. He concludes by emphasizing what he had already represented with regard to the establishment of the detachment of San Pedro, considering it today even more necessary because of what has happened, in view of the fact that this is a nation that dominates by its fierce spirit, and that by controlling it we could promise ourselves the peace of that province. And [he states] that all the experienced persons in that province are of this opinion, for it is a nation respected even by the proud Apaches. He says that he would fail in his duty if he did not represent his opinion concerning it, to which he adds other considerations.

1245. Reflecting upon all the foregoing with the care that the seriousness of the matter demands, there must be ascertained from it, first, the point as to what may be the boundary that divides the territory of the two crowns; and, second, the trade that the French have with the Indians of the pueblos mentioned which are in the possessions of his Majesty, together with what happened during the investigation of this matter, for [determining] the measures that may have to be taken with regard to both.

1246. As to the first point, the *fiscal* considers that notwithstanding the said *auto* of the governor in which he gave an order to suspend and discontinue the proceedings which he was directed to execute in conformance with your Excellency's superior state decree—since he thought that, because of the differences of the witnesses in their depositions, the result of the proceedings did not demonstrate with the requisite certainty, in his opinion, what should be the boundary between the presidio of Los Adaes and the place where formerly stood that of Nachitoos—it is well to carry out the proceeding which was provided for by the said junta and superior decree with regard to demanding of the commandant of Nachitoos in the name of his Catholic Majesty that he abandon and leave free and unobstructed all the land that he might have occupied, and that he retire and limit himself to his own possessions. He should be notified of the result not only of these last proceedings but also of those which the said governor executed previously on this same matter, the governor conducting himself in this particular with prudence and courtesy, after the manner prescribed in the same junta, arranging everything in conformity with its tenor and rules, and reporting to your Excellency the result, so that you may provide for the proper measures, as is also ordered.

1247. For the witnesses of both inquiries give sufficient basis for this proceeding because of the reasons on which they base their statements that they are convinced and are of the opinion that the boundary line is or ought to be the Río Colorado [Red River]. Some of the witnesses of the second group hold this opinion as a result of the admission of the French commandant himself at the time that the soldiers of the Señor Marquis of San Miguel de Aguayo went at his orders to examine the banks of the said river; and [as a result of the incident that occurred] when it was planned to have a Spanish ecclesiastic baptize a child of the same commandant, for in order that it might be done without impediment, he directed that he should cross to this side of the Río Colorado. There are also other things which, according to the witnesses, conduce to and confirm the same opinion, as well as what has already been stated in the junta, of which the governor was informed. Furthermore, when the Señor Marquis of San Miguel de Aguayo went by order of this captaincy-general to dislodge the French who had penetrated into those dominions, he took possession of all of them in the name of his Majesty. Among these lands were included those which the French occupy today, and on which they have settled and fortified themselves, because we had acquired dominion over and possession of them as early as the year 1690, and because they began to form their settlement on our territory subsequent to the possession taken by the said Señor Marquis of San Miguel de Aguayo, while Don Manuel de Sandoval was governor of the province of Texas.

1248. Although Governor Don Jacinto del Barrio ought not to resort to other proceedings than those which he is directed [to carry out] in the said junta, and much less to force of arms, which he has also been ordered not to do for the reason that was stated—the *fiscal* having so requested notwithstanding the royal order cited, and in view of the considerations which he mentioned in numbers 30 and 31 of his reply—yet since these proceedings do not produce the desired effect of causing the French to withdraw to their possessions, the governor will inform himself [further] in the matter of their resistance, and will shed more light on what his Majesty should do and see fit to provide. [This is recommended] particularly in view of the letter which the governor has remitted from the French commandant, Don Cesario de Blans [Blanc], which, although occasioned by the obstruction of his trade, shows also that he desires to appropriate the pueblo which, as the governor wrote him, is located in the center of his [our] province. He brings up the point of the territories of the two crowns and refers the question of limits to the royal deliberation.

1249. In as much as his Majesty has ordered that, if it seems proper to your Excellency, you send the governor one of the engineers who are in this kingdom in order that he may assist and aid him in attaining the restoration of the usurped territory, and in establishing such rules and decisions as may result in preventing in the future the occupation of this or any other place within the possessions of his Majesty, on which important matter he charges you most particularly, expecting from your well-known zeal and love for the royal service its complete fulfilment, the *fiscal* also thinks it proper, in case it is approved by your Excellency's superiority, that the said governor be sent the said engineer for the purposes which his Majesty orders, as the *fiscal* requested in his aforecited reply in number 30, already mentioned. For although arms should not be resorted to in order to dislodge the French from the usurped territory, but rather the pacific means already prescribed—until, an account having been given to his Majesty, he may decide upon what may be his royal pleasure—it is true that the said engineer will be able to contribute a great deal to the end of restoring the usurped territory and conserving that which belongs to his Majesty, aiding the governor in this respect and also in establishing such rules and decisions as may be proper for preventing in the future the occupation of that or any other place that may be within his Majesty's possessions.

1250. As regards the trade of the French with the Indians who are within the jurisdiction of Texas, the freedom of this trade, and the control they have over the Indians, to the point of having named the captain in Nadotes and Nasones; what happened when Lieutenant General Bermúdez went to conduct his inquiry, the repulse that he received from the said captain of Nadotes who it is presumed was influenced by the Frenchman La Flor; and what Father Calahorra certified to regarding that which the captain of Nadotes stated to him, and the rest that has been mentioned and represented by the governor,

1251. In as much as all this must be considered extremely dangerous, and since the proper measures must be applied for its remedy—particularly in view of what also is happening with regard to the same French of New Orleans, who have been attempting to establish their trade in the province of New Mexico since the year '40, as has been verified in the *autos* and dispatches concerning various individuals of the said nation which the governor of that province drew up in the year '51, with regard to which various measures were taken and a report was given to his Majesty, the same thing being done at present in connection with others of this nation who were imprisoned and who came from the same direction and with the same intention, with regard to which the *fiscal* replies separately—

1252. If it is your Excellency's superior pleasure, you will order that a letter be written to the governor, notifying him of what has taken place in the case of the French brought from New Mexico, who came through that region for the purpose of establishing their trade, in order that after he has been informed of it, he may adopt in so far as they apply to him the measures which he may consider appropriate, since he is face to face with the situation, keeping this information to himself and availing himself of it for the measures that he may take on this point.

1253. In the matter of the trade with the Indians under his jurisdiction he shall continue the policy which he has already adopted of attracting the Indians and demanding prudently and with diplomatic arguments that the commandant of Nachitoos and the *alférez*, Don Luis de San Deni or San Dionis [St. Denis] shall not enter nor allow other Frenchmen to enter to trade and traffic with the Indian subjects of his Catholic Majesty living in his dominions, nor shall they go so far as to give them orders or confer titles on them, since these Indians are not vassals of their sovereign. He shall explain to them that it is not right that they should do this against the wishes of our king, when the Spaniards refrain from causing them any uneasiness.

1254. It being true, as it is, that the Indian captain of Nasones is named and placed in this office by the *alférez*, Don Luis de St. Denis, and that according to the proceeding on folio 31 it is presumed that the Frenchman La Flor induced the said captain to make Lieutenant General Bermúdez retire, the governor shall likewise demand that the said *alférez* withdraw the title from the captain of Nasones and advise him that he had conferred it upon him without having authority to do so. Whereupon the governor shall go immediately to confer the title of captain in Nasones and Nadotes upon the Indian or Indians whom he may consider to possess the necessary qualifications for the position, endeavoring to select a person who is not only worthy but also capable of detaching himself and the Indians under him from their proclivity for and trade with the French, and of gaining their affection and commerce for the Spaniards. He shall carry out this plan with the requisite sagacity, prudence and discretion and he will know how to conduct himself in executing it. He shall also make a representation to the commandant of Nachitos [demanding] that he reprimand the Frenchman La Flor for his action in having incited the Indian captain of Nasones to such an unseemly demonstration as to make his own superior withdraw from his own lands. The governor shall likewise give an account of the result of these proceedings and of any others that his zeal may dictate.

1255. The governor insists that the detachment of twenty soldiers and an officer be stationed on the Río de San Pedro—regarding this measure as even more necessary today because of recent events and of other considerations which he presents, explaining that he would not be fulfilling his obligation if he did not represent his opinion concerning it, so that at no time may he be accused of being dilatory in the discharge of his duty, and so that no charges may be brought against him whatever the result, for even with that provision many fears and evident dangers still remain. With regard to this, the *fiscal* likewise insists on his corresponding petition, which is found in number 32 of his said reply. Hence your Excellency's greatness, if it be your superior pleasure, may be pleased to yield to this new importunity of the governor, giving the corresponding orders and commands for its [the detachment's] prompt establishment, as the señor *auditor* has likewise recommended.

1256. The governor should also be written that with regard to the measure concerning trade which he mentions in his *consulta* although he considers it desirable for the reasons given in his report, in view of the fact that such a trade has many prohibitions placed upon it by his Majesty and since it is not opportune at present to attempt to cut off the Indians from their trade with the French and to restrict the latter to their own possessions—your Excellency cannot permit such a step until his Majesty, in view of what the governor proposes, may decide what is his royal pleasure, the governor in the meantime being careful not to engage in this or any other kind of trade, as he states.

1257. Continuing his report to the effect that there is not a single small pueblo that does not have interpreters paid by the king (speaking of his

Most Christian Majesty), if the pueblos to which he refers are those situated in the 'dominions of his Catholic Majesty and in them are the interpreters paid by the King of France, neither the continuance nor the toleration of this practice can be condoned. With regard to it your Excellency will be pleased to order the governor to demand that the commandant of Nachitos withdraw the said interpreters from the pueblos of our sovereign, in case they are subjects of his Most Christian Majesty; and that if the interpreters are subjects of his Catholic Majesty he shall cease to maintain them. The governor on his part shall do everything that his zeal may dictate in order to prevent the continuance of such a practice, conducting himself in this matter with the same prudence and courtesy that he is ordered to exercise in the others.

1258. As regards what the governor also reports concerning the negro slaves of the French and the proclamation that he would like to issue in order to attract the said negroes in case of a break with the French nation [it may be said:] As has been noted, all the proceedings that he is to execute for the purpose not only of making the Frenchman withdraw to his own lands but also of preventing his entering ours to trade and traffic with the Indians, should be courteous, polite, and carried out with the greatest urbanity, without resorting to arms until his Majesty, in view of everything, shall decide what may be his royal pleasure. Nevertheless, since, in the course of events, a break may occur between the court of France and that of Spain, and since this break would have its effect in New Orleans and in the province of Texas, in such an event, and in no other except a break between the two courts, it might be proper and opportune to take this step (in the contingency mentioned) of issuing the proclamation for attracting the negro slaves away from the French.

1259. This plan is especially feasible if one considers the unrest which the French will cause among our Indians in such an event, and the existing discontent with their masters among the negroes belonging to the French, because of their ill-treatment. The governor considers that the measure could be very useful in protecting the province, in view of its sparse population and small forces, as an aid to its defense in case of the outbreak of war. With regard to this your Excellency, bearing in mind all that has been mentioned, will order what you may consider most fitting.

1260. A report should be sent to his Majesty, together with these new proceedings, in order that in view of them and of the measures that may yet be taken, he may be pleased to decide according to his royal will. And, in order that he may also [render a decision upon] what the *fiscal* stated in the cited numbers 30 and 31 about its not being possible at the present time to force the French to withdraw from the occupied lands, in view of the new situation presented by the measures taken by France—and which she is continuing, according to the new *consulta* of the governor—in increasing the forces of that colony; in view of the existing difficulty in assembling men in the province of Texas; and in view of the fact that the officers and soldiers of its presidios, aside from being needed to restrain the Indians, are not considered by the *fiscal* to be adapted to the manner and mode of warfare which it would be necessary to practice against the French troops, together with the rest stated in the said number 31,

1261. Your Excellency may send at the same time a report to his Majesty on the representation of the *fiscal* in number 33 of his said reply with regard to the fact that the garrison of the presidio of Los Adaes should be like that of the port of Vera Cruz, since the province of Texas now has a different status and other requirements than it has had heretofore. If its presidio and soldiers formerly have been chiefly for the defense of the province against hostile Indians, and were established on this basis and for this precise purpose, today they must also give attention to what is occurring and what may occur with regard to the French, for the reasons contained in the said number 33 which the *fiscal* reproduces along with all the rest in his cited reply.

1262. And, finally, your Excellency will be pleased to give an account to his Majesty so that he may deign to order what should be done with the said French deserters or with others who in time of peace or war may come to his Majesty's domains—whether they shall be dealt with in the same manner as has been done in time of peace, that is, arrested, tried as foreigners, and sent under special convoy [to Spain]—so that, in view of it [the report] and of all the *autos* that have been drawn up on this matter and the incidents that have occasioned them, his Majesty may decide and command whatever may be his royal pleasure. Your Excellency will be pleased to order, if you think it best, that the matter be submitted first to a *junta de guerra y hacienda* for its decision. Mexico, July 28, 1753. Dr. Andreu.

Mexico, July 30, 1753. To the señor *auditor*. Signed with his Excellency's rubric.

1263. The señor *auditor* replied as follows (number 358):

Most excellent señor: Since the past year of 1734, when Captain Don Manuel de Sandoval was governor of the province of Texas, the question has arisen as to whether the French established at the presidio of San Juan Baptista [de] Nachitos, founded with a fort on an island in the center of the Río Roxo, or Colorado [Red River], had gone beyond the boundary or dividing line between the territories of the two crowns of Spain and France by the act of having moved the fort to the south margin or bank on this side in the direction of the presidio of Los Adaes, six or eight leagues from that place and about the distance of a musket shot or a stone's throw from the banks of the river. This innovation was imputed not only to carelessness but also to permission and dissimulation on the part of Governor Sandoval, so much so that it was one of the most serious charges which were examined in his *residencia*, and which were formally and specifically brought against him therein. However, in order to clear himself of it, it would have been sufficient to have proven his ignorance of the moving of the French presidio. [This is true] since he was on his general inspection tour of the province and was many leagues from the presidio of Los Adaes, whose lieutenant sent him the news; and, in view of this information, he dispatched without loss of time several letters and demands in the name of his Majesty to the commandant of Nachitos, Don Luis de St. Denis, to the effect that he should return his presidio to its former location on the small island and leave the territory of the kingdom of Spain free and unobstructed. Nevertheless, in the evidence or judicial process which as a result of the judgment was received in this city before Señor Doctor Don Pedro Malo de Villavisencio, *auditor de la guerra* at that time, and which is included separately in *cuaderno* 11 on the eighth written folio of the *autos* of the said *residencia*, which the *auditor* has had before him, he [the governor] proved conclusively by the depositions of six confirmatory, reliable, and unexceptionable witnesses that the said presidio of Nachitos, removed to the south bank of the Río Colorado, was located on territory belonging to the crown of France. [This is a fact] because it was still two and a half leagues, or somewhat more away from the boundary or dividing line of the dominions of the two contiguous crowns, which they [the witnesses] fixed, not at the said river, but at La Gran Montaña or Arroyo Hondo, an equal number of leagues distant from the Spanish presidio of Los Adaes, it being located exactly halfway between the two.

1264. Now it is clear that this was brought out in the said evidence in order to absolve Sandoval from the blame that was ascribed to him with regard to the said permission or dissimulation upon which the charge was founded, even though, in the event that he had had certain knowledge of the transfer of the presidio, he would not have been able to prevent it with his exhortations and demands upon the commandant St. Denis. But, nevertheless, for the discussion of the principal point which is now being examined, the testimony referred to affords important evidence, because of the commendable qualities and the circumstances of the six witnesses who give it— for five of them are eyewitnesses who have seen and been in the presidio and had dealings with the French long before the transfer. Some were on the expedition which the Marquis of San Miguel de Aguayo led during the year 1721, and they saw that they [the French] had some houses and cattle on this side of the river, to which the presidio has been moved, and the said marquis left them in undisturbed possession there. Testimony to this effect is given by the fifth witness, who is Doctor Don José Codallos y Rabal, a canon of the holy Metropolitan Church of Mexico, an individual of extraordinary energy and intelligence, who entered with the marquis and examined all those countries, and took a leading part in the expedition, having twice lodged in a house (St. Denis speaks of this house and another, in paragraph 898) with good accommodations which Monsieur Pierre had on this side of the Río Colorado [Red River], where he had established an hacienda. He [Dr. Codallos], replying with the other witnesses on various matters, declares openly that the transferred presidio is in territory belonging to the French, this admitting of no doubt, and that, on that occasion, by agreement with the French, La Montaña Grande, which is midway between the two points, was designated by the clause "for the present" as the boundary between the presidios of Nachitos and Los Adaes. The other [witnesses] agree to this unanimously.

1265. This evidence becomes even more important with the support which is afforded by some other which Don Prudencio de Orobio Basterra, at that time governor of the province of Texas, took in the year 1740 by virtue of an order from the most excellent señor, the Duke of La Conquista, who was then viceroy of this kingdom, to receive it officially. It also consists of [the depositions of] six witnesses. The orginals run from folios 50 to 60 of the eighth *cuaderno* of the *autos* of Sandoval's *residencia*. And, though all of them do not testify with certainty regarding the boundary or barrier, all agree that the territory to which the presidio was moved belongs to the French and not to our possessions. [They agree also] that before the transfer took place they saw and knew of some houses there belonging to different individuals whom they name. Hence [the evidence of] twelve witnesses, most of them eyewitnesses, some of whom were on the expedition of the Marquis of San Miguel de Aguayo and others of whom lived in that country near the time of the expedition (from which time to the incident of the removal of the presidio thirteen years elapsed without there being even the least inquietude or disturbance of either of the adjoining nations with regard to the overstepping of boundaries and the dividing line) shows conclusively that the presidio, moved southward from the small island to the bank of the Río Colorado [Red River], was erected on territory belonging to the King of France. It must be noted that in view only of what the witnesses testified in the secret [investigation] and of the information received in this city, the señor *fiscal* requested that in the *residencia* Sandoval be absolved of the said charge. Thus, in his opinion, the second [investigation], which was carried out subsequently in order to have that court pass upon the secret charge, was superfluous.

1266. It seems that the controversy was ended in this manner, until, in March of 1744, a letter was received from Don Justo Boneo,[54] governor of Texas, dated in the presidio of Los Adaes on December 16 of the preceding year of '43 and directed to the most excellent señor, the Count of Fuenclara, at that time viceroy of this kingdom. In it was enclosed a royal cedula dated in Buenretiro on July 15 of the year 1740, in which his Majesty ordered him [the governor] to investigate by all possible means the truth of the matter of tolerating the French fort, providing himself for the purpose with the necessary related documents from this capital, and sending a report of the result of his operations so that the said most excellent señor could order him what to do in the matter, which thereupon began to be revived and brought up anew. But after the letter had been shown to the *auditor general de la guerra*, who at that time was the Señor Marquis of Altamira, he stated in his opinion of March 6 of the said year, considering the point as a thing already having been judged and decided in the *residencia* of Sandoval, that the investigation could be dispensed with, though if the

---

[54] Justo Boneo y Morales was governor of Texas from 1743 to 1744.

governor to whom it was committed should consider it proper he might
execute it, since the original royal cedula entrusted this duty to him. [The
auditor] offered to draw up the necessary instructions for the business, based
upon the *autos*, and in fact he did so, making an exact and accurate abstract
of thirty *cuadernos* [of documents], containing complete information about
those lands and territories, and leaving nothing to be desired as regards
precision and guidance. Two certified copies of this instrument were made,
one for the purpose of giving a report to his Majesty, and the other to be
sent to Governor Boneo, and everything contained in this passage appears in
and is drawn from *cuaderno* 32, composed of written folios.

1267. Governor Boneo did nothing in this affair in spite of finding himself so superabundantly informed, for in the entire accumulation of *autos*
there is nothing to show that he might have proceeded with the inquiry which
the said royal cedula directed him to conduct. The matter rested in this
state until the year 1751 when your Excellency's well known zeal, motivated
by a *consulta* of the captain-commandant of the island of Santa Rosa y
Punta de Sigüenza, was pleased to order the present governor[55] of the province of Texas, by a superior decree of February 10 of the same year—marked
number 7, with which the current *cuaderno* begins—to make an inquiry concerning the penetration of the French into lands under the dominion of Spain,
and as to whether or not the Mississippi River was the barrier or boundary
which divided the territories of the two crowns in those very extensive lands.
Your Excellency ordered the governor to report to this captaincy-general the
proceedings that he might execute in the matter, so that an account might be
given to his Majesty. Pursuant to this order, Don Jacinto de Barrios y
Jáuregui, governor of the said province, proceeded to receive evidence separate from that of another inquiry which he was ordered in the same dispatch
to make on various other points. This evidence consists of eight declarations
or testimonies and it runs from folios 36 to 50. Examined in accordance with
an interrogatory which he formed, they [the witnesses] answered almost uniformly in reply to the first question that they knew the French had penetrated into our possessions and that they had heard it commonly said that
the Río Colorado [Red River] was the dividing line of the two monarchies,
which they believed because formerly they [the French] had the presidio of
Nachitos on a small island, and the deserters of both sides enjoyed asylum
and immunity upon touching the respective opposite banks of the said river.
Having taken this testimony, the governor sent the originals with two *consultas*, in which from his own knowledge or judgment he adds nothing applicable to the business, because he fills them entirely with proposals for
various [new] measures.

1268. While this action of Governor Barrio [Barrios?] was pending, your
Excellency received a royal order from his Majesty enclosed in a letter of
the most excellent señor, the Marquis of La Ensenada, dated at Aranjuez on
June 20, 1751. It is concerned with the same matter and prescribes the same

---

[55]Reference is to Jacinto de Barrios y Jáuregui, who was governor of Texas
from 1751 to 1759.

measures as the royal cedula issued at Buenretiro on July 15, 1740, which was directed to Don Justo Boneo, and it was the effect or result of what the most excellent señor, the Duke of La Conquista, had informed his Majesty with regard to the extension of the French colonies into territory of our monarchy. It was sent to the señor *auditor*, the Marquis of Altamira. In view of this, in his opinion of November 27, bearing in mind that nothing new was occurring at that time in the affair to demand special measures, in due fulfillment of the said royal order he reproduced in substance the same opinion that he had drawn up with regard to the content of the royal cedula [already] cited. In conformance with this two certified copies were made for the same purpose, as appears from the sixth *cuaderno* of these *autos*. There are included in the nine written folios of which the latter consists, only this incident and his [the *auditor's*] decision.

1269. The señor *fiscal* of his Majesty reviewed the evidence sent by Barrios, and in his reply of January 29, 1752, he declared that it showed that the Mississippi River should serve as boundary for the French, to keep them within their limits. Notwithstanding this opinion, he requested that *autos* and instruments be sought which might show that the said river had been and ought to be the dividing line between the two crowns, and that it be ascertained whether there were any orders from his Majesty or other confirmatory documents regarding it. Having ascertained that such *autos* and dispatches as he requested were not with the opinion of the Señor Marquis of Altamira, which begins on folio 66 *vuelta* of the seventh *cuaderno*, he formulated his reply, which runs from folios 67 to 68 of the same *cuaderno*. In it he does not defer so completely to the said [governor's] report as not to request additional measures conducive to a better ascertainment of the boundary, the aggressions of the French, and the portion of land which they have occupied with the presidio which was moved to this side of the Río Colorado [Red River]. The Señor Marquis of Altamira subscribed to this in substance in his opinion, beginning on folio 87 *vuelta*. Both officials concluded that for a decision on a matter of such a serious nature it should be submitted to a *junta general de guerra y hacienda*, and, in fact, it was reviewed in the junta which was convoked and held on September 25, 1752, [as recorded] on folio 93.

1270. Eight points were discussed in the junta, of which the third is the one that specifically concerns the case, and with regard to it, even bearing in mind the evidence remitted by Governor Barrio [Barrios?], all those present decided by common accord that it was not possible to ascertain from this evidence what the boundary between New Orleans and [the possessions of] his Majesty ought to be—whether it should be the Río Colorado [Red River], La Gran Montaña, or some other place; that formerly, from the proceedings previously drawn up, it seemed that it was the place of La Gran Montaña or Arroyo Hondo, which is halfway between the French presidio of Nachitos and that of Los Adaes; that neither was the amount of land occupied by them known, nor between what points it lies; and that, in order to arrive at a knowledge of all this, the present governor should be directed to carry out all the necessary proceedings to the end that it might be definitely known what the boundary was [is] that divides the territories of the two monarchies. He was to receive declarations for this purpose and adopt such measures as might be desirable, and if these should make clear what the barrier or boundary was between the two crowns and whether the French have advanced beyond their [territory], he should have recourse to demands sent to the commandant of the presidio of Nachitoos in the name of his Catholic Majesty, to the effect that he should leave free and unobstructed the land that he might have occupied and withdraw to his own possessions.

1271. Two things are inferred from this decision of the *junta general:* first, that the preceding evidence which Governor Boneo sent was not considered sufficient or conclusive for forming the opinion that the Río Colorado was the fixed boundary, as the witnesses declared who took part in the inquiry. Consequently, with the transfer of the presidio to this bank the French had not overstepped themselves, for if the evidence had been held sufficient, the new proceedings, directed by their circumstances to a more thorough and complete inquiry, would have been useless; and second, that the nature of the measures that he was to carry out anew in order to dispatch the demands to the French commandant of Nachitos being left to the present governor, the only steps that he took in the matter, as a result of the dispatch that was sent him in accordance with what had been decided in the *junta general*, were to receive the declarations of twelve witnesses, which are found from folios 105 to 130, without, in view of them, having proceeded to send the three demands in accordance with the orders given him in the dispatch.

1272. This fact implies that the governor, who was face to face with the matter and knew well the quality of the witnesses and the motives for their statements, did not consider the proof which the inquiry furnished sufficient for dispatching the demands with advantage and with hope for a favorable result, or, at least that he doubted its sufficiency and therefore, without doing anything else, he contented himself with remitting it to this captaincy-general. Whereupon the matter presents nothing new to qualify his [the *fiscal's*] recommendation to give the governor orders in accordance with the decision that may be made on this point.

1273. The said evidence having been examined with the care and attention which the serious importance of the matter demands, and it having been compared with the previous evidence on folios 37 to 54, it is found that of the twelve witnesses examined who took part [in the second inquiry], the first, second, third, fourth, and fifth, according to their names and ages, are the third, second, fourth, first, and fifth of the first inquiry, and thus these five are the same individuals. Their testimony was not considered sufficient by the *junta general.* When the witnesses testified with regard to the first question of the interrogatory, they said only [that they understood] by hearsay and common belief that the Río Colorado [Red River] was the dividing line between the two presidios of Nachitos and Adaes, and some of them, as the fifth, eleventh, and twelfth, stated that they had also heard that La Gran Montaña or Arroyo Hondo was the boundary; thus the question has always been a matter of opinion. Therefore, since the evidence has almost the same context and is qualified by the same circumstances as the preceding—which was not estimated or considered sufficient in the *junta general* for deciding positively and definitely that the governor of Texas should have recourse to demands as a means for dislodging the French and [causing them] to abandon the new presidio which their commandant transferred from the small island in the Río Colorado to the south bank, which faces the presidio of Los Adaes—it should receive the same consideration. At least, in the opinion of the *auditor*, considered by itself the evidence is so weak and unstable that it would not be sufficient, without other documents and perfect support, even to adjust a civil case between private parties who might litigate on the boundaries or limits of a stock farm or hacienda. Then what force would it have for erecting a barrier or fixed boundary for the territories and possessions of two crowned heads of the sovereign character of their Catholic and Most Christian Majesties? The establishment of such a boundary demands some exceedingly delicate formalities. These, up to the present, have not been carried out, in spite of the fact that as early as the year 1717, an account and a report was given to his Majesty by Señor Don Juan de Oliván, while he was *auditor general de la guerra.* He pointed out how important it would be for the peace of these dominions and the opportune prevention of the introduction of the French and their clandestine trade to fix as the definite and unalterable dividing line between the two crowns the great Mississippi River, which seems placed by nature for the purpose of separating Louisiana from the province of Texas, as is seen from a copy of his erudite and laborious report which occupies folios 44 to 51 in the seventh *cuaderno* of the *autos* of the *residencia* of Don Manuel de Sandoval. In the thirty-six years that have passed since the date of the above report, it has not produced any result whatsoever which might serve for a precedent on the present occasion.

1274. The belief that the said evidence could make a case is weakened still further, and even destroyed, if it is reviewed and compared with the two reports, so circumstantial and repeatedly attested to, which were cited and dispatched, given in numbers 1 and 2 of this opinion. They were occasioned by the royal cedula, letter, and order issued on the same matter of the encroachment upon boundaries with the removal of the French presidio, and the comparison demonstrates, [with] a little consideration and reflection, the serious and notable difference in point of proof which comes from the witnesses [who testify according to their] beliefs, based upon hearsay—of which type are those of the said inquiry—and witnesses trustworthy for their character and actual experience, and for definite personal knowledge. These last-named witnesses, from what they saw and experienced, concluded without any evasion or doubt that the presidio had been moved to land under the dominion of France, and that the barrier or boundary was not the Río Colorado but La Gran Montaña or Arroyo Hondo. Of this type are the witnesses of the two said official inquiries, who on this occasion are free from the usual suspicion of the passion with which the loyalty of [those of] political nations is wont to interest itself in the extension and expansion of the dominions of their respective sovereigns. And, in any legal judgment, or one given by arbitrators, it is now understood that the evidence which these latter produce, although their number may be smaller, ought to be predominant and superior to that of those others whose number may be larger.

1275. Notwithstanding this, and the fact that to the very governor who received the said evidence it seemed insufficient and wanting in the certainty required for dispatching on a rational basis the three demands to the French commandant of Nachitos—as he was ordered to do in the junta and as he shows in his *auto* of remittance, from folio 130—with regard to what was stated on the point of the boundary, the said evidence has appeared efficacious and conclusive to the zeal and learning of the señor *fiscal* of his Majesty in the preceding reply. For this purpose he expounds it and advances it with various inductions until he reduces to conformity the statements of several witnesses who answered the interrogatory with doubt or ambiguity. Thus, in his opinion, this evidence proves that the barrier, or dividing line, between the two crowns is the Río Colorado; and that, therefore, since the French with the transfer of the presidio have gone beyond its banks for the distance of a stone's throw or a musketshot, as the witnesses in the inquiry uniformly declare, they have usurped lands of the dominion of Spain which they should leave free and unobstructed. He therefore concludes by requesting that the governor deliver the three demands in the name of his Catholic Majesty, conforming carefully to the terms of the decision of the *junta general*, and contenting himself with this measure without proceeding to anything else that may involve [the use of] armed force or a break of the close alliance and harmony with which under the present system the two crowns deal with one another.

1276. The perspicacity of the señor *fiscal* in the notable performance of his ministry immediately discovered in the said evidence the vigor, solidity, and force which the *auditor*, informed with other documents, does not perceive. And since actually the execution of the measure in the terms in which it is conceived would lead to no break whatsoever, he would be of the same opinion as the señor *fiscal*. In fact, however, the proceeding of the three demands of the governor of Texas to the commandant of Nachitos should be considered not only as useless and unprofitable, but in the light of being prejudicial in the situation which we are discussing. That it is not of any use, that from it cannot be expected the good result of their withdrawal to the opposite side of the Río Colorado [Red River] and the demolition of the presidio, is judged from several things. For this legal and politic expedient between two free and independent nations was put into execution eighteen years ago by Don Manual de Sandoval while he was governor of that province, with Don Luis de St. Denis, commandant of Nachitos, with all formality, and without any result whatever. This was at the time when the removal of the presidio had just occurred, and the French commandant in his replies responded to the demands with various arguments on which he bases his title for continuing to hold the site from which it was planned to dislodge him. Two of the arguments further confirm the doubt that a repetition of the demands would have any effect.

1277. The first argument is that the establishing of a fixed barrier, or boundary line, in the dominions of the two adjoining crowns can be done only by a concordat, or agreement, between the sovereigns themselves. The second is that the transfer or removal of the presidio was done in accordance with an order of his Most Christian Majesty which was communicated to him [the commandant] for that purpose. It is inferred from this that the new commandant, Don Cesar de Blans, or the one who may have succeeded him in office, would not stay or go because he would be told by us that the Río Colorado is the boundary; and that, since the French did not receive a contrary order from the Most Christian King, they would not abandon the place. Thus the matter will be in the same state in which it was after the demands of Sandoval, which appear in the seventh *cuaderno* of the *autos* of his *residencia*, where the Latin letters are found, faithfully translated into our language by Don Gerardo Moro. These letters constitute the said commandant's reply, and their contents express a great deal of presumption and readiness to defend the rights of his sovereign, in which the present commandant, Don Cesar de Blans, is not inferior to him, as is seen from his letter on folio 140 of this current *cuaderno* in the matter of the Nadotes and Nasones Indians.

1278. If consideration is again given to the time of Sandoval's demands, and is then fixed upon the present time, and upon the deliberations with regard to issuing other requisitions, it becomes less probable that there will be obtained with the second what was not attained with the first, when the French were not well established on the site to which they transferred the presidio from the small island, and were not as strongly entrenched as they are today. For, in the course of eighteen years, in which they have not experienced the least trouble or uneasiness because of us, *from which inactivity also the French may form an argument,* they have had an opportunity to fortify their presidio, increase the population of their settlements, build houses, plant gardens, establish haciendas, and to have increased their garrison with the troops and families who have come to New Orleans from France, as the present governor reports in his *consulta,* on folio 142. It is most natural that they should be more attached to the country and that, since their withdrawal would be painful because of what they would lose by it, they should not only resist with greater stubbornness but also with greater pride, which may degenerate into disdain or contempt for the one who is making the demands, since they derive confidence from the greater forces and prompt aid that can come to them from the head of their colony, so well provided with trained militia from Europe. There would contribute no little to this [support] the multitude of barbarous Indian nations which, by means of gifts and presents to their liking, they have at their disposal for any emergency.

1279. As for stopping the proceeding only because it might turn out unprofitable in the end, nothing would be risked by trying it, except that it is to be feared that the result might be prejudicial to a nation so sagacious and well informed [as the French, who could] forestall in many ways the dangers contained in the threat. For, aroused by our movement, it is probable that they would proceed with reports to their sovereign which would impress his royal mind and make it averse to an agreement advantageous to the monarchy of Spain whenever the fixing and establishing of a boundary line may be discussed. It is also probable that, having an order meanwhile from their court to draw our forces off and to frustrate our plans, they would persuade and incite the barbarous Indians included in his Majesty's possessions to some outbreak against the Spaniards residing in the province of Texas by skilfully sowing discord that will make them rise in rebellion. This will be very easy for them because of the affection that the Indians profess for the French and the power they have over their spirits and minds. A certain proof of this is the incident [described] on folio 137 which Father Fray José Calahorra, minister of the mission of Nacodoches, certifies to as having occurred with the captain of his pueblo. It is to the effect that when more than five hundred Nadotes, Navidachos, Nasones, and Teguacanas Indians assembled in a junta which the official Don Luis de St. Denis attended, they proposed to kill all the Spaniards, since they were angry with them because of their prohibition against the entrance and trade of the French. They would doubtless have carried this out if the French official himself had not restrained them, threatening them with his wrath if they perpetrated such an outrage. It is understood, finally, that whoever has such authority and acceptance among those barbarians that when they are tumultous and aroused, their respect for him is sufficient to calm them, this person will be capable of inciting them to the contrary whenever it may be to his advantage and may conduce to the protection of his interests and those of his nation, so ingratiated and beloved because of its generosity and the freedom cf religion which it permits to all the nations who deal with the French. The Indians will not resist their entrance into the territory and dominions of the crown of Spain, for whose vassalage their trade engenders aversion rather than affection.

1280. In addition to this, it appears from the last investigation that the twelve witnesses examined in the course of it, on the fourth question of the interrogatory, declared, confirming one another and as a matter well known, that the French have built no other presidio than the one at Nachitos, which they moved from the islet, nor have they usurped more than a stone's throw or a gunshot's breadth of territory from the crown. All of this the eleventh and twelfth [witnesses] affirm, in case the boundary is the Río Colorado [Red River]. This verifies what was stated long before by Dr. Don José Codallos to the effect that the French do not establish presidios except on the banks of rivers because of the convenience in transportation and for the other reasons that he stated. Since the year '34, then, in which they moved the presidio from the islet to the bank on this side of the Río Colorado, they have remained in the same place without expanding or going beyond it, penetrating toward La Gran Montaña. This has been given such a formidable name through pure irony, since it is nothing more than a small hill, or large rock, raised in the center of the plain which extends from the bank of the said river to the presidio of Los Adaes. It is apparent from this that no unusual incident has occurred, the toleration of which may some day be harmful and would remove the impu-tation of untimeliness from the action of those who would make the demands, which would moreover arouse the sleeper, disturbing the peace that he has enjoyed for a period of eighteen years. Because of this fact the matter is in the same state today that it was previously, without any new motive that would justly demand measures which, since it is not expected that they could be useful, would carry with them the presage of being under the circumstances seriously prejudicial to the crown of Spain and its vassals.

1281. The *auditor*, from these motives, finds it proper and is of the opinion that your Excellency's superiority, notwithstanding what has been so diffusely expressed by the señor *fiscal* in his cited reply and of what the new evidence produces, which was sent by the present governor of the province of Texas, should be pleased to order the discontinuance of the measure with regard to the three demands to the French commandant of the presidio of Nachitos. This had been decided upon in the *junta general de guerra y hacienda* on the hypothesis that from the proceedings which he executed it would be clearly and justly shown that the barrier or dividing line between Louisiana and Texas was the Río Colorado and not any other place nearer the presidio of Los Adaes. The said governor shall be ordered to be on the watch with the greatest care and zeal, befitting his obligation and honor, for all the movements of the French that may be directed to expanding or going beyond the site to which they have been restricted since the removal of the presidio. He shall not permit them to make the least unusual move. He shall report to this captaincy-general anything that may occur in order that such prompt and opportune measures may be taken as are needful for obstructing the advancement of their schemes. [The *auditor* also recommends] that after complete and literal certified copies have been made of all the new proceedings that were executed as a result of the *consulta* of the captain-commandant of the island of Santa Rosa, and which are contained in this current eleventh *cuaderno*, a report shall be sent to his Majesty on the first possible occasion, so that, in view of it, his royal will may decide whatever may be its pleasure. The señor *fiscal* likewise requests this in his conclusion with regard to this point of the boundary, which cannot be fixed or established for the purpose of preventing controversies, anxieties, and trouble, except by means of an agreement between the two courts.

1282. In accordance with this plan and in order to be consistent, it is seen that for the present it will be wholly unnecessary to send an engineer to that province as the señor *fiscal* requests in his last reply and as he had requested in the preceding one which he cites, in conformance with the royal order of his Majesty and the special charge to your Excellency. [This is true] notwithstanding that this point had been the second one of the eight that were discussed in the *junta general de guerra y hacienda*, and with regard to which it was decided to take no action. Certainly there does not seem to be the least necessity for sending him. Nor is there contemplated any useful employment that he could engage in or in which he could help or serve the governor of Texas, because nothing new is to be undertaken and things are to remain in the same state in which they have been hitherto until, after examining the certified copies of these new procedings, his Majesty shall order whatever may be his royal pleasure.

1283. The said engineer is not needed either to designate the boundary in question, or to mark off the land which the French are occupying with their presidio, or to demolish their buildings, and even less to construct additional new ones. And, since the royal order upon which the señor *fiscal* bases the

repetition of his request should be understood [to apply only] in case your
Excellency's superiority may consider the presence and assistance of the said
engineer necessary and useful—this not being so under the present circumstances—you will be pleased likewise to order that on this point what was
decided upon in the junta general be observed and fulfilled.

1284. Notwithstanding the fact that the present governor had before him
what the *junta general* had determined with regard to whether a detachment
of twenty soldiers with an experienced and zealous officer should be stationed
on the Río de San Pedro in order to observe the schemes of the French and
the reasons they have had for increasing their settlements; and although this
was the first point which was discussed in the junta—it being decided in the
negative—he repeats the same request in his last *consulta* with such arguments
that they force one to the belief that he judges this measure to be necessary
and conducive to the important ends which he proposes and to which he directs
it. It is not remarkable that the señor *fiscal* is inclined to defer to these
arguments in his next reply when previously, with a less urgent representation,
he requested that the detachment be stationed on the said river. The Señor
Marquis of Altamira, in his opinion, on folio 91, also subscribed to this repeated
proposal of the governor, and the mutual support that the señores marquis and
fiscal have lent to it has inspired in the *auditor* a natural desire to inform
himself fully on the matter. He has succeeded in doing so through the expert
and well informed person of an individual of much experience in those lands
who, because of an office that he has held in them, in the discharge of which
he has traversed and explored them personally, should know all the places of
the province of Texas, in which he resided several years. From the exact
information that the *auditor* has obtained from him, he has learned in substance only that in the whole extent of the province of Asinays, which is
commonly called Texas, no river whatsoever is known or spoken of by the name
of Río de San Pedro, which, because of its situation and location, would be
appropriate for observing the schemes and movements of the French in the
colonies adjacent to it. [He has learned further] that the only place named
San Pedro is the first pueblo of the Navidachos Indians on the other side of
the Río de la Trinidad on the direct road to our presidio of Los Adaes, at
which place it is not apparent what opposition a detachment of twenty soldiers
can make to the French who might be scheming to penetrate into our possessions and introduce their commerce and trade among the nations of the royal
crown, because it is too distant and not appropriately located for the purpose
for which the detachment will be intended.

1285. If, perchance, the Río de San Pedro of which the governor speaks is
the one of this name which the Señor Marquis of Altamira mentions in his
extensive report, already cited, contained in *cuaderno* 32, number 32, between
which and the Río de San Antonio is located the presidio of San Antonio de
Béxar—the latter being two hundred leagues from Los Adaes, which is the
nearest to the French presidio of Nachitoos—it results that opposition to the
ingress of the French into Texas and the observation of their schemes and
movements would be even more difficult. It is possible, therefore, that the

information the *auditor* has received coincides with the notice of the señor marquis, the river and place being one and the same.

1286. This notice and the insufficient information with which the governor in his zealous eagerness persists in the measure concerning the detachment on the Río de San Pedro, the actual existence of which can reasonably be doubted, make the point indeterminable and put it back in its former difficult state, without any new document or evidence which was not available to the *junta general* and which, discussed therein, would have brought about a contrary decision. This is especially true, in as much as the establishment of the detachment would certainly and necessarily be costly to the royal treasury because of the increase in the number of soldiers and their corresponding salaries, and it is very improbable that it would be useful and efficacious for the purpose for which it is created. Its usefulness will be proved only when there may be evidence that the said Río de San Pedro is in the province; that it is located and flows at such a distance and in such a manner that the movements of the French could be observed from the site on which the detachment would be stationed; and that on it there is only one narrow crossing available, by means of which it can be forded and passage found from one bank to the other, and from which alone can be impeded the entrance of the French and the introduction of their commerce into the province of Texas, and the passage of the Indian nations included in its district and vicinity to the presidio of Nachitoos or any other settlement of the French colonies. For it would be of little advantage for the detachment to be stationed at one place if along the course of the river there are many easy and safe passes, or fords, by which to cross without encountering opposition from the detachment. Because, if their retreat were cut off [at the ford] and they should take some other crossing either farther down or higher up, even though it might be at the cost of a short detour, the trespassers would accomplish safely their schemes of trading and intercourse with the Indians of the crown of Spain, and the detachment would be idle and useless, the purpose for which it was created being thus defeated.

1287. It follows from this that until the governor shall designate with a map, or description, which one is the Río de San Pedro, its length, and the other circumstances mentioned in the preceding number, with which procedure he could have furnished information from the beginning regarding his proposal for the detachment, it cannot be either adopted, or rejected on the basis of impending harm to the royal treasury as the result of disbursements for its salaries and the other expenditures that it might entail as a new establishment. In view of this, your Excellency's greatness may be pleased to order the present governor of Texas, Don Jacinto del Barrio [de Barrios] y Jáuregui, to supply the necessary information that is lacking with regard to the nature of the place in which the detachment is to be stationed which he has referred to in his *consultas*. He shall report on this matter very clearly everything that he may find to be most useful and conducive to the royal service in the new examination that he will conduct to this end. Your Excellency may reserve for yourself the final disposition and decision with regard to the matter of the detachment, in view of what the proceedings that the said governor shall remit may show.

1288. As the governor in his *consulta* reproduces his preceding representations, the señor *fiscal* follows his lead. And it seems that he insists on what he had requested in number 33 of his reply on folios 67 to 68 of this current *cuaderno* with regard to the garrison of the presidio of Los Adaes being trained like that of the port of Vera Cruz, for he requests that a report be sent to his Majesty for the reason that he gives. And, in as much as one of the points that was discussed in the *junta general* and that was not approved therein or regarded as convenient was the changing of the form of that militia—for in the manner in which the country permits, as a result of the continual warfare that it wages and the permanent enemies with whom it fights, it cannot be denied that it is trained, as are all the militia companies of the interior presidios of the kingdom—therefore, in order that his Majesty, when a report shall be sent him, may have before him at the same time the reasons of utility and convenience with which the señor *fiscal* supports himself, and the inconveniences and impracticability that militate against the change and on which the junta based its adverse decision, it may be well to state here that a trained troop like that of Vera Cruz at most would be useful and suitable for a war or a defense against the French in case of a break between the two crowns, or with some other of the civilized nations of Europe, who do not use or are not accustomed to fight with anything but trained troops. But for the type of warfare which the Spaniards carry on against the barbarous nations of Indians there has not been found in all these years a militia more fit and adequate to cope with their brutal and indomitable ferocity than that which is now and has always been maintained in all our interior presidios. Experience shows by good results how fitting and useful that discipline is for controlling and checking the invasions and hostilities of the barbarians, to whom each one of our soldiers, mounted on horseback with the offensive and defensive arms that they use, seems a formidable giant in spite of the frequency with which they see them and the fact that they often engage them hand to hand. The French at Nachitoos themselves can be good witnesses to all this, for in the year '31 they requested aid and succor from the governor of Texas, who at that time was Don Juan Antonio Bustillos,[56] because more than five hundred Indian musketeers of the bellicose nation of the Nachies [Natchez], as skilled and ready in handling muskets as the most veteran Frenchman, were coming to surprise their presidio and settlement, after having first destroyed a presidio of Louisiana and killed everyone in it from the commandant to the drummer. With a well-equipped squadron of eighteen mounted soldiers, commanded by a lieutenant whom they detached for the engagement, the Spaniards so terrified the insolent and rebellious Naches that they laid aside their pride and arrogance, and confessing that they were afaid only of the Spaniards, they withdrew and left the presidio unhurt. The latter would certainly have been destroyed without such immediate and timely aid, because of the kind of enemies who were preparing to attack and despoil it.

---

[56]Reference, apparently, is to Juan Bustillo Zevallos, who became governor of Texas in 1730.

1289. It is inferred from this that militia trained after the manner of that of Vera Cruz which might be useful against the French in the possible, though remote, case of a break with that nation, is not and cannot be so against barbarous Indians. And if in preparation for a war that is only a possibility our presidials accustom themselves to this kind of training, they make themselves unfit for the other [mode of warfare] which is constant, permanent, and continuous; and the fear and respect with which the Indians in their barbarity regard our soldiers and their manner of fighting being removed, they will become more daring and fearless. All this is under the supposition that the trained troop could be established and maintained, but the rigor and rawness of the climate, especially in winter, and the severe hardships of these frontier soldiers cannot be borne or sustained by any others than natives of the country, accustomed to it. The detail of guarding the horse drove alone, adding to the heavy weight of the leather and arms all the ice and snow which they endure without being permitted to make a fire to warm themselves, would suffice in itself to terrorize and intimidate outside people, aside from the awkwardness and difficulty they would find in handling the leather shield and the lance as skilfully as necessary without losing control over the reins. It is in this that the military exercise of the frontier soldiers principally consists. It is not easy to learn rules for it, nor is there any other method than the same continuous exercise with which they grow up, accustoming themselves to it. From this proceeds the fact that our presidials are docile, obedient to their superiors, and most long-suffering in the extremities of hunger and thirst, for often they subsist on a few grains of corn, either parched or cooked, and some days they go without food, without desertions or flights from their companies taking place because of it. The same thing cannot be expected from trained troops in difficult and inaccessible countries in which the lack and scarcity of food almost always prevails, for the soldiers would mutiny at every step, impatient with the lack of necessities, or their desertions would be frequent. It might even be feared that in their want they would find a pretext for clandestine trade with the French, who are in a position to supply them as they do the Indians appeartaining to the royal crown [of Spain].

1290. The governor, in his *consultas* of which the señor *fiscal* takes cognizance, states as a fact that there are in New Orleans thirty-six companies of fifty men each and one of Hussars and Swiss of one hundred, and that many ships have arrived with food and war supplies and other material. But with all this, he asserts that the French are not prepared for conquest because of the lack of provisions, the flooded rivers, and most of all because of the scarcity of horses and the fact that these provinces are inaccessible without cavalry. And [he states] that if they intend to commit any hostile action against us it will have to be with the support and protection of the Indians. Thus even when it is considered that the French troops are disciplined, with all this we ought not to make innovations in regard to the character of the troops when their principal opponents are the Indians from whom the French can obtain aid, and when against the former there are no soldiers more effective than those who hitherto have been on the frontier.

1291. The *auditor* does not doubt that today the aspect of affairs in the province of Texas has changed, and that it has come to demand a special attention of another sort than that which it has been given hitherto, because of its proximity to a nation as powerful as the French, because of the large scale upon which the latter continues to establish its colonies, and because of the open and unprotected situation of the pueblos and forts of the said province. This is the just misgiving that prompts our seeking from now on to guard against any schemes that are being considered, not only as possible but also as contingent, but this cannot be accomplished simply by changing the character of our militia, over which that of the French may have some advantages— not in valor and skill but in numbers. These are pouring in every day from European France, well equipped and prepared for any kind of campaign. Thus it seems that the most opportune preventive defense for restraining them and frustrating their schemes would consist in opposing them with a sufficient number of men by strengthening the presidios with soldiers, for that of Los Adaes, distant seven leagues at most from that of Nachitoos, which when first erected contained a hundred men, today has only sixty, on which basis the field marshal, Don Pedro de Rivera, left it after the inspection which he made of it.[57] These are circumstances so serious and so pertinent to the subject that mention of them cannot be omitted, to the end that after they have been weighed in the balance of his Majesty's judgment, together with the señor *fiscal's* arguments, in view of both his Majesty may decide whatever may be his royal pleasure.

1292. Likewise the suggestion of the governor with regard to permitting a limited trade with the French in wines and brandy suffered rejection in the *junta general.* He considered this trade necessary for the maintenance of the presidials because of the rigor of the climate of that region in winter and because of the scarcity and bad quality of these goods and the difficulty with which they are brought to the presidios from other provinces of the kingdom; this was the sixth point which was discussed in the junta, and it was characterized as irregular. The governor nevertheless brings it up again in his *consulta,* and with regard to it the señor *fiscal* requests the proper measure in view of his Majesty's strict prohibitions which exclude indefinitely all commerce, under whatever guise or pretext an attempt may be made to excuse it. Since in this question of commerce there is no insignificant small matter that cannot lead the said commerce to greater excesses, it is not easy [to believe] that the French, who are of a commercial mind and aspire to nothing else than to introduce and spread their trade by every means throughout the possessions of the royal crown [of Spain], will restrict themselves to the small sphere of selling only their wines and brandy, and that our presidials, in order to provide for their necessities during the rigorous seasons of cold, will content themselves

---

[57]For details concerning the recommendations in 1728 of the inspector of the northern presidios, Don Pedro de Rivera, and, particularly, his recommendations regarding the diminution of the presidial force at Los Adaes, together with the approval of his recommendations, see Castañeda, *Our Catholic Heritage in Texas* . . . , Vol. II, pp. 225 and 231.

with their purchase, without going on under cover [of this trade] to supply themselves with other goods and merchandise fraudulently and in contravention of his Majesty's prohibitory royal orders. Their exact fulfillment, without the slightest interpretation that may relax or weaken their complete vigor and force, should be the first obligation in whose discharge the governor is to prove his zeal and assiduity in the royal service. In this particular, therefore, your Excellency will be pleased to accede to the request of the señor *fiscal*, directing that the decision of the *junta general* be observed in conformance with the royal orders, by which the governor shall be guided. He is to conduct himself with the same care and vigilance with respect to these goods that he shows in connection with other merchandise of illicit commerce, not permitting his presidials to give up their horses and saddles in exchange for either, and punishing severely anyone he may find who has committed an irregularity of this sort, by which the French may supply, equip, and strengthen themselves. For, as he reports, they lack these [horses and saddles] in their colonies, while our people relinquish what they have most need of in that region for its pacification and defense.

1293. The same fate as the preceding one should be dealt the suggestion which, among others, the governor makes in his *consulta*, to the effect that he be permitted to issue a proclamation stating that all the slaves of the French presidios and colonies who might escape from them and come to take refuge in the province of Texas shall enjoy their liberty and the king's protection. Their escape may be expected because of the excessive cruelty and harshness with which they [the French] treat and punish them. Since they have an exceedingly large number of slaves, if they are taken away the French will be seriously handicapped, and afterwards the slaves will not be the least of their enemies. This suggestion, dictated by zeal for strengthening our interests through the weakness and decline of a buoyant rival and by the natural compassion which is engendered by the wretchedness of those slaves, treated with such cruel tyranny by their masters, seems even to its own author to be contrary to military usage. In the last analysis, it is in itself contrary to civil laws, treaties, and conventions among monarchs and states which, when they are belligerent, proceed with decorum and rectitude without appealing to the vassals themselves. Such an inducement [to the slaves] with the promise of freedom would be a just motive for war and a break with the crown of Spain, as were among other things the attempts that the British nation made among the negro slaves of La Havana, inciting them with like promises to rebellion and revolt. Furthermore, since this premeditated proclamation could not reach the notice of the slaves of the French colonies without at the same time reaching that of their masters, the latter would take so many precautions that they could never escape, and it is possible that even greater harshness would be exercised to restrain them, keeping them in closer custody than hitherto.

1294. The señor *fiscal*, taking into consideration this suggestion, believes that it would be appropriate only in case an outbreak of war might occur between the two crowns of France and Spain, and in no other. For, with the advent of the many fugitive slaves who it is thought would be attracted by a desire for freedom and royal protection and would be incited against their masters in retaliation for their continuous inhuman treatment, and with those experienced in the uprising in New Orleans which the governor mentions, the forces of our side would be increased and the province of Texas, so deserted and uninhabited, would be placed in a better state of defense, because being closest to the rival colonies it would be the first theater of the war to suffer invasions and hostilities. He nevertheless leaves the decision on the point to your Excellency's just arbitriment. This decision, even in the fatal event that a war be declared, is not lacking indifficulties and obstacles which can be overcome only by a decree of state and by orders from his Majesty, prescribing the kinds of reprisals and hostile acts with which the enemies of the crown should then be proceeded against. But, since at present we are not discussing this extreme case, which is considered improbable because of the well-founded alliance, friendship, and harmony which are being cultivated between the two courts; and, since the governor's suggestion is inappropriate in the present state of peace and tranquility which the two nations are enjoying, in order that he may abandon the idea of the decree which he has considered through fear of a future war, and for which he asks authorization in the understanding that he cannot decide upon it by himself, your Excellency will be pleased to make clear to him that in the present situation such a means is in no way appropriate, just, and decorous, and that on the contrary it will serve to change the minds of the French and provoke the very war that he fears.

1295. The governor does not base his fears solely on the power and forces that the French are acquiring daily, strengthening their colonies notably with trained troops from Europe, munitions of war, and families to settle Louisiana, but also on the blind devotion and partiality that the nations of Indians included in the government of Texas profess for them. They have won over their good will by the profuse liberality which they practice, as some testify, by order of the Most Christian King, whose warehouses are opened to them, and with the merchandise and articles that are so to their liking and taste. With these articles the French maintain their trade in skins with them, which is the one they esteem most because it is the most profitable and lucrative. Those barbarians therefore regard with aversion and disdain the same things from us, with which they could supply themselves, though not as cheaply because all of them cost more than those which the French bring in and dispose of by barter. Thus the latter with their trade are making a silent conquest of the said nations, with whom they fraternize to the stupid extreme of painting themselves and of living in the same licentiousness and heedlessness of religion as they. Thus it is no wonder that the Indians love and respect them and subject themselves to their domination and temptations, escaping from the control which [the Spaniards] do not and cannot have over them. The French go so far as to confer titles of captain on the Indians and to incite them to default in their submission and obedience to the Spanish civil and military officers who govern them. This is proved by what happened to the lieutenant of the presidio of Los Adaes, Don Antonio de Soto Bermúdez, with the *tama*, or captain, of the Nasones who, incited by a Frenchman named La Flor who had gone there with some merchandise to trade, prevented him from entering his pueblo and even dared to intimidate him with the threat that it would go badly with him if he persisted in passing on. For this reason the lieutenant, seeing signs of tumult and hostility, returned to the presidio, as is shown by the judicial proceeding which he set , down, beginning with folio 134. The governor therefore fears with good reason that in case of war breaking out with France the said nations will be partial to and on the side of the neighboring French and against the Spaniards.

1296. The señor *fiscal* touches on this point, and realizing that the trade and communication of the French with the Indians of the royal crown is the source of their pride and insolence, and perhaps in time it may be for rebellion and open hostilities, he considers it a great danger, for whose remedy the most active and efficacious measures should be applied which may tend wisely to draw them away from this intercourse, so that the affection which the governor says in his *consulta* they have for the French, in a superlative degree, may be gradually effaced. For, by reason of being deprived of it for a time, their naturally fickle and mercenary minds are capable of converting their most passionate affection into hatred for the nation. But what are those measures from which such favorable results may be expected? He does not specify them, leaving the adoption of suitable ones to the governor's zeal and prudence, he being informed by a private notice which is enclosed that the French of New Orleans have attempted to establish their trade in New Mexico, whose governor has arrested several persons of that nation whom he has sent as prisoners to this capital. These shall be the measures which the governor ought to adopt for the time being, exerting his powers of discretion, industry, and vigilance in the diplomatic and persuasive manner which the *junta general* enjoined him to use, until a report is sent to his Majesty of everything that has happened and has been done in the matter, and until some other measures may be decided upon. They are the same ones that your Excellency's superiority may be pleased to order and charge him to observe in general, leaving to his prudence the details of putting them into execution in accordance with the occasion and opportunity that may present themselves to him, so that their use may not alarm the suspicions of the Indians and so that no break or misfortune shall come to the good relations which it is important to preserve undisturbed with our frontier neighbors.

1297. The governor includes two other matters in his *consultas:* first, the authority and license that the official Don Luis de St. Denis has taken upon himself to confer titles of captain upon the Indians of the nations subject to the dominion of Spain, as is clearly seen by his having conferred it upon the captain of Nasones and of Nadotes, who had the audacity to make Lieutenant Bermúdez withdraw; and second, the matter of the interpreters whom the Most Christian King keeps in each pueblo. The señor *fiscal* considers both matters, and in spite of the fact that there is no more proof of the first one than the single statement of the interpreter examined by Bermúdez with regard to the sudden change in the captain of Nasones, without his saying whether the title which the French *alférez* conferred upon him was written and in the form of a military commission, or only a verbal nomination [made] with the guileful intent of deceiving his stupidity with this trivial and apparent honor in order to lure him to his side and to do business; and, notwithstanding that there is no more proof of the second than the statement of the governor, whose veracity must not be questioned, he requests what is appropriate and practicable in the present situation, in which the only contention between the two nations must be that of diplomacy and civility. The measures to be applied are courteous demands to the commandant of Nachitoos and to Alférez St. Denis to the end that they may restrain their people within their boundaries—not going beyond to trade with the Indians of the royal crown and to confer titles of captain without authority to do so, revoking the titles that may have been given in the terms and with the statements which the señor *fiscal* suggests as appropriate to the case—and in order to disarm whatever complaint they may make if, after these friendly expostulations, French trespassers should be encountered in the territory of Texas, and their capture and the confiscation of the goods they may be attempting to introduce should be undertaken. As a consequence of this the governor shall remove from the position of captain the Indian whom the French official named, and shall appoint another with the necessary qualifications. He shall attempt to make them understand that since they are vassals of his Majesty and are living in lands under his dominion, no one else but he can confer such titles, nor can they accept them without conniving in treason and making themselves liable to severe punishment. [He shall see] also that the foreign interpreters who may be in our pueblos shall withdraw, whether they are there to make trading easier with their knowledge of the languages, or with some other secret and different purpose, which for the present it is not convenient to investigate. Thus, in regard to these particulars, and the measures for separating the Indians of that government from their inclination for and trade with the French there, if the desired end is not gained from their execution, no harm can result. The *auditor* subscribes fully to what the señor *fiscal* requests in his reply, with which your Excellency's greatness may conform, ordering what he suggests to be done.

1298. The governor also gives an account in his *consulta* of the dispute he has had with the commandant of Nachitoos, Don Cesar de Blans, from whom is the letter on folio 140. He expresses surprise therein that the governor should plan to place a presidio in the country of Nadotes, affirming with excessive presumption that it is included in the dominions of the Most Christian King, his master, to whom belong the sierras in which it is located. For this reason he, in his royal name, exhorts and demands that the governor take no step pending a decision by the two crowns, in which the limits and boundaries of both dominions may be designated. The governor replied to this what is contained in the certified copy of his letter on folio 140, and in a subsequent one, for which he asks your Excellency's approval so that he may never be charged with negligence or carelessness in the matter, and so that the French may not find support in his silence. The said letter is in fact a reply to the demand and exhortation of the French commandant, and is an authentic contradiction of the false and erroneous idea that he has that the question of whether the Nadotes belong to the monarchy of Spain or France is a subject for negotiation and discussion at any time.

1299. Just as the above action merits [official] approbation, so also does the measure the governor adopted in having the two Indian women ransomed by Don Felipe de Rábago y Terán, captain of the presidio of San Xavier, and restored to the bellicose and dreaded Apaches who on this occasion were stirring up disturbances against the Spaniards, thus leaving the Apaches content and quiet. So that he may enjoy the satisfaction of seeing that the zeal and courage with which he conducts himself in these operations in his Majesty's royal service are approved by your Excellency's superiority, and so that such deserved approbation may stimulate him to continue with the same careful attention, you will be pleased to approve what he has done in regard to the said particulars.

1300. In as much as the señor *fiscal* considers none of the measures requested by him effective for dislodging and causing the withdrawal of the French to the opposite bank of the Río Colorado [Red River]; since, as regards the plan that the said river should be the dividing line between the two crowns and that three demands should be issued by the governor of Texas to the commandant of the presidio of Nachitos, supported by armed force, as he was commanded to do in the royal order of June 20, 1751, with which the sixth *cuaderno* begins; and, in order that the powerful motives which have supervened for not executing that extreme measure under the present conditions may be clear to his Majesty, even though the more diplomatic measure of the exhortations may not bring results or have the desired effect of their leaving the land that they have usurped from the royal crown with their new presidio, moved from the small island,

1301. The *fiscal* requests that a report be made to his Majesty, and the *auditor* considers it appropriate and necessary, in order that, at the same time, the reason on which is based his opinion as to the uselessness of the demands and the little advantage that is to be expected from them, may be clear to his Majesty. He requests likewise that the king be sent a report so that he may condescend to prescribe the manner in which French deserters or traders shall be dealt with, who in time of peace or war may come over as fugitives or may be found to have penetrated into his dominions.

1302. This request doubtless was occasioned by a pertinent incident of the same nature as several that are discussed in these *autos*, namely, the capture and sending [to Mexico] of Pedro Malec and three companions,[58] all Frenchmen, which was done by the governor of New Mexico, and the investigation that he made of the direction from which they had arrived at the pueblo of Taos, from the Cumanche nation of that province. Two additional *cuadernos* of *autos* relative to this matter are filed with this one. Notwithstanding that hitherto [such intruders] have been arrested, indicted as foreigners, and sent there under special guard, it will be most important [to make a report to the

---

[58]For frequent references to Pedro Malec, or Pedro Mallet, consult the Index of *Pichardo's Treatise* . . . , Vol. III, p. 594. See particularly *ibid.*, n. 1, p. 298.

king] so that there may be a fixed rule [established] by which to be governed in a matter in which there is perhaps room for a mistaken decision. Thus if it be your Excellency's superior pleasure, you will see fit to provide for it, calling a *junta general de guerra y hacienda* to pass upon what has occurred anew, and also upon what has resulted from the decisions it has already made in the same matter.

1303. In as much as it is well for the junta to have before it for this purpose the two inquiries cited in this opinion and contained in the eighth and eleventh *cuadernos* of the *autos* of the *residencia* of Don Manuel de Sandoval, you will be pleased likewise to direct that they be brought out along with the other things for the junta, so that it may note therein what appertains to the case. Above all your Excellency's good judgment will decide upon what you may consider best, most appropriate, and most opportune. Mexico, September 25, 1753. Don Domingo Valcárcel.

1304. (Number 409.) In the *junta de guerra y hacienda* which the most excellent señor, Don Juan Francisco de Güemes y Horcasitas, ordered convoked and which was held on the 21st and 22d days of January, 1754, . . . attended by the señores Don Francisco Antonio de Echavarri, Don Domingo Valcárcel y Formento, etc., consideration was given to *autos* drawn up at the order of this captaincy-general with regard to investigating whether the French who are at the presidio of Nachitoches have advanced beyond their boundary, moving the presidio into territory of our sovereign under the same name in order to dissimulate it and to come closer to our presidio of Los Adaes, which is located in the province of Texas.

1305. The *autos* begin with those drawn up by virtue of the royal cedula issued in Buenretiro on July 15, 1740, in which his Majesty, on the occasion of having appointed Don Justo Boneo governor of that province, and being informed that while Don Manuel de Sandoval was governor of the said province the commandant of the French colony had moved his presidio of Nachitos to our possessions and to territory of his Catholic Majesty, ordered him [Boneo] to take from this capital the appropriate information and the instructions that he should receive from the most excellent señor viceroy of this kingdom, and to inform him of the truth of this matter and everything else that he might consider worth while. There was considered also the *consulta* in which Don Justo Boneo, reporting the said matter, gave an account to the most excellent señor, the Count of Fuenclara, he being viceroy, governor and captain-general of this New Spain, requesting that he be pleased to order him what he ought to do in view of his report on the subject.

1306. [The junta also examined] the opinion of the señor *auditor general de la guerra*, dated March 6, 1744, in which, regarding the point as having already been adjudged and decided in the *residencia* of Sandoval, he stated that the investigation could be dispensed with, but that if the said governor considered it necessary he might conduct it, for which purpose the cited original royal cedula should be returned to him. This was done, with the necessary instructions on the matter, based upon their respective *autos*. What is deduced from those drawn up in this case against Don Manuel de Sandoval is that the charge that was made against him—with regard to his having given opportunity for the governor-commandant of the French colony to move the fort of his presidio within territory of his Catholic Majesty, without his having impeded or obstructed its construction, because he had made use only of written protests, and that thus the commandant had time to complete his work—remained deferred, pending, and without decision in the *residencia*.

1307. But it is not shown clearly and exactly in the *autos* whether the land to which the presidio was moved belonged to the French or to the royal crown, and for this reason Señor Don Pedro Vedoya, being *fiscal* of this royal audiencia, requested in a reply of September 28, 1741, that there should be received by the then governor of that province the information for which he had asked in his preceding communications, and that he should report whatever might occur in the matter; and that likewise there should be examined in this court all those persons who might have been employed in that province. He deferred recommending the appropriate measures until seeing [these reports].

1308. According to the information that was received in this city in the presence of Señor Don Pedro Malo de Villavisencio, at that time *auditor general de la guerra*, the fact was apparent from the depositions of six leading and unexceptionable witnesses that the presidio of Nachitos, moved to the bank of the Río Colorado, was located in territory belonging to the crown of France, since it was still two and one half leagues or a little more from the boundary and dividing line between the adjoining dominions of the two crowns. This boundary they fixed not at the said river but at La Gran Montaña or Arroyo Hondo distant as many leagues again from the Spanish presidio of Los Adaes, since it is located about an equal distance between the two. From the testimony which Don Prudencio de Orobio Basterra,[59] while he was governor of that province, received at the order of the most excellent señor, the Duke of La Conquista, then viceroy, governor, and captain-general of this kingdom, it appears from the depositions of six witnesses that the territory to which the French commandant moved his presidio belongs to them and is not ours, and that before the transfer they saw and knew of some houses of various private individuals which they state were there.

1309. His Majesty's royal order contained in a letter of the most excellent señor, the Marquis of La Ensenada, dated in Aranjuez on June 20, 1751, was copied literally. Its context is concerned with the same thing and contains the same provisions as the royal cedula issued in Buenretiro on July 15, 1740, directed to Don Justo Boneo. [There was considered also] the opinion which the late Señor Marquis of Altamira, while he was *auditor general de la guerra*, issued on this matter, dated November 27, 1751. In this he stated that since there was no unusual occurrence and had not been any with regard to the usurpation, extension, or penetration of the French, and since their movements were being so carefully watched in order to obstruct any illegitimate scheme on their part that might in some way be unfavorable to or disturb the present friendly alliance between the two crowns, an account should be given to his

---

[59]Prudencio de Orobio y Bazterra was governor *ad interim* of Texas from 1737 to 1740.

Majesty, with certified documents, of what had been done pursuant to the said royal cedula; and [further that] the governor of the province of Texas should be ordered to apply himself with all due, prompt, and zealous watchfulness to check any least irregularity or excess on the part of the French, and to report everything worthy of attention that might occur and that he might note.

1310. Consideration was also given to the *consulta* in which the commandant of the island of Santa Rosa, Punta de Sigüenza stated to the most excellent señor viceroy of this kingdom that he had observed that four ships laden with people, including soldiers, settlers, women, and children, had come to the French colony for the settlement of the many lands which they today possess, always penetrating farther inland and fortifying themselves with various forts in different places, they having already formed a troop of cavalry, which they did not have [previously]. He adds that besides the said four ships, thirty-six merchant vessels had passed; that these were then in the Mississippi River, [laden] with clothing and other articles; that the said French have their annual trade in the region of Los Adaes, introducing their clothing in exchange for meats, silver, and other clothing; that the soldiers of the Spanish presidios take turns in transporting all these articles on rafts, together with the saddles for their horses which they take overland to New Orleans, in order to transport the clothing on their return and to go back to the Spanish places from which they come; and that this trade has been confirmed by the French [Spaniards] themselves on the island of Santa Rosa. For, when, in the year '49, some soldiers and sailors were dispatched from there with an officer in search of provisions, they saw more than forty of the said soldiers and civilians [from Texas] in the villa of New Orleans.

1311. There was noted also the reply of the señor *fiscal* of his Majesty, dated February 1, 1751, and the opinion of the señor *auditor general de la guerra* of the 8th of the same month, to which his Excellency conformed, and ordered the present governor of the province of Texas to proceed with the activity and zeal that a matter of such importance demands, making the necessary investigations of the subject treated in the *consultas* of the said commandant, and with regard to whether the Mississippi River should serve as the boundary of the French nation, so that in view of them suitable decisions may be made.

1312. The same thing was done with the *consulta* with which the said governor sent the proceedings executed for that purpose, in which it is clear, first, that according to the declaration of witnesses examined they have gone beyond the Río Colorado [Red River], which used to serve as boundary prior to the year 1720, penetrating since that time as far as the presidio of Los Adaes. Some [witnesses] added as proof of this the fact that when the French kept within the said boundary they did not follow their deserters across the river, nor were the Spanish deserters pursued beyond it; and that this is not true today with regard to the French, who in the time of Governor Sandoval, without any fault of his, penetrated into our territory. However, even though he had attempted to resist it, he would not have succeeded because of his small forces and the many that the Frenchman has in alliance with the Indians.

1313. Second, it appears that in the years 1750 and 1751, ships arrived from Europe at New Orleans with many regular troops and families. Third, that the troops and families were brought to extend and fortify the settlements of Caudachos, Puente Cupé, Sirinué (that is, Illinoes), and Nachitos, and that they expected to do this as soon as the crops were gathered and the Río Colorado should have more water, for at the time it was low, and therefore the people were being kept in New Orleans. Most of the witnesses added that notwithstanding what had been stated about the said people, some of them had come down by canoe to the presidio of Nachitoos, and some say that they did so with secrecy and caution.

1314. Fourth, that the commandant of Nachitoos has among the many orders with which he finds himself since the arrival of the said people, one which directs him not to impede or obstruct the trade and communication that the *alférez*, Don Luis de St. Denis, has with all the Indians of Nacodoches, Texas, and the rest; and that although the commandant has always had the said order, on this occasion he has again been especially enjoined to this effect.

1315. Fifth, that the paymaster of the royal warehouse of Nachitos has received general orders to furnish the said Don Luis with whatever he may request from the warehouse, and that he is to apply to him for everything he wishes, such as muskets, powder, shot, baize, vermilion, and other things that appeal to the Indians among whom he distributes them, because he is extremely beloved and implicitly obeyed by them. [They add] other like statements.

1316. And sixth, that in the year '50 the said *alférez*, Don Luis, came to ask permission of the [Spanish] governor to go and trade with the Indians, and, angry because it was denied him, he embarked on the Río de los Adaes in a canoe and went to the pueblo of Yatasi, whence he passed to that of Nasones, and craftily continued inland to the rest. In them he so bent the Indians to his will that the captain of the Nacodoches dared [to threaten] with his musket in his hand the missionary father of the said pueblo, Fray José Calahorra, whom, after having offended with insults, he wanted to kill for being the cause, along with the other Spaniards, for Captain Don Luis's being angry with them.

1317. That all the pueblos were prepared to take up arms against the Spaniards, whom they did not want in their lands, desiring only the French because they received everything they needed from them, which was not the case with the Spaniards; and that the Indian captain would have committed his bold act if the said reverend father had not humiliated himself. All this is learned from a certification of the reverend father missionary of the mission of San Miguel de Aguayo de los Adays. The said governor concludes with the statement that he considers it indispensable that a detachment of twenty soldiers with an experienced and zealous officer be established on the Río de San Pedro in order to observe the plans of the French and the reasons they have had for increasing their settlements. The principal care of this officer would be to win over and attract those Indians who control the rest of the nations of that whole province.

1318. A report was likewise made on the *consulta* of the said governor, dated November 8, 1751, which accompanied the preceding one. In this one he requested that he be empowered to advance the soldiers a third of what they regularly need in order that they may be equipped and supplied; and likewise, that he be authorized to trade or buy from the French of Nachitoos as much as six *arrobas* of brandy and eighteen barrels of wine, this step being necessary to prevent the soldiers from doing so by exchanging their horses and saddles for the wine.

1319. A report was also made on the measures requested and acted upon by the señor *fiscal* of his Majesty and the señor *auditor general de la guerra*, with regard to which a *junta de guerra y hacienda* was convoked. In the meeting that was held on September 25 of the said year, it was decided that there was no occasion for the establishment which the governor of the province of Texas requested to be made on the Río de San Pedro of a detachment of twenty soldiers with an experienced and zealous officer for observing the plans of the French and the reasons they might have had for increasing their settlements. [There was] even less [reason] for sending the engineer for whom his Majesty provides in his royal order of June 20, 1751, since, although from the proceedings executed by the said governor it seemed that the French had advanced beyond their territory from the time that Don Manuel de Sandoval was governor of the same province, these proceedings did not show what would be the boundary between New Orleans and his Majesty's territory—whether it should be the Río Colorado [Red River], Gran Montaña, or some other place. On the other hand, from the proceedings drawn up previously it seemed that it was the place of La Gran Montaña or Arroyo Hondo which is midway between the French presidio of Nachitoos and that of Los Adaes, the capital of the province of Texas, and therefore it was not known to what place they should be restricted, or how much land they had occupied, either as to amount or boundaries. In order to arrive at a clear understanding of what lands these were, their amount, bearings, and landmarks, and whether the Río Colorado or some other river was the dividing line between the two territories, it was decided that the present governor should be ordered to take immediately all the necessary measures for the purpose of ascertaining definitely what is the line that divides the two monarchies, receiving for this purpose the necessary depositions and executing all the requisite proceedings. He was to clear up as well the question of the year from which the French have penetrated into the territory of our sovereign; what amount they are occupying; its limits and boundaries; what settlements, forts and presidios they have built; their names, garrisons, state, and present condition. And if it should result from the proceedings that he might execute, that the Río Colorado or some other of the places cited is the boundary of the said territory, and that the French have advanced beyond it with their settlements and fortifications,

1320. He was to demand of the commandant, or governor, of the presidio of Nachitoos in the name of his Catholic Majesty that he evacuate and leave free and unobstructed all the land that he might have occupied, and that he withdraw and restrict himself to his own possessions. To this end he was to demonstrate to him that those lands into which he had trespassed belong to our sovereign, in accordance with the result of the proceedings which he might execute; and he was to repeat this measure as many as three times, presenting to him all the courteous demands that his zeal might dictate. If by force of his reasoning the said commandant should be led to withdraw to his own possessions, in that case the governor of the province of Texas was to go and demolish all the fortifications that he might have constructed, leaving a marker to indicate the limits and dividing line. In case courteous demands should have no effect, the governor was to send a report, along with the proceedings, to this captaincy-general in order that the most excellent señor viceroy of this kingdom, in view of them, might adopt the measures that he should consider most opportune, for which purpose he was to regard the royal order of June 20, 1751, as adequate authorization. A letter was to be written to the said governor enclosing a certified copy of the order mentioned so that he might proceed to put into execution the abovesaid, without having recourse to arms in either case, but making use only of courteous demands.

1321. With regard to the authority which the governor requested to be allowed to advance a third [of their pay] to the soldiers of his company, he was to be ordered to be guided by and to observe the military ordinance. [He was to be ordered] also that he was by no means to introduce the wines and brandy from the French nation that he requested, for supplying his company, and he was to apply himself to discharging his duties with care and to seeing that the soldiers of his company had no trade and commerce with that of the presidio of Nachitoos.

1322. A report was made likewise of the superior decree of conformity, dated September 26, 1752, and of the proceedings which the said governor executed pursuant to the above resolution, along with which he sent a report to this captaincy-general. It is noted that in due fulfillment of what had been decided upon in the said junta, he proceeded to examine twelve witnesses, and it appears from the deposition of the first of these witnesses that he had heard that when the French troops entered the presidio of Nachitos, the Río Colorado [Red River] served as the boundary between the two monarchies, and that this being true, everything on this side of the said river had always been considered as belonging to our Catholic King.

1323. The second witness testifies, also from hearsay, that the French were settling on this side of the river when the Señor Marquis of San Miguel de Aguayo entered, and that on this side of it were three small houses which remained there without any question being raised, aside from that which came up twenty-four years ago upon the occasion of the Reverend Father Fray Francisco Ballejo's going to baptize a child of the commandant of the French colony. When the curate there made objections he persuaded him, but in order that it might be valid, the commandant said that he would take his child to this side of the river, where, since it was on lands belonging to the Catholic King, he should baptize him.

1324. From the deposition of the third witness it appears that the boundary is the Río Colorado, and he gives as the reason the fact that he has heard that when the Señor Marquis of San Miguel de Aguayo entered, Don Luis de St. Denis told him that he could establish his presidio on the bank of the river and that he would take away his ranch house which was there, with two other houses. He adds that this notice was circulated after his captains had gone at the order of the señor marquis with Dr. Don José Codallos, at present canon of this Holy Church, to reconnoiter the banks of the river.

1325. The fourth witness agrees on this point and adds that the houses were not moved.

1326. The fifth witness says that the river is the dividing line, because the French used to pursue their deserters to it; and that today they follow them as far as the Arroyo Hondo.

1327. The sixth witness agrees with the second. The seventh testifies from hearsay that he is convinced that the Río Colorado is the dividing line.

1328. The eighth affirms the same thing and adds that the three houses still remain. The ninth is ignorant of and does not know definitely what the boundary may be, because he has heard it said by some that it is the Río Colorado and by others that it is La Gran Montaña.

1329. The tenth [states] that he does not know positively what the boundary may be. The eleventh declares by hearsay that the commandant of Nachitos had consented to the construction of the presidio on the banks of the Río Colorado and that La Gran Montaña or Arroyo Hondo is the dividing line.

1330. The twelfth [declares] that from common rumor he is convinced that the Río Colorado [Red River] is the dividing line. All agree that the French penetrated into the dominions of our sovereign in the years '34, '35, and '36, as well as that the amount of land usurped by the French is about the extent of a musketshot or a stone's throw, and that from that time up to the present they have not built or fortified any presidio either in their territory or in ours.

1331. It is noted likewise from the said proceedings that the French trade and traffic with the Texas, Nacodoches, Nasones, and Nadotes Indians, included in the province of Texas, and that they supply them with shirts, blankets, and breechclouts, muskets, powder, shot, beads, vermilion, and other articles esteemed by those nations, by which means they win the good will of the chiefs who are their leaders, and that they distinguish the latter by regaling them with laced hats, military coats, and other things esteemed among them. At the same time it is seen that the said governor, in order to confirm what has been stated, gave a commission to his lieutenant general, ordering him to go to each one of the said pueblos with instructions with regard to what he should do. From the proceedings which he executed by virtue of the order it appears that in the pueblo of Nacodoches where a captain of this nation resides, placed there by Don Pedro del Barrio while he was governor of that province, it happened that when he stated to him that it was his intention to settle in his pueblo with other Spaniards, he appeared to be pleased. He mentioned the reasons he had for being grateful; the advantages which would follow for him and his fellow-natives; the manner in which they were trading with the French; and the number of families of which they consist, together with other particulars.

1332. From the proceedings which he executed in the pueblo of Nasones it appears that when the said commissioner arrived there, its chief, or captain, was away from the pueblo, having his residence in the pueblo of Nadotes; and that they have there everything they need from the French, without going to the presidio of Los Adaes. It seems that this [Indian] official is named by the commandant of the French colony, who presented him with a coat, baton, and hat; that no other merchandise enters his pueblo except that from the French; that the said pueblo consists of twenty-four rancherias and forty armed Indian men; that at a distance of twenty leagues toward the north are the Tebancamas, a nation widely distributed and today much larger because of their union with the Pelones; that the Tebancamas are followed by the Tancangueyes, the Yujuanes, the Chicaes, the Aguajuani, the Aguajo, the Tancames, the Asinays, and Guajis, the Guesos, the Tusas, the Enanos, and many other nations, and that all are friendly to the Texas; that some Frenchmen are accustomed to go to the Tebancamas; and that although they do not go to the other nations, the latter are supplied with muskets, shot, and whatever they need from them and from the Tebancamas. It is noted likewise that when the said commissioner and those who accompanied him were ready to go to the pueblo of Nadotes, the interpreter of this nation told him not to do it because if he attempted to, it would go badly with him. To an objection that was made to him, he answered that he [the Spaniard] was by no means to pass on, because he would not permit him to do so; that what he could do was to return, as he did. The commissioner stated that this unexpected occurrence was due to a Frenchman named La Flor, who at an unseasonable hour of the previous night had persuaded them not to be friendly to the Spaniards, as they had promised to do. The instruments which the said governor sent along with these proceedings make clear the love that they [the Indians] profess for the French nation and the enmity that they hold for the Spaniards.

1333. A report was likewise made on the letters sent in reply by Don Cesar Blans, commandant of the presidio of Nachitoos, in which he acknowledges the receipt of those of Don Jacinto de Barrios, governor of the province of Texas. [A report was made] also on the *consulta* with which the latter accompanied the proceedings that have been mentioned, in which, persisting in the requests he had made previously, he added that the freedom of the negro slaves belonging to the French should be promulgated by decree, in order to deplete their forces by this means in case there should be an outbreak of war between the two crowns.

1334. Finally, a report was made on the measures requested and recommended in this matter by the señor *fiscal* of his Majesty and the señor *auditor de la guerra*, and on the superior decree of his Excellency dated the 14th of the current month. In this he ordered a *junta de guerra y hacienda* to be convoked so that in it the following points might be decided:

1335. First, as to whether it will be proper for the governor of the province of Texas to carry out the proceedings that he was ordered to execute in the above-cited previous royal junta as regards his demanding of the commandant of Nachitos in the name of his Catholic Majesty that he evacuate and leave free and unobstructed all the land that he may have occupied, and that he withdraw and restrict himself to his own possessions.

1336. Second, whether by virtue of his Majesty's order the governor should be sent one of the engineers who are in this kingdom, so that he may assist and aid him in obtaining the restoration of the usurped land, and so that a rule may be established to prevent in the future the occupation of that or any other place that may be found in his Majesty's dominions.

1337. Third, whether a squadron of twenty soldiers and. an officer should be stationed on the Río de San Pedro to observe the movements of the French. Fourth, whether the squadron of Texas should be trained in the manner of that of La Nueva Veracruz, and what measures should be taken with regard to the manner in which the French intruders are to be proceeded against. Fifth, whether the soldiers of the presidio of Los Adays should be permitted to trade with the French because of the rigor of the winter and the scarcity of wines and brandy. Sixth, whether a proclamation should be issued promising freedom to the negro slaves of the French in order to deplete the latter's forces in case of a break.

1338. Seventh, whether the trade of the French with the Indians who are within the government of Texas should be entirely prohibited; whether the commandant and *alférez* of Nachitos should be diplomatically requisitioned to the end that the rest of the Frenchmen may not penetrate or be allowed to come in to trade and traffic with the Indians subject to his Catholic Majesty, and much less to go further and confer titles upon them; whether the one that was conferred upon the captain of Nasones should be taken away; and whether the governor, in consequence of this, should go immediately and confer the title of captain of this nation or of the Nadotes upon the Indian or Indians who have the necessary qualifications. Eighth, whether the governor should demand that the commandant of Nachitos withdraw from the pueblos of our sovereign the French interpreters who are in them in case they are subjects of his Most Christian Majesty, or whether, if they are subjects of his Catholic Majesty, he should desist from the measure.

1339. After having considered everything here mentioned with the deliberation, reflection, and attention which the subjects demand, the señor *fiscal* in his turn stated: In view of the fact that he had not had before him the judicial processes which the señor *auditor* cites, nor the other preceding ones which were drawn up on the occasion of the transfer of the French presidio in the time of Don Manuel de Sandoval, it was not just that if the two judicial processes which the señor *auditor* cites, and which are made in favor of the French, are to be filed and considered, that all the preceding ones which were made in favor of the royal crown should fail to be collected, in order that, being submitted to his Majesty together with [a report of] what had been done previously, he may decide on whatever is his royal pleasure. In view of these circumstances it was resolved by common accord

1340. That as regards the first point, the most excellent señor viceroy of this kingdom shall be pleased to order that the measure decided upon in the preceding royal *junta de guerra y hacienda*—in which it was directed that the French commandant of the presidio of Nachitos be requisitioned by three demands to withdraw and restrict himself to his own possessions—be suspended. For these proceedings which Don Jacinto de Barrios y Jáuregui, the present governor of Texas, was ordered to execute, were on the hypothesis that as a result of them it would be apparent and proven that the barrier or dividing line, between Louisiana and Texas was the Río Colorado [Red River], and not some other place nearer the presidio of Los Adaes. The said governor shall also be ordered to be on the watch, with the greatest care and the zeal befitting his obligation and honor, for all the movements of the French that may be directed to expanding or advancing beyond the site to which they have been restricted since the removal of the presidio, not permitting them [to make] the least change. And he is to report to this captaincy-general whatever may occur in order that such prompt and opportune measures may be taken as are needful for obstructing the advancement of their schemes. It was resolved also that after a complete and literal certified copy is made of all the new proceedings that have been drawn up as a result of the *consulta* of the captain-commandant of the island of Santa Rosa, which are contained in the seventh *cuaderno*, a report shall be sent to his Majesty on the first occasion so that in view of it his royal will may decide whatever may be its pleasure.

1341. With regard to the second point. In as much as it was decided in the preceding royal junta that the engineer should not be sent—because certainly there is not apparent the least necessity for sending him, nor is any useful operation contemplated that he could attempt, or in which he can help or serve the governor of Texas, since nothing new is to be undertaken and things are to remain in the same state in which they have been hitherto, until his Majesty, having examined the certified copies of these new proceedings, shall order whatever may be his royal pleasure; and since the said engineer is not needed either to designate the boundary in question or to mark off the land which the French are occupying with their presidio, or to demolish their buildings, and even less to construct new ones—the said most excellent señor will be pleased likewise to order that in this matter the governor must faithfully observe and comply with what was decided in the *junta general de guerra y hacienda* held on September 25, 1752.

1342. With regard to the third point. Since in the whole extent of the province of Asinays, which is commonly called Texas, there is no river whatsoever known or spoken of by the name of Río de San Pedro, which would be at a suitable distance and location for observing the schemes and movements of the French in the colonies adjacent to it; and since the only place named San Pedro is the first pueblo of the Navidachos on the other side of the Río de la Trinidad on the direct road to our presidio of Los Adays, it is not apparent what opposition a detachment of twenty soldiers at this place can make against the French who might be scheming to penetrate into our possessions and introduce their commerce and trade among the nations of the royal crown. It is too distant and not appropriately located for the purpose for which the detachment will be intended, especially if perhaps the Río de San Pedro of which the governor speaks is [the one] between which and the Río de San Antonio the presidio of San Antonio de Béxar is situated, the lattter being two hundred leagues from that of Los Adaes, [which is] the nearest to the French presidio of Nachitos. As a result, opposition to [the

ingress of] the French into Texas and observation of their schemes and movements become even more impracticable, because it is possible that the river
and place may be one and the same. Furthermore, the insufficient information
with which the governor persists in [advocating] the measure of the detachment on the Río de San Pedro makes a decision on the point impossible,
putting it back into its former difficult state without any new document or
evidence which was not available to the said junta and which, discussed
therein, would have brought about a contrary decision. This is especially
true in as much as the establishment of the detachment would certainly and
necessarily be costly to the royal treasury because of the increase in the
number of soldiers, and their corresponding salaries, and it is very uncertain
whether it will prove useful and efficacious for the purpose for which it is
created. Its usefulness will be proven only when there may be evidence that
the said Río de San Pedro is in the province; that it is located and flows at
such a distance and in such a manner that the movements of the French can
be observed from the site on which the detachment would be stationed; and
that there is only one narrow crossing available by means of which it can be
forded and passage found from one bank to the other, and from which alone
can be impeded with convenience and advantage the entrance of the French
and the introduction of their commerce into the province of Texas, as well as
the passage of the nations included in its district and vicinity to the presidio of
Nachitoos or any other settlement of the French colonies. For it would be
of little advantage for the detachment to be stationed at one place if along
the entire length of the river's course there were many well known, easy, and
safe fords by which to cross without encountering opposition from the detachment. [This is true] because, if their retreat were cut off and the French
should take some other crossing either higher up or farther below, although
it might be at the cost of a short detour, the trespassers would accomplish
safely their schemes of trading and intercourse with the Indians of the crown
of Spain, and the detachment would be idle and useless, the purpose for which
it had been created being thus defeated.

1343. It follows from this that until the governor shall designate with a
map, or description, which is the Río de San Pedro, its length, and the other
circumstances just mentioned, with which procedure he could have furnished
information from the beginning regarding his proposal for the detachment, it
cannot either be adopted, or rejected on the basis of impending harm to the
royal treasury as the result of disbursements for its salaries and the other
expenditures that it might entail as a new establishment. The said most
excellent señor will therefore be pleased to order the present governor of
Texas, Don Jacinto de Barrios y Jáuregui, to supply the information that is
lacking with an adequate account of the nature of the place in which the
detachment is to be stationed, which he has referred to in his *consultas*,
reporting on this matter very clearly everything that he may find to be most
useful and conducive to the royal service in the new examination that he will
conduct to this end. The said most excellent señor will reserve for himself
the final disposition and decision with regard to the detachment, in view of
what the proceedings which the said governor shall remit may show.

1344. As regards the fourth point. In view of its having been one of those discussed in the cited royal junta, which failed to approve or to consider feasible the suggestion that the squadron of Texas be trained in the manner of that of La Nueva Veracruz, and still less to consider it proper to change the type of that militia, it was resolved to observe the decision already made on this matter because of the merits and reasons that the señor *auditor general de la guerra* explains diffusely in his opinion of September 25 of the year just past of 1753, until his Majesty, having seen the certified copy of *autos* which is to be sent with the report, shall decide whatever may be his royal pleasure.

1345. As to the fifth point relative to the governor's suggestion concerning the permitting of a limited trade with the French in wine and brandy, which he considers necessary for the maintenance of the presidials because of the rigor of the winter in that region and the difficulty in obtaining, the scarcity, and the poor quality of these articles which are brought to the presidios from other provinces of the kingdom, the said most excellent señor will be pleased to order that there be observed in this case likewise the decision which was made on this point in the said royal junta. To this end the said governor, Don Jacinto de Barrios y Jáuregui, shall be ordered that the commercial measure which he suggests in his *consulta*, although he considers it appropriate for the reasons he gives in his report, is totally opposed to his Majesty's strict prohibitions, which exclude indefinitely all trade, no matter what semblance or pretext might be used to give it an honest appearance. With this understanding and without even the least interpretation that may relax or weaken its complete vigor and force, the governor shall be advised that this should be his chief obligation, in the discharge of which he is to prove his zeal and assiduity in the royal service, conducting himself with the same care and vigilance with regard to these articles that he shows in connection with other merchandise of illicit commerce, not permitting his presidials to lose their horses and saddles in making such exchanges, and punishing severely anyone he may find to have transgressed in this matter.

1346. With regard to the sixth point concerning the permission which the governor of Texas requests to issue a proclamation promising freedom to the negroes belonging to the French who might escape from those colonies and come to take refuge in that province, the said most excellent señor will be pleased to deny this request, giving him to understand that under the present laws in no manner whatsoever is such a measure proper, honest, or decorous, and that it would rather serve to change the minds of the French and provoke the very war that he fears.

1347. Concerning the seventh point relative to whether the trade of the French with the Indians who are within the government of Texas should be prohibited, and the rest that is included in this point, it was decided to inform the said governor that the Frenchmen who had attempted to introduce trade with the Indians of New Mexico have been arrested by its governor. He has sent them to this capital, and they have been sent on to his Majesty under special guard,[60] with a certified copy of the *autos* that have been drawn up on

---

[60]Consult *Pichardo's Treatise* . . . , Vol. III, p. 363, n. 84.

the matter. The governor shall keep this information to himself and have recourse to it on the occasions that may be offered to him, until, after a report has been sent to his Majesty of everything that has happened in that province with regard to this matter, some other decision may be made. He shall pursue this investigation [of the Indian trade] vigorously, using discretion, industry, and viligance, in the diplomatic and conciliatory manner which the said *junta de guerra* held on September 25 of the year just passed of 1752 charged him to employ. This measure shall be recommended to him in general, leaving to his judgment the working out of the details in accordance with the occasions and opportunities that may present themselves, in order that its enforcement may not irritate the indisposed minds of the Indians, and so that no break or unpleasantness may be experienced in the good relations which it is important to keep unimpaired.

1348. Pursuant to the above, the governor shall demand of the *alférez*, Don Luis de St. Denis, that he recall the title which he conferred upon the captain of Nasones and shall advise him that it was conferred by him without his having had authority to do so. Consequently the said governor of Texas shall go immediately and confer the title of captain in Nasones and in Nadotes upon such Indian or Indians as he may see fit, and appoint others having the necessary qualifications. He shall endeavor to impress them with the understanding that since they are vassals of his Majesty and live on lands under his dominion, no one but he can confer such titles nor can they accept them without incurring [suspicion of] treason and making themselves liable to severe punishment. Carrying out the purpose of winning the Indians away from their love for and trade with the French, and of drawing their affection and trade to the Spaniards, he shall act with the sagacity, prudence, and discretion required for accomplishing this end. He shall make representations to the commandant of Nachitoos regarding the act which the Frenchman named La Flor committed; he shall persuade the captain of Nasones to make amends for such an unjustified demonstration; and he shall send a report of what may result, with the judicial proceedings and anything else that his zeal may dictate.

1349. And with regard to the eighth and last point it was decided to order the governor of Texas to demand that the commandant of Nachitos withdraw from the pueblos of our sovereign the French interpreters whom he may have in them, in case these are vassals of his Most Christian Majesty. If they are subjects of his Catholic Majesty, he shall discontinue the measure. On his part the governor shall execute all the measures that his zeal may dictate for preventing such a procedure from being carried out, and shall conduct himself in this matter with the same prudence and diplomacy that he is ordered to observe in the rest.

1350. Also the abovesaid most excellent señor will be pleased to state to the said governor that the discussion which he carried on with the commandant of Nachitoos, Don Cesar Blans, proving to him that the nations of the Nadotes and Nasones Indians are direct subjects of our sovereign, was satisfactory and gratifying to him, as was the ransom of the two Apache Indian women whom he returned to their nation through Don Felipe Rábago y Terán, captain of the presidio of San Xavier. Thus they provided and signed it, with the said most excellent señor.

1351. His Excellency disposed of [the findings of] this junta as follows:

Mexico, January 30, 1754. I conform to the decision made in the preceding royal junta, and by virtue of it let a certified copy of it be made and remitted with a letter to the present governor of the province of Texas for his information and observance, manifesting to him the approbation that he has deserved in what he has done pursuant to the orders that were given him. Let another copy be made in duplicate of the seventh *cuaderno,* as has been ordered in the said royal junta, which shall be accompanied in the same form by the reports received by Señor Don Pedro Malo and Don Prudencio de Orobio y Basterra, and also by the report which, under date of July 28, 1717, was made to his Majesty by Señor Don Juan de Oliván then *auditor general de la guerra,* in order that in the presence of all these documents he may decide whatever may be his royal pleasure. Signed with his Excellency's rubric.

1352. This complete *expediente* occasioned the dispatch of the following cedulas which are found in document 39, number 252, and in the others that are cited therein.

In the letters of February 16 and July 25 of last year your Excellency reports the importunities which the commandant of the province of Louisiana made to you with regard to establishing a cartel with the presidio of Los Adays for the mutual restitution of French and Spanish deserters. Your Excellency refused this on the ground of not having an order from the king, fearing that this would lead to maintaining spies who would go to mark out the land and observe the settlements that are in those dominions. Your Excellency reports also that you had learned from the governor of La Havana and the president of [the audiencia of] Santo Domingo that more than 1,600 troops, a good many arms, and some provisions had been brought to Leogal (it seems that this should read Leogane, which is a French villa in the part of Santo Domingo which belongs to them—see the *Diccionario* of Alcedo under the word "Leogane") and to El Guarico, and that barracks were being built for more than four thousand. While your Excellency considered that there is probably more exaggeration than truth in all this, nevertheless you were taking due precautions, and repeating the request that you had made before to send you six or eight thousand muskets with bayonets.

1353. I have informed the king of the context of your Excellency's letters and of the certified copies of documents enclosed with them. In view of them his Majesty has been pleased to approve the reply which your Excellency gave to the commandant of Louisiana, refusing to establish the cartel which he was soliciting. His Majesty orders me also to advise your Excellency to observe in the future the same practice that has been followed hitherto, in no manner whatsoever permitting the governor of the province of Texas to deliver or return the Frenchmen who under the name of deserters or on some other pretext may come to or enter by way of Los Adaes, or some other part of the territories under his jurisdiction, for your Excellency's suspicion that they may want to obtain information about those settlements and the state of the forces that may be there, is plausible. His Majesty therefore desires that your Excellency and your successors continue to refuse to agree to the mutual restitution of deserters by way of Los Adaes, for the legitimate reason that you are not authorized to do so either by an order of his Majesty for changing the existing practice, or by agreeing to a new regulation.

1354. In a dispatch boat which left Cádiz for Vera Cruz on the 18th of this month, four hundred muskets with bayonets are being sent for your Excellency's disposal, and in the others that may follow and in other vessels which may sail for that kingdom, the remittance will be continued until the six thousand which your Excellency has requested are completed. His Majesty has ordered them sent to your Excellency (for which purpose they are already in Cádiz) so that you may distribute them in the manner which you may consider most conducive to the security of those provinces. At the same time his Majesty charges your Excellency to be constantly on the alert and to give the most vigilant attention to the operations of the French so that if they should attempt to expand or advance in the region of Texas, New Mexico, or some other, demands may be made to them immediately that they desist. Your Excellency is to send his Majesty successive and exact reports of everything that may occur in this particular. You will be guided by the royal order of June 20 of last year, with regard to inducing the commandant of Nachitos by efficacious representations to abandon the second presidio of Nachitoos and the island with the farms, without your Excellency s having recourse for the present to armed force in case he should refuse, so as not to cause immediate disturbance and difficulties in those regions, that may have far-reaching effects in Europe.

1355. His Majesty relies on your Excellency's prudence and distinguished conduct. You shall look upon this matter as of the highest importance, and shall apply your measures opportunely in the proper manner, making a report of what may occur on every occasion, so that his Majesty may be informed. God keep your Excellency many years. Madrid, July 26, 1752. The Marquis of La Ensenada. To the Señor Count of Revilla Gigedo.

1356. (Number 256.) Your Excellency's letter of June 22 has just been received, in which you report that six Frenchmen from New Orleans entered the province of New Mexico[61], and that upon the advice of the *auditor de guerra* your Excellency ordered that governor to send those as well as any others who may still come, to Nueva Vizcaya or to Sonora, where they might be assigned a place to live.

---

[61]For details concerning expeditions of French traders from Louisiana to New Mexico during the middle of the eighteenth century, consult *Pichardo's Treatise . . .* , Vol. III, Chapter VIII.

1357. [Your Excellency states] that when four other Frenchmen afterward arrived in New Mexico with some merchandise[62], the governor sent them from magistrate to magistrate to that City of Mexico, the cost being defrayed by the goods that they carried. After having taken several depositions from them, your Excellency decided, upon advice of the *fiscal*, that they should be sent to Vera Cruz so that they might be dispatched to these kingdoms as foreigners, consigned to the tribunals of the Casa de Contratación. Your Excellency also encloses a certified copy of the four *cuadernos* of *autos* executed in this instance, and as a result of the commandant of the presidio of Pensacola having reported that four ships had arrived at New Orleans with troops and families, who were proceeding inland toward the jurisdiction of Texas and the presidio of Los Adaes. Your Excellency concludes with [the statement] that the preparations of the French arouse strong suspicions that they have hidden designs, because, although they have so much unappropriated land possessed by the barbarian Indian nations, their ambition was leading them to penetrate even the possessions of his Majesty, which have not sufficient garrisons to oppose disciplined and well armed troops.

1358. I have given an account to the king of the cited letter, and bearing in mind what your Excellency was ordered in the decree of July 26 of last year, the original of which was sent to your Excellency in the ship for New Spain, his Majesty instructs me to send your Excellency on this occasion the enclosed duplicate, so that you may carry out everything ordered in it and report the results on the first occasion. Your Excellency will explain to his Majesty the measures that you think should be adopted in the future to prevent the extension of the French into his Majesty's possessions, and the designs that could bring them into their vicinity. God preserve your Excellency many years. Madrid, January 24, 1753. The Marquis of La Ensenada. To the Señor Count of Revilla Gigedo.

1359. (Number 259.) In a letter of June 29 of this year your Excellency states that at the request of the governor of the Texas, Don Jacinto del Barrio [de Barrios] y Jáuregui, your Excellency ordered that seventeen soldiers who were detached at the missions be returned to the presidio of Los Adays. You state also that as a result of the commission which your Excellency gave him it was proven that his predecessor had not traded illicitly with the French of New Orleans as had been supposed; that the latter had crossed the boundary—the farther bank of the Río Colorado [Red River] being their limit— and the bank on this side being the limit of the dominion of Spain; that they had penetrated to both sides of the said river in order to fortify themselves; that the commandant of the presidio of Nachitoos had orders to win those nations to his side by every means, some of which nations have begun to maltreat the Spaniards; that after everything had been examined by the *fiscal* and the *auditor de guerra*, it was decided to hold a junta in which were discussed the eight points which your Excellency sets forth, and with whose opinion your Excellency agreed, the principal decision being to requisition the French as many as three times to withdraw from the usurped land, designating

---

[62]*Ibid.*

the boundary and limits of both nations; and that, after everything had been arranged, the corresponding order had been given to the governor of the Texas, from whom your Excellency had not yet received a reply. You close by stating that what the king had commanded in the order of June 20, 1751, would be duly put into effect, as well as what had been decided upon in the junta, because of the distrust inspired by the French, who are constantly increasing their forces by winning those nations to their side, contrary to the existing friendship and alliance between the two crowns.

1360. I have acquainted the king very minutely with the context of the said letter of your Excellency, and in view of it his Majesty has approved the measures that your Excellency adopted and the commission that you gave to the governor of Texas, together with everything decided upon in the junta which was held as a result of what he had reported. Bearing in mind how important it is that the French shall withdraw from the land that they have usurped to Nachitoos and the Río Colorado, his Majesty orders me to send you the most strict special charge to carry out on your part with the zeal, vigilance, and attention which are such a credit to your Excellency, everything that you have been ordered to do, so as to succeed in defending and preserving the territory and settlements that belong to his Majesty in the said province of the Texas. Your Excellency will apply all the methods, expedients, and orders that you may consider appropriate, and will report on all occasions everything that you may have done in this matter, so that it may be brought to his Majesty's attention, for he awaits it impatiently because of the seriousness of the affair. God keep your Excellency many years. Madrid, December 16, 1753. The Marquis of La Ensenada. To the Señor Count of Revilla Gigedo.

CHAPTER XV

PICHARDO'S CONCLUSIONS, BASED ON DOCUMENTARY EVIDENCE, CONCERNING THE BOUNDARY DISPUTES BETWEEN TEXAS AND LOUISIANA IN THE MIDDLE OF THE EIGHTEENTH CENTURY

1361. Here end all the documents that I have been able to see and copy, which relate to the tumultuous disputes over boundaries that took place in the middle of the past century between the Spaniards and the French, which notices the royal order requires to be collected. By the terms of my commission, I am obligated to express my conclusion and designate the limits from the information that I have acquired in the examination of the books and manuscripts, together with the maps. [In this connection] I am of the opinion that—assuming that his Majesty's cedulas and the orders of the most excellent señor, the Marquis of Casafuerte, in favor of the French have not been revoked, as we have shown above—the French in consequence of the [act of] possession of Monsieur de la Salle which extended to all of the Mississippi and to all of the rivers that flow into it, directly or indirectly, with the lands which they drain, could move their presidio of Nachitoches from the island on which they founded it to the other side of the river on the site where they had erected houses, gardens, and corrals, as territory that was drained by the Red River or, so to speak, was protected by the shield of its current. In as much as the French believed that this protection did not extend over a small area of land, but over a more or less large quantity, according to the way the land lay, they extended their territory in that region to La Gran Montaña and the Arroyo Hondo, through which, as I believe, no waters flow that issue from or enter a river which they had appropriated for themselves.

1362. For, in truth, I perceive from the injustice with which the French appropriated for themselves all the lands of Louisiana, that they observed this maxim based on the procedure of Monsieur Champlain[1] and the rule of Señor Marca,[2] of which we have spoken

---

[1]Reference is to Samuel de Champlain, a French explorer of the St. Lawrence River in the early seventeenth century.

[2]Reference is to Pierre de Marca, Archbishop of Paris, a sketch of whose life is found in *Pichardo's Treatise* . . . , Vol. I, pp. 270–271.

above beginning with paragraph 2, to wit: That all the rivers which entered the Mississippi belonged to them, together with all the other waters, permanent as well as existent only during the rainy season, which enter or leave the Mississippi and the rivers that flow into the latter. In this manner the waters that might issue from these rivers thereby appropriated to France the lands which they watered. Likewise all the lands that might send their rivers or rain waters to some French river were regarded accordingly as a part of the [lands of which] Monsieur de la Salle had taken possession. This is seen clearly in the case of the Missouri, for they appropriated it because it enters the Mississippi. [The same is true in] the case of the Arkansas and the Red, for the same reason that they flow into that great river, to which the ancient Indians gave the name of Meschasipi, that is to say, the Father of Rivers. On the contrary, I would call it their large son, because of the infinity of rivers which combine to form it, flowing into it from both sides, that is, from the east and from the west, to increase its volume. The same Mississippi, as we have seen, by breaking its dikes, diverts its waters, which go to join the Chafalaya, and, united with this river, flows into the sea in the Bahía de la Ascensión. For this reason the French took also the land which lies between the Mississippi and the Chafalaya.

1363. On the contrary, when a territory neither received French waters nor gave them to the French rivers, it remained in the dominions of Spain. For this reason D'Anville proceeded to draw his line with the greatest exactness, especially through the lands that are immediately above the province of Texas from the presidio of Nachitoches, and from the latter down to the sea or Gulf of Mexico. The Arroyo Hondo, in my opinion, carries some water which no doubt is of this last variety, that is to say, which neither comes from French territory nor goes to disembogue in one of the rivers which the French appropriated.

1364. They therefore fixed their boundary at the said Arroyo Hondo. From this comes the fact, as Señor Codallos declared—a declaration to which no one has given consideration—that St. Denis agreed with the Marquis of San Miguel de Aguayo that for the time being the Arroyo Hondo should remain as the boundary between the two monarchies. Thus the señor *auditor de la guerra,* Valcárcel, relates it in these words, copied above in paragraph 1264:

Doctor Don José Codallos y Rabal, a canon of the holy Metropolitan Church of Mexico, an individual of extraordinary energy and intelligence, who entered with the marquis and examined all those countries, and took a leading part in the expedition, having twice lodged in a house with good accommodations which Monsieur Pierre had on this side of the Río Colorado [Red River], where he had established an hacienda. [He, in] replying with the other witnesses on various matters, declares openly that the transferred presidio is in territory belonging to the French, this admitting of no doubt, and that, on that occasion, by agreement with the French, La Montaña Grande, which is midway between the two points, was designated by the clause "for the present" as the boundary between the presidios of Nachitos and Los Adaes. The other [witnesses] agree to this unanimously.

1365. This temporary designation was never confirmed, for neither did the Spaniards think any more of it, nor was it advantageous to the French for it to be decided, because in the meantime they were in possession of the territory. If the Marquis of San Miguel de Aguayo had ordered this incident to be recorded in his diary, or if it had been written in some other instrument which could have been widely circulated, Don José González, Father Ballejo, the other residents of Los Adaes, and the governor of Texas, Don Manuel de Sandoval, would have seen it, and, in view of it, would have taken no action when they noticed that the French were beginning to transfer their presidio. For they would have known that they were making this transfer within territory which the said marquis had conditionally agreed belonged to the French, and that the expression "present boundary" applied only as far as the Arroyo Hondo. This instrument would have favored the said Governor Sandoval and would have served him as a defense against the charge which the judge of his *residencia*, Briseño, brought against him. See above, paragraph 977.

1366. Since the Marquis of San Miguel de Aguayo, however, perhaps, did not give an account to the government of this action of his in favor of the French, or gave it very superficially, it was entirely unknown and was not quoted in any of the proceedings. St. Denis was not ignorant of it and therefore he cited it in his replies to the lieutenant of Los Adaes, Don José González, and to the governor of Texas, Don Manuel de Sandoval. To the first he says in reply to his third requisition (above, paragraph 891):

While Don Fernando de Almazán was governor, the Marquis of Aguayo saw that this land which is in dispute was founded, settled, and inhabited by the French and other Spanish governors have seen the same thing, and none has opposed it.

In reply to the second he writes as follows, as we have seen above in paragraph 897:

But, in fact, in 1715 I had left two Frenchmen in possession of both banks of the Río Colorado de los Nachitoos [Red River] before I left the Asinais. When I returned to them (the Frenchmen) after the founding of the missions had been completed, I found them under the jurisdiction of the captain of a company. Aside from this I found two substantial houses built by two French residents on the same land which you are now disputing and on which our presidio is being placed. Therefore, the title cannot be more publicly known or more certain, and neither the viceroy of Mexico nor any governor will make claims against it any longer.

1367. And [he writes] a little farther on (paragraph 899):

You state that distinct and express orders came from the viceroy now governing as well as from his predecessors, not to permit the erection of or to tolerate any house on the said land. But even though it was of such importance, no opposition has arisen from your predecessors with regard to the said settlements from their founding to the present day. This must be because they knew of the right acquired. . . . Things remained in this state down to the time of the expedition of the Señor Marquis of San Miguel de Aguayo, who was sent to restore the abovesaid missions which in time of war had suffered some damage. The said marquis sent Don Fernando de Almazán to visit the banks of the Río Colorado [Red River], but since he found them occupied and settled by the French, he returned to Los Adays and founded the presidio which flourishes today.

1368. In another letter, above in paragraph 932, St. Denis writes to him [the governor] as follows:

The land of Nachitoos has always been situated as it is today. There the Río Colorado, or Rubro [Red], flows from north to south. I have here on the east side the land of the French, who inhabit it. On the west is an island on which the French presidio was placed in the beginning, and on which it remained until the day of its removal. Between the two is the river itself. The said island most certainly belongs to the disputed land, because on its west side there is nothing except a flat hillock which, when the river is flooded, encloses a branch of it. When the latter is dry it is not extensive and does not form any obstacle. On the contrary, one travels without difficulty from the island to the disputed territory and to the site of the presidio. Perchance the Spanish señores do not know that the Nachitoches Indians had their camp and their homes on the said island, on the west side of Río Colo-·

rado, before the French came to Nachitoches and also at the very time that the said Frenchmen placed their presidio on the said island.

1369. If, before the Spanish and French señores came to these lands, some-one had stated that the said island did not belong to the disputed territory, the Nachitoches Indians would most certainly have objected and have proven that the Nachitoches Indians should at least be conceded as much right to go as far as the Adaes Indians, as the Indians of Los Adaes had to go as far as the Nachitoches Indians; or at any rate that the land should be so divided between both that each Indian nation might enjoy an equal portion of it, as is the case between the Tunicas and the Houmas Indians on the Mississippi River. And no one at any time should claim that the land of the Nachitoos Indians was only that included on the east side of the river. This being true, we should enjoy the rights of the Indians, when in truth neither we Frenchmen nor the Spaniards set foot on these barbarian lands except as they wished it and consented to it.

1370. I infer from this argument of St. Denis that the Nachi-toches Indians were owners of the land which extends from La Gran Montaña or Arroyo Hondo to the Red River, and from the latter to the east. This determines the western territory which I tentatively assigned to the Nachitoches Indians in paragraph 1583 of the [discussion of the] expedition of Hernando de Soto, when I wrote these words:

I judge that all this territory belonged to the Nachitoches Indians, because these Indians inhabited and were the owners of the territory through which the Red River flowed toward the French and Spanish presidios of Nachitoches and Adaes. (See the letter of Monsieur de St. Denis in document 26, num-ber 17.) These Indians, therefore, were masters of the lands to the east and west through which a part of the Red River passed.

In paragraph 936 St. Denis adds:

The French presidio always had the river to the east and the disputed land to the west, and the Spaniards have never attempted to object to its position. This indicates that the status of the French dominion is certain and secure, and we follow the same course in the removal of the said presidio. Then on what basis is the disturbing question now raised? In fact, most illustrious sir, I am today following the same course: I am removing our presidio only a stone's throw from the site where it formerly was. It is a place midway between an adjoining lake and a branch of the river which becomes dry and which has been crossed and is being crossed today without difficulty.

1371. And in paragraph 948 he says also:

It was not without a feeling of surprise that I read this statement in your letter: "*The second [reason] is that French courtesy offered a suitable site for the construction of the presidio [of Los Adaes] on the other side of the land on which today your Honor wishes to introduce himself. It seems that this urbane action, because of its being so well known to all who were present on that occasion, is sufficiently authentic.*" And thus, most illustrious sir, the French through their courtesy offered land to Don Fernando Almazán on which to place the Spanish presidio. Don Fernando did not wish to accept it. Then the French offered what was their own. . . . Then this is in favor of the French. Then this courtesy of the French should not be cited in your support.

1372. It is to be wondered, therefore, since this incident of the declaration of Señor Codallos is brought out in St. Denis's letters, why neither the señores *fiscales*, nor the *auditores de guerra*, nor Sandoval's lawyers should have given any consideration to it. What is more, the said declaration of Señor Codallos is mentioned only in the opinion of Señor Valcárcel. Nor can the truth of this incident be doubted, for it is testified to by Señor Codallos, who accompanied the Señor marquis on his expedition to Texas in the capacity which Bachiller Peña states in number 7 of our document 21, in these words:

A few days later the Señor Doctor Don José Codallos y Rabal, censor and commissary of the Holy Office [of the Inquisition], synodal examiner of the bishopric of Guadalajara, *ex-visitador* of it, and ecclesiastical judge of Mazapil and of Saltillo, arrived from Coahuila at the Río del Norte. He is entering Texas in the capacity of vicar-general, with the delegation of all the powers of the señor bishop of Guadalajara, to whose jurisdiction the said province belongs.

1373. The same Señor Codallos at the end of the said document placed this certification, signed by his hand before an ecclesiastical notary. It reads as follows:

Doctor Don José Codallos y Rabal, censor and commissary of the Holy Office [of the Inquisition], *ex-visitador-general* of the bishopric of Guadalajara, synodal examiner of it, ecclesiastical judge-vicar of the mining camp and mines of San Gregorio del Mazapil and the villa of Saltillo, vicar-general of the provinces of Texas and Nuevas Filipinas, etc. I certify in so far as I am able that the *Derrotero* which Bachiller Don Juan Antonio de la Peña, vicar-general of the battalion of San Miguel de Aragón, has written and signed, dealing with the journey and expedition which the señor Marquis of San Miguel de Aguayo has made to the province of the Texas for its recovery, the restoration of the missions, and the establishment of a barrier with the building of the presidios of Los Adays, Texas, and Bahía del Espíritu Santo—

which have been garrisoned from these dominions of New Spain—is accurate, true, and written with the greatest exactness in every respect. For I was present at all the events since I accompanied the said señor marquis from the time he left the Río Grande del Norte until he returned to this villa of Santiago de Monclova, capital of the province of Coahuila, where, in order that this may be evident, I signed it on June 23, 1722. Doctor Don José Codallos y Rabal. Before me, Antonio de Espronzeda, ecclesiastical notary.

1374. St. Denis would certainly be careful to give a report to his court of the agreement with the marquis and he would perhaps give it with the map of which we have spoken before, in paragraph 49, and which we believe he would have made either by himself or with the help of some other engineers. He would place on it the dividing line passing through the Arroyo Hondo in accordance with the agreement with the said marquis, and for that reason Monsieur D'Anville, considering it permanent, followed it; or rather, he would transcribe the dividing line, making it pass through the middle of the territory between Los Adaes and Nachitoches, which middle point, as we have seen so many times, is found at the said Arroyo Hondo. The result of everything that has been stated is, therefore, that the boundary between Adays and Nachitos passes through the Arroyo Hondo or Gran Montaña. Let me be permitted to make a suggestion here. Was there perchance no other region through which these boundaries would be extended, since no mention is made of them? Is it possible that so many suits against Sandoval, so many opinions of the *fiscales*, so many reports that came out of the *auditoría de guerra*, would be restricted only to this one point of La Gran Montaña?

1375. Why were not the inquiries and investigations extended toward the north and south in order to ascertain what the French had taken in these two regions? Suppose that the French had withdrawn their presidio to the old site and that the Spanish possessions had extended plainly and clearly to the Red River. Then where should this dividing line ascend toward the north? Ought it to go in a straight line, cutting the river? But this could not be, because the Spaniards had already agreed that the Cadodachos, who are to the west of this Red River, should be left to the French. If the Red River remained as the boundary of this nation, notwithstanding that it extends from east to west, it should be considered as the barrier for all the northern lands of the province of Texas, which barrier should retain the said lands, with the exception of the Cadodachos, for Spain.

1376. But for this purpose it should have been agreed that the French might build presidios on the north side of the said river, since the south bank already belonged to Spain. The limits which were to be assigned to the Cadodachos should also have been agreed upon. None of this was discussed, and neither was the question as to the lands through which the dividing line should run from the presidio of Nachitoches south to the sea. It should have been decided whether the same Red River was to continue as the dividing line to its confluence with the Mississippi, and that thus all the southern lands such as those which the Opeluses, Atacapas, etc., occupied, would belong to Spain, or whether, the Red River ceasing to be the dividing line, it should be some other that might be drawn from the river to the sea. But not a single word was said about this in all the discussions that we have seen. The whole controversy centered solely around La Gran Montaña.

1377. Then were these lands to the south and north of this mountain less valuable to Spain, so that she would not protest the Frenchman's taking them? In due time we shall see the efforts that were made to keep the French from establishing themselves in the southern region which the Spaniards claimed as their own. For the present we shall treat only of those lands which the French appropriated in the northern regions. We have seen that they had taken the Arcansas, the Cadodachos, and the Panis even before the expedition of the Marquis of San Miguel de Aguayo. After the Cadodachos they took the others of whom we have treated in the notes which we made to the *Historical Sketches* of Dr. Sibley, and in other preceding places.[3] But, since hitherto we have not spoken a word concerning the proceedings executed by Don Manuel Antonio de Soto Bermúdez, commissioned by the señor governor, Don Jacinto Barrios, we shall discuss them now in order to examine the procedure of Monsieur de St. Denis, the son: Whether or not he acted therein against the Spaniards by penetrating into their lands, or whether he conducted his operations only within the limits which France had prescribed for herself.

---

[3] See *Pichardo's Treatise* . . . , Vol. I, p. 368, n. 2.

1378. In document 21, number 88, it is said that it is well known how St. Denis, the father, dissimulated his regret that the Marquis of Aguayo had recovered Los Adays, because of its being a place to which the French had aspired, as it was very important to them for their communication with the presidio that they have among the Cadodachos. This need of theirs for Los Adays was due chiefly to lack of roads by which to go to the Cadodachos whenever the water of the Red River was low and it could not be easily navigated. Perhaps for this reason his son, St. Denis, finding it necessary to go to the pueblos north of Nachitoches and not being able to do so because of the low water in the Red River, or perhaps for some other reason analogous to this one, submitted to requesting permission from the governor of the province of Texas, Don Jacinto Barrios, to go by way of Los Adays to the said pueblos. This appears in paragraph 1083, in which is stated:

During the past year of 1750, in the month of August, the said *alférez*, Don Luis de St. Denis, irritated because the señor governor had denied him the permission he had asked to go and trade with the Indians, embarked on the Río de los Adaes in a canoe and went to the pueblo of Yatasi, whence he passed on to that of Nasones; and he craftily continued inland to the rest [of the pueblos]. In them he reduced the Indians to his will.

1379. But what were the results of this refusal of the governor of Texas, which was so well justified? It has already been stated in the same place that, irritated by it, he [St. Denis] embarked on the Río de Los Adays in a canoe and went to the pueblo of Yatasi and to the others, and in them subjected the Indians to his will. In this action of St. Denis, the son, it was seen clearly to what anger may lead. What except anger could have led him to go to the Nasonis? This pueblo belonged to Spain and had never belonged to the French, and a proof of this is the mission which the Spaniards had maintained in it, in the founding of which his father, St. Denis, had taken part (see paragraph 763 of Part II, and above, paragraph 897). Father Fray Isidro Felix de Espinosa writes (in his *Chrónica Apostólica y Seráfica de todos los Colegios de Propaganda Fide de esta Nueva España*, book 5, chapter 8, pages 416ff.) :

In the year 1715 two Frenchmen from Mobile arrived at the presidio of San Juan Bautista under the pretext of coming for cattle and provisions. They were sent by the captain to the most excellent señor viceroy, the Duke of Linares. And his Excellency, considering, with his great comprehension, and after consultation with his royal junta, that pernicious consequences might result from the introduction of these Frenchmen into the dominions of his Catholic Majesty, ordered that some missionary religious should go immediately to the province of Texas to found missions, protected by twenty-five soldiers with their officer, in order that by this means the Indians of the said province might be introduced to our holy faith for the spiritual good of their souls, and so that the reduction of the other neighboring nations [might be accomplished]. Thereby the entrances of the French to discover more lands into which to introduce their commerce would be successfully prevented. The viceroy designated Alférez Domingo Ramón[4] as captain. . . . They (the religious) left this college on January 21, 1716, with many good wishes from this holy community. . . .

1380. With a small viaticum by which they were given provisions in the mining camp of Santa María de las Charcas, they continued their journey to the villa of Saltillo where they joined the military men whom the captain had assembled. Having passed Holy Week in the mining camp of Boca de Leones, they arrived at the missions of the Río Grande del Norte after Easter. . . . That afternoon some of the religious began their march, and on the following day all of them assembled and proceeded on their journey to the Texas. . . . Since the expedition opened roads as it went, and as we had no one to guide us by the most direct route, the *entrada* into [the region of] the Texas took more than two months. On June 27, thirty-four Texas Indians came to meet us, five of whom were captains, and all of them embraced us, showing the joy with which they were awaiting us in their country. On the following day, on which we travelled nine leagues, ninety-six persons came with all the captains and principal men, whom we went out to meet with a standard on which were portrayed the images of Christ Crucified and of Our Lady of Guadalupe, which all adored and kissed while on their knees. . . .

1381. We continued our journey, and on July 3 with an Indian woman of the same nation serving as interpreter, she having been reared in Coahuila because her parents had been there a long time when the Spaniards left [Texas] in the year '93, and she spoke fluently—we gave all the Indians to understand the principal reason why we were coming. They settled among themselves the distribution of four missions among the leading nations, which was the arrangement made in the beginning. . . . On the 10th, among the nation of the Nazonis, which lies another ten leagues more or less to the north of La Concepción, the fourth mission was placed with the title of Señor San José. . . . The most excellent señor viceroy and the prelates of the two colleges were sent accounts of everything that had occurred. With the hope that new measures would be ordered, so that that new vineyard might prosper, the religious continued to reside there, undergoing hardships and hoping for better things.

---

[4] See *Pichardo's Treatise* . . . , Vol. I, p. 218, n. 1.

1382. In document 16, number 84, Don Domingo Ramón, leader of the expedition which went to Texas in the year 1716 and founder of the four missions which were erected in Texas, writes as follows:

On the third (of July, 1716), the first establishment of the mission of San Francisco was begun in the pueblo of the Nechas, where I appointed a *cabildo* and gave possession to the said religious in the name of his Majesty. The days of the 4th and 5th of the current month were spent in building the hut. I left on the 6th and on the 7th I arrived at La Concepción, having marched nine leagues through a land wonderful for its abundance of water, pastures, and open groves of beautiful pines and other trees, with many grapevines laden with large green grapes. Crossing a fairly large river toward the east-northeast, we arrived at the pueblo of the Aynais where there are a great many *ranchos* with their fields of corn, watermelons, beans, cantaloupes, tobacco, and a pale yellow flower that they have which is very good to eat but the name of which we do not know. I gave possession to the said religious, named a *cabildo*, and did everything else necessary, the Indians here having devoted themselves with their usual activity to the building of a dwelling and a church. On the 7th I left this place, and on the 8th I arrived at the pueblo of the Nacogdoches, having marched nine leagues toward the east-southeast through a land abounding in springs, pastures, open forests of pines and liveoaks, and many grapevines, the whole country being extremely warm. I named a *cabildo*. A church and a dwelling were built. On the 9th I remained at this place attending to the business that came up.

1383. On the 10th I left this mission, which is located twenty-three leagues farther inland than the place where the first settlement of the Spaniards stood, and on this day I went to the mission of the Nasonis, having marched ten leagues toward the west, passing all the way through land just as fertile as the preceding and thickly populated with the said Indians, in whose villages they entertained us highly with whatever they had. On the 11th the order was given to build a church and a dwelling, and I proceeded to appoint a *cabildo*. All the said people are of a similar nature, pleasant, generous, and fond of teaching their language. Those of this mission especially have good faces. With these measures was concluded what had to be done in founding the four missions, as your Excellency had ordered me to do. . . . Domingo Ramón.

1384. Aside from this, in the same document 16, number 168, the aforecited Father Fray Isidro Felix Espinosa in noting what happened to him during the days mentioned, writes as follows:

On Friday, the third (of July, 1716), all we religious went with the captain to the spring which we had previously examined, and the Indians began immediately to build the house for the first mission. In the meanwhile we spent the day in a hut made of branches. One league was travelled. On Saturday, the 4th, all of us said mass, and the house was completely finished.

Although it is poor and like a farm hut, we moved into it, and we proceeded to distribute what appertained to each mission.

1385. On Sunday, the 5th, the captain appointed alcaldes, *regidores*, and a constable, and subsequently at the spring he proceeded in the name of his Majesty (whom may God keep), to give me, as president, possession of the mission. The customary ceremonies having been solemnized, I named the Reverend Father Fray Francisco Hidalgo,[5] who for so many years has solicited this conversion, as minister of the first mission, which is called Nuestro Padre San Francisco de los Texas, and as his companion I named the father preacher, Fray Manuel Castellano,[6] to whom I committed the spiritual care of the soldiers in the presidio. The greater part of the clothing and other things that were brought for the Indians was distributed, and on this day our captain left with the father preachers, Fray Matías Sans [Sáenz] de San Antonio[7] and Fray Pedro de Santa María y Mendoza,[8] in search of the place of Nacogdoches, in order to establish their first mission for the college of Nuestra Señora de Guadalupe de Zacatecas.

1386. On Monday, the 6th, [we marched] toward the northeast, a quarter to the east-northeast, through open woods—crossing a creek which flows by the first mission. A plain more than two leagues in extent followed, and after crossing three small creeks, we arrived at the first hut of the Aynais Indians, where we halted during the heat of the day and made a repast of green corn. In the afternoon, travelling toward the east through an open forest, after two leagues we crossed a creek with a good deal of water and later we went through many poplars, pecans, and oaks, and in the ravines through many pines. Upon approaching the other house of the Aynais, we met our captain with the fathers of Guadalupe de Zacatecas who had not yet gone on. That afternoon a site was sought for the mission of La Concepción, which was found, although with many trees. We travelled eight leagues.

1387. On Tuesday, the 7th, I went with the captain, and after we had examined two ever-flowing although not very large springs, because they are in the center of this pueblo I was given possession in the name of his Majesty, as is customary, and the captain went with the fathers of Zacatecas to establish their mission, while my two companions and I prepared to move our belongings to the spring. The rest of the day was spent in doing this and in getting the place in order. On Wednesday, the 8th, the building of the straw dwelling was begun, although somewhat late, and Father Fray Benito Sánchez[9] left for the Nasoni rancheria, which had been chosen for the establishment of the third mission for the college of Querétaro.

1388. On Thursday, the 9th, I went with the French captain, Don Luis de St. Denis, to the rancheria of the Nasoni, where we arrived after midday. It

---

[5] See *Pichardo's Treatise* . . . , Vol. I, p. 222, n. 1.

[6] For information concerning the missionaries who accompanied the Ramón expedition to east Texas in 1716, see Castañeda, *Our Catholic Heritage in Texas* . . . , Vol. II, pp. 45–46.

[7] *Ibid.*

[8] *Ibid.*

[9] *Ibid.*

is seven leagues to the northeast from this mission of La Concepción. On the way there are many Indian houses and streams of water with good sites for settlements. Father Fray Benito and I examined a site that afternoon and our captain came from the Nacodoches. On this day he gave possession of the mission of Nuestra Señora de Guadalupe de Zacatecas. On Friday, the 10th, at a creek with quite a bit of water which runs to the north, the señor captain gave me possession of the mission of Señor San José. It comprises the Nasoni and Nacono Indians, and I named as its minister the father preacher, Fray Benito Sánchez. Thus three of our missions had been founded, which include about three thousand people as far as we have seen. I returned to this mission of La Concepción where I minister. . . . Fray Isidro Felix de Espinosa. July 30, 1716.

1389. These four missions having been founded, the venerable Father Margil founded two others, namely, that of Nuestra Señora de los Dolores de los Aix, and that of San Miguel de Linares among the Adaes. This is clear from many printed documents, such as the memorial to the venerable Father Margil which Father Fray Isidro Felix de Espinosa wrote under the title of [El] Peregrino Septentrional Atlante, book 2, chapter 23, page 280; the said Chrónica Apostólica written by the same Father Espinosa; and the second part of this Chrónica which Father Fray Juan Domingo Arricivita published under the title of Crónica Seráfica y Apostólica del Colegio de Propaganda Fide de la Santa Cruz de Querétaro; and manuscripts which are found in this document 16. But to prove it we have chosen only the following letter because it is from the same venerable Father Margil. The original is included in the autos from which we made the copy that is found in document 16, number 255:

Most excellent señor: Long live Jesus and His most sorrowful Mother, and may they keep your Excellency for us, as my companions and I (the unworthy president of these missions of the province of the Texas, which belong to our college of Nuestra Señora de Guadalupe de Zacatecas) request. Amen.

1390. Señor, in as much as the Reverend Father Fray Isidro Felix de Espinosa, president of the missions of this province which belong to his college of the Holy Cross of Querétaro, is informing your Excellency on the present occasion of the state of these missions, I shall not weary your Excellency by repeating it. I merely say that of the six missions which we have founded up to the present, three belonging to each college, only four were established with the funds and ornaments which the most excellent señor, your Excellency's predecessor, sent. The said college of Zacatecas took under its charge three of the said four, because I and my companions saw that the

French were coming in when we went with the captain of our presidio, Domingo Ramón, to Los Nachitoos where we found two Frenchmen already, and today they have their fortress built with a presidio.

1391. Our said captain talked with the Adaes Indians, a nation eight leagues to this side of the said Nachitoos, who received him and requested a mission. They said that they liked the Spaniards. Executing the order which he carried in his commission, he made the chief captain among them governor, and gave them [the missionaries] possession with the usual solemnity. And he charged me, as a missionary and in the name of his Majesty (whom may God keep), with their religious instruction, assigning this mission to our said college of Zacatecas and naming it the mission of San Miguel de Linares. He gave us the usual instrument of possession which is in our hands. Likewise, upon returning over the same *camino real*, about halfway between the said four missions and the above-cited San Miguel he talked with another very populous nation called Aix.

1392. They also said that they wanted a mission and liked the Spaniards, and he gave possession in the same manner as in the said mission of San Miguel, in the name of his Majesty, the authentic instrument of which remains in our hands. He assigned the mission to our said college of Zacatecas, it being named Nuestra Señora de los Dolores de los Ayx. From then on I remained there as the missionary in charge, having left another minister in the mission of San Miguel. Of the other two of the four missionaries from our said college, one has been a minister from the beginning in one of the first four missions assigned us, and the other is my assistant in this said mission of Los Dolores. Thus, señor, we have three missions belonging to us, but these last two have churches adorned with images of their patron saints and sacred vestments received through the alms of their benefactors. I therefore appeal to your Excellency's piety to look upon these two missions and assist them like the rest. By founding these two missions, as I have said, passage was closed to the French, and our captain executed the order that he carried to proceed to make establishments beginning at the place where he might encounter the French.

1393. Although there are so many nations desiring that we go among them, it has been impossible to take another forward step, not only for lack of sacred vestments but also because the supplies which your Excellency was sending us by Governor Don Martín de Alarcón[10] have been delayed. All the people of the presidio and the missions are suffering the need which they describe to your Excellency on this occasion, hoping for help and provisions from your Excellency's great piety, with the promptness that the matter demands, for these people are on the point of perishing if they are not aided quickly. I remain with all my companions praying to God to prolong your Excellency's life prosperously in both respects [i.e., material and spiritual].

------

[10]For earlier references to Alarcón, consult the indices of *Pichardo's Treatise* . . . , Vols. I, II, and III.

Mission of Nuestra Señora de los Dolores, February 13, 1718. Most excellent señor, your most humble servant kisses your Excellency's feet. Fray Antonio Margil de Jesús. To the most excellent señor, the Marquis of Valero[11] viceroy and captain-general of all New Spain and president of the royal audiencia of Mexico.

1394. The said Father Espinosa (*Chrónica*, book 5, chapter 17, page 451) writes that a short time after all these missions had been founded, in the mon h of June of the year 1719, it so happened

that because of the fact that peace had been broken between the two crowns, as soon as the captain-commandant of Nachitos (Don Luis de St. Denis) received the news, and before the Spaniards knew of it, he came in person to the mission of San Miguel de los Adays, which is ten leagues from the said fort, and with many expressions of courtesy he told the lay religious (the priest had left) and the soldier who was with him to give themselves up as prisoners. . . . The commandant took away everything that he could carry from the mission, not excepting the sacred vestments or holy things. As he was returning to his own district he fell from his horse because of a ridiculous mishap, and with this opportunity the lay religious made his escape through the dense forest and ran with such speed that they could not lay hands on him. (We have also described the flight of this religious above in Part I, paragraph 320, in the words of Father Arricivita.) He arrived at the mission where the venerable Father Margil was, and gave a report of everything that had happened and of what some Frenchmen, who had shown themselves friends because of having been acquainted earlier, had told him, to the effect that Panzacola had already been taken by surprise, and that they were expecting a hundred armed men at Nachitoos at any moment in order to go to the other missions and do the same thing that they had done at Los Adaes.

1395. This news was given to all of us by this same religious, and the venerable Father Margil decided to leave with all the sacred vestments of his missions which had escaped the attack. . . . At this unhappy news the captain of the few soldiers that we had became dispirited, for some were boys, on foot, naked, and without arms, and the French were taking advantage of the situation. Added to this was the clamor of the eight wives of the soldiers, who requested urgently that they be allowed to withdraw, even though it might be with two soldiers, and to escape from the French. Everything was confusion and lamentation. But we religious waited in our mission for the venerable Father Margil to arrive with his companions, and after we were all together, we insisted to the captain that he do nothing more until new reports should be received, for the Indians offered to place

_____

[11]Baltazar de Zúñiga, Guzmán Sotomayor y Mendoza, the Marquis of Valero and the Duke of Arión, was viceroy of New Spain from 1716 to 1722.

spies along the roads and to warn us as soon as they learned that the French were coming. The French needed time to arrive at the place where we were because they were more than a hundred leagues from us. Nothing sufficed to stem the tide of this misfortune, and the fears and misgivings were so great that some of the religious were influenced by them, and they so altered the constancy of the venerable Father Margil that he came to believe that the retreat should be made, carrying along the sacred vestments and holy things, and that a report of what had occurred should be sent to Mexico.

1369. The venerable Father Margil also sent a report to the most excellent señor viceroy of this lamentable occurrence in a letter which is found in document 12, number 208. It is of the following tenor:

Most excellent señor: Being depressed by a heavy grief, our hearts seek in their pain to bring to your Excellency's attention the sad state of this poor province, agitated by the activity of the neighboring French who are continuing the execution of their premeditated schemes, to our loss. On the 20th of the past month of June the unfortunate news came to us that the crowns had broken [the peace], and that as a result the French of Los Nachitoches had sacked the mission of San Miguel de los Adays, a soldier who was [there] with a lay religious having been taken prisoner. The religious who was also being taken as hostage escaped through haste or by permission of some Frenchmen known to him. If it had not been for the fact that the missionary priest had come here two days before with some companions to renew friendships and to relieve his loneliness due to the distance from the other missions, they would no doubt have captured him.

1397. There was likewise news that Pensacola was destroyed and that ships had been sent to Vera Cruz, as the said Frenchmen, formerly friends of ours, reported. Because of all this and because according to the same Frenchmen, who showed themselves merciful, they were expecting a hundred men in Los Nachitoos at any moment in order to go and destroy these missions, all we religious decided to unite as soon as possible and to escape, for which [step] the lack of soldiers and beasts would furnish good reasons. [We did this] in order to begin to withdraw and to await reinforcements and supplies together with whatever your Excellency might order us to do in this matter, which we shall await on the road wherever time may permit, provided the activity of the enemy does not give occasion for the obstruction of our withdrawal either in themselves or by means of the Indians who yield easily to their schemes. It can be feared with a good deal of foundation that what the French have done may be an opening for a considerable loss to New Spain, as your Excellency warned beforehand in the order that you entrusted to Governor Don Martín de Alarcón when this province was commended to him, and if your Excellency's orders had been carried out at that time this break, which is regrettable, would not have occurred.

1398. The forces which we have are so weak that the appearance of the boy soldiers on foot, naked, and without arms, causes them to be a laughing-stock of the Indians themselves. The soldier whom the French captured was of this type. Aside from this,, since the departure of Governor Don Martín de Alarcón last November, we have not had even a single letter or notice from our people for our consolation. Our troubles have been increased because of the fact that, the peace between the two crowns being broken, as is shown by the sacking already mentioned, this news was not sent to us here so that the damage might have been less or so that we might have withdrawn in time. This neglect is emphasized by the fact that one after another the plans and fortifications of the French are carried out, while in three years we have not advanced beyond what we settled at the very beginning, and besides have suffered the loss of those who have deserted, died, and become unfit for service because of the destruction or loss of arms and because no new supplies of arms, not even a single musket, have been brought in since that time. Meanwhile we see with our own eyes the hundreds of arms which the French have and are distributing among the Indians. In these missions alone this is evident, from the representation made by Don Martín de Alarcón who was received with volleys from more muskets than we had at that time. And we have [a garrison of] only twenty-five soldiers, whose number is not complete. This past May we expected a reinforcement of men and arms, both of which we failed to receive.

1399. Our anxiety is further increased by the fact that, although in two representations, one made immediately after entering this province in 1716 and the other made in more detail on November 17—besides other private notices to the same effect in letters—we have tried to notify your Excellency minutely of the designs and actions of the French. They are desirous of settling these lands, and, although we have requested fifty men for the Cadodachos, aside from the fifty for this mission center; and although, as we know, your Excellency's pious zeal and generous ardor are empowered to provide most promptly and efficaciously for the welfare of this province, the execution of all this has been delayed so long that it has given an opportunity for the French settlements to be reinforced. So many ships have come to it from Europe that for two years they have had the city of New Orleans established on the Río de la Palizada [Mississippi River], have strengthened the fort of Los Nachitos, *have occupied, to our particular regret, the post of the Cadudachos with fifty-one men,* swivelguns, and a great many munitions of war, and have plans to advance much farther. From all this will come consequences which cannot be stated in detail and which cannot fail to be well known to your Excellency.

1400. Another reason for our grief is the circumstance that, while during the past year the lack of food supplies has been so general that it continues down to the present time, with relief now near because the missions and the presidio have planted everything they could with the few people who are helping us, and with the harvest closely following the planting because of the favorable season, we now find ourselves obliged to leave our missions deserted. The cornfields are exposed to the voracity of the Indians and that which had been gathered together in the way of tools and implements with so much trouble we find partly buried and partly scattered about. Added to this are another considerable assault from the copious floods of the rivers, a shortage of animals, and the fact that the Indians had hidden some of the horses in order to force us to stay, although through the intercession of the *caciques* the stolen animals have been returned once more.

1401. In closing our laborious account, there remains [to present] for your Excellency's most attentive and pious consideration our grief at leaving this new settlement, the many baptized children, so much spiritual and material labor of the priests without any widespread success, and the general regret of these wretched heathen. Although this feeling is based on what interests them among the Spaniard's possessions, as well as on natural affection, they have been and are making efforts to prevent our leaving them, many of them renewing our grief with their own tears. So that they will permit us to go, it has been necessary to assure them repeatedly that our withdrawal is only for the purpose of joining the Spaniards whom we are expecting. Seeing, then, the tears and the needs of these poor people (for whom we had conceived fond hopes), some of us ministers of God almost decided to remain alone (for some still had not gone) and at the risk of everything, but the combination of dangers forces us to follow the withdrawal of our people. All we humble chaplains of your Excellency hope that, bearing in mind the blood of the Son of God shed for these poor heathen, your Excellency will dip your quill in it in order to sign by your hand whatever may be most conducive to the welfare of these souls, to the service of our king and lord (whom may God keep), and to the great consolation of these afflicted missionaries, who desire the spiritual and temporal growth of your Excellency into the heights that are most proper to you and which you deserve. Mission of La Purísima Concepción de Ágreda, province of Nuevas Filipinas de los Texas, July 2, 1719. Fray Antonio Margil de Jesús, president of the missions of [the college of] Santa Cruz de Querétaro.

In a word, because of the invasion and the sacking which the perfidious St. Denis perpetrated on the mission of Los Adays, the religious and the people who accompanied them left this said mission, that of Los Aix, that of San José de los Nasonis, that of Los Nacogdoches, that of La Concepción, and that of San Francisco de Texas—in short, the six missions that had been founded in the province of Texas—and withdrew to San Antonio de Béjar.

1402. The said Fray Isidro Felix de Espinosa mentions the same occurrence in his life of the venerable Father Margil, book 2, chapter 24, and the said Father Arricivita in book 1, chapter 21 [of his work]. We recount this lamentable story above in paragraph 320 of Part I, in the words of the Señor Marquis of Altamira. Finally, in the diary of the [expedition of the] Marquis of Aguayo, Bachillar Peña writes as follows (see document 21, number 1):

Twenty-one years ago the French at the expense of the merchants of Paris settled this region at Mobile, a port on the Gulf of Mexico twelve leagues from our presidio of Santa María de Galve (commonly called Panzacola), and have advanced during this time about three hundred leagues to the Río de Nachitoos, which they call Riviera Rojo [Red River], adjacent to Los Adays of the province of Texas. They extended their settlements about four hundred leagues upstream on the Río de la Empalizada, which they call Misuri (this was a mistake of this author, for the Misuri was never called La Empalizada; the only rivers which received this name were the Mississippi where it enters the Gulf of Mexico and the Red in the region of the Cadodachos, because of the palisades [log rafts] which they have, of which we have spoken above). And, taking advantage of the good faith and the alliance between the two crowns, they surprised the presidio of Panzacola and invaded at the same time the province of the Texas, on June 19 of the past year, 1719. Their superior forces obliged the Spaniards to abandon it by withdrawing with the missionary fathers of the six missions which they had erected to the presidio of San Antonio de Béxar, which is on the border of the province of Coahuila and which is 240 leagues from Los Adays, on the frontier of Texas. Upon receiving this news, his Excellency gave an order for aiding the said province, to the effect that a company of the largest number of men which could be raised in the Kingdom of León, the villa of Saltillo, and Parras, should be recruited as speedily as possible, as the emergency demanded, the task of equipping and provisioning it being committed to the Señor Marquis of San Miguel de Aguayo, as was done.

1403. The said señor marquis actually recovered [in 1721] the entire province of Texas and reëstablished the missions that had been abandoned. This is evident from the same document 21, where the following is stated in number 89:

On Saturday, the second (of August), the señor governor dispatched a detachment . . . to the missions of San Francisco and La Concepción to rebuild the churches and dwellings of the religious of both missions.

In number 97 the following is stated:

On Sunday, the 10th, the señor governor sent another detachment with the Very Reverend Father Fray Antonio Margil de Jesús, president of the missions of the college of Nuestra Señora de Guadalupe [de Zacatecas], and two other religious to rebuild the mission of Nuestra Señora de Guadalupe de los Nacogdoches, of which not a sign of the church had remained nor of the dwelling of the fathers; it is eight leagues from this encampment.

On Monday, the 11th, after the chief captain of all the Texas had united
all the people of the Aynais, who are under the jurisdiction of the mission
of La Concepción, and the eighty Caudadachos, he came with all of them,
many of them having muskets, to his lordship's encampment. After his
lordship had delivered to them the same discourse as to the other Indians,
to persuade them to assemble in a pueblo, and after they had offered to
do so as soon as the crop had been harvested, he gave them clothing. . . . His
lordship visited the two captains who came with the Caudodachos, and gave
them a bundle of clothing and some of the said small articles to distribute
among their Indians in order to win them over to the Spaniards and because
they are allied with the Texas. As a result of this both of them were very
grateful and happy. On Tuesday, the 12th, the señor governor went with
a company to the mission of San José de los Nasonis which is eight leagues
out of the way, and the Indians of that place received his lordship with
many signs of joy. On Wednesday, the 13th, the reëstablishment of that mission was solemnized, and the instrument of possession given to the father
president and to the captain of the Nasonis Indians with the same solemnity
as in the two other missions, etc.

1404. In number 108, the following is added:

On Thursday, the 21st [of August, 1721], the señor governor continued his
journey in the same direction of the east-northeast and over broken land,
containing streams and trees, to a quarter of a league beyond the place where
the mission of Nuestra Señora de los Dolores de los Adays (this is a printer's
error, as we have noted in the margin of number 108 of document 21; it
should read "los Ajx") was located, not a single trace of which was left.
Father Margil had ascertained that there was a better place at the side of
a stream and a spring which comes forth not very far away, because of its
being high clear ground and having a large tract of level land for farming.
We travelled six leagues that day.

1405. (Number 120.) On September first, the *cacique* of the Adays came
with many Indians, showing the greatest signs of joy at the arrival of the
Spaniards. After the señor governor had received him cordially and presented
him with gifts, as he had done with the other captains of the Texas Indians,
the *cacique* explained the special reason which he had for being pleased at
the arrival of the Spaniards, since all the Indians of that country hoped to
live under their protection. They desired this for the reason that when the
French invaded the mission of San Miguel de los Adays, just because they
[the Indians] had shown regret at the Spaniards' withdrawal, the French and
the Indians of Nachitoos had committed many hostile acts against them,
carrying off as prisoners some of their men, women, and children whom they
captured at the time of their retirement. Because of this unusual occurrence
they found themselves forced to abandon that country and to take refuge
in a more distant and rugged land. From there more than four hundred
men, women, and children were coming to see the señor governor. His lordship made them very happy with the quantities of clothing and presents which

he distributed among them, clothing them all as he had in the other missions. And his lordship having assured them of the protection of the king, our lord, and that he would leave a presidio of a hundred men established on that frontier and would reëstablish the mission of San Miguel in their community, they offered to assemble in it.

1406. The reëstablishment of the mission, which is to be placed about a quarter of a league away, was celebrated in its church on the day of the Archangel St. Michael. On October 12, since it was the day of the apparition of Nuestra Señora del Pilar de Zaragoza, the dedication of that church and presidio was celebrated, his lordship choosing her for patron saint and protectress of that frontier. Both feasts were celebrated with the greatest possible solemnity and demonstrations of joy, with repeated salvos from the artillery and from all the companies that were formed in the *plaza de armas*, while Señor Doctor Don José Codallos y Rabal sang mass, after having first blessed the temple and the fortress and carried the image of Nuestra Señora del Pilar in procession; the most reverend father, Fray Antonio Margil, extolled her cult in a very devout and eloquent sermon.

1407. Having seen the reëstablishment of these missions, let us now fix our attention on the following. Father Fray Felix Espinosa in his *Chrónica*, book 5, chapter 19, page 457, writes as follows:

In order to give a complete account of all that happened in Texas I note particularly a clause in the letter of the most excellent señor, the Marquis of Valero, dated July 22, 1721, in which he says that the missions should remain in the places where they were founded, so that it might not happen that, as a result of the actions of the French, that province should be abandoned by the fathers, the captain, and the soldiers. His Excellency could not have known what part the fathers took in this abandonment which was discussed. In order to enable them to give proof to the contrary, in case they might be held responsible for this abandonment, at my request a judicial inquiry was made by order of the Marquis of Aguayo, with four eyewitnesses, as a result of which it is clear that the fathers opposed the withdrawal and that two of them remained for more than twenty days [thereafter] in the missions. . . .

1408. The chief endeavor of the missionaries at all times was to get the Indians to congregate, reduced in pueblos, and in all the *entradas* of the officers and governor this was the principal task assigned to them. Finally, when Brigadier Don Pedro de Rivera[12] went to visit the presidios in 1727, the father president, Fray Gabriel de Vergara, presented him a petition asking that he issue an order that the Indians should be congregated, because if they were not the expenditures which his Majesty was making would be fruitless, for, after all these years, the Indians were as scattered as before and the principal end of converting them was not being attained.

---

[12]See Chapter XIV, note 57. For further information concerning Don Pedro de Rivera consult the indices of *Pichardo's Treatise* . . . , Vols. I, II, and III.

PICHARDO: LIMITS OF LOUISIANA AND TEXAS

1409. What happened was that the brigadier suppressed the presidio which was among our missions, and retired some of the men stationed in that of Los Adays, where he reduced the company from one hundred soldiers to sixty. The college having represented to his Excellency the unprotected state in which the missionaries had been left, in order to see what should be decided upon, the Señor Marquis of Casafuerte requested the opinion of the said Don Pedro de Rivera, and the latter attempted in a long report to disprove everything that the fathers were representing. He stated as an accepted fact that the measure providing for the congregating of the Indians was useless, because during the preceding century Don Alonzo de León[13] and Don Domingo Terán de los Ríos[14] had entered with a large number of people, and in the year '21 the Marquis of San Miguel de Aguayo had entered, and never had the reduction of those Indians to an orderly life been attained. The señor brigadier did not take account of the fact that all these officers were in Texas without making a settlement, and that they entered only to leave again, and never insisted on the obligation of congregating the Indians.

1410. As regards his insistence that the religious are leaving the impression that conversions will have to be obtained by force of arms, this is a manifest error, for it is one thing for the religious to have armed protection in order that the heathen may respect them, and it is another thing for them to receive the faith by force of arms, which no one has considered down to the present. The many examples which he brings out in his *consulta* of the great hardships of certain religious who were badly treated by the Indians, can be used against him, for the Indians would never have been so bold if they had feared the punishment of some nearby presidio. This same fact of seeing the missionaries without defense made them bold and daring. In the beginning of the conquest of this kingdom many religious were killed who went among the heathen without soldiers.

1411. All the missionaries are very well acquainted with everything that has been written on this matter, especially in the instructions of the venerable Father Fray Juan Focher,[15] who wrote on the subject in the beginnings of this New Spain. Later, Doctor Don Juan de Solórzano,[16] Father Acosta,[17]

---

[13]For details concerning several expeditions made in Texas by Alonso de León between 1686 and 1690, see Castañeda, *Our Catholic Heritage in Texas* . . . , Vol. I, pp. 314–356. For earlier references to De León, consult the appendices to *Pichardo's Treatise* . . . , Vols. I, II, and III.

[14]For details concerning the expedition of Domingo Terán de los Ríos, to Texas in 1691–1692, consult Castañeda, *Our Catholic Heritage in Texas* . . . , Vol. I, pp. 361–377. See also *Pichardo's Treatise* . . . , Vol. I, p. 408, n. 1; also consult the indices of *Pichardo's Treatise* . . . , Vols. I, II, and III, under "Terán de los Ríos."

[15]Reference may be to Joannes Focher, author of *Itinerarivm catholicvm profiscentium, ad infidelis couertendos* . . . . This book was published (n.p.) in 1574, two years after the author's death.

[16]For two well-known works of Don Juan de Sólorzano Pereira, consult the bibliography in *Pichardo's Treatise* . . . , Vol. I, p. 564.

[17]Reference may be to Father José de Acosta, author of *Historia natural y moral de las indias* (see bibliography in *Pichardo's Treatise* . . . , Vol. II, p. 531).

and the Most Illustrious Montenegro[18] followed him with great erudition, all of them agreeing that in the missions in which apostolic work was carried on without the protection of arms the ministers perished at the hands of the heathen, or returned in flight. On the contrary, those who proceeded to preach the gospel to them with sufficient escorts and protection from soldiers to check the audacity of the barbarians had good results and made excellent progress. It is one thing to make war on them in order to convert them, which was never thought of, and it is another to have arms in evidence for the defense and protection of the missionaries and to assure the results that are being sought. The Most Illustrious Montenegro testifies to having known a great worker of the Company of Jesus who for a period of twenty-five years had devoted himself to the conversion of heathendom; he had heard him say that only two arquebuses to protect him were worth more than fifty friars who might accompany him.

1412. The religious of Texas did not request the presidio of soldiers because of any fear that they might have had for their lives, for they travelled alone from hut to hut seeking the dying. But they requested it in order that, by a show of arms, they might persuade and stimulate the Indians to congregate, and in order that the fathers and soldiers might aid them with their example, help them to clear the fields, draw water from the streams for irrigation, and build their houses all together. For this is not contrary, but rather is very conformable to what the *Leyes de las Indias* have ordered under the title of "*Reducciones.*" If its provisions had been carried out, I do not doubt that the Indians of Texas would now be assembled, and the fathers would not have found themselves obliged to move their missions to other heathen.

1413. After the religious of this college [of Santa Cruz de Querétaro] had realized that they had taken all the measures that their holy zeal had suggested to them to bring about the assembling of the Indians of the Texas, and that all of them had failed, they requested that the three missions which they had maintained for fourteen years in the center of the Texas be moved to the neighborhood of the San Antonio River, where, owing to the multitude of heathen, it would be easy to congregate them and to pursue their apostolic labors among them. This proposal seemed appropriate to the Señor Marquis of Casafuerte, and with a new opinion of Brigadier Don Pedro Rivera, he dispatched an order to move the missions to the places that might seem most convenient. An order was given to the governor of the province of the Texas, who at that time was Don Melchor de Media Villa y Azcona,[19] to execute this transfer without additional cost to the royal treasury. He did so with such efficiency that he examined the margins of the rivers in person, made himself familiar with the country, and omitted no measure to obtain the end sought by the missionaries.

---

[18]Reference to this author is indefinite.

[19]Melchor de Media Villa y Ascona was governor of Texas from 1727 to 1730.

1414. After he had explored the whole country in company with the father president, Fray Gabriel de Vergara, desirable places were found on the banks of the Río de San Antonio, and, with another *consulta* and order, three missions were established, to the great consolation of the religious. These, although they grieved over the abandonment of the Texas, were comforted by having near at hand three nations of very docile heathen Indians, the Pacaos, Paalat, and Pitalaque, all of whom probably number more than a thousand persons, including children and adults. Toward the end of the year '30 they began to assemble, and from then until the present day they [the missions] have continued to grow. Each one has its two ministering priests; many Indians are instructed in the Christian faith; and it has been possible to baptize many adults, and much larger numbers of the children. I shall make a computation of these when I treat of the spiritual fruit that the apostolic colleges have gathered in all their missions, to the joy of the holy Church.

1415. In order that those missions of the Texas may not complain of total abandonment, Divine Clemency provided that three missions of those that the venerable Father Fray Antonio Margil had founded should remain: the first one, which is that of the Nacoddochis, is in the center of the Texas, dedicated to Nuestra Señora de Guadalupe. In it there is always a minister who maintains it and, as I have learned, he leaves at times to make his apostolic visits among the Indians of the same language, who are all those whom the missionaries of this college had under their charge in three missions. Since up to the present they are not congregated but are scattered over an area of more than fifteen leagues, this missionary has an extensive field in which he can obtain the baptism of many dying ones, for, since the father already has a knowledge of the language, he needs only to visit one band after another. In this he takes no risks since all of them are friends. And God knows that if my strength were not already so spent, I would consider it a singular good fortune to go and serve as a companion to the minister of this mission, for although I might not have any other occupation than to go from house to house all through the year, at the end of it I would have obtained a harvest of dying children and of many adults, whom I could send to heaven since, as I know their language, they would be instructed in the Christian faith. Let me be permitted this short unbosoming of the great affection I have always had for those wretched people and for the love with which they always responded to me; I shall die with the wish that they may all know God and be converted.

1416. There remains also the mission of the Ays Indians, who, although they have a different language, are docile by nature, and among them an abundant harvest of souls is expected. The last mission of the college of Nuestra Señora de Guadalupe is that of San Miguel de los Adays, which is near the Spanish presidio. It serves as a frontier to check the settlements of the French by land. Since the minister of this mission has the post of chaplain of that presidio, he has need of redoubled energy to care for both the Spaniards and the Indians of the mission, who are numerous.

This historian has here told us that three of the six missions, namely, that of San Francisco de los Nechas, or Texas, that of La Concepción de los Ainais, and that of San José de los Nasonis, were abandoned, the religious withdrawing from them and going to found others on the banks of the Río de San Antonio de Béxar.[20]

1417. Father Fray Agustín Morfi in volume 1, book 7, number 7 of his *Memorias para la Historia de Texas*[21] describes this abandonment of the missions in more detail, copying the report of Señor Brigadier Rivera. In discussing it, his words are as follows:

Don Melchor de Media Villa y Azcona succeeded Almazán in the government of Texas, and before the new governor could take a useful measure in the province the field marshal, at that time brigadier, Don Pedro de Rivera, entered it on an inspection of its presidios. He began to exercise his functions as *visitador* in September, 1727. Before beginning a discussion of various points to which this *visita* gave rise, I shall mention certain actions in order not to interrupt the narrative with controversies.

1418. Don Pedro de Rivera carried out his inspection, and after it was finished he returned to Mexico, where he suggested in an extensive report everything that he thought appropriate for reforming and improving the organization of the provinces. In view of this, without sending official copies [of the report] to the governor and captains, and without hearing the missionary fathers, the viceroy issued his decree of April 26, 1729, to the effect that the governor of Texas should discharge from the service the captain and twenty soldiers of the Texas presidio.

(This presidio is the same one of which the same Brigadier Don Pedro de Rivera speaks in number 314 of his diary and *derrotero*, copied in our document 24. He says concerning it that, after the sun had been observed there, it was found to be located in 32° 16′ of north latitude and in 281° 20′ of longitude. It is the same one that the Marquis of Aguayo restored, as is stated in document 21, number 102, in these words: "On Friday, the 15th, after

---

[20]For details concerning the removal of the three above-mentioned Querétaran missions to San Antonio, see Castañeda, *Our Catholic Heritage in Texas . . .* , Vol. II, pp. 240–243.

[21]See *Pichardo's Treatise . . .* , Vol. I, p. 6, n. 3. "References to Father Fray Juan Augustín Morfi and his *Memorias para la Historia de Texas* are numerous, . . . His *Memorias* and his *Historia de Texas* have, up to the present, been indiscriminately referred to as one and the same work. That they are two distinct works, that the first was a collection of data for the second, and that the *Historia* was left unfinished because of his death, are all facts that have been ignored."—Castañeda (trans. and ed.), *History of Texas, 1673–1779, by Fray Juan Agustín Morfi*, Part I, p. 15.

the feast of the Assumption of Our Lady had been celebrated early
in the morning, his lordship left the company of Captain Don
Juan Cortinas, which consists of twenty-five soldiers, reëstablished
in its old presidio, which is located a league from the mission for
the protection and aid of [all] the missions." In number 90 the
following mention is made of the presidio which was founded in
1716 by Captain Ramón: "On Sunday, the third, all the people
crossed, and camp was made near the mission of San Francisco
where the presidio stood the second time, when it was moved in
the year 1716." And in number 84 he speaks of the one that was
founded in 1690, in the following words: "On Monday, the 28th,
the journey was continued in the same direction of the east-northeast to the site of San Pedro, where the presidio and mission were
placed on the first *entrada*—in which the Spaniards did not advance beyond there—in the year '90.")

This was promptly done (continued Father Morfi) on the 30th of the
following June, when their salaries stopped, and forty soldiers in the presidio
of Los Adaes, fifty in La Bahía, ten in San Antonio, and all of the squad of
Saltillo were dismissed.

1419. This order greatly surprised Don Francisco Becerra, captain of the
presidio of the Texas, as well as all the people of the province. But it made
no less impression on the missionary religious of the college of Santa Cruz,
under whose charge were the nearby missions. They saw that with it was
destroyed the fruit, although small, of those conversions, for since their Indians would lack the contact and example of those few Spaniards, their
natural fickleness and the continual seduction of the heathen would make
them forget the religion which so irked them. The enemy nations who were
quiet in order not to expose themselves, finding themselves now without the
slight restraint of that garrison, would see nothing to prevent their profaning
the holy temples, vessels, and vestments or even obliging the ministers to
abandon that territory for the third time. They remembered what happened
on the expedition of Terán, and during the invasion of St. Denis, when it
availed them nothing to have the Reverend Father Espinosa at their head, nor
yet a Venerable Margil, to prevent the abandonment of the province being
attributed to them and their being held responsible for the [loss of] the great
sums invested in those expeditions and establishments.

1420. In order to avert such a calumny they appealed to the most excellent
señor viceroy through their superior, the Reverend Father Fray Miguel Sevillano de Paredes. This prelate begged his Excellency to revoke the measure,
or that, if it were sustained, in view of the little fruit of the missions and
their poor prospects for the future, an order should be given to the ministers
to withdraw, and to go to some other place where their labors might be more

useful. He made this appeal on July 16 of this year of 1729. He repeated his importunity within a few days, enclosing a report which the missionaries sent him, dated the 4th of the same month. But his Excellency answered none of these representations, and the order was irremediably sustained. We shall see its fatal results in the course of these *Memorias*.

1421. So that the reader may be in a position to understand the little reason that Bonilla had to judge the orders of Rivera without finding out, even if only superficially, what the religious thought, it has seemed to me that the best method would be to copy by paragraphs, word for word, the report of that visiting gentleman, adding at the end of each one the considerations which in my opinion weaken his arguments, in order that, the comparison being thus made easy, it may be noted which of the two has justice on his side. I do this not because I am pretending to intelligence in matters that do not appertain to my profession, but because I am persuaded that in view of what I have seen and read, I should have as much liberty to discuss it as any one else. In general I shall have recourse to no other means to argue against him than those which the report itself furnishes. I therefore begin the subject.

1422. Bases for the report of Rivera: After Brigadier Don Pedro de Rivera arrived in Mexico City, having completed his inspection, the viceroy ordered by a decree of August 2, 1728, that after the *autos,* representations, and *consultas* that might have been drawn up, together with all the other papers relating to the general inspection, had been studied, a project should be formed in view of these documents stating the number of presidios that should be maintained, along with the officers and troops of their respective garrisons and their salaries; also which ones should be suppressed, removed, etc.

1423. In obedience to this order Rivera presented an extensive report on December 7 of the same year, and, limiting myself for the time being to that which appertains solely to the province of Texas, I say:

1424. "First point. In the *consulta* of March 23 of this year I represented to your Excellency how unnecessary are the presidio of Los Adaes and the hundred soldiers who garrison it, for although the one that the French have, located on an island which is in the middle of the Río de Nachitoches [Red River], is only seven leagues from the said presidio of Los Adaes, its garrison does not exceed twenty-five men, who serve only to keep possession of that place. And since the reason why that of Los Adaes should have been erected seems to have been none other than that of establishing a boundary line in order that the colony might have a barrier to separate it [from the French], it seems that the sixty soldiers who would be left there would be sufficient in number for its garrison, and especially, since the Indians of the eight tribes, the Adaes, Aix, Nacogdachos, Asinays, Nasonis, Naconomes, and Navedachos, who are the ones who inhabit that province, are so docile by nature that although the French have introduced muskets among them, which they handle skilfully, they respect those soldiers when they see them on horseback with their arms, this submission being a token of their docile spirit. This is the reason why I consider the sixty soldiers, whom I suggested to your Excellency should remain in the said presidio, as sufficient for that garrison."

1425. Discussion. Señor Rivera makes many false assumptions here in order to reach his conclusion. He assumes, first, that the presidio of Los Adaes opposes only that of Natchitoches, forgetting the one of equal strength that the French had in Los Cadodachos; second, that the garrison of Natchitoches serves only to hold that place, for experience had already shown that they served to protect their hunters, to aid commerce, and to introduce it into the nations who are our friends, and to advance their possessions; third, that the Marquis of San Miguel de Aguayo had no other purpose in the construction of the presidio of Los Adaes than to establish a boundary line in order that the colony might have a barrier to separate it [from the French]. This sole object would make the foundation ridiculous, even with the sixty soldiers whom Rivera assigns to it. The boundary was already known. The place called Montaña Grande was admitted as such by both nations. In no part of the world are frontier settlements fortified in order to establish boundaries, but to protect them. In the same quarter the Río de las Netchas is a boundary line, and Rivera did not consider sixty men necessary to establish it. Then if Los Adaes served only to form a boundary, the sixty soldiers assigned to it were also unnecessary. Actually they were not. Then they were destined for another more important purpose, which was to defend the frontier and protect the province.

1426. He assumes falsely that only the eight tribes which he mentions inhabit that province, and that they are as docile as he states. The falseness of the first is shown in book 2 of these *Memorias*. And the falseness of the last is evident on its face. What he calls docility in the Indians is really an indolence which in general makes them incapable of a perfect friendship. But this itself shows that force is necessary, not for using violence against them, which would be inhuman, but for holding their respect. That they should respect our soldiers simply from seeing them on horseback, armed, is another assumption born from judging by appearances. They are acquainted with our arms, and were skilled horsemen before they had any dealings with the Spaniards. In what manner, then, would they respect our courage? Witness Béxar; witness La Bahía, where they came to seek us in order to fight us; witness San Sabá, where, aided by all the Lipan Apaches, they destroyed the mission, killed the ministers and some soldiers, and laid siege to the presidio garrisoned by a hundred men; and witness Parilla, who, wishing to avenge this outrage, found them neither docile nor respectful, as Rivera affirms, but resolute, daring, and brave, as will be seen below.

1427. The falseness of these assumptions having been shown, the inadmissibility of the inference is evident. When the marquis erected that presidio he was aware that he left it exposed to the forces of Natchitoches, whose garrisons could unite easily and quickly to attack it; that it should hold the eight tribes in obedience and many other nations in respect; that if thirty men were occupied in tending the horses and even an equal number in the fort, forty men would remain free to acquaint themselves alternately with their duties in time of quiet or to punish the unruly whenever the need might arise; and that an establishment so distant from our possessions, so far within a restless country, and facing the foreign presidios, should have a garrison proportionately numerous in order to perform so many duties and to fill the places of those who might be out of the service because of desertion, sickness, or death, especially where recruits and replacements were not obtainable. No one will say that for this a hundred men would be an excessive number.

1428. "Second point. The same argument holds with regard to the French, though by inverse reasoning, for if they keep the peace as they are doing at present, the sixty soldiers in the said presidio of Los Adaes are sufficient, and if, through some outbreak of war, they were to become enemies, the hundred men will not be sufficient to check them in case they might attempt to attack them. For if they undertook to do so with trained troops whom they might bring from Mobile and Canada under officers of experience and ability, they would have little trouble in overcoming our men, because of being so well versed in that kind of warfare as well as because the muskets which the French use are of long range and the arquebuses which our people use are of short range; thus they would gain control of the country with little effort."

1429. Second discussion. Allowing for the great variety which exists in the ways of men's thinking, it is still difficult for me to believe that any one of these arguments could have any force. According to Rivera, the eight tribes that inhabit the country are very docile and respectful. Then with regard to them the sixty men are unnecessary; a smaller number would suffice. Why, then, does he want these sixty soldiers while the French are at peace? In order to mark the boundary line? For this alone the mission was more than sufficient. Under his system, therefore, the whole presidio should be withdrawn. The señor brigadier was poorly informed of the geography of this part of America, and even more poorly of the history of the French colonies, when he stated the following: That in case they attacked us in that region, it would be with trained troops which they could have brought from Mobile and Canada. In the first place, in Mobile there were none and in Canada there were very few, but even if they had attempted to bring them, it would not have been so easy to transport them over such vast distances. The trained troops have an advantage over those of the country, I confess, but they are accustomed to short marches, to warm food, to sleeping under shelter, and to other conveniences which those of the country scorn. But leave them with all their advantages. The French did not have the troops and thus the argument is chimerical. Besides this, was not the inspection that he [Rivera] made for the purpose of training those troops? Train them, then, and they will be equal [to the French]. Give them experienced and able officers, and the French will not have the advantage over us. Were we not in exactly the same position in which Portugal found itself in the last war, with few and undisciplined troops? And would the minister at Lisbon have argued reasonably in saying, "The garrisons of our frontier forts will not be able to resist the trained troops of Castile, commanded by officers of experience and ability; thus it is necessary to reduce them by about half?" Not at all. But this is precisely the inference of Brigadier Don Pedro de Rivera. The fact that the French muskets have a shorter or longer range I consider unimportant in this case. The musket could not destroy a stockaded fort, and to the difficulties of him who had to take it would be added in that case the necessity not only of approaching within arquebuseshot but also within range of the blow of the sabre. This is especially true in as much as the French neither have nor could transport easily any artillery to fire on the fort, without a previously planned expedition from Europe, and this could never be so secret that it would be difficult to prepare for it.

1430. "Third point. It is true that the said presidio of Los Adaes, although stockaded, is surrounded by a redoubt. But the French could make themselves masters of the interior country without losing a soldier merely by leaving the said presidio to their left and going along the banks of the Río de los Cadodachos, directing their march to the Nasonis, whence they would dominate the Asinais, Netchas, and Navedachos. And by camping at the site of this last nation they would cut off the convoys that might attempt to go to the presidios. They would surrender to the French from necessity, without any more effort on the part of the latter than that of having placed themselves at the said site of the Navedachos. These circumstances caused me to state to your Excellency in the aforesaid *consulta* how superfluous the forty soldiers who would be dismissed are in the said presidio, and how useful those funds [now used for their salaries] would be to the royal treasury if the soldiers were suppressed as unnecessary."

1431. Third discussion. The señor brigadier assumes that in case of war with the French, the Spaniards in America must play the rôle of an inanimate body which, buried under inaction, only waits to receive blows. The same arguments that he advances in my opinion furnish clear proofs against his view. The French, I would say, can easily occupy the site of the Navedachos. Then the presidio of the Texas in their vicinity should not be withdrawn, but its garrison should be increased in order to keep the French from making themselves masters of that country. They can cut off our convoys, with only twenty-five men from Natchitoches and those whom they may receive from Mobile. Then we, with a hundred men in Los Adaes, the rest of the garrisons from the other presidios of the province—who according to Rivera, in the following paragraph, can join them in two weeks—and with the aid that may be sent them from Coahuila and the New Kingdom of León, not as far from Los Adaes as Canada and Mobile are from Natchitoches, will be able to occupy their banks of this river, intercept their convoys, and without losing a single man, make ourselves masters of that presidio and drive them to the other side of the Mississippi. On paper one marches in silence and without fatigue, rivers are crossed on foot and without difficulty, and mountains are conquered in a moment. But it does not happen that way in practice. No matter how secret the march of the French might be, and no matter how careless the officials of Los Adaes might be, they could never hide themselves from the acute perception of the mission Indians. We have a thousand examples of this every day. The Indians, if not from affection, then for the small consideration of a handful of tobacco, would give the information to the governor.

The news would be communicated immediately to Béxar, and the march of the enemy, if not checked, could be retarded either by sending immediately fifty men to the unprotected Natchitoches, or by posting ambuscades in opportune places; or by a thousand other means, which I do not comprehend, the presidio of Texas which it is now recommended should be withdrawn, could prevent them from making themselves masters of the country. No one believes that the French would plunge themselves heedlessly into the center of our presidios where, in case they could not withstand the troops that might be sent from New Spain, the garrison of Los Adaes would make them suffer greatly on their withdrawal. Let us not grow weary, [for] in the following paragraphs we shall see what may facilitate that which at present is difficult.

1432. "Fourth point. Even in case the hundred men were sufficient to defend the country, if the French should arrive to break the peace, there would still be no reason why they should be maintained in the said presidio of Los Adaes, for if this contingency should arise, it would not be difficult to replace in fifteen days the forty soldiers whom I say should be withdrawn. Since it is customary when a breach of the peace is expected between sovereigns, that soldiers be taken from interior forts to garrison the frontiers, without depriving the former of those necessary for their protection, therefore if at any time it should be convenient for the presidios of Los Adaes to maintain the said hundred soldiers because of fears that peace may be broken, it could be restored to its former strength by adding the forty men, to complete the number of one hundred, in this manner."

1433. Fourth discussion. The marquis never thought that the hundred men would be able to defend the province from the whole power of the French. But he did think, and rightly, that they were necessary for protecting it from outrages similar to the one of St. Denis, and to prevent another such convocation of the nearby [Indian] nations. And if the presidio with only sixty soldiers could be reinforced on fear of a break, why could it not be in like manner, having a hundred? But let us pass on to the method of reinforcing it.

1434. "Sixth point. (Number 27.) At the time that I made my inspection of the presidio of Los Texas, I noticed that it did not deserve this honored name, not only because it consisted of only a few huts of sticks and grass badly put together, but also because in all the time since its erection, its garrison has not served for anything whatsoever, because the Indians who inhabit its environs have remained as quiet as was expected when the troops entered there. It may well be believed that they will continue to do so because of their nature, a circumstance which those soldiers have considered sufficient reason for living without troubling to post any guards or sentries. This is the reason why, under date of March 23 of this year, I suggested to your Excellency that it would be appropriate to suppress this presidio of Los Texas, because since the year 1715 when it was placed there, it has not performed any function that corresponds to the purpose for which it was built, the soldiers occupying themselves only in assisting the three missions which were established near the presidio. The captain who has commanded them has no incumbency to distinguish him as such other than that of naming the soldiers in his company who are to relieve the others who are stationed at the missions. This is done when the religious request it. Since the employment of the said captain and soldiers does not correspond to the occupations which their titles demand, this presidio should be suppressed as unnecessary, the distribution of [men] to aid the missions in which they are employed being made from the presidio of Los Adaes. Two soldiers will be taken from there to attend at each of the three missions, since—because of the fact that they have no Indians settled in the country near them, for those who belong to the missions live at a distance in their rancherias—it is necessary that two soldiers shall assist each one of the said three missions. In this manner the said presidio of Los Texas may be suppressed, so that what is needlessly consumed in paying the captain and twenty-four soldiers of whom it consists, may be applied to other expenditures which may be for the good of the royal service. It is of no benefit whatever for 10,000 pesos to be consumed annually in salaries for the said captain and soldiers, the former with five hundred pesos and each of the latter with four hundred. These are the reasons why, in my opinion, this presidio should be suppressed."

1435. Sixth discussion. That because the presidio of Texas consists only of poorly-constructed huts of sticks and grass, it therefore should be suppressed, is an unjustified inference. If the señor brigadier had ordered to be executed that for which the señor marquis had provided, the presidio would be in a proper state and capable of defense. The fact that Guayaquil, Panamá, Cartagena, Cuba, Vera Cruz, etc., might have been poorly fortified and almost abandoned when the buccaneers sacked them, was not and could not be a reason for withdrawing the garrisons and destroying the defense works. The fact that the presidio of Texas since its erection may not have been of any service whatever because the Indians who inhabit its vicinity have maintained their accustomed peace—by his leave, he is deceiving himself. If someone were told that the prisoners of El Morso [Morro?] and Uloa were always quiet and that therefore the troops who guard them were unnecessary, he would certainly not accept the inference of the señor brigadier, for it is immediately seen that this quietude is not due to their inclination but to the fear that the arms with which they are surrounded inspire in them. But the Indians, he says, are quiet by nature. He little knew them, and this will be seen continuously in the course of these *Memorias*. That the captain should permit his soldiers to neglect guard or sentry duty was a very bad policy. Punish his negligence but do not demolish the establishment. How could a troop be useless which occupied a position so advantageous that, in his own opinion, the first act of the French in case of a break would be to come to take possession of it?

1436. That those soldiers occupied themselves with nothing except assisting in the missions is inconsequential, for he [Rivera] asserted in his special report that they were engaged in tilling the soil. Whether or not this was useful let the Señor Marquis of Altamira say. Speaking precisely of the provinces of Texas in his long report already cited, he wanted to transform this entire troop into farmers without their forgetting, for this reason, the use of arms. As is stated in another place, the soldiers served the missions in the capacity of majordomos, and this in itself is evidence that the missionaries have never attempted to usurp or dispose, as masters, of the possessions of the Indians, for they sought witnesses of their administration and to have the [Indians'] goods distributed by their own hands. Then it was necessary for the presidio of Texas to exist, first, because although it was slack in discipline, it fulfilled the purpose of its erection, which was to keep the Indians quiet, and this purpose was defeated as soon as the troops were withdrawn. Second, because it occupied a place of which the French might on any occasion avail themselves. Third, because those soldiers were gradually forming a settlement and cultivating the soil, so that it was in the power of the señor brigadier to give the place a good recommendation, to make it prosperous, and to maintain it, in order that, the settlement being well established, the presidio could move on to another place where it would produce the same benefits. Fourth, because it maintained peace and trade with the nearby nations, the communication between Béxar and Los Adaes, and the lives of four missionaries, and protected the convoys that were sent to the latter presidio. Fifth, because it impeded or could impede the trade which the French were continuing to introduce among the Apaches and the interior nations, taking arms to them to destroy us. Finally, in order to understand all the advantages of an establishment on that site, read what Señor Mézières says about the pueblo of Bucareli, which found itself in a like case.

1437. In number 60 of the said book 7, Father Morfi concludes his reflections upon it.

In this year of 1731, Don Melchor de Media Villa y Azcona completed his term as governor—out of favor with the viceroy because he had not ceased making representations against the measures of Rivera and because it was suspected that it was he who was inciting the missionaries to continue their importunities. There is no doubt that since the cause was a common one, he perhaps would not be sorry that the missionaries should agitate it, but he had no other part in it than to furnish them the documents which they requested, and which he could not deny them without injustice.

1438. As soon as the Reverend Father Sevillano learned that a report was being requested by the court from the señor viceroy, he knew that the order would stand. For this reason he limited his solicitation to an appeal that his missions be moved to a more advantageous place. The viceroy in effect agreed, and by his decree of May 1, 1731, the three missions which the college of Santa Cruz [de Querétaro] had in the interior of the province were ordered placed on the banks of the Río de San Antonio and in the vicinity of that presidio. These were La Purísima Concepción, Nuestro Padre San Francisco, and San José, which upon its transfer changed its name to that of San Juan Capistrano. This measure increased the labors of the missions which remained in Texas, belonging to the college of Nuestra Señora de Guadalupe de Zacatecas (which were that of Nacogdoches, that of Los Ayx, and that of Los

Adays), because, the extent of their territories being enlarged, they had more ground to cover in order to gather the harvest of dying persons, adults and children, for I have already stated the absolute hopelessness of their conversion.

Down to here we have seen the report of Señor Rivera and Father Morfi's reflections upon it.

1439. All these discussions, even if they should be but anecdotes for other foreigners, could not be such, in any manner, for the son of a Spanish mother of the Ramón family,[22] so well known in Coahuila and Texas, and of a French father, the commandant of Nachitoches, who had founded the missions of the said Texas, invaded that of Los Adays, and had kept up a continuous correspondence with the Spaniards—for a person, in short, having the blood of both nations, who was born and reared in Nachitoches, a place adjoining the Spanish dominions. Consequently, he could not be ignorant of the fact that the Nasonis had always belonged to the Spanish dominions. The Nasonis, who inhabited an area of that territory located west of D'Anville's dividing line (as is seen on our map 19, document 74), are found in 31° 44' of latitude and 77° 48' of longitude. It was of them that his father, St. Denis, had spoken these very words, which are found in his letter copied above in paragraph 930:

[But] notwithstanding that as far as the Río del Norte I did not find any, vestiges of Spanish settlements (if there were such), it does not follow that we Frenchmen claim all the territory to the said Río del Norte for our own. I admit unreservedly that the Spaniards have legitimate possession of it.

And these other words, also copied above in paragraph 939:

Nor would there even be any occasion for raising a question if the French (which will never happen) should attempt to settle and inhabit the country up to and excluding the Lago de los Adaes, because then they would indeed be more truly on the other side of the river than they had ever been. It would be a just matter for controversy if the French should attempt to move beyond the Lago de los Adaes to the vicinity of the Spaniards.

The Nasonis [are] very different from the Nasonitas whom D'Anville places on his map at 34° 25' of latitude and 77° of longitude, on the south bank of the Río de los Cadodachos, and

---

[22]Reference is to St. Denis, the younger—son of Louis Juchereau de St. Denis, who married the granddaughter of Captain Ramón, presidial commander at San Juan Bautista in 1714.

also very different from the Natsoos, located by the same D'Anville near the Nasonitas, but on the north bank of the same river. Both nations without doubt belonged to the French, since they were within the territory embraced by the dividing line of the same D'Anville. Then if he [the younger St. Denis] could not be ignorant of the fact that the Nasonis belonged to the Spaniards, how did he dare to insult the Spaniards by going to their Indians? Was this not perhaps an act of French temerity and an insult committed by a Frenchman against the Spaniards?

1440. In order to prevent the French from penetrating into the dominions of our sovereign, the Catholic King, in the future, the zeal of the governor of Texas, Señor Don Jacinto Barrios, planned to place a presidio in the pueblo of Nasonis and on the banks of the Río de San Pedro, because in effect this place was chosen by him for this edifice, as we shall see later, although the señor *auditor de guerra*, Don Domingo Valcárcel, knew nothing about it and for this reason opposed it. The said governor, above in paragraph 1093, writes about it as follows to the most excellent señor, the first Count of Revilla Gigedo:

Despite your Excellency's unmistakable disposition, I regard it as indispensable that as many as twenty soldiers be stationed on the Río de San Pedro with an experienced, zealous officer, in order to observe the moves of the French and the increase that they are going to make in their post of Caudachos and other settlements. The principal care of this officer would be to reduce and attract those Indians with cunning and skill. They are the ones who rule the other nations in that whole province, and the passion that they have for the French is so blind that they would lose their lives to please them. This is proven by their action in the year just past, [an account of] which is contained in the said judicial proceedings.

1441. When his Excellency requested from the señor *fiscal*, Andreu, his opinion on the *consulta* of Señor Barrios, he replied to him in paragraph 1135 as follows:

With regard to the matter which the governor brings up—stating that he considers it indispensable that as many as twenty soldiers with an experienced and zealous officer should be established on the Río de San Pedro in order to observe the schemes of the French and the increase that they are going to make in their pueblo of Caudachos and other settlements, and that the principal care of this officer should be to win over and attract those Indians with cunning and skill—if it be your Excellency's superior pleasure, you will concur in this measure which the governor suggests. You will give the corresponding orders and commands for its prompt execution, making certain that the officer and soldiers who are selected shall have the qualifications and training that are required.

The señor *auditor de guerra* recommended the same thing, as is seen above in paragraph 1145.

1442. But the *junta de real hacienda*, held on September 25, 1752, stated, above in paragraph 1156, that

there is no occasion for the establishment which the governor of the province of Texas requests shall be made on the Río de San Pedro, etc.

Notwithstanding this refusal, the same Señor Barrios again wrote his Excellency the following words, copied above in paragraph 1221:

I do not withdraw, señor, what I represented with regard to the establishment of the detachment of San Pedro. I consider it today even more necessary because of what has happened, in view of the fact that this is a nation that dominates by its fierce spirit, and that by controlling it, we could promise ourselves the peace of the province. All persons of experience are of this opinion, for it is a nation respected even by the proud Apaches. I would be failing in my duty if I did not represent my opinion concerning it, so that I may on no occasion be accused of being dilatory in the discharge of my duty, etc.

1443. With regard to this the señor *auditor de guerra*, Valcárcel, rendered a conforming opinion, above in paragraph 1284:

Notwithstanding the fact that the present governor had before him what the *junta general* had determined with regard to whether a detachment of twenty soldiers with an experienced and zealous officer should be stationed on the Río de San Pedro in order to observe the schemes of the French and the reasons they have had for increasing their settlements; and although this was the first point which was discussed in the junta—it being decided in the negative—he repeats the same request in his last *consulta* with such arguments that they force one to the belief that he judges this measure necessary and conducive to the important ends which he proposes and to which he directs it. It is not remarkable that the señor *fiscal* is inclined to defer to these arguments in his next reply when previously, with a less urgent representation, he requested that the detachment be stationed on the said river. The Señor Marquis of Altamira in his opinion, on folio 91, also subscribed to this repeated proposal of the governor, and the mutual support that the señores marquis and *fiscal* have lent to it has inspired in the *auditor* a natural desire to inform himself fully on the matter. He has succeeded in doing so through the expert and well informed person of an individual of much experience in those lands who, because of an office that he has held in them, in the discharge of which he has traversed and explored them personally, should know all the places of the province of Texas, in which he resided several years. From the exact information that the *auditor* has obtained from him, he has learned in substance only that in the whole extent of the province of Asinays, which is commonly called Texas, *no river whatsoever is known or spoken of by the name of Río de San Pedro*, which because of its situation and location would be appropriate for observing the schemes and movements of the French in the colonies adjacent to it. [He has learned further] that the only place named San Pedro is the first pueblo of the Navidachos Indians on the other side of the Río de la Trinidad on the direct road to our presidio of Los Adays, at which place it is not apparent what opposition a detachment of twenty soldiers can make to the French who might be scheming to penetrate into our possessions and introduce their commerce and trade among the nations of the royal crown, because it is too distant and not appropriately located for the purpose for which the detachment will be intended.

1444. If perchance the Río de San Pedro of which the governor speaks is the one of this name which the Señor Marquis of Altamira mentions in his extensive report, already cited, between which and the Río de San Antonio is located the presidio of San Antonio de Béxar—the latter being two hundred leagues from Los Adaes, which is the nearest to the French presidio of Nachitoos—it results that opposition to the ingress of the French into Texas and the observation of their schemes and movements would be even more difficult. It is possible, therefore, that the information the *auditor* has received coincides with the notice of the señor marquis, the river and place being one and the same.

1445. This notice and the insufficient information with which the governor in his zealous eagerness persists in the measure concerning the detachment of the Río de San Pedro, the actual existence of which can reasonably be doubted, make the point indeterminable and put it back in its former difficult state, without any new document or evidence which was not available to the *junta general* and which, discussed therein, would have brought about a contrary decision. This is especially true, in as much as the establishment of the detachment would certainly and necessarily be costly to the royal treasury because of the increase in the number of soldiers and their corresponding salaries, and it is very improbable that it would be useful and efficacious for the purpose for which it is created. Its usefulness will be proven only when there may be evidence that the said Río de San Pedro is in the province; that it is located and flows at such a distance and in such a manner that the movements of the French can be observed from the site on which the detachment would be stationed; and that, on it there is only one narrow crossing available, by means of which it can be forded and passage found from one bank to the other, and from which alone can be impeded the entrance of the French and the introduction of their commerce into the province of Texas, and the passage of the Indian nations included in its district and vicinity to the presidio of Nachitoos or to any other settlement of the French colonies. For it would be of little advantage for the detachment to be stationed at one place if along the course of the river there are many easy and safe passes, or fords, by which to cross without encountering opposition from the detachment. *Because, if their retreat were cut off and they should take some other crossing either farther down or higher up, even though it might be at the cost of a short detour,* the trespassers would accomplish safely their schemes of trading and intercourse with the Indians of the crown of Spain, and the detachment would be idle and useless, the purpose for which it was created being thus defeated.

1446. It follows from this that until the governor shall designate with a map, or description, which one is the Río de San Pedro, its length, and the other circumstances mentioned in the preceding number, with which procedure he could have furnished information from the beginning regarding his proposal for the detachment, it cannot be either adopted, or rejected on the basis of impending harm to the royal treasury as the result of disbursements for its salaries and the other expenditures that it might entail as a new establishment. In view of this your Excellency's greatness may be pleased to order the present governor of Texas, Don Jacinto del Barrio [de Barrios] y Jáuregui (he should have written Barrios, for the surname del Barrio was that of the preceding governor, called Don Pedro del Barrio Junco y Espriella), to supply the necessary information that is lacking with regard to the nature of the place in which the detachment is to be stationed, which he has referred to in his *consultas.* He shall report on this matter very clearly everything that he may find to be most useful and conducive to the royal service in the new examination that he will conduct to this end. Your Excellency may reserve for yourself the final disposition and decision with regard to the matter of the detachment, in view of what the proceedings that the said governor shall remit may show.

1447. It seems that Señor Barrios did not fulfill the wishes of Señor Valcárcel, because in all these *autos* there is no evidence of his having satisfied them by marking on a map, or a plan, which one the Río de San Pedro was, its extent, and the other information requested, in order to discuss whether or not to found such a presidio. But it also seems, as we have suggested above, that there is no doubt whatever that Señor Barrios planned the establishment of this presidio in the pueblo of the Nasonis. In his affidavit, above in paragraph 1204, Father Fray José Calahorra speaks as follows:

From this action it resulted that the Indians, seeing their captain (Don Luis de St. Denis) angered, for they respect him as such, became quiet. Those from Nasones concluded [however] by saying that they would give their lives before allowing the Spaniards to place a presidio in their pueblo, because they had abandoned them (they are alluding to what is stated above in paragraph 1438) when they took away the mission which was there, which act was a clear sign of their lack of love for them.

1448. Here I ask: What was the reason for the Nasonis Indians saying that they would give their lives before they would allow the Spaniards to place a presidio in their pueblo? Is this presidio which was planned among the Nasonis perhaps spoken of in some other place? It is not. Then this was the one which Señor Barrios had indicated that he wished to be established on the banks of the Río de San Pedro. And, in fact, if this river passes through the site of the Nasonis, as we shall see [that it does], is it not to be believed that the erection of the presidio was sought on its banks in the vicinity of the pueblo of the Nasonis? But the commandant of Nachitoches, Monsieur Cesario de Blanc, in his letter copied above in paragraph 1206, writes as follows to the said Señor Barrios:

> The Marquis of Baudrevil [Vaudreuil] learned . . . of the decision which your lordship had made . . . for the purpose of placing a presidio at Nadote, among the Panis, and among the Apaches, for no other reason than to check the intercourse which we have with the Indians friendly to his Most Christian Majesty and to cut us off entirely from our means of seeing them. I am greatly astonished that your lordship does not know that Nadotes has been in territory under our control since the founding of the presidio which your lordship now commands. The boundaries will show us the truth of this.

There is mentioned here the presidio among the Nadotes, that is to say, the Nasonis, as Señor Barrios explains this word in the reply which he addressed to him [Cesario de Blanc].

1449. But it becomes necessary in passing to point out that Monsieur de Blanc was very ignorant of the boundaries. For this reason he believed erroneously, or rather, perhaps, maliciously, that the Nasonis had belonged since the beginning to the crown of France, and he did not remember, or perhaps he was feigning not to remember, that his predecessor, St. Denis the elder, had aided in the founding of this mission for these Indians, and that by reason of this he wrote those notable words, in paragraph 1439, with which we have argued against his son, to wit:

> But notwithstanding that as far as the Río del Norte I did not find any vestiges (if there were such) of Spanish settlements, it does not follow that

we Frenchmen claim all the territory to the said Río del Norte for our own. I admit unreservedly that the Spaniards have legitimate possession of it.

And the other words:

Nor would there be even any occasion for raising a question if the French (which will never happen) should attempt to settle and inhabit the country up to and excluding the Lago de los Adaes, because then they would indeed be more truly on the other side of the river than they had ever been. It would be a just matter for controversy if the French should attempt to move beyond the Lago de los Adaes to the vicinity of the Spaniards.

1450. Señor Barrios in his cited reply, above in paragraph 1210, answered him as follows:

I must tell your honor that the Indians of Nadotes and Nasones are immediate subjects of the Catholic King, my lord, and that until the year '31, the mission of San José de Nasones was maintained at that place. In the said year it was withdrawn from that place (in confirmation of what Senor Barrios states here see above, beginning with paragraph 1407) for the purposes considered convenient by his Catholic Majesty. Our ancient [antiquada] possession therefore dates back to its founding in the year 1716.

(He meant to say old [antigua], for according to the Diccionario de la Lengua Española [Castellana], antiquado means to be out of use for a long time, and Spain was actually making use of the possession of those places.)

Then Señor Barrios thought of establishing this presidio among the Nasonis. Then everyone should be forced to see that Señor Valcárcel would not have given special attention (this is stated with due respect to his most illustrious lordship, who was honorary councillor and *electo en propriedad* to the royal and supreme Council of the Indies, from which he resigned, and dean of the royal audiencia of Mexico, etc.) to the three following instruments: the certification, the letter of Monsieur de Blanc, and the reply to it by Señor Barrios, for if he had examined them carefully he would have settled his doubts. In order to go from the pueblo of Texas, that is, from San Pedro de los Navadachos, to the Nasonis it is necessary to cross the river which passes through the same pueblo of the Texas. Father Le Clerc so testifies in the following words, which are found in document 3, number 127:

After having been there among them (the Cenis, or Texas) four or five days recuperating, we continued our journey by way of the Nasonis. It was necessary to cross a large river which runs through the center of the large rancheria of the Cenis.

This is the Río de los Nechas which, as is stated in the diary of [the expedition of] the Marquis of San Miguel de Aguayo (document 21, number 87), Monsieur de St. Denis crossed by swimming his horse when he came to have a conference with the said señor marquis, and which we shall prove later is the Río de San Pedro, concerning which there is this dispute.

1451. In document 11, number 46, Alonso de León writes as follows:

On Friday, the 26th of the said month, I set out with the missionary fathers and some soldiers and officers with the said Indian governor toward the northeast to select the most appropriate site for placing the mission, and, after having seen three small valleys as far as the place where they told us two Frenchmen had died—at a spot where they had wished to settle, and there we saw their graves—we placed a cross on a tree for them. Having arrived at a river, we found no crossing on it except by means of a tree which the Indians had laid across it and a rope by which they supported themselves. We gave the river the name of San Miguel Arcangel (here the Río de las Nechas is called San Miguel by Alonso de León), and from there we returned to the camp, having travelled six leagues.

In document 13, number 23, Father Massanet writes the following:

On the next day we went with the said governor, and he took us to the site which the *French had selected for a settlement,* which is on the banks of the river, very pleasant and a very good site. Because it is removed from the Indians, we did not erect the convent at the said place. They showed us the bodies of two dead Frenchmen who had killed each other by carbine shots. (It seems that since they had died among the Cenis, these two Frenchmen are different from those others whom Father Le Clerc mentions, cited above in Part I, paragraph 205, who killed each other among the Nasonis.) During this whole day we found no place to my liking. On the next day, I went out in the morning with Captain Alonso de León not very far from where we were, and I found a very pretty place next to the creek with pleasant woods. . . . Within three days an adequate and very convenient dwelling and church in which to say mass were built.

In number 26 he adds:

There remained voluntarily, and quite contentedly, with the religious three soldiers whom I requested; they were among those from Zacatecas.

On the map drawn by Father Puelles, number 10 of document 74, this mission is seen above the 31st degree of latitude and at 282° of longitude (which corresponds, in making the computation given in paragraph 677, to 78° 6′). It is marked with the number four and an inscription saying, "San Pedro," and in the margin, giving an explanation of this number, it says:

Number 4. Spanish camp, where on May 25, 1687 [?], solemn high mass was sung on the day of Corpus Christi. The Spanish flag was unfurled; the Indians rendered obedience to the Catholic Monarch; the first mission was established.

From this account of Father Massanet, and from what Alonso de León said a little before, we infer that the French companions of La Salle did not found any fort on the banks of the Río de los Texas, but that they did wish to found one and selected the site for it. It is precisely the one that the missionary religious rejected as being too far from the village of the Indians, and they went to establish their mission on the bank of a stream.

1452. In document 16, number 77, Domingo Ramón in describing his journey said:

On the 28th I travelled five leagues toward the east-northeast through some eminences and valleys of open woodlands of liveoaks, oaks, pines, walnut trees, and grapevines. We arrived at a large clearing in which there are two lakes with fish. Along the edge of it flows a somewhat large river. This afternoon more than a hundred and fifty Indians, many of them captains, came to see me, and about a league before we arrived Don Luis de St. Denis came out to meet us. All the Indians alighted in our presence.

In number 79 he adds:

On the 29th, I stayed in this place to celebrate the day of St. Peter, which was done as well as possible, and because we were waiting for more people who were to come. These, Indians of the Nasonis Nacogdochis nation, who made demonstrations of peace, arrived in the afternoon. . . .

(Even though it were not apparent from many other texts that the discoverers were accustomed to give to rivers, mountains, pueblos, etc., the name of the saint on whose day they discovered some of these places, or the name of some other object or idea which presented itself to them, or of an occurrence which they observed, there is in addition the statement of Father José Acosta in his

Historia Natural y Moral de las Indias, book 1, chapter 13, who says the following: "It has been a very common custom in these discoveries in the New World to give names to lands and ports in accordance with the occasion that presented itself." Our documents show us that the discoverers and settlers of Texas did this. Thus Ponce de León named the vast country that he discovered Florida, because of having made his discovery during the Pasqua de Flores, ó de Resurrección [Easter]. As we have seen in Part I, paragraph 40, the followers of Alonso de León gave the Río de la Santísima Trinidad this name because they crossed it on that day [of the Most Holy Trinity], or its eve. The San Marcos [received its name] for a like reason; and the Arroyo del Cíbolo because they saw some Indians who were skinning some of these cattle [buffalo], as is inferred from Father Massanet's letter, or document 13, numbers 25, 5, and 7. The Señores Marquis of Aguayo and Brigadier Rivera did the same thing, for to everything that did not have a name they gave one in accordance with the event. This is seen from their diaries, copied in documents 21 and 24. Other did the same thing, for, without knowing who their authors were, we still know the names as, for example, the Cerro de la Tortuga [Hill of the Tortoise], because it has the shape of this animal, and that of La Xicarilla because it is shaped like a small chocolate cup. Thus it is that, following this procedure, Captain Domingo Ramón and his companions gave the name of San Pedro to the place on which they celebrated the day of St. Peter, as Father Espinosa testifies in some words of his which we shall see later. Since this place was at the rancheria of the Navidachos, it was thereafter called San Pedro de los Navidachos. Near this place was a river, not very large, as Domingo Ramón describes it, and and it is precisely the same one that Alonso de León named San Miguel Arcangel and which others call the Neches. But losing this name subsequently, it was called Río de San Pedro by everyone, as if they were saying the river that is adjacent to the place of San Pedro, and avoiding circumlocution they call it only Río de San Pedro.

On the 30th (continues Ramón), I travelled four leagues toward the east-northeast over a country most noteworthy for the abundance of springs, fine valleys, and woods with walnut trees and grapevines, together with many pines.

I stopped on the edge of a large clearing because there was a spring of good and cold water, with good pasturage and other springs in the vicinity.

1453. This afternoon I set out with the religious to look for a site suitable for founding the said mission, being accompanied by the great captain of the Indians and some others. An appropriate site was found, selected by the Indians and satisfactory to the father president, whereupon we returned to the said camp.

And in number 84, concluding this account, he says:

On the day of the third, the first establishment of the mission of San Francisco was begun in the pueblo of the Nechas, where I appointed a *cabildo* and gave possession to the said religious in the name of his Majesty.

1454. The days of the 4th and 5th of the current month were spent in building the hut. I left on the 6th and on the 7th I arrived at La Concepción, having marched nine leagues through a land wonderful for its abundance of water, pastures, and open groves of beautiful pines and other trees, with many grapevines laden with large green grapes. Crossing a *fairly large* river (this is the one called Santa Bárbara, in document 21, number 93, by the Señor Marquis of Aguayo, whose words we shall give later in paragraph 1464, because between the Río de San Pedro and that of Santa Bárbara there is no other that deserves the name of *fairly large* and because it is located just this side of the mission of La Concepción de los Aynais) toward the east-northeast, we arrived at the pueblo of the Aynais where there are a great many *ranchos* with their fields of corn, watermelons, beans, cantaloupes, tobacco, and a pale yellow flower that they have, which is very good to eat, but the name of which we do not know. I gave possession to the said religious, named a *cabildo*, and did everything else necessary, the Indians here having devoted themselves with their usual activity to the building of a dwelling and a church. I left this place on the 7th and on the 8th I arrived at the pueblo of the Nacogdoches, having marched nine leagues toward the east-southeast through a land abounding in springs, pastures, open forests of pines and liveoaks, and many grapevines, the whole country being extremely warm. I named a *cabildo*. A church and a dwelling were built. On the 9th I remained at this place attending to the business that came up.

1455. Father Isidro Felix de Espinosa, describing the same journey of Ramón, whom he accompanied, writes as follows in the same document 16, number 164:

On Monday, the 29th, mass was sung in honor of Señor San Pedro, for whom we named this camp. (Here are the words of Father Espinosa with which we promised, above in paragraph 1452, to prove that the place of San Pedro was given this name on the day of this holy apostle.) This was attended by the entire multitude of assembled Indians. About noon others came with eight captains, and in receiving them the same ceremonies were solemnized as on the day preceding, except that in place of the *Te Deum* the *Tota Pulchra*, *etc.* was sung. The last group of Indians brought a pipe (this is the famous calumet of which Father Le Clercq speaks so often in document 3) of bronze adorned with many feathers. He [Ramón] distributed clothing among them as he had done with the others, and they also celebrated his arrival with dances as is their custom.

1456. On Tuesday, the 30th, after three masses had been said for the success of their conversion, we proceeded toward the east-northeast through open woods, until we came to a plain which seemed to our captain to be a suitable place to establish the presidio for the time being. It was on the bank of a very large lake and not very far from a medium-sized river. (This is the San Miguel which was later called San Pedro.) We religious crossed with the captain and some Indians to look for a place for the first mission, and having found the one that seemed to us most appropriate, we returned to the camp. On this day, going as far as the place where the presidio was established, the expedition travelled three leagues.

1457. On Wednesday, July first, the Indians who were still together remained to build the captain's dwelling. It was begun on this day, as was the distribution of the tools and other things belonging to the four missions. On Thursday, the second, the house was covered with grass, and in the meanwhile all of us said mass, and wrote a little of the language of the Asynais. With Don Luis de St. Denis serving as interpreter, the Indians made pacts and settled differences among themselves and apportioned the four missions between them. Availing ourselves of an Indian woman (this is the famous Angelina of whom we shall speak later, in paragraph 1474) of this nation, who knew our language, having been reared in Coahuila, we gave them to understand as well as the opportunity afforded the object of our coming. They immediately informed us that they would not be able to assemble [at the missions] until they had gathered their crops.

1458. On Friday, the third, all we religious went with the captain to the spring which we had previously examined, and the Indians began immediately to build the house for the first mission. In the meanwhile we spent the day in a hut made of branches. One league was travelled. On Saturday, the 4th, all of us said mass, and the house was completely finished. Although it is poor and like a farm hut we moved into it, and proceeded to distribute what appertained to each mission.

1459. On Sunday, the 5th, the captain appointed alcaldes, *regidores,* and a constable, and subsequently at the spring he proceeded in the name of his Majesty (whom may God keep) to give me, as president, possession of the mission. The customary ceremonies having been solemnized, I named the Reverend Father Fray Francisco Hidalgo, who for so many years has solicited this conversion, as minister of the first mission, which is called Nuestro Padre San Francisco de los Texas, and as his companion I named the father preacher, Fray Manuel Castellano, to whom I committed the spiritual care of the soldiers in the presidio. The greater part of the clothing and other things that were brought for the Indians was distributed, and on this day our captain left with the fathers preachers, Fray Matías Sans [Sáenz] de San Antonio and Fray

Pedro de Santa María y Mendoza, in search of the place of Nacogdoches, in order to establish their first mission for the college of Nuestra Señora de Guadalupe de Zacatecas.

Let it be noted that this mission of San Francisco was not placed on the same site on which Father Massanet founded it, but four leagues farther east and closer to the river which Alonso de León called San Miguel. This is evident from a letter which is found in document 16, number 177, from the same Father Espinosa, written to the most excellent Duke of Linares, dated July 22, 1716, in which he says the following:

After two months of travel from the Río Grande del Norte to this desired province of the Asinais, or Texas, the Divine Majesty was pleased to grant us success in the founding of four missions: the first with the name of Nuestro Padre San Francisco, replacing the old pueblo, four leagues farther inland toward the east. . . .

Here we have the first site on which was founded the first presidio and mission of Domingo Ramón.

1460. With the information that these texts have given us, we come into a most clear understanding of the places where Alonso de León and Domingo Ramón founded the missions, and we understand well the text of the diary of the Marquis of Aguayo which reads as follows (number 84):

On Monday, the 28th, the march was continued toward the east-northeast, through the same kind of country thinly covered with trees, as far as the place of San Pedro, where the presidio and mission (the Spaniards had not penetrated beyond that place) were established during the first *entrada* in the year 1690. Since this was a convenient site and there was no other suitable for the purpose as far as the Río de los Nechas, only three leagues were travelled.

Here is the site of the mission and presidio which Alonso de León founded and which we have just seen, in paragraph 460 [1455], was called San Pedro, because Ramón gave it that name. According to this account of the journey of the señor marquis, it is inferred that it is in 30° 50′ of latitude and in 78° 20′ of longitude, and thus it is seen on our map. Taking four leagues of the scale of 25⅗ to the degree (for since it is such a small number we believe them to be equal to travellers' leagues, for which reason we do not deduct their sixth part), if we fix one point of the compass on the crossing on the Río de Nechas and with the other mark off this distance toward the west, we shall find that it falls in the latitude and longitude mentioned.

1461. In number 85 he continues:

On Tuesday, the 29th, the señor governor set out in the direction of the northeast, [and going] through open woodlands of the same kind of trees, over hills and ravines, and crossing the plain on which the presidio was placed for the first time during the *entrada* of 1716, we concluded the day's march on the bank of the Río de Nechas, by the side of a lake fed by a fresh-water spring, having travelled four leagues. Since we found the river very high, the señor marquis ordered a bridge built, the construction of which required six days. It is thirty-two *varas* long and four wide. It turned out to be so well made and so durable that it was given the blessing of the Church.

Here is the site of the first mission and presidio founded by Domingo Ramón, four leagues from the one on which León had founded his, as Father Espinosa has shown us and as is inferred from the account itself. It is deduced from a calculation similar to the preceding one, that it was in 30° 53′ of latitude and 78° 13′ of longitude, and thus it is seen also on our map.

1462. In number 90 he adds:

On Sunday, the third, the bridge having been finished, all the people, baggage, pack animals, and cattle crossed without difficulty. And [after having marched] toward the east-northeast, we made camp near the mission of San Francisco, where the presidio was located the second time in 1716. The day's journey consisted of only two short leagues.

Here we have another site, distinct from the presidio and mission of Ramón, since it had been removed from the place where he first founded it, for he had located it previously on the banks of the river and later had moved it to the other side of the same river two leagues away. Concerning this, Father Morfi, book 1, number 60, says the following:

1463. After crossing the Río de Nechas one traverses two leagues of very good land in order to arrive at the Arroyo de San Francisco, where the presidio of Texas was located on its first removal in the same year of 1716.

But for what reason was this second transfer of the presidio and the mission of San Francisco made from the west bank of the Río de San Pedro to the east bank in one and the same year? Nothing is said in the *autos*, nor does any other author disclose it.

But it is easily perceived from what the said Father Espinosa writes in his *Chrónica*, book 5, chapter 8, namely:

To each of these missions was given its linen of more than two *varas*, together with the saint for whom each is named, and its ornaments, with everything necessary for the holy sacrifice of the mass. Each minister and his companion proceeded with great care to make their churches more adequate and to construct the dwelling that they would need for themselves and for the other religious whenever they should have them as guests. The truth is that the Indians, coming together in each pueblo, built two huts of wood and grass for them, one for a church and the other for a dwelling, of the kind that they themselves use. But these served for only a short time, because the religious, observing the inconvenience which they were undergoing and that they had no protection from the continual rains that fall in that land during the winter, found themselves forced to choose better sites to which to move their missions. They themselves, with two or three soldiers, were the builders who constructed new churches and their poor little convents of wood plastered with mud, in which they could live more comfortably although always burdened with excessive hardships, and these lasted a long time in those early days. An account of everything that had happened was given to the most excellent señor viceroy and to the prelates of the two colleges. The religious sustained themselves with the hope that new measures would be taken in order that that new vineyard might continue to increase, undergoing many hardships and hoping for better things.

In chapter 14 of the same book 5, he adds:

Since the Indians live so widely dispersed, the entire effort of the missionaries was directed to persuading them to assemble. And, although they gave hopes of doing so as soon as they had gathered their crops, so many difficulties arose in putting this into effect that in twenty years not one of the ministers could attain the consolation of having all the Indians of his pueblo together. The missions were moved to more spacious sites for the purpose of congregating the Indians, but the territory was not sufficiently extensive for nearly a thousand persons, who were in each pueblo.

1464. After this mission of San Francisco had been moved by the religious, keeping the same name of its holy patriarch, to a better site, which in their opinion was on the east bank of the Río de San Pedro (where it stood in 30° 56′ of latitude and 78° 6′ of longitude, and thus it is seen on our map—see Part II, paragraph 75), the presidio was also moved near the arroyo which was likewise called San Francisco, after the mission. (See below, paragraph 1471.) For, since the accessory follows the principal object, after the mission had been moved, for the custody and protection of which the presidio had been founded, the latter also was moved. Aside from this, in the same year there took place another transfer of the presidio alone to a site that was exactly a league east of the mission which Ramón founded with the name of La Concepción in the rancheria of the Ainais, or Asinais, as we shall see. In number 93 of the said document 21, the following is stated:

On Wednesday, the sixth, continuing in the same direction through the same kind of forests and plains, we crossed a creek and later a plain about two leagues wide. . A small river was encountered which has permanent water, and most of the year it is so high that the Indians have canoes there in order to cross it, although at this time it was not necessary to use one. Since it did not have a name, his lordship called it Santa Bárbara. It is less than half a league from the mission of La Concepción de Nuestra Señora. In order not to damage the cultivated fields of the settlements that are near there, the señor governor went on and camped a league beyond at a place where the presidio of Domingo Ramón was located at the time the missions were abandoned. The day's journey amounted to five leagues.

These last words show us that the said presidio of Ramón was finally moved to another site which was precisely the place where it was located in 1719 when, owing to the attack of St. Denis upon the mission of Los Adays, the religious and the troops of the whole province of Texas withdrew. We have given the history of this withdrawal above, beginning with paragraph 1394.

1465. Since the main purpose of the expedition of the Marquis of Aguayo to the province of Texas was to reëstablish the missions, at the earliest possible moment he attempted to effect this restoration. Therefore, when he found himself on the banks of the Río de los Nechas, or San Pedro,

he dispatched (as the diarist of his expedition states, document 21, number 89) a detachment to the mission of San Francisco with the father preacher, Fray José Guerra, whose horses swam the river, and another with the fathers preachers Fray Gabriel Vergara and Fray Benito Sánchez to the mission of La Concepción, in order to rebuild the churches and dwellings of the religious at both missions.

In numbers 91 and 95, he adds:

On Monday, the 4th, the señor governor sent new reinforcements of people in order to complete the work on the mission of San Francisco and so that on the following day the festival of the reëstablishment of the holy Catholic faith, which had been discontinued in the country of the Texas, might be celebrated.

On Tuesday, the 5th, learning that the church and the dwelling for the missionary fathers were completed, the señor governor, with the entire battalion, went to reëstablish the mission of San Francisco de los Nechas, commonly known as [San Francisco] de los Texas. This was done with a very solemn celebration. . . . On Friday, the 8th, the señor governor with the entire battalion and the two companies of Don Alonso de Cárdenas and Don Juan Cortinas proceeded to the mission (of La Concepción). . . . A mass of thanksgiving was sung, and the father president of the missions of Querétaro, Fray Isidro Felix de Espinosa, requested title of possession in the name of his college and on behalf of the Indians, and his lordship made this grant to the said father as well as to the Indian governor. . . .

1466. (Number 102.) On Friday, the 15th, after the feast of the Assumption of Our Lady had been celebrated early in the morning, his lordship, for the protection and assistance of the missions, left the company of Captain Don Juan Cortinas, which consists of twenty-five soldiers, reëstablished at the old presidio which is located a league from the mission of La Concepción. He then proceeded with the entire battalion toward the east-northeast, arriving at a very open site on which there were a large ravine and an abundant spring. Here we made camp that day after having marched four leagues. Since the spring had no name, it was called the Arroyo de la Asunción de Nuestra Señora.

Then this mission and the presidio as Ramón removed it for the third time, were reëstablished in the same places on which they were located before St. Denis's attack on Los Adaes. It is noted on our map with the title of "Old Presidio of the Texas," and in Part II, paragraph 75, we found that it was located in 31° 2′ of latitude and 77° 48′ of longitude.

1467. The Señor Brigadier Rivera speaks of these two reëstablished missions and the presidio as follows in his diary, document 24, number 311:

On the 5th, going toward the east, a quarter to the northeast, through the same kind of country and forests that we had traversed on the preceding day, I marched seven leagues, crossing the Arroyo de Santa Coleta, and camped on this day near a plain which is called San Pedro de los Navidachos, inhabited previously by Indians of the nation of this name and at the present time by that of the Nechas, allies of the Aynais, the leading nation of the province of Texas. . . . On the 6th, passing through lands and forests similar to those of the preceding day and continuing the march in the same direction, I travelled six leagues. I crossed the Río de los Nechas, and at a distance of more than a league from it, I encountered some huts where a religious of the [college of Santa] Cruz de Querétaro resides. He is there for the purpose of ministering to the Indians whenever they may wish to become Christians. [The mission] has the name of San Francisco de Nechas. There I halted.

1468. On the 7th I travelled toward the east-southeast over level lands with a somewhat downward slope in the direction of our march, and having extensive hills and plains with abundant pastures and with woodlands in certain sections. After marching eight and a half leagues, I crossed the Río de los Aynais (this is the river which the Marquis of Aguayo called Santa Bárbara, above in paragraph 1464) and at a short distance from its banks I came upon another house of the said reverend fathers of the [college of Santa] Cruz de Querétaro, intended also for ministering to the Aynais Indians at such time as they may wish to come to receive the faith. A short distance beyond I encountered the presidio of Nuestra Señora de los Dolores, which they call de los Texas, where I halted. (This is the presidio which the Señor Marquis of Aguayo founded; see above, paragraph 466.) Having observed the sun in it, we found that it is located in 32° 16′ of north latitude and 281° 20′ of longitude.

What a great difference there is between this latitude and longitude and that which we have given it! But we are convinced that our latitude and longitude are the more accurate. See Part II, paragraph 73 [75?].

Father Fray Gaspar José de Solís, in document 40, number 113, writes as follows:

On the 30th we crossed a stream called Santa Coleta, containing very good water, its banks being very green and overgrown with trees. There are some rancherias of heathen Indians here, in the direction of the Río de San Pedro. Beyond it there is a very large pueblo of the same name settled with Texas Indians.

In number 116 he adds:

We passed this pueblo (of San Pedro de los Tejas) and arrived at the bank of the Río de Nechas, which carries much water and is bordered by luxuriant growth, with many trees.

In these last words it seems that Father Solís falls into somewhat of an error, calling the river which the Marquis of Aguayo had called Santa Bárbara, and which the señor brigadier had just called the Aynais, the Río de Nechas. For the Nechas, as we have seen, is certainly the San Pedro. But his mistake is pardonable, for since this Río de los Aynais joins the Nechas, some people are wont to give it the latter name.

1470. Having now ascertained definitely that the Río de los Navidachos is the same as the San Pedro, it becomes necessary to inquire into the names and the courses of the other rivers of that

province in order that this hydrographical information about that
country may be complete. Father Solís, in document 40, beginning with number 116, in giving an account of these rivers writes
as follows:

We passed this pueblo and arrived at the bank of the Río de Nechas, which
carries much water and is bordered by luxuriant growth, with many trees. . . .
On the day of the first, we crossed a stream called the Alazán, containing good
water. Through a plain which they call Las Carreras, [there flows] another
stream without a name, which was called San Felipe y Santiago. We arrived
at the Río de Angelina which is deep but not very large.

1471. Father Morfi in his *Memorias*, book 1, beginning with
number 59, [writes:]

Netchas. Four leagues to the east flows the Río Nechas, so called after the
nation of Indians of that name who inhabit its banks. It rises, as do all those
of that province, toward the northwest, near the pueblo of the Navedachos
Indians. It flows at a distance of eight leagues from the Río de Angelinas,
with which it later unites, and as the result of this union it enters the sea
large and navigable for small vessels. It ends on the coast between the
province of Texas and Louisiana, its mouth being fifteen leagues from that
of the Trinity, with which it unites by means of a branch. At its mouth it
forms a small island two hundred varas in diameter, this river having only the
one mouth. This island and coastline are well known to the English, who
attempted to establish themselves there. . . . Having crossed the Netchas, one
travels over two leagues of good ground in order to reach the Arroyo de San
Francisco, where the presidio of Texas was located upon its first transfer in
the same year of 1716.

I do not remember that anyone else mentions this Arroyo de
San Francisco, which took the name from the mission of San
Francisco which was founded near it. Perhaps it is the one which
Father Puelles places between the Cerrito and the Río de San
Pedro, and flowing into the latter. See his map, which is number
10 of document 74.

1472. In the distance of two leagues of forests two streams are crossed
(continues the said writer), and at the beginning of a large plain is the stream
of Nuestra Señora de las Nieves.

(These two streams and that of Nuestra Señora de las Nieves
are mentioned in number 92 of the diary of the Marquis of Aguayo,
as follows:

He continued the march between northeast and east-northeast, through open groves of tall oaks and mulberries. Two streams and two plains were crossed, and we went as far as a flowing stream which is at the beginning of another plain, larger than the preceding ones. Here we halted, for it was very late because we had been detained until nearly noon in the mission [of San Francisco]. Today four leagues were travelled, and his lordship gave the said stream and site the name of Nuestra Señora de las Nieves.

But is this Arroyo de las Nieves perhaps the one that Father Solís calls the Alazán, and which Father Puelles shows on his map as flowing into the Río de Angelinas? I believe so, providing it may not rather be the Río Florido of which Father Morfi goes on to speak.)

The same woodlands are followed (proceeds this father historian of the province of Texas) by some open plains. The Arroyo, or, as some say, the Río Florido, is crossed, and five leagues beyond flows the Río de Santa Bárbara, so high that it is not fordable, and the Indians of that region keep a canoe there to facilitate its crossing, although during the severity of a drouth this aid is not necessary. At less than half a league from the ford of this river, the mission of Purísima Concepción de María was located, which is today on the bank of the Río de San Antonio. Angelinas. The Río de Angelinas took its name from a Texas Indian woman, baptized in Coahuila, who, having returned to her country, was very useful to the Spaniards because of her knowledge of our language and the good offices with which she recommended us to her countrymen. This river is almost equal in volume to the Netchas. It flows through territory which the nations known by the name of Texas inhabit. It is not navigable until it unites with the Netchas about twenty leagues from its ford [on the road that leads] to Los Adaes, and it rises an equal distance toward the northwest. It waters extremely fertile lands.

1473. As long as Father Morfi or someone else for him does not prove with good documents that the Río de Angelinas is distinct from the river which the Marquis of Aguayo called Santa Bárbara, I must continue in the belief that they are one and the same, most especially since the Señores Marquis of Aguayo and Brigadier Rivera testify that the mission of La Concepción de los Aynais was about half a league beyond the Río de Santa Bárbara or de los Ainays, going from west to east. This is what Father Morfi states concerning the Río de Santa Bárbara, and it is due to the fact that he depended greatly on the text of the diary of the señor marquis, and did not understand very well what he was saying. He therefore made two rivers out of one.

Almost all the writers agree with regard to the number of leagues
from the Río de San Pedro to that of Los Asinais. Don Athanase
de Mézières in Part II, paragraph 141, places it at eight. Father
Morfi assigns the same number. A slightly greater distance is inferred from the diary of Domingo Ramón, and from those of the
Marquis of Aguayo and the Brigadier Rivera, whose words we
have given above in their proper places. Now: within this distance no river of any size has been mentioned by any of the
writers, to which the name of Santa Bárbara can be given. For
this reason we believe that the one which the marquis called Santa
Bárbara is the same one which others call Los Aynais and Angelinas. The description which Captain Ramón gives of it agrees
perfectly with this, for he calls it "somewhat large," a term not
very dissimilar from the one that Father Solís applies to it when
he calls it "abundant but not very large." And although the same
señor marquis calls it small, he adds nevertheless that it rises so
high the greater part of the year that the Indians have canoes
there in which to cross it.

1474. The name of Santa Bárbara which the señor marquis gave
to this river lasted only a short time, for almost immediately it
was given the name of Angelina, and, as we have seen above,
Father Solís, Don Athanase de Mézières, Father Morfi, and finally
Father Puelles, on his map, cite it by this name. It was so called,
as Father Morfi has said, in honor of an Indian woman of that
name, of whom without stating her name Father Espinosa, in some
words copied above in paragraph 1457 and in his *Chrónica*, book
5, chapter 9, makes honorable mention because of her good offices
in behalf of the Spaniards. He says:

On the third of July, with an Indian woman of this same nation, well-versed
in both languages, serving as interpreter—she had been reared in Coahuila,
since her parents had been there a long time when the Spaniards left [Texas]
in 1693—we gave all the Indians to understand the principal reason for our
coming.

The author of the diary of the Marquis of Aguayo [recounts it]
in this manner:

On this day the *cacique* of the nation of the Aynais, whom all the nations of
Texas recognize as their superior, arrived with eight of the principal Indians
and four women, among them Angelina, an Indian reared on the Río Grande

in Coahuila. She served as interpreter since she spoke the Spanish language as well as that of the Texas.

1475. Giving an account of the reëstablishment of the other missions, in treating of that of Los Nasonis the author of the diary of the Señor Marquis of Aguayo writes as follows in number 96:

On Saturday, the 9th, his lordship sent a lieutenant with a detachment to accompany the father preacher, Fray Benito Sánchez, a missionary assigned to the mission of San José de los Nasonis, which is eight leagues north of that of La Concepción, to build the church and a dwelling for the fathers, both of which were destroyed. (Number 99.) On Tuesday, the 12th, the señor governor left the battalion at this encampment and went with a company to the mission of San José de los Nasonis, which is eight leagues off the main road. On Wednesday, the 13th, the restoration of that mission was celebrated with a sung mass [*Misa cantada*], and after mass the grant of possession was drawn up and given to the father president and to the captain of the Nasonis Indians with the same formality as at the two other missions.

If this mission was reëstablished by the Spaniards, the French did not acquire dominion over that country during the time that passed from the year '19, in which they attacked Los Adaes, to the day of this reëstablishment nor consequently in all the time since then down to the day that France ceded Louisiana to Spain, even though in 1731 all these missions might have been abandoned, because the arms of Spain were protecting that entire land as far as Los Adays, and were making use of their possession.

1476. On this river, then, in the region where it passes through [the pueblo of] the Nasonis or at some other place nearby (for it was not necessarily on the banks of the river itself because of the fact that the Spaniards, as long as they did not need the rivers for trading purposes, did not build their presidios on the said banks except when some other motive obliged them to do so), Señor Don Jacinto de Barrios planned [to establish] a presidio

in order to observe (as he told his Excellency above, in paragraph 1440) *the moves of the French and the increase that they are going to make in their post of Caudachos, . . . and the principal care of this officer would be to reduce and attract those Indians with skill and cunning. They are the ones who rule the other nations in that whole province.*

In another letter, copied above in paragraph 1442, he repeats this same plan, saying:

I do not withdraw, señor, what I represented with regard to the establishment of the detachment of San Pedro. I consider it today even more necessary because of what happened, in view of the fact that this is a nation that dominates by its fierce spirit, and that by controlling it, we could promise ourselves the peace of the province. All persons of experience are of this opinion, for it is a nation respected even by the proud Apaches. I would be failing in my duty if I did not represent my opinion concerning it, so that I may on no occasion be accused of being dilatory in the discharge of my duty, etc.

1477. The señor *fiscal*, Amoreu [Andreu?], in his opinion in paragraph 1136, above, not only acceded to the request of Señor Barrios, but he also added the following considerations:

In as much as this province of Texas and its presidio, as the *fiscal* suggests, now becomes another sphere, and has a status different from that which it has had formerly—because if heretofore its presidio and soldiers were mainly for defense of the province against Indian enemies and were established on this basis and for this precise purpose, today they must be also alert and watchful of what is happening and may happen with regard to the French; and since, for this second purpose, the soldiers of its garrisons are not adequate or suitable, either in number or in the rules, system, defense, and methods that they have observed for protecting the province against Indian enemies, not being disciplined and trained to meet emergencies that may arise with the French; and since we must now take care, for the reasons stated, not only of defense against the Indians but also and simultaneously of whatever may arise with the French—it therefore seemed proper to the *fiscal* that it should be suggested to his Majesty that the garrison of this presidio should be like that of the port of Vera Cruz. For this purpose adequate troops should be raised, established, and trained, and also those which may be considered essential for such protection against and pursuit of the Indians as may be necessary. Thus, these troops assisting the presidio in its defense against the French, they will be equally prepared and prompt in any eventuality and movement against the Indians. On this matter, if it be your Excellency's pleasure, the governor of Texas can report the result of his operations.

1478. In truth Señor Barrios could not have chosen another site more to the purpose because, as we have seen, the Nasonis were located east and a little north of the Nechas. These Indians were the most distant from the Texas and at the same time the ones nearest to the lands of the French. Placed between the two, the squadron of the presidio would check the hostile Indians and the French, preventing their advancing beyond their boundary and attempting to penetrate gradually the dominions of Spain. Thus, just as the presidio of Los Adaes stood against the Indians and the French, and observed the latter's movements and impeded their illicit trade, so that of the Nasonis could serve the same purposes. In a word, this presidio would be in a better situation and location, farther to the north than the very weak post which Alonso de León founded with the three soldiers that he left as a protection for the missionary fathers (see above, paragraph 1454) ; than the ones which Domingo Ramón established; and, finally, than the one which the Señor Marquis of Aguayo founded, which was destroyed because of the report of the Señor Brigadier Rivera. (See above, paragraph 1434.)

1479. It is ascertained, then, which was the Río de San Pedro on which Señor Barrios intended to build a presidio. Thus the well-informed expert, who had so much experience in those lands and who through the office he had held in them, in the discharge of which he had travelled over and explored them personally, was obliged to know all the places of the province of Texas, in which he resided for some years, could not inform Señor Valcárcel that the Río de los Nechas, or San Pedro de los Navidachos, was called also simply the Río de San Pedro. What his most illustrious lordship did gather in substance from all these notices was (see paragraph 1443)

that in the whole extent of the province of Asinays, which is commonly called Texas, no river whatsoever is known or spoken of by the name of Río de San Pedro, which because of its situation and location would be appropriate for observing the schemes and movements of the French of the colonies adjacent to it. [He has learned further] that the only place named San Pedro is the first pueblo of the Navidachos on the other side of the Río de la Trinidad on the direct road to our presidio of Los Adays, at which place it is not apparent what opposition a detachment of twenty soldiers can make to the French who might be scheming to penetrate into our possessions and introduce their commerce and trade among the nations of the royal crown, because it is too distant and not appropriately located for the purpose for which the detachment will be intended.

Even though the first pueblo of the Navidachos may be on the other side of the Río de la Trinidad, travelling toward the east in the direction of Los Adaes, it must not be understood by this that it is on the east bank of this river, but rather a goodly distance beyond it and in the vicinity of the Río de los Nechas, called also for this reason Río de San Pedro, as we have seen. And we

have just noted in the preceding paragraph what opposition a
detachment of twenty soldiers could present to the French and
the benefit that they would bring to his Majesty's dominions.

1480. If . . . the Río de San Pedro of which the governor speaks (continues
Señor Valcárcel) is the one of this name which the Señor Marquis of Altamira
mentions in his extensive report, already cited, between which and the Río
de San Antonio is located the presidio of San Antonio de Béxar—the latter
being 200 leagues from Los Adaes, which is the nearest to the French presidio
of Nachitoos—it results that opposition to the ingress of the French into Texas
and the observation of their schemes and movements would be even more
difficult. Therefore, it is possible that the information the *auditor* has received
coincides with the notice of the señor marquis, the river and place being
one and the same.

In fact this is not true, and the words of the señor marquis are
as follows, found in document 33, number 31:

The said marquis reëstablished the three missions of Los Adays and erected
there the aforementioned presidio of Nuestra Señora del Pilar, seven leagues
on this side of that of Nachitoos. He placed another presidio on the same
road and restored three other missions in the place properly known as Texas,
which gives its name to the entire province and is about in its center, 172
leagues on the other side of the presidio of San Antonio, sixty on this side of
that of Los Adaes, sixty-seven also from the French presidio of Nachitos, and
thirty from the one of Cadodachos, which is likewise French. . . . He moved
the presidio of San Antonio to a better site, establishing it between the two
rivers of San Antonio and San Pedro, with their two missions, to which were
added three others that had been brought from the said place of Texas.

1481. Let us understand well the location of this presidio of
San Antonio de Béjar which the Marquis of Aguayo bettered. It
is precisely the location which we have assigned to it in Part II,
paragraph 664, and therefore we do not repeat it here. But let us
consider whether a Río de San Pedro flows into the San Antonio,
as we state above, in paragraph 661. It is necesary that it be
very different from the Río de San Pedro de los Navidachos. But
Father Morfi, in book 1, number 8, illuminates this point still
further with the following words:

San Antonio. This river rises a league north of the presidio of its name
(San Antonio de Béxar) and of the villa of San Fernando, where it joins the
Arroyo de San Pedro. Before the confluence the water is taken from it that
is necessary for irrigating the [lands of the] five missions that were founded
on its banks, and still it remains so full that it seems that not the least bit of

water has been taken out of it. It joins the Medina and enters the North Sea by way of the Bahía del Espíritu Santo, after three streams and two springs have entered it and after it has flowed six [?] leagues. Its mouth is toward the southeast, twelve leagues from the Río de Guadalupe.

It must be inferred from this that in order that in the future there may be no further mistakes, this stream should never again be called Río de San Pedro but, as Father Morfi calls it, Arroyo de San Pedro. But as for what Father Morfi says here to the effect that the Río de San Antonio flows into the Bahía del Espíritu Santo, twelve leagues from the Río de Guadalupe, it seems that when he wrote this he was guided by false reports. In paragraph 315 of Part II, we proved that the river which Evía called the San Antonio is the Guadalupe, and the one he called San José is the San Antonio. If the mouth of the latter is no farther from the former than six minutes, which consist of three leagues according to the table found in Part II, paragraph 28, there cannot be twelve leagues between the two. Aside from this, if we measure the extent of the entire bay, its greatest breadth hardly exceeds twenty-two minutes, which would equal the twelve leagues after their sixth part had been deducted. Therefore this same distance cannot lie between the mouth of the Río de Guadalupe and that of the San Antonio.

1482. In the same book, number 57, the said Father Morfi, discussing the Río de San Pedro de los Nechas, writes:

Continuing [through] the same kind of land and forests, at three leagues the Arroyo de San Pedro is encountered, on the banks of which the presidio and missions called those of Texas were located. A little farther on, after having passed some ravines and hills also overgrown with woods like the preceding ones, a plain is entered, where the first presidio of Texas was built in 1716, on the bank of a lake of fresh and very good water which comes from a spring in its center.

1483. Four leagues to the east flows the Río Netchas, so called after the nation of Indians of that name who inhabit its banks. It rises, as do all those of the province, toward the northwest, near the pueblo of the Navedachos Indians. It flows at a distance of eight leagues from the Río de Angelinas, with which it later unites. As the result of this union it enters the sea large, and navigable for small vessels. It ends on the coast between the province of Texas and Louisiana, its mouth being fifteen leagues from that of the Trinity, with which it unites by means of a branch. At its mouth it forms a small island two hundred varas in diameter, this river having only the one mouth. This island and coastline are well known to the English, who attempted to establish themselves there, although disastrously, as we shall see in another place.

1484. In Part II, paragraph 70, there is formed a compendium of the diary of the Marquis of Aguayo, and it shows clearly that there are 195 leagues from the presidio of San Antonio de Béxar to the Arroyo de la Asunción, by the road which he followed. After subtracting from these the three before this arroyo, where the said marquis founded the presidio, there remain 192, the number of leagues which, according to the said marquis, there are from Béjar to the presidio which he founded. Therefore when the Señor Marquis of Altamira writes that there are 172 leagues from Béjar to the said presidio, either he is mistaken or, as is more likely, there is a copyist's error on the part of his clerk or of the person who made the copy in my possession.

1485. Nor, in my opinion, were those motives which Señor Valcárcel gives sufficient reason for preventing the establishment of this presidio, when he says, in paragraph 1445:

This notice and the insufficient information with which the governor in his zealous eagerness persists in the measure concerning the detachment on the Río de San Pedro, the actual existence of which can reasonably be doubted (we have already seen that there is a real and actual river called the San Pedro, which flows through the [pueblos of the] Nechas and Nasonis, for which reason its existence cannot reasonably be doubted), make the point indeterminable and put it back in its former difficult state, without any new document or evidence which was not available to the *junta general*, and which, discussed therein, would have brought about a contrary decision. This is especially true, in as much as the establishment of the detachment would certainly and necessarily be costly to the royal treasury because of the increase in the numbers of soldiers and their corresponding salaries, and it is very improbable that it would be useful and efficacious for the purpose for which it is created. Its usefulness will be proven only when there may be evidence that the said Río de San Pedro is in the province (this condition is already needless, for we have seen that there is one); that it is located and flows at such a distance and in such a manner (we have seen its course) that the movements of the French can be observed from the site on which the detachment would be stationed (they could be watched from the Nasonis because they are the nearest to the French lands, just as they are watched from Los Adaes); and that on it there is only one narrow crossing available, by means of which it can be forded in canoes and passage found from one bank to the other, and from which alone can be impeded the entrance of the French and the introduction of their commerce into the province of Texas, and the passage of the Indian nations included in its district and vicinity to the presidio of

Nachitoos or to any other settlement of the French colonies. For it would be of little advantage for the detachment to be stationed at one place if along the course of the river there are many easy and safe passes, or fords, by which to cross without encountering opposition from the detachment. Because, if their retreat were cut off and they should take some other crossing either farther down or higher up, even though it might be at the cost of a short detour, the trespassers would accomplish safely their schemes of trading and intercourse with the Indians of the crown of Spain, and the detachment would be idle and useless, the purpose for which it was created being thus defeated.

1486. The argument which the señor *auditor* has presented here to prevent the construction of this presidio, is the very same one which the Señor Brigadier Rivera made in favor of withdrawing the one of Los Adaes. Let us hear again the words of this señor brigadier, copied above in paragraph 1430, as follows:

It is true that the said presidio of Los Adaes, although stockaded, is surrounded by a redoubt. But the French could make themselves masters of the interior country without losing a soldier, merely by leaving the said presidio to their left and going along the banks of the Río de los Cadodachos, directing their march to the Nasonis, whence they would dominate the Asinais, Nechas, and Navedachos. And by camping at the site of this last nation they would cut off the convoys that might attempt to go to the presidios. They would surrender to the French from necessity, without any more effort on the part of the latter than that of having placed themselves at the said site of the Navedachos. These circumstances caused me to state to your Excellency in the aforesaid *consulta* how superfluous the forty soldiers who would be dismissed are in the said presidio, and how useful those funds [now used for their salaries] would be to the royal treasury if the soldiers were suppressed.

1487. But the Reverend Father Morfi demolished his arguments above, in paragraph 1431, as follows:

The señor brigadier assumes that in case of war with the French, the Spaniards in America must play the rôle of an inanimate body which, buried under inaction, only waits to receive blows. The same arguments that he advances, in my opinion, furnish clear proofs against his view. The French, I would say, can easily occupy the site of the Navedachos. Then the presidio of Texas (this is the one which, as is stated above in paragraph 1453, the Marquis of San Miguel de Aguayo founded, and the same one that was destroyed because of the report of the señor brigadier; see above, paragraph 1453) in their vicinity should not be withdrawn, but its garrison should be increased in order to keep the French from making themselves masters of that country. They can cut off our convoys, with only twenty-five men from Natchitoches and those whom they may receive from Mobile. Then we, with a hundred men in Los Adaes, the rest of the garrison from the other presidios of the province—who according to Rivera, in the following paragraph, can join them in two weeks—and with the aid that may be sent them from Coahuila and the New Kingdom of León, not as far from Los Adaes as Canada and Mobile are from Natchitoches, will be able to occupy their banks of this river, intercept their convoys, and without losing a single man, make ourselves masters of that presidio and drive them to the other side of the Mississippi.

1488. On paper one marches in silence and without fatigue, rivers are crossed on foot and without difficulty, and mountains are conquered in a moment. But it does not happen that way in practice. No matter how secret the march of the French might be, and no matter how careless the officials of Los Adaes might be, they could never hide themselves from the acute perception of the mission Indians. We have a thousand examples of this every day. The Indians, if not from affection, then for the small consideration of a handful of tobacco, would give the information to the governor. The news would be communicated immediately to Béxar, and the march of the enemy, if not checked, could be retarded either by sending immediately fifty men to the unprotected Nachitoches, or by posting ambuscades in opportune places; or by a thousand other means, which I do not comprehend, the presidio of Texas, which it is now recommended should be withdrawn, could prevent them from making themselves masters of the country. No one believes that the French would plunge themselves heedlessly into the center of our presidios where, in case they could not withstand the troops that might be sent from New Spain, the garrison of Los Adaes would make them suffer greatly on their withdrawal. Let us not grow weary, [for] in the following paragraphs we shall see what may facilitate that which at present is difficult.

1489. These replies of Father Morfi to Señor Rivera may very well be used against Señor Valcárcel, for if the French should stealthily outflank the Spaniards of the presidio of Los Nasonis, the latter would eventually learn of it and would prevent their entering even though it might be only with the aid of the troops of the other presidios. Above all, a sentinel such as this presidio, which the French could fear, would be more valuable than anything else, for if the French could outflank them in spite of it, they could do so much more easily if it were not there. It is true that in the erection or conservation of this presidio an additional expense to the royal treasury may be occasioned, but in necessary things it is always essential to make some expenditures. Because of the fact that the presidio was not established in El Quartelejo according to plan, as we have seen above, in number 291, how many times may the French have attempted to take possession of it? With regard to this the señor *auditor*, Don Juan de Oliván, gave the following opinion, above in paragraph 298:

Most excellent señor: [The *auditor*] has seen this *expediente*, and the first *cuaderno* concerning the Apaches, and this representation of the governor of New Mexico, in which he says that from various notices that he has received, he knows that the French have settled in El Quartelejo and Chinali, 160 leagues from the villa of Santa Fé, capital of that kingdom. [He says further] that, with orders from your Excellency, he will go next year to reconnoiter those places if, in view of the information he sent, your Excellency so orders him; but that the number of soldiers which he has in that presidio being insufficient, [he asks] that your Excellency be pleased to order that the captains of the presidios of La Vizcaya detach those necessary for this expedition.

1490. But in accordance with the measure which your Excellency was pleased to adopt at the beginning of April of this year, upon the recommendation of the *auditor* on the reply of the señor *fiscal* and the *consulta* of Brigadier Don Pedro de Rivera, which is in folio 93 of the said first *cuaderno*—in which it was provided that the governor arrange that the Apaches of the valley of La Xicarilla go to settle at the pueblo of Taos, twenty leagues from Santa Fé, thereby making unnecessary the erection of a new presidio, and that kingdom being better protected with this nation assembled at Taos, for the reasons explained and set forth by the brigadier in his *consulta*—another dispatch was issued on April 5, although the governor would not have received it when he wrote his letter on the 30th [of April].

1491. For this reason and also bearing in mind the occurrence of the death of more than forty soldiers, perpetrated by the French and Pananas on the other reconnaissance which was made beyond El Quartelejo in the time of your predecessor for the purpose of learning whether the French had come to that region, because of the war then in progress with their nation—which today is not the case, nor is there fear that they will commit hostilities from this motive in that kingdom at present—it does not appear necessary now that this reconnaissance be made.

(And what if this war should sometime break out, or the French, having recourse to their iniquitous methods, should do what the Marquis of San Miguel de Aguayo mentioned? He is cited in Part I, paragraph 384, as follows:

This is also made evident by the information in some letters from Paris, which were seized. Among many other instructions, they said to the Frenchmen on our frontier that, although the two crowns might be at peace in Europe, they should turn all their attention to estranging the Indians who were the subjects of the Spaniards, and prevail upon them and upon all the other nations to make war on us.

His Majesty had information concerning these letters, as we have stated above, in paragraph 348. It is well known that Virgil's Dido, in the *Aeneid*, book 4, verse 373, said in complaining of

Aeneas, who had acted very perfidiously toward her, *"Nusquam tuta fides,"* that is, "No one is to be trusted." Iodoco Badio Acensio commented as follows on this text:

Virgil pointed out that one should not complain of fidelity because trustworthy faithfulness cannot be found, and consequently cannot superabound.[23]

And concerning the French of those lands the Spaniards could say the same thing: *"Nusquam tuta fides*—there is not a one of them who can be trusted."

Nor does it seem necessary (in order to make it) that the proposed detachment of troops be ordered, nor the expenditures which necessarily would have to be made; for the purpose of the French in coming there must be that of trading to the heathen their clothing, muskets, and arms, as this governor explains in his letter, or that of aiding one nation against another as they are accustomed to do, especially since they are living among the Pananas, two hundred leagues from Santa Fé.

But when the governor of New Mexico says in paragraph 291 that,

on the said Río de Chinali, a short distance from El Quartelejo, on a cove, they have settled and erected some dwellings and there is where most of them are, and [the Indian woman] says that they send out white people from the boundary of the said place where they live, and that those who go out, according to what she has learned, come to settle in these places. Above all, the said captive says that it causes the greatest satisfaction to see people so comely and splendid,

how could the señor *auditor* think that they would come [simply] to aid some nation against some other or to trade their clothing, mukets, and other arms to the heathen? For, although this trade took place, it was the means by which the French proceeded to appropriate those lands. Perhaps if the presidio had been placed even among the Xicarillas as soon as its erection was discussed, it is possible that the French would not have penetrated as far as El Quartelejo, fearful that the Spaniards of that presidio would prevent them from doing so.

1492. In view of all this, and if, through the knowledge that I have acquired of those regions in the exercise of my commission, it is proper for me to express my opinion on a matter of such

---

[23]The above quotation from the Latin was translated by Mrs. Minnie Lee Shepard.

seriousness, I humbly beg our government to fix its most upright vision on those regions and to build there now the presidio which the zeal and patriotism of Señor Don Jacinto Barrios desired so much. [I say this] even though it may be costly to the royal treasury, in order to prevent in time the subjects of the United States from doing in the future what the French had planned to do, and especially since today in the absence of the presidio of Los Adaes, they have a better opportunity to appropriate those lands for themselves in the same manner in which they now plan to take over, because of the absence of the said presidio of Los Adaes, the territory which lies between La Gran Montaña or Arroyo Hondo where, as we have seen, the boundary and limits are fixed, and the Sabine, as we shall later see clearly. When the Señor Brigadier Rivera reported that it would be convenient to abandon the presidio of Texas, he depended upon the one of Los Adaes remaining, although reduced in strength, to observe and even to check the designs of the French upon the Nasonis, Navidachos, etc. But now that there is no presidio, the necessity of protecting that country demands imperatively that the one suggested be erected. But in as much as it is possible that at some time it may be necessary to take up arms against the disciplined troops of the United States, it seems evident that its establishment should be as the señor *fiscal*, Andreu, suggested above in paragraph 1477, namely, like that of Vera Cruz, and with the other features which he states with so much zeal and intelligence.

1493. It seems to me that what I have proposed with regard to the presidio of Río de San Pedro I should also suggest with regard to the presidio of Los Adaes. For, in fact, this presidio of Los Adaes is of the greatest importance, and therefore should again be settled, rebuilt, and fortified accordingly. Because of its having been dismantled and abandoned in 1773, by virtue of an express command of the king, our lord, dated in San Ildefonso on September 10, 1772, as we shall see later, the United States have believed that all the land that lies from this presidio toward the west as far as the Río de Sabinas belonged to Louisiana, and this erroneous opinion and belief induces them to claim it, as included in the part that they bought from France.

1494. Father Fray José María Puelles, a missionary living in Nacogdoches, in a letter written on September 16, 1806, which we shall copy later, says the following:

The United States charge that the settlement of Los Adais was clandestine and without royal permission, and that for this reason his Majesty withdrew it.

But it is a very easy matter to demonstrate to them the legality of this settlement, made with the approval of the king, our lord, and the very excellent reasons that the Spaniards had for making it.

1495. In the diary of the Señor Marquis of Aguayo, document 21, number 1, Bachiller Peña states

that the expedition of the said señor marquis was undertaken because the French had invaded the province of Texas on June 19, 1719 and had, with their superior forces, obliged the Spaniards to abandon it by withdrawing to the presidio of San Antonio de Béjar, and that in order to aid the said province the most excellent señor viceroy gave an order for a company to be raised, consisting of the largest possible number of men.

After this had been done and during the journey that the señor marquis made, accompanied by his troops, at the time that he was near the Río de Nechas (*ibid.*, number 87).

he had a conference with Monsieur de St. Denis, captain-commandant of the French presidio of Nachitoches. In the course of it his lordship told him that in compliance with the orders he had, he would observe the truce, provided that he [St. Denis] would immediately evacuate the entire province of Texas and withdraw with the other Frenchmen to Los Nachitos; and provided that he would not impede, directly or indirectly, the restoration which at all costs was to be made to the forces of the king, our lord, of all he had possessed up to and including Los Adaes. St. Denis agreed to this unreservedly.

In number 118, he adds that:

Don Fernando de Almazán, lieutenant-governor of the said señor marquis, in a conference that he had with the commandant of Nachitoches, told him that the reason why his governor (the said señor marquis) was coming was to occupy the country of the Adaes just as he had taken possession of that of the Texas; and that he was determined to reëstablish the mission of San Miguel (which had been founded by the venerable Father Margil, and which was the one St. Denis had attacked) and to construct a presidio on that frontier on the site that he might consider most appropriate. To this the French commandant replied that he had neither orders to agree to this nor to obstruct it, and that since he knew of the truce that the two crowns had established in Europe, he would observe it in America if the señor marquis would also observe it.

1496. Immediately after this the said presidio of Los Adays was founded. It was established, as has been noted, in order to restrict the French within their boundaries and to prevent them from going beyond them, and it was also extremely useful in keeping the Indians obedient and in inducing them to receive the law of Jesus Christ. The Señor Brigadier Bonilla so states expressly in the following words, in number 151 of his *Breve Compendio de los Sucesos ocurridos en la Provincia de Texas* [*Brief Compendium of the Events which have occurred in the Province of Texas*], which is found in document 42:

> The said presidio of Los Adaes was established with the purpose of serving as a safeguard at the French boundaries, but it has never been attacked by the Indians, etc.

Thus the Spaniards did the same thing at Los Adaes that the Roman emperors did on the frontiers of their empire. Suidas[24] says the following concerning them in his *Lexicon*, article "Limitanaioi," which is in volume 2, page 448, of the edition of K. Küster, published in Cambridge in 1705:

> The Roman emperors, in times past, were accustomed to station in the most remote parts of their territory a large number of soldiers, so that they might maintain the integrity of the boundaries of the Roman Empire. They kept these troops especially on the eastern borders, for the purpose of checking the invasions of the Persians and Saracens. . . .

1497. In paragraph 338, above, his Majesty in a cedula says the following to the most excellent señor viceroy, the Marquis of Valero:

> You had sent the Marquis of Aguayo to the Texas country with armed and well-equipped men to found a presidio on the Río Caudacho. . . .

And in paragraph 345, he says to him also, in another cedula:

---

[24]Suidas, a Greek lexicographer, lived in the eleventh century A.D. The lexicon of Suidas (*Suidae lexicon*) was first published at Milan in 1499. "The first critical edition of Suidas is that of L. Küster (Cambridge, 1705, 3 vols. in folio)."—*Diccionario Enciclopédico Hispano-Americano de Literatura, Ciencias y Artes*, Vol. XIX, p. 736.

[You state] that for the purpose of keeping these lands obedient to me, you sent to them missionaries and likewise families to settle them; that presidios would be founded at suitable points, particularly one on the Río Caudacho, on the French frontier.

He repeats the same thing in the cedula copied in paragraph 348. By virtue of the orders of the most excellent señor viceroy, the said Señor Marquis of Aguayo founded the presidio of Los Adaes near the Río de Nachitoches, which, since it enters that of Cadodachos, the said royal cedulas seem to call the Río de Cadodachos.

CHAPTER XVI

REORGANIZATION FOLLOWING THE CESSION OF
LOUISIANA BY FRANCE TO SPAIN IN 1762

1498. After Louisiana through its cession by France had become a part of the dominions of Spain, this presidio was thenceforth considered useless, since the French, now being vassals of Spain, could no longer commit any hostility or damage whatever against the province of Texas. This uselessness was well known to the most excellent señor, the Marquis of Rubí,[1] and he therefore said in his report (of which a portion is found in document 58, beginning with number 16, with this title: *Copia de los Capitulos 17, 19, 20, y 25 del dictamen que el Exmo. Sor. Marquez de Rubí dió sobre la mejor situación de los Presidios internos [Copy of Chapters 17, 19, 20, and 25 of the report which the Most Excellent Señor Marquis of Rubí rendered on the better location of the Interior Presidios]*) :

How painful and repugnant to many was the proposal that I then made to abandon the villa and the five very prosperous missions of San Antonio de Béjar, situated on the watershed of the river of that name, by withdrawing them to this side of the Río del Norte, within the protection of the line of presidios, as are those of San Juan [Bautista] and San Bernardo with respect to the presidio of San Juan Bautista of the same Río Grande, which has just been discussed. This transfer, which undoubtedly raises sufficient difficulties, could be supported by repeated examples of those executed with other larger colonies in order to procure their progress or security. But I myself do not dare, nor do I trust my own opinion sufficiently, to recommend a step of such moment. Let the presidio and villa of San Antonio de Béjar, then, remain in their present and original location, for the royal treasury has borne so much expense in the conveyance of families from the Canary Islands; in the erection of a temple; which must be sumptuous; and in repeated gratituities to the settlers to provide tools for the *labores* [cultivated fields], which they neglect, and arms for the service, which they do not render except at the cost of many gratuities on the part of the king. The five missions likewise remain in their pleasant valleys. They are composed, not of Indians native to that place, but of those brought from the coast of the colony of Nuevo Santander and from other places farther inland, to which the missionaries go to get spiritual recruits. Since this settlement, however, is more than one degree of latitude farther north than the other presidios placed on a line along the banks of the

---

[1]See *Pichardo's Treatise* . . . , Vol. I, p. 8, n. 1.

Río Grande, it is necessary to guard in the best possible manner against the dangers which its location and its distance of more than fifty leagues from the presidio of San Juan Bautista del Río Grande present.

1499. After San Sabás has been evacuated[2], as has been suggested, and the presidio and worthless settlement of Los Adaes,[3] which is already ending its own unhappy existence, have been suppressed or incorporated into the government of New Orleans, and by removing at the same time to this villa or some other place near it the extremely useless presidio of El Orcoquisac,[4] the villa of San Antonio will remain as our most advanced frontier outpost in the province of Texas. If the rancherias of the Lipanes, who today are inhabiting the banks of the Río Grande, are left in its rear, it will have, as has been stated in the preceding article, a certain inducement for the hostilities of the Cumanche Indians and their other allies in the north, who have already on other occasions entered this villa and committed in it the desecrations befitting their barbarity, on the pretext of coming in to hunt their enemies, the Lipanes. The proximity of the latter who—although they have been pushed back opposite this settlement by the combined forces of all the adjoining presidios—will never go very far away from the said nearby springs and streams of El Cañon, Candelaria, Trancas, Guadalupe, Alarcón, and the rest, will always be an imminent and nearby danger to this settlement and presidio, farther advanced than is conducive to their safety and than all our other settlements in Coahuila, Nuevo León, and the colony of [Nuevo] Santander. Their danger and the inevitable war that it is to be assumed is always alive among the Lipanes, Cumanches, and Norteños [Northern Nations], leading to the total extinction of the first, oblige us to keep this villa in a respectable state of defense until its security has been sufficiently assured by an increase in its population and by those settlements that this same protection may encourage in its vicinity in the future.

1500. This protection, therefore, can now be secured by an increase in the garrison of this presidio [of San Antonio], which consists of only twenty-one men distributed in its detachments, and by placing it on a footing of eighty men, taken from those left at San Sabás, and from the entire suppressed company of Los Adaes. Or perhaps there could be incorporated in it the company of El Orcoquisac itself, if, after a thorough examination, it should be decided to be unnecessary in view of the existence of this presidio and of that of La Bahía del Espíritu Santo, as will be suggested in its place. This

---

[2]The "New Regulation of Presidios" of September 10, 1772 (see *Pichardo's Treatise* . . . , Vol. III, p. 433, n. 5), provided that "San Sabá was to be moved as soon as possible to a more advantageous position on the banks of the Rio Grande, where together with those of Cerro Gordo, Santa Rosa, and Monclova, it was to form a new line of defense between La Junta (Presidio) and San Juan Bautista."—Castañeda, *Our Catholic Heritage in Texas* . . . , Vol. IV, p. 293.

[3]See *Pichardo's Treatise* . . . , Vol. III, p. 426, n. 46.

[4]Reference is to the presidio of San Agustín de Ahumada. For details concerning its abandonment, in conformity with the recommendation of the Marquis of Rubí, see Castañeda, *Our Catholic Heritage in Texas* . . . , Vol. IV, pp. 277–278.

matter would not be decided until it has been examined and the most convenient measure has been adopted.

1501. For the further increase in forces, commerce, and the circulation and consumption of money and goods, it will be convenient for the governor, unhampered by the troublesome charge of Los Adaes, to reside in this settlement [San Antonio] and for the command of the presidio of San Juan Bautista del Río Grande to be added to his. It will have to be taken from the command of the governor of Coahuila, and perhaps the governor of Texas will propose to move it closer to this settlement of San Antonio, in view of the respective distances at which the other presidios located on the banks of the Río Grande will remain, beginning with the one of La Junta at the junction of this river with that of Conchos in La Vizcaya, even though it be at the expense of advancing this presidio of San Juan Bautista a little from its present location on the banks of the river in order to shorten and cut the distance from the latter to the said villa of San Antonio.

1502. The residence of the governor in this villa, aside from the advantage of its larger population, should also be considered in other respects as a favorable circumstance in case of the occurrence of other less probable accidents against which it is always proper for the government to prepare in time.

1503. Let it be supposed, now, that a change should take place in the present friendly disposition of the Cumanches and the other Norteños, who fight today only against San Sabás, regarding it as a fine ally of the Lipanes, and that they should decide to attack also the remaining possessions of the Spaniards, which [however] I do not believe enters into their kind of policy. Let us suppose also, adopting an idea that I have never been able to accept, that, persuaded and aided by other European nations—those closest to us, although they may be very distant from this region, among whom it may even be wished to include the Russians—they might begin to advance in force into those regions that really belong to the king. In either of these two cases San Antonio, always the first and most considerable of our settlements, would be the object of their conquest, and this would likewise be the point for mustering and assembling the troops that we should have to obtain in order to oppose their undertakings. For in any one of the most distant points which we supposedly occupy today from Los Adaes to this place, in all that unpopulated intervening area of 250 leagues, it would be impossible to make a vigorous resistance because of the difficulty of transporting and sustaining over such a distance the people, provisions, munitions, and other necessities for the subsistence of a large body of troops. It would be convenient to leave these same difficulties to the enemies who, weakened by their inevitable suffering, would meet on our frontier the opposition of the forces who would be in course of being assembled and gathered together in San Antonio from their respective nearby governments and provinces. They would proceed to reinforce it and sustain it and give an opportunity to this government to take the most vigorous measures. In accordance with the probability that may be attributed to these fears, it may also not be out of the way to build a small fort in this villa, not only for the protection of its natives but also for that of the war and food supplies, of which this place should always be a depository.

1504. The few and poor families now living in Los Adaes should be moved to this same presidio [of San Antonio], to that of La Bahía, or to other settlements that may be erected in their vicinities, unless it shall be considered more appropriate to permit whoever might prefer it to live in the colony of New Orleans, since it is now under the dominion of the king. This measure will make communication between that colony and this kingdom much more difficult, in accordance with the strict orders of his Majesty, for it would be extremely easy for the governor to impede it since the weather will continue to make the route more difficult, as is the case at present with the San Xavier road, which is impassable.

1505. These considerations and those that will be explained later concerning the nature of the coast of the Gulf of Mexico from the mouth of the Río de Guadalupe to that of the Mississippi in Louisiana, [lead us to recommend] that the presidio of La Bahía del Espíritu Santo be left in its present location on the Río de San Antonio. [This is desirable] alike because it has the beginnings of a settlement with cattle-raising on a large scale, aside from those that may be added to it from Los Adais, and also because of the repeated unfortunate experiences which closer proximity to the coast has always brought to this presidio. Even at the present distance of twenty leagues [inland] it still suffers the effects of the inclemencies of the weather.

1506. It is an error of which we should today be quite undeceived to persuade ourselves that we should occupy by land the coast of the Gulf of Mexico from the Mississippi to the port of Santander in the colony of this name. Nor should we believe that this might be attained, even admitting its necessity, by the costly means of this type of presidio. All the inspections made by sea of this coast have verified its inaccessibility, which is confirmed by the knowledge that repeated shipwrecks have befallen various vessels on the same coast, and very recently by what happened to the two vessels *Nueva Constante* and *Santa Bárbara*, of the last fleet, to which not the least assistance could be given by the neighboring presidio of El Orcoquizac.

1507. On the basis of orders sent him, the governor of Louisiana, Don Antonio de Ulloa[5], ordered the brigantines and schooners which he dispatched to make this same reconnaissance. Far out of sight of land they failed to find navigable waters, and therefore they could not come near enough to reconnoiter it, or the Bahía de San Bernardo[6], which they likewise had been directed to examine. Don Antonio de Ulloa himself has reported this to me.

1508. The same thing has resulted from the efforts made recently by land of Colonel Don Diego Parilla in the region of the mouths of the Guadalupe and San Antonio rivers,[7] which had a difficult connection with the same Bahía de

---

[5]See *Pichardo's Treatise* . . . , Vol. I, p. 411, n. 2.

[6]Reference is probably to present Matagorda Bay. See *Pichardo's Treatise* . . . , Vol. III, p. 163, n. 12.

[7]For details concerning the reconnaissance of this region of the Mexican Gulf coast by Parilla in 1766, see Bolton, *Texas* . . . , p. 106.

San Bernardo. He discovered through this procedure that the great size of the rivers that empty into the Gulf and the circular movement of the waters make the coast less approachable every day and impossible to sound for a distance of thirty leagues. It is not even navigable in canoes, which frequently run aground on the sandbanks and in neap tides that continue far into the sea along the entire coast. Thus it seems that there is no need for placing the said presidio of La Bahía closer to the same coast and that its reconnaissance is of little importance.

1509. The line of presidios, then, being garrisoned, as has been stated, without abandoning the most advanced points in it such as the presidio of the villa of Santa Fé in New Mexico and the one of San Antonio de Béjar in the province of Texas—whence the further conquests will have to be undertaken which may be planned after the vacant or open places are occupied which divide them from our real settlements—there remains only to prepare against the damage which may be occasioned by the great distance that lies between the presidios of San Juan Bautista de Río Grande and San Antonio, as pointed out in articles 16 and 17.

1510. Supposing the war that I have proposed therein should be waged against the Lipanes by all the frontier presidios, and that the former, as was stated in the same place, should not withdraw very far from our frontier because of the immediate resistance that they would encounter from their enemies, the Norteños, it may be feared that in the area intervening between the two cited presidios, by following the course of the Río del Norte they might penetrate as they have already been doing to attack the colony of Nuevo Santander in the rear of the presidios of San Antonio and Bahía del Espíritu Santo. But in view of the fact that this colony [Nuevo Santander] has by itself a sufficient armed force paid by the king to go to check any hostilities with which it might be threatened, this inconvenience has not seemed to me to be of any great moment. For it can be easily remedied by placing in Laredo, or in any other of the settlements of the said colony that are established along the Río del Norte downstream from Laredo, one or several of their fourteen squadrons which are not doing anything in their present locations.

1511. Let us now see, the defense of the line being provided for by means of the seventeen presidios and the detachments of twenty men from that of San Antonio who are on duty in it, what will be the number of troops of which the entire force will consist. After adding to it the extra forces that may be left to the presidios for the protection of such posts as may need it, it will be easy to deduce the saving to the royal treasury that will result from this plan.

1512. This is the place in which it is convenient and fitting to discuss the suggestion noted incidentally in article 17 with regard to evacuating the presidio and the worthless settlement of Los Adaes, and the extremely useless company at El Orcoquisac where it is impossible to establish any settlement whatever, since the introduction of provisions for the maintenance of the troops alone occasions no little worry, loss, and difficulty.

1513. Since the evacuation of these two presidios and of the small settlement of the first one entails the delimiting of some hundreds of leagues of what we call with complete impropriety dominions of the king, there will not be lacking those who, on the pretext of this imaginary loss, may appraise my idea as ungenerous and contrary to the maxims of advancing these dominions, which must be considered in preference to everything else. So that this objection may not be raised immediately, a possibility that I cannot ignore, it is indispensable that in support of my idea I should, by means of the briefest analysis possible, give an exact account of what the king will lose, in losing, as is proposed, the uncultivated deserts of Texas.

1514. From the presidio of Los Adaes, only seven leagues from the fort of Nachitos [of the colony of] New Orleans, there are 240 leagues to the villa of San Antonio de Béjar, which I have left as the most advanced point on our frontier, and slightly less than two hundred to the presidio of La Bahía, the last one of those of our line. On these two lines of communication, which are the only ones that are used in going to Los Adaes, there are two narrow paths which we use in common with the various tribes of the coast Indians. Their suppression leaves this road open to some degree, although not entirely free from their petty thieving. In this entire area as far as the mission of Nacodoches, we have not a single settlement, nor should we promise ourselves one for many years. [This mission is] forty-six leagues from Los Adaes, and there, without a single Indian convert, or pupil, has been stationed a religious since the time of the last expedition, made by the Marquis of San Miguel de Aguayo in the year 1721. There follows this one, at a distance of less than twenty leagues on the same road, the mission of Los Aix, with the appellation of Los Dolores, where the religious live in the same inactivity without a single Indian to minister to. After this mission one reaches Los Adaes, in which, aside from the company whose salaries amount to 27,765 pesos annually, the king maintains another mission with two religious who, frustrated in their principal object of converting the heathen, minister to the spiritual welfare of the presidial troops and the small number of settlers of its nearby farms, which misfortune and scarcity of water are causing to become depopulated, and which at the time of my inspection did not contain thirty families. To the south-southwest of the said presidio and at a distance of some 120 leagues, there exists, amid thousands of difficulties and misfortunes, the presidio of El Orcoquisac with its company of thirty-one soldiers—an imaginary mission without Indians, with two ministering missionaries, and no settlement, for it was found to be impracticable in spite of the offer of erecting it to which the founder and planner of this presidio pledged himself.

1515. The allowances of the two presidios and the stipends of the four missions occasion an expense to the king of 44,157 pesos annually, which, multiplied by the respective number of years since their creation, beginning with the year '21 of this century, will amount to quite a considerable sum, without their compensating this exhorbitant expenditure in any manner, either spiritually or politically. For, with regard to the conversion of the heathen, I say that not only no Christian, but also not a single neophyte will be lost on the day on which the said four missions may be suppressed. As regards the protection of our true dominions, removed from this imaginary frontier two hundred leagues and more, we might substitute for this weak barrier the one that the present governor of that colony [Louisiana], Don Antonio de Ulloa, is establishing on a respectable footing on the Colorado [Red] and Missouri rivers, and thus the communication and trade of that colony with the dominions of this kingdom will be rendered much more difficult, in conformance with the intentions of the king.

1516. Let me be permitted, therefore, to ask now whether in the suppression of the presidios of Los Adaes and Orcoquisac and their imaginary missions the king will lose an exaggerated extent of territory, or will gain the saving of more than forty-four thousand pesos which he is spending for their maintenance. Thus I satisfy this objection which it has seemed to me could not be ignored. . . . This conforms exactly to the originals, to which I certify. Mexico, April 9, 1774. Melchor de Peramas.

1517. As a result of this report these two presidios were ordered suppressed. This is shown by a pamphlet issued in Madrid at the order of his Majesty by Juan de San Martín, in the year 1772. The title of it is: *Reglamento e Ynstrucción para los Presidios que se han de formar en la linea de frontera de la Nueva España. Resuelto por el Rey Nuestro Señor en Cédula de 10 de Septiembre de 1772.*[8] [*Regulation and Instruction for the Presidios that are to be established on the frontier line of New Spain. Ordered by the King, Our Lord, in a Cedula of September 10, 1772*]. In title 14, number 22, page 108, it states:

Since the suppression of the presidio of San Sabá has already been ordered, for the purpose of establishing one with the same name on the banks of the Río del Norte, and in the supposition that the other two of El Horcoquisac and Los Adaes are at present useless, I order the governor of Texas, and the other officers of these two presidios to dismantle them immediately and to abandon the places in which they are located. They are to take care that the few settlers who are in them shall withdraw to the said villa of San Antonio de Béjar or its vicinity where I command that they be distributed lands on which they may settle and maintain themselves. At the same time they are to suppress the useless missions of Nacodoches, Aes, and the rest that have been maintained under the protection of the said presidios, and the soldiers and officers left at the latter are to be retired and their salaries and stipends for the said missions are to be suppressed in favor of my royal treasury.

1518. In the fulfillment of this command of the king, our lord, the most excellent señor viceroy of this New Spain, the *bailío* Fray Don Antonio María Bucareli y Ursua,[9] ordered a decree issued for

---

[8]See *Pichardo's Treatise* . . . , Vol. III, p. 433, n. 5.
[9]Fray Antonio María de Bucareli y Ursua was viceroy of New Spain from 1771 to 1779.

carrying out the abandonment[10] [of these establishments]. In accordance with the decree, the señor commandant-inspector of the Interior Provinces, Don Hugo Oconor,[11] drew up the following instruction (which is found in document 56, beginning with number 57):

Confidential instruction which the Baron de Ripperdá,[12] colonel of cavalry, governor of the province of Texas, will bear in mind for executing and observing in its two presidios the new regulation which his Majesty was pleased to issue on September 10 of last year, and the other points that it contains for the politic administration of the said province, issued to me, Don Hugo Oconor, colonel of infantry and commandant-inspector of the Interior Provinces of this kingdom of New Spain by order of the most excellent señor, Fray Don Antonio María Bucareli y Ursua, viceroy, governor, and captain-general of them.

1519. All the high royal plans of our sovereign have as their most commendable object the eternal and temporal happiness of his vassals. To this end are directed, precisely and strictly, all the lines of his most upright measures. A spirit of religion and piety, of kindness and sagacity incessantly compels his Majesty to take new measures that may facilitate the attainment of such sacred ends, and with his power and authority he accomplishes even those that have been judged impossible because of insuperable obstacles.

1520. One of the greatest hindrances is the extremely vast area of his happy dominions, for in many cases if this has not been impeded, it has delayed measures most conducive to their better government, they being suppressed maliciously or through the indolence of those who for so many reasons are obligated to execute them.

1521. His Majesty (whom may God keep) has been well acquainted with and promptly informed of such irregular proceedings, as well as of the number and daring of the barbarous Indians and of the extremely serious damage and injurious ravages which his vassals are suffering in their lives and property on the frontiers of the Interior Provinces. His royal piety, desiring to attend immediately and efficaciously to their complete relief, alike with vigorous steps to punish the nations that are attacking them as well as with methodical, solid and appropriate measures which in the future may assure their calm and peace, which are so important, he has been pleased to order in a cedula of September 10, 1772,[13] the formation of a new line which the old presidios are to cover, and which will change the basis, pay, and economic administration of them. He likewise provides through special secret instructions for the

[10]For details concerning this abandonment, see Bolton, Texas . . . , pp. 377–446, and Castañeda, Our Catholic Heritage in Texas . . . , Vol. IV, pp. 273–302.
[11]Don Hugo Oconor was ad interim governor of Texas from 1767 to 1770. By the "New Regulation of Presidios" of September 10, 1772 (see n. 2, supra), an inspector comandante was established. Oconor was made the first inspector comandante. See Bolton, Texas . . . , p. 108.
[12]The Baron de Ripperdá was governor of Texas from 1770 to 1778.
[13]See n. 2, supra.

better establishment, control, security, tranquility, and even remuneration of the settlers and their settlements.

1522. The most excellent señor viceroy of these kingdoms, being no less impelled by an active desire that the sovereign plans of his Majesty be completely fulfilled, than to manifest a superior exemplary submission to his royal decisions, has, with extraordinary promptness, given all the corresponding orders so that they may be put into complete effect. These actions should arouse our implicit obedience to give, in so far as it concerns us, the most exact and punctual observance that we owe, considering it a very special honor and particular good fortune to find ourselves in a position to be able to do our sovereign a service that is so pleasing to him. Therefore:

1523. As soon as the honorable governor shall receive this order, without allowing any imaginable pretext to prevent or delay him, he shall proceed to carry out the suppression of the four missions of the college of Nuestra Señora de Guadalupe de Zacatecas named Nuestra Señora del Pilar de los Adaes, Nuestra Señora de los Dolores de los Aix, Nuestra Señora de Guadalupe de los Nacodoches, and Nuestra Señora de la Luz del Orcoquisac, because this is the will of his Majesty, stated in article twenty-two of the royal regulation which treats of the location of presidios, and because the most excellent señor viceroy orders its prompt fulfillment in his superior decree of March 10 of this year.

1524. As soon as the governor of Texas, the Barón de Ripperdá, received this order, he duly fulfilled it, as is clearly shown by the following letter[14] which is found in document 58, number 2:

Señor Governor Don Hugo Oconor. Señor: Being moved by the wretchedness in which we find ourselves, I decided for myself and in behalf of the whole body of former inhabitants of the suppressed presidio of Los Adaes, humbly, in the presence of your lordship's greatness and with the consolation that you have always looked upon us and treated us as children, to lay before you all our misfortunes, which are those that I shall report to your lordship by means of this letter which I am sending to you from the valley of Santa Rosa by Señor Don Roque Medina, from whom I have received every favor. I have told him of the purpose that brought me as well as Gil Flores,[15] the two of us being vested by our settlers with power of attorney, which they gave us in the presence of the señor governor in order that we might come

---

[14]The author of this letter was Don Antonio Gil Ybarbo. For further details concerning him, see *Pichardo's Treatise* . . . , Vol. II, pp. 61–62 and the indices of Vols. II and III, *ibid.*

[15]After the Spanish settlers had been evicted from east Texas by Governor Ripperdá in 1773, they were finally congregated at San Antonio. They had, however, no other desire than to return to their former homes. "On December 7 [1773], representatives of the one hundred and twenty-seven families appeared before Ripperdá and appointed Antonio Gil Ibarbo and Gil Flores their legal agents to proceed to Mexico and solicit permission from the viceroy to found a settlement on the abandoned site of Mission Dolores de los Ais."— Castañeda, *Our Catholic Heritage in Texas* . . . , Vol. IV, pp. 305–306.

before your lordship and the most excellent señor viceroy in their name to beg
the favor that we be conceded [permission] to establish a pueblo at the
mission which formerly was that of the Aix Indians, without its occasioning
the least expense to his Majesty except that of a chaplain for a period of ten
years. After that his stipend would be paid by us. By being near our
abandoned dwellings we might be able to recover a little of so much that we
left, lost because of the short time that was given us. For the señor governor
had hardly arrived at Los Adaes, when he had an order issued that within five
days we should begin our march. During this time we found ourselves without
piovisions for food, nor were there any in Nachitos. And with our corn partly
in ear and partly beginning to form ears, seeing that it was necessary to obey
such a superior order, with complete submission we gave it its due fulfillment,
abandoning our belongings, crops, cattle, and houses. For, since the señor
governor had left Los Adaes as soon as he had given the orders and had left
the señor lieutenant, Don José González, to act in his place with the order
that we should leave on the day designated, the latter, as soon as the day
arrived, mounted his horse and began, house by house, to eject the people, all
of whom attempted to get out their children on their backs and, women as
well as men, to take the road on foot, without anything to eat, leaving behind
kitchen utensils and everything that they had in their homes, for they hardly
got out with the clothes on their backs. They began their march at the time
of the greatest scarcity of drinking water along the way. Our hardships
started on June 25 and lasted until September 26, when we arrived at San
Antonio, having suffered on the way as much thirst as hunger. The majority
of the people came on foot as far as the three [rivers of the] Brazos de Dios,[16]
where the aid reached us which the señor governor had sent us, consisting of
beasts and food. These scarcely sufficed to relieve the worst effects of thirst
and hunger, and many had become ill with swollen legs and feet. Including
children and adults, thirteen people died on the way, and the food relief
barely reached us in time, for it found us so weakened that everyone was sick.
Of these, down until the last day that we left it, there had died in San Antonio
thirty children and adults. On the day that I left they buried María Antonia,
the wife of Miguel de la Cerda, and the daughter of Tadeo Ramos, and God
knows how many since.

1525. Señor, I can assure your lordship that in Texas and in San Pedro
they sold not only their rags but even their reliquaries and rosaries in order
to buy food. And with the few possessions with which they arrived at San
Antonio, these poor people have continued to sustain themselves. Now they
have nothing more to sell. Many of them are begging. They go around like
worms from mission to presidio asking for food. There is no one to help
them since the most anyone has is a shirt. These pitiful creatures wake up in
the morning crying and they retire at night in the same manner. Then, señor,
two days after we reached San Antonio, the Indians carried off the few beasts

---

[16]Reference probably is to the present Navasota River, the present Brazos
River, and the present Little River. Consult the index of *Pichardo's Treatise
. . .* , Vol. I, p. 575.

that we had brought for the alleviation of our ills. The señor governor two days after our arrival at San Antonio, promulgated an *auto* in our favor in which he said that we should request lands on which to establish ourselves in a place where we would not harm the settlers and missions, and that we should install an irrigation system at our own expense. In view of the fact that the region from San Antonio to the Guadalupe is overrun with cattle belonging to the missions and the settlers, and in order to prevent quarrels and complaints against us, because necessity would finally force us to steal, and [to prevent] what may result from this, as well as because we find ourselves without property, we answered him with a written statement, a copy of which we are sending to your lordship, enclosing a copy of his decree, in order that you may see it and acquaint yourself with it.

1526. Señor, as soon as I saw the very severe order which the señor governor gave us, the loss of my property that I was to suffer was not as painful to me as the fact that my mother had been in bed for ten years expecting death daily, as well as the fact, that I had a sister very ill with cancer, and that the wife of my brother, Juan Antonio, had been in bed ten months at the point of death from an abortion. Since it was impossible to move them until they recovered or died, it was necessary for me to inform the señor governor in order that he might grant me permission to leave them in my farmhouse until they became well or died, as well as to leave another family to assist them. It was difficult for me to obtain this permission from him. It was necessary for that purpose to present him with a written statement in order that his lordship, accompanied by a religious and other witnesses, might go and certify to the state in which my patients found themselves. Thus, in view of these conditions and because of the intercession of the missionary, he had to grant me the said permission in order that I might leave the said patients and a son of mine to take care of them. Now, along with the other families, I find myself in San Antonio undergoing the same hardships as the rest. And seeing that we cannot support ourselves here in any way whatsoever, we beg your lordship's greatness that, as our father, who has always looked kindly upon us, you interest yourself in our welfare and not let our loss be greater. In consideration of all this, and in case we do not obtain the site we desire, a pueblo [might be erected] beyond the Brazos de Dios, where all of us can serve our sovereign in something. There will be no expense except for the minister, as I have already stated. Someone from among the settlers themselves can be named as the head, with the duty of carrying out the orders that might be given him. Your lordship should know that at present there are Frenchmen living in each of the interior nations for the sole purpose of trading. They have built houses and stocked them with goods of all kinds. This is the case with the Orcoquizac, the Vidais, [at] Paso de Tomás, in Texas, [at] San Pedro, [with] the Quichas, the Nacodoches—among the Aix there is an Englishman—and all the other nations to the Brazos de Dios, along the San Xavier road. This fact which I call to your lordship's attention will be confirmed by everyone, and the señor governor knows it well. We had no sconer come [away] than the French settled among all those nations, as we were advised by a Spaniard who, being ill, had remained there and had come on later. Also we were so informed by a Frenchman, one of the said traders, who arrived with some Indians.

1527. Knowing your lordship to be the principal center of the entire province, I left, señor, with the intention of going to place myself at your lordship's feet in order to beg you for myself and for all of us to favor us with your support and to give us a letter of recommendation for the señor viceroy. With it and with another letter that we are carrying from the señor governor, the señor viceroy might take pity on our hardships and concede us what we requested as a favor. After having arrived at this valley of Santa Rosa with the intention of passing on to see your lordship and of going from there to Mexico City, we have had the counsel of Señor Don Roque, who tells us that there will be great difficulty in seeing your lordship because of this danger from the Indians, the latitude in which your lordship is at present, the hardships of the road, and the poverty which overwhelms us. For this reason I am sending your lordship these letters by his hand and I am going on to the City of Mexico in order that, after presenting myself to the señor viceroy, he may immediately send our request to your lordship so that you may give your opinion on the matter. I shall be expecting this reply, as well as that his Excellency will see fit to allow our petition. I am begging him to permit me to go to Nachitoos just long enough to see the end of my sick ones. I therefore beg your lordship, prostrated at your feet, to have pity on these poor people. I shall be grateful for your lordship's kindness until the last day of my life. I remain ready for your lordship to make use of my uselessness as you may please, and I remain praying to God to preserve your lordship's life the many years that I desire. Santa Rosa María, January 8, 1774. Your most humble servant is at your lordship's feet. Antonio Gil Ybarbo. To Señor Commandant Don Hugo Oconor. I defer in everything to Señor Don Bernardo, who will inform your lordship on other matters concerning which I am not writing to you.

1528. These wretched people, expelled from the presidio of Los Adaes, after having sought with the diligence demanded by their unhappy condition of not having a place in which to establish themselves, found a spot on the banks of the Río de la Santísima Trinidad[17] which at first sight seemed extremely convenient for them. But experience later showed them how greatly they had deceived themselves in choosing it. Their settlement on the banks of the Río de la Trinidad is apparent from the following evidence, which is in document 58, beginning with number 42:

[17]Reference is to the colony of Nuestra Señora del Pilar de Bucareli which was founded by the erstwhile refugees from east Texas on the Trinity in 1774. The settlement remained there for five years, after which the settlers returned to east Texas. Secondary accounts of the history of this settlement are found in Bolton, *Texas . . .* , pp. 405–431, and Castañeda, *Our Catholic Heritage in Texas . . .* , Vol. IV, pp. 312–316.

Most excellent señor. Señor: In obedience to your Excellency's superior order, dated May 17, last, which Don Antonio Gil Ybarbo and Gil Flores, as representatives of the residents of the suppressed presidio of Los Adaes, delivered to me, I ordered that they should go and establish their settlement directly on this side of the Río de la Trinidad on the road leading to the said Adaes and Orcoquizas. I heeded the particular warning which your Excellency gives me to the effect that under no circumstances shall these settlers be transferred to Nachitoches, and that your Excellency had been pleased to declare to them verbally that you desired them to establish themselves a hundred leagues from the said post, at which distance they might go to any place that they may have selected in the direction and region designated. But the poverty of the said settlers being great, only a few of the families, aided by the provisions which these missions gave them, have been able to go, although nearly all those who came are thinking of doing so as soon as they may be able to get horses, provided a favorable location is found. I have ordered to this end that it shall have the special advantage of an easy extraction of water [for irrigation], and thus, so that he may establish them in my name, I have sent the lieutenant general, aided by a corporal and three soldiers, with an order to go immediately with Don Antonio Gil y Barbo to the Vidais, Texas, Quichuixes, and Yscanis nations, and, if it were not a great detour, to the Taovacanes and Jaranames, returning by way of the Tahuacanas (for the Taovayas and Ouachitas are far away), since it has been recognized that it will be appropriate to notify all the surrounding nations of the establishment of this pueblo and to tell them that this place had been selected so that the Spaniards might live near them.

1529. Likewise, seeing that settlement distant from all the others and without any troops whatever, I inform your Excellency that I have ordered the establishment of a company of militia formed from its settlers, composed of fifty officers and soldiers. As captain I have appointed the said Don Antonio Gil y Barbo, he being *justicia mayor* of the pueblo (since he is the best suited and most acceptable to his companions), as lieutenant Don Gil Flores, and as *alférez* Don Juan de Mora, together with a sergeant. I gave them these commissions to promote activity and discipline, on the usual condition that they are provisional, pending your Excellency's approval if you see fit to give it. The said people are very justly grateful to your Excellency for the charity with which you have seen fit to look upon them, and they are beginning to manifest it by attempting to immortalize your Excellency's illustrious name among their posterity by calling their pueblo *Nuestra Señora del Pilar de Bucareli*. They take refuge in your Excellency's protection, hoping that you will always look upon them as dependent upon the piety which is so notably an attribute of your Excellency, and that from now on you may furnish them the consolation of a priest who, as the parish curate, will take care of their spiritual needs for ten years—the length of time they will ordinarily require to be able to support him by themselves. They have no other object than that of service to both Majesties and the exact fulfillment of whatever your Excellency may see fit to order me. I desire to merit your approval, and again beg of you to see fit to take care of these poor, destitute, but obedient inhabitants who I hope will establish the pueblo of Nuestra Señora del Pilar de Bucareli in the midst of their destitution. I desire to render to your Excellency my most humble respects, and that our Lord may preserve your most excellent person many years. San Antonio de Béjar, September 1, 1774. Most excellent señor, your most respectful and faithful servant kisses your excellency's hands. Juan María, Barón de Ripperdá. To the most excellent señor *bailío*, Fray Don Antonio María Bucareli y Ursua.

1530. Extract: Obeying your Excellency's superior order, dated May 17, last, for the settlement of the residents of the suppressed presidio of Los Adaes, they proceeded to execute it on this side of the Río de la Trinidad, closer to this presidio than to Nachitoches. This presidio is defending them in accordance with what your Excellency has commanded me to do and was pleased to tell them. Several families went there, aided by the corn which these missions are very charitably giving them for their sustenance. Other missions should do likewise, for they have the horses for which they are asking. I sent my lieutenant general for this establishment, aided by a corporal and three soldiers, and they went immediately with Gil y Barbo to the neighboring nations to inform them of it. As that settlement found itself without any troops whatever, I ordered that a company of fifty militiamen be formed from it, and granted them by way of greater stimulus commissions of *justicia mayor*, of *teniente*, and of *alférez*, made provisionally from among them until they receive your Excellency's approval, provided they merit it. They desire to immortalize your Excellency's illustrious name in their pueblo by calling it Nuestra Señora del Pilar de Bucareli. They take refuge under your Excellency's protection, hoping now to obtain a parish priest for ten years and your powerful protection forever.

Mexico, February 13, 1775. To the señor *fiscal* with the previous documents on the matter. El Bailío Bucareli.

1531. *Most excellent señor. Señor:* I inform your Excellency that my lieutenant general has returned from establishing the new pueblo of Nuestra Señora del Pilar de Bucareli. Since they did not find a place for taking out water [for irrigation], although they found all the other conveniences that they might have desired, they established themselves on the said site about midway of the lower road that goes to Los Adaes, three regular days' [journey] from the coast, on the bank of the Río de la Trinidad, at Paso de Tomás.[18] They intend to cultivate their fields on the other side of the said river where there are some permanent lakes, though their poverty will not allow them to plant all that they need. For the present they find themselves detained here, most of them for lack of horses on which to travel. They comprise now seventy men capable of bearing arms, but many are without them. I therefore beg

---

[18]Bolton is of the opinion "that Paso Tomás was at the crossing of the San Antonio road and the La Bahía road over the Trinity . . . . This place has in modern times been identified with the crossing known as Robbin's Ferry at the old village of Randolph in Madison County."—Bolton, *Texas* . . . , p. 406.

your Excellency to see fit to order at least sixty or eighty muskets and the corresponding ammunition to be sent to them, provided your Excellency may find it proper to do so. I have obligated myself to supply them for the present with an *arroba* of powder and two of shot.

1532. The lieutenant general for lack of horses could not make the round of all the neighboring friendly nations in order to notify them of the establishment of the said settlement, and he was only among the Vidais (some of whom live near the pueblo) and among the Texas. I repeat to your Excellency my respects and desire to employ myself in whatever way may be most to your liking. I pray our Lord to keep your most excellent person many years. San Antonio de Béjar, November 15, 1774. Most excellent señor, your Excellency's most respectful and faithful servant kisses your hand. Juan María, Barón de Ripperdá. To the most excellent señor *bailío*, Fray Don Antonio María Bucareli.

Extract: My lieutenant general has returned, leaving the pueblo of Nuestra Señora del Pilar de Bucareli established on the Río de la Trinidad, at present with seventy men, most of them without arms. For this reason I ask your Excellency for them and for ammunition.

1533. After this settlement had been founded, the following complaint was made concerning it (document 58, number 45) :

Most excellent señor: I am the only captain in this province and, consequently, the second-in-command in it, as my inspector-commandant has notified me. For this reason, and by virtue of the order which your Excellency has sent me to the effect that I should give you an account of everything that may occur in the said province, and since I am complying with my duty and the devotion that I profess for the king's service in preventing the usurpation of his royal interests, I notify your Excellency that when some residents of this presidio under my charge left to hunt buffalo on the other side of the Río de Guadalupe, they encountered several subjects of the presidio of San Antonio de Béjar who were coming from a settlement established a short time ago on the Río de la Trinidad by a man named Gil Ybarbo. Having learned, it seems, that they were bringing back some French tobacco, they succeeded in acquiring a little. But when I discovered it on their return, recalling that with which your Excellency has charged me in this matter so carefully guarded by royal orders, I conducted the most secret investigations in order to verify it and to apprehend the transgressors. Having discovered that it was a small amount that one of the said settlers brought, I availed myself of the strategy of dissimulating it in order that without arousing fear, I might learn from whom he had acquired it by having him buy me some even though it were only a handful. He offered to do it for me, went to San Antonio, and brought me an amount weighing four pounds, nine ounces, and four *adarmes*, costing three and a half pesos. He delivered this to me intact, along with a piece that he had bought for himself at the same time. As I now talked to him with the seriousness that was proper in a matter of this nature, he confessed it to me, being fearful of the bad results that might befall him in case he should be discovered.

1534. Assured of what I had suspected in this matter, I proceeded to the examination of the other residents of this presidio, who informed me that it was true, that those of San Antonio brought back a good deal of tobacco on the said occasion, and that they heard them say that in the said pueblo of the Río de la Trinidad there was a large amount, the trade in which was in the hands of some Frenchmen who traded also with the Indians of the Northern Nations. This is all [the information] that I have been able to acquire. I advised the governor of the province of this matter, and despite the fact that in his zeal he probably did all that was proper, he answered me that all of them denied it and only one confessed to having sold two handfuls.

1535. Since your Excellency's pious and upright superior zeal may perhaps with its Christian good faith have a different idea of the existing conditions in the said settlement, because of its remoteness, I can do no less than call to your Excellency's attention the fact that it seems that the only purpose the settlers have who go to live there is to smuggle and to be out of reach of justice, since, for their sustenance, they have everything they need in these presidios and their jurisdictions, and also are able to avail themselves of the spiritual aid which they lack there, it being a hundred leagues away with five rivers in between, three of which are quite large, a fact that seems to show that they are opposed to our true religion. As I regard all the above as contrary to the service of both Majesties, I would consider myself a poor servant of the king and no less a poor Catholic, if I did not bring to your Excellency's attention what I have mentioned in this, my disinterested, honest, and candid representation, which is occasioned likewise by the pious opinions that I have heard on this point from the missionary religious of these missions under my charge, who foresee the perdition of many souls if the said system is continued. Another quite notable detriment will result to this province: that is the fact that the Indians waging war as they have been doing on these presidios, the latter will need many men for their defense, because of the lack of troops, and in time they may be depopulated, for many of the people long to go to the said settlement, both because it is well known that the said Indians are kept quiet there by means of the barter or trade that they have with them, and because it is understood that they live there with liberty of conscience. From this, unfortunately, it may be expected that in the course of time, and not much of it, they will become uncivilized apostates, finding themselves among the Indians, intercourse with whom is as welcome to those inhabitants as it seems to me it is prejudicial to these dominions of the king.

1536. Your Excellency, if you should consider that the arguments I have advanced have some basis, will take such measures as may be to your superior pleasure, and if not, I hope that your Excellency will be good enough not to hold them against me and will consider them as the result of my honest and upright intentions in the fulfillment of the duty with which I am charged. May our Lord preserve your Excellency's life many years. Royal presidio of La Bahía del Espíritu Santo, May 14, 1775. Most excellent señor. Señor, your most respectful subject kisses your Excellency's hand. Luis Cazorla. To the most excellent señor *bailío*, Fray Don Antonio María Bucareli y Ursua. Mexico, July 10, 1775. Let this be sent to the señor *fiscal* together with the *expediente* in which the settlement was decided upon. The Bailío Bucareli.

Most excellent señor: Although the señor governor of Texas, the Barón de Ripperdá, in his letters of September 1 and November 15 of last year, concerning the order that was sent him to effect the establishment of the residents of the suppressed presidio of Los Adaes, reports that he has done so in the vicinity of the Río de la Trinidad, where some families have settled whom others are likewise to follow as soon as they can supply themselves with horses, it seems that this settlement presents some dangers requiring a remedy, so that they may not increase, and may be cut off at the root in time. For, notwithstanding that the señor governor ordered the forming of a company of militia of fifty men for their better protection, and requests that your Excellency allow them a parish priest to minister to and catechize them at the expense of the royal treasury for a period of ten years, which is the usual time that they require in order to be able to support him themselves, and, notwithstanding that at the same time he requests you to furnish them arms and ammunition, the captain of the presidio of La Bahía del Espíritu Santo, Don Luis Cazorla [in a letter of] May 14, last, exposes the contraband trade that is being carried on there in tobacco with some Frenchmen and with the Indians of the Northern Nations. He explains the means he used to verify it by obtaining an amount weighing four pounds, nine ounces, and four *adarmes*, which he has in his possession. He says also that the only occupation of the settlers seems to be fraud and license, for they have not even the benefit of a minister. They are about a hundred leagues away from the spiritual aids which they could enjoy, and in that distance there are five rivers, three of which are quite large. From this may result the perdition of souls, and also the possible depopulation of the presidios, for many people long to go to the settlement [of Bucareli] not only because of the quietness [of the Indians] there, but also because of the lack of subjection in which those people live.

1537. These points, which are delicate in view of the bad consequences that they entail if illicit commerce and insubordination in the new pueblo named Nuestra Señora del Pilar de Bucareli should continue, demand a serious decision whereby, putting an end to the dangers that are feared, the settlers may be quieted, will not carry on such continual smuggling, and may live in a Christian and politic manner. To enable your Excellency to make the proper dispositions in this matter, you will order that the señor governor of Texas be told that you have been informed of those things that have been mentioned, that on each point he shall inform your Excellency exactly and promptly of everything he may know, and that until he shall receive further orders, he is to watch carefully to see that God and the king be not insulted, that they be not defrauded of their interests, and that no commerce be permitted with foreign nations. If there is no other way of checking such serious abuses, he shall try to get the settlers to move nearer to the center of the province and to the missions in order that they may not lack religious instruction and teaching. The captain of the presidio of La Bahía del Espíritu Santo will be sent an acknowledgment of the receipt of his *consulta,* and told that the zeal with which he endeavors to attend to the better service and to the loyalty of the vassals of those territories is pleasing to your Excellency, and that he is to continue to do so without failing to fulfill the orders that the señor commandant-inspector may have given him. And, whereas, in the *junta de guerra y real hacienda* held on May 25, 1774, the sending of a complete certified copy of the *expediente* to Don Hugo Oconor was ordered— so that he might provide for the permanent settlement of the former residents of the presidio of Los Adaes in the mission of Los Aix, if he should see fit to do so, and if not to report what may seem best to him, the results of which not yet have been noted—your Excellency will order that he be sent similar certified copies of the representations of the señor governor of Texas and of Don Luis Cazorla, so that in view of everything he may express his opinion as to the final decision that is to be made. Mexico, July 13, 1775. Areche.

Mexico, July 15, 1775. As the señor *fiscal* says in everything. The Bailío Bucareli.

1538. As a consequence of what the señor *fiscal* requested, the Señor Barón de Ripperdá (*ibid.,* number 67) rendered his report in the following manner:

Most excellent señor. Señor: In obedience to your Excellency's worthy order, dated July 26, last, which I have received (with too much delay), to the effect that I should inform your Excellency exactly and promptly in so far as I am able with regard to each one of the points which your Excellency has been pleased to present to me, concerning the pueblo of Nuestra Señora del Pilar de Bucareli which I established on this side of the Río de la Trinidad in fulfillment of the order which your Excellency was pleased to send me, dated May 18, 1774, the settlement being made with residents of the suppressed presidio of Los Adaes: In compliance, then, with this order I must state to your Excellency that Don Antonio Gil Ybarbo and Don Gil Flores, who had the honor of presenting themselves and rendering you obedience in person, and of obtaining from your kindness the said settlement, [were selected] as commissioners by the same residents because they (especially the first-named) were highly regarded by them. They have some farming implements [*bienes de campo*] and the zeal so essential in leaders, for the service of both Majesties and for the prosperity of their people. Pending your Excellency's approval, or superior decision, I have named him [Gil Ybarbo] captain of militia and *justicia mayor,* the second [Gil Flores] lieutenant, and Don Juan de Mora *alférez,* and have enlisted fifty men of the said settlement for militiamen, including a sergeant and four corporals. I had the honor of informing your Excellency of this, as I now also have of assuring you that the said *justicia mayor* up to the present is doing his duty creditably and does not allow any trade in tobacco with the French or with the Indians. Reports to the contrary could have been circulated only because of the fact that there remained in the extinguished [settlement of] Los Adaes three Frenchmen, old settlers and married to Spanish women. The wives of two of them, called Nicolás Beausolcille and Carlos Grande, being here, while Ramón Terio stayed [there] with his wife, [the two former ones] began to engage in the Indian trade, along with others from Nachitoches. The first [Nicolás Beausolcille] was found when we went to establish Nuevo Bucareli. He had articles to trade among the Vidais who live near there. This he did until Monsieur Lemee, intrusted with the trade of the said nation, made him withdraw. When he returned and asked for a place to settle, the *justicia mayor* granted it to him on condition that he withdraw from the said trade, and to his companion on the condition that he continue it only until he could collect from the said Vidais what they owed them. During this time there went with the señor curate to the said settlement Jacinto de Mora, who among others was accompanying him. Through the agency of one of those Vidais Indians, he purchased two or three handfuls of left-over tobacco which the said Beausolcille had, as is clear from the proceedings drawn up against Mora, which I sent to your Excellency. Because of this summons the former was brought in chains to this presidio, as were Carlos Grande and a brother of the said *justicia mayor* (who had also become involved in it). When the presidio was suppressed, I had permitted him to remain in order to take care of his mother and wife, for I saw for myself the many infirmities from which they were suffering. The *justicia mayor* himself had them restore the goods which they had with them, and withdrawing from the trade entirely, they went back to the pueblo without any goods. Ramón Terio, who still remained with his family at the former mission of Nacodoches, was trading with the Texas, and when the *justicia mayor* passed by there, going at my orders to recover in Los Adaes some artillery equipment which still remained there because there had been no way of transporting it, and some nails from those houses to be used on their own, being unable to make use of force in the presence of the heathen, he enjoined him [Terio], in the best possible manner, to come with his family to the pueblo, which he promised to do, and he does not doubt that he has done so, because of his wife. Aside from this, the zeal of the said *justicia mayor* is proven and the royal treasury saved from being defrauded by the seizure which he made of contraband goods which Don Marcos Vidal of this settlement brought from Nachitoches, as I reported to your Excellency. He sent him to me, secured with shackles, with a party of militia in charge of his lieutenant, together with the said Nicolás Beausolcille, a deserter, and another miscreant. The first and last fled together from this guardroom. The second one died. And when Don Agustín Grevenverge [Grevembert], the captain of militia of Atacapas, passed through Bucareli with the message which he brought me from his governor and which I sent on to your Excellency, as I did—see number 110—with the invoice of the goods which (being ignorant of its prohibition) the said captain was bringing here in order to obtain some horses, they were seized by the captain of militia of Bucareli. We are keeping the goods intact pending your Excellency's decision, and likewise those smuggled in by Vidal, already mentioned, with the exception of the tobacco. With regard to this, proceeding in accordance with the royal instruction conforming to the order which his Majesty was pleased to issue in Spain on July 22, 1761, promulgated in Mexico February 5, 1768, I sent an order that it be distributed for account of [*de cuenta de*] the royal revenue, a tobacco shop being established in the best manner possible in view of the dearth of money in that settlement. It was placed in charge of the *justicia mayor* as the most reliable person, and the settlers who wished to come were given two or three pounds of the said tobacco for their journey (among them being some of those enlisted as militiamen). When a corporal went with six of these men to take their horses to the pasture of this presidio which was near the one of La Bahía, they passed it while using some of the said tobacco. I had not warned them to carry a permit stating that, despite its quality, the tobacco was no longer contraband, and believing it to be such the captain of the said presidio surprised them, and finding among them two pounds, less fourteen *adarmes*, in pieces, after having detained them for three days he sent them to me as prisoners (although they were innocent). Because of such contingencies, and even before this one, recognizing the misfortune of that poor settlement [Bucareli] because of the rivals who solicit its destruction, and in order to avoid all motives for comment, the above-mentioned *justicia mayor* had requested me to bring the said confiscated tobacco to this depository [at San Antonio] even if it were at his expense, giving him cigarettes to distribute in that settlement without risk of having them mistaken for tobacco from Nachitoches, and making it easier for him to discover whether anyone is using the latter.

1539. The distance from Bucareli to this presidio is more than a hundred leagues, but in between there are only three rivers, called the Brazos de Dios, the Colorado, and the Guadalupe, which most of the year afford passage without any impediments or obstructions other than the risk of Comanches on this side of the Guadalupe on the lower road, and on this side of the Colorado by the more direct one.

1540. The suffering of the said settlement for lack of a parish priest is as evident as are the constant requests of its inhabitants to obtain from your Excellency's piety the payment at royal expense of [the salary of] a priest for ten years, as they ask in their representation, which I am sending to your Excellency with my report. Meanwhile, eager for spiritual consolation, they obtained one last year through the well-known zeal of this señor parish priest. And since the reverend father president here also has an order from the reverend father *guardián* of Zacatacas to help as much as possible in the same matter, on this occasion, by agreement with the said señor curate, several reverend missionary fathers of these missions went for some days to Bucareli, for missionary purposes and to look for apostates. As soon as its *justicia mayor* had finished founding the pueblo, he built a decent chapel there and the said señor curate placed in it its most holy Patroness of El Pilar. There he [the *justicia mayor*] assembled the people daily at the sound of the bell to recite the holy rosary in unison, together with other prayers, and also in the mornings on feast days. When two residents of Nachitoches came there with the proper passport from their governor-general to collect some debts of past years, one of them, called Don Nicolás de la Mata, who has proven his long devotion to this image, as a further proof of it offered to build her a temple twenty-five varas in length and of the corresponding breadth and to send this year two carpenters who will build it of wood in accordance with the custom and resources of the country. They already have the permission of the señor bishop of Guadalajara for this.

1541. That settlement lives in due obedience, its *justicia mayor* correcting and punishing those who deserve it. For this purpose he provided from the beginning an adequate guardroom as well as stocks and fetters, at his own expense. In the same way he had brought from Los Adaes four small bronze cannons and two iron ones, four-pounders, which I had left behind because they were burnt out [*desfogonados*]. He hopes that your Excellency will grant them to his pueblo and that the blacksmith will bush them. He likewise transported with his mules as far as his pueblo, three *tercios* of old guncarriage iron, leaving eight *tercios* of the same material deposited where he had the Rancho de Lobanillo[19] and more than seven hundred balls of the same calibre buried at Los Adaes until he could get them. At my order he has sent [a party] to the coast of the former on this side of El Borcoquiza [Orcoquiza] which is two or three long days' journey distant, to inquire whether the English disembark on it to trade with the Indians or for any other purpose, and at the same time to gain the good will of the Carancaguas nation, which inhabits the said coast and island of La Culebra, and who formerly have not been united as they are now beginning to be. Some of them have come to the pueblo. Also a negro and an Apache have obtained the right to live there and be free. They were slaves in Louisiana, whence they fled years ago. All these things, as well as the visits (not counting the neighboring Vidaes) of the Texas, Quitseigus, and Tancagues Indians, who live two or three days' journey away, occasion him unavoidable expense.

1542. With regard to the depopulation of these presidios because many people wish to live in that settlement, it cannot be done without the governor's consent, and this permission I give only to those who were in Los Adaes, and many of them still remain [in San Antonio] because their poverty has burdened them with debts as if they were vagabonds. But the permanent settlers are by no means allowed to leave. A wretched mulatto or negro overseer of blanketmakers, who was useless because of his bad conduct, has been taken by the said *justicia mayor* with my permission, because he wants him at least to teach the making of them and, if possible, of cotton cloth [*manta*] like that of Puebla. For this purpose he is taking wool with which

---

[19]Antonio Gil Ybarbo "was owner of a large ranch 'already a pueblo,' at El Lobanillo, on the highway west of the Sabine. He was also a trader, and during the reform administration of Oconor as governor *ad interim*, he had been imprisoned on the charge of contraband trade with Louisiana. Nevertheless, he was generally regarded as a substantial, trustworthy man, and was spokesman for his fellows. He was a type of the able men which the Spanish as well as the English frontier sometimes produced."—Bolton, *Texas . . . ,* pp. 113–114.

to begin, sheep for its continuance, and cottonseed for growing the amount necessary for the said work which he is trying diligently to establish. For he realized the evident advantages that the people will gain from them, without for this reason failing to take advantage of the unusual fertility which that beautiful country affords not only for the raising of horses, cattle, and sheep, but also for the production of tallow and lard from the many wild cattle, and from the buffaloes which are found in abundance a day's journey distant. This can facilitate for these presidios the making of soap, which is now being brought from Saltillo. That river furnishes good fish in abundance. Its water can easily be taken out and the territory through which it flows is very good for the planting of maize, wheat, rice, and other crops. After their experience last year of losing by a severe flood their first crop of maize, which they had planted on the other side of the river, the Vidais Indians showed them a favorable place for planting on this side without risk from floods, and they harvested some maize, of which they brought me samples of ears a third of a vara long and of a good quality of grain. They also planted some fields of cotton which grew luxuriantly, as did the vegetable gardens and the other things that were put out in such a short time. As a beginning in the growing of wheat, they have sown a *fanega* of it. All of this has not prevented the construction of twenty houses which the pueblo now has, made of hewn wood and placed in a symmetrical manner similar to the plan of the new presidios. These do not include the chapel and the guardhouse, nor various huts of those who have not yet been able to build regular houses, which is still being done. Nor does the *justicia mayor* cease coöperating in everything, not only by example but also by furnishing them implements, oxen, and everything that his resources could supply for the benefit of that community. He has just made an agreement with a merchant from here, called Don Juan de Ysurrita, to supply him with the most necessary goods, for which he will pay him with products of that country. He is taking from him on this occasion a supply of what is most needed, with the idea that the entire pueblo may have the actual necessities, and thus avoid the use of whatever may come by way of Louisiana.

1543. As for that settlement being free from attacks of the enemy up to the present, [it may be stated that] it is not due to their having less trade or communication with them, but because the Comanches are farther from them than they are from us. This is the only enemy nation that this province knows today, and fortunately they have not discovered them [at Bucareli] because of the great obstacle afforded by the Taovacanas and Tancaoves nations who are practically in front of them and who have lately been at war with the Comanches. They are friendly to us, as are the others who surround the settlement of Nuestra Señora del Pilar de Bucareli. I must report to your Excellency that I found this settlement of great usefulness, not only to its settlers who deserve consideration because of the loyalty with which they suffered the depopulation of Los Adaes and their hard journey to this capital without the least assistance, but more particularly because of the good opportunity that that location presents for the better service of the king, since it is near to a coast which is as extensive as it is defenseless. That militia not only can reconnoiter it frequently but can also obtain information through the same friendly Indians if any foreigners should land there, and thus can surprise them. They can make secure the peace with the neighboring Indians who are persuaded that your Excellency has sent those Spaniards at their request in order that they may live in their vicinity as before, over which they have shown themselves very happy. Many of them are also happy at being able to die Christians, for those who live nearby call a Spaniard to baptize them before they die. There is also hope that several families of apostate Indians from these missions may assemble there, such as the Cocos and others who have been living in that region for many years and are beginning to visit the settlement. The latter is also conducive to preventing the smugglers from Louisiana coming inland, and to supplying these presidios in the future with horses and with some articles that [now] come from outside, provided the tranquillity which it is enjoying today and the special diligence which its *justicia mayor* is displaying, continue. These circumstances make him worthy of the kindness of your Excellency, under whose obedience I respectfully remain, eagerly awaiting your commands and praying that our Lord may keep your most excellent person many years. San Antonio de Béjar, January 25, 1776. Most excellent señor. Señor, your most respectful and devoted servant kisses your Excellency's hand. Juan María, Barón de Ripperdá. To the most excellent señor *bailío*, Fray Don Antonio María Bucareli y Ursua.

1544. The former inhabitants of Los Adaes had hardly established themselves on the banks of the Río de la Trinidad when they found themselves obliged to abandon this settlement because of a most dreadful flood which descended upon them, brought on by the waters of that very large river, which, not being able to keep within its banks because of the abundance of rains, overflowed the fields and reached to that recently-established settlement, its entrance leaving it uninhabitable. Therefore they again had to seek another place where they could settle, and after many hardships, they found one at the abandoned mission of Nacodoches where they established themselves with the permanence which they desired, for that pueblo still exists today.

1545. All this is clear from the following letter which is found in document 62, number 42:

Señor commandant-general. Señor: This entire body of inhabitants and militia presented itself in my house on the first and eighth of January, 1779, and I granted them permission to move with their families to the vicinity of the pueblo of the Texas Indians, since they had become terrified by the hostile Comanches to such an extent that the families were suffering, the men being unable even to go out to butcher meat, because of not wishing to leave their families exposed to the Indians' barbarities. [These hostilities] also have left them practically afoot and with little time, what with the constant agitation over defenses and guards, to support themselves, and with no hope of being able to plant crops for the same reason, and also because their fields are scattered and at a distance, and because of the scarcity of arms and ammunition for defending them. They believe that there [at the Texas pueblo] they could plant crops and support themselves until, your lordship being informed by my governor and by me, you may decide what you consider best with regard to the matter. Therefore, since all the arguments they advanced were obvious to me; and considering that, if I did not give them the permission, I exposed them to a serious risk and that if I did permit them to move farther away, to a greater one, and that the friendly nations would feel hurt; and in view of the grave necessity and danger as well as the long delay [occasioned] by applying to your lordship's superiority, particularly with the lack of means that I have for doing so, notwithstanding the amount of work that we have done in our pueblo—I decided to allow them to move and to give an account of it to my governor at once. They began to do this on January 25, while I remained with twenty men until these could return with their baggage and belongings. It was found that their fears had not been groundless, for it happened that on the night of February 14, the river went out of its banks and inundated everything on both sides, drowning most of the few horses and cattle that remained. Its waters rose to about the middle of the houses of the pueblo, endangering the domestic animals there and causing the loss of the poor things that the sudden flood gave no time to free, because of the necessity of attending to the women and children who remained. These were got out on boards and doors and taken to the highest point in the vicinity, where a few days later the Comanches fell upon us. They displayed their courage by surrounding our camp throughout the night. Being unable to kill us, on the following day (at about six in the morning) they carried off thirty-eight horses which had been saved from the waters in canoes with a great deal of trouble, and which could not be defended because we were unable to leave the families unprotected. Thus we were left entirely on foot. They [the Indians] went without taking leave, and encountered not very far away eight friendly Indians of whom they killed six. Two escaped and in fleeing came to our camp. When the crossing of the families to the other side of the river was begun in canoes on the wide-spreading, flooded waters (which on occasion lasted for eighty days at a time), there was heard, between seven and eight in the evening of the day on which the crossing was completed, a volley of shots from the direction of the place which we had left. Consequently, on the following day, when some people were sent to see what it had been, there were visible only a great many footprints of the enemy, who had left the said place after firing their shots. It must be added that if most of the families had not left on the said 25th of January, there is no doubt, señor, but that there would have been a greater loss because of the flood, for many children as well as some invalids disabled by disease would have been drowned. Continuing with all of them to the vicinity of the pueblo of the Texas Indians, two days' journey distant, more than a hundred days were spent on the road in getting the people together, and because of the many floods, which were general. There they suffered unspeakable hardships, until we saw the place of Los Texas and the old mission of the Nacodoches, which is three leagues farther inland. Since there was a small chapel in it, where the reverend missionary father could administer the holy sacraments, and a house in which he lived, as well as sufficient water, lands, and building materials, I took advantage of these things to enable us to raise crops and sustain ourselves while awaiting your lordship's superior decision. I humbly beg your lordship to think well of my decision, it being impossible to return to the old site or to the banks [of the Trinity] below or above it, because they are lowlands, or to go farther inland because of the greater risk. No better place can be found here than this one and the one that was granted us by the most excellent señor viceroy. This place is situated conveniently for watching the movements and operations of the friendly nations and for controlling the traders, as well as for acquiring information from the coast, a matter with which I have been charged by my governor.

1546. For this reason, in behalf of this entire pueblo as well as myself, I beg your lordship to be pleased to take pity on us for the hardships that we have been suffering since the suppression of Los Adaes, where we so obediently abandoned our belongings and our houses. We continue in this obedience and offer ourselves for whatever we have been ordered to do in the service of his Majesty, as we have done [hitherto] at our expense. After having had to move three times, we are now hoping that your lordship's piety will look upon us with your paternal love and will order us what you may consider best with regard to our settlement, for which purpose we beg that your lordship will bear us in mind in giving your orders. With regard to them, I do not omit telling your lordship that of the two places this one has more advantages. May our Lord keep your lordship's life many years. Nacogdoches, May 13, 1779. Your most attentive and grateful subject kisses your lordship's hand. Antonio Gil Ybarbo. To Señor Commandant-general Don Teodoro de Croix.[20]

1547. The last historian of the province of Texas, the Reverend Father Fray Agustín Morfi, did not forget to insert in his *Memorias* the history of the abandonment of the presidio of Los Adaes and of what happened to its inhabitants, for in book 11, number 2 and following, he gives us this narrative:

The time arrived in which the *autos de visita* and the reports of the most excellent señor, the Marquis of Rubí, were examined in a *junta de real hacienda*. In consultation with it and in accord with the most excellent señor

[20]"In 1776 the Interior Provinces of New Spain were put under a *comandante general* with his capital at Chihuahua. The first *comandante*, El Cavallero de Croix, arrived on the frontier in 1777. As his first great task, he set about checking Indian hostilities, particularly those of the Apache. It is indicative of the importance of that frontier that he began with Texas."—Bolton, *Texas* . . . , p. 124.

viceroy, Don José de Gálvez,[21] at that time *visitador-general* of New Spain, the
Most Excellent Señor de Croix decided that—since the villa of San Antonio
de Béjar was at that time the place most exposed to the invasions and attacks
of various nations of hostile Indians from the north who were warring upon
that settlement, its haciendas, and opulent missions, in the course of their
pursuit of the Lipan Apaches who are their hated enemies—in order to reinforce the said settlement in the manner needed, its company should be increased to eighty men. Included in this number were two lieutenants, an
alférez, two sergeants, and six corporals. [He also decided] that the governor
of the province should be its captain, with an increase in salary of a thousand
pesos over the 2,500 which he was receiving. He was to establish his residence in the province, which he had formerly had at the useless presidio of
Los Adaes. From its company and from that of Horcoquisac, which was to
be withdrawn, he was to choose men to complete the said villa.

1548. [He ordered also] that twenty men were to be detached from this new
company, under the command of one of its lieutenants. They were to be
stationed permanently on the banks of the Arroyo del Cíbolo to protect the
ranchos belonging to various settlers as far as San Antonio, and in order to
leave less unprotected the intervening distance of about fifty leagues between
that villa and the last presidio of La Bahía del Espíritu Santo. Parties from
these two places could be mutually aided by the said detachment and by
acting together could check the entrance of enemies who might penetrate
into that area, under the supposition that because of their pusillanimity and
poverty, very little or nothing need be feared from the heathen who inhabit
the land in the direction of the sea. To this last point the most experienced
men of the country and those having greatest knowledge of its Indians, such
men as Lieutenant Colonel Don Athanase de Mézières, Colonels and Governors
Barón de Ripperdá and Don Domingo Cabello,[22] and the captain of that
presidio, Don Luis Cazorla, do not agree.

1549. The presidio of La Bahía del Espíritu Santo, the eastern terminus of
the cordon proposed by the most excellent señor, the Marquis of Rubí, and
approved by the most excellent señor viceroy, should continue in its present
status on the same site on which it is now located and with the same purpose
as that for which it was built, and in order that its detachments and those of
the villa of San Antonio de Béjar may mutually aid one another. Its company
should, like those of the other presidios of the line, with the exception of the
one of San Antonio already mentioned, be composed of a captain, a lieutenant,
an *alférez*, a chaplain, and fifty-three soldiers, including a sergeant, two corporals, and ten Indian scouts with a corporal of the second class.

1550. The presidio of San Sabá should be suppressed in order to erect one
of that name on the banks of the Río del Norte on the new line (as was

---

[21]José de Gálvez never was viceroy of New Spain, although as visitor-general
of New Spain, he had powers superior to those of the viceroy at Mexico City.
For a biography of Gálvez, see Priestley, *José de Gálvez, Visitor-General of
New Spain (1765–1771).*

[22]Domingo Cabello was governor of Texas from 1778 to 1786.

actually done by locating it between the new presidios of La Bahía and San Carlos, although with the name of San Vicente) and, of course, to reinforce with its men the detachments of the *comandante de campaña* of Nueva Vizcaya. And in the indubitable supposition that at present the other two presidios of El Horcoquizac and Los Adaes, the latter seven leagues from the one of Nachitoches, are also useless, because the colony of Louisiana is under the dominion of his Majesty, the governor of Texas and the other officials of these two presidios were ordered to dismantle them and abandon them immediately the places on which they stood, taking care that the few settlers who were in them should be withdrawn to the said villa of San Antonio de Béjar or its vicinity where, they were likewise ordered, lands were to be distributed to them on which they could settle and maintain themselves. At the same time [orders were given] to extinguish the useless missions of Nacogdoches, Aix, and others that have been maintained under the protection of the said presidios without any Indians whatsoever and against the wishes of their missionaries; and to retire the surplus officers and soldiers from these, abolishing their salaries and the stipends of the said missions in favor of the royal treasury.

1551. I have already said that at the same time that the depopulation of Los Adaes was ordered, it was provided that the settlers at that presidio be sent to San Antonio de Béjar, distributing lands and water among them in order that they might subsist. But when these people could not adapt themselves to the land of San Antonio, more because of fear of the land and the petulance of its people than for any other just cause—since, as we have seen, that territory is capable of maintaining many thousands of settlers—they appealed to the most excellent señor viceroy through their deputy, Don Antonio Gil Ybarbo, who, accompanied by another citizen, went to Mexico, aided by a favorable report from the governor. The negotiations were brief, and they returned to the province carrying an order to the same governor to establish them where it might be most convenient for them and of the greatest advantage to the entire colony. With this order the Barón [de Ripperdá] formed a new town with them on the banks of the Río de la Trinidad, with the name of Nuestra Señora del Pilar de Bucareli. He formed a company, the command of which he gave to Gil Ybarbo, making him at the same time his lieutenant-governor for the administration of justice throughout the jurisdiction of the new pueblo. Later, in the name of the same señor viceroy, he sent an official letter of request and command to the reverend father president of the missions of that province, asking that he designate one of his religious for the administering of sacraments in the new pueblo, which was done immediately. This settlement would have been of untold advantage, but the new settlers had the misfortune of establishing themselves on land subject to inundation (although they had many other lands available), which occasioned its abandonment.

CHAPTER XVII

AGGRESSIONS OF THE FRENCH TO THE SOUTH-SOUTHEAST OF NATCHITOCHES

1552. Now that we have shown hitherto what the French appropriated for themselves north of their presidio of Nachitoches and west of the Mississippi, the only thing that we lack is to point out, as we promised to do above in paragraph 60, what they took from this same presidio toward the south, or rather toward the south-southeast, as far as where the Río Chafalaya[1] entered the sea by way of the bay which the Spaniards have always called La Ascensión.[2] But the geographer D'Anville[3] shows us most clearly the extent of all the land that was taken by the French, designating it with his line[4] which he ends at the Cabo del Norte,[5] which is the point closest to the said Río Chafalaya, the banks of which are contiguous to the said cape and to the line mentioned. Consequently, all that territory which the Río de Nachitoches [Red River] drains and the settlements in the vicinity of this river belong to the French, as do also those that are on the west bank of the Mississippi as far as its entrance into the sea, commonly called Paso del Sudoeste [Southwest Pass][6] because it is the one farthest west, and all the land that lies to the south of the same Río Nachitoches and between the Chafalaya and the Mississippi, because D'Anville's line includes all this.

[1]The present Atchafalaya River. As previously stated *(Pichardo's Treatise* . . . , Vol. I, p. 354, n. 2): "In the transcript of the Pichardo text from which this translation has been made, the form 'Chafalaya' is used continuously and that form . . . has been retained, the modern form to the contrary notwithstanding."

[2]The Rio Chafalaya enters the Gulf of Mexico "by way of the bay which the Spaniards have always called La Ascensión."—*Pichardo's Treatise* . . . , Vol. I, p. 359.

[3]See *Pichardo's Treatise* . . . , Vol. I, p. 24, n. 7.

[4]D'Anville's dividing line, referred to above, is indicated on Pichardo's map published in *Pichardo's Treatise* . . . , Vol. II, following Index.

[5]For numerous references to Cabo del Norte, consult the Index to *Pichardo's Treatise* . . . , Vol. I, p. 606, and also the map published in Vol. II of the same work, following the Index.

[6]Reference is to one of the well-known mouths of the Mississippi River. Southwest Pass is located on the map published in *Pichardo's Treatise* . . . , Vol. II, following Index.

1553. But this does not seem to be true, because the Spaniards themselves confess that the district of Louisiana included the lands of the Atacapas[7] and Opelusas,[8] and extended as far as the east bank of the Río Nechas, called also, as we have seen in Part II, Río Mexicano.[9] In fact, the governor of Texas, the Barón de Ripperdá, cited in Part II, paragraph 142, says that

the Río de Nechas is the one that divides this province (of Texas) from Louisiana, on the coast.

In paragraph 160 he says also

Apeluza . . . is a coast belonging to Louisiana.

Don Luis Cazorla, captain of the presidio of La Bahía del Espíritu Santo, writes also (ibid., paragraph 163):

. . . the other side of the Río de Nechas, in the jurisdiction of New Orleans.

And many other Spaniards assert the same thing, as may be seen in Part II, from paragraph 142, and beginning with 838, in which the Orcoquizas are discussed.

1554. But we shall see that during the entire time that France was mistress of Louisiana, she never went beyond the dividing line of D'Anville, and she never owned the lands of the Atacapas and Opeulsas Indians, nor did she know the course of the Río de Nechas. If she had dominated those lands and had known the course of the said stream, D'Anville and the other Frenchmen would not have erred so seriously in their description of the coast lines, especially in the parts where the Nechas and Sabinas rivers flow into the sea. And if France had possessed these lands, D'Anville would have drawn his line through them and would not have moved it so far to the east, ending at the Cabo del Norte.

1555. Unfortunately for Spain, in the same year of 1763, in which France ceded Louisiana to her, Don Ángel Martos de Nav-

---

[7]The Atacapas Indians and other members of the Attacapan family lived on the lower Trinity, Neches, and Sabine rivers.—See *Pichardo's Treatise* . . . , Vol. I, p. 379, n. 6.

[8]For frequent references to the Opelusas Indians who lived on the Louisiana coast west of the Mississippi River, consult the indices of *Pichardo's Treatise* . . . , Vols. I, II, and III.

[9]Pichardo (*Treatise* . . . , Vol. I, p. 398) identifies the Río Mexicano as the "San Pedro de Navidachos, also called Río de Nechas."

arrete[10] was governor of Texas. As we have proven in number 14, of the note we attached to document 70, which contains the representation made by the same Governor Martos Navarrete to his Majesty with regard to the limits of Louisiana because of the fact that the governor of New Orleans had asked for aid, this man Marcos Navarrete, in about the year 1759, plotted the abominable crime of giving to France the lands of the Atacapas and Opelusas and of taking them away from Spain by permitting and consenting, for reasons of his own, that the French come to settle on them, going beyond D'Anville's line. In as much as he feared the just accusations of our government against such permission and consent, he attempted to defend himself beforehand, so to speak, by representing to the most excellent señor viceroy, the Marquis of Las Amarillas,[11] that the French had introduced themselves into those lands against his will and without his being able to resist it, and that although this was very painful to him, he could not remedy it, for if he tried to do so and did not succeed, the unfortunate result might be a war between the two crowns.

1556. But what was to prevent his remedying this condition? The French were in his district without arms or any defense whatever, and therefore in a state to be made prisoners and sent to Mexico to the most excellent señor viceroy, as his predecessor, Don Jacinto Barrios, had done with Blancpain.[12] In pursuit of his plan to give France the lands of the Atacapas and Opelusas, following Massé[13] and Cortebleu,[14] in time other Frenchmen began to come in, recognizing not the Spanish government but that of Louisiana. During this interval came the year 1763, in which France ceded Louisiana to Spain.[15] The most excellent señor, Don Antonio de Ulloa, came as its first governor, and when his Excellency saw that there were French subjects in his district in the lands of the Atacapas and Opelusas. Furthermore, being new to

---

[10]Don Ángel Martos y Navarrete was governor of Texas from about 1759 to 1766.

[11]Agustín de Ahumada y. Villalón, the Marquis of Las Amarillas, was viceroy of New Spain from 1755 to 1758.

[12]See *Pichardo's Treatise* . . . , Vol. I, p. 376, n. 3 and p. 380, n. 2.

[13]See *Pichardo's Treatise* . . . , Vol. I, p. 376, n. 2.'

[14]See *Pichardo's Treatise* . . . , Vol. II, p. 202.

[15]Louisiana was ceded by France to Spain secretly on November 3, 1762. For further details see *Pichardo's Treatise* . . . , Vol. I, p. 3, n. 2.

that country and ignorant of the fact that in reality and in truth these lands belonged to the government of the viceroyalty of Mexico, since there was no protest either from the court of Spain or from the said viceroyalty, he began to extend and exercise his authority over them, and his successors continued to do so to the last, when Spain returned Louisiana to France.

1557. It is clearly inferred from all this that the French never were owners of the lands in question. For even the most learned among them knew nothing whatever about them, and the penetration of one or two Frenchmen, clandestinely and unjustly, could not prejudice the rights of Spain. Thus, if any loyal vassal had denounced Governor Navarrete in time for having permitted and allowed the French to penetrate into lands of our Catholic sovereign, as had been done against Don Manuel de Sandoval, our government would have applied the proper remedy or at least the injury would have lasted only until the arrival of his successor who would have corrected it. But notwithstanding the fact that while Spain was ruling Louisiana the lands in question were governed by a Spanish governor, nothing was done to put an end to the injuries that resulted to the most excellent señores viceroys of New Spain, to the royal subordinate magistrates, to the most illustrious señores bishops of Guadalajara, and to the Holy Tribunal of the Inquisition. Indeed, things remained in the same state. If the French were never owners of the lands of the Atacapas and Opelusas, they could never be retroceded to them, and, consequently, the United States can never have a right to them nor can they transgress D'Anville's line. Then this line marks the true French limits. Then, although the Señor Barón de Ripperdá and Don Luis Cazorla may have said that the Río de Nechas is the one that separates this province from Louisiana along the coast, that El Apelusa is a coast belonging to Louisiana, and that the other side of the Río de Nechas is in the jurisdiction of New Orleans, they did not thereby prejudice the right of Spain, for their assertion should be understood as referring to Spanish Louisiana and not to French [Louisiana].

1558. Let us go into the details and into an explanation with regard to all this. Supposing that, as we have seen, the Bermel-

lon[16] is west of D'Anville's line, which begins at La Punta de
Venados, or Cabo del Norte, then this river should belong to the
Spanish dominions. And in reality D'Anville's line should not cut
it, as in fact it does not at any point, provided we understand
the system of division of limits adopted by the French. According to the rule of Señor Marca, explained above in paragraph 2
and 1362 (followed no doubt by Monsieur de la Salle when he
came to explore the Mississippi, and later by St. Denis and other
geographers who drew the map by which D'Anville guided himself in order to draw his own), the waters that fall or flow from
the eminences are the ones that should form the dividing line
of districts and provinces. Therefore, the waters that flow from
the hills and other frontier eminences to the rivers and marshes,
already recognized as belonging to France, appertain to the possessions of this power. Conversely, the waters that flow from similar places to Spanish rivers and marshes should be Spanish, together with all the places from which they descend. It may be
gathered from this that the waters which enter the Bermellon, a
river that enters the sea and thus flows through the lowlands,
doubtless come from high lands, that is to say, from Spanish lands,
and consequently are waters that cannot come from any French
river, for naturally no waters can flow through lands higher than
themselves. Then the entire course of the Río Bermellon should
belong to Spain. This is inferred from D'Anville's map (as we
shall see), on which, although it does not show the Río Bermellon, it is easy to recognize the place where it should be and even
to locate it there. On Evía's map[17] there is a distance of thirteen
minutes of an equinoctial degree between the Cabo del Norte,
which he calls Punta de Venados, and the mouth of the Río Bermellon. Therefore, if we count thirteen minutes toward the west,
beginning at the Cabo del Norte, we shall see that wherever they
may end the mouth of the Río Bermellon should be located on
D'Anville's map. Now, if we measure on Lafon's map[18] the distance down to the sea of the arc of the meridian which passes through

---

[16]The Río Bermellon is shown on Pichardo's map, published in his *Treatise*
. . . , Vol. II, following the Index, as entering the Gulf of Mexico west of
the Bay of La Ascensión (see note 2, *supra*).

[17]See *Pichardo's Treatise* . . . , Vol. II, p. 196.

[18]See *Pichardo's Treatise* . . . , Vol. I, p. 42, n. 2.

the pueblo of St. Landri, where it seems the Río Bermellon rises, we shall find that from the sea to the said pueblo there are only forty-eight minutes. Let us now take these forty-eight minutes on D'Anville's map and fix them on the arc of the meridian which passes through the mouth of the Río Bermellon, from this mouth to the north, and we shall find that the source of the Bermellon lies not only west of D'Anville's line, but even far to the south of it, and thus it is seen on our map, number 19 of document 74. Having explained this, let us now hear what our pilot, Evía, adds concerning the Río Bermellon in his words copied in Part II, paragraph 101, to wit:

That the Río Bermellon communicates with the Atacapas.

The post of the Atacapas of which Evía speaks, from what I understand, is the said pueblo of St. Landri. We have seen that this pueblo is not cut by D'Anville's line. Then this pueblo belongs to the possessions of Spain, a consequence so legitimate that D'Anville himself plainly admits it by locating the "Atacapas or Anthropophagi, nomadic Indians" west of his line. In view of all this the French cannot claim that the Atacapas belong to them. But, since these Indians are nomadic and do not inhabit any fixed territory, they would belong to France only in case, having crossed the dividing line, they should continue to reside between it and the Mississippi. But if they wish to remain west of the line, it is indispensably necessary for them to recognize our Catholic King as their legitimate sovereign.

1559. Perrin du Lac,[19] in his [account of his] journey to the two Louisianas, upper and lower (see document 64, number 81), drew up a good description of the coasts that lie west of the Mississippi and on which the Atacapas and Opelusas have their settlements, but without telling us how far they extend toward the west. He writes as follows:

The upper part of the Punta Cortada [Pointe Coupée] as it approaches the Mississippi, in inhabited by the Acadians[20], who abandoned their country in the year 1714, when France ceded Acadia to England. . . . Forty miles below the Punta Cortada the cultivation of the soil is divided between cotton and rice. . . . A large part of those who engage in this cultivation are Germans,

[19]See *Pichardo's Treatise* . . . , Vol. I, p. 23, n. 3.
[20]See *Pichardo's Treatise* . . . , Vol. II, p. 7, n. 19.

for the most part old inhabitants of the colony, who support themselves
comfortably by the fruits of their lands. Their houses, commodiously built,
are much cleaner and better furnished than those of the Acadians. Like them,
they are kindly and hospitable, and prompt to aid the travellers whom business
or bad weather obliges to disembark on their coasts; these have retained the
name of German Coasts [Costas de Alemanes]. The inhabitants of Louisiana
gave the name *bayú* [bayou] to a species of canal which extends from a river
to the sea, and which, when the said river is not flooded, nearly always remains
dry. It is possible to go by way of one of these canals from the Mississippi
as far as the Atakapas, and from there to the Apelusas (others call them
Opelusas). These two settlements, which are held to be the most considerable
of all those in the inland region of Louisiana, extend to the west almost as
far as the Nachitoches, with whom they have intercourse. The Apelusas [who
are] in a low unhealthy country, number around eight hundred inhabitants,
while the Atacapas, whose lands are rich, high, and healthful, have at least
2,000, who live in the greatest comfort and convenience. These two settlements produce a large quantity of cotton, as well as maize, rice, and some
excellent legumes. The inhabitants, among whom are many Americans, are
active, industrious, and good workers. If they were able to obtain labor
[*brazos*] at small expense, there is no doubt that this section of the colony
would become speedily of the greatest importance. From the Atacapas there
are obtained peltries of medium quality, and some cattle for consumption in
New Orleans. In each one of these establishments there is a garrison of fifty
to sixty men, whose commandant is a captain or a lieutenant colonel. The
profitable trade of these posts, as well as that of all those which are on the
banks of the Mississippi, causes them to be solicited with much activity by the
superior officers, almost all of whom, after having resided there some years,
retire with a considerable fortune.

1560. On Lafon's map these German Coasts are seen to the west
of the Mississippi, and the coast of the Atacapas and Opelusas is
somewhat beyond the Río Bermellon . But because of this circumstance of their being beyond the Río Bermellon, can the French
say that they are in the territory of Louisiana? By no means. For
although the act is certain, the right does not exist. I mean that,
although iniquitous Frenchmen, by going beyond the Río Bermellon, occupied the territory of the Atacapas and Opelusas, they
did so unjustly and without any right and by trespassing the
dividing line which they themselves had established in accordance
with the rule of Señor Marca concerning the divergence of the
waters that flow toward their rivers. When D'Anville drew his
map, he ran the line on it in such a way that the Atacapas and
Opelusas Indians remained in the dominions of Spain, and he
even had so little information about them, that he could say only

that the Atacapas Indians (of the Opelusas he does not say even a single word because, as is inferred, he had not the least knowledge of or information about them) were nomads and anthropophagi, that is to say, they were accustomed to eat human flesh. But Monsieur du Pratz,[21] in spite of having lived many years in Louisiana, also had not the slightest knowledge of the Opelusas, and for that reason did not say a single word about them. I infer this from the fact that throughout his *Diccionario de América,* Señor Alcedo[22] makes not the slightest mention of these Indians, and he would have done so without doubt if he had found some mention of them in Du Pratz, as he did with all the others which Du Pratz noted, he being the guide who led him to all the Indians belonging to Louisiana of whom he treats, just as the *Teatro Americano* of Villa-Señor[23] was his guide in all the articles in which he treats of the settlements of New Spain belonging to her viceroyalty. Even of the Atacapas he had merely some very superficial notions, such as those that the same Señor Alcedo reveals to us in his article "Atacapas," in which he writes as follows:

Atacapas: A barbarous nation of Indians of Louisiana which inhabits the seacoast to the west. They are called thus because they are cannibals, and in their language the name means "eaters of human flesh." Although they trade and communicate with the Europeans, little is known of their customs, except that the French have persuaded them to cease the barbarous custom of eating their fellowmen.

1561. When Señor Alcedo says that these Indians belong to Louisiana and that they inhabit the seacoast to the west, it must not be understood that he is speaking of all the Atacapas Indians living west of the Río Bermellon, because Du Pratz did not know or treat of these. Neither he nor any Frenchman of his time entered their lands, with the sole exception of the lands of those who were accustomed to withdraw to the banks of the Mississippi and to live between this river and D'Anville's line. These were not many in number, nor was their stay there prolonged. For that reason, although they traded and communicated with the Euro-

---

[21]For frequent references to Le Page du Pratz, consult the indices to *Pichardo's Treatise* . . . , Vols. I, II, and III.

[22]For frequent references to Antonio de Alcedo y Bexarano, consult the indices to *Pichardo's Treatise* . . . , Vols. I, II, and III.

[23]For frequent references to José Antonio de Villa-Señor y Sánchez, consult the indices to *Pichardo's Treatise* . . . , Vols. I, II, and III.

peans, the latter knew little about their customs. On the contrary, they would have known a great deal if these Indians had been numerous and had remained for a long time in that part of Louisiana.

1562. According to the Military Gentleman,[24] the author of the short treatise which is found in document 72, number 18, Monsieur Du Pratz lived in Louisiana from 1718 to 1734, in which year he returned to France, and in 1758 he published his *Historia de la Louisiana* [*Histoire de la Louisiane*]. Although in the twenty-four years that elapsed between his return to France and the publication of his work, the French could have acquired the information about these Indians that Du Pratz could not obtain, because of their having penetrated as far as their posts located a long distance to the west of the Río Bermellon, it is clearly shown that this trespass of the French did not take place, at least not in the twelve years that elapsed between 1734, when Du Pratz returned, and 1746, the year of the publication of D'Anville's map, because in this case D'Anville would have known of these circumstances. If the lands of the Atacapas and Opelusas had been already occupied by the French, he would have drawn his line farther west and would have made it pass through these lands. He did not do so; therefore the French during the said twelve years did not occupy the lands of the Opelusas and Atacapas.

1563. Moreover, in the six years elapsing between 1746 and 1752, in which the English reprinted D'Anville's map with corrections, as we have stated above in paragraph 50, this trespass still had not taken place, for otherwise the English, in order to improve D'Anville's map and to give it greater value, would have changed the dividing line, and would have fixed with greater exactness the location of the Atacapas and Opelusas. They did not do so; furthermore, there appears in our documents absolutely no report or complaint to indicate that the French might have penetrated as far as the said Indians.

1564. In the following five years from 1752 to 1757, in which Señor Don Jacinto Barrios was governor of the province of Texas, there is found not the least indication that the French might have trod the path from the Río Bermellon to the lands on which

---

[24]See *Pichardo's Treatise* . . . , Vol. I, p. 23, n. 4.

usually the Atacapas and Opelusas were living. Although it is most certain that the French, toward the end of the government of Señor Barrios, began to attempt to settle on the lands of the Indians in question, the zeal of that governor did everything possible to expel them from there. Let Monsieur Blanplain [Blancpain], whose story we give in Part II, beginning with paragraph 847, confirm this. But even this Frenchman did not come by land. He penetrated mostly by way of the Río de la Trinidad as far as the place on the banks of this river that he chose for his settlement. But he was taken from it and expelled in 1757 by the said Señor Barrios, even though he determined that his establishment was not made as a vassal of the king of France, but upon becoming a vassal of our Catholic monarch, by permission of Governor Barrios, as Father Morfi states, cited in Part II, paragraph 853. A presidio was even placed there for the purpose of preventing other such entrances of Frenchmen, a presidio that had been proposed for the same purposes, as Señor Bonilla told us in Part II, paragraph 847, in the time of Governor Don Prudencio de Orobio y Basterra, who governed from 1737 to 1741.

1565. During the time of Governor Don Angel de Martos y Navarrete, the successor to Señor Barrios, toward the end of the year 1757, two other Frenchmen came in, I do not know whether by land or sea (I believe it was rather by land, leaving from Nachitoches), and went beyond the meridian of the mouth of the Río Bermellon. These were, as we have seen (*ibid.*, paragraph 852), Monsieur Massé and Monsieur de Cortableau. Monsieur Massé established himself in a rancheria which, according to Señor Navarrete, was to the east, and according to Father Morfi, to the north, of the Río de Flores, which was east of the Río de los Adaes, or Sabinas, and Monsieur Cortableau settled a short distance from him. French audacity and effrontery led these men to occupy Spanish territory without any more authority or title than the one that they themselves formed and that the perfidious consent of the señor governor, Navarrete, gave them. In order to conceal from our government this consent which he had given them, the latter reported (see document 70, number 4) that he had feigned ignorance of their settlement, because of the fact that perhaps if he had opposed them and told them to go back to their Louisiana and they had turned a deaf ear to him, it might have been necessary to expel them by force, and this might have brought about some bad consequences between the two crowns of Spain and France.

1566. This condescension, consent, and consideration on the part of Governor Martos was the cause of the French, by going beyond the dividing line, having proceeded to establish themselves in the lands of the Atacapas and Opelusas, especially after Louisiana came into the possession of Spain. For from that time on they settled there in great numbers and they even dared to occupy the land from the Río de Sabinas to the Río de Nechas, particularly when at the order of his Majesty the presidio of Los Adaes was abandoned. This is what Don Antonio Gil Ybarbo stated to Señor Don Hugo Oconor, above in paragraph 1526, in a letter whose words are as follows:

Your lordship should know that at present there are Frenchmen living in each of the interior nations for the sole purpose of trading. They have built houses and stocked them with goods of all kinds. This is the case with the Orcoquizas, the Vidais, [at] Paso de Tomás, in Texas, [at] San Pedro, [with] the Quichas, the Nacodoches—among the Aix there is an Englishman—and all the other nations to the Brazos de Dios along the San Xavier road. This fact which I call to your lordship's attention will be confirmed by everyone, and the señor governor knows it well. We had no sooner come [away] than the French settled among all those nations, as we were advised by a Spaniard who, being ill, had remained there and had come on later. Also we were so informed by a Frenchman, one of the said traders, who arrived with some Indians.

1567. This same condescension and compliance was the cause of the said Martos' meddling where he had no business—for the matter appertained solely to the sovereigns of Spain and France—and doing what resulted in notable damage to the possessions of our Catholic monarch. I refer to the forming of boundaries between the dominion of Spain and France in order to conceal his perfidy in having given the French his permission to establish their said settlements when the said limits already existed, admitted at any rate by France on D'Anville's map. Let us hear what the same Señor Martos wrote on this point to the most excellent señor viceroy, the Marquis of Las Amarillas (*ibid.*, number 3):

In my reply on this article, which your Excellency will find in the cited testimony, I have indicated and denied to the governor of New Orleans what I considered improper, with the caution that this matter of limits demands. Your Excellency will find that everything that may tolerate the French nation making settlements on this side of the line which I established along the Río de los Adaes, or Mexicano, to its mouth, without any prejudice to the other rights of our sovereign, will in the future clearly expose to evident danger the entire frontier of the Mexican Gulf.

What hypocrisy! What perfidy! In order to conceal his ineptness in having permitted these French settlements, he attempted to show himself a loyal vassal and good governor by designating to the French a dividing line very hurtful to the rights of the king, his master. And who authorized Señor Martos to form of the Río de los Adaes, or Mexicano, to its mouth a dividing line beyond which the French could not go? If the lands which were to the east of this Río Mexicano were recognized as belonging to our Catholic sovereign even by France herself, by this same act of adopting D'Anville's line—which, far from taking them from Spain, left them to her, since they fell west of the line—why did Señor Navarrete cede them to France? The very few Frenchmen who had begun to settle on them should have been arrested and sent to Mexico to the most excellent señor viceroy, as Señor Barrios had done with Blanpain. This would not have been difficult since there were so few. He should have investigated carefully to find all those who had come to inhabit those lands and should have cleared them of that entire brood, so pernicious to our possessions. Because it was not done in subsequent years, the number of Frenchmen in those lands grew so fast after Louisiana was given to Spain that the señores governors of New Orleans extended their command to the Río Nechas.

1568. But for a perfect understanding of what Señor Martos ceded to the French, let us examine the location of the places on which the Frenchmen Massé and Cortebleau settled. Let us also ascertain the river to which he gives the name of Los Adays. Above in paragraph 725, while discussing the Adaes, we found that those Indians lived near the Río de Sabinas. This is the one that D'Anville calls Río de los Adays and which he also calls Mexicano where it enters the sea. Señor Martos, like D'Anville, called the Río de Sabinas by these names. Consequently, when he says that Massé and Cortableau established their *ranchos* on this side of the Río de los Adays (in order to understand this phrase

of Señor Martos we should know that he was speaking in his
representation to the most excellent señor viceroy of New Spain,
whose capital is in Mexico City, located south-southwest of the
presidio of Los Adaes where Martos had his residence, and since
this presidio is east of the Sabinas and Flores rivers, he was speaking correctly when he used the words "on this side of the Río de
los Adaes and before reaching the Río de las Flores") he meant
that these *ranchos* were near the Río de Sabinas.

1569. Although at first sight it seems that Señor Martos left the
impression that these Frenchmen settled in the same parallel as
the presidio of Nachitoches, in reality he says nothing except that
they were found in the parallel of the entrance of the Red River
into the Mississippi. As a matter of fact, he could not say that
they were in the parallel of the presidio of Nachitoches, because
this presidio, as we have said in Part II, paragraph 832, is in
31° 50′ of latitude. Hence the *ranchos* of Massé and Cortableau
should have been in the same latitude, assuming that they were
in the same parallel. But this could not be, for the presidio of
Los Adaes, being in 31° 40′ of latitude, thus would necessarily
be to the south of these rancherias. And at what distance? The
presidio of Nachitoches, with relation to the presidio of Los Adaes,
is ten minutes farther north. These equal four leagues according
to the table in Part II, paragraph 28. Consequently, if the *ranchos*
of Massé and Cortableau were in the same parallel as Nachitoches,
they would be ten minutes north, or rather northwest, of the presidio of Los Adaes, or, which is the same, four leagues distant.
Therefore these Frenchmen and the others who may have come
to establish their *ranchos* near theirs, in spreading toward the
south, which was what they chiefly desired to do, not only would
have taken the lands of Spain north of the presidio of Los Adaes,
but even the road itself, which connected Béjar with the said presidio of Los Adaes.

1570. The Most Reverend Father Morfi knew better how to de-
'scribe the French establishments, when he wrote as follows, as we
have seen in Part II, paragraph 857:

Before sending this report, his Excellency received a dispatch from Governor
Barrios, in which he advised him that the French, not taking warning from
the death of Blanpain, continued to enter our possessions. For to the south
of Los Adaes, and to the north of the little Río de las Flores, Monsieur Massé

had settled himself on a rancheria, . . . as had Monsieur de Cortableau a short distance away. . . .

1571. Father Morfi's gainsaying that those rancherias were south [north?] of Los Adaes shows that Señor Navarrete was trying to leave the impression that they were located on the parallel of the mouth of the Red River, since, as is seen on the maps, the parallel of this mouth is found to the south of Los Adaes. But notwithstanding the fact that from the place that we have called the ford of Señor Rivera to Los Adaes there are nineteen leagues, there ought to be that many, or almost as many, from the same river to the meridian that passes through the presidio of Los Adaes and continues toward the south. Consequently, once these rancherias were located near the Río de los Adaes and the Río de las Flores, they would not fall to the south of Los Adaes, as Father Morfi says, but rather south-southwest, or approximately in that direction, and what Señor Martos might truthfully have said to the most excellent señor viceroy [was that they were] on this side of the Río de los Adaes and before reaching the small Río de las Flores.

1572. If the location of the said *ranchos* was to the south, as Father Morfi states, or rather to the south-southwest [of Los Adaes], as we have inferred, the other Frenchmen could very well extend their settlements by descending and spreading from the parallel of Monsieur Massé toward various points on the coast. For this is the same parallel that passes through the entrance of the Red into the Mississippi (which is in 30° 54′ of latitude) and should terminate in the same latitude on the Río de Sabinas. This parallel will be a kind of line with which will be determined the northern limits of the possessions which Señor Martos gave to the French. From this elevation [*altura*] of the pole another line must be drawn to the banks of the same Río de Sabinas [and along it] as far as its entrance into the sea; and these will be the western limits. The southern limits will be the entire coast of the Gulf of Mexico from the mouth of this same river to the mouth of the Mississippi at the entrance called Pasa del Sudoeste [Southwest Pass], which is the westernmost entrance; and the eastern limits [will be] the same Mississippi from the said Pasa del Sudoeste to the said mouth [of the Red River]. For

in truth all this vast territory, with the exception of the area between D'Anville's line and the said Mississippi River, which already
belonged to France, Señor Martos took from the viceroyalty of
Mexico and gave to France. This line is indicated on our map
19, of document 74 with red dots, but we confess that we did
not designate Massé's rancheria, because we did not know exactly
where the Río de Flores rises or how it flows, and if perchance
this is the river which others call the Carcasiu,[25] the source which
we have given it should be brought down to a place south of the
said parallel, in order that Massé's said *rancho* shall be north of
the Río de las Flores; or if the Río de las Flores is the one that
Pilot Evía does not name and whose mouth he locates east of
the Mermentao, this latter [stream?] should be so drawn that
Massé's rancheria lies to the north of it.

1573. Thus this line, which Señor Martos discussed with the
greatest confusion and apparently without wishing to be understood, is explained with complete clarity. He had previously proposed another which is exactly the same one that we have given
for the eastern limits. And since he believed, or rather suggested
to our government, that the French could never consent to this
line because it was very prejudicial to them—taking from them
the territory between the Mississippi and D'Anville's line as well
as the lands of the Atacapas and Opelusas which he wished to
cede to them—he drew them the line that they desired and by
virtue of which they were to obtain, as in fact they did obtain,
possession of the lands of the Atacapas and Opelusas. With this
line drawn to please the French he harmed Spain. And he attempted to deceive our government, which he wronged severely
by supposing it to be extremely ignorant of the location of those
lands, and that, because of its ignorance, it could not know of the
harm which his dividing line would cause in case the French would
not consent. For, necessarily, they were not going to consent to
the first one that he proposed to them, which would have run along
the west bank of the Mississippi from its entrance into the sea
by way of the mouth called Paso del Sudoeste [Southwest Pass]
to where the Red River enters it.

---

[25]Pichardo on his map published in his *Treatise* . . . , Vol. II, following the
index, locates the Río Carcasiu [Calcasieu] directly east of the Sabine River.

1574. That this line as we have described it would be the same one which Señor Martos proposed with so much confusion and obscurity is shown by the following words, which are clearer and less confusing and involved, and which are an explanation of other previous ones with which he described his line (see document 70, number 17):

I consider it beneficial to the welfare of the state and for the preservation of peace between the two crowns to transfer the presidio of Los Nachitoches to the other side of the Mississippi and to let this river serve as the boundary in that region from its entrance into the sea to where it receives the Colorado [Red], and if this may not be possible, let this line be altered in favor of France by setting it at the Río de los Adaes, or Mexicano, as far as the entrance of the latter into the Río Colorado [Red River].

1575. That statement "and if this may not be possible, let this line be altered in favor of France by setting it at the Río de los Adaes or Mexicano as far as the entrance of the latter into the Río Colorado" explains sufficiently Señor Martos' line. Because he states clearly enough that from the mouth of the Río de los Adaes, or Sabinas, this line follows the banks of this river northward up to a certain point, and from there turns directly toward the east, to the entrance of the Red into the Mississippi, which is exactly what we have found out. The point on the Río de Sabinas up to which the line has to go from its mouth, is the one found in latitude 30° 54′, which is the same latitude as the aforesaid mouth [of the Red River], and the same, without doubt, in which Massé's *rancho* was located. In order to understand better with how much malice and confusion Señor Martos wrote, attention need only be called to those words "to transfer the presidio of Los Nachitoches to the other side of the Mississippi and to let this river serve as the boundary in that region from its entrance into the sea to where it received the Colorado."

In another suggestion that he makes with regard to the establishment of this line he states, as we shall see, that the presidio of Nachitoches should be moved to the east bank of the Red River in order that the west bank of this river, from its entrance into the Mississippi to where it divides into two branches, etc., may serve as limits for Spain, so that all the territory bounded by this line may belong to this power. Here, changing his tune, he wants the presidio of Nachitoches to be moved beyond the Mississippi in order that this great and famous river may be the one that forms the limits.

1576. But, comprehending Señor Martos' scheme, [one knows that] his desire was not for the Mississippi to be the boundary, beginning where the Red River enters it, but that it should be the Red River itself. First, because the French were certainly in possession of all the territory which lies between the Red and the Misssisippi and it would not be probable that they would give it up. Second, because he expressly states that the first dividing line should be the Mississippi from its entrance into the sea to the entrance of the Red River into it; and that the second dividing line should be the Red River from its entrance into the Mississippi to where it separates into two branches. Thus either he was a man who absolutely did not know how to express himself, or he spoke very maliciously and did not wish to be understood. But the impression he wished to leave was that the presidio óf Nachitoches, located east of Los Adaes, where he lived, should be moved farther east, that is, to the east bank of the Red River, in order that the west bank might remain free from French settlement, and might serve as boundary for the Spanish territories.

1577. The other words in which he treats of his said boundaries are as follows (document 70, number 8) :

I believe that the Mississippi River would be, under the present conditions, the most appropriate boundary for both sovereignties as far as the Seno Mexicano is concerned, at least from the latitude in which the Río Colorado [Red River] joins it. This is about forty or fifty leagues from New Orleans. In this case they should transfer the presidio of Los Nachitoches, located today forty leagues from the Mississippi and facing ours of Los Adaes, to the other side of the same principal river (this is, as we have said, the Colorado [Red]). Thus the three barbarian nations of Chitimacha, Opelusas, and Atacapas, who live from the Mississippi to the Río de la Trinidad, would remain [on our side], and the whole region that comprises the Seno Mexicano, from the said confluence of the two rivers, where I fix the first line, would be considered as belonging to these possessions. . . .

1578. If France should object to being deprived of the area from the mouth of the Mississippi to where it receives the Río Colorado [Red River], either because within this region (that is, the region of the Río Colorado—a useless explanation but, on the other hand, very necessary to avoid errors) they have established their presidio of Nachitoches, and on its parallel (that is, on the parallel of the entrance of the Red River into the Mississippi) Monsieur de Massé and Monsieur de Cortableau have their rancherias;

Or perhaps because, having travelled over all that area as far as the Río de los Adaes, or Mexicano (this is false, because they had always kept within D'Anville's line, and only during the last days of the government of Señor Barrios, who protested vigorously, had they begun to travel over those lands, Massé and Cortableau being the first ones), they may claim it as belonging to their colony:

I believe that—substituting for my first dividing line that of the same Río de los Adaes from its mouth, past our presidio of the same name, to the point on the second line on the Río Colorado [Red River] (that is, beginning at the entrance of the Río de los Adaes, or Sabinas, into the sea and ascending along its bank as far as latitude 31° 54′ and then turning east, making it pass south of the presidio of Los Adaes, and continuing as far as the entrance of the Red into the Mississippi—and if this explanation be not admitted, let another be given which may explain completely what Señor Martos is discussing here), and fixing unchanged the others that I am proposing (of these other lines which Señor Martos suggests here we shall speak later in a more appropriate place)—it would be much more advantageous to suspend our plan for making new advances along the coast of the Seno Mexicano.

In effect, the Gallo-Spaniards of Louisiana advanced along this coast, for they penetrated as far as the Río de Nechas. For this reason the Señor Barón de Ripperdá, Don Luis Cazorla, and others said above, in paragraph 1553, that this Río de Nechas separates Louisiana from the province of Texas in the coast region, and that the other side of the Río de Nechas is under the jurisdiction of New Orleans.

1579. Here we have the two lines. The first is the one that begins at the mouth of the Mississippi and ends at the entrance of the Red River into it. The second begins at this entrance and follows along the Red River as far as a certain point of which we shall speak later. And in case the French should object to the first, as it was clear they would do because of the harm it would mean to them, he [Martos] suggested the one conceived by his perfidy and agreed upon with the commandant of Nachitoches. It is the one that would run along the parallel of the entrance of the Red into the Mississippi, and of Massé's *rancho,* and descend by the east bank of the Río Sabinas to its mouth.

1580. But what should be noted most particularly is that, while the line of Señor Martos took from Spain all the territory lying between the east bank of the Río de Sabinas and D'Anville's line south of the parallel of Massé's *rancho,* it gave to her everything that falls north of the said parallel and terminates at the Red

River. Hence by this line Spain should be mistress of the land that extends north from the entrance of the Red into the Mississippi, running along the east bank of the Red. But in their iniquity the French of Natchitoches, in taking possession of the territory which Señor Martos' line gave them, neither removed their presidio of Nachitoches nor did they leave to Spain the territory agreed upon, beginning at the entrance of the Red into the Mississippi. Instead, they kept it.

1581. The oldest document that I can remember having read, which mentioned the Opelusas, is this one of Señor Martos Navarrete, in which, in his number 8, he writes the most excellent señor viceroy of Mexico the following, which has already been copied, to wit:

> I believe that the Mississippi River would be, under the present conditions, the most appropriate boundary for both sovereignties as far as the Seno Mexicano is concerned, at least from the latitude in which the Río Colorado [Red River] joins it. This is about forty or fifty leagues from New Orleans. In this case they should transfer the presidio of Los Nachitoches, located today forty leagues from the Mississippi and facing ours of Los Adaes, to the other side of the same principal river. Thus the three barbarian nations of Chitimacha, Opelusa, and Atacapas, who live from the Mississippi to the Río de la Trinidad, would remain [on our side], and the whole region that comprises the Seno Mexicano, from the said confluence of the two rivers, where I fix the first line, would be considered as belonging to these possessions. . . .

> 1582. If France should object to being deprived of the area from the mouth of the Mississippi to where it receives the Río Colorado [Red River], either because within this region they have established their presidio of Nachitoches, and on its parallel Monsieur de Massé and Monsieur de Cortableau have their rancherias; or perhaps because, having travelled over all that area as far as the Río de los Adaes, or Mexicano, they may claim it as belonging to their colony: I believe that—substituting for my first dividing line that of the same Río de Los Adaes from its mouth, past our presidio of the same name, to the point on the second line on the Río Colorado [Red River], and fixing unchanged the others that I am proposing—it would be much more advantageous to suspend our plan for making new advances along the coast of the Seno Mexicano.

But at the same time that he mentions the Opelusas he also states that the lands of these Indians, as well as those of the Atacapas, had already been explored by the French, and that, for this reason, the latter could claim all this territory for their colony.

1583. The very fact that the information concerning the Opelusas was so scarce, down to the time of Señor Martos, that neither
the French nor the Spaniards spoke of them in all the documents
that we have collected, tells us clearly that neither the Spaniards
nor the French had penetrated into that territory. The Spaniards
had not done so, because from San Antonio de Béjar they went
only as far as the presidio of Los Adaes, and settled only that
strip of land with the four missions which they placed on it. Thus
they did not go south of Los Adaes and of the missions of Los
Aes, of Los Nacodoches, of La Concepción los Aynais, and of San
Francisco de los Nechas, in order to reconnoiter the land and inquire about the nations of the Atacapas and Opelusas. There is
not the slightest evidence to the contrary. Rather, all the diaries
tell us that the expeditionaries and travellers who went to Los
Adaes went neither to the right nor to the left of the road that
they took. Nor is it clear that those who lived in the missions
spread to the north or south of them for the purpose of recon-
noitering the lands and inquiring as to the Indians who inhabited
them. The urgency of arriving at their desinations gave the travellers no opportunity for these detours, and the many occupations
of the missionaries and of the few people whom they had with
them did not give them time to make these reconnaissances,
although it is true that it is evident that our missionaries left
their districts and made extremely long journeys to give spiritual
aid to the Indians who solicited them or to go and seek and bring
back to their homes the apostates and fugitive Indians. See Part
I, beginning with number 419.

1584. But this failure of the Spaniards should not prejudice
them or be the cause for their losing the lands of the Opelusas
and Atacapas, or for the French taking them away from them. The
Spaniards, as we have seen in Part I, beginning with paragraph
419, need many things for settling among the Indians, and by
their laws, as we there state, beginning with paragraph 142, they
could not make any new settlements until those they might be
making at the time were perfected. Consequently they were in no
condition to go and occupy the lands of the Opelusas and Atacapas, although they were anxious to do so whenever they might
have an opportunity for it. And for the reasons which we gave

in paragraph 132, they should not have lost their right to those lands, nor should the French have acquired it in order to settle them. Is it not a surprising and detestable thing that the French should attempt to acquire dominion over the lands which in all justice and right belonged to the Spaniards, just because of the fact that one worthless and despicable little Frenchman, leaving the comfort which civilization furnishes in the settlements, should, because of a most sordid interest, go to live in a hut among the barbarian Indians with whom he cannot enjoy even the least of the comforts which is available in the settlements? Then, just because this profligate Frenchman, I say—by hiding from the Spaniards, mingling with the Indians, nourishing their vices, embracing their perverted habits and customs, adapting himself to their barbarous manner of living, dressing, and eating (see what we have said in this regard in Part I, paragraph 425)—goes to live among them, the French should be allowed to acquire a title to that land? What is this? Where is our good faith? Where the law of nations? Where the good feeling that they should maintain among themselves?

1585. How aptly might we have used these expressions of Don Martín de Alarcón,[26] cited above in paragraph 331, when he writes the following words:

> During the time that the government was in my charge, I always exercised all the care and vigilance possible to prevent the French from trading in the places that I had reduced. This, I understand, has been their purpose, and not settlement, and I earnestly believe that they would have succeeded, had it not been for the opposition I offered, in order to dislodge them. Finding myself in a certain place, and being informed that they were six leagues away, I sent two soldiers with a letter for the leader of the said French to find out whether the news I had was correct. It turned out, in fact, to be true, but there were only twenty-five Frenchmen—five men and twenty naked and barefoot boys, who were lodged in some huts without any sort of shelter or protection. They saw in another hut much clothing, whose value at a conservative estimate would be about 200,000 pesos.

What a fortune to be guarded by such few and poorly-equipped men, and in such miserable buildings! Aside from this, in the letter cited above in paragraph 678, that military officer, an eyewitness, said to his friend:

---

[26]See *Pichardo's Treatise* . . . , Vol. II, p. 101, n. 2.

From the Río de Sabinas, which the American wants, to the Arroyo Hondo, there are probably over twenty-five leagues of pure forest, settled only by one or two French ranchos, which have only four cows, corn enough for their use, which they plant, and a piece of land in tobacco. This is the territory in dispute.

1586. In truth, just because two French vagabonds, Massé and Cortableau, were seized by the desire to come and settle south of Los Adaes, next to a river which Señor Navarrete calls the Adaes, or Mexicano—and which is the Sabinas—without any other authority or title than they themselves drew up, or rather with the disloyal and perfidious consent of Señor Martos Navarrete, the French claim that the territory is theirs and that, consequently, everything that lies east of it as far as the Mississippi is theirs also. Thus other Frenchmen came after these, and they continued to settle in various places of that common territory, as in a country belonging to their nation or irreclaimable by the Spaniards.

1587. Spaniards! Reject the unworthy procedure of Governor Martos. Living in Los Adaes, he would certainly have information concerning the day and the hour in which the settlement of the daring Massé and Cortableau was begun. Consequently, he should have torn up this spreading venomous plant in order that it might not propagate by growing and strengthening itself. If he had done this by apprehending them and confiscating their goods, and had sent them to Mexico to the most excellent señor viceroy, all the subsequent damage would have been avoided. In my opinion—and it may be that I am mistaken, and may God grant that it be so—Governor Martos was a traitor and a hypocrite. Bound to the French because of the trade that he had with them, as we shall see later, he attempted to deceive our government with plausible words to the effect that in order to avoid bad consequences between the two crowns of Spain and France, he had found himself obliged not to expel Massé and Cortableau. Also, that in order to keep the French from making further advances he had designated the Río de los Adaes, or Mexicano, as the final boundary for them. [And, finally,] in order to make their activities less conspicuous and more excusable, he proposed the limits that he schemed to establish between the two crowns. These were fixed on the banks of the Mississippi from where it enters the sea to the place where the Red River, or the Nachitoches, flows into it (the first dividing line proposed by him); thence, from the said mouth, following the right bank (one supposes here, as one should, that on descending this river from the north, its left bank is the one that lies toward the region of Los Adaes) of the said Red River as far as the fort of Nachitoches—and in order that this line might not be deflected, the French should move their fort to the left bank, so that all the land that lies between the presidio of Los Adaes and the right bank of the Red River would fall to Spain; thence, following the same bank to the place where the Río de los Cadodochos enters the Red (near this junction the Nasotites are found on one side and the Natsos on the other; to the west of the latter and on the same river are the Quirereches; and on the bank of the same river and in the same westerly direction are found the Canecis Indians—see the maps of D'Anville and Michel), the second line proposed by Señor Martos ends, at the confluence of these two rivers. In another more opportune place we shall give an explanation of the other lines that ascend toward the north.

1588. Because of the calculated and most criminal negligence of the said Señor Martos Navarrete in not dislodging the French from the Opelusas and Atacapas, when, following its cession by France to Spain, Louisiana entered into the dominions of our sovereign, the first governor of Louisiana, the Most Excellent Señor Don Antonio de Ulloa, mistakenly believed that they belonged to his government. As a result he began to exercise the acts of jurisdiction that did not belong to him, for the will of the king, our lord—when he received Louisiana—was that the governor of it should govern precisely and solely the lands which had been legally, clearly, and manifestly recognized as belonging to the French possessions; that all the [other] lands should be governed by the most excellent señores viceroys of this New Spain; and that the Laws of the Indies should not be in force in Louisiana. Thus by separating, without the king's consent, the lands that lie east of the Río de las Adaes, or Mexicano—that is, the Sabinas— from the government of new Spain, the enjoyment of their jurisdiction and command in those lands was taken from the said most excellent señores viceroys with notable injury to their authority, just as it was later taken from the señores commandants-general of the Interior Provinces. The same injury was occasioned to the royal subordinate magistrates; to the most illustrious bishops of Guadalajara, and later to those of the kingdom of Nuevo León, because the territory of their diocese was diminished; and finally, to the Holy Tribunal of the Faith [the Inquisition], because the authority which it had freely and promptly to apprehend and prosecute the criminals of whom it might learn was restricted.

1589. Let us hear the following cedula, issued on these matters, which is found in document 39, number 290:

> My viceroy, governor, and captain-general of the kingdom of New Spain, and president of my royal audiencia of Mexico: Having named the naval captain of my royal armada, Don Antonio de Ulloa, so that he may go as governor of the province of Louisiana—which has been ceded to me by the Most Christian King, my cousin, and has been added to my crown—to take possession of it by virtue of the dispatches of that sovereign, which will be sent to you by my *Secretario del Despacho de Estado*, with the corresponding orders; and, having decided that the system of government in this new acquisition shall not be changed for the present, and, consequently, that in no way shall it be subjected to the laws and rulings which are observed in my possessions in the Indies—it shall be considered as a separate colony, even as regards trade with them [the Indies]. It shall enjoy the same independence of the Ministry of the Indies, its Council, and the other tribunals connected with it, everything appertaining to it to go through the Ministry of State, and only by this means shall the said governor report everything that may occur relative to his charge and receive in the same way the orders, instructions, and everything the government and direction of that new independent possession may embrace. You will hereby take note of it and will inform the tribunals, governor, and others to whom this may apply in the district of that viceroyalty. Given in Aranjuez, on May 21, 1765. I the King. Don Julián de Arriaga.

1590. In volume 9, page 290 of the representations to the court by the viceroyalty of Mexico, is found the copy of a letter of the most excellent señor viceroy, the Marquis of Cruillas,[27] written to the most excellent señor *bailío*, Fray Don Julián de Arriaga, the tenor of which is as follows:

> *My dear señor:* As soon as Don Antonio de Ulloa may ask me for the support of troops (or any other aid), for the settlement he is going to establish at the place of Cheli Manchac [Chetimachas] for the pacification of several Indian tribes on the confines of Louisiana and New Mexico, according to the project of Don Antonio de Olivera, I shall furnish him with them as your

[27]Joaquín de Monserrat, the Marquis of Cruillas, was viceroy of New Spain from 1760 to 1766.

Excellency is pleased to direct me in your letter of October 22 of last year. God keep, etc. March 17, 1776. Señor Arriaga.

1591. We learn from this letter that the Most Excellent Señor Ulloa established a settlement, or a presidio with troops, in the pueblo of the Chetimachas Indians, of whom we have spoken in Part II, paragraph 94, for the purpose of keeping at peace various Indian tribes on the confines of Louisiana and New Mexico in accordance with the project of Don André de Olivera. This presidio, since it had been placed among the Chetimachas, should have served principally for keeping at peace the Atacapas and Opelusas Indians, who were the ones adjacent to it. We see here how the government of Louisiana was extending its authority over these Indians. I do not know whether the same most excellent señor, Ulloa, placed a lieutenant-governor at a post belonging to the Atacapas and Opelusas, in order that he might govern the French who have settled there and keep the Indians down with his troops, so that they would not attack the vassals of our Catholic King, but I do know that his successor, Señor Don Luis de Unzaga y Amézaga, placed one there.

1592. In document 44, number 31, a letter is found, written to the Barón de Ripperdá, of the following tenor:

My dear señor: It having been the pleasure of Señor de Unzaga,[28] governor-general of this province, to appoint me, in the name of his Catholic Majesty, his lieutenant-governor of the two posts called Atacapas and Opelusas and their dependencies, for the purpose of upholding the military discipline so necessary to good order, as it is so little known among the people who inhabit these parts, I flatter myself that I am carrying out his intentions. I shall see to it that in the future no one under my orders goes into the territory of that government without your honor's permission. Señor de Mézières pointed out to me upon my arrival those persons who had ventured to do so, and I have not hesitated to punish them severely, in such manner that they will always regret their error or excess.

1593. The bearer of these presents is a good and brave subject, an old colonist in the service of France, and at present captain of one of the two companies under my command. Upon his arrival he will be pleased to comply with all the orders which your honor may see fit to give him with regard to the number of mules, horses, asses, etc., so much needed in the capital of this

[28]"In 1769, when O'Reilly set out for Louisiana, he brought [Luis de] Unzaga [y Amézaga] along to be governor of the province, a capacity in which the latter served for approximately seven years."—Caughey, *Bernardo de Gálvez in Louisiana, 1776–1783,* p. 43.

province which, by his Majesty's orders, must supply each year for Havana a quantity of lumber and eighty thousand sugar casks, under a contract made with the king.

1594. I have likewise charged this officer who will have the honor to be near you, to make known to the red men, or Indians, whom he may encounter on his route the advantages there will be in living in peace and subjection to your honor's orders. He is to give you information about all those whom he may encounter in the territory of that government without a passport from your honor. I have the confidence to flatter myself, because of the zeal that I recognize in him, that he will fulfill his charge exactly, and this makes me request your honor's kindness in his favor. I am enclosing or sending along two letters from the señor governor of Louisiana, with which he favors me and which he requests that I send on to your honor.

1595. It would flatter me infinitely to be informed of your needs, so that I might send you aid by water, in view of your present difficulties in carrying it by mule train or on pack horses. To be of service to you would be a great honor to me, and I shall always regard correspondence with you as a good fortune. Moreover, I have the advantage of knowing your honor's noble family. I am from Flanders, allied to the house of Rupelmonde, a neighbor and friend of that of Bakelaer and of Creubec. If these names are known to you, I can give you further information on another occasion.

1596. I request, my governor, that you be pleased to give a passport to this officer for the safety of his return journey and for a second trip, which I shall not have him make unless it is your pleasure. In default of this I shall sooner see the province do without the said stock, though they are so badly needed for the preparation of the said supplies for Havana. Your honor will please order that all the animals from the jurisdiction of that government be countermarked, or branded, in order that I may be enabled to confiscate those in the territory under my command which are found without this mark, the lack of which will be sufficient to indicate them as stolen, in which case I shall have the honor to advise you of it.

1597. I shall agree to everything that you may consider necessary, both as regards the men who drive the mules, and as regards the purchase price. I should be pleased if two of the same color can be sent, distinct or separate from the others, for the señor governor, and I shall agree to everything that you may wish to specify. Please do not fail to send your orders likewise, for I shall esteem it a pleasure to be of use to you and to carry out your commands exactly, and you may count upon their fulfillment. Believing that I am complying with your honor's desires, I have written a letter to Señor Ysbarbo (he means Gil Ybarbo), commandant on the Trinity, asking that he provide an escort for the bearer of these presents so that he may arrive more safely. I am happy to be, with consideration and respect, señor governor, your honor's very humble and obedient servant. El Caballero de Clovet [Clouet.][29]. Atakapas, November 10, 1774.

[29]See *Pichardo's Treatise* . . . , Vol. III, pp. 465–468.

1598. It may be seen from this letter that Señor Unzaga named the Caballero de Clouet as his lieutenant-governor, and it is necessary to give very particular attention to the clause that says

for the purpose of upholding and enforcing in them the military discipline so necessary to good order, as it is so little known among the people who inhabit these parts.

If this good order was not known by the people who inhabited that region, it is an evident proof that the Spanish governor of Louisiana was the one who planned to introduce it. Then before France ceded Louisiana to Spain it had not been introduced. Then the French government had no governor or military officer there. Then it did not govern there. Then those lands were not French.

1599. In fact, the governor of Texas, Don Ángel Martos Navarrete, during the very few years that intervened from the beginning of his government to the cession of Louisiana and until Spain took possession of it, or, speaking more accurately, from the year 1763, in which the cession of Louisiana by France to Spain was confirmed,[30] most criminally permitted the French to occupy that country as far as the limits that he designated for them, that is, as far as the Río de los Adaes, or Mexicano. I admit freely that the opinion I have formed with regard to the conduct of Señor Martos may be wrong, but it will not be hasty, for in forming it I have been given more than enough reasons by his crimes, which are mentioned by the following cedula, found in the secretariat of the viceroyalty, in volume 92, page 221, of the royal cedula:

The King. [My] viceroy, governor, and captain-general of the provinces of New Spain, and president of my royal audiencia which resides in the City of Mexico. In a letter of June 27 of the past year, you acknowledge the receipt of a royal cedula of December 15 of the preceding year (1766) in which you were ordered to conclude and pass sentence, in conformance with the ordinances and laws, on the case that was pending in your tribunal concerning the investigation which, by order of your predecessor, Sargento Mayor Don Hugo Oconor, was to make with regard to what happened between Don Ángel Martos de Navarrete, governor of the province of the Texas, and Don Rafael Martínez Pacheco, captain of the presidio of San Agustín de Ahumada— reporting the results to me. Subsequently, in another letter of the following July 24, you have given me an account, with a certified copy of documents, of what the said Don Hugo had informed your predecessor concerning the

---

[30]See note 15, *supra.*

peculiarities of the said governor of the Texas, and, among them, that he had offered him thirty thousand pesos to get rid of Captain Pacheco. This letter either did not reach your hands or it was overlooked in the accumulation of business of that viceroyalty. But [you state] that when the duplicate reached you, you sent it on to your *asesor*, who took the deposition of the courier and of another witness to whom the latter referred him. He took steps to acquaint himself with Oconor's procedure, and he reported to you that this procedure was proper for ascertaining Martos' conduct while in office. You therefore ordered him to draw up instructions on the basis of which witnesses could be examined, and you gave a commission to the same Oconor for this purpose. You also issued an order for the arrest of Don Manuel de Soto, a Spaniard (who because of his misdemeanors had withdrawn to the presidio of Nachitos to live), for being the one whom the governor of Texas had charged with apprehending Pacheco and who was the cause for the burning of the presidio of Ahumada. And you add that in fulfillment of this commission, Don Hugo Oconor received adequate evidence and took reports from the fathers of the missions, who gave their testimony with the permission of their superiors. As the result of this the bad conduct of Don Angel Martos was clearly proven. He does not pay the soldiers even a fifth of their salaries and what he pays them is in goods, for which he charges them three or four times their regular prices. He carried on an illicit trade with the French and even with the idolatrous Indians. He had a store with its cashier for the sale of merchandise, and through this cashier he warned Don Manuel de Soto that he could not be arrested by the sargeant whom Don Hugo Oconor sent for that purpose. Because of this information and in view of the respective documents, you say that with the advice of your *asesor* you took the measure of ordering the said governor to present himself in that city within a month and for the cashier to be arrested and the goods of both to be confiscated, especially those of the store. The fulfillment of this order and that of seeking anew to arrest De Soto you entrusted to the same Don Hugo. You concluded all the above by telling me that you were informing me of it, as you had likewise proceeded in the whole matter, with the requisite secrecy and caution, because Martos had quite a number of friends and connections in that capital.

1600. Your cited letter and certified copies of documents, together with the antecedents of the matter, having been considered in my Council of the Indies, and having been explained by my *fiscal*, I have decided in a *consulta* of February 26, last, to order and command you (as I am doing) to hear fully and decide the said case as quickly as possible in accordance with law and in consultation with the *visitador*, Don José de Gálvez.[31] [You will] have it carefully considered also, in accordance with the procedure ordered to be observed, by the *auditor de guerra* of that captaincy-general, with the concurrence of the *fiscal* of that audiencia (steps that are lacking in the beginning and in the prosecution of this case). All this having been done, you will give me an account of everything in this form and in no other, so that in view of it an opinion may be formed and whatever may be considered as appropriate may

---

[31]See Chapter XVI, n. 21, *supra*.

be decided upon, for that is my will. Dated in Aranjuez, on April 21, 1768. I the King. By order of the king, our lord. Don Tomás del Mello. Here three rubrics.

1601. It is clear from this cedula that the governor of Texas, Don Ángel Martos Navarrete, was a man so shameless that he had the boldness and temerity to offer thirty thousand pesos to the judge investigating his case, Sargento Mayor Don Hugo Oconor, to get rid of or to arrest for the most serious crimes his enemy Don Rafael Martínez Pacheco, captain of the presidio of Orco-quizac. He had previously ordered him arrested, giving rise to a very notorious scandal with the most lamentable results, an account of which is given by Father Fray Juan Agustín Morfi in his *Memorias*, book 11, number 23, as follows:

For very trifling reasons, which were not concerned with the royal service, Governor Don Angel Martos de Navarrete became embittered against Don Rafael Martínez Pacheco, captain of the presidio of San Agustín de Ahumada or Horcoquizac. He wanted to arrest him at San Antonio de Béjar but his soldiers decided not to do it, and let him leave for his presidio. The governor sent a large enough group of soldiers after him to assure his arrest, with orders so rash and imprudent that as soon as they arrived at the presidio of Orcoquizac they laid formal siege to it and invested it several times in attempts to take it. Pacheco defended himself resolutely, and when the besiegers saw the poor results of their attacks, they set fire to it in several places. As all of its buildings were of wood, a fierce conflagration broke out which proceeded to reduce everything to ashes. Pacheco, to escape burning up, left by a private door accompanied by a Catalonian, and left an order with his brother, who was already wounded in the hand, to surrender. The besieging soldiers clearly saw him leave, but either because they were frightened by his courage or because they themselves detested the task with which they were charged, they gave him time to escape. Pacheco travelled many leagues with his faithful companion, on foot and without any food except that supplied by their muskets with which they made fires and killed some birds for sustenance, being all the time exposed to the danger of encountering their enemies. More than a hundred leagues from the burned presidio they met a party from Los Adaes who, ignorant of the governor's orders, gave them some food, two horses, and two bad saddles. With this aid Pacheco arrived in Mexico City where he presented himself before the señor viceroy, and after he had been held prisoner for a long time in the houses of the *cabildo*, after several reports of the act and its origin had been received, after Don Hugo Oconor had been commissioned to conduct the preliminary hearing, and after many other judicial proceedings, too long to discuss, Pacheco was reinstated in his position and in his presidio, and Martos was discharged from the governorship.

There was left pending the decision as to which of the two should reimburse the royal treasury for what had been burned and destroyed in the fire.

1602. It is also clear that the said Don Ángel Martos was a man so avaricious and unjust that he paid the soldiers only a fifth of their salaries. Even this payment was made in merchandise, [for which] he charged them three or four times more than the regular prices. And he was so corrupt and so disobedient to the laws and orders of the king, his master, that when his Majesty prohibited all trade with the French of Louisiana he, in spite of this prohibition, engaged in it and even extended it to include the idolatrous Indians who were enemies of the Spaniards. Without doubt, in the course of this trade he sold or exchanged to them for their goods, arms and munitions with which they could make war against them [the Spaniards], thus causing them to become more intractable toward subjecting themselves to the teachings of the gospel and to recognizing our Catholic monarch as their king. From this illicit trade with the French there came to him no doubt the idea of permitting the French to advance as far as the Río do los Adaes, or Mexicano, to settle, and that they should fix their boundaries there in order that he might open his trade with them more easily, aside from the gratuity which in my opinion the French might have promised him and that he would expect from them in return for giving them such permission.

1603. The duties of his office obliged him to reside in the presidio of Los Adaes, and at this post he found himself with the French facing him in Nachitoches, on his left in Cadodachos and the other northern posts, and on his right were those whom he had permitted to settle among the Atacapas and Opelusas. Surrounded by so many Frenchmen, how large and extensive would be his trade with them? In order, therefore, to keep the good will of this nation; in order to enjoy greater facility in acquiring goods from them and to shorten the transportation to San Antonio de Béjar, to Coahuila, to the New Kingdom of León, to Parral, and to the other provinces where he was thinking of selling them; and in order to realize from them the said gratuity that they promised him, he allowed not only Messieurs Massé and Cortableau and the rest to remain on the banks and in the vicinity of the Río Mexicano, but also the others who might go as far as the Río de Nechas, that is, the San Pedro de los Navidachos. This is the one called the Río Mexicano, because the Río Atoyaque, as we have seen, enters the Angelinas and the latter enters the Nechas. For in truth, as we have seen and proved with good documents, on this Río de los Nechas between the pueblo of San Pedro de los Navidachos and the sea at the place where this river has its mouth, the French established the post that they called Atacapas and Opelusas, and it seems that it is the same one in which the lieutenant-governor of Louisiana later resided.

1604. Supposing, then, that the French did not possess the territory of the Atacapas and Opelusas; that because of the temerity of Massé, Cortableau, and all the other Frenchmen in having established themselves as far as the Flores and Sabinas rivers, and because of the corruption of Governor Martos Navarrete, France could not acquire any right to those lands, nor could Spain lose them by the laws *Improba possesio* and *Ex libris Sabinianis*, cited in Part I, paragraphs 139 and 140. Since even natural reason so dictates, when France ceded Louisiana to Spain, she did not cede to her the lands in question because she did not recognize them as hers, or that she had ever possessed them. Neither did Spain receive them from her, because she held them as her own. Then when Spain recedes Louisiana to France, she must not recede these lands to her, because they were never ceded to Spain. Then France, when she sells Louisiana to the United States, sells it without these lands. Then the United States bought Louisiana from France without these lands. Then Spain ought not to give the United States these lands. Then the United States must neither ask for these lands in good faith nor plan with bad intentions to take them from Spain. Then [their territory] must extend as far as D'Anville's line. Then they should receive Louisiana as bounded by the Cabo del Norte.

1605. If Spain by chance had desired to do so, and had put into effect the idea that its governor in Louisiana should have governed not only there, but also in Texas, New Mexico, Coahuila, Chihuahua, Sonora, the Californias, Cuba, and even in other islands, when Louisiana was ceded back to France would she be obligated and could she be made to cede with it all the said territories, under the extremely false pretext that the governor of Louisiana governed all of them? The veriest madman would not say that.

Then not even a stupid person can say that Spain should recede Louisiana to France with the lands of the Atacapas and Opelusas just because the governor of Louisiana governs them. Then they should return these lands to the respective Spanish authorities, ecclesiastical as well as secular. Then, finally, the Indians who came in from elsewhere, such as the Conchattas and others, and the French and Anglo-Americans who inhabit them today, should withdraw to their old and legitimate possessions and abandon these lands, or if they wish to remain on them, they should recognize our Catholic sovereign as their king and subject themselves to all the laws of the Indies.

1606. Following all this, let us inquire as to what settlements and lands belong to the French, north of the coasts of the Seno Mexicano and south of the presidio of Natchitoches. In order to make this inquiry most methodically, let us not omit the *Rasgos Históricos* [*Historical Sketches*] of Dr. Sibley, who says (see Part II, paragraph 1018) concerning the Boluxas, that they

are emigrants from the fort of Pensacola. They came to the Red River about forty years ago. . . . They settled first at Avoyel [Avoyelles], then moved higher up to Bayuco Rapido [Rapide Bayou]—whence they passed to the mouth of . . . the little stream of El Buen Dios, . . . which is a branch of the Red River—about forty miles below Nachitoches, where they now live.

Since the territory on which they settled has all these characteristics, it indubitably belongs to the French.

1607. Concerning the Apalaches, the same Dr. Sibley says that

they are likewise emigrants from West Florida, and come from the river that bears their name. They settled on the Red River, at about the same time as the Boluxas [Boluscas] and afterwards passed above the Bayuco Rapido [Bayou Rapide].

For the same reasons they belong to the French.

Concerning the Alibamis he adds that

they are also from West Florida, from the Río Alibami [Alabama River], and they settled on the Red River about the same time as the Boluxas and Apalaches [Boluscas and Apalachies]. Part of them have lived on the Red River, about sixteen miles above the Bayuco Rapido [Bayou Rapide] . . . and later they went to live near the Cadodachos [Caddoques] . . . who are their friends and have no objection to their settling nearby. . . . Another party of them have their village on a small creek in the Apelusas [Opelusas] district,

about thirty miles northwest from the church of the Apelusas [Opelusas]. . . .
They have lived there ever since they came from Florida. . . .

Dr. Sibley does not tell us who these Cadodachos were, whether
they were the modern or the old ones. If he is speaking of the
old ones, the Alibamis Indians who live near them will certainly
belong to France, but if he is speaking of the modern ones, it is
probable that they belong to Spain. The latitude and longitude,
the direction in which, and the distance at which, they are found
with respect to the Cadodachos will decide the question. With
regard to the others who live thirty miles northwest of the church
of Los Opelusas, they undoubtedly belong to Spain, because we
have seen that the Apelusas do.

1608. Concerning the Conchattas, Señor Sibley tells us that they
live on the east bank of the Río Sabinas, almost south of Nachitoches, and at a distance of eighty miles from this fort. If from
the eighty miles that Señor Sibley suggests, we take their sixth
part, there will remain sixty-seven, and if we reduce them to
leagues by dividing them by three, we shall have twenty-two
leagues in the quotient. Now, if with an agle of the compass equal
to twenty-two leagues we fix one point at the fort of Nachitoches,
and with the other seek the east bank of the Río de Sabinas, it
will show us a point a little below the crossing of Señor Rivera
on the Río de Sabinas, and in 31° 20′ of latitude and 76° 36′
of longitude. Therefore these Indians certainly belong to Spain,
since this spot is found far to the west of D'Anville's line.

1609. Concerning the Pacanas,[32] Señor Sibley says that they live
on the banks of the Río Quelqueshoe which empties into the bay
between Atacapas and the Sabinas, whose source is on a prairie
called Cooko, about forty miles southwest of Nachitoches, and that
their rancheria is about fifty miles southeast of the Conchattas.
In order to understand the location of the rancherias of these
Indians, it is necessary to ascertain which river is the one that
Dr. Sibley here called Quelqueshoe. This is made very easy by
looking at the map of Lafon (see this map, number 14 of document 74), on which the Río Carcasiu is the one nearest the Río
de Sabinas on the east, and rises on a meadow that he calls Yanne
Coucou, a word which Señor Sibley converts into Cooko. He adds

---

[32]See *Pichardo's Treatise* . . . , Vol. II, p. 271.

that the source of this river is about forty miles from Nachitoches, toward the southwest. If their sixth part is subtracted from these forty miles, thirty-four remain. If these are divided by three, eleven leagues and a third remain, a number which we may change into twelve leagues, because Dr. Sibley is considering [the distance as] more than forty miles. If a point of the compass is placed on Nachitoches, and with an angle equal to twelve leagues we seek with the other a spot which falls southwest of the said Nachitoches, we shall find it in 31° 29′ of latitude and 76° 8′ of longtitude, and here we shall locate the source of the Río Quelqueshoe, or Carcasiu. According to Dr. Sibley, the Pacanas Indians are fifty miles southeast of the Conchattas. If their sixth part is taken from these fifty miles, forty-two remain. Dividing these by three, we shall have fourteen. If we fix a point of the compass on the spot on which we have found the Conchattas to be, and if with an angle equal to fourteen leagues we seek with the other the east bank of the Río Carcasiu, or Quelqueshoe, we shall find it in 30° 56′ of latitude and 76° 16′ of longitude. Then these Indians are also located on Spanish lands.

1610. Concerning the Atacapas,[33] Dr. Sibley writes that their village "is about twenty miles to the westward of the Atacapas [Attakapas] church, toward the Río Quelqueshoe," and concerning the Opelusas Señor Sibley adds that "their village is about fifteen miles west from the Opelusas church." Therefore, supposing that the Río Quelqueshoe, or Carcasiu, belongs to the dominions of Spain, these Indians also should belong to those dominions, and we have proven this sufficiently. We say the same thing with more reason with regard to the Opelusas, who are west of the Atacapas, as is seen on La Fon's map.

1611. Concerning the Tunicas, Pascagoulas, Tenisaws, and Chactoos,[34] Dr. Sibley writes, first, with regard to the Tunicas that "they live at Avoyel"; concerning the Pascagoulas that "they live in a . . . village on the Red River, about sixty miles below Nachitoches." Since the Red River belongs entirely to the French, these two Indian nations will belong to Louisiana. Concerning the Tenisaws, he says that

---

[33]*Ibid.*
[34]See *Pichardo's Treatise* . . . , Vol. II, p. 272, for Sibley's comments on these four tribes.

they used to live on the Red River . . . and their village was within a mile
of that of the Pascagoulas (for this reason they belong or used to belong to
the French), but that they . . . are moving or are about to move to the Bayuco
Buey [Bayou Boeuf] which is twenty-five miles south of where they lately lived.

And concerning the Chactoos, he says that

they live on the Bayuco Buey [Bayou Boeuf], about ten miles south of the
Bayuco Rapido [Bayou Rapide].

As the same Dr. Sibley, discussing the Chactoos (See Part II,
paragraph 1029), says of the Bayuco Buey that

it falls into the Chaffelí, or Chafalaya, and discharges through Apelusas and
Atacapas [Opelusas and Attakapas] into the Bahía del Bermellon [Vermillion
Bay]

we cannot deny that these Indians belong to Louisiana. (The Spaniards, speaking more accurately, call the bay into which the Chafalaya empties Bahía de la Ascensíon—see Part II, paragraph 102.)

1612. Concerning the Washas,[35] the said Señor Sibley states that
they used to live on an

island to the southwest of New Orleans, called Barritaria (D'Anville, Evía,
and others called it Barataria). . . . They afterwards lived on the Bayuco la
Fosh [Bayou de la Fourche].

There is no doubt that the island of Barataria belongs to the
French. Hence the old Washas belonged to them. Concerning the
present ones, settled on the Bayuco la Fosh, we shall say nothing,
since their small number of five persons is not worth noting. We
do not remember, if we have ever known it, the location of this
lake.

1613. Concerning the Chaslaws [Choctaws], he says

that they live on the west bank of the Mississippi, . . . that twelve miles above
the Oacheta [Ouachita] post . . . there is a small village of them, . . . and
that they likewise have another settlement on the Bayuco [Bayou] Chico, in
the northern part of the Apelusas [Opelusas] district.

As for these Indians, it is incontrovertible that those who live
on the Vachita, called the Oacheta [Ouachita] by Sibley, belong
to France, but concerning those who live on the Bayuco Chico,

---

[35]See *Pichardo's Treatise* . . . , Vol. II, p. 273.

we cannot say anything either because we do not know the latitude and longitude of the said bayou.

Finally, Dr. Sibley adds concerning the Arcansas that "they live on the Río Arcansas [Arkansas River]." There is no doubt that these Indians have always belonged to the French since the latter discovered the Mississippi.

With this the demarcation of the limits between the province of Texas and Louisiana is complete. It has been shown by the clearest demonstrations that the line which D'Anville drew on his map is most exact, and that the Spaniards as well as the Anglo-Americans should approve, adopt, and accept it in all its parts, because it designates to each nation the boundaries which it should not cross. In Part IV we shall show that those who do not conform to them will be acting unjustly.

PART IV
OF THE WORK WRITTEN BY FATHER
JOSÉ ANTONIO PICHARDO
ON THE VERIFICATION OF THE TRUE LIMITS
OF THE PROVINCES OF
LOUISIANA AND TEXAS

CHAPTER I

REFUTATION OF OBJECTIONS ON THE PART OF ANGLO-AMERICANS TO THE BOUNDARY BETWEEN LOUISIANA AND TEXAS AS PROPOSED BY D'ANVILLE

In Part IV the objections are refuted which have been raised against accepting the limits proposed by D'Anville's line. [This is the case] alike on the part of the Anglo-Americans, as well as on the part of those Spaniards who consider them illegal and claim that they should be contracted, or who, because of not knowing them, wish to withdraw them on the one hand or to extend them on the other, in contravention of the agreement between the two powers whereby Spain retrocedes precisely that which was ceded to her, without any addition or diminution.

1. In the first place, the Anglo-Americans do not conform to the limits which D'Anville's line designates for them, because they claim that this line should be moved so far west as almost not to leave Spain any possessions up to New Mexico. Even to the north of it they wish to despoil her of all the lands that extend to the Pacific Ocean—unjust and reprehensible claims, and claims founded on false principles and on fabulous histories and anecdotes that existed only in the heads of their authors, and, finally, claims with which they are wronging the Spaniards. They believe them entirely ignorant of the geography of those lands, of their discovery, and of the military and political events there. They think the Spaniards are wholly unprovided with documents with which they may present their evidence, even without D'Anville's line, as regards what they left to the French and allowed them to possess and what they kept for themselves. They consequently consider the Spaniards incapable of defending and stating their rights and as unable even to understand the damage that they are attempting to do them.

2. All this is clearly seen in a paper that was published in the *Mississippi Messenger*,[1] number 121 of volume three, dated December 23, 1806, the title of which is "Limits and Extent of Louisiana: A Treatise taken from some Manuscript Notes on Louisiana,

---

[1]See *Pichardo's Treatise* . . . , Vol. I, p. 23, n. 4.

made by a Military Gentleman who has Resided in Mississippi
since the Spring of the year 1803." In document 72, we give a
copy of it in the English language, in which it was published,
and, following it, our translation into Spanish. Father Doctor
Fray Melchor de Talamantes[2] also produced another translation
of this paper and he added to it some critical notes. This translation is the first treatise of the eight by this religious which we
present along with our documents, and of which we speak in
paragraph 32 of our Introduction. Notwithstanding the fact that
since Father Talamantes had made this translation, ours seemed
superfluous, we nevertheless undertook to make one because it
seemed to us that in some places he had not perceived the full
sense of the English text, and that, therefore, it was not correct.
I am giving the English text in order that it, rather than these
translations, may be referred to whenever it may be judged convenient; and I am including Father Talamantes' translation in
order not to present his critical notes by themselves, for in this
way it will be better undertsood to what words of the author
they refer. But it is now time to hear the said Military Gentleman, author of the paper which we are discussing, in which he
writes as follows:

I

3. Spain never considered that the discovery of the Mississippi, made by
Hernando de Soto in the year 1541 (A) clothed her with all the authority
necessary for aspiring to the dominion of that country, but this power recognized (B) finally the subsequent discoveries and settlements made by the
French.

NOTES

4. (A). And why should not Spain consider the journey of
Hernando de Soto on the plains of Cíbola sufficient basis for aspiring to dominion over them? These plains were hers because of the
general possession that Columbus took of all of the New World
on the first island that he discovered; because of the other specific
acts of possession that she proceeded to execute subsequently
through her vassals; because of the bull of Pope Alexander VI;[3]

---

[2]See *ibid.*, pp. xv–xvii.
[3]See *ibid.*, p. 28, n. 5.

and for the other reasons presented in Part I, beginning with paragraph 7. In fact, the journeys of Francisco Vásquez Coronado and of all the others, whom we mention in the dissertation on La Quivira, who went to La Quivira or to these plains, and of all those who entered Florida, such as, among others, Hernando de Soto, and the possession that they took of all these lands, give Spain an indisputable right over them since they were her vassals—the first discoverers of those lands, and the first ones to explore them. (See everything we said in the cited dissertation on La Quivira and on the journey of Hernando de Soto.)

5. (B). If Spain recognized the discoveries and settlements of the French, it was only in the quality of mere usurpations or infractions of her rights. If she consented to their retaining what they had appropriated, it was due to the Christian piety of her king, Señor Don Felipe V,[4] who, in order to prevent the shedding of French and Spanish blood in the wars that would have developed between the Spaniards in defending their possessions, and the French in taking them away from them, ordered that no war be made against the French and that they be permitted to keep all the lands that they might have taken down to the date of the last cedula issued on this matter, as we proved in Part III, beginning with paragraph 327.

II

6. Among civilized nations the right derived from a discovery as well as the right of purchase is conclusive and decisive. (A). The discovery of the Mississippi by the French goes far back, for they discovered it in 1673. (B). In 1680, they navigated it from its mouth to the Río de San Francisco [St. Francis River], about sixty miles above the falls of San Antonio [St. Anthony]. (C). In 1683, they established settlements in the vicinity of the Ylineses [Illinois], on Isla Delfina [Dauphine Island], and above the mouth of the Río Mobila [Mobile River]. (D). In 1685, Monsieur de la Salle established a colony on San Bernardo Bay, not very far from the Río Bravo. (E). In 1699, Iberville[5] was appointed governor of Louisiana, he being the first to obtain this position. He established his capital at the mouth of the Mobile, where it remained until 1720, when New Orleans was founded.

---

[4] Philip V, the first king of the Bourbon dynasty in Spain, ruled from 1700 to 1746.

[5] See *Pichardo's Treatise* . . . , Vol. I, p. 232, n. 1.

NOTES

7. (A). If among civilized nations the right derived from a dis-covery as well as the right of purchase is conclusive, the discovery by Spain of this entire New World should consequently, accord-ing to this principle, give her a right to it as conclusive as if she had bought it.

8. (B). If the French discovered the Mississippi in 1673, it was not as far back as the discovery of the Spaniards who, as this writer states, discovered it in 1541.

9. (C). This author does not explain very well the voyage that the French made in 1680, for he says that they navigated the river from its mouth, by which it seems it should be understood that they navigated it from the entrance of this river into the sea as far as the mouth of San Francisco [St. Francis]. This is false, for Father Hennepin, who navigated it in this year, began his voyage at the mouth of the Río de los Ylineses [Illinois River] and continued it toward the north (see document 2, number 128), and La Salle and those who accompanied him went toward the south.

10. (D). It is false and very false that the French established settlements in 1683 on Ysla Delfina [Dauphine Island] and at the mouth of the Río Mobila [Mobile River], for when La Salle sailed through the Gulf of Mexico he not only did not establish settlements at these places but he did not even do so on the Mississippi, for which he was bound, because he went on as far as the Bahía del Espíritu Santo which he called at that time San Luis [St. Louis]. The first Frenchman who entered the Gulf of Mexico with the intention of entering the mouth of the Mississippi was D'Iberville, but he did not come until the year 1699, and it was at that time that he took possession of the mouth of the Río Mobila and of Ysla Delfina, as Prevost says, whose text we give below, beginning with paragraph 41, in note (B) of Number VIII.

11. (E). It is also false that La Salle established Fort Luis in 1685[6] on the bay of San Luis, for as we have proved in Part I, paragraph 175, he founded this settlement in 1683.

---

[6]For a statement concerning the alleged falsity of this date, see *Pichardo's Treatise* . . . , Vol. I, p. 151, n. 1.

III

12. By the treaty of October 1, 1800, Spain promises and obligates herself to cede to the French Republic six months after the full and complete fulfillment of the conditions and stipulations contained therein relative to the Duchy of Parma, the colony or province of Louisiana, with the same extent that it now has in her possession, which is exactly the same that it had when France possessed it, and with that [extent] which it may have in conformity with treaties subsequently made between Spain and other powers. This clause was confirmed and strengthened by another treaty made later in Madrid on March 21, 1801, and this same clause is likewise embodied in the treaty of cession drawn up on April 30, 1803, between the French Republic and the United States (A), and it is cited very particularly as it is the one that describes and designates the boundaries. These boundaries underwent no changes while Louisiana was in the hands of Spain, with the exception of the dividing line agreed upon between that power and the United States (B), so that the sole object of the present discussion is to ascertain what were the boundaries of Louisiana while this province was in the hands of France.

NOTES

13. (A). It is true that Spain ceded Louisiana to France, but it is also most certain that it was upon the strict condition that she would never transfer it. The supreme Junta Central so tells us in a paper, printed in Cádiz and reprinted in Mexico, which has the following title: *Demostración de la lealdad española.*[7] It is found also on page 140 of volume seven of the *Colección de infinitas poesías*[8] that came out in Spain against the French and the perfidy of Napoleon. Its words are as follows:

And what in the way of compensation has Spain received from the alliance previous to the disgraceful break? Two equally fatal maritime wars; our squadrons sacrificed at the whim of our allies; important colonies lost; the principal nerve of our industry cut by the interruption of our relations with America; *Louisiana ceded to the French in exchange for Etruria and sold immediately by them, contrary to the express stipulated agreement never to transfer it;* Etruria, the price of this cession and of huge sums of money, finally torn violently from the prince who possessed it; a torrent of silver and gold that ran without ceasing from Spain to France to quench the insatiable covetousness of its rulers; finally, the incompetent administration of the favorite which, sustained and protected by them [the French] is another of the bitter fruits that their friendship has produced for us.

[7]The full title of this work, published in Madrid and Cádiz in 1808–1809, is given in the bibliography, *infra.* No reference has been found to the Mexican reprint of this work.

[8]No reference has been found to this work.

14. (B). As a matter of fact this boundary has not suffered any other change under the control of Spain than the one given by the Military Gentleman, and it is precisely the one that became the boundary line between Spain and the United States. We speak of this line in Part I, paragraph 1.

IV

15. The limits claimed by France can be determined in part by referring to the concession of the trade of Louisiana made in the year 1712 to Crozat. (A). This document is of the greatest importance since, as is seen, it contains the first formal and official recognition of these limits, but we shall cite from it only those words which are most useful in explaining these limits.

NOTES

16. (A). Here Father Doctor Talamantes inserts a note of the following tenor:

From a pamphlet published in Mexico in 1719, at the order of the government, it is shown that the king of France informed the king of Spain of the claims of Crozat[9] and that, the matter being referred to the Council of the Indies, our sovereign denied the claims. This reply obliged the king of France to assure the king of Spain that if the French remained at some points on the Gulf of Mexico, it was not as possessors of that land, but for the purpose of aiding the Spaniards against the inroads that the English might make. France thereby admitted how groundless were her claims and the heedlessness with which she had proceeded to give Crozat the privilege of trade in lands which did not belong to her and which nevertheless she was attempting to take away fraudulently from Spain by abusing her good faith. It may be inferred from this what value a concession would have that is made without any real authority and over the formal protest of the legitimate owner.

17. I have had this pamphlet in my possession for many years. It was bound by its former owner with the old *Gacetas de Mexico*[10] which began to be published in January, 1722. Father Doctor Talamantes took a copy from it, which is the one in document 19, and in Part I, paragraph 349, I transcribed what is said in it concerning Crozat.

---

[9]See *Pichardo's Treatise* . . . , Vol. I, p. 126, n. 1.
[10]See *ibid.*, p. 41, n. 2.

V

18. Louis,[11] by the grace of God king of France and of Navarre. To all who may see these presents, greeting: The care that we have always taken to secure the happiness and prosperity of our vassals has induced us to seek out everything that may contribute to the augmentation and extension of the commerce of our American colonies, notwithstanding the almost continuous wars that we have been forced to wage from the beginning of our reign. Therefore, in the year 1683, we issued our orders for undertaking the discovery of the lands and countries situated in North America, between New France and New Mexico.[12] Señor de la Salle, to whom we entrusted this enterprise, comported himself therein so happily that he succeeded in confirming us in the belief that communication could be established from New France, or Canada, to the Gulf of Mexico, by way of the west. But the outbreak of a new war in Europe[13] shortly thereafter has deprived us up to the present of the possibility of deriving from that new colony the profits that might have been hoped for from that time forward, because private persons who were engaged in maritime trade had obligations in other colonies and could not abandon them. While on the contrary we are persuaded, because of the reports that we have received concerning the nature and situation of the said regions, known at present by the name of the province of Louisiana, that a considerable commerce could be established in them, the more advantageous to our kingdom in that up to the present it has been necessary to secure from foreigners most of the commodities that can be obtained from that country, and because, in exchange for them, we shall not be under the necessity of taking there anything except commodities produced and manufactured in this our kingdom, we have decided to concede the commerce of the country of Louisiana to Señor Antonio [Antoine] Crozat, our councillor and secretary of cámara, state and hacienda, to whom we entrust the execution of this project. We have chosen him the more readily because his zeal and the extraordinary knowledge that he has acquired in maritime commerce inspires us to hope for a result as successful as that which he has obtained heretofore in the various

---

[11]Reference is to Louis XIV, king of France from 1643 to 1715.

[12]On February 6, 1682, the well-known La Salle reached the upper Mississippi from Canada. He descended that stream, arriving at its mouth in April, 1682, where he took formal possession of the great valley, naming it in honor of Louis XIV, king of France. From there La Salle returned to Quebec. "La Salle now planned a colony at the mouth of the Mississippi River, as a means of developing the fur trade, controlling the Mississippi Valley, providing a base for commanding the Gulf, and, in case of war, for attack on the coveted mines of New Spain. France and Spain were on the verge of war, . . . La Salle's proposals were favored, therefore, by Louis XIV. In the summer of 1684 La Salle left France with a colony of some four hundred people. . . . La Salle missed the mouth of the Mississippi and landed on the Texas coast at Matagorda Bay."—Bolton and Marshall, *The Colonization of North America*, pp. 98–99.

[13]Reference is to the War of the English Succession—as it was known in Europe—or to King William's War—as it is known in American history. This war lasted from 1688 to 1697.

private ventures that he has made in his trade. By means of this he has succeeded in bringing into this our kingdom large amounts of gold and silver, sometimes under such circumstances, that we could do no less than view them as extremely opportune. For these reasons, desiring to manifest to him our favor, and to arrange the conditions upon which we have proposed to concede him the said commerce, after having deliberated upon this matter in our council, of our own and certain knowledge, full power, and royal authority, by the presents signed by our own hand, we have named and do name the said Señor Crozat as the one and only person who may go to trade in all the territory that we possess, which borders upon New Mexico and the lands of the English in Carolina (A), that is to say, *to all the settlements, posts, bays, rivers, and particularly the post and bay of La Ysla Delfina, formerly called Masacra, or Matanza; to the Río de San Luis, formerly called Mississippi (B), from the coast to the country of the Ylineses; as well as the Río de San Felipe, which formerly was named the Missouri; and that of San Gerónimo, to which was formerly given the name of Ouavache, or Ohio, with all the . . . rivers that flow directly or indirectly (C) into any part of the Río de San Luis.* Our will is that all the abovesaid lands, countries, rivulets, large rivers, and islands shall be and remain included under the name of the Government of Louisiana.

VI

19. Here is a solemn decree of Louis XIV with regard to a part of what he took in Louisiana, and we shall see very quickly how solidly this possession was confirmed by actual occupation and settlement. It is not apparent why the trade of Crozat was limited on the north by the Ylineses and at the same time by the Missouri, though it is to be supposed that this was done in order to avoid any clash with the commerce of Canada, which extended to the Mississippi above the falls of San Antonio by way of the Río Ouisconsing [Wisconsin River].

NOTES

20. (A). The same Father Doctor Talamantes inserted the following appropriate note at this place:

What would the title of possession of Louis XIV have been in this vast territory which he wished to call Louisiana when he placed it at Crozat's disposal? Would it perhaps have been discovery? But the Spaniards were the first discoverers, and even the notice that was received in France about this country in 1673 was brought by a Spanish immigrant. (1). Might it have been the reconnaissance that La Salle made of some part of these lands? But this could never grant the title to all of them, and in case reconnaissance should be considered as an act of real possession, no property or territory in the world would be safe. Might it have been that the Pope granted to the king of France, in 1685, the spiritual conquest of that district? (2). But such a grant had already been made long ago in Spain to the Catholic Kings by Alexander

VI, and had been ratified by subsequent popes, and privileges granted to monarchs by the Apostolic See are by their nature permanent, according to the principles of our law. Might it have been the settlement made by Monsieur de la Salle on the lake, or bay, of San Bernardo? (3). But this settlement was opposed and destroyed by the Indians, the original owners of the country (4), who notified the Spaniards of the destruction and sent for them in order to give them possession of their lands. Might it have been, finally, the settlements made by France on the Mobile and on Dauphine Island? But these settlements were made during a turbulent war in which Spain could not watch all the places in her colonies. They were made in the capacity of subsidiary shelters for the French ships, which at that time sailed these seas as friends. They were made as an aid for the Spaniards themselves against the English, the enemies of the two allied nations, and aid should not become a prejudice to the persons aided. Above all, it is strange that these settlements, as wretched and precarious as they were, should warrant possession of the great territory of which this patent speaks, as if title to the kingdom of Chile could be based on settlements on the Straits of Magellan (5).

21. (1). Who was this Spanish immigrant who in 1673 gave a report of the province of Texas in France? From what we wrote in the dissertation on La Quivira, in paragraph 1488, which is found in Part II, we know that it was Don Diego de Peñalosa,[14] but we do not believe that the French would have had from him the first reports of the land that the Mississippi waters, because Prevost[15] contradicts it when he discusses Father Marquette and Monsieur Joliet.

22. (2). With regard to this concession see paragraph 345 of Part I, where the apostolic briefs of his Holiness are given.

23. (3). La Salle made no establishment on the lake, or bay, of San Bernardo, but on the bay of Espíritu Santo, which he called San Luis. See Part II, beginning with paragraph 254.

24. (4). I proposed this argument in the essay that I wrote for the Holy Tribunal of the Inquisition, in the following words:

Returning to Fort Luis, established by Monsieur La Salle on the bay of Espíritu Santo, I say that on seeing the way in which it was established, it was inevitable that it should come to the end that it did. A chief who made

---

[14]For frequent references to Don Diego Dionisio de Peñalosa Briceño y Berdugo who was governor of New Mexico from 1661 to 1664, and who later, after being exiled from New Spain, sought aid of Louis XIV to exact revenge on Spain in the New World, see the indices of *Pichardo's Treatise* . . . , Vols. I, II, and III.

[15]For frequent references to Prevost, consult the indices of *Pichardo's Treatise* . . . , Vols. I, II, and III.

himself hateful to his subjects, subjects of whom the greater part was composed of unhappy people reduced to begging alms, many of them lame or deformed and not knowing how to handle a rifle; of artisans of whom not a single one knew his profession; of men living on bad terms among themselves (see Prevost, volume 23 of the translation of Señor Terracina, page 83), and of men whose numbers continued to diminish either through death or by desertion, to the point that La Salle left for the Ylineses with no more than sixteen men, and with only twenty persons in the said Fort Luis, which number consisted of seven women, two religious, and eleven men. Were these people capable of sustaining the fort against the attacks of the savages? What wonder, therefore, that the latter destroyed them! Then this fort was now left to the Indians. Then in the end the Spaniards could take possession, and particularly because it was located in their territory, of which they had been despoiled furtively and contrary to all justice.

25. Farther on I added:

The Very Reverend Father Fray Agustín Morfi reports that when the French transferred their garrison of Nachitoches to the west branch of the Red River, the commandant of the presidio of Los Adaes, when he attempted to prevent this transfer, was told by Monsieur St. Denis, among other things, that the French had succeeded to the rights of dominion over that country of the Nachitoches Indians, and that the latter possessed lands not only on the other side of the Red River, but on the west side as well, without the Adaes Indians, whose rights the Spaniards inherited, having ever contested their possession (Morfi, *Memorias para la Historia de Texas*, book 7, number 73). And I say now that when the Clamcoest Indians, as Prevost calls them, or Quems, as the missionary Massanet calls them, killed the few Frenchmen who remained in Fort Luis, they recovered dominion over that country and site of which they had been tyrannically despoiled by the French. Then when these Indians handed themselves over to the Spaniards, they permitted them in their country and consented to their settling it with them. In a word, when the Spaniards inherited the rights of domain over that country from the Quems Indians, they remained absolute owners of it, and the French thus lost their rights, if they had them, and cannot now reclaim them. Nor can those who have succeeded them in Louisiana claim the dominion which the French lacked.

26. It is apparent, therefore, that Father Doctor Talamantes took this argument from my cited papers, because it is certain that he read them, as is shown by the following letters:

I am informed of the reply which your reverence wrote on August 31, last, to my communication of the 28th of the same month, and I am sending herewith for your reverence in two *cuadernos*, six papers prepared by the Reverend Fathers Doctor Don José Peredo and Don José Antonio Pichardo of the Congregation of San Felipe Neri, and by the two senior secretaries of the Secreto of the Holy Tribunal of the Faith, all intended to afford very useful information for making clear the true ancient limits of the provinces of Texas and Louisiana. I charge your reverence to make the proper use of all this in carrying out the commission to which I have appointed you. God keep your reverence many years. Mexico, September 11, 1807. Iturrigaray.[16] To the Reverend Father Doctor Fray Melchor Talamantes.

27. I have received with your Excellency's official letter of the 11th of the present month, the six papers sent to your Excellency by the Holy Tribunal of the Faith, one prepared by Father Doctor José Peredo (this paper is found in document 67), two by Father Don José Antonio Pichardo, two documents which accompany this last one (these are in our documents 13 and 19), and a certification drawn up by the two secretaries of the Secreto (this is found in document 68). These have come in the form of certified copies and I have examined them carefully for the use that you charge me to make of them and that I had suggested myself when I sent you my official dispatch of February 3 of the present year. God keep your Excellency many years. Mexico, September 18, 1807. Most excellent señor. Fray Melchor Talamantes. To the most excellent señor viceroy, Don José de Iturrigaray.

28. (5). I also presented this argument in the following words in *La Luisiana del Abate Raynal*,[17] a paper I wrote at the order of the most excellent señor viceroy:

He who is the owner of a river which does not rise in his lands does not have authority except on that part which flows through his lands. The Portuguese never have claimed to be owners of all the lands through which flows the Tagus. Neither because this river disembogues in their possessions have they wished to appropriate it to themselves in such manner that they set up claims as far as the mountain ranges of Cuenca where it rises. Neither has Spain endeavored to make herself owner of Portugal because the river which rises in her mountain ranges of Cuenca flows through that kingdom [of Portugal]. It would be a ridiculous and scandalous thing if those on the Black Sea should claim ownership over all those parts of Germany which the Danube bathes on the ground that this river disembogues into their sea; similarly if the English should also claim ownership over all Spain because of the fact that they have occupied Gibraltar; similarly if the Dutch, because they are owners of the Cape of Good Hope, should wish to be owners of all Africa.

29. (B). The said Father Dr. Talamantes placed here the following note:

At another time—that is, when it was unknown to the French—called Río de la Palisada by the Spaniards, and then also Mercharripi by the natives who inhabited its banks, which name was later corrupted into Misisipi.

---

[16]José de Iturrigaray was viceroy of New Spain from 1803 to 1808.
[17]See *Pichardo's Treatise* . . . , Vol. I, p. 16, n. 2; and for a reference to Raynal's *La Louisiana*, see *ibid.*, p. 125.

30. The French, in order to change everything, changed also the name of the river which they knew the Indians called Mechasipi, to the Río Colbert (see Father Hennepin, document 2, number 134), in memory of Monsieur Colbert,[18] just as they called the Ylineses the Río de Segnelay, in honor of the Marquis of Segnelay, the son of Monsieur Colbert. And as is seen from this royal patent, they changed the name of Colbert to that of San Luis. According to Juan Coles, cited by the Inca Garcilaso in his *Historia de la Florida*, book 4, chapter 3, the Indians called it the Río Chucagua. Concerning its name of La Palizada, see what we say in discussing the itinerary of Hernando de Soto, paragraph 1698. Don Carlos de Sigüenza[19] wrote as follows in his *Trofeo de la Justicia Española* (see document 7, number 15):

It must not be thought because of this that we lack absolutely all information about those lands. For, although it may be thought so from the account which Father Hennepin,[20] the French Capuchin, wrote in his *Louisiana* [*Description de la Louisiane*] concerning a part of them, he might have read in the history which the Inca wrote of the experiences of the *adelantado* Hernando de Soto in Florida, and which is translated into his [Hennepin's] language, that the land which he called Louisiana consisted of the provinces of Cofachiqui, Chicara, Chisca, and others. And [he might have read that] the large river which he (La Salle) called Colbert was the one which Governor Luis Moscoso de Alvarado navigated for a distance of five hundred leagues and is now called La Palizada. But this is not the first time nor will it be the last that the French have gloried in the prodigality of the Spaniards to their advantage and have proven it anew. We may thank the Xannas, Tohos, and Caocosies Indians for having saved us the trouble of punishing them [the French] for meddling in what did not concern them.

31. (C). This grant to Crozat tells us nothing except of the possession that La Salle took of the Mississippi. Because of this fact, we have stated in paragraph 39 of Part III that this grant is a commentary upon that possession. I therefore do not know why the Military Gentleman, author of this paper, thought that he would find a good basis for the extension of the limits in this patent of Louis the Great, for it contains nothing more than the account that Father Le Clercq gave of the possession that La Salle took

---

[18]See *Pichardo's Treatise* . . . , Vol. I, p. 153, n. 3.
[19]See *ibid.*, p. 146, n. 2.
[20]See *ibid.*, p. 246, n. 1.

of the Mississippi (see Part III, paragraph 39). In the said paragraph 39, we wrote as follows:

> The best exposition of this act of possession is indubitably the concession made by the Most Christian King, Louis XIV, to Monsieur Crozat, granting him a monopoly of trade in the country of Louisiana. Regarding this concession, the author well remembers a paper that was published in *The Mississippi Messenger*, or *Mensagero del Misisipi*. . . .

After having copied his words and the patent of Louis XIV, we added in paragraph 44:

> note carefully the terms of this concession: With all the countries, territories, inland lakes, and with all the rivers that flow directly or indirectly into any part of the Río de San Luis. Herein it is given to understand that all the rivers that enter directly into the Mississippi belong to the crown of France, such as, on the east side, that of the Ylineses [Illinois], and the Ouavache [Wabash], and on the west, the Missouri, the Acansas [Arkansas], and the Red, or Nachitoches. It includes also those that enter indirectly, that is, that flow into one of these rivers and discharge their waters through it into the Mississippi. Such are, on the east, the Ohio and the Cumberland which, uniting with the Ouavache, flow into the Mississippi, into which, from the west, by means of the Missouri, flow the Río de los Cances, the Vermellon [Vermilion], and the Osages; and likewise, through the Red, the Cadodachos, the Roxo [?], and others enter it. For this reason all the countries watered by these rivers that in this direct or indirect manner flow into the Mississippi are regarded by the French as their own.

And now we add that D'Anville's line delimits the territory to which Crozat's grant extends:

VII

32. There is no doubt that the French extended their claims to the lands that the English occupy in Carolina because of the settlements that they established in 1562[21] near the city of San Agustín in Florida and because of their wish to circumscribe the claims of their neighboring rivals. But these settlements lasted only five years (A), because the repeated attacks of the Spaniards obliged the French to abandon them, and never subsequently did they try to renew them. The Spaniards were established so strongly that they could not be easily removed. (B).

---

[21]Reference is to the well-known efforts of Jean Ribaut and René de Laudonnière to establish a settlement for French Huguenots on the Florida coast between 1562 and 1565.—See *Pichardo's Treatise* . . . , Vol. I, p. 74, n. 1.

NOTES

33. (A). Father Talamantes in his note at this place says of these five years:

Then what claim could be based on that [establishment] of Monsieur de la Salle, which lasted a shorter time?

34. (B). In confirmation of what the Military Gentleman says here, let us listen to what the Englishman, W. Winterbotham, writes, cited in Part I, paragraph 122, to wit:

All the attempts to establish settlements on this continent which were made by the Dutch, French, and English, from its discovery to the present time, which has been 110 years, proved ineffectual. The Spaniards only, of all the European nations, obtained happy results; and it is not related that there may have been one European family, at this time, that is to say, in the year 1602, in all the vast extent of coast from Florida to Greenland.

35. With regard to this we said in the following paragraph:

This ingenuous confession of an Englishman is confirmed by that of the Frenchman, Prevost, who speaks as follows (book 6, chapter 13, which, in the translation of Terracina, is found in volume 26, page 52):

"Since the year 1549 we have seen the French entirely disinterested in settlements in America; in fact, we know of no other undertaking of theirs than that in Brazil and that in Florida, accounts of which we have given. Until the year 1598, after fifty years of civil war, and until the peace which they began to enjoy anew under the government of one of their best and greatest kings, they did not redevelop an interest in their colonies."

36. Accordingly we have seen thus far that the Spaniards discovered all the land in Adelantado Menéndez's jurisdiction of Florida, in which is included (says Señor Barcia in his introduction to the *Ensayo Cronológico*) all that which there is from the Río Pánuco to Bacallaos Point [Codfish Point] which is in forty-eight and one-half degrees, and from there as far as 73 degrees north, as Herrera states in the aforesaid chapter 8, in which is included all that which the foreigners occupy. Also we have seen that these foreigners entirely abandoned the colonies which they had established in the northern part of this America and they abandoned them in such a manner that not a family of them remained in all the vast extension of coasts from Florida to Greenland, and only the Spaniards obtained happy results. Consequently, we shall have to acknowledge that, by force of the discovery of these lands by the Spaniards and by force of not having abandoned them, they remained the sole owners of them. And even if, by virtue of the discovery of Columbus and of the bull of Alexander VI, they were not owners of them, they would become such because they discovered them later and established themselves in them in a manner so permanent that never have they abandoned them, even entering

into the rights of the foreigners (if, by chance, they had such, which they never had) on account of these having entirely abandoned them.

VIII

37. In 1683, the French established settlements at the mouth of the Mobile and on Dauphine Island, and no power ever attempted to expel them there-from. (A). In 1699, Iberville was named governor of Louisiana, he being the first one, as we have noted, who held this position, and the capital of the government was placed at one of these establishments. The Spaniards did not suffer with patience the settlement of the French in those new regions. On the contrary, they took new measures to check them, and one of them was to found the presidio of Panzacola in the year 1696[22] (B), about thirty-four miles east of Mobile. This proximity of settlements caused many disturbances between them. They attacked each other, and the very danger that they brought on for themselves, together with the loss of some people, impeded the prosperity of both nations. (C). The last one of these contests took place in the year 1718, when Panzacola changed masters three times in the short space of one year.[23] (D). In 1719, peace was concluded between France and Spain. From this time to the year 1763, the Río Perdido (E), about twelve miles west of the bar of Panzacola, was considered as the line of demarcation between the two nations. (F). The French occupied the western part and the Spaniards the eastern. The acts of sovereignty of the two were limited to their respective possessions, and both nations were kept within their boundaries. This fact, together with the uninterrupted possession of the French down to the year 1763, that is, for a space of forty-four years, it seems fixes the limits of the two Floridas on a solid foundation that does not permit any challenge. (G). All these things may be proposed as unanswerable arguments against any present claim of Spain to a greater extension of her rights. (H). After the grant made to Crozat in the year 1712, various other treaties were concluded, and finally the peace treaty of 1719, in the drawing up of which Spain concurred, on her part. But in none of these treaties were the rights of France diminished.

NOTES

38. (A). This is false and very false. We have written the contrary in our Part I, beginning with paragraph 442 [449], where we said:

But while the French and other foreigners have endeavored to despoil Spain of her territories, the Catholic Kings have managed to prevent them, by taking the most vigorous and effective measures. In document 39, we have copied a great number of cedulas in which these said measures are to be

---

[22]The Spaniards did not fortify Pensacola until November, 1698.—See *Pichardo's Treatise* . . . , Vol. I, p. 224, n. 1.
[23]See *Pichardo's Treatise* . . . , Vol. I, p. 230, n. 3.

found. . . . In cedula 56 of the said document 39, his Majesty notifies the viceroy of New Spain by means of a statement sent him by the *maestro de campo*, Don José Fernández [de Córdova] of several declarations which he caused to be taken from some prisoners, who stated that they heard it said that the French were about to settle the bay of Espíritu Santo. Because of this the king ordered the said señor viceroy of New Spain to be on the look-out and to take all possible care to prevent it. In that of number 84, the king charged the señor viceroy of New Spain that, if he judged it expedient to fortify Panzacola, as the result of the representations made by Don Andrés de Pez, he might do it in this case. Note that in this cedula his Majesty ordered that if possible the French should be prevented from taking the bay of Espíritu Santo, and that the coast and all the interior country should be reconnoitered.

39. In the cedula in number 94, the king, because of the viceroy of New Spain having reported the execution of his royal order concerning the recon-naissance of the bay of Santa María de Galve and the coast of the Mexican Gulf because of its having been resolved in the council of war that it was necessary that the said bay be fortified, orders that the fortification that might be needed for the defense of the said port of Santa María de Galve be erected at once. That of number 136 says the same thing about this matter and adds that, notice having been received that the French persist with greater vigor in the enterprise of securing a port on the Mexican Gulf, and, because of this, his Majesty orders the viceroy of New Spain to take the most prompt and effective measures to prevent the contingency of the French anticipating the occupation of the bay of Panzacola. And note that this appears to refer to Iberville, when he came to enter the Mississippi. . . . In that of number 181, the king resolved to order the viceroy of New Spain to take care to extend his dominions and the holy gospel in the new reductions, and to take the measures necessary for forcing the French to abandon La Masacra, Movila, and other territory that they occupy in that region, without any right or title, as he has done with other places that they used to occupy. And observe in this cedula those most conspicuous words which say, "and with respect to La Mobila, Masacra, and other territory that pertains to my royal crown, which the French occupy in those parts, without any right or title whatever, etc."

40. (B). The founding of the presidio of Panzacola actually took place in this year. It is called also Santa María de Galve by the Spaniards, as is clear from the following words which Señor Barcia wrote in his *Ensayo Cronológico*,[24] decade 19, page 316, concerning the year 1696:

General Don Andrés de Arriola,[25] first governor of Panzacola, left Vera Cruz with some vessels of the windward armada and some landing troops to settle

---

[24]For a reference to this work see the Bibliography of *Pichardo's Treatise* . . . , Vol. I, p. 546.
[25]See *Pichardo's Treatise* . . . , Vol. III, p. 477, n. 4.

on the bay of Santa María de Galve and to build a fortress on the ravines that
are called Santo Tomé, which are within the bay and port which the Spaniards
call Santa María de Galve, because they went to make this settlement by order
of the Count of Gálvez,[26] the viceroy of New Spain, who had an order from
his Majesty to that effect.

41. Having told of these beginnings, we now state that after
La Salle's companions had been killed by the Indians and their
Fort Luis had been burned and destroyed by the Spaniards, as
we have stated in Part I, paragraph 167, that entire section of
the Seno Mexicano remained, as it had been before, with no European settlements whatever. But the Spaniards in 1696 settled the
bay of Santa María de Galve and founded the fort of Panzacola,
and after the Spaniards found themselves already settled there,
Monsieur D'Iberville came to the Gulf of Mexico. His story is told
thus by Abbé Prevost (volume 26 of Terracina's translation,
page 97) :

Even though until the end of the century it may have seemed that the
French were resting upon the discoveries of La Salle, it will very soon be seen
that before his death, or at least before it was known in Canada, the Caballero
de Tonti[27] had come down as far as the mouth of the Mississippi with the hope
of meeting him there, and that he had ascended the river, disappointed at not
having been able to discover any trace of him. But it was in 1697 that a
gentleman from Canada, already noted for various expeditions, excited the
attention of the minister with regard to Louisiana. On his insistence the idea
was conceived of building a fort at the mouth of the river [the Mississippi]
which this officer, named D'Iberville, expected to discover.

42. The Count of Pontchartrain,[28] at that time Minister of Marine, had two
warships, the *François* and the *Renommée*,[29] outfitted at Rochefort, the com-

---

[26]The Count of Gálvez was not viceroy of New Spain at the time of the
occupation of Pensacola Bay by the Spaniards. Instead, the viceroy who gave
support to the project of Don Andrés de Pez for the occupation of Pensacola
Bay was Gaspár de la Cerda Sandoval Silva y Mendoza, the Count of Galve,
who occupied the viceregal throne from 1688 to 1696.—See Leonard, "Don
Andrés de Arriola and the Occupation of Pensacola Bay," p. 83.

[27]See *Pichardo's Treatise* . . . , Vol. III, p. 284, n. 23.

[28]The French Minister of Marine, the "Count de Ponchartrain, . . . sent
Iberville to establish settlements on the lower Mississippi."—Caughey, *Bernardo de Gálvez in Louisiana* . . . , p. 2.

[29]According to Fortier (*A History of Louisiana*, Vol. I, pp. 34–45), "Ibei-
ville's fleet sailed from Brest on October 24, 1698; it consisted of two small
frigates—the *Badine*, commanded by Iberville himself, and the *Marin*, commanded by the Chevalier de Surgères—and two store-ships. At Santo Domingo the Marquis de Châteaumorant, commander of the war-ship *François*,
a nephew of the great Tourville, joined the expedition and accompanied it to

mand of which he gave to the Marquis of Chateau Morand [Chateaumorant][30] and to D'Iberville. On October 17 of the following year they sailed, and on January 27, 1699, they discovered the lands of Florida. Since prudence did not permit them to approach too closely a coast that they did not know they sent one of their officers to obtain water and to reconnoiter. Upon his return he told them that they were opposite a bay called Panzacola, where three hundred Spaniards who had come from Vera Cruz had just established themselves.

43. The French officer had entered the port,[31] and after having presented himself to the governor, he had requested permission to obtain water and firewood. The Spaniard, having asked on whose behalf he made this request, had contented himself with telling him that he would reply [directly] to the commandants, and had at once sent with him [the Frenchman] his *mayor*, to present his compliments to the two captains. This courtesy was accompanied by a letter from the governor, which stated that the two French vessels were free to obtain water and firewood, and even to choose an anchorage, but that he was expressly forbidden to receive any foreign vessel in the port. Nevertheless, since it might happen that bad weather would oblige the French captains to enter the bay, he was sending them a pilot to conduct them to it. They answered the governor through the same *mayor* that since the sea was so turbulent and they despaired of finding any other shelter, they found themselves obliged to accept his offers. Beginning on the following day, they sent Lorenzo de Graaf[32] to sound the entrance of the port. He was a notorious freebooter who had made himself terrible to the Spaniards under the name of Lorencillo (we have given the story of the cruelties which this freebooter, or pirate, committed in Vera Cruz, by reason of which he had made himself so dreaded by the Spaniards, in document 4, number 120) and whom they had taken aboard while passing Cabo Francés [Cap François].[33] D'Iberville also went in his longboat with the Caballero de Surgères,[34] and he found twenty or twenty-two feet of water in the shallowest place. But the governor, who had

its destination. Iberville took as pilot Lawrence de Graaf, a celebrated buccaneer, and on January 25, 1699, anchored before the island of St. Rosa. . . . On his second voyage to Biloxi, Iberville commanded the frigate *Renommée*, and Surgères the frigate *Gironde*."

[30]On March 23, 1700, Don Andrés de Arriola in a letter to Iberville referred to a "Marquis de Chatermoran [Chateaumorant] who commanded a French squadron of five vessels which stopped off the Bay of Santa María de Galve in January, 1699."—See Leonard, "Don Andrés de Arriola and the Occupation of Pensacola Bay," p. 105; see also note 29, *supra*.

[31]For further details concerning this incident, see Leonard, *op. cit.*, pp. 92–93.

[32]"In 1683, however, these filibusters of Hispaniola carried out a much larger design upon the coast of New Spain. In April of that year eight buccaneer captains made a rendezvous in the Gulf of Honduras for the purpose of attacking Vera Cruz. The leaders of the party were two Dutchmen named Vanhorn and Laurens de Graaf."—Haring, *The Buccaneers in the West Indies in the XVII Century*, p. 241.

[33]Cap François, a cape on the northeastern extremity of the present Dominican Republic.

[34]See note 29, *supra*.

had time to consider the matter further, suddenly changed his mind and sent to request the French to seek other shelter.

44. The two ships took leave and continued their voyage. D'Iberville, who had gone on ahead in order to explore the coast, anchored south-southeast of the eastern point of La Mobila, a large river parallel to the Mississippi. On July 2, he disembarked on a nearby island which is four leagues in circumference and which at that time had a very adequate port, where five fathoms of water could be found at all seasons. Today, however, its entrance is filled with sand. D'Iberville called it Massacre Island,[35] because toward the southwest point he discovered the skulls and bones of about sixty persons, who, he believed, had been killed there. From this island, which henceforth was called Dauphine (or Delfina) Island, he went on to the mainland and discovered the Río de los Pascagoulas, where he encountered many savages. There he embarked in two longboats with Bienville, his brother; Sauvole, a naval ensign; a Recollect father; and forty-eight men, to look for the Mississippi, of which the Indians had talked to him under the name of Malbouchia,[36] and the Spaniards under that of Empalizada,[37] although it has already been noted that its historians name it Cucagua (not this, but Chucagua, as the Inca states).

45. At length he had the satisfaction of entering it [the Mississippi] on August 2,[38] and finding the mouth entirely filled with logs which the current drags along to it ceaselessly, he decided that this was the origin of the name that it had received from the Spaniards. After having explored carefully the places that he had sought for so long a time, he went to give the good news of his discovery to Chateaumorand, who was following him slowly and who, since he had come to accompany him only until he obtained this happy report, took leave on the 20th in the ship that was under his orders.

46. As soon as he had set sail, D'Iberville again entered the Mississippi in order to ascend it, and he did not go very far without realizing that the account attributed to the Caballero de Tonti, and especially those of Father Hennepin, which had already been published, were of very little value. (He was not at all surprised at this, because he had found them defective in Canada and in Hudson's Bay, as he had reported to the minister in a letter which is in the Marine archives.) He arrived at a dwelling of savages called Bayagoulas, who conducted him to a strangly decorated temple. . . .

47. From there the French ascended to the Oumas, where they were well received. Nevertheless, D'Iberville still doubted that the river which he was navigating was the Mississippi, for though there were some indications that might make him believe that the Caballero de Tonti had visited the country

---

[35]According to Fortier (*A History of Louisiana*, Vol. I, p. 35) the Iberville expedition reached Massacre Island between January 25 and February 13, 1699.

[36]Fortier (*A History of Louisiana*, Vol. I, p. 37) refers to the Mississippi River as "the large and fatal river, the Palissada of the Spaniards, the Malvanchaya of the Indians of the Gulf coast."

[37]See preceding note.

[38]Fortier (*A History of Louisiana*, Vol. I, p. 37) says that the Iberville expedition "sailed until March 2, and on that day the mouth of the great Mississippi was re-discovered."

of the Bayagoulas, he did not find others which are mentioned in the account that he attributed to him. A letter which an Indian *cacique* delivered to him informed him completely. It was from the same *caballero* and was addressed to Monsieur de la Salle, governor of Louisiana. Tonti wrote him from the village of the Quinipisas on April 29, 1688, that since he had found the posts on which La Salle had set up the king's arms thrown down by the battering of the tide, he had had others set up on this side, about seven leagues from the sea, and that he had left a letter in a tree nearby. [He also wrote] that all those nations had received him well and had shown great fear of him, which fact he attributed to the terror that La Salle had instilled into them, but that it was with an exceedingly troubled spirit that he returned without having met him, after having had two canoes visit the coasts toward Mexico for thirty leagues and those toward Florida for twenty-five. These notices caused D'Iberville to return to the bay of Biloxi, located between the Mississippi and Mobile. There he built a fort three leagues from the Pascagoulas, left Sauvole in it as commandant and Bienville as lieutenant, and returned direct to France.

48. He made so short a stay in France that he was already back in Biloxi on January 8, 1700. On his arrival, he was informed that toward the end of September an English corvette of twelve guns had entered the Mississippi; that Bienville in going to sound the mouths of the river had encountered the English in the bend that the river makes, afterwards called Detour aux Anglois [English Turn];[39] that he had told them that if they did not with-draw, he had enough forces to oblige them to do so, and that this threat had produced results; but that upon withdrawing, they had told him that they would return very soon with larger forces, that they had discovered those lands more than fifty years previously, and that they had more right to them than the French. D'Iberville learned also that other Englishmen, who had come from Carolina, were in the country of the Chierchas [Chickasaws?] where they traded for furs and slaves.

49. These reports made him decide to renew the taking of possession by La Salle, since which time twenty years had already elapsed. Then he ordered a small fort built on the bank of the river, where he placed four

---

[39]Bienville, while exploring, on order of his brother, Iberville, the lower Mississippi River, "at the distance of about eighteen miles below the site where New Orleans now stands, . . . met an English vessel of 16 guns, under the command of Captain Bar. The English captain informed the French that he was examining the banks of the river, with the intention of selecting a spot for the foundation of a colony. Bienville told him that Louisiana was a dependency of Canada; that the French had already made several establishments on the Mississippi; and he appealed, in confirmation of his assertions, to their own presence in the river, in such small boats, which evidently proved the existence of some settlement close at hand. The Englishman believed Bienville, and sailed back. Where this occurrence took place, the river makes a considerable bend, and it was from the circumstance which I have related that the spot received the appellation of the *English Turn*—a name which it has retained to the present day."—Gayarré, *History of Louisiana*, Vol. I, pp. 60–61.

pieces of artillery. He put it in charge of St. Denis, a gentleman from Canada. This fort, which was situated almost at the mouth of the river on the east side, did not last long. While it was being constructed, D'Iberville had the pleasure of seeing Caballero [de] Tonti arrive with some twenty men from Canada, [who were] settled in the lands of the Ylineses. He did not fail to tell him of the account published under his name, but Tonti denied having any part whatever in it, and told him that no doubt it was the work of some adventurer, who after having composed it from defective sources, had attempted to give it authority by attributing it to Tonti. The historian of New France observes that Father Hennepin could not deny in the same way his third account, because it was known that he himself was the editor and that it was from his reports that the English were enabled to enter the Mississippi. . . .

50. Let us note with the historian that the Spaniards did not declare their opinion as openly (we have already seen that our kings issued orders against the French) as the English against a settlement that did not fail to cast many shadows on their thoughts, but that they conducted themselves with greater astuteness in order to check its progress. For a long time they have succeeded, with the attraction of a trade of little importance, in restricting the French to the area between the river, which they did not see fit to occupy, and Panzacola—to the sandy coast of El Biloxi, to Dauphine Island, which was not worth much more, and to the Río de la Movila, of which, in truth, it was not useless to take possession, but which did not deserve so much attention. With regard to this they add that on this occasion D'Iberville changed his mind, or that if he did have more ambitious ideas, other expenses dissuaded him from them. After having built his fort on the Mississippi and after having ascended this river to the Natchés, where he planned to found a city by the name of Rosalía[40] (in honor of the Countess of Pontchartrain, who was so named), he returned to Biloxi Bay, which he made the center of his new colony. The Spaniards opposed nothing. On the contrary, the governor of Panzacola, when he was asked permission to enter his port, responded that he had orders to prevent the English or any other company from establishing themselves in the vicinity of the Mississippi but not to refuse entrance into his port to French vessels. He requested likewise that they show him papers of the commandant so that he might be assured that he was in the service of France. Because of this D'Iberville observed to the court that Louisiana would never be settled if trade were not free to all merchants of the kingdom. At that time there were two principal objects especially designated in his instructions, namely, the wool which could be obtained from the cattle [buffalo?] of the country, and pearl fishing. Although the pearls that had been presented to the king might not have been either of a good lustre or of beautiful shapes, it was hoped that others would be found, and D'Iberville had orders not only to bring all he could, but also to explore the places that seemed promising

---

[40]"Peace was afterward with the Natchez, and Fort Rosalie was built in their country."—Fortier, *A History of Louisiana*, Vol. I, p. 62.

for this fishing and to make trials of them personally. It had been recognized very quickly that this object merited little attention, but it still seems strange that the other purpose should have been laid aside, not only because of the hides but also the wool, and that no attempt should have been made to raise the Louisiana cattle in France. D'Iberville, before returning, gave several orders with regard to this which were not carried out. . . .

51. In the following year D'Iberville made his third voyage to Louisiana and started a settlement adjacent to Mobile Island, laying the foundation for a fort[41] to which a short time later Bienville, commander-in-chief of the entire colony owing to the death of Sauvole,[42] transferred all that remained in El Biloxi, the fortress of which was abandoned.

52. In 1702, D'Iberville returned for the fourth time and ordered warehouses and dwellings to be built on Massacre Island. Since this island had a good port, it was much easier to ship to it the goods that came from France than to send them in small boats to the fort of La Movila. It was at this time that this island was given the name of Isla Delfina [Dauphine Island]. It was gradually settled. On it a fort and more adequate warehouses were built several years later, and unintentionally it has come to be the general headquarters of the colony.

53. We are shown by this text of Prevost that all the French settlements of the Gulf of Mexico were [made] subsequent to the Spanish settlement of Pensacola; and we are shown also the very honorable, courteous, and polite manner, so in accordance with international law and the harmony that nations who are at peace should preserve among themselves, in which Monsieur D'Iberville sought and found the entrance of the Mississippi; the voyage he made on it, and the settlements that he established. Oh, D'Iberville, wicked emulator of La Salle! For your perfidy you shall be execrated by all nations, and not only by civilized ones but even by the barbarous; you shall be anathematized by them and they shall not mention your name except with horror!

54. (C). The French (says Father Talamantes with regard to this) were always the aggressors, lacking in good faith and making attacks on our ships and possessions without a previous declaration of war.

But whether or not there were disturbances between the Spanish and French owing to the proximity of their settlements, is easily

---

[41]Reference is to Fort Louis de la Mobile.—Fortier, *A History of Louisiana,* Vol. I, pp. 47–48.

[42]"On August 22, 1701, Sauvole, the first governor of Louisiana, died of fever."—Fortier, *A History of Louisiana,* Vol. I, p. 46.

perceived by what is stated in the cited document 19, which literally says the following:

*Relación de la sorpresa hecha por los franceses de la Mobila en el Castillo
San Carlos, y Punta de Sigüenza, y su restauracion por las Armas de Su
Magestad (que Dios guarde) el dia ciete de Agosto de este año de 1719.
Copiada de la que de Mandato del Exmo. Señor Marquez de Valero se imprimó
en Mexico por los Herederos de Juan José Guillena Carrascosa en la Alcaisería.* [*Account of the surprise attack by the French of La Mobila on the
Castle of San Carlos and Punta de Sigüenza, and its recovery by the arms of
his Majesty (whom may God keep) on August 7 of this year of 1719. Copied
from the account which at the order of the Most Excellent Señor Marquis of
Valero was printed in Mexico by the heirs of Juan José Guillena Carrascosa
in the Alcaicería.*]   At the beginning of the cruel, bloody, and long-drawn-
out war which for many years kept raging in Europe with treacherous tena-
city—the dominions of his Majesty (whom may God keep) in particular
suffering most vitally and cruelly from it, until it was ended for a time by
the peace finally agreed upon in the congresses of Rastadt and Utrecht[43]—
a merchant of Paris named Crozat conceived in his avaricious mind the scheme
of introducing people of his nation into this kingdom [of New Spain] by way
of the north.   Although the ministers of this court despised, or paid no heed
to, the first proposals which he made with this purpose, he insistently presented
them, with repeated petitions of such apparent reasonableness that he persuaded the mind of the Most Christian King (who, by virtue of Divine Mercy,
lives in a better kingdom) that it would be of great service to both Majesties
to permit him to transport French troops, at his expense, to the vicinity of
Panzacola, and that they should be kept, without further extension, in Mobile,
at that time a small port.   His knavish vigilance was not employed in this
business only, for he likewise persuaded his Most Christian Majesty that it
would be of the greatest advantage, alike to the interests of that crown and
to those of the crown of Spain, that these troops should also garrison the
fort of Santa María de Galve.   This pretext, communicated by the Most
Christian King to his Majesty (whom may God keep), obliged his royal
benignity to lay it before his Council of the Indies, asking an opinion concerning business of such importance.   Having condescended, with this purpose,
to attend the just, zealous, representations which his ministers submitted to
his high consideration, setting forth the difficulties which were possible,
natural, and even necessary accompaniments of such a proposal, the answer
of the king, our lord, was in accordance with the clauses which the report
of the council contained.

55. In view of this intelligence, King Louis XIV (of glorious memory)
desisted from this purpose, and informed his Majesty that his vassals had
occupied the aforementioned territory, not to possess it, but in order to aid

---

[43]"The Treaties of Utrecht (1713), Rastadt, and Baden (1714), . . . concluded the War of the Spanish Succession, . . ." which lasted from 1702 to
1713.—Higby, *History of Europe (1492–1815)*, p. 194.

Panzacola in case the English should conceive the idea of attacking its fortifications; for, once peace was reëstablished, they would be obliged to abandon it. Because of the profits derived by Crozat, the proximity of this rich country [New Spain], and, above all, the very regrettable and generally lamented death of the royal personage [Louis XIV], they never did leave, as they ought to have done, in compliance with that stipulated [in the agreement]. These conditions gave rise to the most infamous, aggressive, ambitions, which, assisted by the Duke Regent,[44] and not examined into by the Council of the Regency, were pushed through, [urged by] many weighty considerations, which [they said] ought not to suffer opposition in their observance. Abusing the indulgent dissimulation which allowed the residence of the French in the said place, they so facilitated these new cunning designs that, with the permission of an individual of the crown of France, and without the knowledge of those who represent its great authority, Crozat established an armed company of merchants to which he gave the name [Company] of America, he being obligated to bring each year a number of families and troops. It was his aim that, in this way (legal because of the friendly intercourse that has marked the reciprocal and perfect union that happily has obtained between the two crowns) these French should be slowly extended by way of the Mississippi River and its confines, forming in separate settlements a province more than a thousand leagues distant from New France, with the specious name of New Orleans. They constructed several forts with the object, which they openly revealed, of getting possession of the rich minerals of Santa Fé and all this kingdom. More disturbing, even to those who are less concerned with civil rights and natural laws, was the act of bad faith by which the French of Mobile, commanded by their governor, Monsieur Bienville, on the day of May 14 of this present year surprised the castle of San Carlos and Punta de Sigüenza, which was being placed in a state of regular defense in accordance with more elaborate plans, at the order of the most excellent señor, the Marquis of Valero, viceroy of this New Spain. With due precaution against the occurrence of such an accident, he was facilitating all the zealous measures that were calculated to prevent it, not only by having increased a short time previously the number of men in the garrison of that presidio, but also by having it abundantly provided with several months' supply of provisions, munitions, and war materials. But, influenced by the fact of having the French as allies in arms, while this

---

[44]"The death of Louis XIV in 1715 and the youth of his successor and grandson, Louis XV, made necessary the establishment of a regency. For the next eight years the Duke of Orleans, a nephew of the late king, controlled the Government of France as regent. He reversed the foreign policy of Louis XIV and broke down many of the accepted standards. In foreign affairs he allied France to England, the United Netherlands, and Austria, the Powers with which it had just been at war, in an effort to prevent Philip V of Spain from regaining the Kingdom of the Two Sicilies for Spain, from acquiring the Duchies of Parma, Piacenza, and Tuscany for the son of Elizabeth Farnese, his second wife, and, in case Louis XV should die, from establishing himself on the throne of France."—Higby, *History of Europe (1492–1815)*, p. 343.

did not oblige one to live without the least suspicion of them, at any rate one felt a security not justified by their [later] indecorous operations. Favored by this indifference, and with the security which military courtesy afforded, in loyal relations with neighboring allies, on the 13th of the said month of May they captured La Punta de Sigüenza with a hulk of a warship and several pirogues, which overcame the small garrison of that fort.

56. This unexpected event caused the governor, Don Juan Pedro Matamoros de Isla, the greatest [astonishment], and especially so in view of the fact that he could not comprehend the motive that occasioned it and the end to which it was directed. Being in this perplexity, he dispatched a canoe with a trustworthy officer and some soldiers, who were made prisoners. And at daybreak on the said May 14, three vessels of considerable size flying French flags were sighted from the castle of San Carlos. The bastions of the castle fired on them, and the combat continued vigorously and on equal terms for three hours. But such a superior force could not be resisted any longer and thus Maestro de Campo Don Juan Pedro Matamoros de Isla ordered the surrender. The surrender was preceded by repeated councils of war, through the deliberations of which the terms to be stipulated for the capitulations were decided upon. These were most honorable (Señor Barcia gives them word for word in his *Ensayo Cronológico* under the year 1719, page 349) and contained even greater advantages than are customary. Thus the transfer of the fort to the troops of France was fully executed and effected under these terms, although with the protest (which was first made) that such an act of hostility was strange in time of peace. To this they [the French] gave assurances that war had been declared between the crowns of Spain and France since the 14th of January, but it was recognized that this assertion was entirely false, since such a declaration had not been made previously. For, even though the duke regent has managed to disturb the peaceful, tranquil, and precious friendship based upon the closely identified interests of the two kingdoms, the action of one individual should not be regarded as the action of France. But even though the proclamation of war was made, these Frenchmen still were not free from the imputation [of being] insincere violators of good faith, since always after war has been declared, two months must pass before either side, without incurring censure, can begin hostilities. The first report of the loss of Santa María de Galve that reached the most excellent señor viceroy was the one given in a letter of May 26, by Don Gregorio Salinas,[45] governor of the bay of San José,[46] which he received on the night of June 29. This unfortunate, unforeseen, calamity occasioned his zeal inevitable grief, it being the more regrettable in that it was unexpected; and because of the considerations involved in it and the important influence exercised upon the royal service by the interests of our religion, which

---

[45]For frequent references to Don Gregorio Salinas Varona, consult the indices of *Pichardo's Treatise* . . . , Vols. I, II, and III.

[46]This bay previously has been identified with present Espírito Santo Bay— a northeastern arm of present San Antonio Bay on the Texas Gulf coast. See *Pichardo's Treatise* . . . , Vol. I, p. 420, n. 3, and p. 472, n. 1.

suffered noticeably in such a contretemps, this genuine affliction could make
no other impression on his Excellency's mind than that of anxiety. For
from that instant the continuous toil of his zealous activity did not cease [put-
ting into execution] all the measures dictated by the proper discharge of his
duty of punishing the daring, violent action of these Frenchmen, of maintaining unblemished and in due respect the honor of the arms of his Majesty
(whom may God keep) and the glory of the nation, as well as of checking the
facile plans of the opposing nation which (according to the declaration of
the father *guardián* of Panzacola) they were making public—not omitting the
fact that their special purpose, which motivated them to make themselves
masters of this presidio, was to succeed in penetrating from such a base into
the vast province of New Mexico. The earnest desire of the most excellent
señor viceroy to obtain all these ends caused him to begin his measures by
sending a succession of couriers to ports of the kingdom for the purpose of
assembling maritime forces, prosecuting this laborious task not only for this
purpose but also for the preparation of vessels in Vera Cruz, the recruiting
of soldiers, and for preparing five·thousand daily rations for a period of four
months, which were to be ready within a few days after the order was given.

57. The great and obvious difficulty which is experienced in this kingdom
in making such arrangements was increased by the lack of vessels, and had
prevented the success [of these plans], when on July 5, three warships destined
for the windward fleet, under its commandant, Don Francisco Cornejo, of the
Order of Santiago, cast anchor in Vera Cruz. When they, with others, were
ready to set sail, the governor of Havana, Don Gregorio Guazo Calderón,
reported in a letter of July 19, that when a fleet had left that port on the
4th of the same month, consisting of fifteen vessels well manned and armed,
in charge of Don Alfonso Carrascosa de la Torre, on an expedition in the
royal service, they discovered two frigates which were crowding all sail
in an effort to escape. But when the said fleet set its course in pursuit of
the said frigates and gained the windward, they made them strike colors and
it was learned that they were French vessels which were going to leave on
the coasts of Havana the governor, officers, and garrison of the captured
presidio of Santa María de Galve. Don Gregorio Guazo Calderón, being informed of this calamity in this way, convoked a council of war in which it was
declared that the frigates were legitimate prizes, since he who does not observe
a treaty and attempts by force to dispossess others, contrary to all right and
reason, of immemorial dominion which he can under no pretext claim, should
not be protected by military exemptions. And it was decided to change the
destination of the fleet of fifteen vessels, and to direct its full strength toward
Santa María de Galve, as a more urgent objective, for which place it sailed
on the same day as the date of the governor's letter, July 19. This voyage
was facilitated in a great measure by the military provision which the most
excellent señor viceroy has ordered for that port in supplying it with everything for quickly assisting the rest, as a place close to all of them. On this
occasion 1,200 landing troops embarked as volunteers, among them many
people of distinction, and 150 infantry from the garrison of that fort.

58. The news that the arms of the king, our lord, were already engaged in this undertaking further animated the tireless persistence with which war-like preparations were being made in Vera Cruz. Indeed, it was only a matter of moments until the results were [expected] to be seen of the work on the formidable armed fleet that was to proceed to the aid of the one from Havana, when, on the night of August 25, the rejoicing with which the people's affectionate and humble loyalty was celebrating the joyous annual festival of the happy birthday of his most serene highness, the prince, our lord (whom may God keep), was completed by the favorable news which Don Alfonso Carrascosa de la Torre sent in a letter of August 7. He reported that the arms of his Majesty, (whom may God keep), of which he went as commandant, had arrived at the presidio on the 6th of the same month and that it had been restored to submission to his Majesty on the 7th, after some resistance made by two warships anchored in the port, aided by the castle. But they became terrified when our vessels continued to enter, and finding themselves pursued by the latter, one of them was set afire and the other surrendered with its crew, followed by the post itself in its former state, with some additions, there being in all about 350 men. They surrendered at discretion as prisoners of war, together with their governor and officers. They were sent immediately to Havana (with the exception of forty men who came over to our side), in order that they might be sent from there to Spain.

59. This occurrence, deserving universal applause because of its importance, and because of what it obtained for the nation, promises other greater successes. The residents of Havana deserve particular approbation, their loyal courage almost having caused that island to be left depopulated, since the desire to sacrifice themselves in the service of his Majesty was, to their credit, strong in all of them; and their glorious, never-emulated ardor had to be tempered by the fitting prudence of the governor with considerations worthy of his zeal. The hope for these further successes changes to certainty in as much as the fleet has continued its voyage to La Masacra and Movila with the intention that the French should feel the force of [our] reasonable irritation. There adds to this certainty the considerable force that left Vera Cruz in good time with the same destination, consisting of the warships in charge of the commandant of the windward fleet, Don Francisco Cornejo, of the Order of Santiago, and of those that arrived later from Havana under Don Francisco Guerrero, of the Order of San Juan. No doubt remains concerning the most complete restoration, with which will be obtained very shortly the complete extermination of the French settlers in this kingdom. Their ill-conceived haughtiness has brought on their ruin. Their anxiety for his Majesty's arms, interesting in view of their bad faith, is a justifiable cause which fittingly demands that royal magnanimity should not continue to be tolerant and merciful, as it has been hitherto. The End. At the order of the Most Excellent Señor Marquis of Valero, viceroy of this New Spain, etc. In Mexico. For the heirs of Juan José Guillena Carrascosa in the Alcaisería.

60. (D). Father Charlevoix,[47] in Prevost, volume 26 of Señor Terracina's translation, page 35, explains these changes of possession in the following words:

Such was still the condition of this garrison in the year 1719, when the French under the command of Monsieur de Serigny[48] laid siege to it in the name of the Company of the West,[49] which took advantage of the occasion of a temporary break between the two crowns to acquire the only port on the entire Florida coast from the Bahama Channel to the Mississippi. In one and the same year the fort of San Carlos was taken by Serigny, recovered by the Spaniards, and retaken by the French who held it peacefully when we arrived, but it was found in such bad condition that it seems that they had no desire to preserve it.

And Señor Barcia, in decade 9, under the year 1719, gives this entire history at great length, especially the French recovery of this port after the Spaniards had taken it away from them. The following cedula, which is found in document 39, number 197, discusses the restitution that should be made to Spain following the conclusion of peace:

The King.[50] The Marquis of Valero, relative, gentleman of my bedchamber, viceroy, governor, and captain-general of the provinces of New Spain, and president of my royal audiencia of Mexico. As a consequence of what has lately been agreed upon between this crown and that of France, the Most Christian King,[51] my nephew, and the Council of Marine of that kingdom, on August 20, last, issued the two enclosed orders for Monsieur de Bienville, commandant-general of the colony of Louisiana, in which he orders him to deliver to the Spanish bearers thereof the fort, or presidio, of Panzacola, named also Santa María de Galve, and the rest of the lands that the French might have conquered in those, my dominions, during the last war with this nation, with everything in the state in which it may be at present, with the artillery, stores, and munitions of war which were found there when the French troops made themselves masters of it the first time, without excepting or reserving anything that may have been there at that time.

61. So that the said provisions may be carried out immediately, the French restoring the presidio of Panzacola and the other places, provinces, and territory that they might have acquired since the day that war was declared with France in the past year of 1719, on the east side of Mobile as well as on the west side

[47]See *Pichardo's Treatise* . . . , Vol. I, p. 215, n. 4.
[48]The Sieur de Serigny was the brother of Iberville and Bienville.
[49]For details concerning the French Company of the West, see Fortier, *A History of Louisiana*, Vol. I, pp. 63–68.
[50]Reference is to King Philip V of Spain.
[51]Reference is to King Louis XV of France.

beginning with the Mississippi, leaving those places in the same state in which they were when they occupied them, withdrawing the arms, munitions, and equipment that they had in them,

62. I have decided to send you with this dispatch the two cited original orders and to command you (as I do) that as soon as you receive them, by taking definite and specific statements from the military and royal treasury officials of that kingdom who might have been in Panzacola at the time of the first surrender of that presidio in the year 1719, you shall draw up an account of the artillery, arms, munitions, and stores which at that time existed in it, and shall ask the same officials if they know whether, since the French occupied it, they have taken over any other place in the vicinity of Panzacola. . . .

63. After taking these statements with the greatest promptness and exactness possible, you shall inform the said commandant of Louisiana of them, sending him copies of the enclosed orders of the court of France, so that in conformance with them, he may take the necessary measures to the end that when my troops arrive with the persons whom you may send for the delivery of Panzacola and the rest that is to be restored, there may be no delay in executing it. The letters that you shall write with regard to this to the said commandant you shall send to him by an officer—who is in your confidence, intelligent, active, and capable—who is to be sent to the post of La Movila in sloops or a brigantine which you will direct to be prepared for this purpose.

64. You shall also give an order (upon receiving the reply of the commandant of Louisiana) for one of the companies of infantry which the squadron under the command of Don Baltasar de Guevara left in that kingdom to garrison it, to go and occupy the presidio of Panzacola. With this company you shall send the said original orders of the court of France and a person of integrity and zeal who with all care will receive the artillery, arms, munitions, and stores which were in that presidio at the time that the French first attacked it in the year 1719. He shall make an inventory of whatever may be left to be delivered (if thus it should happen) setting forth clearly and distinctly the things that remain there.

65. Likewise you shall order to be sent to Pensacola with the said company the engineer, Don José de Berbegal, together with such workmen and criminals sentenced to prison by that audiencia as you may see fit, and with the necessary tools, so that as soon as the Frenchmen shall have handed over that presidio, they may undertake and carry out the work of cutting through the isthmus made by the island of Santa Rosa, between the sea and the bay of Panzacola, at the narrowest and most suitable place, in order that its current may be discharged by way of the channel that is thus opened for it, and so that by taking in this way a large portion of water from the principal channel, the latter may become shallower than it is at its entrance, making it impossible for warships to enter it. This will make unnecessary the heavy expenditures for fortifying and maintaining that bay, without any benefit whatever to my royal treasury or to my vassals, and with the evident risk of losing it upon any assault of enemies, as the facility with which it was lost and won three times

in the year 1719 testifies. But if the said bay cannot be rendered useless in the manner stated, in order to prevent any foreigners from occupying it, you shall have the engineer who goes there and the workers who are to accompany him, construct under his direction on the Punta de Sigüenza of the said island of Santa Rosa, and nowhere else, a fortress capable of being garrisoned with 150 men of both infantry and artillery, in order to prevent the entrance of enemy vessels into that bay by forcing their way in with artillery. In view of the situation of La Punta de Sigüenza, this purpose may be attained most readily by placing the fortification there, rather than at its former site or at any other place that may be newly fortified in a different part of the bay. To this is added the difficulty of attacking the one of La Punta de Sigüenza without first making a landing, which was not the case at the old fort, and would not be at one that might be built on another site on the bay, for they could go to it by land from La Mobila.

66. In either of the two cases stated, either of rendering the said bay useless, which is the matter in which the greatest care must be taken and all possible effort made, or of constructing the fortress on La Punta de Sigüenza, the one on the bay must be destroyed and razed since it is worthless, indefensible, and in a poor location. If the first object is attained, the artillery, arms, munitions, and stores which the French may deliver will be taken to that kingdom [New Spain]. But if it should be necessary to construct the new fortress on La Punta de Sigüenza, there shall be left in it whatever of these articles may be necessary, together with an adequate garrison and an officer who will serve as governor, they being supported from that kingdom with salaries and provisions, as was done in the case of the Panzacola garrison, and the engineer and the workmen and other persons who may have gone to that presidio, except the criminals, will be returned after one of the two operations described shall have been executed.

67. And in as much as I have been informed that the bay of San José, which was occupied about three years ago at your orders, is useless, unhealthy, and incapable of being placed in a state of defense because of the width of its mouth or entrance; and that it cannot be of benefit to this crown or to the French because it is located a long distance from La Mobila, for which reasons not only they but also my vassals have neglected it in the past, I order you to have it abandoned, withdrawing the garrison, artillery, arms, and munitions to the port of Panzacola, holding them there as if in bond until it is seen whether it is possible to prevent large ships from entering. For by saving in this way the excessive expenditure which the maintenance of these two presidios has occasioned, with only a fourth of that amount the fertile province of Apalache, which is on the same Gulf of Mexico opposite Havana and communicates by land with the presidio of San Augustín de la Florida, may be put in good condition. This will be demonstrated by the many good products in which it abounds, as was the case twenty years ago, and there will not be felt there the scarcities and hardships which have been experienced during the said time that the province of Apalache has been without a settlement of Spaniards.

68. All this I order you to observe and have executed exactly and promptly, without any objection or delay whatever. You shall give me a special report

on its fulfillment and on everything which you may order to be done concerning it, so that I may be informed, for such is my will. Dated in Balsain, on September 20, 1721. I, the King. Don José Grimales.

69. (E). Río Perdido. This is not the correct name of that river; it should be Río de los Perdidos. This is shown by Father Charlevoix, in Prevost's volume 26 of Señor Terracina's translation, page 36, when he discusses the reason why it was given this name:

> At midnight (he says) we set out from Panzacola and at four in the morning we left on our right the Río de los Perdidos, celebrated as the site of the wreck of a Spanish ship, whose loss, with its entire crew, caused the river to be given this name.

And Señor Barcia, under the year 1693, page 312, speaks of it in these words:

> Toward the west-northwest, outside the bay and at a distance of three leagues from the Gulf of Mexico, there enters the mainland [on which is] the castle another river or arm of the sea which they call Los Perdidos, which also extends toward the north-northeast. One goes by way of it to La Movila, the settlement of the French, located north-northwest of the presidio of which we spoke, at a distance of some twenty-two or twenty-four leagues.

It is true that our Military Gentleman is not the only one who fell into the error of calling it the Río Perdido, for among others who did so were D'Anville, on his map of North America; Monsieur Robert and his son, Robert Vaugondy,[52] on map 102, which is the one of North America in his *Atlas Universal,* printed in Paris in 1757; the Englishman, Michel[53] [Mitchell], on his map 6 (which is number 148 of the *Atlas* of Le Rouge)[54] of North America; the map of Señor Lángara;[55] Alcedo[56] in his *Diccionario de America,* under the article "Perdido"; and many other Spaniards.

[52]For frequent references to Monsieur Robert and his son Robert Vaugondy, see the indices of *Pichardo's Treatise* . . . , Vols. II and III.

[53]For frequent references to John Michel [Mitchell], consult the indices of *Pichardo's Treatise* . . . , Vols. I, II, and III.

[54]For frequent references to George Louis Le Rouge, consult the indices of *Pichardo's Treatise* . . . , Vols. I, II, and III.

[55]For frequent references to Don Juan de Lángara and his map, consult the indices of *Pichardo's Treatise* . . . , Vols. I and II.

[56]For frequent references to Antonio de Alcedo y Bexarano and his dictionary, consult the indices of *Pichardo's Treatise* . . . , Vols. I, II, and III.

70. (F). Everyone is of the same opinion, and the celebrated D'Anville enclosed all the country of the Spaniards called Florida with a dotted line in the following manner. The line begins at the entrance of the Río de los Perdidos into the sea, which is located in 30° 20′ of latitude and 69° 55′ of longitude, and ascends toward the northeast to 34° 30′ of latitude and 66° 56′ of longitude. (In map number 20 of document 74, which we have drawn by computing it from those of D'Anville and Señor Lángara, the entrance of the Río Perdido is found in 30° 17′ of latitude and 70° 32′ of longitude, because it is found on the map of Señor Lángara in this latitude and longitude.) Thence it goes east, with a slight inclination toward the north, to 34° 35′ of latitude and 66° 16′ of longitude, and from here it descends toward the southeast until it ends on the coast of the Atlantic Ocean, above the city of San Agustín in 30° 38′ of latitude, almost at the mouth of the Río Alatama. Therefore everything that is included within this line as far as the tip of Florida was assigned to the Spaniards. The same line is seen on the cited map number 6 of Michel [Mitchell], which, as we have stated, is number 148 of Le Rouge's *Atlas*. Consequently, everything that lies west of the Río de los Perdidos was part of Louisiana and belonged to the French, and everything that lies to the east was a part of Florida and belonged to the Spaniards. The following royal order (which is found on page 292 of volume 67 of the royal cedulas and orders which are kept in the secretariat of the viceroyalty) also states that the Río de los Perdidos was the boundary between Louisiana and Florida.

In a letter of January 25 of this year [1747] your Excellency encloses a certified copy of what has been done as a result of the commandant of the presidio of Santa Rosa, Punta de Sigüenza, having reported that a Frenchman named Cuartier[57] had settled on the Río de los Perdidos, pretending to fish for tuna and erecting buildings and warehouses. You stated that from the

---

[57]"In the last year of the War of the Austrian Succession the king learned with great concern from the viceroy of New Spain that a Frenchman named Cuartier [Martier] had settled on the Perdido River, feigning as an excuse that he was fishing for tunny, and that there he had 'constructed buildings and storehouses.' The viceroy, upon receipt of this information, requested in writing the French commandant of Louisiana 'to have the aforesaid Martier retire and to keep within its boundaries those of his nation.' "—Hackett, "Policy of the Spanish Crown Regarding French Encroachment from Louisiana, 1721–1762," in *New Spain and the Anglo-American West*, p. 120.

reports received it was shown that the land on which they are being built belongs to his Majesty, and that in view of this, your Excellency wrote to the commandant of the French colony in order that he might make the said Cuartier withdraw and restrict those of his nation to their limits. And your Excellency ordered the commandant of the presidio not to permit the usurpation of the cited territory and to prevent the French from expanding, your Excellency offering to report the results. I have given the king an account of these reports, and he is awaiting one concerning the results that may have been produced by the measure which your Excellency says you have applied. But [the king states] that if the result has not been the recovery of that territory and the expulsion of the said Frenchman who established himself on the Río de los Perdidos, your Excellency shall proceed to have him arrested and to have the buildings which he may have built destroyed, this last to be done in any case. And his Majesty orders me to advise your Excellency that in cases similar to this one and in which there is no doubt that land belonging to his royal crown [is involved], your Excellency shall begin by executing [the offenders] as if they were pirates on land and sea, for only in that way may the end be achieved, and the sovereign of those captured will not object. If demands are made, they [the Spanish officials] will immediately be sent patents [for this purpose], which they will use. I advise your Excellency of this for your observance. God keep your Excellency many. years. Madrid, September 28, 1747. To the Marquis of La Ensenada. Señor Don Juan Francisco de Güemes Horcasitas.

71. (G.) With regard to this Father Talamantes states:

This is the principle on which the solution of this question should be based. The question does not reduce itself to inquiring into what the French should possess, but what in fact they did possess. If justice is adhered to, France does not possess a span of territory there. If fact is adhered to, the limits of Louisiana are very much reduced.

72. (H). The same father inserts here a note of the following tenor:

De facto possession is one of the most solid arguments Spain has on which to base her claims, which cannot appear exhorbitant except to those who are interested in increasing their possessions at the expense of the Spaniards.

IX

73. For all these reasons it is difficult to understand the basis for the assertion that no part of West Florida, with the exception of the island of Orleans, is included in Louisiana. If the original discovery and the settlement which the French made in it (A), if the name of Louisiana which they themselves gave it (B), if recognizing it as his by the Most Christian King (C), if the establishment of a government and the administration of the laws, if the unin-

terrupted possession of eighty years and the consent of Spain at least in the last
half of this period (D), if all these things, I say, are not sufficient to give
France an indisputable title, territorial rights of nations are completely uncertain. The claims of Spain to West Florida have no antecedent with which they
can be sanctioned and they engender a distrust of all those principles which
commonly direct the conduct of civilized nations.

NOTES

74. (A). It seems that the Military Gentleman is of the opinion that the French were the first discoverers of West Florida
and the first also who established themselves there. But in order
to be able to discuss this assertion, it becomes necessary to explain what is meant by West Florida. W. Winterbotham,[58] on
page 65 of volume 4 of his work, cited in Part I, paragraph 101,
discusses the history of the Spanish dominions in North America,
and he begins with East and West Florida, of which he says:

that East and West Florida are located between 25 and 31 degrees of north
latitude and between 5 and 17 degrees of longitude west of Philadelphia; that
they are nearly six hundred miles in length and nearly 130 miles wide; that on
the north they are bounded by Georgia, on the east by the Atlantic Ocean, on
the south by the Gulf of Mexico, and on the west by the Mississippi River,
and he adds that they form the shape of a capital letter L.

The *Diccionario* of Alcedo, under the article "Florida," states
the following:

After the French had established themselves in the part which they called
New France, or Canada, and in Louisiana, and the English in Carolina, they
both proceeded to found various provinces, or colonies, setting boundaries,
and giving them names. Because of this the old name of Florida remained
only to the territory in which the Spaniards were settled. It is a peninsula or
point of land opposite the island of Cuba, which extends a hundred leagues
north along the coast and is twenty-five leagues wide. It forms the mouth or
entrance of the Gulf of Mexico and one side of the Bahama Channel. It is
bounded on the northeast by Virginia and on the southwest by the province
and nation of the Apalache Indians. Although the Spaniards made various
settlements, only those of Panzacola and San Agustín, which is the capital,
remain, since this country has been the site of almost continuous warfare
between the Spaniards, the English, the French and the natives. The first-
named ceded it to the English in the year 1762 by the peace of Versailles, and
they took possession of it, dividing it into East and West Florida. The first

---

[58]For frequent references to W. Winterbotham, consult the indices of
Pichardo's Treatise . . . , Vols. I, II, and III.

consisted of the Spanish peninsula and was bounded on the north by Georgia and on the west by the Río Apalachicola. The second extended from this river and had as its limits the Gulf of Mexico on the south, the 31st parallel of latitude on the north, and Lakes Maurepas and Pontchartrain and the Mississippi River on the west. Its extent was more than eighty leagues. In the peace of the year 1783 they again ceded it to its first possessors, who still have it today.

Treating of the governors in Florida, he says concerning Don Lucas Fernando Palacios that

he was appointed governor of Florida in the year 1758, and he held this position until 1762, when he was killed by the Indians in a sally he made against them. He was the last governor, for in the following year the court ceded that country to the king of England in the peace of Versailles, and although it recovered it later in the peace of Paris of 1783, this government continued under the authority of the commandant-general of Louisiana.

Don Antonio Vegas,[59] in his *Diccionario Geográfico Universal,* printed in Madrid in 1795, under the article "Florida" also says:

Florida was ceded to England in the peace of 1763 and was divided into East and West Florida. The last was reconquered by Spanish arms in 1781, and by the peace of 1783 Great Britain ceded East and West Florida to Spain.

75. Finally, in our document 39, number 279, is found an extract from the treaty of peace of the year 1762 [1763] between France and England and between Spain and England also, the frontispiece of which is the following: *Tratado definitivo de Paz concludido entre el Rey N.S. y su Mag. Cristisima por una parte y S.M. Britanica por otra en Paris á 10. de Febrero de 1763 con sus articulos Preliminares y la accesion de su Mag. fidelisma á ellos y al mismo Tratado como tambien las Ratificaciones Plenipotencias y demas actos de las Potencias interesadas De orden de S.M. En Madrid: En la Ymprenta Real de la Gaceta. Año de 1763.*[60] [*Definitive Treaty of Peace concluded between the King, our Lord, and His Most Christian Majesty on the one hand and*

---

[59]For references to Don Antonio Vegas and his dictionary consult the indices of *Pichardo's Treatise* . . . , Vols. II and III.

[60]The Spanish text of the treaty of 1763 as given above by Pichardo has not been available to the editor. A French text "taken from the original manuscript of the French ratification in the London Public Record Office, St. Pap. For., Treaties, no. 124," is found in Frances Gardiner Davenport and Charles Oscar Paullin, *European Treaties Bearing on the History of the United States and its Dependencies*, Vol. IV, pp. 92–98.

His Britannic Majesty on the other, in Paris on February 10, 1763, with its preliminary articles and the accession of His Most Faithful Majesty to them and to the same Treaty, as well as the Ratifications, Plenipotences, and other acts of the interested Powers. At the order of his Majesty. In Madrid, at the Royal Press of La Gaceta. 1763.] In it are read the articles that we copy here.

Article six. In order to restore peace on solid and durable bases and to preclude forever all motives for disputes with regard to the limits of the French and British territories on the continent of America, it has been agreed that in the future the boundaries between his Most Christian Majesty's lands and those of his Britannic Majesty in that part of the world shall be fixed irrevocably by a line drawn in the middle of the Mississippi River from its source to the Río Iberville, and from there with another line drawn in the middle of this river and of Lakes Maurepas and Pontchartrain to the sea. To this end the Most Christian King cedes the most complete ownership, and constitutes himself guarantor to his Britannic Majesty, of the river and port of La Mobila and of all that he possesses or should have possessed on the left side of the Mississippi River with the exception of the city of New Orleans and the island on which it is located, which shall continue to belong to France, with the understanding that the navigation of the Mississippi River shall be equally free alike to the vassals of Great Britain and to those of France, in its entire width and along its entire course, from its source to the sea, and especially on that part which is between the abovesaid island of New Orleans and the right bank of that river, as well as entrance and exit at its mouth. It is stipulated also that the vessels belonging to the subjects of either nation may not be detained or searched or obliged to pay any duty whatever. The stipulations inserted in the second article in favor of the inhabitants of Canada will hold good likewise with regard to the inhabitants of the countries ceded by this article. . . .

Concerning this article it seems that it is clear that France ceded to England all the country that falls east of the Mississippi, beginning at the source of this river, the boundary line being drawn along the middle of it to the entrance of the Río Iberville, along the middle of which another boundary line was to run east, traversing Lakes Maurepas and Pontchartrain to where the latter empties into the sea. Consequently France ceded to Spain all the territory which lies west of the Mississippi from the same source of the said river to the points through which D'Anville's line should have passed and did pass, running the boundary line of the lands ceded to Spain along the same middle of the said Mississippi so that the western half of this river belonged to Spain and the other half, the eastern, to England. This Spanish boundary line, however, should not have ended in the Río Iberville, but should have continued to the entrance of the Mississippi into the sea, as did the one of the English. And on the east it should have continued along the south side of the Río Iberville [and Lakes] Maurepas and Pontchartrain, to the sea, because in this way the island on which New Orleans is located was given to Spain and was excluded from the part of the French lands given to England. England, by force of this cession, remained in possession besides of everything that is located farther north—of that piece of Louisiana which, beginning at the middle of the entrance of the Río Iberville into the Mississippi and ending at the dividing line that ascends from the Río Perdido, separating Florida from Louisiana, embraces, from the said Río Iberville, La Punta Cortada [Pointe Coupée], Baton Rouge, Manchac, Biloxi Bay, La Mobila, and La Punta Lassar, all of which are seen encircled with a yellow line on our map. After France had ceded all this land to England in 1762,[61] she turned her attention to Spain in 1763[62] and began to treat with her concerning the lands which she was ceding to her, which were exactly the same ones that we have described, that is, all that part of Louisiana that falls west of the Mississippi and east of this river only the island on which New Orleans was located, which was called an island because it was enclosed by various waters, that is, by rivers, by lakes, and by the sea, for on the north it was bordered by the Río Iberville and by Lakes Maurepas and Pontchartrain, on the west by the Mississippi River, from the said Río Iberville to the sea, and on the south and east by the said sea. This is clearly seen on our map 20. Concerning Lake Pontchartrain Alcedo writes as follows in his *Diccionario:*

Pontchartrain. A lake in the province and government of Louisiana in North America. It is seven to eight leagues long, empties into the sea through a narrow channel, and is fewer than four leagues from New Orleans.

---

[61]Preliminaries of peace to end the Seven Years' War (1756–1763) were signed at Fontainebleau on November 3, 1762. The definitive treaty of peace was signed at Paris on February 10, 1763. From France, England received Canada, St. John's, Cape Breton, and all of the former French province of Louisiana that lay to the east of the Mississippi except the island of Orleans.— See Hayes, *Modern Europe,* Vol. I, pp. 312–319 and pp. 359–360; Bolton and Marshall, *Colonization of North America,* pp. 369–383; and Thwaites, *France in America,* pp. 266–380.

[62]See note 15, Chapter XVII, *supra.*

And since this lake ends in the sea, it is said that the line that left the Mississippi and passed by way of the Iberville, Lake Maurepas, and Lake Pontchartrain reached the sea but did not end there, continuing along the coast to the mouth of the Río de los Perdidos where the French lands ended.

76. These treaties being concluded, Spain and England began to draw up theirs, which were conceived in terms stated in the eighteenth and nineteenth articles of the said *Definitive Treaty of Peace*, which are as follows:

Article eighteen. The king of Great Britain restores to Spain everything that he has conquered on the island of Cuba, including the fort of Havana. This fort, as well as all the others of the said island, will be restored in the same state in which they were when they were conquered by the arms of his Britannic Majesty. Article nineteen. In consequence of the restoration stipulated in the preceding article, his Catholic Majesty cedes to his Britannic Majesty full ownership and constitutes himself guarantor, of everything that Spain possesses on the continent of North America east or southeast of the Mississippi River, and his Britannic Majesty agrees in granting the inhabitants of this country, ceded above, the free exercise of the Catholic religion, etc.

From this article nineteen we learn that Spain ceded to England everything that she possessed east or southeast of the Mississippi River, which consisted precisely of Florida, just as we have described it above in paragraph 70, in accordance with D'Anville's map. England combined with Florida, which Spain had ceded to her, all the land that she had received from France and which began from the middle of the Mississippi. Consequently England became the possessor of these two French and Spanish territories, now united, and it was at this time that England gave the name of Florida to this entire territory composed of the two said sections, and took its name from [that part formerly belonging to] Louisiana. When under this name of Florida she divided it all into East and West Florida, West Florida began at the Mississippi and extended as far as the Río Apalachicola, and East Florida from this river to the Atlantic Ocean, the peninsula of land which extends as far as a point opposite Havana being included in the latter. From all this we see clearly that France never ceded to Spain that part of Louisiana which is above New Orleans and in which are included Manchac, Baton Rouge, La Mobila, etc. For when France ceded Louisiana to Spain, she had already ceded this part of it to England. This power possessed the said Floridas until the time that the most excellent señor, Don Bernardo de Gálvez,[63] who was later viceroy of this new Spain, governed Louisiana. When his Excellency died in Mexico, the honorary printer to the *cámara* of his Majesty, Don Manuel Antonio Valdés, a writer and founder of the *Gaceta* of this city, composed a poem which he published in the year 1787, under the following title: *Apuntes de algunas de las gloriosas acciones del Exmo. Sor Don Bernardo de Galvez, Conde de Galvez, Virrey, Governador, y Capitan General que fué de esta Nueva España, etc. Hacialos en un Romance Heroico Don Manuel Antonio Valdes, Autor de la Gaceta Mexicana.* [*Notes on some of the glorious deeds of the Most Excellent Señor Don Bernardo de Gálvez, Count of Gálvez, former Viceroy, Governor, and Captain-General of this New Spain, etc. Composed in heroic ballad style by Don Manuel Antonio Valdéz, a writer of the Gaceta Mexicana.*] And since poets cannot always explain all their material in verse, they are wont to add some marginal notes in which they state what they could not put in metrical form. For this reason Señor Valdéz attached some similar notes to his poem. Those that relate to our subject are the following:[64]

After his Excellency had filled the position of governor *ad interim* in Louisiana, with the rank of colonel of its permanent regiment, beginning in the year 1776, he received in 1779 orders relating to the outbreak of the war, together with the title of possession of that government. His Excellency having made the heroic decision to attack the English in their own fortifications, notwithstanding the fact that it had been thought that he would simply stay on the defensive until reinforcements were received from Havana, such a fierce hurricane arose that it sank almost all the vessels his Excellency had, together with the supplies for his campaign. But despite such an adverse circumstance, he knew how to keep the troops and settlers of that capital under such obedience that instead of becoming discouraged, they offered themselves with greater determination for the undertaking. Several vessels were raised from the bottom of the river, and, after assembling as many as seven hundred troops, his Excellency began his march and took the fort of Manchak by a surprise attack, its garrison being made prisoners of war. The fort of Baton Rouge was the place where the troops of the enemy had assembled and fortified themselves, but

[63]See *Pichardo's Treatise . . .* , Vol. I, p. 381, n. 2.
[64]A detailed account of the events summarized in the following document is to be found in Caughey, *Bernardo de Gálvez in Louisiana, 1776–1783*, pp. 135–214. The two accounts differ in certain particulars, principally as regards numerical data.

by ordering trenches built and batteries established, his Excellency succeeded in distracting the enemy's fire to the place of a false attack, and, finally, in reducing their fort and making it necessary for them to ask for a capitulation, which was granted them on the condition that the troops (which consisted of 500 men) should become prisoners of war and that the fort of Panmure de Natchez be handed over, which had an equally large garrison and was in a dominant position.   Subsequently he took the posts of Tompson [Thompson?] and Smith, together with the other establishments which the English had on the east bank of the Mississippi, and he captured on its waters eight vessels which were coming from Panzacola to the aid of the said forts.   This under-taking and its respective operations were so well directed that its great success is shown by the surrender of a thousand Englishmen and the fact that 430 leagues of the most fertile lands, settled by various [Indian] nations, came under the dominion of our Catholic monarch without any more bloodshed on our side than the wounding of one man.   The conquest of La Movila was no less glorious. His excellency embarked for it with 1,200 men, setting sail on the Mississippi on January 14, 1780, with fourteen ships of various tonnages. His valor overcoming all the misfortunes that befell the troops on sea and land (which would have been sufficient to cause another less hopeful leader to abandon the undertaking), he succeeded in making them surrender the fort by capitulation, the garrison, consisting of 307 men, becoming prisoners of war in the presence of their General John Campbell, who withdrew precipitately with the loss of a captain and sixteen dragoons, who likewise became prisoners. See the cedula of May 20, 1783, in which the king is pleased to grant his Excellency the honor of Titulo de Castilla.   Who is capable of praising justly the one exploit alone which his Excellency accomplished in having undertaken on his own responsibility to force an entrance into the port of Panzacola against the unanimous opinion of all the naval officers, who considered the enterprise impracticable, and in succeeding in doing so in full view of the army, fleet, and convoy, and of the enemy, despite the stubborn fire which the castle kept up from the heights!   See the said cedula.   In one of the engagements that took place during the siege of Panzacola, his Excellency was also wounded in the stomach and in the left hand; but, although this misfortune terrified the army greatly, it did not keep him from continuing to direct the respective operations. The surrender of the fort on the half-moon was the deciding event of that famous expedition, for when Divine Providence willed that a grenade discharged from the batteries of our camp should set fire to the powder house of that fortress, blowing up a section of it with 105 Englishmen who were guarding it, the result was that its defenders asked for a capitulation and that Fort George and other fortresses were surrendered.   They contained 153 mounted pieces and the corresponding arms and stores, and the garrison, which consisted of 1,400 men with their respective officers, among the Field Marshal John Camp-bell, commander-in-chief of the troops, and Vice-Admiral Peter Chester, gov-ernor and captain-general of the province, who became prisoners of war.

As a result of these most glorious acts of the Most Excellent Señor Gálvez, Spain recovered Florida. which she had ceded to the English, and she also made herself mistress of the part of Louisiana which France had ceded to the same English and in which were located Baton Rouge, Manchac, Movila, etc. This was confirmed by the treaties of peace of the year 1783, to which Señor Alcedo, cited above in paragraph 74, alludes in the following words:

But in the peace of the year 1783, they again ceded it to its first possessors who still have it today.

But it must be admitted that England did not return to Spain all the land of Florida which she had ceded to England, for England kept that part which extended from the 31st parallel north to 34° 35' of latitude, where it ended. For this reason the cited Winterbotham makes the two Floridas, East and West, end at the 31st parallel, although Señor Alcedo limits expressly only West Florida to this parallel. After all this has been explained with the clearness that is noted, the crass ignorance or, rather, the malice of the Military Gentlemen, poured forth in those statements which are found at the beginning of the paragraph which we are going to discuss, is unmistakable. They are as follows:

Because of all these reasons it is difficult to understand the basis for the assertion that no part of West Florida, with the exception of the island of Orleans, is included in Louisiana.

Just because the English gave the name of West Florida to the area of land which lies between the Río Apalachicola and the Mississippi, having taken the name of Louisiana from the territory which extends from the Río de los Perdidos to the said Mississippi, Spain received from the English all this area of land called by the name of West Florida and did not recognize in it the name of Louisiana, which a certain part of it bore for some time. Thus she affirms with complete truth that no part of West Florida, except the island of Orleans, is included in Louisiana. And for this reason in the proclamation of May 18, 1803, by

Señores Don Manuel Salcedo[65] and the Marquis of Casa Calvo,[66] which we shall mention below in paragraph 399, these gentlemen say:

Article one. That the transfer of the colony and island of New Orleans should be made to General Victor or some other official authorized by the [French] Republic. It will take place under the terms by which France ceded it to Spain, and the limits were fixed in accordance with article seven of the treaty of peace signed in Paris on February 10, 1783. Thus the territory from Mancak [Manchac] to the American line remains a part of the dominion of the king, annexed to West Florida.

(The American line is the one that runs along the 31st parallel, as is seen on our map 20, marked in the red color, and of which the treaty of peace of October 27, 1795,[67] cited above in paragraph 14, speaks.) And, in truth, if Spain is to retrocede to France only what the latter ceded to her, would she be obliged to give her the land of Manchac and Baton Rouge, even though she did not receive it from her? Then it is unjust for the Military Gentlemen and for all those who follow him in his mode of thinking to lay claim to this country of Manchac and to want Spain to transfer it to the United States, since she acquired it not from France in the cession of Louisiana which the latter made to her, but by her arms in the battles she won from England. Thus it has been shown clearly that the country in question, on which the fort of Baton Rouge is located, should in no wise be handed over by Spain to the United States, for, since she did not receive it from France, it should not be a part of the restrocession agreed upon with France. And since Spain took over the rights of England acquired by Article six of the treaty of February 10, 1763,

[65]"Governor Salcedo . . . had been appointed governor [of Louisiana] on October 24, 1799. He had been the King's Lieutenant in the island of Teneriffe, and was brigadier-general of the royal army. He arrived in New Orleans in June, 1801, and Casa Calvo, who had been governor ad interim from the death of Gayoso de Lemos, sailed for Havana."—Fortier, A History of Louisiana, Vol. II, p. 228.

[66]"On September 13, 1799 . . . the Marquis de Casa Calvo had taken possession of the military government of Louisiana, having been appointed to that office by Captain-General Marquis de Someruelos. . . . On May 7, 1803, the Marquis de Casa Calvo arrived to act as commissioner with Salcedo in delivering the province to Captain-General Victor."—Fortier, A History of Louisiana, Vol. II, pp. 175–225.

[67]Reference is to the treaty of friendship, boundaries, commerce, and navigation negotiated with Spain on behalf of the United States by Thomas Pinckney. A copy of this treaty is in Malloy, Treaties, Vol. II, p. 1641.

she should preserve them and engage in the same navigation freely
without the United States being able to disturb it. Finally, the
only thing that she should retrocede is the island of New Orleans.
Spain therefore is obligated to retrocede to France only the land
that extends west of the Mississippi from the source of this river
to its entrance into the sea as far as D'Anville's line, and the island
of New Orleans east of the same river.

77. This being settled, let us return to the text of our Military
Gentleman, who would not say that the French made the original
discovery of Florida (as I understand his statement, he declares
that the French were the first discoverers) if he had read the text
of the very old Spanish [writer], Gómara, cited in Part I, paragraph 48, in which he describes it with the greatest accuracy. This
perforce compels one to believe that the Spaniards were the first
discoverers of West Florida. And in the same Part I, paragraph
48, I wrote the following words by which I attempted to prove,
by the text that I had cited and was citing, that Francisco de
Garay traversed the entire [coast of the] Gulf of Mexico in the
year 1519, and even that it was he who named the bay of Espíritu
Santo. Juan Ponce de León discovered Florida (in 1512), but he
saw only a very small part of it, and after he had discovered it,

Francisco de Garay explored further, following the coast as far as Pánuco.
This he did in 1519, as Herrera narrates (dec. 2, lib. 6, cap. 1). This
[individual] was without doubt the one who, on passing through it, gave the
name to the bay of Espíritu Santo, because when Alvar Núñez Cabeza de Vaca
set out from Spain in 1527 to make a voyage to Florida, the bay of Espíritu
Santo, which the Spaniards also call La Culata, was already named. . . . Afterwards it was called San Luis by Monsieur de la Salle.

Then it is false that the French were the first who discovered
West Florida. Then when Monsieur de la Salle, who was the first
Frenchman to enter the Gulf of Mexico, went there in 1683, for
the purpose of exploring its coasts, at least 164 years had passed
since the Spaniards had begun to explore them.

78. As to the French being the first who made settlements in
West Florida, I say that this also is false, because as we have
said, just above, in 1696 the Spaniards founded the presidio of
Panzacola and later D'Iberville arrived. If it is desired to cite
the settlement of La Salle on the bay of Espíritu Santo as the
means of the acquisition of some right by the French, we have

seen that all this right, if they acquired any at all (which they
did not) they lost by the fact that some of them returned to
France and the others were killed by the Indians, and not a single one remained to sustain it.

79. (B). The French called Louisiana only that part which they
occupied.

80. (C). The Most Christian King Louis XIV did not recognize Louisiana as his, at least not the part east of the Mississippi,
as is stated in document 19, copied just above, and his successor,
Louis XV, recognized as his only what was called Louisiana. This
is proven by the fact that the Duke of Orleans, who was governing for him, restored to the King of Spain the presidio of Panzacola which he had unjustly taken from him.

81. (D). Since the French were never the owners of West
Florida, unless it were during the time that they occupied the
presidio of Pansacola, they could not establish there any government and administration of laws. Consequently, it is false that
they would have possessed it for eighty years without any interruption whatsoever, and it is most untrue that Spain would have
given her consent to this possession for a period of forty years.
The Military Gentleman makes unwarranted assumptions. Everything that happened with regard to Louisiana he wishes to apply
to West Florida. I agree that the French established themselves
in Louisiana, that they gave that land its name, that the Most
Christian King recognized it as his, that they established a government in it and the administration of law, and that they possessed it for eighty years.

X

82. If the matter is examined accurately, it will also be found that the
claims of France to the lands on the west, or opposite, side of the Mississippi,
between the Gulf of Mexico and the Río Bravo, called also at times the Río
del Norte, and west of the Mexican Mountains, are likewise little susceptible
to objections. (A). The rivers which flow directly or indirectly into the
Mississippi as well as some other discoveries of the French are included in
Louisiana, and for this reason they claimed them, on indisputable bases.
During the period of eighty years in which the French were in possession of
that country, they were the only people (with the exception of the Indians
who inhabited it) who subsequently ascended the large rivers that empty
into the Mississippi and Missouri from the western side. They ascended some

of these rivers to their sources, especially that of the Arkansas, that of the Osages, that of the Cances, and the Somano [Somero] or Chato [Platte]. (B). These rivers, as is known, have their origin among the Mexican Mountains, which are distinct from the Rocky, or Shining Mountains, and are prolonged from near the Gulf of Mexico, and divide the waters which flow into the Río Bravo from those which enter the Mississippi and the Missouri. (C).

NOTES

83. (A). Let us examine the matter closely and it will be found that from D'Anville's line west the French cannot claim one span of territory. I agree that owing to the possession of La Salle and the permission of the king of Spain, the rivers that flow directly or indirectly into the Mississippi as well as some other discoveries of the French are included in Louisiana. But because of this they should not claim as theirs all the territory west of D'Anville's line, and if they did so, they would not be supported by any indisputable bases but by their caprice, injustice, and avarice. Let us hear the bases which, according to our Military Gentleman, the French can cite. Those, for a period of eighty years, during which they were owners of that country, were the only ones, with the exception of the Indians who inhabited it, who ascended the large rivers that flow into the Mississippi from the west. It is true that they ascended them, but we deny that they were the only ones and [we deny] that they ascended them to their sources, especially the Acansas, the Osages, the Cances, and the Chato.

84. For, as our author confesses, if all these rivers have their origin in the Mexican Mountains, since no Frenchman reached them, none could have arrived at the sources of these rivers. If they had reached them, they would have explained clearly the location of each one of these sources and their geographers would have placed them on their maps in their correct longitude and latitude. But into what errors did they not fall with regard to this? First, it still is not known where the Missouri rises; then the French, while they possessed Louisiana, did not ascend to the source of this river. It is well enough for our Gentleman to confess below that in fact they did not ascend to the source of the Acansas. We have discussed this sufficiently in Part II, beginning with paragraph 557, where we have shown even the evidence that the French did not pass the place where D'Anville ends it [the

Arkansas], and after some irrefutable and most convincing proof, we concluded as follows:

From all this we must conclude that the Río Napestle, or Arcansas, which rises in the Sierra de las Grullas, has its source far to the northeast [north-west] of the villa of Santa Fé, and that as D'Anville's line cuts this river at the point only to which the French had reached, this river to its source could not belong to them on any other grounds than the presumptuous claim of La Salle in having taken possession of the Mississippi and of whatever rivers enter it, from their sources.

85. If they did not know the source of the Río de Arcansas, neither would they know those of the Osages, the Cances, and the Chato. Then these are fanfaronades and not truths which our author proclaims with regard to this matter.

86. (B). In Part III, paragraph 372, discussing this river, we expressed ourselves as follows:

The river that the French call the Plate, a name which some Spaniards, as Father Talamantes (see his *Opúsculo I*, number 11), but little versed in the French language, translate *La Plata*, should be translated *Plano*, or *Chato*, or as the English translate it (on page 116 of the English work cited in Part II, number 561) *Shallow*, which means *Río Somero*, or one of little depth. And in fact this river is so; although it is wide, its waters are not deep. On a Spanish manuscript map it is given the name of Río Chato, a name which we have adopted in many instances.

In citing Father Talamantes in this text we had in mind the one in which he translates the word *Plate* used by the [Military] Gentleman into the *Río de la Plata*. See his *Opúsculo I*, number 11.

87. How poorly our author knew the Mexican and Shining Mountains! I do not remember having read at any time—and if I have read it I accuse myself of having a bad memory—that the French might have made this distinction between the Mexican and Shining Mountains, nor even that they may have crossed the Sierra Blanca. For that reason I am of the opinion that the Anglo-Americans are the ones who have given them these names, but without knowing where the ones end and the others begin. They call the ones in which the Río de Acansas rises the Mexican Mountains, but the Spaniards call the range in which this river rises the Sierra de las Grullas. Southeast of this range is found the one which the same Spaniards call Los Taos. Southeast of the Sierra de los Taos is found the mountain range of

Los Pecos, concerning which Father Fray Agustín Vetancurt, in his *Teatro Mexicano*, part 4, treatise 3, chapter 6, number 56, says that it extends for more than a hundred leagues. Southeast of the Sierra de los Pecos lies another range which the Río del Norte bathes on the south and on which dwell the Indians called Faraones. For this reason it is customary to give it the name of these Indians and to name the range the Sierra de los Faraones. And on Señor Lafora's map,[68] which is the eighth one of document 74, it is called Sierra del Capirote. These mountains, then, from those of Los Faraones to the Sierra de las Grullas, are the ones which our writer calls Mexican Mountains, no doubt because they are found in the vicinity of New Mexico. See everything that we have written above, beginning with paragraph 639 of Part III, concerning the Mexican and Shining Mountains.

88. Toward the east of the Sierra de las Grullas is found another range, entirely separated from it, which the Spaniards call La Sierra Blanca. Concerning it Father Posadas (document 9, number 8)[69] says the following:

Since the villa of Santa Fé, the center of New Mexico, serves us as a guide for obtaining a knowledge of the lands and nations which are in that region, it must be noted that following the ranges that are immediately beyond the said villa and are in 38°, directly north at a distance of thirty or forty leagues, there is a very high range that is called Sierra Blanca.

The *alférez*, Don Bartolomé Garduño, said above in Part III, paragraph 310, that

the Sierra Blanca, as the witness believes, is seventy leagues from the villa of Santa Fé. . . . The Canceres live on the eastern end of the Sierra Blanca, which runs from west to east. They have their rancherias on its southern slopes, as well as their cultivated fields. On the northern slopes are the Yutas and Comanches.

And on this range, according to Señor Valverde, cited there also in paragraph 311, are located the Carlanas Indians. From all this we infer the following result in the same paragraph 311:

---

[68]See *Pichardo's Treatise* . . . , Vol. I, p. 71, n. 3.

[69]Reference is to the Posadas report which is referred to in *Pichardo's Treatise* . . . , Vol. I, p. 30, n. 1. The above quotation from that report is found in Cesáreo Fernández Duro, *Don Diego de Peñalosa*, pp. 59–60.

It follows from this that the said Carlanas Indians inhabit [the country] from the Sierra Blanca to the crossing of the Río Napestle. If this is not true, either Governor Valverde or the *alférez*, Garduño, was deceived.

89. Therefore, to sum up, above Santa Fé toward the 38th parallel there is a range which the Spaniards call Sierra Blanca; this runs from west to east. It seems that it extends to 79° 30′ of longitude and 38° 55′ of latitude, in which longitude and latitude D'Anville places the Cances, who, according to Garduño, live on its eastern tip on the southern border. From this range perhaps rise the Río de los Osages, the Cances, and the Somero, or Chato, but not the Acansas, for as we have proven it rises in the Sierra de las Grullas. But, since it traverses it or passes near it, the French believed that because the other rivers had their sources in its center, this one would have also.

90. That this range is separated from the one of Las Grullas and the one of El Almagre, which is a range divided from the other by only a canyon (Señor Anza[70] states this in document 46, number 38), is seen most clearly from the expedition which the same Señor Anza made against the Cumanches (see document 46), owing to the fact that the battle he fought with them was in an open field located east of the said Sierra del Almagre. Such a field would not exist if the Sierra Blanca were joined to it; and, in a word, if the itinerary of Señor Anza and that of Uribarri,[71] which is found in document 17, are carefully considered, it will be found that the Sierra Blanca does not join either the one of Taos or the one of Los Almagres, or, consequently, the one of Las Grullas. It is to be believed from this that the Sierra Blanca begins in the west at a point not very far from the place through which Uribarri passed to the Napeste [Arkansas], which distance, with little difference, is probably the same one that all the rest cover who go from Santa Fé to El Quartelejo. And since this Sierra Blanca is so far separated from the ranges contiguous to the kingdom of New Mexico, it should not be included among the number of the Mexican Mountains nor be taken as one of them. Thus all those who place it among them fall into a very great error, since this mistake has arisen from the fact that the French succeeded only in

---

70See *Pichardo's Treatise* . . . , Vol. II, p. 44, n. 75.
71See *Pichardo's Treatise* . . . , Vol. I, p. 35, n. 3.

visiting the eastern point of the Sierra Blanca where perhaps they would have seen the sources of the said rivers, of the Osages, the the Cances, and the Somero, or Chato. Furthermore the Indians who gave the first Frenchmen the information concerning these rivers would tell them of this sierra, and the French, since they saw the mountains to be nearer to New Mexico than to the Mississippi River, would think them very close or, rather, to be the same ones as those of New Mexico.

XI

91. The French were also the first to ascend the Red River to its source, and they are settled on its banks (A) ; they were the first to explore the country to the south and southeast which lies between this river and the Bravo (B), and to establish a settlement in the territory of the Asinays, about 150 miles southwest of Nachitoches. (C). The perfidious trick of which the Spaniards availed themselves in order to establish a settlement at this place, and expel the French from it, has already been detailed in the historical part, and Spain cannot infer from this settlement of hers any legitimate claims, since the French did not consent to this violation of good faith. On the contrary they protested against it and kept their claims alive by means of a representation and only watched for the means of again gaining possession of the territory of which they had been defrauded. (D). Before the United States bought this country, the Spanish and French commissioners had some heated disputes over the limits of their lands. The former alleged that he was authorized to give possession only of the land that is east of the Río de Sabinas, which is nearly 110 miles from Nachitoches. The other contended that the claims of his nation extended to the Río Bravo, and among other things he produced proofs that the French at a certain time kept a garrison on this river, that the works were still visible, and that there still existed there some old cannon which were of French manufacture. Finally, he declared that many of the outstanding landmarks between the Red River and the Río Bravo, such as the capes, bays, lakes, and inlets, were known by French names. (E). All this tends to prove that the French were the first who explored the country, because the names of things and places in general are derived from the language which the first discoverers spoke. (F).

NOTES

92. (A). In commenting on the ignorance of the French with regard to the sources of the Misuri, Acansas, and Colorado rivers, we said the following in Part II, paragraph 642:

It is then conceded and demonstrated by the evidence that the French never knew the whole course of these three rivers, namely, the Missouri, the

Arkansas, and the Colorado [Red], nor did they know the precise and definite places where they originated, nor at any time did they even approach them. In view of this, I shall always commend the prudence and modesty of the Englishman Michel, because on map number 5 of his *Amérique Septentrionale,* which is number 147 of Le Rouge's *Atlas,* he confesses that he does not know the places where the Red River of Nachitoches, the Arkansas, and the Missouri rise, as is seen from these words of his: "The sources of the rivers, and the lands beyond, to the west of this map, are unknown." We must therefore wonder at the effrontery of the Military Gentleman, author of the treatise published in the *Mensajero del Mississippi* [*Mississippi Messenger*], and copied by us in document 72, number 10, when he says: "During the period of eighty years in which the French were in possession of that country, they were the only people (with the exception of the Indians who inhabited it) who subsequently ascended the large rivers that empty into the Mississippi and Missouri from the western side. They ascended some of these rivers to their sources, especially that of the Arkansas, that of the Osages, that of the Cances, and the Somero, or Chato [Platte]. These rivers, as is known, have their origin among the Mexican Mountains, which are distinct from the Rocky, or Shining Mountains, and are prolonged from near the Gulf of Mexico, and divide the waters which flow into the Río Bravo from those which enter the Mississippi and the Missouri. The French were also the first to ascend the Red River to its source, and they are settled on its banks." If by this source our Military Gentleman understood the place where the Canecis lived, as it appears he learned it from the map of D'Anville, or from others, I agree entirely with him that the French ascended the Red River to its source. But if he believes that the true source of the said river lies in the Sierra de los Taos, I say plainly that he is deceived, because the French never dared to go to this sierra, nor would the Spaniards have permitted it, because of its being so close to their settlement of San Gerónimo de los Taos.

93. In his Number XIV he adds:

"Nobody has imagined that the Spaniards at any time discovered or explored any of the rivers that enter the Mississippi from the west, or into the Missouri. The attempts which they made in the year 1720 to form a settlement on the Missouri came to grief. The adventurers were surprised by Indians who were allied with the French and none of them escaped death unless it was the father chaplain. (On this point see what we have already said above in Part I, beginning with paragraph 258.) The French, on the contrary, ascended by all these rivers, with the exception of the Misuri, to their sources, and opened up a trade with the Indians. They always claimed and even exercised acts of sovereignty over the whole country that lies between the Mexican Mountains, the Mississippi, and the Misuri. They made treaties with the Indians, gave land to settlers, and exclusive privileges to traders, and, finally, they maintained a post many hundreds of miles distant, on the Arkansas River, another on the Missouri, and another near the head of the Osage River, all of which were in the very center of the country.

94. (B). It is true that the French explored the land on the south and southeast side, which lies between the Red River and the Bravo, but they did it furtively, secretly, at intervals and at different times, in fear of falling into the hands of the Spaniards. But they were not the only ones, for the Spaniards also explored the province of Texas and established themselves on those lands as their own. If the exploration of a country were to give the right of appropriating it, how many travellers who have explored countries could assert that their nation had become owner of them through their explorations!

95. (C). I should like for this writer to show me the time at which the French established this settlement among the Asinays, or even to cite me any writer who may give this information, even without designating the date. In document 3, in which is found the history of Father Le Clercq,[72] we have seen that when La Salle found himself in Fort Luis, very short of men and supplies, he tried to make a journey by land to Canada for the purpose of providing himself with what he needed, and in number 122 he [Le Clercq] writes the following words, which are the same as those of Father Fray Anastacio Douay,[73] who accompanied La Salle on this journey:

Then, always proceeding to the east, we entered regions much more beautiful than those which we had crossed, and found peoples who were barbarous in name only. We encountered, among others, a very courteous and civil savage who was returning from the chase, with his wife and family. He presented Señor de la Salle with one of his horses and a quantity of meat, and he and all his party begged him to go to his house. In order further to constrain him, he left with us his wife and family, and the results of his hunting, as a sort of pledge, while he went to his rancheria to tell of our arrival. Our hunter and one of Señor de la Salle's lackeys accompanied him, so that at the end of two days they returned with two horses loaded with provisions, and accompanied by many captains, who came followed by warriors dressed very decently in tanned skins adorned with plumes, bringing the calumet very ceremoniously. We met them three leagues in front of the rancheria, and we saw that they were coming out to meet us. Señor de la Salle was received there as if in a triumph, and lodged in the house of the chief captain. . . .

---

[72]Pichardo (Vol. I, p. 519) accredits to Father Anastacio Douay the authorship of a narrative by Father Chrétien Le Clercq. In this connection see also *Pichardo's Treatise* . . . , Vol. II, p. 150, n. 23.

[73]See preceding note.

96. This rancheria is called that of the Cenis, and is one of the most considerable that I found in America, and one of the most populous. It is at least twenty leagues long, not continuously settled, but with rancherias of ten or twelve huts, which are like cantons, or districts, each having a different name. . . . After having been there four or five days resting, we continued our journey to the Nasonis, and it was necessary to cross a large river which flows through the center of the great rancheria of the Cenis. These two nations are allied and they have more or less the same characteristics and customs.

There is nothing in this entire text to show that La Salle may have established a fort among the Cenis, or Asinays, whom he saw for the first and only time in his whole life on that occasion.

97. La Salle being dead, some Frenchmen returned by land to Canada, among them the same Father Douay, who writes of it. In number 148 he writes these words:

They chose as their leader the assassin of Señor de la Salle, and, finally, after much deliberation, resolved that we should all go together to the famous nation of the Cenis. We journeyed, then, for many days, crossing rivers and torrents . . . and reached without accident, as planned, the said place. . . . We had already passed the Cenis, where we stopped for a short time, and we were even among the Nasones where those four deserters of whom I spoke on our first expedition joined us. . . .

98. And are there found, perhaps, in this account any words from which it may be inferred that the French companions of La Salle might have established a settlement among the Cenis? Even granted that they might have done so, just as they established Fort Luis on the bay of San Luis, upon the death of most of them and upon the capture by Alonso de León, governor of Coahuila, of the few who remained in that entire country (see document 11), they completely lost all their title, if they had acquired any. In reality they had not acquired it, since all those lands belonged to the dominion of Spain. Before the French could have returned to the Cenis, the Spaniards went to the Asinais, or Texas. Father Massanet (document 13, number 23) and Alonso de León in document 11, number 46, whose words we have copied above in Part III, paragraph 1451, say that they went with the governor to the place that the Frenchmen had selected for a settlement. It is one thing to select a site for settling, and another to settle. Then they did not settle.

99. Father Le Clercq in the following words (document 3, number 150) says that some Frenchmen had plans to settle among the Cenis:

> In this manner, Hiens continued to be leader of the unfortunate group. It was necessary for them to return to the Cenis, where they proposed to establish themselves, not daring to return to France for fear of punishment.

But even though they might have settled there as French deserters, that settlement could not have been considered as belonging to France, since it would have been established by some rebels (see Part III, paragraph 74), who had fled from there.

100. If it is said that the French built this fort of the Cenis at the beginning of the eighteenth century, then I ask in what year and under what leader. In document 15, number 4, we have a declaration made by Don Luis de St. Denis, examined at the order of the government by Licenciado Don Gerardo Moro,[74] who drew it up in the following manner:[75]

> Don Luis de St. Denis and Don Medar Jalot, natives of New France, also called Canada, in the northern part of this continent, being with me at the order of his Excellency for the purpose of making clear the motives for their entrance into this kingdom, the itineraries they made, and other particulars which his Excellency communicated to me for the investigation on the matter of their ingress, they said in the French language what is given in the text of the following account:
> 101. That the said Don Luis de St. Denis found himself captain, in the name of his Most Christian Majesty, of a presidio called San Juan, forty leagues west of La Movila; that the said presidio is so called because it is on the bank of a small stream of this name, which is navigable in canoes and is only two leagues long, from its source in the large river called Mississippi, alias La Palizada, to its mouth in Lake Pontchartrain, sixteen leagues from the Gulf of Mexico, into which flow the fresh waters of this lake, nine leagues in circumference; and that sloops and other small vessels can enter it from the sea.
> 108. That when he was summoned by Monsieur de la Mota Cadillac,[76] governor of that French colony, he gave him the commission which is in your

---

[74]"Moro, whose name doubtless was Gerard, or Gerald More, or Moore, was an Irishman, one of that large group who in the eighteenth century resided in Spain and in France, often distinguishing themselves in military or government service. He was described in 1724 as a native of 'the city of Dingle in the kingdom of Ireland,' Licentiate in Laws of the Universities of Paris and of Mexico, and *abogado* of the Royal Audiencia of Mexico."—Shelby, "International Rivalry in Northeastern New Spain, 1700–1725," p. 130, n. 51.

[75]This declaration is found in A. G. M., Provincias Internas, Vol. 181.

[76]See *Pichardo's Treaties* . . . , Vol. I, p. 218, n. 1 and 3.

Excellency's hands, containing a declaration of the reasons for undertaking
his journey, in consequence of which he left La Movila about a year and nine
months ago, more or less, appointed by the said governor as head of twenty-
four Canadian soldiers who went under his command; and that in order to
follow with greater clearness the details of his itinerary, there must be noted
the five stages into which it may be divided.

103. The first, from La Mobila to the said presidio of San Juan, forty leagues
along the Mississippi River toward the west.

104. The second, from this presidio of San Juan to the Red River, forty
leagues along the said Mississippi River toward the north.

105. The third, from the Red River to Nachitoches, eighty leagues toward
the west along this same Red River.

106. The fourth, from Nachitoches to Asinay, overland on foot toward the
southwest, forty leagues.

107. The fifth, from Asinay, alias Los Texas, to the presidio of Captain
Ramón on the bank of the Río Grande del Norte, always toward the west-
southwest, on foot and overland, crossing many rivers in this distance of 120
leagues. There are 160 leagues by water and 160 leagues by land.

108. Leaving La Mobila, then, embarked in their canoes, they went on
their way, coasting the mainland toward the west to the mouth of the Mississippi, or Río de la Palizada. They continued their navigation to the said
presidio of San Juan, finding the seacoast without any settlement whatever
except two pueblos of Indians, a cleanly people supplied with muskets, one
called Pascagoula and the other Bilocsi, allies of the French. After he had
returned to his presidio, which consists of a garrison of twenty men, he went
with the men under his command forty leagues toward the north on the
Mississippi River, always in his canoe, as far as the mouth of the Río Rojo
del Espíritu Santo (let it be noted that the French at the beginning, it seems,
called the Red River, or the Nachitoches, the Río del Espíritu Santo), which
flows into the Río Grande [Mississippi] where the first mission was founded
which the French have along this bank. It is called [that of] the Tonica
nation and is governed by a French cleric. Its trade consists of animal skins,
and fowls, corn, beans, pumpkins, cantaloupes, melons, etc. From there,
changing his course, he navigated eighty leagues in his canoe on the said Río
Rojo del Espíritu Santo [Red River] toward the west, with much trouble
because of the difficulty with twenty-two dams which the said river has built
up naturally with driftwood in this distance, as far as the nation called Nachitoches. The French have traded with these people for fourteen years in this
region for the abovesaid articles and also for salt, which they extract with great
skill from three abundant and inexhaustible salines. It is very white and
better than the salt of France. This nation uses the bow and arrow and is very
rational. The captain left there the canoes in which he had navigated from
La Mobila. He had found everywhere on this entire route of 160 leagues a
great abundance of buffaloes, turkeys, chickens, fish, deer, corn, and the fruits
of the Indies and of Spain, which the land produces naturally and without

cultivation or irrigation. He did not discover any mines on this journey because he does not know anything about mining.

109. From there he continued his course toward the southwest on foot, over level lands wooded with groves of trees, to the nation called Asinay, or Texas, belonging to the crown of Spain.

(Let it be clearly noted that in the year 1715, before the expeditions of Ramón and the Marquis de Aguayo to Texas could have been made, St. Denis states that the Asinay, or Texas, belong to the crown of Spain. When, then, did the perfidious trick take place, of which the Spaniards availed themselves in order to establish a settlement in this region and drive the French out of it, of which our Military Gentleman speaks above? The Spaniards who journeyed to Texas at the end of the preceding century found no French fort there, as we have seen a short while ago; they found only, at most, the place which they had selected for a settlement. After these no other Spaniards came to Texas until Domingo Ramón, as is shown in document 15. Then the French did not build a fort among the Asinays. Then the Spaniards did not eject the French from it. Then they did not avail themselves of any perfidious trick when they built the presidio of the Texas, or Asinays. Then it is a most false charge which our Military Gentleman makes here against the Spanish nation. Then he should retract it and in the future speak with more decorum of such an honorable nation which always tries to act in good faith.)

This region was inhabited in olden times by the fathers of the mission of La Cruz de Santiago de Querétaro, who abandoned it twenty-six years ago. The nation consists of eleven pueblos. Its head is Asinay, and its confederates are called Nabenacho, Nacao, Namidó, Nacodoches, Acnay, Nadacoco, Nasonis, Nacitos, Nachoeos, and Cadojodachos. Among them there are even today some individuals who have continued in our holy religion, such as their governor, Bernardino, whom all obey.

110. Their land is extremely fertile and, owing to the intercourse that they had with the Spaniards, is well cultivated. There are nowhere in the world fruits of any kind more delicious and more abundant, with the most prodigious vineyards that have ever been seen, of different qualities and colors and in such quantities that the country is covered with clusters of grapes which are the size of a cannon ball, of twenty-eight to thirty pounds each, as well as fields so extensive and covered with such fine hemp that it can supply rigging for all the fleets of Europe.

111. The residents charged him to request in the dominions of his Catholic Majesty that they be sent, among others, a missionary called Father Fray

Francisco Hidalgo, a religious of the Cross of Querétaro who had lived among them and had an unusual knowledge of their customs and language, and that there be sent to them also a layman called Captain Urrutia, who had been among them ten years contemporaneously with Father Hidalgo. (If the French had had a fort among the Asinays, these Indians would not have made such requests of the Frenchman St. Denis, nor would he have suffered such an affront as was thereby committed against his nation.)

112. From the capital of this nation their settled possessions extend a full forty leagues toward the north-northwest. At ten leagues there are lead mines, but the captain does not know whether there are any of gold, silver, or quicksilver. Toward the south there is a multitude of nations, friends of these, well governed and industrious according to the account that the Indians gave him. It was at this place that twenty-one of the twenty-four men under his command took leave of the captain in order to return to La Mobila. And because these natives still maintain such a deeply-rooted veneration for the Spanish name, hoping for the restoration [of the missions], they respect it (let our Military Gentleman note this well) to the point of not killing the cattle, which, in this interval of the absence of the Spaniards, have increased to thousands of cows, bulls, horses, and mares, with which the whole country is covered.

113. After the captain had left here with the three men, he and his followers were accompanied by twenty-five Texas under the command of Governor Bernardino. Desiring to find Father Hidalgo, he began his journey toward the west-southwest, doing 120 leagues on foot, to the presidio which is under the command of Captain Ramón, two leagues from the large river called Río del Norte.

114. On this journey he crossed a river which is called Trinidad, fifteen leagues from El Asinay, which flows from north to south, without having investigated its origin, although he did [explore] its mouth on the Gulf of Mexico. He also crossed another river, called Río Rojo (this is the one which we call the Brazos de Dios), eighteen leagues from the latter, and from there the San Marcos,[77] another fourteen leagues distant, together with many other streams, all flowing from north to south, and emptying into the Gulf of Mexico. As for settlements, there are none from the Asinay nation to this Río de San Marcos, and indeed on its banks he encountered only some two hundred outlaw Indians from the seacoast, who are accustomed to go inland to plunder and steal livestock, there being no assurance as to their movements, except only of their attacking the pueblos of the Asinay, they being always their chief enemies. The captain, together with the Texas Indians of his following, had a bloody encounter with them from eight in the morning until two in the afternoon, in which twelve men and a woman of the enemy died, not to mention those who may have fallen dead or wounded in the depths of the forest which was near the field of combat. Two of the Texas were slightly wounded. The captain followed in pursuit of the Indians who had fled to their rancherias, where in fear of their imminent destruction, they made peace on the terms of the Texas,

---

[77]Pichardo called the present Colorado the San Marcos, and the present Brazos the Colorado.—See *Pichardo's Treatise* . . . , p. 492.

who withdrew on the day following the fight, twenty-one of them returning to their homes since they were no longer needed for an escort to the captain, who found himself beyond the dangerous places that could have checked the speed of his journey. The other four, including the governor, two captains, and another, remaining with him, they crossed the river named Guadalupe, eighteen leagues from the preceding one. This is a region inhabited by Indians allied with the Spaniards, and along the route of their march, ten leagues away from there, is the spring of water which they call San Antonio, in a region also friendly to the crown of Spain. It is beautiful and rich, very suitable for a settlement, and worthy of a good presidio (in fact one was placed there—the one of San Antonio de Béxar). From there they traversed the last stage consisting of fifty leagues in the direction of the west-southwest to the Río Grande del Norte, to the Spanish presidio of Captain Ramón. (St. Denis himself calls this captain Ramón. Then the French, Prevost among them—see volume 26 of Terracina's translation—erred in calling him Villescas.) The four Texas had not left him. It must be noted that from Asinay to this presidio the country is most delightful. It all consists of plains, with groves of trees at intervals between varicolored fields of flowers, many small rivers of fine water everywhere, and an untold number of wild animals and of all those species known to us. But no mines of gold, silver, or quicksilver were discovered.

115. But it has been about ten years since the captain made this trip entirely overland and by road, [a distance] of no more than 280 leagues, as is shown by the following stages (no one, as far as I know, mentions this journey of St. Denis to the presidio of Río del Norte, made, as is inferred, in the year 1705, and on this journey and in this year neither was any fort built among the Asinays, because he would have said so and would not have admitted that the Asinays belonged to the crown of Spain):

116. The first, from La Mobila by land to the Chacta, composed of thirty-two pueblos consisting of 18,000 men, fifty leagues toward the west-northwest.

117. The second, from here to the nation which they call Nache, consisting of eleven pueblos, thirty leagues toward the west, a quarter to the northwest. This nation, together with the foregoing one, is under the protection of his Most Christian Majesty. Their trade is similar to that of the other Indians described above.

118. The third, from here to Nachitos, forty leagues toward the southwest.

119. The fourth, from here to Asinay, and from there 160 leagues to the Spanish presidio of Captain Ramón on the bank of the Río Grande del Norte. This is the same route that was given above.

120. From La Mobila to the abovesaid presidio, overland and by a level highway, there are 280 leagues.

121. Hence the two routes join at Nachitos. In the land up to that place no discovery of mines has been made, and indeed it is only a road through many delightful groves of uncultivated and fruit-bearing trees. Gerardo Moro.

122. The patent of La Mota Cadillac, of which mention has been made in this declaration and which is found in number 2 of the said document, is of the following tenor:

Antonio de la Mota Cadillac, lord [señor] of Dauaquet[78] and of Moderet,[79] governor of Delfina Island, Fort Louis, and Biloxi, of the country and province of Louisiana. We permit the lord of St. Denis and the twenty-four Canadians who are with him to take at their choice the number of Indian savages which he considers necessary to go to the Red River and wherever he thinks best, to search for the mission of Fray Francisco Hidalgo, Recollect religious, according to his letter written to us on the 16th[80] day of January, 1711, in order to buy oxen, horses, and other cattle for the colony of the province of Louisiana. We pray all those that, in doing this, it may be to our purpose to permit the said lord of St. Denis and the other members of his party to pass, without offering them any obstacle. In testimony of which we sign this and cause it to be sealed with our arms. Countersigned by our secretary. Done in Fort Louis, Louisiana, September 12, 1713. La Mote Cadillac. By me, the secretary, Olivier. Sealed with red sealing wax.

123. This is a transcript, faithfully made, of the original patent, which Monsieur de St. Denis [?] wrote in the French language to the most excellent señor, the Duke of Linares, the señor viceroy of this kingdom. It is in my hands, and at the order of his Excellency I translated it into the Spanish language in Mexico, on June 6, 1715. Francisco de Abascal y Sorrilla.

From the said declaration and from the entire document 16— which contains [an account of] the expedition that Ramón made with some troops and religious to the province of Texas, for the purpose of settling it and founding missions there, accompanied by the said St. Denis who, with a salary of 500 pesos, was appointed conductor of provisions and of everything else needed (see document 15, number 78)—the Señor Marquis of Altamira took the account that we have copied in Part I, beginning with paragraph 327, in which he gives the complete history of the experiences of St. Denis.

124. But Abbé Prevost in volume 26 of Señor Terracina's translation, page 105, relates as follows this arrival of St. Denis at the presidio of Río del Norte:

[78]This name is spelled elsewhere "Douaguet" and "Davaguet."—See *Pichardo's Treatise* . . . , Vol. I, p. 219.

[79]This name is spelled "Monderet" in *Pichardo's Treatise* . . . , Vol. I, p. 219.

[80]Elsewhere the date is given as the 17th day of January, 1711.—See *Pichardo's Treatise* . . . , Vol. I, p. 219.

The governor of Louisiana promised himself the most certain success in the attempt made by land in the interior, but it turned out no better. Truly the singularity of some incidents to which it gave rise deserves to be related more in detail. St. Denis, the same one whom D'Iberville had left in charge of the fort of Mississippi, son of a father who by his valor had made himself worthy of nobility, was placed in charge of this new expedition. La Motte Cadillac gave him goods valued at 10,000 francs, and he made an agreement with him to leave them on deposit among the Nachitoches, a savage nation living near the Río Bermejo [Red River], with whom an alliance had been made in the year 1701. Many of these Indians had gone to settle on the Mississippi in the vicinity of Colapissas.

125. St. Denis thought it well to take these Nachitoches with him, making the proposition to them through a French ship's carpenter who had accompanied Le Sueur to the copper mine and who, having made many other voyages along the Mississippi, understood the languages of almost all the savages of Louisiana. He was the same one who had persuaded the Nachitoches to migrate, and the confidence that they had in him made them follow him easily. But the Colapissas, who had received them well, became so offended at seeing them leave without informing them that they pursued them, killed seventeen, and took a large number of women from them. The rest saved themselves by fleeing through the woods. They fortunately reached St. Denis, who was waiting for them at El Biloxi and who left with them. Having passed on his journey through the pueblo of the Tunicas, he persuaded the leader of this nation to follow him with fifteen of his most able hunters.

126. The pueblo of Nachitoches is located on an island in the Río Bermejo [Red River], forty leagues from its confluence with the Mississippi. Having arrived at the pueblo without mishap, St. Denis ordered a house built for some Frenchmen whom he wanted to leave there; he succeeded in getting some other savages to join the Nachitoches, assuring them constant protection; and he also had implements distributed among them for the purpose of cultivating their lands, and seeds for sowing them. Later, selecting twelve Frenchmen among those whom he had brought, and some savages, he left the Río Bermejo, which ceases to be navigable above the Nachitoches, and set out toward the west.

127. In twenty days he reached the Assinais, neighbors of the Cenis, who, it is believed, are of the same race, very near the place where La Salle had been killed. These savages did not remember ever having seen Frenchmen, and they knew no other Europeans than Spaniards, who went about naked among them and led a very wretched life. (Is there another such lie as this: As if the Spaniards were like the French, who dress in Indian style, that is, go about naked). They did not fail to give guides to St. Denis, with whom he went another 150 leagues to the southwest before arriving at the first Spanish settlements. Finally, he found on the bank of a large river a fort that had the two names of Fort of San Juan Bautista and Presidio del Norte. Don Pedro de Villescas (not this, but Diego Ramón, was his name, and all his descendants and relatives had the same surname), who was in command there, received him

with great kindness. He lodged him in his house, together with Medard Jallot, his surgeon, and Penicaut, and ordered other lodgings given to the people of his company. After several days passed in resting, he began his negotiations. St. Denis declared that he came on behalf of the governor of Louisiana to propose to the Spaniards a regular trade with that colony, and that he was empowered to propose the conditions. Don Pedro replied that he could take no steps without first receiving permission from the governor of Caoues (there is no place in all the vast country which has this name, although the French commonly apply it, through a most crass error, to Coahuila) to whom he promised to send a messenger to ask for orders. Caoues (that is, Coahuila) is sixty leagues from the Presidio del Norte, on the road to the capital of Mexico. Having received the dispatch of Villescas, the governor sent twenty-five cavalrymen after St. Denis. He examined his commission carefully and advised him to go to Mexico to confer with the viceroy. St. Denis consented to this, but he did not leave until the following year, when he took Jallot with him and ordered the Frenchmen who had remained in the Presidio del Norte to return to the Nachitoches. From Caoues to Mexico the distance is 250 leagues. These he travelled accompanied by an officer and an escort of twenty-four men.

128. As soon as he arrived at the capital of New Spain, he was taken to the house of the viceroy, to whom he presented his commission and passport. This gentleman read them and returned them to him, but being unwilling to give him a hearing, he sent him immediately to prison, where he stayed three months. Perhaps he would never have got out if some French officers employed in the service of Spain, who knew D'Iberville and who knew that his wife was a niece of St. Denis, had not interceded for him. He was freed and the viceroy ordered three hundred pesos given him and invited him many times to his table. The esteem in which he was held, growing with this treatment, the viceroy used all possible means to persuade him to prefer the service of the Catholic King to that of a poor colony. The officers who had obtained his liberty for him also importuned him strongly to follow their example. At that time he had no rank in Louisiana. He was offered a cavalry troop, and this offer was sufficiently seductive to a gentleman from Canada, whose resources were quite small, but he, nevertheless, continued firm in refusing it.

(I wonder if this seductive offer would be what our Military Gentleman calls a perfidious trick, assuming that perhaps St. Denis, seduced by the most excellent señor viceroy, consented to the Spaniards' establishing a settlement among the Asinays and driving the French from them? Since I do not know what he calls a perfidious trick, I cannot assert that he is alluding to the said seductive offer, but almost everything that Prevost writes concerning the journey of St. Denis is false, as may be seen by the said documents 15 and 16, by the account of the Señor Marquis of Altamira, and by the one of Dr. Velasco which is found in document 16, number 314.)

The viceroy told him, "Your honor arouses in me even greater wonder in that I consider you as half a Spaniard, because I am not ignorant of the fact that you are aspiring to the daughter of Don Pedro de Villescas." St. Denis did not deny that he loved that young lady, but he pretended that he had not promised himself that he would get her. "But you will get her," replied the viceroy, "if you will accept my offers, and I am giving your honor two months to consider it. At the end of this time he repeated his persuasions, and finding him inflexible, he placed in his hand a purse containing a thousand pesos. "These (he told him upon taking leave of him) are for the expenses of the wedding, because I hope that the daughter of the viceroy (this is the way it is given in the translation of Señor Terracina, but it should read "of Villescas," as in the French original, the text of which I asked for) will have more power than I to keep your honor in New Spain. With regard to the trade with Louisiana, which your honor has come so far to solicit, I cannot grant it." On the following day he sent him a very beautiful bay horse from his stables and had an officer and two gentlemen return him to Caouis.

129. There St. Denis found Jallot, whose skill in his profession had gained him great esteem and favor.

(At first Prevost said that St. Denis took Jallot to Mexico, and now he writes that he found him in Coahuila practicing his profession as a surgeon, in great esteem and favor. Why did he not state when and how Jallot had returned from Mexico? But such contradictions and errors are found in Prevost's work. What is certain is that Jallot came with St. Denis to Mexico, and together they returned with Ramón to Coahuila and from there continued their journey to Texas.)

From there they went together to the home of Villescas, whom they found in the greatest excitement because he had just learned that all the inhabitants of four settlements of savages had abandoned the country to seek other habitations (this incident is not verified by any of our documents), and his whole fear was that he would be held responsible for this desertion, which moreover reduced his post to the direst need, since the garrison was supported solely by the work of these Indians. He told his difficulties to St. Denis, who offered to march immediately in pursuit of these barbarians and make all efforts to reduce them. Don Pedro embraced him affectionately, but advised him that he would be exposing himself to great danger to go alone. But this did not stop the valiant Frenchman from mounting his horse, accompanied only by Jallot. Without much trouble he reached the savages, whose march was very slow because of the baggage and the women and children, and as soon as he had discovered them, attaching his handkerchief to the end of a stick like a flag, he advanced toward the caciques, who made no difficulty about waiting for him. He told them in Spanish of the danger to which they were going to expose themselves by settling anew among some people of whom they knew very little or whom they must regard as a poor sort and not very friendly. Later, urging them to return to their old home, he promised them, on behalf of Villescas, not only that no Spaniard would ever again enter their pueblos without their permission, but also that in their trade they would receive no cause for dissatisfaction from the garrison of the fort. His promises were sufficient to persuade them. Don Pedro, joyful at seeing his guest return with all the savages, confirmed these promises. The barbarians were happily restored to their settlements, to which Spaniards were prohibited from going, without special permission, on penalty of death. A service of such importance resulted in St. Denis' winning the daughter of the commandant of the Presidio del Norte. He spent six months with his wife and his father-in-law, but finally, being unable to delay any longer going to render an account of his commission, he left for Mobile with Don Juan de Villescas, the uncle of his wife, leaving her with child. After some time had passed she went with him to Louisiana, where she had the satisfaction of finding him decorated with the rank of captain and the cross of St. Louis through the good offices of the Count of Champmeslin, commander of the fleet, who had sent the Council of Marine a very favorable report of his conduct and valor.

130. While his journey and his negotiations were taking place, La Motte Cadillac made several settlements among the savages. He subjected several nations and put a stop to the habit that the English of Carolina had formed of coming to incite wars among these barbarians in order to make occasion for capturing slaves. Bienville, after having had some difficulty in reducing the Natches, made them construct at their expense in their large settlement a fort with warehouses and the lodgings necessary for the garrison and the employees. This fort was named Rosalía, in lieu of the city that it had been planned to found there with the same name. Since at the same time St. Denis had returned from the Presidio del Norte, and the reply that he brought from the viceroy of New Spain took away all hope of open trade with the Spaniards, it seemed also that some precautions should be taken to prevent them from coming too near the colony. For this purpose a fort was ordered built on the island of the Nachitoches.

Thus far Prevost, whose account must not be given credence because it contains almost nothing that actually happened, and among the few facts that it does contain there are many mistakes.

131. But in deference to the truth it is necessary to admit that St. Denis conducted himself toward the Spaniards with great honor, probity, and skill, as is shown by the following paragraphs from letters found in our document 16. In number 252 of this document, Father Fray Francisco Hidalgo writes as follows to the most excellent señor viceroy on April 18, 1718:

During the time that the mail has been detained in this mission of San Francisco, which has been for fifty-six days, without our knowing yet when it will leave, the Indians who are dying without holy baptism have been and are innumerable, because they live far removed from each other and there are rivers and creeks between them, which in time of rain, such as we are having at present, rise to such heights that there is no human strength that can cross them.   The measure of bringing these people together is necessary, for otherwise the way cannot be cleared for the principal purpose for which your Excellency, in the name of his Majesty, sent us here, which is to plant the holy faith among these heathen.   Of all things this is the most necessary.   The most prompt and efficacious remedy will be for your Excellency's greatness to send to this province with any title whatever, Captain Louis de St. Denis, a Frenchman for whom these Indians hold a special affection.   They promised him to assemble when he should come with his wife.   I do not find any difficulty in this, since he is a man of good blood, a vassal of our king and very devoted to him, married to a Spanish woman, and withdrawn from all trade. This is all that I have for the present to represent especially to your Excellency's greatness, whose person may the Divine Majesty keep for His glory, the propagation of the holy faith, and the extension of the royal crown.   From this mission of Nuestro Padre San Francisco de los Texas, April 18, 1718.   Your most lowly chaplain and humble servant kisses your Excellency's feet.   Fray Francisco Hidalgo.   Most excellent señor, my señor.

132.   In another letter which the same father writes to the father *guardián,* Fray José Diez, dated March 11, 1718, he states the following (in number 262 of the said document) :

In view of the information that your reverence already has concerning the want that is experienced here and the need which also exists for families in order that this province may develop and advance, concerning all of which the father president has probably informed your reverence, I cannot refrain from presenting for your reverence's consideration a most important point in order that you may apply the measures that you may consider most to the service of God.   This is that all these people and the nations as far as the Río Grande are clamoring for the French captain, Don Luis de St. Denis, because of the great love that they have for him and because he promised to assemble at a mission those on the road from the Río Grande to this place, or at least to make an effort to do so.   And he gave his word to these to come with his wife and live among them whenever the Spaniards might come and the Indians gave him theirs to assemble in pueblos whenever he might come with his family. This is the point.   I consider it certain that if this gentleman does not come, sent by his Excellency with whatever title he may think appropriate, these Indians will not assemble except at the cost of many years [of effort], of many Spanish people, of great expenditures, and, what is worse, of many souls that will be lost and that might be saved if they were assembled, for many are dying without baptism.

133.   The señor doctor *fiscal,* Espinosa, under date of June 25, 1718, in number 258, gave his opinion on this matter as follows:

With regard to the request that the French captain, Don Luis de St. Denis, be sent to that region because of its being very conducive to the assembling of those nations, now that they are being reduced to our holy faith (as Father Fray Francisco Hidalgo reports), the *fiscal* repeats what he has said in his various former replies, which he has given in the *autos* on this matter. Mexico, June 25, 1718. Doctor Espinosa.

But what had the señor *fiscal* said in his previous replies? This is what we do not know, because his replies are not found among the *autos*. He may perhaps have given them in the *autos* that were drawn up against St. Denis because of his being unjustly accused of contraband trade. See Part I, paragraphs 329 and 339, in which the Señor Marquis of Altamira and Señor Bonilla speak of this false accusation and the bad results of it.

134. In view of these documents relating to the journey of St. Denis, is there anyone who would persuade himself that the French had made a settlement among the Cenis during the period that elapsed from the time that they abandoned the missions founded at the end of the seventeenth century down to the date of this journey? For if there had been one, surely St. Denis would have mentioned it in his statements and would have designated it on the map which he presented to our government and would have spoken of it in the *autos* copied in our documents 15 and 16; and certainly the señor fiscal at least would not have passed it over in silence. And St. Denis would not have stated to Señor Governor Sandoval (see above, paragraph 930):

Notwithstanding that as far as the Río del Norte I did not find any vestiges of Spanish settlements (if there were such), it does not follow that we Frenchmen claim all the territory to the said Río del Norte for our own. I admit .unreservedly that the Spaniards have legitimate possession of it.

And neither would he have said the following (see Part III, paragraph 939):

Nor would there even be any occasion for raising a question if the French (which will never happen) should attempt to settle and inhabit the country up to and excluding the Lago de los Adaes because then they would indeed be more truly on the other side of the river than they had ever been. It would be a just matter for controversy if the French should attempt to move beyond the Lago de los Adaes to the vicinity of the Spaniards.

Thus far, therefore, we have proven that neither before the journey of León nor before the founding of the missions, at the end

of the seventeenth century, is it apparent that the French founded
any settlements in the country of the Cenis. Let us see also why
they did not do so after the year 1714, in which St. Denis arrived
in Coahuila.

135. In document 15, number 31, the Señor *fiscal*, Espinosa,
under date of August 15, 1715, states the following to his Excellency:

> First, that the *fiscal* foresaw the seriousness of this matter and feared the
> most pernicous and extremely obnoxious consequences that might result from
> such expeditions, and explained them in the reply that he gave, as he believes,
> two years ago or a little less, to a *carta consulta* and representation which
> Captain Don Gregorio de Salinas Varona, governor of the presidio of Santa
> María de Galve, made to your Excellency, notifying you that the French of
> La Mobila, in canoes and with friendly Indians, armed and bringing clothing,
> had entered the bay of Espíritu Santo and the Mississippi River, exploring the
> dominions of his Majesty. The *fiscal* explained the grave danger that this
> entrance was producing, which was very harmful because the French were
> examining the interior lands of this North America.

136. In number 40, in a *junta de guerra*, the following is also
stated:

> . . . and of his Excellency's decree of June 22, in which he ordered that
> this account be sent to the señor *fiscal* together with the preceding *autos*, the
> patent of the governor of La Mobila, and the map made by the two Frenchmen
> who came, in order that in view of everything he might request what he con-
> sidered appropriate, bearing in mind the seriousness of the matter and the
> consequences that might follow from such entrances, and the reply of the
> señor *fiscal* of his Majesty of the fifteenth of the current month, in which as
> the first point he requested that they bear in mind, as they did—and I, the
> lieutenant of the chief notary of *gobernación y guerra* made note of it—that in
> the *junta general* of February 7, 1714, in *autos de providencias* with regard to
> the presidio of Santa María de Galve, called also Panzacola, as its ninth and
> last point, an account was rendered of the report which the governor of that
> presidio, Don Gregorio de Salinas Varona, gave to his Excellency in a letter of
> August 29, 1707, to the effect that on the twenty-second of the same month of
> August it had come to his attention that the governor of La Mobila had sent
> twenty-eight Canadians, with their muskets, and one hundred Indians of those
> he had under his orders, to explore the land of the dominions of our king and
> lord with the intention of introducing goods and merchandise into the Nuevo
> Reyno de la Vizcaya, the Nuevo Reyno de León, and the province of Coahuila,
> which they call Nueva Extremadura, taking along for that purpose two pirogues
> loaded with clothing.

(It seems that this date [August 29, 1707] is wrong and that it should be 1713. Even the month seems to be incorrect, inasmuch as the señor *fiscal*, cited in the preceding number, says under date of August 15, 1715, "that the *fiscal* feared such entrances, discussing them in a reply which he gave, as he believes, two years ago or a little less, to a letter, etc." And since the patent of La Mota Cadillac is signed on September 12, then it is probable that the delivery of the patent would precede the departure of St. Denis for Texas and the Presidio del Norte. As we shall see later, in paragraph 138, Father Morfi says that the governor of Louisiana, aside from sending St. Denis to the Spanish missions and presidios, also made an attempt by sea to gain control of the bay of Espíritu Santo. Now the date of the patent which this governor gave to St. Denis is September 12, 1713. Then in this year Salinas would have written the señor viceroy. Aside from this, the Señor Marquis of Altamira, who perhaps saw the report given by Don Gregorio de Salinas, says—cited in our Part I, paragraph 329—that, "The suspicions against him—against St. Denis—were increased by the information which the governor of Pensacola gave to the effect that the Frenchmen who in the year '13 had left Mobile, returned there with many cattle, announcing that they had gone as far as Coahuila." Then this notice or report is subsequent to the year '13 or is of the same year, and not of the year '07.)

137. In another junta, the one of December 2, 1716, it is stated—in the same document 16, number 202—that

In the *autos* from the presidio of Santa María de Galve, in which by the ninth and last point therein was presented the report of August 29, 1707 (regarding this date see the preceding paragraph), communicated to his Excellency in a letter from the governor, Don Gregorio de Salinas, to the effect that on the twenty-second of the same month of August (these dates do not coincide with those that we have verified in the preceding paragraph, so it seems that they were given incorrectly by the one who recorded the proceedings of this junta), it had come to his attention that the governor of La Mobila had sent twenty-eight Canadians, with their muskets, and one hundred Indians, to explore the land of the dominions of our king with the intention of introducing goods and merchandise into the Nuevo Reyno de la Vizcaya, [the Nuevo Reyno] de León, and the province of Coahuila, which they called Nueva Extremadura, taking along for that purpose two pirogues loaded with clothing.

138. Father Morfi in his *Memorias para la Historia de Texas,* after having recounted the expedition of St. Denis to Coahuila, writes as follows in book 6, number 4:

Not content with the incursion committed to St. Denis, the governor of Louisiana also made an attempt by sea to gain control of the bay of Espíritu Santo. But they found so much opposition from the Carancaguases upon whom they looked with horror since La Salle's tragedy, that to their sorrow they saw themselves forced to give up this undertaking forever. This expedition was not known in Mexico, since there were no Spaniards on the bay and no communication whatever with the Indians who frequent it, even though that site gave some anxiety, as we shall see later.

139. He adds in number 18, enlarging on the matter he mentions:

Without doubt, prior to the last dispatches the viceroy had had some information of the new attempt the French had made on the bay of Espíritu Santo, for in the confidential instructions which he enclosed for the Marquis of San Miguel de Aguayo, he charged him that as soon as he could he should occupy that bay as effectively as possible, as he considered this very important to the development of the entire province. For this purpose and upon the occasion of the expedition of Almazán, the marquis also sent Captain Diego Ramón with forty men, and with the special order that, not tarrying in San Antonio or detaining himself with any other matter, he should go to the said bay and lay the foundations of a settlement there, until such time as the marquis himself could go and establish it with the formalities which should be observed, giving him a prompt report of the execution of this order or of the hindrances that might delay it, so that he might be able to furnish him with the means of overcoming them.

140. When Almazán arrived at San Antonio, he learned from Captain García that after he had sent the said report of the proximity of St. Denis to the marquis, he had ordered the Indian, Juan Rodríguez, to go with another highly-trusted man of his nation to explore and reconnoiter the site on which it was said the French were found, and that upon any new occurrence he should return and report to him. In effect, Rodríguez left on his mission and returned on February 25, saying that he had covered all the country to the bank of the Río de los Brazos de Dios, and in this area he not only had encountered not the least sign of the French, but also not a single Indian, not even those of the Ranchería Grande, who frequently live a good distance on this side of that river. Because of this he believed that since they were missing from their country, it was owing no doubt to the fact that they were attending the junta which was being held. He did not dare to go any farther. After he returned to the presidio, his own Indians told him that they had encountered a Jana [Sana?], from whom they had learned that the Ranchería Grande was in the French convocation, that they had many horses, that all the Indians were armed

with muskets, and, finally, that the junta had been held between the two branches of the river that has this name [Brazos], to the left of the road that leads to Texas. This Juan Rodríguez was a Jana [Sana] Indian. One of the most distinguished captains of the Ranchería Grande, a few days previously, attracted by the preaching of the venerable Father Margil, presented himself at the presidio of Béxar with fifty families of his following, requesting a mission. But the venerable Father Margil from the start did not greatly rely on his sincerity, as he did not press or even approve his wishes.

141. Don Gabriel de Cárdenas or, rather, Señor Barcia, knew all this very well, for in his *Ensayo Cronológico*, decade 21, page 328, under the year 1716, he wrote the following, alluding, it seems, to the journey of St. Denis and to the attempt by sea:

The extraordinary care and diligence with which the French were transporting innumerable people and everything necessary for settling in many places, sparing no effort and care in obtaining the friendship of the Indians, kept Don Gregorio de Salinas, the governor of Panzacola, in great anxiety. The French had even succeeded in winning the devotion of all the barbarian nations from La Masacra and Palizada to the provinces of the Texas and of New Mexico, for more than five hundred leagues. He knew that they were building fortifications in the principal sites, and one of greater importance in the province of the Cirinues Indians (read Ylineses; but it is not even near New Mexico nor are mines worked in this country), which is near or in New Mexico, a place north-northwest of Mobile where silver mines are worked, in what they call Louisiana on the Gulf of Mexico. Although Don Gregorio recognized that none of this was conducive to friendship and good faith, the close union between Spain and France sufficed to cause him to conceal his suspicions, and thus, in order not to reveal them or occasion distrust, he did not dare to send demands to the French officials and governors to withdraw from the land that they were usurping from the king.

142. But he could not omit notifying the viceroy of New Spain of all their pretensions, urging very strongly that Santa María de Galve and La Punta de Sigüenza, upon which in any case depended the security of the country, be fortified, for if La Punta were fortified, it would be easy to prevent the entrance of vessels into the port of Santa María de Galve, which otherwise would remain outside the range of the artillery of the castle of San Carlos, which even though it might be all mounted and ready, would not succeed in preventing the enemy's entrance. What disquieted him most was to learn that in La Masacra (whose port the sea had filled up a short time before) and in La Mobila, the idea was being entertained that the port of Santa María de Galve did not belong to the Spaniards, because the French had been settled there a long time previously, and that it was necessary to take it if they [the Spaniards] did not give it up, in order to make up for the port that the sea had filled with sand. Since this idea was untrue, he feared that if an open controversy were to occur, they would decide to besiege him. He tried to place his presidio in the best state

he could to prevent their using the rumors as a pretext for attempting a surprise attack.

143. But, if the Carancaguases Indians, as Father Morfi has told us, killed the French sent by the governor of La Mobila to the bay of Espíritu Santo, it is clear that they could not make any settlement on it, and much less, consequently, in the territory of the Cenis. Nevertheless, it seems that what Doctor Velasco, the counselor of the most excellent señor viceroy, the Marquis of Valero, states in number 289 of his report copied in document 16, beginning with 283, is in favor of the author of the *Rasgos*[81] namely:

In view of the information which Alonso de León gave in another letter, which he sent, together with a declaration of an Indian who had reached the Texas, in which the latter said: that some Frenchmen had settled on their lands, whom they were helping with the settlement because of the good treatment which they were receiving from them; that they had already built three wooden houses and that they were going to bring families; that they crossed an arm of the sea in houses of wood, by means of which they brought pieces of artillery, catapults, and other things; that they had given some Indians appointments as governors and had given them arms; that the settlements of the Texas would be a day's swift travel from where Alonso de León encountered the governor of the Texas and the Frenchmen; that the French had tried three times to settle on the coast and that the Indians had killed them, for which reason they have now gone to settle among the Texas since they are good people; and that the governor told them he would send immediately one of his brothers, together with other Indians, to ask the Spaniards to come and bring religious to teach them—[in view of all this], together with the reply of the señor *fiscal*, it was decided in the *junta general*, on September 10, 1689, that Captain Alonso de León should go with the number of soldiers and religious he might consider sufficient to reduce the Indians who lived from Coahuila to the Texas, and to learn whether the declaration of the Indian were true.

144. But this report of Alonso de León is branded false by Father Massanet in document 13, number 12, where he writes as follows:

Aside from the information that we had brought when we returned from the bay of Espíritu Santo, Captain Alonso de León had already reported that after our arrival an Indian had come and said that among the Texas were eighteen Frenchmen; that they had built houses; that they had livestock, including goats and sheep; and that others had returned to their country to bring women

---

[81]Reference is to the *Rasgos Históricos* [*Historical Sketches*] of Dr. John Sibley. See Vol. I, p. 368, n. 2.

and more men. I do not know what purpose Captain Alonso de León might
have had in making the said report to his Excellency, because I saw the Indian
and talked with him before he saw Captain León. He told me that he came
from the interior and that he had told him that among the Texas six Frenchmen
were wandering around as if lost.

In truth, when León returned to the Texas with the same Father
Massanet and other religious, they did not find any settlements
of Frenchmen; only, at most, a place that they had selected for
making them, as we have stated above in paragraph 98, in this
same note (D) of Number XI.

145. This text of Señor Velasco, therefore, presents nothing in
favor of the French settlement among the Cenis. Although, as I
have already said many times, I have not been able to obtain the
work of Du Pratz, either in French or in the English summary, I
believe, nevertheless, that he is the one who invented this settlement, because of the fact that Don Antonio Alcedo, who, as I
understand it, took from this work everything that he publishes
about Louisiana in his *Diccionario de America*, writes as follows
under the article "Cenis":

Cenis. A pueblo of Indians of the province and government of Louisiana,
located on the road that leads to Mexico. It has a fort which the French
built when they possessed the province.

146. If by Cenis the French understand some settlements made
by them near the Asinais of Texas in the lands which they appropriated, as among the Cadodachos, Acansas, and others, I will-
ingly agree with them in admitting it. But when did the Spaniards
expel the French from these settlements? For if they did not expel them, why is the following insult, so execrable, hurled against
the Spaniards?

The perfidious trick of which the Spaniards availed themselves in order to
establish a settlement at this place and expel the French from it, has already
been detailed in the historical part. . . .

Perhaps the writer of these *Sketches* also wrote this historical
part and gives in it the details of the perfidious trick of the
Spaniards. Would that some one would place these details in
my hands so that I may examine them and see the bases on which
he depends in deducing that the Spaniards were treacherous!

(Father Talamantes in a note concerning these details or this history says that it is probably a novel disguised with the name of a history.) Must this nation, which is so generous (and so noble in its conduct), which comports itself with such good faith in its actions, suffer such an insult? If the writer of these *Sketches* is quoting the work of Du Pratz or some other, let it be understood that they deserve no credence and that from their untruths cannot be deduced any taunts as irrational and insulting as those which he pours out against the Spaniards. I repeat that I have not seen the work of Du Pratz, but I am convinced that this author imagined that when Don Luis de St. Denis captured and sacked the mission of Los Adaes when he came in 1719 to make an attack on it, he also passed on to the Texas to do the same thing in their missions.

147. Let us hear what Father Morfi writes about this in his *Memorias* [*para la Historia*] *de Texas* (book 6, number 1):

The royal cedula, in which St. Denis was exiled with his entire family to Guatemala, had hardly reached Mexico, when he appeared in Texas with his arms in his hands. When war broke out with France during the regency of the Duke of Orleans, the French from La Mobila surprised the castle of Panzacola on May 19 of this year of 1719, and on the same day of the following June, St. Denis, with the troops he could assemble from Nachitoches and Cadodachos, entered the province of Texas, and immediately made a surprise attack on the mission of Los Adaes (and captured the missionary). Notwithstanding the care with which he was guarded, he managed to escape and give warning to the other missions of the coming of the French. The missionaries well thought that if the troops who were with them would fortify themselves in one of the settlements, the French could not overpower it with the men they were bringing, and that while they were asking for aid from Louisiana it was natural that help would come to those besieged. They presented this idea to the military chief, but all their eloquence was not sufficient to persuade him. Without seeing the face of the enemy, he shamefully retreated, abandoning the missions anew.

148. The religious remained alone with the Indians, but with the Reverend Father Margil at their head. He thought that by waiting for the arrival of the enemy the sacred vessels and ornaments might run some risk, for even the most pious leader among Christian nations is likely not to be able to prevent such disorders. Thus, guarding against these sacrilegious acts, he proceeded to retreat just ahead of the oncoming French with all the ornaments of worship and the other ministers, for it was painful for him to leave those children who, although ungrateful, had cost him innumerable hardships. First they stopped at the place which they called Real de Santiago, and finally they took refuge in Béxar. Thereupon St. Denis remained master of the entire province, if the

recently-founded presidio of San Antonio and its missions are excepted, a small feat, which he could have performed with only six men owing to the terror which took hold of our people.

The venerable Father Margil reported all this to the most excellent señor viceroy, the Duke [Marquis] of Valero, in a letter which has been copied in Part III, paragraph 1396. (And beginning with paragraph 1394 and citing various authors, we drew up an account of these lamentable occurrences.)

149. Let us continue this history with the account of Father Fray Juan Domingo Arricivita, who in his *Crónica . . . del Colegio del Santa Cruz de Querétaro* (which is the second part of the *Chrónica* of Father Espinosa), book 1, chapter 21, writes as follows:

Now, at last, with the restoration of the abandoned missions in the province of Texas, there came to an end the anxieties which most afflicted the heart of the Venerable Father Margil, because the people who were to reëstablish them arrived in San Antonio. . . . At his orders they proceeded to reëstablish the missions, which received the same status they had formerly had. A new presidio was placed among the Adays, with a garrison of a hundred soldiers who were also to be settlers. For this reason many brought their wives and families. This presidio was on the French frontier and was the boundary of the Spaniards. As missionary of the mission of San Miguel, an eighth of a league away, Father Fray Antonio was the chaplain of all of them.

150. Here the historian alludes to the expedition which, at the order of the most excellent señor viceroy, the Marquis of Valero, the Señor Marquis of San Miguel de Aguayo made to the province of the Texas, the *derrotero* of which was written by Bachiller Don Juan Antonio de la Peña, who was the chaplain of those troops; it is copied in our document 21. It is a work of the greatest importance in the matter that is being discussed concerning the dividing line between the province of Texas and Louisiana, because, in truth, a large part of the limits in question may be determined from this publication. I am going to designate all the paragraphs in it that seem to me the most interesting and that should be chiefly borne in mind, because in them are discussed the motives of the expedition of the señor marquis, the reconquest of the land that he proceeded to make, the joy with which the Indians received him, the disputes he had with the French,

and other very notable occurrences. They are numbers 1, 2, 35, 81, 83, 88, 93, 117, 118, 119, 120, 124, 142, and 143.

151. Here we have an old document, entirely trustworthy and published with all the formalities of public law and not surreptitiously, perhaps even at the order of the government and for the instruction of the whole world in this matter—a document which gives us in great detail all the operations of the Marquis of Aguayo on his journey and all the places through which he passed, but which gives nowhere, in any part, the information that there might have been a French settlement among the Texas. And this is due to no other reason than that there was none. If St. Denis took the mission of Los Adays and those of Texas, these were not French but Spanish, even though they were taken from the latter by the former at a time when Spain and France were at war. But did this hostile act give them a perpetual title, so that the Spaniards could never recover these lands from them? The Spaniards at that time marched with a strong force, and they found themselves in a position to be able to expel the French from Nachitoches, and if they did not do it, it was only because of orders to the contrary from the king, who directed that his troops should recover only the province of Texas. And is it possible to find in the entire diary of the Marquis of Aguayo any perfidious deceit or villainy on the part of the Spaniards?

152. For a good reason, then, Father Talamantes said the following in a note that he inserted to impugn our Military Gentleman, with regard to the statement that the French established a settlement among the Asinais:

> This statement (says Father Talamantes) is false in all respects. The French never established settlements among the Asinais. They did establish one on the Río de Cadodachos which was not permanent, usurping this land from Spain, who had explored it and taken solemn possession of it in 1692, the leader of this expedition being Don Domingo Terán de los Ríos.

But Father Talamantes was wrong concerning this second point, for it is true that the French founded a presidio among the Cadodachos and maintained it permanently, even though they established it unjustly, for they despoiled Spain of this land on which Spanish religious had already lived. See everything that we have said above in Part III, beginning with paragraph 90.

153. (D). The Spaniards founded their presidio among the Texas, or Asinais, because they were lands belonging to them and, as has been shown, the French had never established settlements on them, nor could the Spaniards treacherously expel the French from a settlement that they did not possess. And I ask, where is the claim, or what writer of good reputation points it out, by which it may be shown that the French did not consent to this breach of good faith? And where is the protest that they made against it? The truth is that their treachery was always watching for opportunities for taking Spain's land from her, at times with secret expeditions to them and at other times by alleging fantastic titles and acts of possession which had never taken place.

154. Father Talamantes, in the corresponding note, says the following with regard to this point:

These representations are as imaginary as the act which is here referred to. For the rest, this sentence, to be accurate, should end as follows: ". . . availing themselves only of convenient means for maintaining themselves in a territory which they had stolen." Further on these means will be indicated.

155. (E). Father Talamantes in his corresponding note writes as follows concerning this point:

There is not a single word of truth in the account which is given of this dispute. While Louisiana was in the possession of France, no commissioners were ever named by it and by Spain to treat of its limits. The French have never claimed to extend to the Río Bravo; never have they had a settlement on this river; never have any traces of them been seen there; and never have such cannon existed. These traces and the cannon are those which remained at the bay that La Salle called San Luis. Also, the Spanish commissioners could not assert that they were authorized only to recover the country to the Río Sabinas, for Spain has always occupied, without opposition from France, not only this river but also twenty leagues of territory east of it to the abandoned presidio of Los Adaes.

156. (F). The same Father Talamantes, refuting this, writes as follows:

This derivation is not very general. America took its name from an individual who had little or no part in its discovery, and the same fate has befallen many of its provinces and territories. There are fortunate names which, favored by circumstances or perhaps by the ease with which they are pronounced, prevail over legitimate names, and even these vary in form with the passing of time. But, if that argument has any strength, will it not be in favor of Spain, who, before Monsieur de la Salle navigated the Mississippi, already called it the Río de la Palizada, already knew the territory of Louisiana in the region of Florida, was already calling the bay which the French called San Luis, the lake of San Bernardo, or bay of Espíritu Santo, and also had long since adopted the name of Maubila, or Mobila, given to the bay and to the river? What difference does it make if she may not have named all the points in that territory with Spanish names provided she had already named and designated the most important points and places?

157. This is how Father Talamantes argues against these two texts of our writer, but we have much more to say. Therefore, admitting that Spanish and French commissioners were never named to designate limits between the two nations, we say also that it is most untrue that the French at any time have maintained a garrison on the Río Bravo. I ask the Military Gentleman, on what part of the Río Bravo did the French have this garrison? Perchance at the entrance of this river into the sea? But we have ascertained in Part II, paragraph 242, that Monsieur de la Salle reached only the mouth of the Río de las Nueces by way of the lake called Yma which, according to Father Le Clercq, he took to be (maliciously or erroneously?—I say that he maliciously announced this information among his companions in order to deceive them) the bay of Espíritu Santo, and that from there he went back as far as the bay of La Culata, or Espíritu Santo, as the Spaniards call it. Even if he had descended to the mouth of the Río Bravo and had believed that the bay into which this river enters was that of Espíritu Santo, it cannot be said that he made a settlement on it, for as we have stated, he turned back in search of La Culata. I challenge the Military Gentleman to name me another author more trustworthy, as a contemporary and as having written on the basis of the memoirs of Fathers Fray Zenobio Membré and Fray Anastacio Douay, than Father Le Clercq, upon whose accounts we have based ours, one who describes the journey of La Salle and explains how his Fort Luis on the bay of La Culata was built, as I know is done by Father Le Clercq, a writer whose work he [the Military Gentleman] doubtless has not seen or heard of.

158. Neither did La Salle place a fort in the interior country which the Río del Norte waters, for Father Le Clercq would have noted it. Aside from this, it was impossible that La Salle would come without the knowledge of the Spaniards and, concealing him-

self from them, would have dared to build a fort on the Río Bravo, for he necessarily would have feared that the Spaniards of Coahuila and of the Nuevo Reyno de León would hear of it, become alarmed, march against him, and deprive him of all the fruits of his iniquity. If there was no such fort, how can the remains of it still be visible, to say nothing of the old cannon of French manufacture? Consequently, when the Military Gentleman again sets out to accumulate arguments with regard to limits, let him see to it that he manufactures information and stories so that they are somewhat more plausible and are not based upon such insecure foundations. The information about the two Spanish and French commissioners is wholly of this nature, as are the proofs of their assertions which his imagination concocted here, desirous of deceiving the Spaniards with idle tales, to induce them to cede to the United States all the area to the Río Bravo.

159. As for the other argument of the French commissioner, which our Military Gentlemen added, to the effect that the capes, bays, lakes, and inlets were known by French names, I say that if the bay of Espíritu Santo, or Culata, the Río de Guadalupe, the San Marcos, the Brazos de Dios, or Colorado, the Santísima Trinidad, the Nechas, or Río Mexicano, the Sabinas, the Cabo del Norte, etc., are French names, I shall admit that he is telling the truth, but since everyone will say that these words are Spanish, everyone should say he made a mistake in this regard.

160. It is incontrovertible that La Salle reached the bay of Espíritu Santo, that he entered the country adjoining it, and that he named various rivers, such as the Robec, the Cannes, or Cañas, the Sablonier [Sablonnière], the Maligne, and several others, but it is also beyond doubt that since the departure of La Salle's companions from that country, the French have not returned to learn what rivers had these names, and we believe that we have ascertained them with approximate correctness. See Part II, beginning with paragraph 356. If it is true, as he says, that the names of things and places are generally derived from the language which the first discoverers spoke, it is inferred that the Spanish names of Río Grande, Nieves, Flores, Culata, bay of Espíritu Santo, and Río Bravo, or Río del Norte, which were given by the companions of Hernando de Soto to the Mississippi, by the pilots of whom Gómara speaks, and by the ancient poet, Villagrá, in his poem

on the conquest of New Mexico, not to mention the rivers of San Pedro and San Pablo, etc., which Francisco Vásquez Coronado named, indicate that the Spaniards were the first explorers of this land. And if the Spaniards, according to the French, did not acquire any rights to the lands that these rivers water in spite of the fact that they discovered them, neither should the French have acquired any right to the Río Bravo, or to the bay of Espíritu Santo, or to the rivers on which they placed, let us say, an ephemeral settlement, such as they made on the bay of San Luis, for in fact we may well call it temporary because of the very short time that it remained in existence before the Indians destroyed it and killed its founders. If Monsieur de la Salle did not found any presidio on the Río Bravo, neither did the French who followed him do so, for who could it be? Not St. Denis. Perhaps some other? If so, when and at what place on this river?

XII

161. From this we have a solid basis (A) for believing that the general claim of France to all the country enclosed by the Mississippi, the Río Bravo (B), and the Gulf of Mexico, was of the highest order, that is, more solid and better founded than that of Spain, and that it never was extinguished. From the year 1717, the Spaniards had a garrison or presidio called San Juan Bautista on the west bank of the Río Bravo (C), located in 29° north latitude, but they never made any settlements on the opposite side of the said river until they established the one of Los Asinais (D). A possession which is fraudulent can never be made legal, nor can it be made legitimate between nations, especially if the injured party refuses to rescind its claims and does not permit the injustice which has been dealt it (E). The treaty of 1763 put an end to all the disputes regarding boundaries between France and Spain, but up to the present it has not invalidated the claims of the United States, because now the only question which exists is what were the boundaries of Louisiana before this epoch? (F).

NOTES

162. (A). If with solid bases such as this France lays claims to other countries, she will certainly lose them, because fallacious claims are no claims.

163. (B). Father Talamantes made a mistake when he asserted in the preceding note that the French have never claimed to extend as far as the Río Bravo, for it is certain that at one time they expanded their claims to cover even that. Let us hear, for our amusement, the following letters which the Señor Brigadier

Don Antonio de Bonilla copied from their originals, which according to this statement are found in the secretariat of this viceroyalty, and copies of which he kept, together with other very important papers relating to the province of Texas, in a bound volume which with many others is in the possession of Señora Doña Manuela de Torres, his widow:

164. *My dear señor:* I have received a letter from the very reverend father president of these missions, Fray José Calahorra, in which he tells me that as soon as he arrived at the pueblo of the Tehuacanas, he took note of the fact that on the flagstaff, below our flag, was the standard of his Most Christian Majesty. After having rested, he asked what flag that was, which he had not seen on the other two occasions that he had been there, and the captains answered him that some Frenchmen (or Canos as they call them) had been there and had given it to them, together with a title for a captain, a thing which has surprised me, for despite the fact that everyone knows that it is in the dominion of his Catholic Majesty, they have gone to introduce their control into that kingdom. Believing that your honor is not responsible for it, I am informing you of it in order that you may give directions for taking the flag away, and if not, so that I may report the incident, and your reply, to the most excellent señor viceroy of this New Spain. May our Lord prosper your honor's life the many years that I desire. Adaes, August 31, 1763. Your most affectionate and humble servant kisses your honor's hand. Don Ángel de Martos y Navarrete. To Señor Bartolomé Macartis.[82]

165. The governor of Nachitoches, Monsieur Macartii,[83] replied to this letter of the governor of Texas as follows:

My dear señor: I am informed by your honor's letter dated August 31, last, that on the last journey which the Very Reverend Father Calahorra made to the Teuacanas he noticed what he had not previously seen, namely, that on the flagstaff in the said pueblo the flag of his Most Christian Majesty was placed below that of Spain, a thing which has caused you no little surprise, and that since you believe it is not my doing, you are reporting it to me so that I may give an order to take it away, and that if I do not do so, upon my reply, you will report it to the most excellent señor viceroy, etc. [In reply] I say to you that as soon as the Spanish religious of the seraphic habit [of St. Francis], at the command of the Duke of Linares, then viceroy of New Spain, and guided and protected by Don Luis de St. Denis, the commandant of Nachitoches, came into these lands on this side of the Río Bravo, which everyone knows had been occupied and settled in the year 1685, at the order and at the expense of the

---

[82]Bolton (*Athanase de Mézières and the Louisiana-Texas Frontier, 1768–1780*, Vol. I, p. 31, n. 18) refers to one Maċarty as "Commandant at Natchitoches" in 1763.

[83]See preceding note.

most invincible king of glorious memory, Don Luis XIV, great-grandfather of our kings (what everyone knows is that in the year 1683, unknown to the Spaniards and concealing himself from them, Monsieur de la Salle erected a presidio on the bay of Espíritu Santo and another among the Arkansas, west of the Mississippi), Don Bernardo de la Harpe, captain of infantry, went to discover the American nations scattered throughout this jurisdiction, and having encountered somewhat above the Cadodachos (in whose territory he founded a presidio, with their permission, and left in it a garrison which is kept there even today) the numerous heathen community of the Tabayas, Teuacanas, Yscanis, and Ouedeitas, located on a large river called the Akansas (if it is true that all these nations inhabited the banks of the Río de los Akansas, east of the place where D'Anville's line cuts this river, we admit that they belonged to the French), which flows into the Mississippi, he made an alliance with them and told them by means of signs of the protection and patronage of his Majesty (for they declared themselves his vassals with the customary solemnity). The flag of France was then unfurled in the center of their pueblo. And in the long period of more than forty years (for this took place in 1720) it has been regarded by them with a great deal of respect, for whenever it has been torn through the inclemencies of the weather, they have requested that it be replaced by a new one. Then. when the Tuacanas had separated from the rest, they came alone to establish rancherias on the banks of our Río Colorado, or Nachitoos, hopeful of benefiting more readily from the contact with the French, their discoverers, friends, and protectors. (If the Tuacanas came to settle on the Red River east of D'Anville's line, we also admit that they came under the control of France.) There they lived, happy and favored, until, because of the incursions of certain Indians from the north, they found themselves forced to move farther south, to the place where they are living today. (The places where they are living now are on the banks of the Río de la Trinidad and the second branch of the Brazos de Dios, as we have demonstrated in Part II, and as they are shown on our map 19 of document 74. These places are far to the west of D'Anville's line. By the act of moving from the Río Acansas and the Red River, these Indians attempted to withdraw from French dominion and place themselves under the dominion of Spain, and now in this location they could no' longer ask for aid and protection from France, nor benefit from the lands of Spain and from French dominion [at the same time]. Furthermore, I believe that these alleged migrations of the Indians are untrue, for it seems that they have always resided where they now have their pueblos. In the *derrotero* of Hernando de Soto we have found that the Tuacanas are the same ones as those whom the Inca Garcilaso calls Guacanes. They used to live west of Naguater [Naguatex?], that is, west of the Nauadachos, and north of and not very far from the bay of Espíritu Santo.) Having decided upon this third location, they sent envoys to Don Cesar Blan, my predecessor (may he rest in peace), begging him with great anxiety to aid them, as the custom had been, with a detachment of soldiers who would reside in their pueblo. This was granted them, the detachment being placed under the command of the *alférez*, Don Luis de Cur. It was kept there until, when it was ascertained from letters of Don Jacinto de Barrios y Jáuregui that the said Indians had taken part in the outrages committed against the new presidio of San Sabá, it was ordered withdrawn. The said governor (even without his demanding it) was thus shown such evident proof of the good relationship to which all of us of this troop aspire, the like of which will certainly be found very rarely in the intercourse of men, for who, out of kindness to another, would go so far as to abandon his possessions?

(The French did not abandon their possessions in withdrawing from the Tuacanas. What is clearly seen is that they abandoned a pueblo in which they wanted to establish themselves, in order that they might not be accused before their monarch for having taken part with the Tuacanas in the atrocities perpetrated in New Mexico, [and in the] presidio of San Sabá. To my mind they would have participated in these by means of exhortations and aid that they might have given the Indians, just as they had done with the Taobayaces when they defeated Don Diego Ortiz Parrilla.) [84]

166. Shortly thereafter (it was at the beginning of your lordship's able and prosperous government) the report was divulged by some letters which your lordship sent officially to the Señor Marquis of Cerlerec [Kerlérec] [85], the governor of Louisiana, that Don Luis de St. Denis, an *alférez* of our troops and a son of the commandant of the same Christian name and surname, who, while he was living, did his best to serve the Spaniards, had incited the coast nations to destroy the royal presidio of San Agustín de los Orcoquisas. This officer [St. Denis], accompanied by another and by a squad of Spanish soldiers, went to inquire of the Vidais what basis they had for this rumor [of an action] which was being falsely attributed to him, a rumor which is quite contrary to the opinion that is held here of the birth, good breeding, and notable talents of the said gentleman—a rumor, I say, which, although your lordship gave it full credence, was found not only in the investigation but also in the irrefutable testimony of the times, to have not the slightest support of truth. Even though your lordship is agreed in this, you still have not done us the favor of inflicting upon the known slanderer the punishment that his daring malice deserved. But what reason have I left to complain, when never has there been a better example of the fact that from evil itself the greatest good often comes?

167. When these officials, then, with my consent and a passport to your lordship, arrived in the vicinity of Nacodoches, they learned that the minister of the mission established in that pueblo was daily exposed to the insults and threats of the heathen around the mission. Thereupon, carried away by their zeal, they convoked the leaders and principal men and gave them such admonitions that the minister had the consolation of their returning with signs of

---

[84] For references to Don Diego Ortiz Parrilla, consult the Index of Volume II.
[85] Kerlérec arrived in New Orleans on February 3, 1753, to assume the governorship of that French province.—Fortier, *A History of Louisiana*, Vol. I, p. 135. See also note 53, Chap. XIV.

the most sincere repentance and with the respect that they owe him, as is best shown by the authentic certification which the very reverend fathers, Fray José de Calahorra and Fray Francisco de Paula Caro, gratefully gave to the said officials. These documents are now on deposit in these archives. From this convocation originated the fact that the Tuacanas, learning of the solicitude with which the French nation was acting in trying to reëstablish general quietude, did not hesitate in asking for peace, and after it was concluded, the Reverend Father Calahorra went to their rancheria with an interpreter whom he requested of us, and who was furnished to him.

168. I have stated all the above in order that your lordship may see how many years the Teuacanas in this region have known and loved us. With regard to what your lordship assures me to the effect that these Indians are included in the dominions of Spain, it seems to me that the contrary is true, for, passing over the discovery made by us and the natural right that all free nations have to place themselves under the overlordship which they like best, how could we otherwise have kept regular troops among them, who even in the transportation of their supplies directed their route by way of the presidio of Los Adaes, without your lordship's predecessors having presented the least opposition, which they would not have failed to do if our undertaking had been irregular? I shall not dwell upon this any longer, for since the boundaries have not yet been designated (indeed the limits were designated on D'Anville's map, and it is unbelievable that Monsieur Macarti [Macarty] should not have seen it, and for this very reason he should have abstained from trading with the Tuacanas), from which the course may be pointed out to us that we must observe in order not to make mistakes in such a difficult matter, I am convinced that only by an agreement and decision of our courts will a definite route be opened to us; meanwhile, when rumors and controversies spring up, they can occasion unfortunate consequences.

169. Finally, since the esteem which the Indians have professed for us has been the cause of so much commotion, I shall be able to point out, with your permission, since you are thoroughly acquainted with the success of the steps that we have taken to quiet the said Indians, that anyone would be somewhat unreasonable were he to show himself jealous because of the fact that favorable results may redound to him. On the other hand it is possible to extol among these barbarians the favorable conditions produced for them by the marriage of the two flags of France and Spain (a bad marriage and one that could not be tolerated, since it would be adultery) when the Family Compact, which our masters have lately concluded (he is referring to the Family Compact of which we have spoken in Part III, paragraph 324), is bringing about such general harmony in the whole political world as that which originates under the protection of two powerful monarchs who from the height of their thrones are showing us the obligation which we owe to the sacred bonds of consanguinity which unite them. Thus your lordship will pardon me if I cannot take the liberty which you suggest of ordering the French flag to be withdrawn from the pueblo of the Tuacanas, for since this, according to my information, is one of the principal idolatries of the Indians, so greatly do they venerate it, its withdrawal could do no less than offend their devotion to such an extent that capital harm

would befall the unfortunate messengers. (A false pretext; reason dictates that he should have explained to the Tuacanas that they were vassals of Spain and not of France, and that therefore the French flag should not be displayed there.) And if I should conduct myself so imprudently as to inform the Indians of the reason that impels me to give them such rebuffs (it was neither an imprudence to give the Tuacanas the said notice nor a rebuff to take from them the flag of France which should not have been there, since those lands belonged to Spain), it would mean that I was giving them to understand that we French and Spaniards no longer professed to have a happy union, the assurance of which, as I have said, caused them to lose their pride and ask humbly for peace, the benefits of which we are enjoying. With the breaking of the peace it would not be long before the same errors would appear that have been experienced previously. (Here is a scarecrow which he sets up to keep from doing what is demanded of him. Why could not those expressive admonitions of the French officials who reduced the Nacodoches Indians to their duty be employed with the Tuacanas Indians?) God keep your lordship the many years that I desire. Nachitoches, September 10, 1763. Your chief and most devoted servant kisses your lordship's hand. The Chevalier Macarti. To Señor Governor Don Ángel de Martos y Navarrete.

170. Acknowledging receipt of this dispatch, Don Ángel Martos wrote him the following:

My dear señor: When they delivered to me your honor's letter of September 10, in reply to mine of August 30 [31?], I found myself prostrated in bed with a relapse of the troublesome illness from which I was still suffering. For this reason, as I told your honor on the 27th of the said month of September, I left whatever might occur to me with regard to that letter until such time as God might be pleased to grant me relief. Being now somewhat better, I am answering it. I say that the nation of the Asinais is so numerous that it extends toward each of the four cardinal points for a distance of a hundred leagues. Its northern boundaries are the banks of the Río Misuri, which flows into the Palizada. (Later, in a more opportune place, we shall speak of these boundaries that he here gives to the Asinais.) It contains many different divisions, and one of them is that of the Tehuacanas, which is located northwest of it on the headwaters of the Río de Sabinas, about sixty leagues away. (It seems that Señor Martos made a mistake here, for no one, as far as I can remember, has said that the Tuacanas lived on the headwaters of the Río de Sabinas, but rather in the places that we have explained on the Río de la Trinidad and the Brazos de Dios.) That the nation of the Asinais and its divisions belongs to the Catholic dominions is confirmed by very old proofs, which I omit in order to avoid prolixity, and I shall say only what is necessary at this time. This is that in the year 1690, which was the time in which these lands were settled at the order of the most excellent señor, the Count of Galve,[86] Don Alonso de León took possession of them in the name of the Catholic

---

[86]See note 26, *supra*.

Majesty, and after founding the first mission, with the name of San Francisco, among the Asinais themselves, the Reverend Father Fray Damián Massanet celebrated the first mass in it on May 24 of the same year.

171. This being settled, it is apparent that your honor's statement to the effect that the first religious who came into these lands came under the guidance and protection of Don Luis de St. Denis is a very great error. It is made more evident by the certainty that this gentleman did not enter them until the year 1715, at which time, when he continued his march to the royal presidio of San Juan Bautista del Río Grande on the pretext that he was looking for cattle, he was sent by its captain to the most excellent señor, the Duke of Linares, who was at that time viceroy of this New Spain. I readily realize that this mistake may be due to the fact that when Señor de St. Denis entered by way of these lands, he found them uninhabited by Spaniards. Since this was undeniably true, I shall proceed to give the cause for their abandonment. In the year 1691, while the said most excellent señor, the Count of Galve, was governing this New Spain, the governor of Coahuila, Don Domingo Terán de los Ríos,[87] made at his command another *entrada* with land and naval forces. On October 26 of the same year, he arrived at the mission that has been mentioned. From here he continued his journey to Caudachos, where he entered on November 29, and after having sounded the river for three leagues in an Indian canoe, the pilots took bearings and found that the Caudachos were located fifty-six leagues from Los Asinais, the capital of all these tribes. Having completed this task, and since supplies were becoming short, the said Terán returned to his province, and the religious of Texas, finding themselves entirely without provisions, abandoned the mission in the year 1693, as did all the soldiers who were there, and the land remained uninhabited until the said year 1715, at which time at the command of the cited most excellent señor, the Duke of Linares, it was again settled. The said Señor de St. Denis accompanied this expedition.

172. From this account it is quite clear not only that the religious of whom your honor speaks are the ones who entered during the third expedition into this province, but also that the tribe of the Caudachos belongs to the king, my lord. And if it belongs to him, as may be gathered from what has been said, no one can doubt that that of the Tehuacanas, since it is about forty leagues (and much more, as is seen on our map, even if the distance is measured between Cadodachos and the source of the Río de Sabinas) to the west-south-west of it, should belong to the Catholic possessions, from which right they cannot be dispossessed by what your lordship says to the effect that during the time of your predecessor, Don Cesar de Blan, a French garrison was placed there. For aside from the fact that, as they said, this happened recently, there was no legitimate basis for it and even less for the statement that the supplies for it passed through this presidio without any objections from my predecessor, because this could have been done under the pretext that they were going to Caudachos. This is the same thing that happened with Sargeant Alexi who, having presented to me his passport to this nation, went to that of the Tehuacanas, delivered the flag, and ransomed the Indian woman Isabel. This he

---

[87]Domingo Terán de los Ríos was governor of Texas from 1691 to 1692.

would not have done if it had been stated in the said passport that he was going to do it, for then I should have returned him to your presidio. For this reason, in the name of his Catholic Majesty (whom may God keep) I demand of your honor for the first, second, and third time that, notwithstanding the excuses you give, you order the flag to be taken away and not permit any person of your nation to enter the pueblo of the Tehuacanas, since this is conducive to good feeling between the two nations. Otherwise your honor will be responsible for all and any bad consequences that may result. . . . May our Lord preserve your honor's life many years. Adaes, November 5, 1763. Your most affectionate and devoted servant kisses your honor's hand. Don Ángel de Martos y Navarrete. To Señor Don Bartolomé Macartii.

173. Monsieur Macartii replied to this letter as follows:

My dear señor: I thought that in my letter of September 10, last, replying to yours of August 31, I had justified sufficiently my reason for not causing the Tuacanas mortal offense by taking from them the French flag which has been displayed in their pueblo for more than forty years, but the new importunities which your honor is making to me and the demand which you sent me on the 5th of the month in the name of his Catholic Majesty to the effect that I should give your honor the most prompt satisfaction with regard to both points, force me to take up my pen again. It is with no little mortification from the thought that in such disputes we continue losing the time that should rather be dedicated to the gratification and joy with which we should celebrate the Family Compact that so closely unites our two nations. Nevertheless, I am confident that with what I shall tell you, your honor will be convinced of the validity of our rights, and in whatever mind this my discourse may leave your honor, I humbly beg of you to be so kind as to send my letters to the most excellent señor viceroy of those kingdoms just as, for my part, those of youŕ honor will be sent to Señor Don Santiago de Abadie,[88] commandant-general of this Louisiana, for the matter that we have undertaken seems to me such an exalted one that only with the prudent decision of our respective courts shall we be able to detect and correct the error. And for my part, although I aspire to nothing more than to do my best in the service of my sovereign, I confess that my zeal grows lukewarm from being forced to argue with your lordship with contentious dispatches, when on the contrary, in view of the sacred union of our masters, I would wish to pledge my strength and sacrifice my person in the common defense of the dominions that are in our care.

---

[88]"The King of France continued to act as the possessor of Louisiana, since the treaty of Fontainebleau of November 3, 1762, was still kept secret. . . . On March 16, the King announced that . . . he had established there [at New Orleans] a director and commandant. D'Abbadie was appointed to that office and arrived in New Orleans on June 29, 1763. . . . In October, 1764, Director-General D'Abbadie received an official communication announcing the cession [of Louisiana] to Spain and ordering the transfer of the province to the Spanish officials. . . . On February 4, 1765, D'Abbadie died, greatly regretted by everyone in Louisiana."—Fortier, *A History of Louisiana,* Vol. I, pp. 144–151.

174. I am not ignorant of the fact that in 1690 and in the following year, at the order of the most excellent señor, the Count of Galve, viceroy of New Spain, the Spaniards went into the interior of the lands located east of the Río Grande, and by sea into the bay to which they gave the name of Espíritu Santo. It is also clear to me that they founded a mission among the Asinais, that later they proceeded to go inland as far as the Cadodachos, and finally, that there they had to turn back, not because they lacked supplies, but in truth—and it is the truth that should be inseparable from history—because the said Cadodachos, incensed by the continual insults with which their guests were harassing them, advised them earnestly to leave their territory.

(If truth should be inseparable from history, Monsieur Macarti should not have written these untruths. If the Cadodachos had expelled the religious from their land, Father Massanet would not have praised them as he did—see Part III, paragraph 133—and would not have written the following words, found in the said paragraph 133: "I placed a cross on the door of the house of the said captain—of the Cadodachos—as a sign that I would return, because all of them wished me to remain.")

This territory is the most fertile, most fruitful, and most abundant in game that can be found. But your lordship omits this incident to which many old people will still bear competent witness. (If these old people did bear such witness, it would be false witness.) You conclude with the statement that all that country belongs to the Catholic monarchy, because it had taken possession of it in the said year 1690, which I shall be unable to dispute if I cannot cite for you another act of possession on the part of my kingdom, of prior date and more valid.

175. It is well known to everyone and it is confirmed alike by the accounts of an infinite number of writers, as well as by royal cedulas and other trustworthy documents that are deposited in the Marine Archives, that in the year 1678 (in Part I, paragraph 176, we proved that it was in the year 1681), after Monsieur de la Salle, a captain of our troops, had explored the extensive lands that are watered by the Mississippi River lying to the south and west with respect to New France, from 29° 5′ of north latitude, where it empties into the sea, to the falls of San Antonio de Padua, which lie in 45°, a place still very far from its source—after he had, I say, explored this river and the others that unite with it from both sides, he reported his discovery to Don Luis XIV, of glorious memory; may he rest in peace. This truly Christian prince— showing himself less inclined to perceive the temporal advantages that he would obtain if he should become master of the beautiful regions concerning which he had received the report, than the celestial treasures that presented themselves by enlightening with the evangelical light the extensive heathendom which was wandering about in those regions, gone astray through the darkness of the most irrational idolatry—ordered immediately that they be settled and honored with

the name of Louisiana. He designated as their governor the said Señor Don Roberto de la Salle, who set sail with two frigates of war, a supply ship, and a brigantine, with four hundred soldiers or sailors, thirty nobles, some young women, many servants and persons of various employments, a Canadian family, three clergymen destined to be chaplains of the troop, and four seraphic religious [Franciscans] who were to gather the apostolical harvest. Finally, they had large amounts of all kinds of stores, artillery, merchandise, and money, in order to succeed in an enterprise worthy of the most illustrious king in Christendom. The fleet had a successful voyage and dropped anchor in the year 1684 (in Part I, paragraph 173, we have proven that it was in the year 1683) a hundred leagues, more or less, west of the Mississippi, on the bay of San Luis, which is the same one that seven years later—as your lordship explains it—the Spaniards called Espíritu Santo. (The Spaniards called it the bay of Espíritu Santo beginning at least in the year 1519. See above, paragraph 77, which is note (A) of Number IX.) Señor de la Salle went ashore with the royal standard in his hand and, enchanted by the beauty of the country, which he learned from the mouths of the natives had never been travelled over or settled by any other Europeans down to that time, he ordered a presidio built a short distance from the said bay and between two rivers which flow into it farther to the east. He also gave it the name San Luis (he did not call it San Luis, but Fort Luis) because of the special pleasure he took in attributing all his successes to the majesty of his most invincible monarch.

176. Later, after having given an order to the naval force to return to Europe, he occupied himself with exploring the coast and the interior, in making alliances with the Indians and especially with the Asinais, from whom he received a good deal of help; and, finally, while marching with the intention of visiting the posts which he had founded previously far to the north of the Ylineses [Illinois], he was killed by his servants not far from the place where the Spanish mission of Nacodoches is maintained today. (We have proven in Part II, paragraph 444, that it was at a place west of the Río de la Trinidad.) Thus he sealed with his own blood the new dominions which he had acquired for his country with so many hardships and fatigues, a destiny indeed lamentable and one which has been common among the famous heroes of America— the Balboas, the Almagros, the Pizarros—who so rightly inspire general emotion, for to the admiration which is due them for their deeds is added the compassion which their misfortunes arouse.

177. After this parricide had been perpetrated, the members of Monsieur de la Salle's following (with the exception of those who had plotted his unfortunate death, among whom a few days later strife arose over the distribution of the spoils, and who perished at each other's hands, for it is well known that Divine Providence does not let the crimes of wicked persons go unpunished even when committed in places where treason seems most commendable) left the Asinais. They went to Cadodachos, from there they took the road to the Akansas, then they went straight to the Ilinues, and embarking in canoes with the intention of crossing the dangerous lakes of Canada, they arrived after unbelievable hardships at Kebec [Quebec], and

finally in France. Therefore it is not surprising if, because of so many misfortunes and calamities, Louisiana experienced neglect from our court (if neglect of the court does not prejudice the right of France to these lands which La Salle discovered, why should it injure Spain who discovered them through Ponce de León, Alvar Núñez Cabeza de Vaca, Francisco Vásquez Coronado, Hernando de Soto, and many others whom we mention in the dissertation on La Quivira) until in the year 1689, the outcome [of the war] being determined, Monsieur de Iberville, captain of naval forces, was ordered to seek the Mississippi, enter it, and station troops on it, which he accomplished successfully.

178. Meanwhile the colony which Monsieur de la Salle had left, learning of the deplorable end of their leader and lacking all kinds of supplies, found itself in the most pitiful straits. Some members of it took refuge among the Asinais. Others, who thought of reaching Canada, died of fatigue on the long road. The rest, gathering from their desperation no other fruits than cowardice and pusillanimity, because of their lack of caution fell into the hands of a maritime nation, the most ignorant known, by whom they were all destroyed or condemned to a captivity worse than death. (Here we have the country abandoned by the French and the Indians recovering their land, which had been unjustly invaded by [people of] a nation which was so odious to them that they came to assassinate them.)

179. It was probably at that time (it was indeed at that time) that the most excellent señor, the Count of Galve, hearing of the settlement of San Luis, despatched Don Alonso de León in order to confirm the report. Finding our Frenchmen scattered among the Indians, León persuaded them to follow him, and when the heart of this general was softened more by the beauty of a French maiden whose rescue he achieved than by their misfortunes, he came to lose the merit of his generous conduct through an act which I shall leave untold but which was the cause for him, far from being rewarded, to be discharged from his duties.

(Here is a most false accusation hurled against one of the greatest Spanish captains whom these lands have had. If this fault of León had been true, Father Massanet, who was no great partisan of his and proclaimed his failings—see especially document 13, in which several of them are presented for consideration—would not have kept quiet about it, and the noted Don Carlos de Sigüenza y Góngora would not have included the following eulogy of him in his *Trofeo de la Justicia Española,* [chapter] 11 [12], page 70: "(The Señor Count of Galve) entrusted this duty (of going to Texas) to Governor Alonso de León who, at the time that I am writing this (he wrote it in 1691), is resting in peace in the home of that immortality which received his spirit; his name will

always be formidable to all the barbarous nations who were subdued and subjected by his strong arm." Therefore his death and
not his crimes was the thing that discharged him from his duties.)

Of the French whom he brought back with him, those who were grown men
were sent to the mines, where, shut up like criminals in the subterranean
abysses, they must have longed for their previous condition, unhappy as it
was. (Beginning with paragraph 224 of Part I, we impunged this tale, con-
trived only to make the conduct of the Spaniards appear odious to other
nations. Only three youths escaped. These, as soon as they had reached adult
age, were embarked on the *Cristo*, flagship of the small armada. Thus when
the Chevalier des Augiers, an officer of his Most Christian Majesty, captured
it (for breaks had occurred between the two crowns) they obtained their
freedom and told of the incidents that I have mentioned.

(These incidents, for the most part very untrue, together with
the story of the three youths, are given practically in the same
terms by Prevost in volume 28 of Terracina's translation, page
96, and since they were related by persons who had witnessed them
while they were very young, their version was very inaccurate
or, rather, entirely false.)

180. With regard to the sea expedition of the Spaniards which your lordship
mentions, it is true that one Don Gregorio Salinas left Vera Cruz, entered
that bay of San Luis, and left again, carrying back with him the artillery
and other articles belonging to his Majesty, which the destroying Indians had
left behind either because they seemed to them of no use or because they
were very heavy.

181. This being settled, your lordship can do no less than admit yourself
convinced not only of our rights to the bay of San Luis but also of the fact
that if we draw a line from there running straight north, the lands that fall
east of the said line will belong to the Most Christian dominions.

(When the claim of this Frenchman is compared with that of
the Military Gentleman, the author of the *Notes on Limits*, there
naturally comes to mind that celebrated description which Virgil
of *Aeneid* fame makes in book 4, verse 175: "Nurtured by motion,
she [Report, Gossip] gains strength at every step."[89] Macarti
wished to fix the limits of Louisiana with a line drawn straight
north from the bay of Espíritu Santo so that all of the province
of Texas would belong to France, because it lies on that side.

---

[89]The above quotation, the Latin text of which was given by Pichardo, was
translated by Mrs. Minnie Lee Shepard.

The Military Gentleman desires the limits to be partly on the Río Bravo and partly in the Mexican Mountains. Someone else will probably want them to be on the coasts of the Pacific Ocean, and perhaps in the south at the Isthmus of Panama and even at Cape Horn. Thus it will turn out that this claim, "nurtured by motion, gains strength at every step.")

And even though by this fitting decision the territory of the Asinai is found far within the boundaries, I think it is no more than proper to confute the idea (without foundation) to which your lordship gives credence, namely, that it is the head of the other tribes and that its jurisdiction extends for a hundred leagues in each direction. Is it possible that you note with such little attention the usages, customs, and laws of so many different pueblos; the manner in which they make their headdresses and paint their faces and bodies; whether they are sedentary or nomadic; whethey they cultivate the soil or are content with wild fruits; and, finally, how some cremate their dead, others bury them, and the majority of them leave them in the open field without worrying about the fact that they may serve as food for vultures or voracious animals?

(If Monsieur Macarti had known that there were Indians who were allied with the Asinais, as we have seen in Part II, paragraph 813, through the instruction of Father Casañas, and that because of this alliance or friendship all of them called themselves Texas, he would not have been surprised at the statement of his opponent, Señor Martos. When nations are allies, their alliance is not hindered by the diversity of usages and customs and even of religion. In the holy book of the Maccabees we see that the people of God made an alliance with the Romans and with the Lacadaemonians—Maccabees, book 1, chapter 12. And Señor Martos' saying that the Asinais were the leaders or the head of the other friendly nations, did not mean that the Asinais commanded the others in the capacity of chiefs and lords, but that they were the ones of greatest renown among the Texas. It is true that he did err in confusing the Texas and the anti-Texas, making them all one, and, consequently, in saying that the limits of the Asinais extended to the Río Missuri and that the Tuacanas are included among the Texas, because we have seen in Part II, paragraph 815, that the enemies of the Texas extended as far as the Misuri and that the Tuacanas were included among them and not among the Texas. But none of this prevents the Tuacanas from belonging to Spain since they are located west of D'Anville's line, which is the sole and universal rule for the demarcation of limits.)

Answer me, señor. Is perhaps such a notable diversity of customs a sign of the harmony which the individuals of one and the same state profess to exist between themselves, such a state as we see established in the other parts of the world and such as, in the days of the Spanish conquest, were maintained among the nations of this New World, which the Mexicans and Peruvians held as vassals? I affirm that in this vicinity there is no rancheria, however weak and unfortunate it may be, that regards itself and is regarded by others as free and independent, that did not in former days have a certain river, small stream, or mountain designated as its boundary, which was never trespassed without bringing about cruel and bloody wars.

(This is not a very general custom among those Indians. In the statistical tables which we have copied in Part III, beginning with paragraph 569, we often read that the Indians under discussion do not claim as their own the land which they inhabit and that they have no fixed limits.)

Thus it was until the time of the entrance of Don Luis de St. Denis, who dedicated himself to knowing our natives, and persuaded them to live in peace and friendship, the blessing being that after they had experienced afflictions, through his efforts they received the benefits of peace, which they had not known hitherto, and for which they are grateful. Wretched in truth and very like the beasts hiding in the same thickets which they inhabited, all of them were close together, all enemies, and all looking upon each other with the greatest hatred, all bemoaning their fate and thinking of no other way to do away with such great misfortunes than the continual practice of the hostilities that were destroying their species. (This is not very accurate, for those who were Texas, or friends, did not make war upon each other. Neither did those who were anti-Texas do so, but war was waged between the Texas and the anti-Texas. See Part II, paragraph 813.) This should be more clear to your lordship than to anyone else, for incessantly and before your eyes, the Bidais, Asinais, Nacodoches, Nasones, and Aices come to beg us to take care (to use their words) that the roads which the said Don Luis de St. Denis cleared may not grow new thorns and that the sky which he dressed in blue, may not be darkened by sinister clouds and frightful omens of the tempests that have assailed them.

(It is true that the French have sown flowers in the path of those Indians, but flowers of intoxication, of hatred for the Spaniards, of aversion for the holy law of Jesus Christ, and of the other vices which have encouraged their passions; and it is true that the Spaniards have sown them with the thorns that the Christion religion and the holy truths of its laws bring with them. For that reason the Indians, induced as much by the example as by the words of the French, refuse Spanish jurisdiction, which is incomparably more beneficial to them, not only for their bodies but for their souls, than the French. For that reason, yielding to human weakness, they love and adapt themselves more to the French than to the Spaniards. But Spain does not therefore cease to be the one who should command them, and she cannot lay aside the right that she has to those lands and their people.)

182. Nevertheless, if there is a tribe that is the basis for inspiring your lordship's contention, it is no doubt the one of our Cadodaches, for they have left the country in which the said Nazones, Nacodoches, and Asinais still remain, together with the Yatasi and Nachitoches. This fact becomes apparent if it is noted, moreover, that they speak the same language; that they are divided into four clans, namely, the Beaver, the Otter, the Wolf, and the Lion; and that all of them happen to believe that on a hill two leagues from Caodachos a woman whom they call Zacado, and consider a goddess, created their first parents, proceeded to teach them the arts of hunting, fishing, planting, building houses, and dressing themselves, and that as soon as she saw that they were instructed, she disappeared. They regard this hill with special devotion, which, since it came from deception, ignorance alone would have permitted, and it is no wonder that superstition and credulity should continue to develop it. Who doubts that in olden times in our kingdoms, now so flourishing and enlightened, even more senseless superstitions may have held equal sway? And supposing that the superstition I have mentioned has such influence upon these barbarians, it seems only reasonable that they should venerate the Cadodachos as ancestors and founders. This is the most loyal and firm obedience.

(Here Monsieur Macarti takes issue with Señor Martos and wants the Cadodachos, since they are regarded as the progenitors of all those nations, to lead all the others after them. And since they are subjects of the French, he thinks all the others should be also. But this argument is very futile. That which constitutes the dominion of a sovereign is lands, and through the lands their inhabitants. Consequently the nations who live on lands of Spain belong to its crown, and whenever they leave them and go to make their homes on lands of another sovereign, they will belong to them. On the contrary, those who may abandon the lands of their sovereign and come to live on those of Spain necessarily will have to live subject to her laws.)

183. Now that I have had the opportunity of discussing at length with your lordship what my predecessors have done, I am convinced that your lordship would have a very poor opinion of me if I were to consent to the destruction of what I have found accomplished by them.

(It is untrue that it has been established that the Tuacanas, who are the subjects under discussion, should belong to France. The attempt of the French to send troops and to raise their flag there did not give them any right to take over these Indians.)

And since it is my intention not to allow the least innovation to be introduced, I hope through this procedure to win for myself your valuable esteem and that of my superiors. If your lordship will be so kind as to fix your attention closely upon the present critical position of this province, you will see clearly how very important it is to us for me to direct all my efforts toward flattering the Indians more and more by visiting them and enticing them in order that if the occasion [should arise] they may join us in opposing the invasion of the English, whose ambitious schemes have become more apparent through what we have recently seen of their pride and boldness.

(What hypocrisy! Under this pretext of preventing the invasions of the English, he wishes the Indians to be at peace with the French, and by means of this diabolical peace to appropriate them, taking them away from Spain!)

Are you perhaps ignorant, señor, of the fact that the English are already masters of the east bank of the Mississippi; that they may freely enter, leave, and navigate this river; that all the natives who surround us are amazed at the rumors of the settlements that they are planning among the Ylinues, among the Chicaza, and among the Natche; that their well-known greed will stimulate them in a short time to proceed to enter these neighboring provinces; that if they do this, the large rivers which come from these provinces in full view of them will invite this invasion; that with the smoothness of their words and much more with their gifts a revolution equal to the one that has ruined Canada, Florida, and Louisiana will be fomented, to our detriment? Can you be ignorant, señor, of the fact that only forty leagues remain for the Englishman to cross in order to reach your New Philippines?

184. I deduce from this that the most effective course we can follow is for me to avail myself of the great friendship which the Indians profess for us (it would be well to avail himself of this great friendship but not by harming Spain by taking her lands and Indians from her) so as to check the advance of the common enemy whenever the occasion may arise, and so that from the beginning they [the Indians] may feel such hatred for him, as the result of my counsels, that they may be capable of defeating any scheme to which he may have recourse. And now tell me: How shall I succeed in this under-

taking if my own advance is impeded by your lordship's attempting to expel
me from the Tuacana, and by your demanding that I take away the flag of the
king, my lord, from among the Indians, or rather that I should incite them
to wage a most treacherous war against us?   Then what shall we gain after
so much expenditure, trouble, and work?   By what route shall we have any
contact with our upper presidios in the future, if by closing to me the interior
lands discovered, explored, and pacified by us, your lordship will force us to
pass only along the Mississippi and in the midst of the English who will
proceed to learn our movements and plans?   Where shall we be able to settle
the Frenchmen loyal to their prince, from La Mobila, El Alibamon, El Marcet
[Manchac?], and El Ylinues, who will ask for asylum, not hesitating to leave
forever their rich haciendas, to avoid suffering the indescribable anguish of
finding themselves subjected to laws other than those of their master?   Would
it be based on justice and good policy for us to say to them, "Brothers, you
are no longer anything but our enemies, for the only section of unfortunate
Louisiana that we thought would remain to us is inaccessible to you because
of the opposition of the Spaniards, and therefore what we advise you to do
is to render prompt obedience to the tyrant, and may the time not come soon
in which, your country being united with his, we as well shall see ourselves
forced under his detestable yoke."

185. I say again, señor, that the matter we are discussing is so delicate that
prudence demands that we submit to the respective decisions of the two courts
whose authority resides in us, not because we might undertake something
that could result in harm to one or the other, but in order that we may both
be on the alert in the reciprocal preservation of their rights.   Therefore, in
the name of Señor Don Luis, the Well-beloved, whom may God keep, I insist
and demand of your lordship, one, two, and three times, that you suspend all
and any plans you may have with regard to the Tuacana or any other tribe
located north of the Spanish settlements, especially those of San Sabá and
Los Adaes, since the lands that lie between the ranges where the three rivers
of Cadodachos, Akensa, and Misuri rise, and the west bank of the Mississippi,
which they join, belong legally to France.

(D'Anville's line does not indicate this. The sierra of Las Grullas and the one of Los Taos, in which the Acansas and Cadodachos,
or Red, rivers rise, have always belonged to Spain. And to France
has belonged, by consent of Spain and because France agreed to
it and never crossed this line, that which this line, passing along
the Cadodachos, Acansas, and Misuri rivers, left to them, on the
east.)

By acting to the contrary, your lordship will be responsible for the ill
consequences that may result. . . . There being nothing else [to discuss], I
pray that God may preserve your lordship's life many years.   Nachitos,

November 7, 1763. Your chief and most devoted servant kisses your lordship's hand. The Chevalier Macarti. To Señor Don Ángel de Martos y Navarrete.

186. Señor Martos replied as follows to this letter:

My dear señor: Monsieur le Dour, captain of infantry, has placed in my hands your letter of the 17th of this month in reply to mine of the 5th of the same month. Having informed myself of its contents, I have to say, finally, that what I have written to your honor in my cited letter is evident from the description of this province of Texas and is so well known that it has been published. (I know of no other printed description of Texas to which Señor Martos might be referring than that of Father Espinosa, of which we shall speak at the proper time.) I would have omitted it, had not your lordship's [letter] of September 10 forced me to write it. And since I realize that by continuing this matter nothing will be gained aside from accumulating arguments uselessly, I refrain from doing so. I offer my services to your honor to use as you see fit, praying that God may grant you a prosperous life for many years. Adaes, November 18, 1763. Your most affectionate and humble servant kisses your lordship's hand. Don Ángel de Martos y Navarrete. To Señor Don Bartolomé Macarti.

187. In these letters of Monsieur Macarti we have seen almost everything that is contained in the *Notes* of our Military Gentleman. Therefore his work is almost a repetition of the letters of Macarti. Let us try to find out as far as it may be possible for us do so, the source of the extent which the French give to Louisiana. Don Antonio Alcedo in his *Diccionario* under the word "Louisiana" writes as follows:

Louisiana. A province and government of North America, one of the two which make up New France. It is bordered on the south by the Gulf of Mexico; on the north by the Río Ylinois and the territory of the barbarous nations of Indians called Paniasas, Padoucas, Osages, Tronontes, Tecaguas, Cahvanons, and others; on the east by West Florida, Georgia, and Carolina; and on the west by New Mexico and New Spain. It is almost fifteen degrees in extent from north to south, that is, from 25° to 40° of north latitude, and ten or eleven degrees from east to west, from 86° to 96° of longitude, its limits not being yet definitely determined. Monsieur Delisle gives it a much greater area, especially in the northern region where it adjoins Canada, and according to him it borders there upon New York, Pennsylvania, and Virginia, and on the west upon the Bravo and Salado rivers. One writer adds that Delisle ends his boundary at New Mexico.

188. This description I believe is not taken from the account of any writer, but in my opinion only from the map which Du

Pratz offers and the map drawn by Delisle who, as is seen in the *Diccionario* of Moréri, under the article "Lisle, Guillaume," published a world map in 1700 and some maps of Europe, Asia, Africa, and America. Later he brought out a new and much more perfect edition. He died on January 25, 1726. I regret that he has not told us the year of the new edition of his maps, but I believe that it was subsequent to the year 1712, in which the concession was made to Crozat, and that in as much as it is stated therein that he might go to trade in ". . . all the territory that we possess, which borders upon New Mexico, . . ." taking this sentence literally, he extended the limits to New Mexico. I have before me a French map which has the following inscription: *La America Meridional y Septentrional levantada sobre los Nuebos descubrimientos y ultimas relaciones de los mejores navegantes de este tiempo conformes á las observaciones astronomicas publicada por el Señor Guillermo Danet, impreso en Paris por Depvoix el año de 1751.* [*South and North America. Drawn from the new discoveries and latest accounts of the best navigators of this day, in conformance with the astronomical observations published by Señor Guillermo Danet. Printed in Paris by Depvoix in the year 1751.*] On this map is seen a line drawn with small dots which begins at the southern mouth of the Río Bravo and follows it, apparently, to where the Sierra de los Apaches Faraones ends. From here it ascends until it passes near the villa of Santa Fé. And from a point a little above this villa it turns west until it joins the Río Colorado which enters the Red Sea of the Californias. All the land which is east of this line he calls Louisiana. It is seen, therefore, that it is to a certain extent a copy of Monsieur Delisle's map.

189. But if the French even in these most recent times have not been able to make an exact map of all the country that lies between the Mississippi and the sierras of the Apaches Faraones and Las Grullas, can it be believed that Delisle's map would be exact even in its second edition? Why, then, does it serve as the model to the French for the demarcation of the limits of the lands that they have taken? But he who has a bad cause avails himself of all kinds of arguments, however futile they may be. To return to Macarti, I believe he is the first one who proposed

all these arguments which he heaped up in defense of the limits that he invented. If I am to speak candidly, I say that in my opinion the apparent conflict that sprang up between the governor of Texas, Martos Navarrete, and the commandant of Nachitoches, Macarti, over the Tuacanas, was one of contrivance. Beginning in 1762, France tried to cede Louisiana to Spain, but these matters were not settled until 1765, in which year the first Spanish governor, the Most Excellent Señor Ulloa, arrived at New Orleans.[90] Martos was found delinquent for having allowed the establishment of Massé, Cortableau, and the others on the banks and in the vicinity of the Río Sabinas, as we have seen above in Part III, paragraph 1555. In the representation which we mention in the said Part III and in the cited paragraph 1555, in which he gave an account of these establishments to the most excellent señor viceroy, he showed himself very prudent and circumspect for, as he told him,

I have desired to pass over this penetration [by the French] without noticing it, even though it is against the opinion I expressed to the governor of Orleans, for to move it [the settlement] for friendly spoliation it was necessary not to institute a lawsuit.

But at the same time that this señor governor showed so much prudence and circumspection with regard to such settlements, he made a great show of bravery and, with sword in hand, so to speak, he quarreled with the said Macarti over the fact that the French had raised the flag of his Most Christian Majesty in the pueblo of the Tuacanas, and exhorted him to give an order to have it removed. Yet in his last letter it seems that he shows himself persuaded and leaves the field to his opponent, infamously withdrawing from it.

190. Therefore I believe that in order to deceive the Spanish government, he made a show of his loyalty, patriotism, and vigilance over the lands which had been entrusted to him to govern and protect, arguing with Macarti in defense of the Tuacanas, where perhaps there was nothing to fear, because it was certainly

---

[90]According to Bolton (*The Spanish Borderlands*, pp. 237–239): ". . . on March 5, 1766, Juan Antonio de Ulloa arrived at New Orleans as first Spanish Governor. . . . Ulloa was coldly received in New Orleans and was soon up to his ears in trouble with the turbulent and dissatisfied *habitants*."

evident and well known that the lands which the Tuacanas inhabited belonged indisputably to Spain since they were located on the banks of the rivers of the Brazos de Dios and Santísima Trinidad, far away from Nachitoches and almost on the very road by which one went to Texas. Perhaps the French would not have raised their flag among the Tuacanas except with the consent of Martos and for the purpose of giving a basis for these disputes, and in order that the said Spanish governor might have something with which to try to delude his government, which, seeing the defense that he was making of the Tuacanas, would not notice the establishments of Massé, Cortableau, and the rest.

191. On the other hand, Macarti, promoting the claims of France to all those lands, would gain the good will of his court and of his entire nation, and thus could hope for rewards. If he were to enter the service of Spain, he would not lose his worth to her for having conducted himself in that dispute as a good servant of the king, his lord, and as a good Frenchman; that is, as very desirous of promoting the interests and welfare of his countrymen, and he would glory in the fact that although they might be separated from the crown of France, they would succeed in reaching the Río de Sabinas.

192. In a word, I am of the opinion that Martos and Macarti agreed to quarrel over the lands of the Tuacanas in order to cover their crime of the extension [of the French] to the Río de Sabinas, and especially so since they would already have known that France had ceded Louisiana to Spain and that Spain would lose nothing in those quarrels, for by the cession she was to be the peaceful owner of all the plains of Cíbola, of which she was to take complete possession in the following year of 1764. Finally, I am also of the opinion that Macarti was the first one to adduce all those futile arguments with which he attempted to prove that France should dominate all the country that extended to a straight line drawn north from the mouth of the Río Bravo, because previous to him no other Frenchman had advanced them, neither St. Denis when he was arguing with Don Manuel de Sandoval, nor Monsieur Cesario de Blan [Cesaire de Blanc] when he quarreled with Don Jacinto de Barrios, and we have no information that there might have been any other dispute between the governor of

Texas and the commandant of Nachitoches. For this reason we are justly convinced that these letters of Macarti were the ones that furnished the greater part of the material used by our Military Gentleman, author of the *Notes on Limits* published in the *Mississippi Messenger*.

193. (C). Here Father Talamanes places the following note:

The presidio of San Juan Bautista del Río Grande is the oldest of the interior ones of New Spain. It is contemporary with the discovery of New Mexico and after the uprising in this province, the Spaniards withdrew to it in 1680,[91] thirty-seven years prior to the time at which this author believes it to have been founded.

But this reverend doctor was mistaken in this (as he was also mistaken in believing that the English words "western side" in the text meant *orilla oriental* [eastern bank], and so put it that way in his translation), because the presidio of San Juan Bautista del Río del Norte was not founded in the year 1680. The one that was founded in that year was the one at the place which they call El Paso del Río del Norte, located on the banks of the same river. This is evident from, among other documents that we have seen, the following cedula,[92] which is found in our document 39, number 37:

Count of Paredes, Marquis of La Laguna, relative, member of my Council, *Cámara*, and *Junta de Guerra de Indias*, my viceroy, governor, and captain-general of the provinces of New Spain, and president of my royal audiencia

---

[91]Talamantes was in error in saying that the Spaniards after the Indian uprising in New Mexico in 1680, withdrew to the presidio of San Juan Bautista del Río Grande, in the vicinity of present Eagle Pass, Texas. After the Indian rebellion in New Mexico in 1680, approximately 2500 settlers of that province withdrew southward to the vicinity of present El Paso, Texas. By October, 1680, the refugees had reached the monastery of Guadalupe in present Juárez, State of Chihuahua, Mexico. A census taken of the settlers there that month showed that there were 1946 soldiers, servants, women, children, and Indian allies at that site. Thus, after reaching Guadalupe "at least several hundred of the refugees crossed into Nueva Vizcaya after having been listed. . . ."—Hackett, *Revolt of the Pueblo Indians of New Mexico and Otermín's Attempted Reconquest, 1680–1682*, Vol. I (*Coronado Cuarto Centennial Publications, 1540–1940*, Vol. VIII, p. cix). Later a presidio was established near the monastery of Guadalupe. With reference to two conflicting estimates concerning the population figures of New Mexico in the year of the Indian rebellion in 1680, see Hackett, *Historical Documents Relating to New Mexico, Nueva Vizcaya, and Approaches Thereto, to 1773*, Vol. III, pp. 327–328, n. 133.

[92]A translation of another copy of this cedula is printed in Hackett, *Historical Documents Relating to New Mexico, Nueva Vizcaya, and Approaches Thereto, to 1773*, Vol. III, pp. 349–350.

of Mexico, or to the person or persons in whose charge its government may be. In a letter of December 22 of the past year of 1682, you mention having given me a report of the miserable state in which are the provinces of New Mexico because of the uprising of the hostile Indians, confederated with many of the converts, and that you undertook two armed *entradas* in our name in order to attempt by this means to recover a part of what has been lost, supplying the necessary funds for that purpose.

194. You likewise ordered that a presidio be formed with fifty soldiers at the pass which they call El Río del Norte, having considered it indispensable for defending and protecting the convent of Franciscan religious which is in that place, and the three missions of Sumas Indians, who are the only ones who have remained in the said *custodia* and new conversion, and also for the safety of the Spaniards who withdrew [from New Mexico] and assembled at that site. The latter, and the Indians who came out on the first occasion, and those whom they brought out the last time from the place called La Isleta, apparently numbered more than 1,300 persons.[93] Since there was no presidio to restrain those who have come out in the first and second withdrawals, it was to be feared because of their inconstancy that they might go back with the apostates, impelled thereto by the attraction of their country, their relatives, and their [desire for] freedom.

195. And the missionary religious and the Spaniards who are in the said place, being without this protection and defense, might abandon the site, likewise leaving exposed to loss the new conversion of the two nations called Zumas and Mansos, with danger to other new conversions as well, in the place called Casas Grandes and all those which follow along one side of the province of Sonora, so that the entire frontier of Parral would remain exposed. In this area the most serious damage and hostilities were feared and expected, with evident danger to those who remain there and the attendant misfortune of losing entirely the hope of restoring the province [of New Mexico] if once that post were dismantled. It also would be necessary to abandon the new conversions and many others in the province of Sonora, and furthermore the whole kingdom of [Nueva] Vizcaya would be more exposed to the hostilities of the enemy. [You state that] in the maintenance of the presidio and the expenditures made you were influenced and persuaded by the cedula issued on June 25, 1680,[94] in which it was ordered that if it seemed evident to you that the conversions in the said provinces were progressing and that the ministers of the doctrine were complying with this obligation, you were to employ all possible means for their assistance and defense, in the form that you might consider most advantageous, to ·accomplish the reduction of the Indians to our holy faith and the conservation of that which had been discovered and might be discovered. In consideration whereof you had ordered (with the assent of a *junta general*) that the said presidio be

---

[93]See note 92, *supra*.

[94]This cedula is translated into English in Hackett, *Revolt of the Pueblo Indians of New Mexico and Otermín's Attempted Reconquest, 1680–1682*, Part I, pp. 234–236.

maintained in the place mentioned until I, having received this information
(which was given more fully in the *autos* which you remitted), might order
whether it is to be maintained and the recovery of the said provinces of New
Mexico continued. You had not proceeded with the latter in order not to
increase the expenditures of my *real hacienda* without having my specific order
to that effect.

196. There having been examined in my royal Council of the Indies the
contents of your letter, the arguments which you set forth in it based upon
the accompanying *autos,* and especially upon the report of the *junta general*
which was held in the City of Mexico on July 28, 1682, and bearing in mind
the cedula cited, of June 25, 1680, and what my *fiscal* recommended with
regard to all this in his report made to me after examination of the matter,
I have decided to approve (as by these presents I do approve) the formation
of the said presidio with the fifty soldiers whom you mentioned, in the place
which they call Río del Norte. It is my will that it be preserved and maintained in the form and manner that you have directed and that was decided
upon in the *junta general* cited, so that by this means not only the missions
and conversions that have been established hitherto and that may be established
in the future may be protected, together with the Spaniards and Indians
assembled there, but also so that the safety of the provinces of New Mexico
and of those of El Parral, whose preservation and progress are so important,
may be assured.

197. As for the recovery of what has been lost in the said provinces, I
order and command you to attempt with all the application which is expected
from your zeal and attention in my service to take the measure that may seem
most appropriate to you in order to accomplish this restoration, at the greatest
possible saving to my *real hacienda,* and that for both purposes you issue at
once the necessary orders. You will advise me of the receipt of this dispatch
and of what you may be doing in compliance therewith so that I may be
informed of it, and my accountants who assist in my royal Council of the
Indies, and the royal officials of that City of Mexico will take cognizance of
the present order. Dated in Madrid on September 4, 1683. I the King. By
order of our lord, the king. Don Francisco de Salazar.

198. The presidio of San Juan Bautista del Río del Norte
was founded in 1701, as we have stated at length in Part
II, paragraph 647. Therefore it is seen that our Military Gentleman erred also when he wrote that until 1717 the Spaniards did
not have this presidio, located on the west, or rather south, bank
of the said Río Bravo. In 1718, the Spaniards through Don Martín de Alarcón founded the presidio of San Antonio de Béxar,[95]
as we have stated in Part II, paragraph 662, and it was of this
presidio that our Military Gentleman was attempting to speak,

---

[95]See *Pichardo's Treatise* . . . , Vol. II, p. 102, n. 5.

even though, since he knew so little of our history, he fell into such a crass error, not only in the designation of the year in which the presidio was founded, but also as to its name.

199. (D). What damage will the Spaniards suffer because of their failure to establish settlements across the Río Bravo, this side of the Asinais? Alonso de León left Coahuila for the Asinais and founded among them the mission of San Francisco de los Nechas at the order of his government and on lands that did not cease to belong to his king just because the covetous La Salle and some of his companions travelled through them. Spain would have founded this settlement among the Asinais with the same right if before settling Coahuila, the Nuevo Reyno de León, and the other provinces and places that lie between them and Mexico, she had sent there another captain from this city. If Cortés had sent Pedro de Alvarado to Texas rather than to Guatemala, Pedro de Alvarado would have founded in Texas with the same right a city and other settlements just as he founded them in Guatemala. And if Francisco Vásquez Coronado, sent by the most excellent señor viceroy of Mexico to all those lands, if Espejo and all the others who visited them many years before La Salle was born, had established some town, would the French still say that they had a right to those lands because their La Salle had entered them? Now then, even though he entered them, the entire result of his entrance was that his own followers killed him; that his assassins killed each other; that the Indians destroyed their fort, sacked it, and killed all his companions; and that of the very small remainder that survived, a part proceeded to escape to France and a part were captured by Alonso de León.

200. Let us compare the monuments raised on the plains of Cíbola by Francisco Vásquez Coronado and by Robert de la Salle. When that Spaniard entered Quivira, as we read in [the work of] Señor Herrera, decade 6, book 9, chapter 12, he placed a cross there with an inscription which said that Francisco Vásquez Coronado had arrived there. And when La Salle entered the bay of Espíritu Santo, he erected a small fort of wood. The Spaniards withdrew from Quivira and for that reason the French say that they lost the right to it. Will the Spaniards not also say that since the French abandoned Texas entirely through flight and

death, they lost all their rights, if they had acquired any, to this province? Why, then, do the French wish to revive their rights after having abandoned this province, and do not wish those of the Spaniards revived, especially since Coronado did not abandon Quivira forever but was determined to return to it? But the dead Frenchmen in Texas never made a promise to return to settle it. We could present a similar argument on the entrance of Hernando de Soto, who remained settled in the pueblo of Vtiangue more than five months, as the Inca relates in the first part of book 5 of the *Historia de la Florida*, chapter 1. Finally, we can make the same argument with regard to the other *entradas* to La Quivira and to the Jumanos, made from New Mexico and mentioned by us in the dissertation on La Quivira.

201. The French having lost their rights, if they had them, that is, which they never did, that province remained (let us suppose for a moment that Spain had no right to it) open to conquest by anyone else who might subjugate it. Now then, Spain was the one who took advantage of this occasion. She entered after the extermination of the French; she won the good will of those Indians; she brought them under her control; and she founded the mission of Los Nechas among the Asinais. In all this there was no perfidious trick, as our Military Gentleman has previously stated. Then she should incur no prejudice for having made a settlement among the Aisnais before having made any others on the west [east?] bank of the Río Bravo.

202. (E). All this is most certain, and Spain desires that this theoretical truth be put into practice. She asserts that her possession is not fraudulent but that that of the French is; that for the same reason her possession may be converted into a legal one; and that it should be [recognized as] legitimate among nations. She refuses to rescind her claims because she finds herself injured, and she does not consent to the injustice that is attempted against her, despoiling her of other lands besides those which by the cedulas and orders of her king and lord, she consented to have taken from her east of D'Anville's line.

203. (F). By the treaty of 1763 France ceded Louisiana to Spain; hence, the disputes which had existed between the two crowns over limits were ended. The foolish, futile, and ambitious

claims of the French ceased. They had been expounded lastly by Macarti, but more with the idea of freeing the Spanish governor, Martos, from the penalty to which the latter had become liable for having consented to the establishments of Massé, Cortableau, and others, than to win advantages for the French, for he would have known very well that D'Anville's line designated the French limits. Now, therefore, when the Military Gentleman asks the question, "What were the limits of Louisiana prior to 1763?" I reply in two words that they were those designated by the line which Monsieur D'Anville drew on his map of North America.

XIII

204. Spain ceded Louisiana to France with the same extent that it had when France possessed it. (A). Now, if the limits were to be established between these two powers, would France perhaps not maintain that her claims extended to the Río Bravo? (B). To prove their validity she would cite (C) the settlement made by Monsieur de la Salle and his people on the bay of San Bernardo in 1685, the recognition of their forethought in the concession granted to Crozat in the year 1712, the erection of the fort on the Río Bravo, the various discoveries made in that part of the country before and after these dates, and, finally, she would allege with good effect that the right of simple discovery without making any settlement was superior to and of greater force than that of fraudulent possession. (D). The rights of France, whatever they may be, have devolved upon the United States (E), and for the same reason we find ourselves forced to determine and to uphold them.

NOTES

205. (A). For that reason she returns it to her with the same extent with which she received it, which is the one designated by D'Anville's line.

206. (B). She would not maintain them, just as she never maintained them while she possessed Louisiana, and Macarti, as we have seen, is the only one who, in the last days of his French government, promoted this nonsense.

207. (C). If France had found that she should cite all this, she would not have slept and would not have failed to cite it. But, on the contrary, St. Denis, without any subterfuge, declared to Don Manuel de Sandoval that the entire province of Texas belonged to the Spaniards.

208. (D). If this is true, as it is, the right of simple discovery of all the plains of Cíbola, even though the Spaniards may

have made no settlements on them, is superior and of greater force than that of the fraudulent possession of the French. And how far does the avidity of our Military Gentleman go in proposing arguments, and why is he not ashamed to propose this one which is against him and against all the French? Then does a simple discovery give the French a strong claim, and none at 'all to the Spaniards? Might the discovery of Juan Ponce de León have been a simple discovery? And that of Alvar Núñez Cabeza de Vaca, that of Francisco Vásquez Coronado, that of Hernando de Soto, and those of all the others who journeyed to La Quivira and to the Jumanos, especially those who went to the former, who covered the area between Santa Fé and the Jumanos and between the bay of Espíritu Santo and La Quivira. On the basis of their reports the Most Illustrious Señor Benavides[96] wrote his account, which Laet[97] translated into Latin, and which may or may not have guided Monsieur de la Salle in his discovery. By this fact alone, according to the doctrine of the Military Gentleman, Spain should have more right to those lands than France, because of the fraudulent or unjust possession that La Salle took of them.

209. (E). It is undeniable that all the rights that France had to those lands have devolved upon the United States. But the rights that France did not have could not have devolved upon the United States. France's right extended only as far as D'Anville's line, which delimited them. With reason Father Talamantes, in the note attached to this text, said:

The poor United States! If only there had passed to them rights other than the original ones of France over Louisiana! France had no other right than that of the possession permitted by Spain, and as this possession was a fact limited in itself, it also left the limits of Louisiana fixed.

XIV

210. No one has ever believed that the Spaniards at any time discovered or explored any of the rivers that flow from the west into the Mississippi

---

[96]See *Pichardo's Treatise* . . . , Vol. I, p. 34, n. 2.

[97]"In 1633, John de Laet added a short abstract of the [Benavides] *Memorial* to the Latin edition of his *America*, first published in 1625. . . . Cap. XXVI of Liber Quintus, pp. 315–316, is headed 'Recentissima Novae Mexicanae *descriptio, è commetariis* Alfonsi de Benavides *Franciscani.*' The description is a condensed summary of the geographical information in the *Memorial*, filling a folio page and a half. . . ."—*The Memorial of Fray Alonso de Benavides, 1630* (Ayer trans.), p. 193.

or the Misuri. (A). The attempts that they made in the year 1720 to establish a settlement on the Misuri came to naught. The adventurers were surprised by Indians who were allies of the French and not one of them escaped death except the father chaplain. (B). The French, on the contrary, ascended by all these rivers, with the exception of the Misuri, to their sources, and opened up a trade with the Indians. (C). They always claimed and even exercised acts of sovereignty over the whole country that lies between the Mexican Mountains, the Mississippi, and the Misuri. (D). They made treaties with the Indians, gave lands to settlers and exclusive privileges to traders (E), and finally, they maintained a post many hundreds of miles distant, on the Arkansas River, another on the Missouri, and another near the head of the Osage River, all of which were in the very center of the country. (F).

NOTES

211. (A). This is calumny and a falsehood. The Spaniards explored these rivers from the beginning of the eighteenth century. Ulibarri, who crossed the Napestle in 1706 (see Part II, paragraph 544), writes as follows to the governor of New Mexico in a letter which is found copied above in Part III, paragraph 167:

The third point was that they gave full information concerning many other nations which, both toward the north, and toward the east and the south, are living on five large and important rivers. These rivers, beginning with the first one, which has been mentioned, are the ones that they call Napeste in their language (the French call this Río Napeste the Río de Arcansas; see document 55, number 24), to which I gave the name of Río Grande de San Francisco; the second, Nisquisandi; the third, Citascahe—on this one live the said Pananas, in two large rancherias—; the fourth, Daenasgaes; and the fifth, Nasatha. The Apaches say that this last one is much larger than the first, the Napeste, or Río Grande de San Francisco. (From this we can conjecture that it is the Misuri, which certainly is larger than the Arcansas.)

212. In Part III, paragraph 215, is found the following opinion:

Opinion of the chief war-captain, José Naranjo. Captain José Naranjo, who is the war-chief of the natives of this kingdom, with a commission from the superior government, said: That having been informed of the superior dispatch of his Excellency, and of the above *auto* drawn up by me, the said governor and captain-general, [he declares] from his own experience and the four *entradas* which he has made to the said country of El Quartelejo, and for some distance beyond, as far as the great river which he named the Jesús María, that the said river is about seventy leagues distant more or less. . . .

Here it is seen that Naranjo saw the nations and rivers of which the Indians told Ulibarri. Don Antonio Valverde y Cosío,[98] governor of New Mexico, crossed the Napestle and went much farther on (see Part I, paragraph 265), and Don Pedro Villasur[99] necessarily crossed it when he went to the Pananas. See this account in Part I, beginning with paragraph 271. Don Juan Bautista de Anza[100] left New Mexico with troops to attack the Cumanches and also crossed the Río Napestle. See Part II, paragraph 553. And I do not know how many Spaniards may have travelled the same road, for neither is everything written, nor do I claim to have read everything that has been written about it. Then the Spaniards have explored the rivers which enter the Mississippi or the Misuri from the west, not once, but many times.

213. Father Talamantes writes as follows in a note concerning this:

From some *autos* that exist on this matter in the superior government of Mexico, the motives and the success of the expedition which is mentioned here, are evident. The viceroy of Mexico, the Señor Marquis of Casafuerte (it was not he, but the Señor Marquis of Valero), learning of the settlement that the French were planning to make among the Pananas Indians located on the banks of the Río de Jesús María, near the Misuri, and having definite orders from our court to prevent these new settlements, decided that the governor of New Mexico, Don Antonio Valverde, should go himself or send his lieutenant to ascertain the truth and to reconnoiter the country, taking along the necessary escort. The said lieutenant, having been put in charge of the expedition owing to the governor being occupied with other matters, left the villa of Santa Fé on June 14, 1720, and, having arrived in sight of the settlement of the Pananas, he sent them an interpreter, whom they detained. This procedure, some other hostile acts that were noted, and the knowledge that they were being incited by the French who had penetrated there and with whom he did not want to have the least cause for an encounter, led the lieutenant, after a

   [98]Antonio Valverde y Cosío was *ad interim* governor of New Mexico from 1717 to 1722.

   [99]Consult *Pichardo's Treatise* . . . , Vol. I, Part I, Chap. VI.

   [100]"Late in the century after 1763, when Indian attacks on all the northern provinces of New Spain became acute, Charles III took extensive measures to meet the menace by erecting the Commandancy-General of the Interior Provinces. The execution of the royal policy in New Mexico was placed in the hands of Governor Juan Bautista de Anza, who successfully established in 1786 a peace with the Utes, Navajos, and Comanches, and used these Indians, now reconciled with one another, against the Apaches."—Thomas, *After Coronado*, p. 47. Anza was governor of New Mexico from 1778 to 1789.—*Pichardo's Treatise* . . . , Vol. II, p. 44, n. 75.

council of war which he held on the matter, to decide to withdraw. This was done in the best order, without having been preceded by the least trouble with the Indians, and our expedition halted, on the banks of a river not very far away, called San Lorenzo. Our troop consisted of fifty Spaniards from among those famous soldiers who reconquered New Mexico, and some friendly Indians. While all of them were resting, guarded by the sentries, who on this occasion failed in their duty, they were surprised during the night by five hundred men armed with muskets, lances, and bows and arrows. It was impossible to resist the first impact. Thus almost all of our people perished, the captain with thirteen men and some Indians saving themselves. This is a brief statement of the event, according to the unanimous declaration of those who escaped, and it is not strange that the French have concealed the circumstances which do them little honor. But it is true that this offense was not so much the work of the Pananas as of the French themselves, who on this and other occasions have failed in good faith and have disturbed the Spanish possessions in various ways. Whatever may have been the result of this expedition, it was not the only one [made], as the writer of this article attempts to infer.

We have given this history in great detail in Part I, beginning with paragraph 262, having taken it from the *autos* which Father Talamantes has cited, and we mention this text of our writer there also, in paragraph 316.

214. (C). We have seen that it is untrue that they ascended to the sources of these rivers, so that the trade that they opened with the Indians was only with those who are east of D'Anville's line.

215. (D). Without notifying (says Father Talamantes concerning this) or obtaining the consent of Spain, to whom belonged the right of recognizing the titles on which these acts of sovereignty were based. . . .

And I add that it is untrue that they had exercised these acts in the territory lying between D'Anville's line and the Mexican Mountains.

216. (E). But all this they did in the area enclosed by D'Anville's line, and they never went west of it, for D'Anville would have then set back his line to that point.

217. (F). It is true that they had these presidios and even additional ones, and we admit it above in paragraph 361. But the maps of Bellin and of others also show us their location, and D'Anville's map shows them to us east of his line. Since the line of this geographer does not go straight to the north pole from

the Cabo del Norte, where he begins it, but turns several times toward the northwest and later to the north it need not be surprising that some Indians should be to the west [of it], and if one wishes to say so, in the very center of the country. But everything that falls to the south of them does not thereby belong to the French, since they are outside of the line and west of it.

XV

218. It is even more than probable that Spain in times gone by consented to these western limits (A), and the facts that we are going to cite cause us to conceive a strong presumption of such consent. When Louisiana was in the possession of France, some traders from the Mississippi ascended the Río de los Acansas and built a warehouse on the eastern slope of the Mexican Mountains[101] (B) for the purpose of trading with the Spaniards located between these mountains and the Río Bravo. The Mexican traders who monopolize the trade of that country (C) under the protection of exclusive privileges, were inclined to believe that this was a violation of their rights, and consequently they seized the persons and goods of these supposed intruders and dispatched them to Havana in order that they might be tried there. (D). The supreme tribunal absolved them of the charge and ordered also that their goods be returned to them since the warehouse of the traders from the Mississippi was located within the limits of Louisiana. One of the persons interested in this negotiation is still alive, and he is the one who has related all this in great detail to the writer of these *Notes*. (E). Another event that happened in 1772 also furnishes us with additional evidence on this matter and corroborates everything we have said. A gentleman engaged in the fur trade at a place located near the source of the Río de los Acansas (F) had a man employed for this who was at that time about sixty years of age. This man in his youth had been a soldier, and he told his master that during that time he was sent by his chiefs to explore or reconnoiter the line of demarcation between the French and the Spaniards. He added that beyond the mouth of a small river which came from the west, at its source [in fact] where the said line crossed it, there was an object of curiosity which consisted of a very thick tree on whose trunk the officials and land surveyors made some marks and signs, and on which they fastened a broad tablet of lead or some other metal on which they engraved some inscriptions. (G).

NOTES

219. (A). With regard to this Father Talamantes says:

Toleration is not acquiescence or consent. Spain tolerated to a certain extent the daring enterprises of the French out of regard for the House of Bourbon

---

[101]For the location and a description of the Mexican Mountains, see *Pichardo's Treatise . ...* , Vol. III, pp. 200, 403–404.

which ruled both nations, and it must be carefully noted that the same thing that induced Spain to a policy of dissimulation and tolerance would serve the French in increasing their possessions at the expense of our own. This is the true and only basis for the rights of France in Louisiana and what furnished her the means of maintaining them: Spanish toleration. Spain, later recognizing her danger and consulting her own interests, thus obtained Louisiana by a secret family compact in the same manner in which, out of consideration for it [the Bourbon family], she had tolerated for some time the dismemberment that had been made of her in this important part of her dominions.

220. What I say, aside from this, is that Spain indeed consented to the limits designated by D'Anville's line, because they [the French] had taken the territory up to it, and she consented to their keeping all they had taken. See Part II, paragraph 352.

221. (B). Now, if our Military Gentleman repeats to us this same thing at each step, we shall also incessantly repeat that it is most untrue, as we have already said, that the French, after they had occupied Louisiana, would have reached the Sierra de las Grullas,[102] which our writer calls the Mexican Mountains.

222. (C). Here the said Father Talamantes placed a note which reads as follows:

The inland trade is permitted to all the inhabitants of that country without any reservation, but their poverty is the real reason, as in all places, for the monopoly which the rich exercise. Such is the only privilege which the latter enjoy.

But it is noted that he did not understand the meaning of the text which he was refuting. The text says that the Spanish government would not consent that foreigners should trade with the inhabitants of New Mexico. In this it was acting as a good vassal who obeyed the laws of its sovereign, which prohibited his subjects from trading with foreigners. And when the government desires Spaniards to trade only among themselves, our Gentleman calls it monopolizing.

223. (D). When we discussed the French merchants who introduced themselves into New Mexico, and what happened to them, we wrote as follows in Part III, paragraph 386:

We are going to give most convincing proof that the French never extended their dominion beyond the dividing line drawn by their geographer, D'Anville. In the extracts which we have made from documents 34, 35, and 36, and which

---

[102]For references to the Sierra de las Grullas, see the Index to *Pichardo's Treatise* . . . , Vol. II, p. 575, under "Grullas, Sierra de las."

we have inserted here as a continuation of the foregoing, it is seen very clearly that the first Frenchman (see below, number 486) who crossed this line was a merchant named Pedro Mateo [Malec], who reached New Mexico. He did not believe himself to be travelling through lands belonging to his nation on this side of the [D'Anville] line, but was coming as a merchant to the lands of the Spaniards with the intention of selling his goods among them. And even this trip does not date very far back, since it did not take place until the year 1739, as the governor of New Mexico, Don Gaspar Domingo de Mendoza, states in document 36, number 82, which we have copied below in number 502, although in the *autos* the year 1740 is given. These documents show also that after this, other Frenchmen came in the same capacity; that, apparently, the French extended their alliances with the Indians as far as the nation of the Panipiques which, according to the deponents, was called also Jumana; and finally, that the Spaniards knew of all the principal French settlements, in both Canada and Louisiana, from reports given by these French merchants and by the Spaniard, Felipe de Sandoval—the declarants in the original *autos* from which we took the said documents 34, 35, and 36—and from what was learned from other printed sources, both French and Spanish.

224. The governors drew up cases against all the French merchants who were captured in New Mexico, and sent them, together with the culprits—with the exception of some who were permitted to stay there—to the captaincy-general of this kingdom, as is shown from the account that we gave beginning with the paragraph following the one cited just above.

225. (E). The Military Gentleman relates that a person who had been concerned in it, had himself told all this to him, who was the writer of these *Notes on Limits*. But Father Talamantes, since he did not comprehend the meaning of the text, translated it as follows:

One of the persons concerned in this matter is still living and he describes it in great detail to the notary of the case.

He added a note which is of the following tenor:

What has been done consistently in New Spain with all foreigners who have been apprehended introducing illicit commerce into the interior of the provinces has been to conduct them to Mexico to be tried by the captaincy-general. For many years the practice was followed of passing sentence and sending the case, together with the culprits, to be disposed of by the king (this is most true, and we have seen it very clearly above in Part III, paragraph 526), but when his Majesty noted that the protection of the ambassadors of the other nations impeded the course of justice, he ordered subsequently that cases of this kind be concluded in America and that the criminals be sentenced here likewise, according to the seriousness of the crime. Since this was generally known in New Spain and much more so in the Interior Provinces, where cases of this nature have been requent, is it credible that the merchants of New Mexico would have arrested the French traders in order to send them to Havana, an unqualified tribunal, if they had one nearer and legally qualified in Mexico? How could their governors have tolerated it? And even if both had been capable of such irregularity, why would the government of Mexico have tolerated it, before whom the said criminals had to be tried? How is it possible, finally, that a purely criminal case, involving a crime against the state such as the introduction of contraband, should pass through civil channels at the sole instance of the merchants of New Mexico? It is no less false that the tribunal of Havana would decide the question of the ownership of the site on which the warehouse had been placed, for if this action, the date of which is not given, was prior to the year 1763, at which time Louisiana was in the possession of France, the matter would have been discussed in the captaincy-general of Mexico and its final solution, since the question of limits was involved in it, would have been referred to the king for decision. If it was subsequent to the said year, that is, when Louisiana belonged to Spain, the governor of Louisiana, having been notified by the viceroy of Mexico of the transgression of his subjects, would have sent them to him if circumstances had permitted it, so that they might be punished, and an account would have been given to the minister of state in whom resided all the authority with regard to the civil, political, and military government of Louisiana. Aside from that, how does the question of limits enter in a criminal case regarding the introduction of contraband? If it is true, as the author of this discourse admits, that the said Frenchmen were trying to trade in New Mexico, was anything else besides this single fact needed to [be able to] prosecute and punish them? Let the warehouse be located on Spanish soil or French—what difference did it make as long as they were guilty and should be punished as disturbers of the public order of a neighboring nation? It is unbelievable, therefore, that their goods should have been ordered restored to them, for the confiscation of goods of illicit trade is the first penalty which a smuggler suffers, and this same penalty has been applied on various occasions to Frenchmen. The expression of "supreme tribunal" is equally strange, for in the Americas, in judicial matters, it cannot be any other than the royal audiencia. But there has been no other audiencia on the island of Havana than the one which was moved from the island of Santo Domingo to Puerto Principe in 1799.

226. Father Talamantes alludes here to the following cedula which is found on page 196 of volume 77 of the royal cedulas and orders which are kept in the secretariat of the viceroyalty:

Notwithstanding the fact that under the date of August 20 of the year just past your Excellency was informed that his Majesty had approved the sending to these kingdoms of the two Frenchmen, Elias Georgon and Antonio del Faro, and two negroes, Bernardo and José, apprehended by the governor of Texas at the landing place of the Río de la Trinidad, and that the king still had not made any decision with regard to the other points which the cited letter contains, his Majesty commands me to tell your Excellency that if in the future the apprehension of any other Frenchmen by the said governor of Texas or by the governor of New Mexico should occur, your Excellency shall order that as soon as their clandestine trade may be verified, or the fact that they have come to his Majesty's dominions without an adequate license, your Excellency shall have them conducted under secure guard to the fortess of San Diego of the port of Acapulco, and that they be kept in it with the same security. They shall be sent from there to El Realejo in order that at the first opportunity they may go with a special charge, which your Excellency shall make to the viceroy of Peru, in order that he may have them placed on the island of Juan Fernández or in the presidio of Valdivia and kept there in safety, thus avoiding the incessant appeals that are being made by the ambassador of France for the freedom of those who are sent to these kingdoms of Spain. May God keep your Excellency many years. Madrid, June 19, 1757. The *bailío*, Frey Don Julián de Arriaga. To the Señor Marquis of Las Amarillas.[103]

227. The royal audiencia of Santo Domingo could take cognizance of cases and business relative to Texas and New Mexico only if they should be presented to it by an unforeseen accident. In the following cedula we see that the French made slaves of three Indians and that they took them out of Mississippi to carry them to other colonies of theirs. The vessel fell into the hands of the Spaniards, I do not know for what reason, and the royal audiencia of Santo Domingo, having information that those Indians were slaves, granted them their liberty. This was approved by the piety of our Catholic monarch, Señor Don Fernando VI.[104] How do we know but that it is true that the person concerned who spoke with our writing Gentleman and told him his story was one of these Indians, who garbled the incident in the unbelievable manner in which he relates it? And how do we know also but that because of another unforeseen incident, a case concerning merchants came before the royal audiencia of Santo Domingo? Since the matter is so vague and is presented only with every aspect of fiction, we cannot determine anything with certainty. We can only state it plainly as it is presented to us, and refuse to admit this argument on limits which is stated to us.

---

[103]A somewhat different translation of this cedula is to be found in Hackett, "Policy of the Spanish Crown Regarding French Encroachments from Louisiana, 1721–1762," in *New Spain and the Anglo-American West: Historical Contributions Presented to Herbert Eugene Bolton*, Vol. I: New Spain, pp. 140–141.

[104]Ferdinand VI was king of Spain from 1746 to 1759.

The King. In as much as, with regard to a *consulta* of my Council of the Indies, I was pleased to decide (among other things) to approve the action of my royal audiencia of the island of Española, which resides in the city of Santo Domingo, in having set at liberty three Indians who were apprehended in a French brigantine which was making a voyage from the Mississippi to the French colonies of that island; and to send it orders that in no case, place, or time could the Indians of America who were not cannibals, suffer slavery, as was ordered by the law that deals with this subject, [I order] also that the same thing he understood and practised even in regard to the Indians of colonies possessed by foreigners, in view of it [freedom] being implicit and natural to them and unable to be changed without breaking the contracts from which proceeds with greater reason the individual welfare of those [people] of New Orleans and of other places occupied by the French in those regions, by virtue of the fact that the contrary has never been allowed nor has the usurpation of this country been consented to; rather, indeed, it has been protested. It is very improper to call them savages, under which abusive term the natives of the said places should not be included, since their protection, defense, and liberty has been the greatest and most scrupulous solicitude of my crown since providence placed them under my charge. This same decision shall be communicated in general to all the persons who should observe it. Therefore I command my viceroys of New Spain, Peru, and our kingdom of [New] Granada, the audiencias, governors, and officials of my royal treasury of those kingdoms and the others, whom ever they may be, and the justices of the said provinces upon whom may devolve and to whom may belong the fulfillment of my said royal decision, to observe and execute it, and order it observed, fulfilled, and executed precisely and promptly without allowing it to be violated in any manner whatsoever, because this is my will. I the King. By command of the king, our lord. José Ignacio de Goyneche. Signed with three rubrics.

228. (F). This statement being proffered, our author can continue his fable no longer, because we already know that the French never penetrated as far as the vicinity [of the source] of the Río de los Arcansas, unless what they call its vicinity is some place near D'Anville's line, where the tree would be found (which I doubt) on which they fastened the plate and made some signs.

229. (G). The narrative which our writer has given us here is similar to the one that a certain Spanish poet gave in a ballad which says:

"En la iglesia no se de onde
está yo no sé que santo
que en rezando no se que
se gana no se que tanto."[104a]

For, in truth, it is exactly like this narrative: a man whose name
he does not know, who served a man whose name he does not
know, told him, I don't know when, that at the mouth of a small
river there was a very thick tree—I do not know whether it was
an elm, or an oak, or some other tree—and on its trunk the officials and land surveyors placed I don't know what kind of marks
or signs; and they fastened on it a plate of lead, or of I don't
know what other metal, on which they engraved some inscriptions of which I do not know the contents. (In a note at this
place Father Talamantes says: "And what were the contents of
these inscriptions which are not given here? . . . An unfortunate
cause that needs for its support gossip and happenings that do
not merit a place in the most despicable gazette!") All this happened in I don't know what year, for although in 1772 he was
sixty years of age, from which it is inferred that he would have
been born about 1712, and that since he was a youth of I don't
know whether fifteen or sixteen or more years when he made this
reconnaissance, it is deduced that it would have taken place in
1727 or 1728, or in I don't know what other year. But such arguments deserve a laugh and contempt rather than the labor of criti-
cizing and refuting them.

230. Above in Part III, paragraph 986, we mentioned this text
of our Military Gentleman in the following manner in connection
with some words of the señor governor of Texas, Don Manuel de
Sandoval:

Another reason is that there is also a map which at [the conjunction of]
54° [51°] of north latitude and the bank of the Mississippi indicates a tree
on which, it says, the royal arms are cut. (Perhaps this map gave the Military
Gentleman, who wrote the treatise on limits which is found in the *Mississippi
Messenger,* his motive for inventing the extremely false anecdote which he
gives us in Number XV of his work, copied in Part IV, number 218, and he
did not cite the map because everyone recognizes the unlikelihood of the

---

[104a]"In I know not what church, is I know not what saint; there, praying I
know not what prayer, one gains I know not what favor."

royal arms having been placed on a tree. Rather, he availed himself of the
statement of a man whom he does not name, in order to make his report
more plausible; and if this map was not what inspired him, some other
similar thing probably did so.) It seems more than unsuitable that a matter
which for reasons of state is of such great importance, should be established
by the most fragile and perishable landmark of a tree, in danger of suffering
complete destruction with the inclemencies of the weather and in the course
of a few years, or likely to conceal the arms within itself as a consequence
of its procerity and growth.

XVI

231. These incidents, although seemingly of little importance, merit investigation in as much as they may lead to important discoveries and, in
fact, it seems strange that the historians of this country do not mention them.
(A). But two circumstances may be cited to prove their truth and accuracy.
The first is that after 1734, about which time it is thought that these limits
were established, no disturbances occurred over the western limits of Louisiana
(B), and the most rational way to explain the cause of such a long calm,
which lasted nearly thirty years, is to suppose that the two nations agreed on
some peaceful solution. (C). The second is that the greater part of the
transactions between France and Spain, particularly those that took place
following the peace of 1763, remained enveloped in a deep secrecy. (D).

NOTES

232. (A). The historians of this country cannot mention occurrences that never took place nor anecdotes that took form only
in the fancy of writers, such as our Gentleman, who amass in
defense of their cases everything that comes to their minds even
though it may be evident lies and fables which everyone recognizes as such.

233. (B). How little this writer knew of our history! It is a
well-known fact that with regard to these lands which the French
had taken from our throne, many cedulas favorable to them were
issued, but it is also certain that before and after these, others
came out much opposed to them. See Part III, paragraph 348.
Señor Don Felipe V[105] (may he rest in peace), in order to avoid
war and the effusion of Spanish and French blood, consented in
several cedulas that the French should keep the lands that they
had occupied up to the time at which the cedulas were dated,
although in some cedulas statements were also made to the contrary, as we have seen above, in Part III, paragraph 334, 348,

---

[105]Philip V was king of Spain from 1700 to 1746.

1005, 1009, 1013, and 1014. Señor Don Fernando [VI], far from favoring them, was very antagonistic to them, as is seen in the cedula dated June 20, 1751, of which we give an account above, in Part III, paragraph 1098. And in the cedula which we have just seen in paragraph 227, which is note (E) of Number XV, his Majesty states:

. . . from which proceeds with greater reason the individual welfare of those [people] of New Orleans and other places occupied by the French in those regions, by virtue of the fact that the contrary has never been allowed nor has the usurpation of this country been consented to; rather, indeed, it has been protested.

234. With regard to what our author says to the effect that it is supposed that the limits of which he spoke were established about the year 1734, I say it is a most false supposition in all its parts, because there was no such establishment of limits and, as we have seen, the stories he cites are fabulous. For in the year 1734 the disputes with the French over limits were not ended, nor were the limits established at that time. On the contrary, in the following year of 1735 the lieutenant of Los Adaes, Don José González (see Part III, paragraph 874), signed the first requisition which he made to St. Denis concerning the transfer of his presidio to the west bank of the Red River. Although these disputes with the French usually ended by being more or less forgotten, they were revived from time to time with fervor. We have seen this lately in the cedula of June 20, 1751, which we have just mentioned, and in the resistance that the governor of Texas, Don Jacinto Barrios, made to the Frechmen Blanpain, Massé, and Cortableau, in preventing them from settling at the places we have noted.

235. (C). Such a long calm never existed, and there were always disturbances between the two nations which lasted not thirty years, which, as may be inferred from our writer, should be counted from 1704 to 1734, but from the time that La Salle entered those lands until France ceded Louisiana to Spain; until, in short, the dispute that we have seen just above between Governor Martos and Commandant Macarti. Therefore it is a mistaken supposition to assume that the two nations agreed to any peaceful measures.

236. (D). These transactions between France and Spain never took place. The only thing that happened was that his Majesty, Señor Don Felipe V, allowed them to keep all the lands they had taken, which D'Anville's line embraces. And his Majesty, Don Fernando VI, although he said that in Spain the usurpation of this country had never been consented to, but on the contrary had been protested, did not order the French attacked or expelled, out of respect to the king, his father [grandfather], and because they were already considered the possessors, although unjustly, of that country; but he always resisted the extension of their possessions. Therefore, transactions which never took place, could not remain shrouded in a profound mystery.

237. Here Father Talamantes places the following note:

The time has now arrived to be able to speak more freely of those mysteries in which the negotiations of France and Spain with regard to Louisiana were enveloped: mysteries worthy of Spanish honor and directed solely at the honor and integrity of France.

238. In the last half of the seventeenth century, the French established in Canada, accustomed already to the trade with the Indians and practised in making long journeys by land, made the most energetic efforts to acquire a settlement near New Spain in order to examine into its great riches by means of trade. The first enterprises were directed toward the Pacific Ocean where they expected to communicate with Mexico—see the patent of Louis XIV of May 12, 1678, document 2, part 1 of the collection of documents (in this citation he is referring to his *Opúsculo VII*, number 2)—but being informed by Don Diego de Peñalosa,[106] who had been governor of New Mexico and who after his disgrace had taken refuge in France—see the cedula of Carlos II,[107] document 1, *ibid.*—they turned their attention to the Gulf of Mexico,[108] a place more to the purpose for their schemes. As is shown from their history, the first attempts were disastrous, because fate opposed designs that did not have justice as their foundation, and also because Spain, who at that time felt no great regard for the French, did not neglect a single point in the defense of her colonies in spite of the frequent wars that molested her. The viceroys and governors, under compulsion of the repeated efficacious orders of the king—see the collection of cedulas and royal orders, Part Four (Father Talamantes thought of making a collection of cedulas such as he describes in his *Opúsculo VIII*, number 1, but he did not get to make it; in our document 39 will be found many more of the cedulas which he intended to collect, because not only in our document but also on these points we have added many to those which he had copied from the volumes of cedulas that are kept

---

[106]See *Pichardo's Trtatise* . . . , Vol. I, p. 369, n. 90.
[107]Charles II was king of Spain from 1665 to 1700.
[108]See *Pichardo's Treatise* . . . , Vol. I, p. 369, n. 90.

in the secretariat of the viceroyalty)—were especially careful in protecting
the coasts, without sparing expense or labor, and by this activity they succeeded
in preventing the French from getting a foothold on the Gulf Coast and on the
island of Santo Domingo, where they attempted to do so in vain several times.

239. The system of our government continued under this plan until the
death of Carlos II. At this time, the two nations being reunited in a common
cause and the reasons for the antipathy that had formerly existed between
them having ended, we proceeded on our part with a great deal of condescension and too much confidence, while on the part of the French there was
all the diligence and astuteness necessary for taking advantage of the
circumstances. In fact, from that time on they were established at Mobile
under the pretext of being our allies and protectors. Under the same title
they took lands on the island of Santo Domingo, and when Felipe V—who in
the course of his long reign gave sufficient proof of not having been entirely
unmindful of national feeling—took up the Spanish sceptre, attempts were
no longer made to harass them and expel them as in the preceding years.
All the orders of that time relating to the French, both those which emanate
directly from the ministry, and also those of the supreme and subordinate
tribunals of the nation, breathe love, kindness, and condescension toward the
French, very different from those others in which shine the spirit of precaution, vigor, and resistance.

240. This was at the time that Louis XIV,[109] already near the end of his
long life, surrounded by a court which interested itself energetically in the
aggrandizement of France, carried away by the flattering and incessant proposals of Crozat, and relying also on the complacency of his grandson, Felipe
V, issued that famous concession of 1712[110] which has been copied in part
in this discourse as a statement of the limits of Louisiana. Spain, who could
not openly disregard, and who in fact did not disregard, this concession, so
offensive to her rights and so prejudicial to her interests, overlooked at least
the settlement which the French had made at Mobile. This toleration was
pernicious to Spain herself, because the French, now able to count upon a
safe place from which they could leave on their discoveries and explorations,
built a new settlement on Dauphine Island and, navigating the Mississippi
in order to explore its banks, selected the points which they judged most
convenient for building other settlements, dominating the intervening land
and erecting a new province. Thus they were suddenly seen established at
Natchitoches, advancing to the Cadodachos, and covering without obstacle the
long distance that lies between Mobile and a large part of the Río Colorado
[Red River].

241. However great Spanish complaisance toward the French might have
been, our government could not remain quiet in view of the excessive activity
and energy of the new neighbors in increasing and extending their recent
settlements and in coming closer to ours. While in the midst of a most
profound peace and while we were united by a close alliance, they did not

---

[109]Louis XIV was king of France from 1643 to 1715.
[110]See *Pichardo's Treatise* . . . , Vol. I, p. 126, n. 1.

hesitate to abuse the confidence that had been, shown them, penetrating daily farther and farther into our lands. When war was declared in 1719,[111] they threw the veil off of their ambition and unexpectedly surprised our settlements, and in order to extend themselves east and west, took Panzacola and drove us out of the province of Texas. A prompt reconciliation between the two nations put an end to their hostilities. But, since our court was favorable to them, even though orders were given to recover what had been lost it was ordered strictly that they not be disturbed in the settlements they had possessed prior to the war. What! If these settlements had been considered as property of the French, would it have been necessary to order so strictly that they not be molested? And does not this same recommendation in their favor, made in time of peace, prove that the French owed their residence in that country to the generosity of Spain? Be that as it may, it was the first concession made by Spain in favor of the French with regard to her new portion of Louisiana and its limits. From that time on they remained peacefully settled at Natchitoches and Cadodachos, whence they could have been easily expelled in 1719. But they were forbidden to extend beyond the last point, on which matter the most active and rigorous orders were sent to the government of New Spain.

242. If we gather together now all the facts that have been brought out in this brief history that we have formed, considering them as so many parts of a whole, we note that the French in one and the same period entered the island of Santo Domingo and the land of the Mississippi, both Spanish possessions. It was only our kindness that gave them protection in both places. It was our generosity that allowed them to extend farther. But it was also our justice and the general interest of Spain which made it necessary to restrain them and to place a fixed limit on their possessions. Thus if the limits of the French colony on the island of Santo Domingo have depended absolutely on the will of Spain, the only one who has always been owner of the said island, the same rule should have been followed in designating the limits of Louisiana with regard to which Spain has had the same rights. It is only to the donor that the right belongs to place the limit upon or designate the measure of his favors.

243. We are far from maintaining the invalidity of the original rights of France in Louisiana because the kindness of Felipe V, who acted in the matter more as a private individual than as a king, could perhaps not have been considered a national consent; because this same kindness might not have been legal in itself since it had not been duly authenticated and sanctioned; and because the same Frenchmen might have extended themselves

---

[111]"At this time a brief period of war ensued between Spain and France, due to the ambitions of Elizabeth Farnese and her adviser, Alberoni. An expedition from Mobile captured Pensacola, but it was soon after retaken by the Spanish, who also attacked Mobile. Shortly afterward the French again captured Pensacola, but at the end of the war it was restored to Spain. At the same time the Spaniards were driven out of eastern Texas and an expedition under Villazur was defeated by French allies on the Platte River."—Bolton and Marshall, *The Colonization of North America, 1492–1783,* p. 279.

much farther than they had been permitted in the beginning. The respect which is due our kings and the sacred regard which we owe their memory forbid us to enter into such discussions, however advantageous they may be for us. Spain also will not regret having been generous with a nation that knew how to mingle its blood with ours in the famous war of [the Spanish] Succession,[112] and which at present looks upon our interests as its own. But this is no reason why that same generosity should be turned now to our detriment, giving arrogance to our adversaries.

244. The French having settled in Louisiana in the manner that has been mentioned and with the extent that we have noted, experience showed later that their nearness might be fatal to us. Although, in order not to make accusations, we would gladly believe that the government of that province was always honest and friendly toward us, there was noted nevertheless in individuals in it the desire to travel through the far interior of the continent; to attract to their side the barbarian nations, to warn them against our usages and customs, to provide them with arms and munitions with which they waged terrible warfare against us, to lead their expeditions against us and to direct them at times in battle according to European tactics, to allow them to raise the French standard during their combats, to attempt by every means available to introduce contraband goods into our possessions; and to change from mere guests, which they were in that country, or rather from permitted owners, into arbitrary possessors who attempted to spread freely to all sections and to dispute the rights of their benefactors.

245. These actions, which occasioned very just complaints on the part of Spain, forced her to think of taking advantage of the first opportunity that might present itself to recover Louisiana, ending in this way all dispute and removing from its midst a fountain of discords which might have altered the good relations and friendship of both nations. This happy moment arrived in 1763, at which time Spain, entering into possession of Louisiana, obtained the reward of her prudence and long patience.

246. With the wisest precautions, in spite of the energetic and frequent representations of the government of New Spain with regard to establishing the limits of the French possessions, Spain abstained for many years from pronouncing the least decision. She seemed to be blind to her own interests and to overlook her advantages with great negligence, because her intentions, as hidden as they were prudent, were to put an end once for all to all quarrels and misunderstandings by taking over that province, but by taking it over on the same terms and with the same secrecy with which she had ceded it.

---

[112]Philip of Anjou, grandson of Louis XIV, king of France, was named by the dying king, Charles II of Spain, as sole heir to all of his dominions on October 3, 1700. Ultimately an alliance to prevent Philip from retaining the Spanish throne was formed; this alliance, forced in 1701, consisted of England, the Protestant Netherlands, Austria, and the Holy Roman Empire. War between the allied countries on the one hand and Spain and France on the other actively began in 1702 and was terminated by the Treaty of Utrecht (see *Pichardo's Treatise* . . . , Vol. II, p. 206, n. 25) in 1713.

XVII

247. Some light may be thrown on this by consulting the latest Spanish and French maps. In 1799 the Gulf of Mexico was explored and a map was made of it under the authority of the king of Spain, by Don Juan de Lángara,[113] secretary of state and of the *despacho universal*. This map embraces all the seacoasts between the eighteenth degree of north latitude and the Río de Santa María in Georgia, and includes also the Gulf and all the islands and places whose depths were sounded between the thirtieth and twenty-ninth degrees of longitude west of Cádiz, but only on one point is it applicable to our present case, and that is that it seems to consider the Río de Sabinas (whose entrance into the sea is located at 29° 53′ of north latitude) as the boundary between Louisiana and the Interior Provinces. (A).

NOTES

248. (A). Father Talamantes says here in his note:

Now, since the writer of this discourse wished to consult maps in order to decide the question of the limits of Louisiana, why did he not have recourse to those that were published in France when Louisiana belonged to that power? Why did he not go to the great French atlas and to the many others that, copied from it, were published in other nations? Is he to be excused for not consulting, at least, the maps of Abbé Raynal,[114] whose work is cited below, produced by the hydrographic engineer, Monsieur Bonnet, and generally accepted in France? For on all these maps it is seen that the dividing line of Louisiana begins at that point on the coast which is called Cabo del Norte, in 285° 28′ of longitude [west] of the Island of Hierro, leaving the Río de Sabinas about ten leagues to the west. The map of Lángara, purely maritime and drawn at a time when the question of limits was not important, should not be cited in this case, and the writer of this discourse knew it very well, as is indicated by the lack of confidence with which he mentions it.

249. This is the opinion of Father Talamantes, but we cannot refrain from pointing out that our Military Gentleman understood very little about maps. Señor Lángara's map does not begin at 30° of longitude west of Cádiz, because, since he attempted to give on it only a description of the Gulf of Mexico, there was no need for beginning it at this degree which is found far to the east of the said Gulf; rather, it begins at exactly 72°. The author of this map adopted the curious procedure of dividing each degree into six parts and each part into ten minutes, and

---

[113]A section of the Lángara map of 1799, corrected in 1805, is reproduced in *Pichardo's Treatise* . . . , Vol. I, opposite p. 350.

[114]See *Pichardo's Treatise* . . . , Vol. I, p. 16, n. 2.

in as much as half of the degree consisted of three of these
parts, which together amounted to 30 minutes, at each half degree he placed the number 30, which denoted half of a degree,
or thirty minutes. Consequently the first number 30 which is west
of the number 72, does not indicate that the map begins at the
30th degree, but that there is found the degree 72 and one-half.

250. Neither does he end it at the 92nd degree, but at 94° 50'.
The meridian of the 92nd degree is found six minutes west of the
meridian that passes through the westernmost bank of the Laguna de
Tamiagua, and from the said 92nd degree to the last point of the map,
the author says, are found the colonies of Nuevo Santander and
part of the kingdom of Mexico. And he even locates the City
of Mexico at 94° 24'. Aside from this our Gentleman erred also
in having believed that the most excellent señor, Don Juan de
Lángara, secretary of state and of the *despacho universal de marina*,
had been the author of this map. What really took place in this
case was that at the order of the king the said most excellent
señor directed that it be made in the naval hydrographic station.
The one who drew it was the engineer, Don Felipe Bausa, and the
engraver was Don Fernando Celma. All this is clear from the
map itself.

251. The real author of the portion of this map which begins
at the mouth of the Mississippi and goes to the Río de Tampico,
was the *alférez* and chief pilot of the royal navy, Don José de Evía,
as we have stated in Part II, paragraph 80.

252. Our Gentleman wishes this map to be applicable to the
present case of the demarcation of limits, because the lands inhabited by the Atacapas and Opelusas begin from the east bank
of the Río de Sabinas, and there is found on them a line which
reads "Louisiana." But we have already written above, in Part
III, paragraph 1566, that

The condescension . . . of Governor Martos was the cause of the French,
by going beyond the dividing line, having proceeded to establish themselves
in the lands of the Atacapas and Opelusas, especially after Louisiana came
into the possession of Spain. For, from that time on they settled there in
great numbers. . . .

Therefore the map of Señor Lángara is not applicable to the
case in question, and the only thing that is applicable is D'Anville's
line, which begins at the Cabo del Norte.

XVIII

253. Monsieur Du Pratz,[115] who resided in Louisiana from 1718 to 1734, during which time he exercised the office of superintendent of the settlements of colonists, and who travelled extensively throughout that entire province, crossed most of its rivers, and acquired exact knowledge of its civil and natural history, published after his return to France, in 1758, the *Historia de la Louisiana* [*Histoire de la Louisiane*], in several volumes. (In three duodecimo volumes, says the *Diccionario* of Moréri,[116] under the title "Louisiana.") A small volume was also published in English which contains an abridgement of this work. This author included in his history a map on which are found described the limits claimed by his sovereign, in which is included that part of Florida that lies between the Mississippi and a line extending toward the south from the end of the Appalachian Mountains to the Gulf of Mexico, at a considerable distance east of Panzacola, notwithstanding which he recognizes in his history the Río Perdido as the line of demarcation (A). He continues this line from the mouth of the Mississippi along the Gulf to the mouth of the Río Bravo, located by the Spaniards at 25° 53' of north latitude. From here it ascends along the east side of the said river to the parallel 29° 25', where it is noted that it makes a very large curve, and then diverges from the river and runs almost parallel to it for a distance of more than 40 [?] miles, and ends in the 46th degree of north latitude.

NOTES

254. (A). We have spoken of this above in paragraph 70.

XIX

255. The same Du Pratz places [on his map] a chain of mountains which begins near the 31st degree of north latitude, not far from the Red River, and continues toward the west until it joins the Mexican Mountains (A), which begin at a certain distance from the Gulf of Mexico and continue almost parallel to the Río Bravo. This chain in some places is one degree of latitude from the Gulf, in some a degree and a half, and in some three degrees. In this area are found no fewer than eleven large rivers, and five of them, among which is counted the Sabinas, it seems have their sources at the foot of this range. This author went into such detail that he added all the rancherias and nations of Indians and other objects worthy of attention, and included all this in the territory bounded by the Mississippi on the east, by the Gulf of Mexico on the south, by the Mexican Mountains on the west (B), and by the parallel of the 46th degree of latitude on the north. And

---

[115]See *Pichardo's Treatise* . . . , Vol. I, p. 215, n. 3.
[116]See *Pichardo's Treatise* . . . , Vol. I, p. 153, n. 1.

let it be noted carefully that since Du Pratz located the limits near the Gulf of Mexico and between the Red and Bravo rivers, his authority is of great weight (D).

NOTES

256. (A). It seems that the traveller Santiago Fernández[117] (see document 53, number 39), is speaking of this chain of mountains which begins near the 31st degree of latitude, not far from the Red River, and continues toward the west, in the following quotation:

On the 5th, we marched at six in the morning in the said direction (east), through plains with abundant pastures, firewood, and water. We stopped at six in the evening at the end of a forest of oaks called El Largo, because it is larger than the one of number 28 (this is the day) of the previous month. That is, its width is greater, for we crossed it only transversely and its entire length is a little more than a quarter of a league. We advanced eight leagues. On the 6th, we left at seven in the morning, going south over good land, and at twelve noon we arrived at the great forest of Nachitoches. We stopped at six in the afternoon. This forest is composed of many cedars, walnuts, royal cypresses, oaks, and other timber. We stopped on the bank of a stream which is here and which we named San Diego.

Concerning the other forest which he mentions here he says the following in number 32:

On the 28th, we left at six in the morning in the said direction (east) and arrived at the large wood called Monte Grande. It is probably more than two hundred leagues long, according to those natives.

257. Concerning this Monte Grande, Don Athanase de Mézières[118] says the following in document 41, number 95:

It is well to note that from the Río de los Brazos on which the Tuacanas are settled, until we arrive at the one which bathes the pueblo of the Taobayaces, there is seen on the right a wood which the natives with good reason call El Monte Grande. It is very dense but not very wide, and seems to be there to guide even the most inexperienced and to give shelter along this dangerous stretch to those of small numbers and courage who want to go from one pueblo to the other.

And further on he adds:

---

[117]See *Pichardo's Treatise* . . . , Vol. I, p. 528, n. 4.
[118]See *Pichardo's Treatise* . . . , Vol. I, p. 349, n. 1.

Firewood may be gathered by hand from the great wood of which I have spoken, which is eighty leagues long, one or two in width, and even more in places, in which bears and javelinas thrive.

But in spite of the extent of this great forest—eighty leagues according to De Mézières and more than two hundred according to what the Indians told the traveller, Fernández—I do not know how anyone can say that it joins the Mexican Mountains, or the Sierra de las Grullas, when at most it might be possible for it to adjoin the Sierra Blanca of which we spoke a short while back; and even if they do unite, from where D'Anville's line cuts this range [the country] would belong to the French.

258. (B). Let us concede that Du Pratz bounds this territory with the Mexican Mountains on the west. Other geographers describe Louisiana and New Mexico in another way, and they give them such limits as they please. Thus there are hardly two maps alike. Therefore to their authors may be applied, without temerity and with little variation, that proverb which Father Godefrido Henschenio testifies hold true in the literary world, to wit: That it is easier to synchronize all watches, making them show the same hour, than to make the astrologers agree in their chronological tables:

So that not without reason is the saying held proverbial that all clocks can be more easily synchronized than all astrologers reconciled.[119]

See the great work entitled *Acta Sanctorum*,[120] volume one, of April, in the first discourse on the first catalogue of the Roman pontiffs. For, by changing the word "astrologers" to "geographers" it can be said that it is easier to synchronize all watches than all of the maps of geographers, because the latter always disagree as to the latitude, longitude, and location of places, and at times—that is, when the boundaries of kingdoms, provinces, territories, etc., are not definitely fixed—in the partitioning of them. But because Du Pratz bounds Louisiana on the west with the Mexican Mountains, are we therefore necessarily obliged to accept

---

[119]The above quotation from the Latin was translated by Mrs. Minnie Lee Shepard.

[120]"A collection of the lives of the saints, arranged day by day according to the calendar, and compiled by the Bollandists, Belgian Jesuits. The work, first conceived at the commencement of the seventeenth century, has been carried on ever since, save during the period of the suppression of the Society of Jesus in Belgium."—*The Encyclopedia Britannica* (Fourteenth Edition), Vol. I, p. 137.

it? Then we should rather be forced to accept, because they are more to the liking of the French, the map of Roberto Vaugondy,[121] which is number 102 of the *Atlas Universal* published by his father and him in 1757, and the one of Monsieur Janvier, which is number 31 of an atlas which was printed in Paris in 1762 under the title of *Atlas Moderno ó Colección de Cartas de todas las partes del Globo terrestre, levantado por muchos autores [Atlas Moderne ou Collection de Cartes sur toutes les parties du Globe Terrestre. Par Plusieurs Auteurs.]* For these maps terminate Louisiana at the Pacific Ocean, in the region of Monterrey and Cape Mendocino, or what the Englishman, Drake, called New Albion. And would it be just, because a French geographer says so, without any more support than his whim, that Spain should have to cede all its lands which are west of D'Anville's line as far as the Mexican Mountains and even to Monterrey, a port on the Pacific Ocean? Why did the Military Gentleman not make use of D'Anville's map in order to argue with the Spaniards? Because he and all the French geographers do not remember that mandate which the Lord gives to his people in Deuteronomy, chapter 19, verse 14:

Thou shalt not take up and remove thy neighbor's landmarks, which they of old time have set in thine inheritance, which the Lord thy God shall give thee in the land that thou shalt receive to possess.[122]

Neither do they remember that curse which is pronounced in chapter 27, verse 17, of the same holy book, against those who change their boundaries, and which says:

Cursed be he who removeth his neighbor's landmarks, and all the people shall say, Amen.[123]

And they forget that Saint Job, reviewing the crimes and iniquities of men in his chapter 24, verse 2, names as the first of them that

They have removed the landmarks.[124]

---

[121]See *Pichardo's Treatise* . . . , Vol. I, p. 171, n. 2.

[122]The above quotation from the Latin, as transcribed by Pichardo, was translated by Mrs. Minnie Lee Shepard.

[123]*Ibid.*

[124]See *Pichardo's Treatise* . . . , Vol. II, p. 2, n. 6.

What I have said in refuting [the claim] that the Mexican Mountains are the boundaries of the French territory, I extend also to other boundaries or limits that do not conform to D'Anville's line.

259. (C). Concerning this eulogy of Du Pratz, Father Talamantes says:

> The weight that Du Pratz's authority should carry in the present matter, France herself must say. Her maps, which we have already cited, follow a partition of limits very different from the one which this writer gives. For the rest, his work is honeycombed with falsehoods in the historical part, as it may well be also as regards geography.

260. We bore in mind this eulogy which our Gentleman gives of Du Pratz, and also the fact that from his map he claims to establish the whole extent of the French lands, when we wrote these statements above, in Part III, paragraph 57:

> This prince (the Duke of Orleans), then, so wise, so religious, and so interested in geography, ordered the chief geographer of his time to make the map of America, sparing no expense in informing himself perfectly on everything included in America, and on the location of the various places in it. As a Frenchman he would charge him to employ the greatest exactness in the demarcation of the dominions belonging to France. As a very religious man, he would not claim that lands should be annexed to France of which she was not the owner, nor that she had any rights to them, on a map for which he paid, which was made by his order and at his expense, to the end that the French and the rest of the world might know the lands in North America that belonged to the French crown. Lastly, as a very inquiring [scholarly?] man, he would procure the original or a copy of St. Denis' map, so that D'Anville could make use of it. And does not a map drawn under these most noteworthy circumstances deserve more confidence than all those made by other hands, less powerful than those of this prince, and less skilful than those of this geographer—a map not drawn in accordance with the ideas of the authors alone, without criticism, without correct information, and without knowing the principles upon which the French depended for claiming the ownership of those regions; and a map, in short, drawn perhaps by authors not carried away with flattering their rulers, and with national pride, which would induce them to extend their possessions, so that, by force of these circumstances, they would assert rights that they did not have? For, in fact, many persons (like our Military Gentleman), taking their arguments from maps of untrustworthy, flattering, and ignorant authors, claim for France rights that have never been nor can be accorded her. This we shall see presently.

261. In view of this, one comes to a complete understanding of the fact that for us Du Pratz's authority is of little weight, that his territorial dividing lines do not merit our regard, and that to a hundred thousand like Du Pratz with all their maps we prefer a single D'Anville with his, because this geographer drew his map with the help of good documents and at the order and expense of a wise and just prince. Du Pratz and the other Frenchmen who have drawn maps proposed to flatter their nation by making her the possessor of more lands than those which her ambition had taken from Spain.

XX

262. When Du Pratz lived in Louisiana, the French had ascended only the Mississippi, as far as the mouth of the Río de San Francisco, that is, sixty miles above the falls of San Antonio[124] in 46 degrees of north latitude, and only nine hundred miles above the Misuri. This probably is the reason which induced him to locate the northern limits of Louisiana at the said degree. But between that date and 1763, the French penetrated to the source of the Mississippi (A), and followed the Misuri to 48 degrees of north latitude, or, what is the same, almost 1,650 miles, and established an indirect trade with the Indians near the Shining Mountains.[125]   As' far as the Spaniards are concerned, they have never visited these regions and down to the present have remained ignorant of them (C), although it is true that they have travelled from Santa Fé to the sources of the Río de los Cances[126] (D) and of the Somero, or Chato[127] (E), and here it is seen that their discoveries in that territory have been limited to these rivers only (F).

NOTES

263. (A). What will Abbé Raynal say about this? For in volume six of his *Historia Filosófica y Política* [*Histoire philosophique et politique*], book 16, chapter 16, he wrote thus:

The source of the famous river (the Mississippi) which cuts this immense country [of Louisiana] from north to south into two almost equal parts, has not yet been discovered. The most daring voyagers have scarcely ascended more than some hundred leagues above the Falls of Saint Anthony, which interrupt its course with a very high cascade, at about 46° of latitude.

---

[124]See *Pichardo's Treatise* . . . , Vol. II, p. 2, n. 6.
[125]See *Pichardo's Treatise* . . . , Vol. III, pp. 404–405.
[126]See *Pichardo's Treatise* . . . , Vol. II, p. 26, n. 16.
[127]See *Pichardo's Treatise* . . . , Vol. II, p. 25, n. 9, and *ibid.*, p. 32, n. 44.

Now, Abbé Raynal published his work in 1770, that is, seven years after 1763, as is read in the supplement to the secret history of the court and cabinet of San Clout [St. Cloud?], and in this year, according to him, the source of the said river still had not been discovered.

264. Likewise, what will the most excellent señor, Don Antonio de Ulloa, the first governor of Louisiana, say?   In his *Noticias Americanas*, printed in Madrid in 1772, *entretenimiento* 2, number 27, he writes as follows:

> The origin of the Mississippi River is not known, nor is its course known to 43 degrees. But from accounts of Indian nations which inhabit those far inland territories, it is inferred that the river comes from the west and that it rises in the chain of mountains which extend toward the sea above California. The lands of these nations, although they are contained within the kingdoms of New Spain, have not yet been sufficiently explored and therefore the reports that have been acquired in this matter are confusing.

265. (B). Perrin Du Lac[128] on his map (which is the seventh of document 74) describes this river only as far as the 47th degree of latitude. It seems, therefore, that until his time, that is, down to 1803, this river had not been ascended as far as the 48th degree. For this reason it cannot be true that the French established an indirect trade with the Indians near the Shining Mountains.

266. (C). Father Talamantes put the following note at this place:

> The Montañas Brillantes [Shining Mountains] were known to the Spaniards by the names of Sierra Blanca and Cordillera Nevada, from the first years of the conquest of New Mexico. Father Fray Alonso Posadas,[129] who lived in this province from the year 1660, gave an accurate description of them in the report directed to the king in 1685. Now, see how long a time before the French, the Spaniards had explored and travelled over those places and how unfounded are the reports which the writer of this discourse is relating!

We have spoken above, in paragraph 87, which is note (C) of Number X, of the Shining Mountains, proving that the Spaniards had much information about them, and we here admit, because we have proposed never to deny any truth or even to pass it

---

[128]Consult the indices of *Pichardo's Treatise* . . . , Vols. I, II, and III, under "Perrin Du Lac."

[129]See *Pichardo's Treatise* . . . , Vol. I, p. 30, n. 1.

over in silence, that it is most certain that they never reached the
falls of San Antonio which are formed by the Mississippi River,
or much less ascended above these falls, nor yet to the highest
reaches of the Misuri, because they never had time for this, having been detained, by force of their laws, in the exploration and
settlement of other lands. The French, since they began their discoveries by way of the Mississippi and did not settle any other
region with settlements that merited the name—for their forts
were nothing more than the residences of a few merchants and
warehouses for keeping their goods, and their discoveries were
made by very few men, as, for example, Father Hennepin and
his two companions who discovered the falls of San Antonio and
whose journey is seen in our document 2—had the opportunity
and the time to penetrate as far as they could, which was not
very far. For when did they establish in so short a time as the
Spaniards settlements comparable to Veracruz, Puebla, Guatemala,
Mexico, Guadalajara, and all the other innumerable towns which
they founded as soon as they discovered this New World?

267. (D). I remember that in the *Polyanthea Novicima* of
Langior,[130] under the word *mendacium* [falsehood], I read, now
many years ago, a maxim attributed to Titolivio, which says, "A
liar should have a good memory,"[131] and I believe that it could
be applied to our Military Gentleman, because he here admits
that the Spaniards have travelled from Santa Fé to the source of
the Río de los Acansas, and above in Number XIV he said:

No one has ever believed that the Spaniards at any time discovered or
explored any of the rivers that flow from the west into the Mississippi or the
Misuri.

And in Number X he said also:

During the period of eighty years in which the French were in possession
of that country, they were the only people (with the exception of the Indians
who inhabited it) who subsequently ascended the large rivers that empty
into the Mississippi and Missouri from the western side. They ascended some
[of these] rivers to their sources, especially that of the Arkansas, that of the
Osages, that of the Canses, and the Somero. . . .

---

[130]No reference has been found either to this writer or to the above-cited
work.
[131]The above quotation from the Latin was translated by Mrs. Minnie Lee
Shepard.

268. (E). Concerning this river Father Talamantes in his corresponding note says the following:

> The Río Plata, which has been spoken of here so many times, seems to be the same one that the Spaniards of New Mexico have known for many years by the name of Napestle. The variety of names in the rivers and places of this vast territory causes considerable difficulty in understanding the maps.

In all of this he has shown that he did not know the meaning of the word *Platte,* or that the Río Napestle was the one the French call Arcansas. *Platte* means shallow, level, or low. See what we said about this above, in paragraph 86, which is note (B) of Number X.

269. (F). Father Talamantes in the corresponding note states very well the following with regard to these discoveries:

> The Spaniards have explored the countries surrounding Santa Fé in New Mexico in all directions: to the southeast, east-northeast, north-northwest, and east, and in our archives are preserved the proofs of most of these journeys, in which care was always taken to take possession of the land in the name of the king.

XXI

270. It is seen from this that the limits in question are not as problematical as it seems they are supposed to be (A). Louisiana, then, has as its limits on the south the Gulf of Mexico; on the southwest in part the Río Bravo and in part the Mexican Mountains; on the northwest the Shining Mountains; on the north a part of Canada; and on the east the upper part of the Misuri as well as the lower Mississippi as far as the 31st degree of north latitude, where the line runs almost at right angles to the river, and embraces all that part of Florida west of the Río Perdido (B).

NOTES

271. (A). They cannot be more problematical and they reach the point of being completely false, because, as we have seen, Louisiana does not have as its limits all of the Gulf of Mexico, but only that part to the Cabo del Norte. Neither does it have its limits on the southwest partly on the Río Bravo and partly in the Mexican Mountains, nor on the northwest in the Shining Mountains. To the north, it is true, it is bounded by a part of Canada, and to the east it is true also that it is bounded by the part of the Misuri which runs from where D'Anville's line cuts it to its entrance into the Mississippi, as well as by this great river.

272. (B). Father Talamantes did not understand the meaning of our author, for he makes this comment concerning him:

This means that all the province of Texas and part of Coahuila and of the Nuevo Reyno de León belong to Louisiana. The French never carried their claims to such a degree of extravagance. Here the same words could be applied to this writer which he himself employs in his discourse, namely, that the rights of nations are extremely precarious if the administration of laws, the establishment of a government, and possession for many years, etc., are not sufficient for investing Spain with an indisputable title. But from premises as false as the foregoing what could result except a monstrous conclusion?

And, in truth, when our Gentleman discusses the Río Perdido, or de los Perdidos, which empties into the Gulf of Mexico near Pensacola, why is he accused of trying to extend the limits of Louisiana to Coahuila and the Nuevo Reyno de León? What has the Río de los Perdidos to do with these provinces? Our writer claims in his text that the limits of Louisiana should extend on the east to the Río de los Perdidos. The fact is that on some manuscript maps Father Talamantes perhaps saw some river by the name of Perdido flow into the Gulf of Mexico in the region of the kingdom of [Nuevo] León.

XXII

273. The form or shape of Louisiana is triangular, because it is a little narrow on the south but becomes wider as it leaves the Gulf. If we can find its length and central width, it will be easy for us to calculate the size of its territory. We know that the Mandan Indians who live above the Misuri are located at 47° 21′ 47″ of north latitude, and from the information which they give of the lands that are farther up, that is, to the north of this river, we have sufficient data to infer that its source, which is in the Shining Mountains, is found at about 57° 30′ of north latitude. From this it is deduced that Louisiana embraces, between these mountains and the Gulf of Mexico, twenty-eight degrees of latitude, to which we must add fourteen degrees of longitude. Therefore its length can be computed at around 2,284 miles (A). If the latitudes and longitudes of San Luis, a town which is found on the banks of the Mississippi, and of Santa Fé, the capital of New Mexico, are given accurately, San Luis and Santa Fé will [be found to] be divided by a distance comprising 692 miles. But, since Santa Fé is located about forty miles west of the Mexican Mountains, or from the source of the Río de los Acansas, the width of Louisiana at San Luis (which will correspond to its width minus the forty miles, which exceed it) is about 652 miles (B). Abbé Raynal calculates it at 600 miles (C). Now, if these data are correct,

Louisiana contains 1,489,163 square miles or 953,067,520 acres (C). Perhaps this estimate or computation may cause some to hesitate to believe it (E), especially since the territory that falls west of the Shining Mountains is not included, but if they will take the trouble to examine the long courses of the rivers and to consult the statements of various travellers, they will have different ideas. If Spain should at some time be capable of depriving us of the territory west of the Red River, we would not greatly feel this dismemberment, but it would wound us much more in our honor than in our pocketbook (F).

NOTES

274. (A). Throughout the context of the present paragraph we find errors of the printer and of the writer. Thus many perhaps would not understand from whence comes this quantity of 2,284 miles. When 28° are added to 14°, they amount to 42°. When the 2,284 miles are divided by 600, which is the number of miles in a degree, the quotient will be 38¼ degrees, or 38° 15', which is the same. But these should be 42°. Then the calculation is wrong. But, subtracting the 14° from the 38¼ degrees, there remain 24¼; but there should remain 28°. Then the calculation is erroneous. The same error will be found by taking 28° from the 38¼, because the remainder will be 10¼. But this leads us to the discovery that the writer adds to the 28° of latitude not 14° of longitude but 10¼ degrees. Thus the error of the printer is revealed, who printed 14° instead of 10¼ degress.

275. (B). When these 652 miles, which the writer calculates are in the degrees of longitude between the meridians of San Luis and Santa Fé, are divided by 60, the quotient will be 10 52/60 or 10 13/15 degrees. If this fraction is discarded, even though it lacks little of being a whole, only 10° remain. This proves the same thing that we have said: That the printer erred and instead of printing 10° he put 14°. With regard to what our writer affirms to the effect that Santa Fé is located forty miles west of the mountains, or of the source of the Río de los Acansas, I say that he erred signally, because as we have seen in Part II, paragraph 554, Santa Fé lies east of the Sierra de las Grullas in which the Río de los Acansas rises. And above, in paragraph 90, which is note (C) of Number X, we have seen also that the Sierra de las Grullas

is not the same as the Sierra Blanca. The latter, it is true, falls east of Santa Fé and of the Sierra de las Grullas, but not at such a short distance as that of forty miles, or 13⅓ leagues, for although we did not venture above, in the said paragraph 90, to give this distance definitely we designate it now as being much greater. For, according to Uribarri, there are 120 leagues from Santa Fé to the Río Napestle, and we believe that its western terminus is found near the place where Uribarri crossed it.

276. (C). In book 2, number 146, of *De Divinatione* Cicero wrote the following words, which should always be borne in mind:

. . . Since as a rule we do not believe a liar even when he tells the truth.[132]

And Diogenes Laertio [Laertius] in his *De Vitis Dogmatibus et Apohthegmatibus Clarorum Philosophorum,* book 5, chapter 1, number 11, testifies that Aristotle asked:

What, pray, do liars gain? Seeing that they are not believed, he said, though they have told the truth.[133]

And what will it be when the liar speaks a truth enveloped in a lie? Our writer, noted by now for the lack of veracity in his writings, says that Abbé Raynal estimates at six hundred miles the distance or extent between the meridian of San Luis and that of Santa Fé. Let us hear what Abbé Raynal himself has to say in his volume 6, book 16, chapter 16:

Louisiana (he says) is a vast country which is bounded on the south by the sea, on the east by Carolina, on the west by New Mexico, and on the north by that portion of Canada whose unknown lands should extend to Hudson's Bay. It is not possible to establish its length exactly, but they assign it a breadth of about two hundred leagues between the English and Spanish settlements.

277. If the two hundred leagues which Abbé Raynal gives here are multiplied by three miles, they will amount to six hundred, the same number, our writer says, as that given by Abbé Raynal. Then he is telling the truth. This is clear, but this truth he mixes

---

[132]*Ibid.*
[133]*Ibid.*

with the falsehood that Abbé Raynal places these six hundred leagues between San Luis and Santa Fé, which he does not do, but rather places them between the English and Spanish settlements.

St. Louis and Ste. Genevieve (writes Perrin Du Lac, cited in Part II, paragraph 466) forty years ago were inhabited only by some hunters who in the proper season went in search of animals as do the savages, with whom they traded.

Let us take these forty years from the year 1805, in which Perrin Du Lac printed his work, and we shall have 1765; or if we wish, we may take them from 1801, in which he began his journey, and we shall have 1761. Then in neither of these years, one prior to the cession of Louisiana to Spain and the other subsequent to it, had San Luis been founded. Then Abbé Raynal could not have been speaking of this place. Aside from this, San Luis was never a possession of the English or a settlement founded by them. Then for this reason Abbé Raynal could not have been speaking of San Luis when he placed two hundred leagues between the English and the Spanish settlements. Finally, if Abbé Raynal in speaking of Spanish settlements had meant the villa of Santa Fé and had given the distance between this villa and the English establishments, he would not have given the distance of 600 miles, but that of 1,518, because upon measuring on D'Anville's map the distance between Santa Fé and the line of dots which separates North Carolina, or Carolina Septentrional, from the French lands which lie west of it at a point not very far from the Cherakis [Cherokees], it will be found to be 422 leagues measured by the scale of French and English marine leagues of 2,850 fathoms. After their fifth part is added, they amount to 506, which, multiplied by three miles, give the said 1,518 miles. Then Raynal was speaking of other Spanish and English establishments.

278. In fact, the Spanish settlements nearest to the English of which Raynal may be understood to have been speaking, are those of Los Adaes, which are some 200 leagues from Georgia, for if the distance between Los Adaes and the boundary line of Georgia and Florida is measured on the same map of D'Anville and

with the same scale, it will be found to be 176, an amount similar to the one of about 200 leagues or a little more if its fifth part is added to it, because then it will amount to 211.

279. (D). Here is a printer's error. The English admit that a square mile contains 640 acres. This being true, I state the following: If 640 acres equal one square mile, how many square miles will 953,067,520 equal? The fourth term is 1,489,168. This quantity shows me that the printing which gives 1,489,163 is wrong. And if I extract the square root of the number 1,489,163, I shall have 1,220 linear miles.

280. The said 28° of latitude and 10¼° of longitude produce respectively 1,680 and 615 [miles]. Added together, they amount to 2,295. But our writer gets 2,284 because he thought that the fourth of a degree was four minutes, or four miles, while it really equals 15 minutes, or 15 miles, because each minute equals one mile. And if these 2,284 are multiplied by 652, the product will be 148,916, which, multiplied by 640 acres, amount to 953,-067,520 acres. But our Gentleman should have noted that Atkinson, cited in Part II, paragraph 36, says that about 69½ common miles of 5,000 feet each make a degree, whereas in the practice of navigation 60 miles are counted in a degree. Therefore he should not have multiplied the degrees of longitude and latitude, since they were terrestrial, by 60 miles but by 69½. I therefore accuse him of having erred in this also.

281. I accuse him likewise of error in having added the degrees of longitude and latitude and then having multiplied the sum by the longitude. I mean that he should not have added the 1,680 miles, equal to 28° of latitude, and the 615 miles, equal to the 10¼° of longitude, and he should not have multiplied the sum, 2,284, again by 652, which he found after he made the correction of 692, in order to obtain the product 1,489,168. I do not know geometry or how triangles are measured, but in the second part of *El Inginiero, o Arquitectura militar*,[134] a work written by Captain Don Sebastián Fernández de Medrano, prop-

---

[134]This work was originally written in Spanish; it was rewritten in French by the author.

osition 33, I learn how the area of an isosceles triangle is obtained, its sides being known, because the writer presents the following:

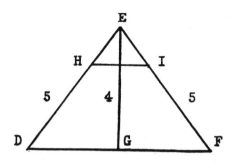

Let the triangle be DEF, in which each of the equal sides contains four [five?] feet and the base DF six. The base will be divided in half at G, and from the angle E the line EG will be drawn which will be perpendicular to DF and will leave the proposed triangle divided into two equal right triangles, DGE and EGF. This being true, the value of the perpendicular EG will be sought by squaring the base DG, and its square of 9 will be taken from 25, the square of the diagonal DE, leaving 16 for the square of the perpendicular. The square root 4 will be the feet contained in this line. These, multiplied by the 3 of the base DG, make 12 for the area of the whole isosceles triangle DEF, and each of the right triangles will contain 6.

282. Applying this principle to the triangle which is made, according to our Military Gentleman, by the shape of Louisiana, the difference will be only in the figures. The sides are equal and each will be supposed to equal 28°, that is, 1,680 miles, and the base 10° 52', that is, 652 miles. Half of 652 is 326. The square of this amount is 106,276. The square of 1,680 is 2,822,400. Subtracting the former from the latter, there remain 2,716,124. Its square root, 1,648, is the length of the perpendicular. Then multiplying 326 by 1,648, the product, 537,24[8], will be the number of square miles which Louisiana contains. Then it is not 1,489,168, as our Gentleman states. Subtracting the smaller quantity from the larger, there remains 951,920, which is the number of [square] miles that he gives to Louisiana above the number

that it has, even assigning to the sides [of the triangle] the length
that the covetousness of our writer may desire.

283. In order to find out the number of acres that Louisiana
contains according to the surmise and data of our author, we shall
state that if a [square] mile equals 640 acres, 537,248 [square]
miles will equal 343,838,720 acres. *Acre* is a word which the English use as much as the French, although, as Abbé Prevost states
in his *Manual Lexicon ó Diccionario Portátil de las palabras fran-
cesas, etc.* [*Manuel Lexique, ou dictionnaire portatif des mots
françois* . . .],[135] it passed from France to England and means
a definite measure of land, which, according to Harris in his *Lexicon Technicum,* volume 1, contains 43,560 English square feet. In
an English work, the title of which is *The Universal Library or
Compleat Summary of Science, Containing above Sixty Select
Treatises,* in the treatise on weight and measures, page 396, it is
stated that an acre of land, called thus from the German word
Acker, which is turn comes from the Latin *ager,* is forty perches
long and four wide, and that a perch, or *pértica,* contains 16½
feet. Therefore, if the forty perches of the length are multiplied
by the 16½ feet, the product is 660 feet. And likewise if four
are multiplied by the same 16½ feet, the product is 66. Therefore it is seen that an acre is a piece of land measuring 660 feet
in length by 66 in width. If the 660 are multiplied by the 66,
the 43,560 square feet of which Harris spoke are given. If we
want to know how many Castilian feet equal these English feet,
we must believe what is stated on D'Anville's map[136] of North
America, translated and copied by the English (see our document
66, number 9) and by other writers, namely, that the French foot
is longer than the English in the proportion of 15 to 16. Therefore 15 French feet equal 16 English, and, as we have stated in
Part II, paragraph 1, six French feet make seven plus Castilian
feet. Therefore we state the following proportion: $6:7::15:17\frac{1}{2}$.
From this we infer that 16 English feet equal 17½ Castilian, or,
what is the same thing, and in order to remove the fraction, that
32 English feet equal 35 Castilian. Now let us state the following proportion: $32:35::43,560:47,643\frac{3}{4}$. This fourth term tells

---

[135]This work is an adaptation of the English dictionary of Thomas Dyche
with additions and modifications.

[136]See *Pichardo's Treatise* . . . , Vol. I, p. 24, n. 7.

us that an English acre contains 47,643¾ [square] Castilian feet, which, divided by three, gives 15,881¼ [square] yards [*varas*]. Therefore it seems that what Boyer says in his *Diccionario Real Inglés y Francés* [*Dictionnaire royal françois et anglois . . .*] is not very certain when, defining the word *acre*, he writes that it is a measure of land differing in various countries and that the *acre* of England ordinarily is 720 feet in length by 72 feet in width.   The same holds true when Don Francisco Álvarez in his *Noticia del establecimiento y población de las Colonias Inglesas* writes in chapter 1, page 45, that an acre is a portion of land that is 720 feet in length by 72 in width. If he took it from Boyer he made a mistake, or if he spoke correctly it was in alluding to some part of France that measures its acres in the manner which he describes.

284. But the Military Gentleman says that the shape of Louisiana is triangular because it is somewhat narrow in the south but increases in width as it leaves the Gulf.   If Louisiana is somewhat narrow on the south and does not end in a point, it will have the shape of a trapezoid, which results from an isosceles triangle with one angle cut off by a line, HI, parallel to the base, so that the shape of Louisiana would be the trapezoid DFIH.   Then he should have made his computation by considering the lands as a trapezoid.   But how can he say that it is somewhat narrow on the south and grows wider as it leaves the Gulf if he bounds it on the south partly by the Gulf itself and partly by the Río Bravo as far as the Mexican Mountains?   The line that may be drawn from the entrance of the Mississippi into the sea to the Mexican Mountains, far from being shorter than the one that may be drawn from San Luis to Santa Fé, will be either as long or longer, because the Mississippi turns very far to the east when it enters the sea. But let us state fairly that the writer here retracts what he has said previously and admits that Louisiana becomes very narrow toward the south, on the coast of the Gulf of Mexico. And, indeed, this is the truth.   D'Anville with his dividing line scarcely gives Louisiana the coast from the Cabo del Norte to the east, to where Louisiana ends in this direction, and from here the land begins to broaden, so that it really forms a triangular figure, or rather a trapezoid formed of this triangular figure, since a small

part has been taken away from its sides where they come together
in an angle, by a line drawn along the coast parallel to the base.

285. (E). This will not only shake the belief of the Spaniards
and even of sensible foreigners, who are instructed by good geographical and historical reports of that country, but it will demolish it, for belief can never be maintained on unbelievable and
extremely false propositions that rest upon the most crass errors,
such as we have seen.

286. (F). Spain, always faithful in her contracts, recedes to
France the same that France had ceded her, and from France the
Anglo-Americans should receive what Spain recedes to her. Therefore, the refusal to deliver to the Anglo-Americans all that they
claim will not be depriving them of what the French possessed.
The latter possessed as far as D'Anville's line designates, and this
same amount is exactly what she should recede to France, and no
more.

XXIII

287. This is the proper place to note that the Mexican Mountains and the
Shining Mountains are entirely distinct, though they are generally confused.
The first begin at the Gulf of Mexico and continue toward the northwest,
to the eastward of Santa Fé. The place where they terminate has not yet been
ascertained. The others are spurs, or prolongations, of the Cordillera of the
Andes, which extends from the Straits of Magellan along the Pacific Ocean
to about 58° of north latitude, where they end (A). The distance from Santa
Fé to these mountains, is not yet exactly known, but the caravans loaded with
precious ores regularly take thirty days in going from one place to the other
(B).

NOTES

288. (A). Father Talamantes places the following note here:

This is very old information to the Spaniards, from whom foreigners have
taken it. It is so well known in Peru and New Spain that there are probably
few men of any intelligence who are ignorant of it.

In confirmation of what Father Talamantes states here let us
add that Fray Juan de Torquemada in his *Monarquia Indiana*, volume 2, book 14, chapter 39, writes as follows:

Along the North Sea, which is the one that those take who sail from
Spain to these Indies, run some mountain ranges more than two thousand
leagues in length, and although in this part of Mexico, around the province

of Pánuco, they are very wide, they become so narrow in the land of Nombre
de Dios and Panamá that there this said North Sea and the South Sea are
nowhere more than fifteen leagues apart. Beyond this said narrow place,
these ranges form two branches. One of them follows the same coast of the
North Sea for very long distances. The other goes around the land of Peru
in very high and very rugged ranges. They are so high that many who
have seen them say that neither the Pyrenees nor the Alps nor any other
ranges of the known parts of the world are higher, and they even think that
these excel all others in grandeur, and are the richest in gold and silver and
the most abundant in the necessities of life of all those in the universe.

289. And [we may add also] that Don Antonio Alcedo in his
Diccionario de America, under the article "Andes," states that

> The Cordillera of the Andes [goes] by way of the isthmus of Panamá,
> crosses the kingdom of Nicaragua, passes to those of Guatemala and Michoa-
> cán and the province of Sinaloa, and continues through the other unknown
> lands of North America.

Therefore, the Cordillera of the Andes, entering by way of the
isthmus of Panamá, comes in this North America and divides into
two branches, one of which goes to join the frontiers of the Río
del Norte and the other those of the South Sea. But our Gentleman, as is inferred [from his statement], was the only one who
knew about it.

290. (B). Father Talamantes in his note says the following
about this:

> Then the Spaniards know very well the brilliant, shining, or luminous
> mountains (Shining Mountains), for they have in them mines from which
> they obtain the precious metals which they take to Santa Fé in caravans that
> require thirty days [for the journey]. How then, as this writer has just stated,
> can it be that the Spaniards are to this day ignorant of those places? This
> is a contradiction which shows fully the excessive incompetence of the writer
> and the lack of merit of his work. The truth is that the supposed ignorance
> of the Spaniards with regard to the Sierra Blanca and Cordillera Nevada is as
> false as are the mines which they are supposed to be working there and the
> caravans that are employed in bringing back the gold and silver. Du Pratz[137]
> is the one who has published this piece of news, among the many nonsensical
> statements with which he sowed his famous history of Louisiana.

291. In contradiction of what our Gentleman says about the silver mines let us repeat here what we stated in Part II, paragraph

---

[137]See *Pichardo's Treatise* . . . , Vol. I, p. 215, n. 3.

611, concerning the account which Brevel gave to Dr. Sibley, namely:

I likewise understood (these are Brevel's words) that other similar small towns, or missions, were within certain distances of each other, for a great extent southwardly, towards Mexico, and that the inhabitants were mostly christianized Indians and mestizos [Maitiffs], and that the mines in that settlement afforded very rich ores, which were taken away in large quantities. (Here is an entirely false statement. If there only had been such an output of metal that country would not have been so poverty-stricken! For, in fact, though there are mines, they are not worked. It is from this, no doubt, that the Military Gentleman, author of the treatise published in the *Mensagero del Misisipi* [*Mississippi Messenger*] . . . took these words: "The distance from Santa Fé to these mountains, is not yet exactly known, but the caravans loaded with precious ores regularly take thirty days in going from one place to the other.") They were transported on mules (these are the same Brevel's words), and had the same appearance of those we encountered about the headwaters of the Red River.

And if you wish, see paragraph 548 of Part II, and document 46, number 30.

292. In Chihuahua some notes were made on this paper of our Military Gentleman, which were sent to Father Talamantes. We give them in document 72, immediately following the said paper of the Military Gentleman. They are as follows:

Notes on some points in the English gazette, the numbers of which correspond to its paragraphs, with regard to what it says about the limits of Louisiana. First, Fernando de Soto discovered the Mississippi in the year 1541. We know that the said discovery was made by land, and consequently he crossed the province of Texas 132 years before the French would have known Louisiana. . . .

293. Third. He says that Spain promises to deliver Louisiana to France with the same extent that it had when the latter ceded it to the former. It is evident that during the time France possessed Louisiana, Spain had established the site of the government of the province of Texas at Los Adaes, five or six leagues from Nachitoches, and that it remained there until the delivery of Louisiana to the latter power. If she had not been the legitimate owner of that country, France would not have consented for such a long time to the peaceful possession of it, so near to Nachitoches.

294. Fourth. This cession in no part treats of or includes the province of Texas.

295. Fifth. I cannot understand the reasons on which he bases his statement that Louis XIV by his grant to Crozat establishes the limits of Louisiana. His words are: "We, etc., name Crozat the sole trader in all the territory

. . . which borders upon New Mexico, the . . . English in Carolina, Canada, and the Gulf of Mexico." It is clear that Louisiana is located between the said provinces and the Gulf. But Louis XIV by the said grant does not say that Louisiana extends to the capitals of the said provinces, and even if he did say it, the approval of their legitimate owners would be lacking. It cannot be denied that Spain discovered and settled New Mexico many years before France settled Louisiana.

296. Sixth. He says that the possession of the French for a period of forty-three years in the part of Florida which is in dispute, makes them the owners of it, yet he is unwilling that peaceful possession of the province of Texas on our part for a period of 119 years should make us the legal owners of it.

297. Seventh. He makes no mention of the conquest of the Floridas by the Count of Gálvez,[138] which included the part in dispute. He will also assert that between civilized nations the right of the conqueror is null and void.

298. Eighth. He says that the French ascended the Red, Arkansas, and Chatoc [Platte] rivers to their sources. It is well known that they have not done so up to the present.

299. Ninth. The fort that he says the French maintained on the Río Bravo is probably the one which La Salle built on the Río de San Antonio, twenty leagues from the Bay of San Bernardo, where he perished with his people at the hands of the Carancaguases; and from that time on the French never thought of returning to settle the said place. It is clear that the names of the rivers are Spanish and that the Río de Sabinas, aside from having a Spanish name, is known on the old maps as the Río Mexicano.

300. Eleventh. Spain has done the same thing throughout the province of Texas, granting land to settlers as far as the Arroyo Hondo which is two leagues from Natchitoches, and giving exclusive privileges to traders.

301. Twelfth. It is impossible that several men with only a tent could have penetrated to the environs of New Mexico, not only because of the danger from the Indians, but also because of the great expense such a long trip would involve, it being necessary to transport their effects a long distance by water and another long distance by land. With regard to the incident of the man who in his youth assisted in running the boundary, it seems altogether improbable to me. He himself admits shortly after that it is strange that no mention has been made of these surveys in the histories that deal with Louisiana. We know positively that a demarcation was made between Nachitoches and Los Adayces [Adaes] by the governor of Los Adayces and the French commandant of Nachitoches.

302. Thirteenth. During this period Texas belonged to Spain.

---

[138]Reference is to Bernardo de Gálvez, who became governor of Spanish Louisiana in 1776. Upon the death of his father, Matías de Gálvez in 1785, "he was sent to Mexico City to succeed him as Viceroy of New Spain. His full title had now come to be: Conde de Gálvez. . . ."—Caughey, *Bernardo de Gálvez in Louisiana, 1776–1783*, p. 252.

303. Fourteenth. With regard to the maps, many of them place the entire province of Texas under the government of the Interior Provinces, and [there are few] which do not give a very limited breadth to the province of Louisiana. On the map[139] of Longehamps [Longchamps?] and Janvier, French geographers, made in the year 1754, the limits begin on the Gulf of Mexico east of the Río de Sabinas, run near Nachitoches, and from the vicinity of the said post they follow a northerly direction, a little inclined to the west, passing more than a hundred leagues from New Mexico. Another map made by Don Tomás López[140] in Madrid in 1762, which was copied from another made by D'Anville, a Frenchman, has placed Los Adayces, together with several missions and the Río Sabinas, under the name of Mexicano.

304. Fifteenth. The history of Du Pratz cannot serve as proof of what he says because it is very inaccurate, even in the most important things.

305. The distance which he gives between the Río de Sabinas and Nachitoches and the time he says is required by the mule trains loaded with precious metals from the Sierra de los Adaes [?] and Santa Fé show his ignorance. This is a copy. Chihuahua, March 10, 1807. Fray José María Rojas.

---

[139]No other reference has been found to this map.
[140]See *Pichardo's Treatise* . . . , Vol. I, p. 37, n. 1.

CHAPTER II

REFUTATION OF OBJECTIONS ON THE PART OF SPANIARDS TO THE BOUNDARY BETWEEN LOUISIANA AND TEXAS AS PROPOSED BY D'ANVILLE

306. The Spaniard Don Ángel Martos Navarrete,[1] governor of the province of Texas, either ignorant of D'Anville's line or disregarding it, boldly intervened on his own authority and without having any commission for it, to establish a dividing line between the French lands of Louisiana and the Spanish lands of Texas. That is what he describes in his representation (see document 70, beginning with number 8), and even though in Part III, beginning with paragraph 1587, we have explained a part of it, it seems appropriate here to repeat what we stated there for the purpose of giving a complete explanation of all of it. In the cited place we saw that from the entrance into the sea of the Mississippi, called Paso del Sudoeste [Southwest Pass], it should ascend along the west bank of the said river to the entrance of the Red River into the same Mississippi. Therefore the province of Texas should have extended to the said Mississippi, and, in case the French might not consent to this line, as they most certainly would not do, since it took from them all the land from D'Anville's line to the said river, he invented another line by which he took from Spain a large part of her lands. And he gave to France what he pleased for his individual interests and in accordance with the agreement that we have supposed he had made with the French. This line was to begin at the entrance of the Río de Sabinas into the sea and ascend by way of its west bank to 30° 47′ [54′?] of north latitude. From there it was to continue east along the same parallel to the entrance of the Red River into the Mississippi, which is found in the same latitude of 30° 54′. Both lines are indicated on our map in red color, with no other distinction than that the one which begins on the Río de Sabinas ascends by way of its banks and ends at the mouth of the Río Colorado [Red River], is shown by a continuous line, whereas the one that begins at the entrance of the Mississippi, or at Paso del Sudoeste

---

[1] Don Ángel Martos y Navarrete was governor of Texas from 1759 to 1766.

[Southwest Pass] and ascends to the said mouth of the Red, is made with small red dots.

307. From the said mouth of the Red the line should first follow along the south bank of this river to the fort of Nachitoches, which, in order that the French might not have any land on the said side, it was necessary to move to the opposite, or north, bank. From Nachitoches it should continue now along the west bank of the said river to where the Río de Cadodachos joins the said Red River, which is at 34° 18′ of latitude and 76° 21′ of longitude, and this line Señor Martos called the second. The third began at this junction and continued toward the north along the northernmost branch (these are his words) of the said Río Colorado [Red River] to where, in the same direction, the Río Acansas is encountered, the source of which he believes to be in the ranges of Santa Fé beyond New Mexico. And the fourth line began at the Río Acansas and [continued] to the Misuri.

308. Let us hear the words with which he describes these lines (document 70, number 8):

I believe that the Mississippi River would be, according to the present conditions, the most appropriate boundary for both sovereigns in the region of the Seno Mexicano, at least from the latitude where it is joined by the Río Colorado [Red River], which is at about forty or fifty leagues from New Orleans. In this case the presidio of the Nachitoches, located today forty leagues from the Mississippi and on the frontier of ours of Los Adaes, ought to be moved to the other side of the same principal river. Thus the three barbarous nations of Chitimacha, Opelusas, and Atacapas, who live from the Mississippi to the Río de la Trinidad, would belong to us, and all this region which is included in the Seno Mexicano from the said junction of the two rivers, where I fix the first line, would be recognized as belonging to this dominion.

309. Ascending by way of the same Río Colorado [Red River] to where it separates into two branches, one finds the last establishment of the French, in the country of the Cadodaquis, their allies, neighbors of the Apaches. From there the lands continue to spread out, not only toward the region of the Missisisppi, but also toward our frontiers among the Apache nation, and this is the second line that I am proposing.

310. A third line is given by going from this latitude by way of the northernmost branch of the said Río Colorado [Red River] to where, in the same direction, the Río Acansa is encountered, the source of which is believed to be in the ranges of Santa Fé beyond New Mexico.

311. Crossing the Río Acansa and continuing north, one finds the Río Misuri, which like the preceding ones empties into the Mississippi. By way

of it the French penetrated almost a thousand leagues, although they abandoned their explorations and settlements. And to this river I place another, or fourth dividing line.

312. Therefore it is seen that if the dividing line of Señor Martos is drawn on D'Anville's map, as we have drawn it on ours, it ends on the north at the Río Misuri, in 77° 35′ of longitude west of the Island of Hierro. But, since this river is to be the boundary, we have continued the line to where, according to our information, this river runs. But can there be a more absurd line than this one? Says Señor Martos:

If by a provisional or definite agreement, therefore, the French nation should be restricted beyond the complete line which results from the four into which I divide it, contenting themselves with the very extensive lands that would fall to them to the north, the country of the three nations of the Chitimacha, Opelusa, and Atacapas would without dispute come under the dominion of his Majesty in my proposed [region of the] Seno Mexicano by the first division of the line; also the extensive country of the Apaches, who are on the frontiers of the Cadodaquis, in which I formed the second division; and the country of the Paducas and Canesies, who although they are united with the Apaches, are different from them. (The Canecis are not different from the Apaches according to Monsieur de St. Denis, cited in Part II, paragraph 876.) All of them are enemies of the Panis Laitas [?] and the nations that live in the ranges of Sante Fé and its frontiers; and the first extend to the Río Acansas, and in conflict with their enemies they extend even to the fourth line on the Misuri.

313. By these words Señor Martos revealed the judgment he was forming with regard to the lands that were to remain to France, whereby both Spain and France were greatly injured; for this reason they could never consent to his line. From the presidio of Nachitoches to the Cadodachos it was to be the right bank of the Red River, a line which would have taken from France the extensive country of the Apaches who border on the Cadodachos; and from these to the Misuri [it would have taken] the lands of the Apaches who live between the Cadodachos and the Río Acansas, the country of the Paducas and Canecis, and the country of the Panis Laitas and the nations who live in the ranges of Santa Fé and its frontiers. But would France consent to the loss of these most extensive lands, and especially when she was in possession of all of them, as D'Anville's line indicates? By ending his line at the Misuri, Señor Martos indicated that this

great river should be the dividing line on the north of the lands
that remained to Spain. Thus Spain could not possess any land
north of the Misuri. And would Spain consent to the loss of a
country as extensive as is that from the other side of the Misuri
to the pole?

314. In the letter which he wrote to Macarti, cited above in
number 170, Señor Martos shows also that his northern line was
the great Río Misuri, because in it he states that

> The nation of the Asinais is so numerous that it extends toward the four
> cardinal points for a distance of a hundred leagues in each direction. Its
> northern boundaries are the banks of the Río Misuri, which flows into the
> Palizada. It contains many different divisions, and one of them is that of
> the Tehuacanas, which is located northwest of it on the headwaters of the
> Río de Sabinas, about sixty leagues away.

In my opinion, Señor Martos obtained this information from
Father Fray Isidro Felix Espinosa, who in book 5, chapter 9, page
419 of his *Chrónica* writes as follows:

> This Asinais nation contains many tribes, so that, in order to avoid con-
> fusion, I shall not name them in their own language. It extends toward the
> four cardinal points for a distance of more than a hundred leagues in each
> direction, as far as the banks of the Río Misuri which empties into the
> Palizada, drawing its peoples from the north where there are many civilized
> nations who till the soil. And from one which is settled upstream on the
> Río Misuri, information has been obtained of the Arricara nation which
> consists of forty-eight pueblos within a distance of ten leagues. Among such
> a multitude of nations only those who had the benefit of six missions that
> were established in the years 1716 and 1717, have been subjected to the
> rule of the Catholic King.

315. But it must be confessed that Señor Martos did not study
Father Espinosa's text very well. It certainly is not very clear
and does not give many of the facts. On D'Anville's map, from the
Cenis, or Asinais, to the Misuri by a direct line, it is a distance of
10° 50′, which contains 189 leagues of those of 17½ to the degree, and with their fifth part, 226; and 288 leagues of those of
26⅗ to the degree (which are smaller than the preceding ones),
and with their fifth part 345. Then it is not a hundred leagues, as
Señor Martos states (disregarding the "more" of Father Espinosa,
which amounts to not less than 126 of the longer leagues and 245
of the shorter) from the Asinais to the Río Misuri.

316. But if Señor Martos, scorning D'Anville's line, formed at his caprice a line by which at the same time he gave to and took from Spain and France their lands, by which act he harmed both nations so that neither of them could consent to it, the reverend father missionary of the missions of Nacogdoches, Fray José María de Jesús Puelles,[2] also drew a line by which he likewise took away from Spain and France some lands which indisputably belonged to them, for which reason it is necessary that the Anglo-Americans should disregard it and that Spain should not agree to it. But before explaining this line, it is necessary to see whether or not the map which this missionary-geographer drew and which we present in document 74 as number 10, is accurate, because by the fact that we are presenting it, it might be thought that we approved it in all its parts when, indeed, we are very far from doing so.

317. In April of 1809, Señor Don Francisco Viana (*ayudante sub-inspector* in the province of Texas, who arrived in Mexico in an extremely serious condition from the illness which finally caused his death in this city) furnished this map and another drawn also by the same Father Puelles for a friend of his, who showed them to me. I made copies of them, which I present in numbers 9 and 10 of document 74, and the defects that they may contain originate from the fact that perhaps these copies of Señor Viana were not very accurate. Father Talamantes saw others, probably more accurate, but the copies that he made of them did not reach my hands. It is clear that he saw them from the following letter, sent to him, the original of which I found among his papers:

Will your reverence be so kind as to accept my thanks for the expressions with which you show the kindness of your heart toward my unworthiness, and for the receipt of the papers which you sent me under date of the 10th of the current month?

318. I am enclosing the maps of Father Puelles, which the señor commandant-general (Don Nemecio Salcedo)[3] has been kind enough to furnish me in order that your reverence may see them, and, after having copied them, may return them to me. His lordship added the favor of showing me a paper, of which the one that is being sent with the number 1 is a copy (this paper

[2]See *Pichardo's Treatise* . . . , Vol. I, p. 378, n. 1.
[3]See *Pichardo's Treatise* . . . , Vol. I, p. 6, n. 2.

is the one found in document 71), in order that your reverence may take notes from it. He offered me also for the next weekly publication [*semanario*] a map, even though it is in rough draft, of the whole interior country—most exact, detailed, and modern—in order that with it before you, your reverence may know that the port by the name of Columbia which the Anglo-Americans in the speech [made] in Congress affirm is theirs, is beyond doubt the one explored by us which is located adjoining the cape of San Roque with the name of Entrada de Eceta [Heceta],[4] as shown on the maps of Mala Espina [Malaspina].

319. The map which your reverence tells me you desire to see and which you believe is in the possession of Father Garza, adviser of Señor Bouset, will be sent as soon as I can obtain it, for since he is my master, I am availing myself of the trust he places in me to write him and request it, while in the meantime I have the honor of again offering your reverence my obedient regards. May God, our Lord, keep your reverence's life many years. Chihuahua, April 21, 1807. Fray José María Rojas. To the Very Reverend Father Doctor Fray Melchor Talamantes y Baeza.

320. With this letter he sends him the following paper:

Catalogue of the papers which Father Fray José María Rojas is sending today, April 21, 1807, to the Very Reverend Father Doctor Fray Melchor Talamantes y Baeza. Number 1: Translation of the message of the President of the United States to the Congress on December 2, taking from it only the articles that refer to Spain. Number 2: Topographical map dedicated to the señor commandant-general, Don Nemecio Salcedo, by the Señor Captain Don Joaquín Ugarte. Number 3: Geographic map of the settlements, source, course, and entrance into the lagoons and the sea of the Río de San Antonio de Béjar, dedicated to the señor commandant-general, Don Nemecio Salcedo, by the señor governor, Don Juan Bautista Elguezábal.[5] Chihuahua, April 21, 1807. Fray José María Rojas.

321. To this letter Father Talamantes replied as follows:

When I received your reverence's highly esteemed dispatch of the 21st of last April, I was occupied with the writing of a very important work, which I must present to the most excellent señor viceroy very shortly. Being desirous of completing it, and also of considering with more deliberation and attention the points which your reverence brings up in your cited dispatch, I have delayed answering it until now.

---

[4]The Spanish explorer, Heçeta, sailing up the coast of North America north of San Francisco in 1775, "reached 49°, discovering Trinidad Bay and the mouth of the Columbia River on the way (1776)."—Bolton and Marshall, *Colonization of North America*, p. 395.

[5]Juan Bautista de Elguezábal was governor of Texas from about 1800 to 1805.

322. First of all I must recognize and strongly commend your reverence's promptness and diligence in furnishing and sending me the two maps made by the Reverend Father Fray. José María de Jesús Puelles. They have confirmed my opinion of his talent, knowledge, and consecration in the office he held. Both [maps] appear to be very fine, and I have taken the care to examine them minutely. But it seems to me that I should give preference to the one of the rivers of San Antonio de Béxar and Guadalupe, not only because it is more detailed, but also because of a certain greater neatness, clarity, and precision. This last map is being copied, and I shall return it before finishing the copy of the other, which I cannot deny has served me greatly, since I have used it with more confidence than many others that have been available to me. (The copies of these maps of the rivers of San Antonio de Béxar and of Guadalupe, and the other drawn by Captain Don Joaquín Ugarte, have not reached my hands although Father Talamantes had them copied; nor have I been able to obtain copies of them elsewhere.) Because of all this, your reverence will be so kind as to transmit to the señor commandant-general expressions of my obedience and gratitude for his repeated favors.

323. I am eagerly awaiting the other general map of the interior of the kingdom which the señor commandant has promised me through your reverence, in order to inform myself from it as to the location of the Columbia, and more particularly in order to rectify or confirm my ideas on a certain project that I have formed. A person sufficiently versed in matters of the secretariat, with a good memory, not a great deal of talent, and with a character of somewhat undeserved importance, employed at present away from this capital, has written that the mariner Eceta [Hezeta] who named that entrance, did not go beyond 43 degrees. But in this particular I am indebted to the account that has been given me by the captain-of-frigate and assistant in my work, Don Gonzalo López de Haro,[6] from whom the señor commandant-general has some maps. He has explored a large part of that coast, surveying it with great accuracy, and he tells me that the bay of Eceta [Hezeta] and the entrance of the Columbia are one and the same, and that he encountered the Anglo-American vessel of the latter name and talked with its captain and officers. I inform your reverence of this in order that you may bring it to the attention of the señor commandant and give him the satisfaction of seeing his inferences confirmed by the testimony of an eyewitness.

324. The merit of the Reverend Father Garza is too great for it to be possible that his name should remain hidden in the district of Arispe, and

[6]"In 1786 a famous French voyage of exploration, under the command of the Conte de Lapérouse, passed down the coast to Alta California. Lapérouse informed the Spanish authorities that the Russians had several establishments in the far northwest. . . . So, in 1788, the *Princesa* and *San Carlos* under Esteban José Martínez and Gonzalo López de Haro was sent to the north. This time the Russians were found; Martínez and López de Haro reported that they seemed bent on pushing as far south as Nootka Sound, off the west coast of what is now called Vancouver Island. Information was also received that the English had pretentions to that port."—Chapman, *A History of California: The Spanish Period*, p. 344.

your reverence may count among your honors that of having such a laudable
person as a teacher. The recourse that your reverence has had to him cannot
be more fortunate, and it is to be hoped that if his occupations allow him
to form an association with us, we may obtain not only his maps, but also
much important information. I should appreciate it greatly if your reverence
would make known to him how highly I regard him and that I am ready to
enter the ranks of his most humble disciples. May God keep your reverence
many years. Mexico, May 13, 1807. Fray Melchor Talamantes. To the very
reverend father and apostolic preacher, Fray José María Rojas.

325. The said Father Puelles, on his cited map, places a number 1 a little above the entrance of the Río Sabinas into the Gulf
of Mexico, at about 29° 35′ of latitude and 283° 50′ of longitude, and, in an explanation in the margin, he states:

Number 1. Place where a valorous Spaniard, Lucas Vásquez de Ayllón,[7]
the discoverer of the interior of this province of Texas in 1520, was killed by
the Indians while fighting with them.

Here Father Puelles revealed that he did not know that this
señor *oidor* of the island of Santo Domingo discovered only what
may properly be called Florida, which is that tongue of land that
faces Havana. It was there that a land was found which was called
Chocora [Chicora?][8] and Gualdape by the Indians and later Cabo
de Santa Elena and Río Jordán by the Spaniards, as Gómara,
writing as follows in his *Historia de las Indias*, chapter 42, states:

Seven citizens of Santo Domingo, among whom was Licenciado Lucas
Vázquez de Ayllón, *oidor* of that island, fitted out two vessels in the port of
Plata in 1520 in order to go to the Lucayos Islands for Indians, as I stated
above. They went, but found no men on them to barter for or capture to
bring back for their mines, ranches, and farms, and therefore they agreed
to go farther north to look for a land where they might find some and not
return empty-handed. They therefore went to a land which they called
Chocora [Chicora?] and Gualdape, which is in 32 degrees [of north latitude],
and is that which they now call Santa Elena and Río Jordán.

And Señor Herrera, in decade 2, book 10, chapter 10, also writes
as follows:

---

[7]Lucas Vásquez de Ayllón was *oidor*, or superior judge of Española, who,
between 1521 and 1526, promoted exploration and personally attempted
colonization of the Atlantic coast north of present Florida. For further details,
see Bolton, *The Spanish Borderlands*, pp. 12–19.

[8]Bolton (*op. cit.*, p. 13) says that Chicora "seems to have been near the
Cape Fear River on the Carolina coast."

They came upon a land called Chicora and Guadalupe (this is a printer's error; Gómara, as we have seen, gives Gualdape, and Herrera himself calls it Gualdape in a place that we shall cite shortly) which is in 32 degrees and which they now call Cabo de Santa Elena and Río Jordán, because Jordán was the name of one of the captains or masters of those vessels and it was the custom of discoverers to give their names to rivers and to other places, or those of the days of the saints on which they discovered them, or other names at their will.

And in decade 3, book 8, chapter 8, in discussing the events of the year 1525, he adds:

Licenciado Ayllón equipped three vessels and arrived with them at the Punta de Santa Elena, a hundred leagues north of Florida, where there was a pueblo which, since it was named Orista, they called Chicora, because the Spaniards never hesitated to corrupt words somewhat. Another place which was also there and which was called Guabe, they named Gualdape, and it is in this region that the Río Jordán is found, to which the pilot of a vessel who discovered it gave his name, just as the Punta de Santa Elena was given the name of the [saint on whose] day it was found.

Anyone who knows well where the cape of Santa Elena and the Río Jordán are located must consider Father Puelles' explanation as fabulous and untrue, and cannot believe that Señor Ayllón died in 1520 on the banks of the Río Sabinas.

326. In the next line the same Father Puelles adds:

At this time the Spaniard Juan Pardo[9] crossed the interior of this province of New Spain.

I do not recall any of the earliest writers who discussed the conquest of these West Indies, who speaks of the expedition of the Spaniard, Pardo, aside from Señor Herrera who in his treatise of the *Descripción de las Indias Occidentales*, chapter 8, recalls him in these terms:

Concerning this [territory], it has been explored and discovered from the Río de las Palmas to Santa Elena Point and the Río Jordán, which distance comprises about six hundred leagues. It is a part of the mainland, is of a

---

[9]In 1566, Pedro Menéndez de Avilés, colonizer of Spanish Florida, "sent Juan Pardo with twenty-five men 'to discover and conquer the interior country from there to Mexico.'" He got as far northwest from present Florida as "a stream near the foot of the Alleghenies. . . . He had thus extended the work of De Soto by exploring a large part of South Carolina and adding considerably to the knowledge of North Carolina."—Bolton, *The Spanish Borderlands,* pp. 152–153.

good climate, fertile, and in many parts thickly settled, as those learned who went through it with Hernando de Soto in the years of 1536 and 1537, and even later. And furthermore, Juan Pardo, a native of Cuenca, went by land from Florida to New Spain in less than two years.

The very fact that Señor Herrera places the expedition of Juan Pardo following that of Hernando de Soto indicates to us that this journey was subsequent to the one of 1539, in which, as the same Señor Herrera states in decade 6, book 7, chapter 9:

On the last day of May, Soto and his companions anchored in the bay of Espíritu Santo of the province of Hirrigua.

Consequently, we fix the expedition of the Spaniard, Pardo, at a year subsequent to that of 1539, and reject the statement of Father Puelles, who says it took place in the year 1520.

327. In the same way (continues the cited Father Puelles) the Spaniards, Alvar Núñez Cabeza de Vaca[10] and his companions, who were saved in the shipwreck of Pánfilo de Narváez,[11] traversed it and discovered the region as far as New Mexico.

In the dissertation on La Quivira we have seen quite clearly that Alvar Núñez Cabeza de Vaca travelled through the provinces of Texas, in addition to the island of La Culebra, from the bay of Espíritu Santo west as far as the pueblo which is now called El Paso del Río del Norte, and that he never ascended north as far as what is properly called New Mexico. Therefore, from the bay of Espíritu Santo he did not ascend by way of the plains of Cíbola toward the north until he reached New Mexico, nor yet did he go from El Paso del Río del Norte, crossing this river, even one palm's length along its banks toward Santa Fé.

328. In the year 1536 (continues Father Puelles) the region from New Mexico to Florida and Mobile was explored by the Spaniard, Hernando de Soto, later by other Spaniards, and also by a party of Spanish troops.

We have seen that Hernando de Soto reached the bay of Espíritu Santo of the province of Hirrigua, but we never saw that a party of Spanish troops explored it, going from New Mexico to Florida and Mobile. What troop was this? Not the one of Francisco Vásquez de Coronado or of any of the others who entered by way

---

[10]See *Pichardo's Treatise* . . . , Vol. I, p. 35, n. 1.
[11]*Ibid.*

of New Mexico, because these scarcely reached La Quivira, which is west of the Mississippi. Nor is the topography which he gives us here correct, for if they travelled from New Mexico by way of the plains of Cíbola and the province of Texas, after having crossed the Mississippi, they would have first entered Mobile and later Panzacola and then the tongue of land which is properly called Florida, since Mobile is northwest of that tongue of land. Therefore it is wrong to say that that troop of Spaniards explored those lands from New Mexico to Florida and Mobile, for if this had taken place, it should have been written from New Mexico to Mobile and Florida. It has been necessary to make these remarks in order that one may not come to believe, upon reading all these absurdities on the said map, that because of one bad critic all our documents are full of other similar errors.

329. Father Puelles certainly read the paper of Don Domingo Cabello[12] of which we have given a copy in Part I, paragraph 89, in which this governor of the province of Texas states very incorrectly that

Roberto de la Salle . . . , with two companions, escaped from the havoc which the Indians wrought upon his people. Continuing his journey by land, he reached the Mississippi River, which he crossed on a raft which he and his two companions made. He went on to the port of Mobile which had already been founded by the French.

But it is untrue that La Salle survived the massacre of the French, his companions, in Fort Luis, that he escaped to Mobile, and that the French had already founded a fort on the mouth of this river. All these things we have already proved in their proper places. Father Puelles, by making a very incredible metamorphosis of this flight of La Salle into a journey of the Spaniards from New Mexico to Mobile, showed that he did not abstain from writing untruths as long as they gave him arguments with which to show that the limits he proposed were correct. But Spain does not need to avail herself of lies in order to show where her rights extend in those lands, and she should place her landmarks and boundary lines on them.

330. The señor commandant-general of the Interior Provinces, Don Nemecio Salcedo, in his letter copied in document 73, be-

---

[12]Domingo Cabello served as governor of Texas from 1778 to 1786.

ginning with number 2, relying upon the reports of others—as the Señor Fiscal Sagarzurrieta states in his opinion, copied in our Introduction, paragraph 16—seems also (I speak with the respect due his lordship) to have transformed the journey which Don Domingo Cabello supposes La Salle to have made to Mobile, into another which he supposes Don Domingo Terán de los Ríos[13] to have made to the same Río de Mobila, when he wrote as follows in number 4:

Continuing his march, Don Domingo Terán de los Ríos arrived at the Mississippi River, which he crossed on a raft, and he passed on to the post of Mobile where there was already a French establishment.

Above in Part I, we have seen the whole route of Don Domingo Terán, and that he never reached Mobile, nor had D'Iberville, who was the one who founded the Fort of Mobile, at that time arrived on the Gulf of Mexico. Perhaps Father Puelles was alluding to this supposed journey of Terán when he imagined the expedition of the Spaniards from New Mexico to Mobile.

331. The same Father Puelles places a number 2 at about 29° of north latitude and 281° 43′ of longitude, on a small island near the bay of San Bernardo, and commenting on it in the margin, he writes as follows:

Number 2. Place where the French captain, Roberto de Sal [de la Salle], who came to settle the Mississippi, arrived in the year 1685, having lost his way. He built a small fort for defense against the Indians and stayed there two years, until on March 20, 1687, a soldier, Duján, killed him. Some of the rest left and others dispersed into the interior and were captured by the troops of Coahuila who with their governor, Don Alonso de León, came to expel them. They placed their camp there in the year 1687.

Concerning the epoch of the arrival of Monsieur de la Salle at the bay of Espíritu Santo, we have noted above, in Part I, that it was not in the year 1685, but in 1683. The place on which he erected his fort we have designated in Part II, paragraph 278. When, where, and by whom he was killed have been stated in Part I, paragraph 201, and in Part II, paragraph 444. And the *entrada* of Alonso de León has been related in the said Part I. From this it is seen how far this missionary religious departed from the truth:

---

[13]Domingo Terán de los Ríos was governor of Texas from 1691 to 1692.

332. In the note to number 4, Father Puelles also says:

Spanish encampment where on May 25, 1687, solemn mass was sung on the day of Corpus Christi.

Father Cristóbal Clavío [Clavius] in volume 5 of his *Obras Matemáticas* [*Opervm mathematicorvm*] in which he discusses the Roman calendar, changed by his Holiness, Señor Gregorio XIII, states in the table of the movable feast days, chapter 22, page 383, that in the year 1687 the day of Corpus Christi fell on May 29, and that in the year 1690 it fell on the 25th of the same month. From this is seen also the mistake of Father Puelles and the fact that this mass was sung on the second entrance of the said Captain León which took place in the year 1690, as he himself states in his journal (document 11, number 45):

On Thursday, the 25th of the said month (of May, 1690), the feast of the most holy sacrament was celebrated with due solemnity and a procession, etc.

333. In [note] number 8 of this map Father Puelles adds:

In the year 1693, toward the end of October, the province was abandoned because it did not have forces with which to resist the French who, it was stated, were coming to attack the Spaniards. This was not true, for the French were not yet on the Mississippi.

With these words it seems that Father Puelles wishes to contradict Father Fray Isidro Felix Espinosa, who in his *Chrónica*, book 5, chapter 7, wrote as follows:

Returning to the missionaries of Texas, it is certain that they underwent considerable suffering trying to sustain themselves until the year 1693, in which, hope having been lost for the coming of reinforcements from the outside, and there being at the same time repeated reports that Frenchmen were coming to take possession of that country, and with this fear gaining control over the few soldiers who were there and who incessantly wished to leave the fathers by themselves, the religious found themselves forced to abandon those people. For this purpose they put all the sacred ornaments in places of safety and hid the bells and many other objects of iron in the ground, in order that they might be found if [Spanish] people should come there again. Finally, toward the end of October, 1693, with great regret at leaving that vineyard, still uncultivated, and escorted by the few soldiers whom they had, the religious took the road for Coahuila, etc.

334. But even more untrue is the statement that there would have been no Frenchmen on the Mississippi by that year. If only they had not been there at that time or ever! See Part III, paragraph 61, where we have proved that the unjust French began to settle the plains of Cíbola from the day that Monsieur de la Salle arrived at the rancherias of the Acansas, at which time they reached them by navigating the Mississippi. But why did he [Puelles] refute Father Espinosa when he was the guide who led him by the hand to some of the places which he showed on his map, as is noted in what he states concerning the places and dates of the founding of the missions by Domingo Ramón in 1716, for it is clear that all this is taken from book 5, chapter 8, of the *Chrónica?* I do not know, but I do know that the note to number 17 is apocryphal.

335. Father Puelles placed the number 17 on the south bank of the Río de Cadodachos and next to it a legend which reads, *French fort.* Explaining it in the margin, he says:

Number 17. Small French fort which they established on their own authority and which after many years was ordered destroyed by the most excellent señor viceroy of Mexico because it was an encroachment, etc. But the campaign came to naught. It did not reach the place, and the French had already abandoned it.

In order to be believed Father Puelles should have gone further and given the year of this occurrence, the name of his Excellency, and the name of the captain who went in command of that expedition. (However, in a letter which we shall copy later, he explained himself more fully, because he declares that the leader of this expedition was Parrilla. But with regard to the text of the said letter we shall note that this expedition was not against the Cadodachos, but against the Taobayaces.) The French, as we have seen beginning with the said paragraph 61 of Part III, took over the Río de los Cadodachos, and founded a fort on it. But this foundation was subsequent to the *entrada* of Don Domingo Terán de los Ríos, as is gathered from Father Massanet, who accompanied this captain and wrote to the most excellent señor, the Count of Gálvez [Galve] the following words, copied in Part III, paragraph 133:

Concerning the French, the news was that they live far down the river; that during the past year six Frenchmen in a canoe came to the pueblo of the Yatas [Yatasis] Indians; and that the French captain has one hand missing.

But this was prior to the year 1721, in which Señor Marquis of Aguayo, entered, for in his diary (document 21, number 88) it is said that

Saint Denis agreed that the said señor marquis should recover for the arms of the king, our lord, all that the French had occupied to Los Adaes, although his regret at their recovery of the said Adaes was well known, since it is a place to which the French have aspired because of its being very important to them in communicating with their presidio among the Cadodachos. . . .

336. Now, there is not the least proof or indication whatever that in the time which elapsed between the *entrada* of Don Domingo Terán and the one of the Señor Marquis of Aguayo, as may easily be seen in all our documents, there would have been any expedition against the French presidio of Cadodachos and, in fact, there could not have been any, because from the time that the missions were abandoned in the year 1693 to the year 1716, in which Don Domingo Ramón entered, accompanied by St. Denis, not a single matter concerning the province of Texas was discussed, so completely forgotten was this province. Nor was there any such expedition from this year 1716, to that of 1719, in which our Spaniards abandoned that province because St. Denis had attacked the mission of Los Adaes. Then the expedition which Father Puelles cites was subsequent to the year 1721, in which the Señor Marquis of Aguayo made his *entrada*. But in all our documents and histories not another expedition against the French will be found, either successful or unsuccessful, except the one which Captain Don Diego Ortiz Parrilla[14] made against the Taobayaces, of which we have spoken in Part II, beginning with paragraph 926. On this expedition, however, far from defeating the French, we lost our artillery. Father Puelles should have noted all this, and with this information, he would have abstained from placing such a ridiculous note here. Because of it foreigners may take the liberty of ridiculing all our documents and histories and

---

[14]See *Pichardo's Treatise* . . . , Vol. II, p. 233, n. 4.

may exhibit to the whole world this *ex ungue leonem*,[15] in order
to show that if this history which is so well known was written
so inaccurately, all the rest of less note and not so celebrated,
will have been written the same way. We therefore have thought
it our duty to show the inaccuracy and untruthfulness with which
the said Father Puelles wrote this note.

337. He fell into a similar error when he placed the number
26 at 31° 45' of latitude and 285° 40' of longitude, and explaining it in the marginal note, said the following:

> Number 26. Place where the arms of France were buried in the time of
> Governor Sandoval,[16] according to the old people. The *alférez* of Los Adaes,
> Felipe Muñoz, and Sergeant Juan Regino Muñoz de Mora were the witnesses.

As he shows here, Father Puelles gave much credence to the
tales of old people [i.e., gossip]. In document 26, number 122,
there is the following judicial declaration, given in some depositions that there were made against the governor of Texas, Don
Manuel de Sandoval. It has been copied in Part III, paragraph 976.

> In the royal presidio of San Antonio on the 31st day of the month of
> May, 1738, before Don Juan José Briseño y Zúñiga, *juez de residencia* of the
> said Señor Sandoval, Mateo Antonio de Ybarbo, soldier of the presidio of
> Los Adaes, thirty-six years of age, under burden of an oath, stated . . . in
> reply to the eleventh question of the interrogatory, that it is clear to him, and
> he knows it very well because he has seen it, that the French have a new
> settlement and fortification on our lands. (He was speaking of the presidio
> of Nachitoches, removed to the west bank of the Red River to lands which in
> the opinion of this witness belonged to Spain.) But he knows also that from
> the time they intended to make it and came to this side to examine and
> designate the land, the lieutenant general, who at that time was Don José
> González, advised the señor governor of this movement, and later he advised
> him on two more occasions after they were already building it. He said
> that what he heard the above-cited lieutenant say was that the governor replied
> to him that he could not come in person because he was occupied with other
> matters relative to the royal service which were detaining him. He said that
> he also knows that the said lieutenant called the French commandant to
> account on the basis of those lands belonging to Spain, and that he replied
> that they first belonged to France and that if it were necessary, he would
> come and show him where they left the *fleurs de lis* buried, when they took

---

[15]"The lion is recognized by the claw."

[16]Manuel de Sandoval became governor of Texas in 1734.

possession in the name of his sovereign, which place is where the Spaniards later put the presidio of Texas. . . .

338. When Señor Sandoval replied to the charges [against him] in a written statement which he presented, he refuted this fable of Ybarbo as follows (see Part III, paragraph 984):

That which the ninth witness, Mateo Antonio de Ybarbo, a soldier of Los Adays, points out to the eleventh question . . . is not true when he says that the French commandant (called to account by my lieutenant) replied that if it were necessary he would come and show where the *fleurs de lis* of France were buried when possession of those parts was taken in the name of his sovereign, and that this place was where the Spaniards later put the presidio of Texas. [My explanation is more probable] first, because Commandant Don Luis, in his spirited reply to the demand of my lieutenant, González, in folio 115, indicates the contrary [of that pointed out by Ybarbo], by requesting that he be shown genuine titles [of Spain's] ownership of the territory which runs from Los Adays to Nachitoos along the banks of the Río Colorado [Red River]. He again demands [proof] of him there on this point, specifying that because of lack of the said titles, my lieutenant would be responsible for anything that happened if it came to a resort to arms. He would not say this if there had existed *fleurs de lis* that would make the ownership of those dominions certain, for this would be a titular indication that everything that was not ours was theirs.

339. From this we must deduce that if the arms of France were never buried there, Felipe Muñoz and Sergeant Juan Regino Muñoz de Mora could not have been witnesses of it. Moreover, the same Mateo Ybarbo would have known that they had been witnesses and would have cited them in confirmation of this story, and especially so since they were living at the time that he gave this declaration. Finally, if they had been present at the burial of the French arms in question, they would have so stated frankly in the declarations that they gave on different occasions on the same matter of the transfer of the presidio of Nachitoches, which we discussed in Part III, paragraph 1043, and in other numbers in which we referred to it. They did not mention it. Then it is untrue that they were witnesses of the said burial [of the arms].

340. Since we are convinced that Father Puelles did not write here with the critical examination that he should, one may suspect that he was misinformed also when he wrote the note designated by the number 22. At the point of 33° 48′ of latitude and 285°

6′ of longitude, on the banks of the Río de los Ouachitas, he placed the number 22 and, giving an explanation of it in the margin, he says:

Number 22. Here Monsieur Fabri, a Frenchman, buried the arms of his nation in 1759, as a marker of the French limits.

I confess freely that I have not the slighest information about this burial of the French arms, but speaking frankly, I consider it a fable, because for what purpose would Monsieur Fabri bury these arms? Perhaps in order that they might serve to designate the limits of France as Father Puelles asserts? From the time that the French appropriated Louisiana they took the Río Ouachitas, but they did not fix this river as their limits; rather they spread west over all the land from the Río de los Cadodachos and from there successfully to the points through which D'Anville's line passes. Nor did Spain, after they established themselves, ever dispute with them a single palm of land to the banks of the Río de los Ouachitas. Since, as we have seen in Part III, beginning with paragraph 327, the king, our lord, permitted the French to keep everything that they had taken, they now remained the possessors of that whole vast territory. Therefore there was no need for Monsieur Fabri to have buried the arms of France in order to fix her limits. But it was convenient for Father Puelles to consider that this act of possession was performed in order that the dividing line which he placed on his map and of which we shall speak later, might be considered accurate.

341. In the same place, then, at which this line cuts the Río Ouachita, Monsieur Fabri, according to Father Puelles, buried the French arms as a sign to everyone at all times that the French possessions extended to that place, and that the region north and west from there belonged to Spain. On seeing this absurdity might one not say with Horace (*De Arte Poetica* [*El Arte Poética*], verse 5): "Could you, my friend, refrain from laughing?"[17] Would a Frenchman, that is, a member of the nation which was eager to appropriate that whole country as far as the Pacific Ocean—and if it failed to do so it was only because it could not, and at least it went as far as it could, which was to where D'Anville located

---

[17]The above quotation from the Latin was translated by Mrs. Minnie Lee Shepard.

his line—would he, this Frenchman, curtail his limits to the point of placing them on the banks of the Río Ouachitas? I say the same as the cited Horace (book I, *Sem. Sat.*, 5, verse 100): "The Jew Apella may believe this, not I."[18] And what terrible charges should his whole nation have made against Monsieur Fabri for this act!

342. I omit other comments that I might make on this map because some have been already included in the body of these notes and the others do not merit the time it would take to make them, for we are trying to be brief. But, because it is of the greatest importance, we shall not fail to repeat those words of Señor Martos, copied above in paragraph 311, which state:

By way of it (the Río Misuri) the French penetrated for almost a thousand leagues, although they abandoned their exploration and settlements.

In my opinion the señor commandant-general, Don Nemecio Salcedo, read these words with a great deal of attention, and because of them he was convinced (I repeat that I am speaking with the respect due him) that the French at the time Louisiana was ceded to Spain, did not possess any land along the Misuri, nor did they navigate by way of it. I shall explain my manner of thinking about this, in which I admit freely that I may be mistaken throughout. The señor commandant wrote the following words (see document 73, number 5) to the most excellent Señor Iturrigaray:[19]

The most reasonable decision that could have been made on the demarcation of its western limits was the one that I showed to the commissioners, Don Manuel de Salcedo[20] and the Marquis of Casa Calvo,[21] in an official dispatch of October 4, 1803, which his Majesty' was pleased to approve by the royal order of April 17, 1804, after he had heard the report of the Junta de Fortificación y Defensa de Indias and an opinion of the señor generalissimo to the effect that the limits mentioned should be fixed from the coast which lies between the entrance into the sea of the Río Carcaciut [Calcasieu] and the said Mermentao, in a straight line by way of the vicinity of the post of Nachitoches to the Red River, or Colorado, observing in the remainder of the country article four of the treaty concluded with the government of the

---

[18]*Ibid.*
[19]José de Iturrigaray was viceroy of New Spain from 1803 to 1808.
[20]Manuel de Salcedo was governor of Texas from 1810 to 1813.
[21]See *Pichardo's Treatise* . . . , Vol. I, p. 5, n. 2.

United States on October 27, 1795 (he is referring to the treaty of peace of
which we have spoken in Part I, paragraph 1) concerning the matter of the
boundary of the respective states being placed along the channel or main bed
of the Mississippi River.

343. I have not seen the royal order of April 17, 1804, which
the señor commandant-general cites here, but I believe that its
contents would be similar to those of another confidential royal
order of April 6 of the same year copied below in paragraph
400, in which, after having marked off the limits that should be
fixed from a point on the Red River to the coast of the Gulf of
Mexico, it adds:

> Our commissioners will also maintain that the new possessors of Louisiana
> who may enter from the Mississippi to navigate by way of the Red River, may
> not penetrate farther upstream than the precise point at which the dividing
> line, which should pass between Los Adaes and Nachitoches, reaches and cuts
> the said river in the vicinity of this last post; and likewise that they cannot
> claim any right to the navigation of the Río Misuri, since it never was con-
> nected with Louisiana.

344. The contents of this royal order seem to be exactly those
limits which the señor commandant-general proposed, and it seems
that Father Puelles served as his interpreter, designating these
same limits on his map. Although this map does not extend beyond the latitude of 34° 23′, and therefore it cannot be known
how far Father Puelles intended to go, nevertheless in a letter
which we shall give later, he explains himself as follows:

> From here (from the Arroyo Hondo), ascending toward the north about
> twenty leagues, they will cut the Red River of the said post, which they mis-
> takenly call the Río Colorado, by a diagonal line running northwest, which
> ends at the mouth of the Misuri.

Therefore it seems that the mouth of the Misuri should be the
end of navigation for the Anglo-Americans, and that they cannot
turn there to enter the Misuri and continue navigating by way of it.

345. In fact the confidential royal order does not desire that
the Misuri have any connection with Louisiana, which seems to indicate that the French did not possess it and that consequently
they did not navigate it. This, in my opinion, is inferred from
the said words of Señor Martos:

By way of the Río Misuri the French penetrated for almost a thousand leagues, although they abandoned their exploration and settlements.

For from their act of abandoning it, it is inferred that they lost the claim that they had acquired to it by penetrating along it as far as a thousand leagues, and that after this claim had been lost, the Misuri no longer had any connection with Louisiana.

346. Now, in order to understand the dividing line which Father Puelles drew, let us hear the following letters of his, on which we shall make some comments.

Reply of Father Puelles to the señor governor of Texas, Don Simón de Herrera.[22] *My dear señor:* In reply to the esteemed dispatch of the señor commandant-general which your lordship does me the honor of sending to me with yours of the 11th of the present month, to the effect that I explain the reports that I gave to the Señor Marquis of Casa Calvo concerning what the limits of this frontier include, as well as the documents with which I informed him or to which I referred him, and everything else that I related on this matter, I state: Honor, respect, patriotism, and religion are, señor, the things that impelled me to break my silence. When I saw the said señor marquis desirous of obtaining information on this subject, I stated to him what I knew and this same material I place before the high consideration of the señor commandant-general in view of what he is ordering me to do. The first thing that I showed was the ecclesiastical archive in which are kept the parochial books which legally authenticate the age of the missions and presidios of this frontier, which were Nacogdoches, Los Ais, Los Adais, and El Orcoquiza. The first entry of baptisms in the books of Nacogdoches is that of August 6, 1716, the year in which it was founded (one year, so they say, before the villa of Orleans was settled). The last entry is that of February 12, 1773, in which year the said mission was abandoned by superior order. The same dates, with little difference, are contained in the burial books.

347. In the parochial books of Los Adais, the entries begin at the end of November of the year 1721, and end on June 2, 1773, two days before it was abandoned by superior order, as is clear from the dates of the dispatch in which the commandant of the said presidio communicates it to the governor of Orleans, which dispatch is in the hands of the Marquis of Casa Calvo. But, señor, it is to be noted here that the mission of Los Ais was founded in the month of January of the year 1717; that of Los Adays in the month of March of the same year. I believe that it was at the same time that the Señor Governor Sandoval and the French commandant, St. Denis, made the agreement fixing the limits at the Arroyo Hondo. This was rejected by our

---

[22]Simón de Herrera was offered the commandancy-general of the Eastern Interior Provinces, but "he lost his life at Béxar during the revolution before taking the office."—Bolton, *Guide to Materials for the History of the United States in the Principal Archives of Mexico*, p. 76, n. 35.

superior government (A). The said French officer and his detachment was subject to orders from Mobile, not only in temporal but also in spiritual matters, for in this year our venerable Father Margil received permission of the vicar-general to give spiritual aid to the troops of the French detachment. Mobile (a part of the Floridas, focal point of disturbances between the Spaniards, their ancient discoverers, and the English and French) was illegally founded by the latter in 1700, and in 1719, in which year peace was broken between Spain and France, orders were given to the detachment of Natchitoches to invade and attack the province of Texas. This was done at Los Adays, and according to letters which were taken from several individuals, they wanted to make efforts to reach even the missions on the Río Grande del Norte. As a result of this attack Los Adays was occupied for the second time and fortified with a presidio in the year 1721, at which time its parochial books begin.

348. The books of the presidio and mission of Orcoquiza begin on March 23, 1759, and end in 1770. Their being founded and maintained without opposition during the time that France ruled Louisiana indicates the fallacy of its claims (which the American Cabinet has advanced) on these coasts of San Bernardo, for they affirm that they are theirs because Monsieur La Salle discovered them. While it is true that he built a small fort of wood on the islet which the French mistakenly call San Luis, and which I on my map name La Culebra, this was done clandestinely, and it was destroyed by the Carancaguases Indians before our troops arrived, who were coming by sea and by land to do the same thing. These coasts were discovered and were given the name of Floridas, as were the others discovered in 1512 by the Spaniard, Juan Ponce de León, and later they were explored by other brave captains of our own nation. The same was done with regard to Louisiana, which was also included under the name of Floridas. From this I infer that since the Spaniards had discovered and were masters of the circumference or coasts [of the Gulf], they were of the interior also, as its first possessors; and thus whatever settlements other nations made later, they were without legal character and prior right.

349. For further clarifying that which I have explained, I am enclosing, señor, what I call the second document. It is the [record of the] episcopal inspection (B) made by the most illustrious Señor Marín, bishop of Nuevo León and prelate of this diocese, begun on April 28 and concluded on May 21 of the year 1805. The said señor visited the settlements of Bayupier and was at the boundary, called Arroyo Hondo, two and a half leagues west of Nachitoches, and he was not opposed or requisitioned by the American Government. Rather, indeed, his person and his escort of troops were respected as if they were treading on our own lands.

350. The third document which I presented to the Señor Marquis of Casa Calvo was the life of our venerable Father Margil, written by Father Espinosa of the Apostolic College of Querétaro. In it are clearly shown the apostolic journeys of this holy man in this province and its frontier of Los Adays. But the place where your lordship's high comprehension will best inform itself

on this subject is in the chronicle of our apostolic colleges written by the same author, who, discussing in detail the various events, settlements, and limits of this province of Texas, does not leave out Louisiana, to which he concedes scarcely fifty leagues of extent along the banks of the Mississippi. Since the latter flows in the form of a curve, this should also be the line of its limits (C).

351. And conforming to the opinions of the old settlers, which they inherited from their elders, I say that the said limits should be on the Bayuco Mermentao, or farther to the west on that of Carcasiut (D). These limits, dividing the land by means of a curved line drawn to the northwest as far as the Arroyo Hondo, will ascend from Nachitoches toward the north about twenty leagues and from there will cut the Río Colorado [Red River] of the said post by a diagonal line running northwest, which will end at the mouth of the Misuri.

352. Aside from this opinion, which is founded on the peaceful and ancient possession of the said lands and on the well-known tradition of the old people, we know that the government of Louisiana even during the time that Spain possessed it, always respected these limits and never permitted settlements west of the Calcasus [Calcasieu], since it did not belong to it (E), and indeed [permission to settle] was only conceded on the east, about 1798, to Don José Piernas. In Upper or Greater Louisiana the French never went farther than the Islas Negras east of the Mississippi (F), and scarcely or never during the time of their government did they reach the mouth of the Misuri. Its wretched settlements (G) had only one courier a year, who spent the whole time in going and returning to Orleans. The fact that the French explored to that point during their discoveries is clear from the archives of New Orleans (H).

353. I told the señor marquis and brigadier, Casa Calvo, that the fifth [fourth] piece of evidence could be furnished by that which the religious of the evangelical province of Mexico, in company with the Spaniards, explored and have been exploring east and west of New Mexico from the time that it was settled, which was in the year 1595, to the present day, as may be seen in the chronicles and archives of the said provinces and of their *custodia*, and in those of the government of Santa Fé itself. They will show the many apostolic and military expeditions that have been made, extending along the banks of the Misuri as far as those of the Mississippi (I), without its being known at times exactly and precisely what latitude they reached. The expedition of 1773 was outstanding, for it is inferred that on it they reached the lagoon from which the Mexicans set out to settle this kingdom, and on which they travelled many leagues east on the Misouri (J).

354. The fifth proof that is favorable to us, señor, is the *Diccionario Geográfico* of this America, written by the Señor Colonel Don Antonio Alcedo, who asserts that the limits of New Mexico, which was discovered in the year 1581 by Antonio Espejo, a Spaniard, nearly 150 years (this is doubtless an error of the copyist—it should be 100 years) before Louisiana was settled by the French, were Canada to the northeast, and what we today call Florida on

the southeast (K), which is where its first discoverers landed. They were the ones who were saved from the shipwreck of Pánfilo de Narváez and who, traversing these vast lands, reached Mexico. They told what they had seen and settlements were begun (L). From that time on the said government of New Mexico and later that of Coahuila, which is nearer, kept watch over the encroachment of foreigners on these lands, as was seen when the French entered by way of the coast and by way of the Río de Nachitoches [Red River]; immediately measures were taken to check and dispossess them.

355. There will serve your lordship as a sixth argument [the account] which has been published of the expedition of the Señor Marquis of Aguayo, when he entered with a commission to expel the French who were attempting to penetrate into this province. It is shown therein that the Spaniards placed their presidio seven leagues west of Nachitoches. There it is stated that in 1700 the settlement of Mobile was begun; that on June 19, 1719, the French invaded this province of Texas and forced the fathers of the frontier missions to withdraw to Béjar; and that all of this was recovered by the zeal of the señor marquis, together with other interesting facts that are given there concerning this matter (M).

356. The seventh [piece of] evidence which we have against them is our peaceful and uninterrupted possession of these frontiers of Los Adaes (N) for so many years. There are still eyewitnesses of this who lived there and who saw the señores governors, the ecclesiastical ministers, and the troops, all paid by our monarch. And some are still living who were soldiers and were detached on the Arroyo Hondo, making the French who had their garrison on the other side respect our limits. Their testimony destroys the biting calumny of the United States against us, to the effect that the settlement of Los Adaes was made furtively and without royal permission, and that therefore his Majesty had it withdrawn.

357. The eighth charge that I make against the Americans informed by the French is that, although it is true that the latter had a small fort among the Cadós, where they lived many years with families, troops, and a few military stores, and that it was about five days' travel northwest of Natchitoches on the river of the same name, at 33½ degrees of latitude—as the American engineer, Freeman,[23] observed last July and as he told those of our expedition which, sent out by your Excellency and commanded by the señor *ayudante inspector*, Viana, made his intruding and suspicious squadron retire about ten leagues above the said fort on the day of July 29 of the present year—nevertheless, against it I state that the said settlement was considered clandestine, unauthorized, intrusive, and prejudicial to the ancient rights and possessions of our sovereign, and as such it was decided to destroy it. This was to be done by means of a campaign which was called [the campaign] of Parrila [Parrilla] (O), who was the leader. He did not accomplish anything because of the reverses that he suffered and because the French, already harassed by the Indians, had abandoned the settlement. This I know is shown in the

[23]See *Pichardo's Treatise* . . . , Vol. III, p. 262, n. 13.

archives of Monterrey. I say the same thing with regard to the rumor which is current in Natchitoches to the effect that a Frenchman (I do not remember his name), at the time that France ruled Louisiana, buried the arms of that nation on an *arroyo* at the headwaters of the Sabinas (P). Nothing else occurs to me, señor, concerning which I might have informed the Señor Brigadier and Marquis of Casa Calvo. It only remains for me to proffer the señor commandant-general and your lordship my most respectful gratitude for the opportunity you have given me to be of service to you, and to place myself anew at your command. May God keep your lordship's life many years. Nacogdoches, September 16, 1806. Señor, your humble servant and chaplain kisses your lordship's hand. Fray José María de Jesús Puelles.

REMARKS

358. (A). In Part III, beginning with paragraph 847, we have presented with complete clearness and in detail the truth concerning the exchanges that took place between the señor governor, Sandoval, and the French commandant, St. Denis. In this entire history there is no evidence that there might have been an adjustment of limits at the Arroyo Hondo, for the person who made it, with the qualification "for the present," was the Señor Marquis of San Miguel de Aguayo, when he entered the [land of the] Texas and reached Los Adaes in about August of 1721. Our government did not reject these limits on the Arroyo Hondo, but it did, finally, by the royal cedula of June 20, 1751 (see the said Part III, paragraph 1098), disapprove the removal of the presidio of Nachitoches to the other side of the Red River, notwithstanding the fact that previously it had declared that the said Sandoval had not been at fault in permitting this transfer.

359. (B). We have spoken of this inspection in Part III, paragraph 711.

360. (C). Father Espinosa, in the work cited here by Father Puelles, says only the following, in book 5, chapter 15, page 443:

> During the month of March the rivers gave him (the Venerable Father Margil) an opportunity to go across to the Adays Indians, who are more than fifty leagues from the mission of Los Dolores (de los Ais), toward the east— it is the one nearest the fort that the French now have, with only ten leagues between them—and there he founded a third mission on behalf of his college, and dedicated it to Prince San Miguel.

This is the only passage in Father Espinosa's entire work in which it is stated that there are more than fifty leagues from the

Ais to the Adays, who are ten leagues from Nachitoches. Where is it shown, then, that Father Espinosa concedes an extent of fifty leagues to Louisiana along the margins of the Mississippi? As for the life of Father Margil written by Father Espinosa under the title of *Peregrino Septentrionale Atlante delineado en la exemplarisima vida del V. Padre Fray Antonio Margil de Jesus*, printed in Mexico in 1737, this author, in book 2, chapter 23 and following, does in fact discuss the travels of this apostolic man and his founding of the mission of Los Adacs.

361. (D). In Part III, beginning with paragraph 1558, we have proved that the Río Mermentao and the Carcasiu belong to Spain and that the French limits on the coast are at the Cabo del Norte, as is shown by D'Anville's line. Therefore, Father Puelles should not have begun his line at any of these rivers, even though the confidential royal order might have so prescribed, for it emanated from an error, but he should have shown that the truth demanded that it be begun at the Cabo del Norte. From this procedure of the confidential royal order in having given such a command, it is inferred that the line proposed by the señor comandant-general, Don Nemecio Salcedo, was adopted therein. But I cannot imagine where his lordship would get the idea that the Mermentao should be set as the boundary, nor how his line can proceed to divide the land by a curve drawn toward the northwest as far as the Arroyo Hondo, from Nachitoches, for both rivers are located west of the meridian that passes through the Arroyo Hondo, as is seen on our map; unless it may be that the line was drawn toward the northeast. Father Puelles' error was due to the fact that because of ignorance of how the coast line of the Gulf of Mexico runs, he placed the mouths of these rivers east of the said meridian of the Arroyo Hondo, and thus with respect to them the Arroyo Hondo lies to the northwest. And let it be noted that here Father Puelles' line (which is the same one that the señor comandant-general proposed and which was ordered established by the said confidential royal order) begins to be explained, the explanation continuing in the following words:

362. (E). We believe that we are speaking with better evidence, there explained, when in Part III, paragraph 1588, we said the following:

Because of the calculated and most criminal negligence of the said Señor Martos Navarrete in not dislodging the French from the Opelusas and Atacapas, when, following its cession by France to Spain, Louisiana entered into the dominions of our sovereign, the first governor of Louisiana, the Most Excellent Señor Don Antonio de Ulloa, mistakenly believed that they belonged to his government. As a result he began to exercise the acts of jurisdiction that did not belong to him, for the will of the king, our lord, when he received Louisiana, was that the governor of it should govern precisely and solely the lands which had been clearly and manifestly recognized as belonging to the French possessions; that all the [other] lands should be governed by the most excellent señores viceroys of this New Spain; and that the Laws of the Indies should not be in force in Louisiana. Thus by separating, without the king's consent, the lands that lie east of the Río de los Adaes, or Mexicano—that is, the Sabinas —from the government of New Spain, the enjoyment of their jurisdiction and command in those lands was taken from the said most excellent señores viceroys with notable injury to their authority, just as it was later taken from the señores commandants-general of the Interior Provinces.

If only what Father Puelles states were true, namely, that the government of Louisiana even during the time it belonged to Spain herself, always respected these limits and never permitted settlements west of the Carcasiu! For then what the Señor Barón de Ripperdá said in Part II, paragraph 142, would not be true, as it now is, namely, that "the Río de Nechas . . . is the one that divides this province (of Texas) from Louisiana, on the coast"; nor [what] Don Luis Cazorla [said concerning] "the other side of the Río de Nechas, in the jurisdiction of New Orleans." (*Ibid.*, paragraph 163.)

363. (F). I here confess quite frankly, as I should, that I am most grossly ignorant of the location of the Islas Negras. I find myself lost in such ignorance by reason of the scarcity of maps and histories of those lands, and perhaps also because of my bad memory. However, from another source I have the following report on these islands. The Frenchman Luis del Fierro declared, as we have seen in Part III, paragraph 390, that from San Miguel Michilimakinac he

continued his journey to a place called La Isla Negra, which is on the banks of the Mississippi; and that on the said island his nation has a presidio with two companies of infantry; he has heard it said that the post has been there sixty years; there are no other inhabitants than the companies and three *hacenderos*, whose fields [*labores*] produce maize and wheat, with some cattle and horses. They are accustomed to obtain the horses by bartering with the hostile Indians; he does not know where the Indians obtain them.

And in [Part III], paragraph 459, Pedro Malec said:

I, Pedro Malec, state that in the year '40, together with eight other companions from the city of Canada, being desirous of seeing the country and of seeking employment or occupation for our families, and encouraged by reports of the nearness of the Spaniards, came by way of Isla Negra, or an Indian pueblo in New France, to this kingdom of New Mexico, and from there to the city and locality of Santa Fé, etc.

In an unsigned letter which I have before me, and which was written to the señor governor, Don Antonio Cordero,[24] from Nacogdoches on September 10, 1807, the one who writes it tells him the following:

The American captain, Monsieur Pike,[25] and Doctor Robinson (with six soldiers of the same nation), men instructed in mathematics, astronomy, and natural history, a short while ago left Las Islas Negras. They explored all of the Sierra Madre [and] the source of the Río Misuri. They travelled south, with the same sierra serving them as a guide, for more than six hundred leagues. On this journey they examined at their leisure the sources of all the rivers that water these provinces. When they were on the Colorado they crossed the Gran Sierra and they learned of the other Río Colorado which runs toward Sonora. They then crossed the Río Grande del Norte, where our troops of New Mexico encountered them and took them (to their sorrow) to Santa Fé and from there to Chihuahua.

364. W. Winterbotham,[26] describing the Mississippi River, volume 1, page 186, says only:

A large number of islands, some of which are of great size, obstruct or keep back this mighty river.

As far as I know, Don Antonio Alcedo had no information about these islands or about the French fort that is on them, if there is one, because he did not see them on any map or in any history, since he does not mention them anywhere in his dictionary. In confirmation of what W. Winterbotham has said, I shall state that on D'Anville's map are found six legends on the banks of the Mississippi. The one farthest south, and south of the Misuri, says *Isles aux Canadiens;* the one next above it, *Isles a la Sonde;* the one that follows, *Isles a la Course;* above these, *La*

---

[24]Antonio Cordero y Bustamente was governor of Texas from 1805 to 1810.
[25]See *Pichardo's Treatise* . . . , Vol. III, p. 262, n. 13.
[26]See *Pichardo's Treatise* . . . , Vol. I, p. 24.

Grande Isle; above the Misuri, at 41° 22' of latitude, another which says *Isles aux Canots;* and at 43 degrees of latitude, another reading *Isles a Tewi* [*Tessier?*].

365. But in as much as the Frenchman, Luis del Fierro, leaving the island of Michilimakinac, which according to D'Anville is located in 45° 8' of latitude, arrived at La Isla Negra and later among the Arcansas, as we see in the continuation of his cited declaration, we are convinced that La Isla Negra lies north of the mouth of the Misuri and that perhaps it is either one of those which D'Anville calls Isles aux Canots or one of those called Isles a Tessier, unless it is the one that D'Anville calls La Grande Isle (and this is what we think most probable), which is found south of the Misuri in 37° 50' of latitude.

366. Modern geographers divide Louisiana into Upper and Lower Louisiana, but I do not know in exactly what place Upper Louisiana begins and extends northward, although I do know that Perrin du Lac, cited in Part II, paragraph 464, says that the settlement of Ste. Genevieve is "the first establishment of any importance in Upper Louisiana," and that he adds in his *Viage* [*Voyage dans les deux Louisianes*] that "the Cape Girardot [Cape Girardeau], which is located south of Ste. Genevieve and north of the Ohio (see Arrowsmith's map,[27] from which we took it to place it on ours), is the first post of any importance found upon descending the Mississippi." Supposing that this writer, as soon as he entered the Mississippi from the Ohio and began to navigate it toward the north, regarded himself as already in Upper Louisiana, I believe that this Louisiana is considered as beginning at the mouth of the Ohio and that the said Cabo Girardot is found near the southern boundary of it. Therefore New Madrid, which is located south of the mouth of the Ohio, belongs to Lower Louisiana. Granting also that the said Isla Grande is located south of the mouth of the Misuri, I understand that this Isla Grande, and not the others, Aux Canots and Tussier, is the one to which Father Puelles is referring when he calls them Islas Negras. This geographer religious did not want the French to have any part of the Misuri, and for that reason it seems that he says that when they navigated the Mississippi from New Orleans north, they

---

[27]See *Pichardo's Treatise* . . . , Vol. I, p. 42, n. 3.

did not pass into Upper or Greater Louisiana of the Islas Negras, and scarcely or never during the time of their government did they reach the mouth of the Misuri. But how opposed to this religious do all writers show themselves who assert unanimously, as we have seen in Part III, beginning with paragraph 373, that the French navigated the Misuri almost from the time they discovered it. Even the most excellent señor, the Marquis of Rubí,[28] noted this in the year 1767 (see Señor Bonilla's *Compendio*, document 42, number 142), and for that reason said the following in his report copied in Part III, paragraph 1515:

As regards the protection of our true dominions, removed from this imaginary frontier two hundred leagues or more, we might substitute for this weak barrier the one that the present governor of that colony [Louisiana], Don Antonio de Ulloa, is establishing on a respectable footing on the Colorado [Red] and Missouri rivers, and thus the communication and trade of that colony with the dominions of this kingdom will be rendered much more difficult, in conformance with the intentions of the king.

Then, if the Most Excellent Señor Ulloa was constructing a barrier on the Misuri in 1767, the French of Louisiana were navigating this river as if it belonged to them.

367. (G). Of what wretched establishments is Father Puelles speaking here? Of those of the Misuri? Then he confesses that they had them. If he is speaking of others, why does he mention them here if they do not bear on the question?

368. (H). As long as Father Puelles does not cite the specific words of some document of the archives of New Orleans [to show] that the French explored as far as the Islas Negras by means of their discoveries, and did not explore the country farther north, neither the Spaniards nor the French need to give credit to this assertion of his, because there are a great many other documents against it.

369. (I). I am certain that there is not mentioned in these chronicles and archives a single apostolic or military expedition which was made by way of the banks of the Misuri to those of the Mississippi. In order to have spoken the truth, his reverence should have cited at least one. For my part, I have seen only the

[28]See *Pichardo's Treatise* . . . , Vol. I, p. 8, n. 1.

one of Pedro Vial,[29] when he journeyed from Santa Fé to the Ylineses [Illinois]. His account is found in document 55.

370. (J). Why did not Father Puelles tell us what expedition this one of the year 1773 was? The lack of judgment and veracity that we have noted in him, makes us doubt that there was such an expedition. Perhaps that of Fathers Fray Atanasio Domínguez and Fray Silvestre Vélez Escalante,[30] begun in 1776, concerning which we present a copy in our document 45, is the one that he proposed to discuss, even though he antedated it to the year 1773. On this journey, in numbers 115 and 278, the said fathers speak of the lagoon of the Timpanocuitzis, from which Father Puelles perhaps thought the Mexicans went forth to settle this kingdom. But nothing is seen on this journey indicating that the said fathers travelled many leagues toward the east on the Misuri. Rather, on the contrary, it is seen that their journey was directed toward Monterrey [California] and that all along their route they travelled far to the west of the Misuri.

371. (K). It seems that Father Puelles proposed only to deceive fools with this fifth argument, and not to present the truth. If he had given entire the quotation from Alcedo's *Diccionario*, anyone could have shown him the fallacy of this argument. Alcedo, then, in his *Diccionario*, volume three, page 183, having finished speaking of Old Mexico, says the following:

Another extensive kingdom has the same name with the addition of *New*. It is the northernmost part of the dominions of New Spain in America. It is bounded on the south by the provinces of Sinaloa, Nueva Vizcaya, and the Nuevo Reyno de León; on the south and southeast by Florida; on the northeast by Canada, or New France; and on the west, northwest, and southwest by the Californias. Toward the north its limits are still unknown. Its extent is from 260° [to 275°] of longitude, and from 28° to 45° of latitude. It is 350 leagues long from north to south, and 150 wide from east to west.

If we subtract 260 from 275 degrees of longitude, there remain 15. Then, according to Alcedo, New Mexico is enclosed in fifteen degrees of longitude. But since this kingdom is bounded by California, the fifteen degrees begin to be counted in the Californias or, which is the same thing, 260° is found in the Californias,

---

[29]See *Pichardo's Treatise* . . . , Vol. I, p. 528, n. 4.

[30]For a statement concerning Fathers Domínguez and Vélez Escalante, see *Pichardo's Treatise* . . . , Vol. II, p. 29, n. 36.

west of Santa Fé, and 275° will fall to the east of this villa. Count the fifteen degrees from wherever may be desired in California, and they will end west of Santa Fé. But they will end in a meridian far from the westernmost part of Florida. We have seen in Part II, paragraph 50, that there are fifteen degrees from Santa Fé to Los Adaes. But Los Adaes does not reach Florida. Then much less will it reach a meridian in which the fifteen degrees terminate, which are counted from a meridian located in the Californias. Unless I am mistaken, Señor Alcedo in thus describing New Mexico had Father Alzate's[31] map before him, because, in truth, on this map the 260th degree, passing through the parallel 30° 40′, touches the old Californias, and if we count the leagues from this point to the [2]75th meridian, taking the measurement on the scale that this map uses of 17½ leagues to the degree, we shall find that there are 258. If we multiply the 17½ leagues by 15, they will amount to 262½, a quantity 112 leagues greater than the one which Señor Alcedo says is the width of New Mexico. Therefore it is known that the 150 is the printer's error, and should read 250 leagues. It is known also that he measured this distance from another different point, 12 leagues to the east of the one that we have given, but without noting that by giving it exactly 15 degrees, he should also give it 262½ leagues. The 275th degree on Father Alzate's map passes almost east of San Sabá and of Cerralvo, a villa and presidio of the Nuevo Reyno de León.

372. We infer from all this that Señor Alcedo encloses the kingdom of New Mexico between the border of Old California and the presidio of San Sabá. For that reason he also makes the Nuevo Reyno de León the boundary on the south. Consequently, by saying that New Mexico is bounded on the south and southeast by Florida, he calls the province of Texas, Florida, and by this name he did not mean to signify only the tongue of land that is so called, but also what was formerly called the government of Florida, even though it was dismembered of all the land from the meridian of San Sabá west to the Sierra de los Faraones, or Capirote. (See Part I, paragraph 38.)

373. (L). The true history of the companions of Pánfilo de Narváez and of the lands they traversed is related in detail by

---

[31]See *Pichardo's Treatise* . . . , Vol. I, p. 316, n. 2.

Alvar Núñez Cabeza de Vaca in his *Naufragios* and we have touched on this matter in the dissertation on La Quivira and in the [account of the] journey of Hernando de Soto.

374. (M). We presented this journey in document 21, in order that what it contained might be seen in its entirety, and the limits of Texas ascertained up to certain points.

375. (N). In Part III, beginning with paragraph 1494, we have proved this possession sufficiently.

376. (O). The French always occupied the old post of the Cadodachos, as we have shown in Part II, beginning with paragraph 647. And Don Diego Ortiz Parrilla did not carry on a war against these Indians but against the Taobayaces. See what we have said above concerning this, in paragraph 336, when we spoke of the map of the same Father Puelles. I do not believe that the falsehood written here by the said father can be proven from the archives of Monterrey.

377. (P). This rumor which at the present time is current in Nachitoches, according to Father Puelles, is untrue, and it never circulated in former times, for Macarti would have mentioned it in his letter to Señor Martos.

378. From this letter, by altering and varying it somewhat, and taking from it and adding to it a little, he formed the following one which he wrote to some person whom I do not know, for in the copy I have it is not indicated. I insert it here in order that from it there may be corrected some errors of the pen which are in the copy that was sent from Chihauhua to Father Talamantes. It is as follows:

My dear señor: The documents on the limits of this frontier, which I gave to the Señor Marquis of Casa Calvo, were the following: First, I showed him the ecclesiastical archives in which are preserved the parochial books which legally authenticate the age, location, and territory of the missions and presidio of this frontier, especially those of Nacodoches, Los Aises, Los Adaes, and El Orcoquizac. The first entries of baptisms and burials in the archives of Nacodoches are of the month of August of the year 1716, and in those of Los Adaes, in November of the year 1721. The last entries are of June 2, 1773, two days before they were abandoned by superior order of this government, as is clear from the dates of the dispatch in which the commandant of Los Adaes communicates the matter to the governor of Orleans, the original of which is in the possession of Señor Casa Calvo.

379. But it is to be noted here, señor, that the mission of Los Aises was founded in the month of January of the year 1717 and that of Los Adais or Adaices in the month of March of the same year, in which our troops, seeking the Río Colorado [Red River], came with orders to check the French who were entering. The Spanish troops left for the place which today we call Bayupier, and from there they descended, in prosecution of their mission, to Los Adaes, where the commandant received a warning from the French chief of Nachitoches to restrain himself if he did not want to be the cause of the shedding of blood. This led them to reach an agreement, and our Governor Sandoval and the French commandant, St. Denis, fixed the Arroyo Hondo as the limits. This the French cabinet has always respected.

380. Mobile, a part of the Floridas and focal point of the war between the Spaniards, their ancient discoverers, and the English and French, was illegally founded by the latter in 1700, and in the year 1719 in which peace was broken between Spain and France, hostile orders were given to the detachment of Nachitoches to invade the province of Texas. This was done at Los Adaes, and, according to letters which were taken from several individuals, they wanted to make efforts to reach the missions of the Río Grande del Norte. This resulted in Los Adaes being occupied for the second time and fortified in the year 1721, which is the same year in which the entries begin in its parochial books.

381. The said books of the presidio and mission of El Orcoquizac, founded and maintained for so many years without any opposition, during the time that France ruled Louisiana, indicate the fallacy of the claims that the American Cabinet has advanced to these coasts of San Bernardo by asserting that they are theirs because of the Frenchman, La Salle, having discovered them. Although it is true that he built a small fort of wood on the islet which the French mistakenly call San Luis (A), and which on my map I have named La Culebra, he did this clandestinely, and it was destroyed by the Carancaguaces Indians before our troops could arrive, who were coming by land to do the same thing. These coasts were discovered and were also given the name of Floridas in 1512 by the Spaniard Juan Ponce de León, and later they were traversed by other brave captains of our own nation.

382. Second, for further clarifying what has been expressed, I furnish him the [record of the] episcopal visit made by the most illustrious Señor Marín[32] in this Nacogdoches in the year 1805. He visited the settlements of Bayupier as dependents of this diocese. He was at the boundary or place called Arroyo Hondo without being opposed by the American Government. Rather, his person and escort were respected as if they were treading on our own lands.

383. The third document is the life of our Venerable Father Margil, in which his apostolic journeys into this province and frontier of Los Adaes are clearly shown; and also the chronicle of our apostolic colleges, written by Father Espinosa, who, discussing in detail the various events, settlements, and limits

---

[32]See *Pichardo's Treatise* . . . , Vol. III, p. 439, n. 18.

of this province of Texas, does not leave out Louisiana, to which he concedes scarcely fifty leagues of extent along the banks of the Mississippi, which, flowing in a curve, should also be the line of its limits.

384. And if I conform to the common and ancient opinion, the said limits should be on the Bayuco Mermentao or on the Calcasiu. They divide the land by a curved line drawn to the northwest as far as the Arroyo Hondo, and ascending from Nachitoches toward the north for some twenty leagues, they will cut the Red River of the said post, which they mistakenly call the Río Colorado (B), by a diagonal line running northwest, which ends at the mouth of the Misuri.

385. This opinion is based on the fact that the government of Louisiana even during the time of Spanish rule never permitted settlements west of Carcasiu, as an area that did not belong to them. And when the Señor Governor Miro[33] asked the court of Spain for an extension of limits for the said province, it was denied him (C). In Upper Louisiana the French never passed beyond the Islas Negras, west of the Mississippi, and scarcely reached the mouth of the Misuri during the time that France governed it, as is clear from the archives of New Orleans.

386. The fourth matter that I referred to was the explorations that the Spaniards, together with the religious of El Santo Evangelio, have made east of New Mexico since 1595, some of our parties having traversed these vast territories and gone as far as Florida without any opposition. This is clear from the archives of this commandancy-general.

387. The fifth [piece of] evidence, señor, is the *Diccionario Geográfico* of this America, which asserts that the limits of New Mexico, which was discovered in 1581 by Antonio Espejo,[34] nearly 150 years before Louisiana was settled by the French, were on the north, Canada, and on the southwest [southeast], Florida, where its first discoverers landed. They were the ones who were saved from the shipwreck of Pánfilo de Narváez on the said coasts and who, traversing these vast lands, reached Mexico. They gave reports on these countries, which began to be settled. From that time on this government and later that of Coahuila kept watch over the encroachment of foreigners on these lands, as was seen when the French began to enter by way of the Red River of Nachitoches, for immediately measures were taken to check and dispossess them.

388. The sixth proof is the [account] which has been published of the expedition of the Señor Marquis of Aguayo, when he entered with a commission to expel the French who were attempting to penetrate into this province. It is shown therein that the Spaniards finally placed their presidio seven leagues west of Nachitoches. There it is stated that in 1700 the settlement of Mobile was begun and likewise that in 1719, on June 19, the French invaded this province of Texas and forced the fathers of the frontier missions to withdraw to San Antonio de Béjar, and that all this was recovered through the zeal

---

[33]Don Estevan Mirò was governor of Spanish Louisiana from 1785 to 1791.
[34]See *Pichardo's Treatise* . . . , Vol. I, p. 70, n. 1.

of the señor marquis, together with other interesting facts that are given concerning this matter.

389. The seventh [piece of] evidence which we have in our favor is our peaceful and uninterrupted possession of this frontier of Los Adaes for almost a hundred years. There are still eyewitnesses of this who lived there, who saw the señores governors, the ecclesiastical ministers, and the troops, all paid by the king; and many of them are still living who were soldiers and who were detached on the Arroyo Hondo, making the French who had their garrison on the other side of the said stream respect the boundary. Their testimony destroys the biting calumny of the United States against us, to the effect that that settlement of Los Adaes was made without royal permission and that therefore his Catholic Majesty ordered it withdrawn.

390. The eighth evidence is that, although it is true that the French had a small fort among the Cadoos on the same Río de Nachitoches [Red River], and that it was about five days' travel northwest of it [Natchitoches], and that they lived in it many years with families, troops, and a few military stores, I nevertheless state against this that the said settlement was considered clandestine, unauthorized, intrusive, and prejudicial to the ancient possessions of our monarch. For that reason it was decided to drive it out. This was to be done by means of a campaign that was called [the campaign] of Parrilla. He did not accomplish anything because of the reverses that he suffered on the expedition and because the French, already seriously harassed by the Indians, had abandoned the settlement. This I know is shown in the archives of Monterrey.

391. But the same unhappy result was not experienced on the campaign which was made in the past year, 1806, to the same place and under superior orders, by the señor *ayudante inspector* and commandant of this post, Don Francisco Viana, to whose skill and military talent it was entrusted. For when the Americans had attempted to ascend the Río Colorado [Red River] even after their request had been denied by our government, and when their expedition was at the said place of the Cadoos, at 33° of north latitude, according to the observation of the American engineer, they were expelled very readily by the said señor as violators of Spanish territory.

392. The same things that I stated above confirm the rumor which is current in Nachitoches to the effect that a Frenchman (I do not remember his name), during the time that France ruled Louisiana buried the arms of his nation as a perpetual memorial at the headwaters of the Río de Sabinas, called and known on our old maps as the Río Mexicano. Nothing else occurs to me concerning which I might have informed the Señor Marquis of Casa Calvo, and it only remains for me to express my gratitude for this occasion which your honor has afforded me to be useful to you and to place myself anew at your command. I was asked for a copy of this, and I sent it to the señor commandant-general, Don Nemesio Salcedo, on September 12, 1806. Your honor will pardon the many errors of the copyist. God keep your honor's life many years. Nacogdoches, March (my copy does not have the day), 1807. Fray José María de Jesús Puelles.

REMARKS

393. (A). La Salle did not found his Fort Luis on the island but on the same site on which the Señor Marquis of Aguayo erected his. And if the French call the island of La Culebra, San Luis, they probably mean by this that it is an island which is found in front of the bay of San Luis. Aside from the fact that I do not find any map on which this island is called San Luis, and that where it is found, the name falls on the bay and not on the island, the pilot, Evía, cited in Part II, paragraph 195, gives the name San Luis to the island that is found adjoining the bay of San Bernardo, and thus these two islands are seen on our map with the names that have been given them.

394. (B). Where is the error? Why, just because there is a river in the province of Texas which they call Colorado, and which is the Brazos de Dios, cannot the same name be given in Louisiana to another river? Furthermore, the French do not call it by the Spanish name, *Colorado*, but by the Fench name, *Rouge*. They gave it this name because, as Doctor Sibley, copied in Part II, paragraph 566, states,

On entering the mouth of the river, I found its waters turgid and of a red color. . . .

And according to Monsieur Dunbar, copied there also, in paragraph 617,

The Red River derives its name from a rich, fat earth, or marl, of the said red color. . . .

395. (C). Concerning this we speak in Part III, paragraph 801, as follows:

From this *expediente*, all the Anglo-Americans should know and understand that the said territory extending from the Arroyo Hondo to the Río de Sabinas was denied by their king and lord to the vassals of Spain residing in Louisiana; and that consequently the French never were owners of it, as they did not own Los Adaes which, according to the marquis of San Miguel de Aguayo, was located, as we have seen repeatedly, to the west [east?] of the said river; and that if his Catholic Majesty did not desire to separate it from the province of Texas in order to give it to his subjects living in Louisiana, much less will he be willing to detach it from the said province for the purpose of handing it over to those who are not his subjects, especially since this land extends

from the point which we have named De Mézières' Crossing to the source of
the said river. If, after passing this source, they should desire to follow the
line which this river would form had it continued northward, would there not
be danger that they would desire to appropriate the Taobayaces pueblos as
well, and who knows how much more territory? Extending southwest [south-
east?] from the said crossing of De Méziéres there is another expanse of
territory of which Spain would necessarily be deprived, which would be a
great misfortune.

From the horizontal line of which we have spoken above in
paragraph 306, which Señor Martos drew from the Río de Sabinas
to the entrance of the Red into the Mississippi, as far as the coast,
there were Gallo-Hispanic lands, that is, lands settled by the inhabitants of Louisiana at a time when this province still belonged
to Spain, as we have stated in Part III, beginning with paragraph
1553. Consequently, it seems to me that the claims of the commandant of Nachitoches and of Señor Miro to the effect that to
their possessions should be added the territory that extends to the
Río de Sabinas, included all from the said line of Señor Martos
north to the source of this river, first, because this land was near
and fronting Nachitoches, and, secondly, because the Gallo-Spaniards no longer needed to claim, since they already possessed it,
all the land from the said line of Señor Martos to the coast. Therefore, it is known that Father Puelles was not accurately informed
as to what the Señor Governor Miro had requested of our court,
nor [did he know] that the government of Louisiana, even under
Spanish rule, not only permitted but also made settlements west
of Carcasiu and even as far as the Río de Sabinas, and also to
the Neches, beginning with the horizontal line of Señor Martos.
(See Part III, from paragraph 1566.)

396. In these letters, then, our geographer religious discusses
the line that he drew. This line originates at the entrance of the
Río Mermentao into the Bahía de la Ascensión, and, ascending
toward the northwest, it crosses the Arroyo Hondo. From there,
ascending toward the north some twenty leagues, it reaches the
Red River and cuts it. And going northeast, it ends at the mouth
of the Misuri. It is shown in that form on his map, although
the latter is very imperfect and confusing because its rivers and
lakes are so badly described. On our map we have shown this

line in yellow more accurately and clearly. But, since it was impossible to run it in the vicinity of the coast in the manner in
which Father Puelles drew it, because the Mermentao does not enter
the sea east of the Arroyo Hondo but west of it, and since it
also does not flow into Ascención Bay but into its own bay at
29° 42' of latitude and 76° 40' of longitude, we have divided the
line into two branches, designating it with yellow dots: one running from the mouth of the Mermentao toward the northeast to
a point on the Arroyo Hondo which is found in 31° 43' of latitude and 75° 53' of longitude, and the other going from the
mouth of the Chafalaya (which Father Puelles undoubtedly took
for the Mermentao), which is found in 30° of latitude and 75°
of longitude, toward the northwest as far as the said latitude and
longitude of the Arroyo Hondo in something of a curve, as its
author desires. We have drawn these two lines for no other purpose than to show how greatly Father Puelles erred in drawing
his line, for it should begin neither at the Río Mermentao nor at
the Chafalaya, for the reasons that we have given.

397. From the said point on the Arroyo Hondo we drew it
directly north for a distance of twenty leagues, or, which is the
same, for 45 minutes, and at the end of these it cuts the Red River.
From there it proceeds straight toward the northeast as far as the
mouth of the Misuri, which is found, as we have said in Part II,
paragraph 508, in 39° 26' of latitude and 72° 10' of longitude.
In this space it crosses the Río Vachita (at the spot where he
believes Monsieur Fabri buried the arms of his nation in order
that they might serve as limits), although it is not in the latitude of 33° 48' nor in the longitude of 285° 6' (which, reduced
to west longitude, is 74° 54'), which Father Puelles assigns to
it, but in 33° 31' of latitude and 75° 19' of longitude. Hence it
is seen that our map differs from his on this point, by 17 minutes
of latitude and 25 minutes of longitude. We have described the
Río Vachita in accordance with the opinion of D'Anville, which
we regard as most reliable in this matter. Since this river has
been so useful to us for verifying the route that Hernando de
Soto took through these lands, we shall make an effort to describe
it, copying from the writer who seems to us the best in this case.

398. In as much as this line took from the French the control which they had of one side of the Misuri and conforms to a confidential royal order of which I have spoken before, in order to determine the limits with the requisite accuracy and not to expose myself to error in a matter of such great importance, I addressed the following *consulta* to the most excellent señor viceroy, Don Francisco Xavier Venegas:[35]

Most excellent señor: Don Juan López Cancelada,[36] former editor of the *Gaceta* of this court, as much out of curiosity as for the purpose of obtaining materials to publish in his gazette, succeeded in acquiring many papers and reports on the Interior Provinces, and knowing that I was commissioned to designate the limits between the provinces of Texas and Louisiana, he had the kindness to furnish them to me with permission to make copies of all of them, or of those that might be most useful. I did so, and among them I copied the following: "On the delivery of Louisiana. Royal dispatch of October 15, 1802. Extract. His Majesty commands that as soon as the said dispatch may be presented by General Victor[37] or any other official authorized by the French Government, the colony of Louisiana, its dependencies, and the island of New Orleans shall be delivered to him with the extent that it now has and that it had when it was ceded to Spain, in order that they may govern it as a personal possession. The soldiers and employees shall leave for Spain or other points in the dominions of the king, and those who may desire shall remain in the service of France. The records and expense accounts shall be taken to Spain, except those that treat of limits and demarcations, ports [posts?] and Indian alliances, which will be delivered to the French governor."

399. Another extract from a proclamation of May 18, 1803, by Señores Don Manuel Salcedo and the Marquis of Casa Calvo, brigadiers, authorized and acting together for the delivery of the province: "Article I: That the delivery of the colony and island of New Orleans shall be made to General Victor or any other official authorized by the Republic [of France]. This delivery will take place on the terms under which France ceded it to Spain; and the limits were fixed in accordance with article seven of the treaty of peace signed in Paris on February 10, 1783. The territory from Manchak to the American line thus remains a possession of the king, attached to West Florida."

---

[35]Francisco Javier Venegas was viceroy of New Spain from 1810 to 1813.

[36]See *Pichardo's Treatise* . . . , Vol. I, p. 368, n. 3.

[37]"The treaty of peace between France, Spain, and England was signed at Amiens on March 25, 1802, and Bonaparte made preparation to take formal possession of Louisiana. . . . Bonaparte appointed General Victor captain-general. . . . He remained nearly six months in Holland, . . . until May, 1803. In the meantime the peace of Amiens between France and England was broken, the expedition to Louisiana was abandoned, and Victor never reached the colony of which he had been named captain-general."—Fortier, *A History of Louisiana*, Vol. II, pp. 179–181.

400. And the one that follows, which is marked "confidential copy"; *"Most excellent señor:* I am returning the *expediente* which by royal order your Excellency was pleased to send me on February 12, last, for examination by the Junta de Fortificaciones y Defensa de Indias, because of the doubts which have arisen concerning the limits of Louisiana, among those commissioned to designate them and the commandant-general of the Interior Provinces. I am enclosing the opinion of the junta which, having been seen by the señor generalissimo, was returned to me at his order by the chief of staff, Don Antonio Samper. It states what I am copying: *'Most excellent señor:* The generalissimo, the Prince of the Peace, has informed himself concerning the opinion which the Junta de Fortificaciones y Defensa de Indias has drawn up, which your Excellency sent him on last March 18, regarding the best system that could be adopted in the demarcation of limits of Louisiana, on the west and north of this province; and as a consequence he has been pleased to point out that the entrances into the Gulf of Mexico of the Sabinas, Caricut, and Armenta rivers are found to be located with considerable variation on the maps, without one's being able to ascertain definitely their true position, and that for lack of a solemn agreement or definitive treaty to authorize the limits between the provinces of Texas and Louisiana, we should recur to the possession which we have always had of the Río Caricut along its entire course until it empties into the sea, and of the abandoned presidio of Los Adaes which was the capital of the province. Since the post of Nachitoches, which was dependent upon the government of Louisiana, is located at a distance of eight leagues from this presidio, our commissioners may establish a title of possession to include within the territory of the province of Texas, as points well known, the Río Caricut along its entire course and the presidio of Los Adaes. And since the dividing line, be it straight or curved, may pass between Los Adaes and Nachitoches to where it cuts the Red River, our people may claim that the said line runs to the east as near as possible to the Red River until it ends on the sea coast, unless the commissioners of the other contracting party should show authentically that France may have had permanent settlements in the area lying between Texas, the west banks of the Red and Mississippi rivers, and the seacoast, aside from the post of Nachitoches and some other points of lesser importance on the bank of the Red River. It might even be disputed whether or not these should be considered as a part of Louisiana, notwithstanding the fact that they had been subject to the government of New Orleans, for in like manner our province of East Florida is dependent on the island of Cuba, and Florida is not for that reason a territory of Cuba.

401. " 'Our commissioners could maintain likewise that the new owners of Louisiana who may enter from the Mississippi to navigate along the Red River, shall not be able to penetrate farther upstream than to the exact point where the dividing line that should pass between Los Adaes and Nachitoches may cut the said river in the vicinity of this last post, and also that they shall not be able to claim the least right to the navigation of the Misuri, since it never had any connection with Louisiana. By these precau-

tions there will be averted the prejudices that might otherwise result to our Interior Provinces, as is shown clearly enough by the enclosed, and I add that perhaps it might be well that at certain suitable points on both rivers a fort be placed for better insuring exclusive navigation.

402. " 'With regard to the demarcation the señor generalissimo finds it preferable that the true limits be indicated simply by a straight or curved line rather than by a strip of our land between the possessions of the two nations. I report all this to your Excellency by direction of the said superior chief and for the purposes that it may serve. I am returning all the documents which your Excellency was pleased to include in your cited official dispatch. These remarks are communicated to your Excellency with the knowledge of the junta in order that you may be be so kind as to present them to his Majesty at the same time as the *consulta*. May our Lord keep your Excellency's life many years. Madrid, April 6, 1804. Most excellent señor. Frey Francisco Gil. The most excellent señor, Don Pedro Ceballos. This is a copy with a rubric. It is a copy of the original which is in the secretariat under my charge and administration, to which I certify. New Orleans, September 10, 1804. Andrés López Armento. This is a copy. Chihuahua, April 22 [2?], 1805. Bernardo Villamil. This is a copy. Herrera.' "

403. The said Don Juan Cancelada assured me that these papers merited complete confidence, because they had been copied from good originals, and that they bore the signs of authenticity. The same Don Juan Cancelada in the *Gaceta de México* of Saturday, July 12, 1806, published the note with which the Señor Marquis of Casa Yrujo accompanied his circular letter to all the foreign ministers officially accredited to the government of the United States, and in it one reads that *"Louisiana was ceded to France upon the same terms* that France had ceded it to Spain."

404. On making the serious reflections that I should upon these papers, I found myself submerged in a great sea of confusion, and I shall not be able to come out of it without molesting your Excellency by presenting this *consulta* to you. If in the cited royal dispatch, in the proclamation of the Señores Salcedo and Casa Calvo, and in the note accompanying the circular letter of the Señor Marquis of Casa Yrujo,[38] it is asserted that Louisiana will be returned to France upon the same terms that France had ceded it to Spain, how can it be said in the confidential copy, "Our commissioners could maintain likewise that the new owners of Louisiana who may enter from the Mississippi to navigate along the Red River shall not be able to penetrate farther upstream than to the exact point where the dividing line that should pass between Los Adays and Nachitoches may cut the said river in the vicinity of this last post, and also that they shall not be able to claim the least right to the navigation of the Río Misuri, since it never had any connection with Louisiana?" For, in truth, France, throughout the period that she held Louisiana, from the time she took possession of it until she ceded it to Spain in 1762, considered as one of her possessions the whole of the Red or

---

[38]See *Pichardo's Treatise* . . . , Vol. I, p. 41, n. 1.

Nachitoches River and all the lands near it and near the Río Misuri from its entrance into the Mississippi to a place far above it. This is clearly shown from the *Historia General de los Viages* [*Histoire générale des voyages*] of Monsieur Prevost, from all the French books that treat of Louisiana, and even in the *Diccionario* [*Dictionnaire*] of Moréri[39] a place was given to an article that begins, "Misuri: A large river of Louisiana." The Spanish writers who treat of the same province admit openly that the Misuri belongs to Louisiana. Colonel Don Antonio de Alcedo in his *Diccionario Geográfico de America* did not forget to include the following article: "Misouri: A pueblo of Indians of the province and government of Louisiana, located on the bank of the river of their name, on which there is a fort built by the French for the defense of that settlement. The said river, which is large and carries much water, has its origin in New Mexico. It flows many leagues to the southeast and, changing its course later to the east, it enters the Mississippi. Its current is so swift that it seems incredible." And in addition to many other printed Spanish books, the many *autos, expedientes,* and papers which were delivered to me from your Excellency's secretariat and from one of the offices of the superior *gobierno y guerra,* at the request of the señor *fiscal,* for the discharge of this commission, testify to the same thing.

405. I do not believe that it was ignorance but rather excessive attention to what is said in the confidential copy, that led the Most Reverend Father Fray José María de Jesús Puelles, missionary religious of the province of Texas, to make a map of this province and of a part of Louisiana on which he proposed a dividing line for these provinces which, going from the Bayupier toward the northeast and passing through 286° 40′ of longitude and 34° 22′ of latitude, should end at the mouth of the Misuri, as he himself states in the following words in a letter addressed to an unknown person, which I found among the papers of the said Cancelada: "And if I conform to the common and ancient opinion, the said limits should be at the Bayuco Mermentao or on the Calcasiu. These limits will divide the land by means of a curved line drawn to the northwest as far as the Arroyo Hondo, and ascending from Nachitoches toward the north some twenty leagues, they will cut the Red River of the said post, which they mistakenly call the Río Colorado, by a diagonal line running northwest, which ends at the mouth of the Misuri."

406. By this line of the Most Reverend Puelles (since it cuts the river which the French call Le Rouge and which in Spanish is called Rojo [Red] or Colorado) the Cadodachos Indians would be wholly excluded from Louisiana, a fact which is entirely contrary to the undeniable possession which the French had of these Indians from the first days that they entered by way of the Mississippi into the lands which they called Louisiana. This is told not only by the same Frenchmen, but even by our Spaniards in the cited books and manuscripts, which are not recent and of these last days, but of an age contemporary with the first entrance of the French, as I show in my work by quoting them.

---

[39]See *Pichardo's Treatise* . . . , Vol. I, p. 153, n. 1.

407. But the French possessed not only the Cadodachos, but other Indians who are far to the west of them, such as are all the Panis and the Padoucas, who are the ones farthest west. This is clear from their writings and from our old documents prior to the cession of Louisiana to Spain. How many Frenchmen may still be living who were born in these French forts and settlements? And would not they and even the Indians themselves testify that those lands always belonged to France? Furthermore, in the royal dispatch it is ordered that the records and expense accounts shall be taken to Spain, except those which deal with limits, demarcations, posts, and Indian alliances, which will be delivered to the French governor. And may there not be in these papers some direct or indirect evidence that the French were owners of those lands? And will not the United States be able to use them as arguments?

408. It is also clear from the cited Prevost that from the Misuri toward the north the lands of the Sioux and other Indians were occupied by the French, and that at the order of Iberville, Monsieur Le Sueur founded a fort among these Indians in the year 1700 at latitude 43° 50′. It is deduced from all this that if a line is to be drawn in accordance with the documents we have, and which may be acceptable to the United States, I shall be forced to represent to your Excellency that what is stated in the confidential copy cannot be put into effect; on the contrary, it is certain that the work which is being expended in designating the limits according to its ideas will be fruitless. In order not to fall into these errors, and to establish a line which the United States must perforce accept, I adopted the dividing line which the French geographer, Monsieur D'Anville, placed on his map, drawn in 1746 at the order and expense of the learned Duke of Orleans. [I did so] first, because this line is entirely in accord with the papers that are found in your Excellency's secretariat, with the *autos* and *expendientes* which are in the said office of *gobierno,* and with the French writers; second, because D'Anville's map was copied by the English in 1752 with the same line, without the least alteration in its longitude and latitude, by which action the English showed that they were convinced that this line divided accurately the Spanish and French lands, since, although they corrected D'Anville's map along many other lines, they left this one unchanged; third, because when France ceded Louisiana to Spain, the Spanish geographer, Don Tomás López, copied only the portion of the same map of D'Anville which showed Louisiana, and he placed on it this inscription: *La Louisiana cedida á el Rey Nuestro Señor Por Su Magestad Christianisima . . . construida sobre el Mapa de Monsieur D'Anville. . . . En Madrid año de 1762* [*Louisiana. Ceded to the King, Our Lord, by His Most Christian Majesty. . . . Based on the Map of Monsieur D'Anville. Madrid, 1762*]. It is noted thereon that the Misouri and everything to the north, south, and west as far as the Paducas Indians, is shown among the lands of Louisiana. Therefore Don Tomás López recognized as belonging to Louisiana all the land which D'Anville attributes to it, and if this is an acknowledgment that it was ceded by France to Spain, it seems by logical inference that one must admit that Spain should return the same

to France. Fourth, [I adopted this line] because, as I have stated, it is in conformance with what the Spaniards and the French say; fifth, and last, because in the sixteen years that elapsed between 1746, when D'Anville drew his map, and 1762, when France ceded Louisiana to Spain, this line was not altered, as I prove in my work.

409. This line of D'Anville sets limits to the excessive claims of the United States, for since it continues as far as the pole, it should restrain them so that they may not go by way of the Columbia River as far as the Pacific Ocean and establish themselves on it, as in fact they have done, and have attempted to form such a settlement in these last years as is stated in some accounts published by them which I have before me, and which I shall give word for word in my work.

410. In this work, most excellent señor, I comply with the order of May 20, 1805, in which his Majesty requests that as many documents and historical and geographical accounts as possible be collected to prove the dates of our settlements at the various points of the Interior Provinces of New Spain, especially in the province of Texas and the adjoining coast, and that notes be extracted from them of everything of importance with reference to these settlements, together with the corresponding citations. [Pursuant to this order] I have assembled seventy-three documents, taken from the said papers of the secretariat of your Excellency and from the ministry of the superior government, and from many other manuscripts and published materials which my diligence, stimulated by zeal for the service of God, of the king, our lord, and of our country, has furnished me; and from almost the whole of four books, very rare, although printed, one in Italian, two in French, and the other in English, which I have translated from their own languages into Spanish. To all this I have added fifteen maps (after the date of this report others were added). The first fourteen are exact copies of the publications of D'Anville, of Don Tomás López, of Father Puelles, and of others, and the last was made by me in accordance with trustworthy accounts of which I availed myself. It is not added to the other maps, but is inserted in the work itself in the proper place. (Thus I had thought to do at that time, but later it seemed better to place it with the rest, and it is found as number 18 of document 74.)

411. This work is none other than the notes prescribed by the royal order and taken from the documents that I have collected and concerning which I have had the honor of reporting to your Excellency in my official letter of last January 27. These notes are divided into three parts. In the first I show with most forcible arguments that Spain was the legitimate, sole, and absolute owner of all the land on which the French founded Louisiana, and that consequently the latter acted with great injustice and iniquity in settling it when they discovered it. In the second I showed what the French took and what the piety of the Catholic King, in order to avoid wars and the effusion of human blood, permitted them (although with grief in his heart) to keep, and consequently the limits of the lands usurped and left to France by permission of the king of Spain were established. In the third the objec-

tions are removed which are raised against accepting these limits, alike on the part of the United States as well as on that of those Spaniards who consider them illegal and claim that they should be contracted, or who, because of not knowing them, wish to withdraw them on the one hand or extend them on the other, in contravention of the agreement between the two powers whereby Spain retrocedes precisely what was ceded her, without any addition or diminution.

(I had divided my work in this manner when I whote this *consulta*, but later, considering it most necessary to give a description of those lands, and noting that each one of these parts was becoming very long, I changed the division of them in the way that is seen in the work as a whole.)

412. The first of these three parts is entirely finished. The second is almost done, for of the twenty parts about eighteen are already written. The third is entirely lacking, but since the replies [to the objections] have been already prepared in what has been written, not much time will be needed for assembling it. Therefore at the latest I shall complete all of my work (as I have promised your Excellency) before the end of the next March. (I thought I could finish it in this manner; but the description of all the plains of Cíbola which I considered most! necessary and indispensable for a perfect understanding of everything relative to the demarcation of limits, and the insertion of many other accounts which I acquired later, have forced me, up to the present, to defer the fulfillment of my word.) For, aside from what I still have to write, I shall need to revise and correct my entire work which, in truth, is somewhat long. But circumstances and the material demanded this.

413. It seems, however, that I really should not continue until I know your Excellency's decision on the subject of my report, which is whether I should conform to that which was ordered in the confidential copy with regard to excluding the Misouri from the French possessions, and to cutting the Río Rojo de Nachitoches [Red River] by the dividing line, for according to D'Anville and the texts of the writers whom I have cited, this river not only cannot be cut there but it cannot even be cut in any other part, because its source is not beyond the line and limits which D'Anville prescribes. (When I wrote this report I did not yet know exactly where the Red River rises, but having now ascertained the place where its source is located, I must state that D'Anville's line cuts this river, as is seen on my map, at 82° of longitude [west] of the Island of Hierro. Nor should I have drawn my map or described the plains of Cíbola.) For by cutting it, the Indians living from the Cadodachos to the Padoucas would also be excluded from Louisiana. And if I do not cut this river or exclude the French from the Missouri, our government will perhaps look upon it unfavorably and consider me a criminal for not having obeyed its instructions and commands, which God forbid, for

I have the joy of counting myself among its most humble and obedient subjects.

414. Notwithstanding the fact that I am aware that my work is of no value and that nothing will be lost if it should fail, I shall continue it in accordance with the plan proposed of not cutting the Red River or excluding the Misouri from what should be ceded, so that in case it should be your Excellency's pleasure to order me to proceed according to this plan which I have begun, time may not be lost and delay may be avoided. Consequently, I beg your Excellency to be pleased to turn your attention for a moment from the very many and extremely important matters which are demanding it, and to grant it to me in order to command me what I ought to do. May God keep your Excellency's most important life the many years that I desire and that your Excellency deserves, for the good of this entire kingdom. Royal Congregation of the Oratory of San Felipe Neri of Mexico, February 8, 1811. José Antonio Pichardo. To the Most Excellent Señor Don Francisco Xavier Venegas.

415. His Excellency having received my report, he was pleased to send me the following official dispatch:

In order to resolve with certainty the doubts which your honor presents to me in your official dispatch of the 8th of this month with regard to fixing the correct ancient limits of the province of Texas, the commission for which is in your charge, it is necessary for your honor to report to the señores *fiscales* orally, agreeing on the days and hours that may be most convenient, in order that, being informed concerning the documents which your honor cites, they may recommend to me the proper decision in this serious and delicate matter. God keep your honor many years. Mexico, February 21, 1811. Venegas. To Señor Don José Antonio Pichardo.

416. The señores *fiscales,* Don Ambrosio Sagarzurrieta and Don Francisco Robledo de Alburquerque, after our conferences replied as follows to his Excellency:

Most excellent señor: The royal treasury and civil *fiscales* state that they have conferred with the father commissioner, Don José Antonio Pichardo, and have seen the drafts, documents, books, and part of the work which has been done on the limits of Louisiana and Texas, and as a result they have formed the same opinion as the said father, of its being impossible to support by title of possession the dividing line designated in the confidential royal order of April 6, 1804, which leaves as possessions of Spain the territories of the Cadodachos Indians, of the Panis, of the Paducas, of the Sioux, and the others which, it seems, the French possessed. In the opinion of the *fiscales,* the dividing line traced in the said royal order is more a project of the claims or desires of our court than a definite admitted fact of which our commissioners must not lose sight in the demarcation of limits, for they

are told to conform to it in their claims unless the commissioners of the
other contracting party shall show authentically that France may have had
permanent settlements in the area lying between Texas, the west banks of
the Red and Mississippi rivers, and the sea coast, aside from the post of
Nachitoches and any other point of lesser importance on the banks of the
Red River.

417. But be this as it may, since Father Pichardo's commission ends with
the collection of all available documents and historical and geographical
accounts to prove the dates of our settlements at the various points of the
Interior Provinces of New Spain and especially in the province of Texas
and along the adjacent coast, and with taking notes of everything of importance with reference to them, this is the thing that should be borne in mind,
even though the result may not be as favorable as we might wish to the
project or plan of limits of the cited royal order. The *fiscales* have seen
with pleasure the many papers, books, and reports which Father Pichardo has
collected in the fulfillment of his commission, as well as the care, diligence,
and industry displayed in his work. And although his dividing line, which
is the same one that the French geographer, Monsieur D'Anville, places on his
map, drawn in the year 1746 at the order and expense of the Duke of Orleans,
greatly curtails on the west and northwest the lands which the other line of
the royal order granted us, in spite of all this, if the former is extended
to the pole, we shall succeed in turning the Anglo-Americans away from the
northwest coast of America, the region to which they are chiefly directing
their designs. This could be very prejudicial to us.

418. From the conferences with Father Pichardo the *fiscales* have learned
that he had no account of the disputes which occurred in the year 1763
between the Chevalier Macarti, the governor of the French presidio of
Natchitoches, and Don Ángel de Martos y Navarrete, governor of the Spanish
presidio of Los Adaes, concerning the freedom of an Indian woman and
control over the Tuacana, or Tehuacana, located north of the Río Misuri
[?] at the headwaters of the Sabinas, about sixty leagues distant. The
originals of these should be in the Secretaría de Cámara of this viceroyalty
and copies of them in volume one of the late Señor Brigadier Bonilla's
[documents concerning] Texas, from which the *fiscal* of the royal treasury
took an extract. They contribute greatly to showing not only that the lands
of the Tuacanas Indians, included by D'Anville in Louisiana, were owned
by Spain as part of the province of Texas in the said year of '63, our flag
having been placed in their pueblo long before that—or at least to making
the possession of the French doubtful and contentious, they having also
placed their flag there, although seemingly clandestinely—but also they indicate that the dominion of the French over the pueblo of the Cadodachos
was uncertain, for in order to go to it from Nachitoches they obtained permission and a passport from our governors of Texas.

(I did not, in fact, have the slightest information about the disputes between Monsieur Macarti and Señor Martos. But the widow

of the Señor Brigadier Bonilla placed in my hands the volume which the señor *fiscal* cites here, and I took from it the copy which I have given above, beginning with paragraph 164. The disputes over the freedom of the captive Indian woman do not supply anything in particular with regard to limits, and the things which are given concerning the Tuacanas are sufficiently well presented in the copies. For this reason and for the sake of brevity I omitted them.)

It is important, then, to find this *expediente* in the secretariat and send it on to the said father commissioner, and likewise the catalogue of the papers which were sent to the commandancy-general of the Interior Provinces when their independence of this viceroyalty was declared, in order that he may make use of their contents and notify your Excellency of those which he may see fit to request from the said commandancy. It also will be well for your Excellency to issue an official letter to the widow of Brigadier Bonilla, which may be given to Father Pichardo, requesting her to permit him to examine the papers of her late husband relating to the Interior Provinces, and make certified copies of what he may consider conducive to ascertaining their limits with Louisiana.

(The most excellent señor viceroy saw fit to accede to this request of the señores *fiscales,* as is shown by the following official letter which he addressed to me: "To the Señora Doña Manuela de Torres, widow of the Señor Brigadier Don Antonio Bonilla, I am sending under this date the following: 'Since Father Don José Antonio Pichardo is commissioned to ascertain the true ancient limits of the provinces of Texas and Louisiana, and since I have information that among the papers left by your ladyship's husband, the Señor Brigadier Don Antonio Bonilla, there are some maps, drafts, and other documents that may facilitate that work, I charge your ladyship to show them to the said father commissioner in order that he may obtain the copies conducive to the said purpose.' I am enclosing it to your honor for your information and guidance. May God keep your honor many years. Mexico, September 6, 1811. Venegas. To Father Don José Antonio Pichardo.")

419. Father Pichardo has made only informal copies of the confirmatory documents to which he refers in his work, but it is necessary that certified copies be made in authentic form so that they may be attested.

(As I intended the copies which I have taken from the originals only for rough drafts, because with the constant use that I was to make of them in the composition of my work they would necessarily be greatly maltreated, I made them on ordinary paper and full of corrections, always postponing the making of copies on stamped paper, legalized by notaries, in order that they may be certified as the royal order of May 20, 1805, commands, and as the señores *fiscales* here request.)

Your Excellency therefore will be pleased to order that he be sent the necessary stamped paper and that as soon as the said documents have been certified by one of the notaries public of the government, they may be legalized thereafter by three others, the said father commissioner being instructed that each document shall be sent by itself and separated from the rest, in order that our court may make use of and show to the Anglo-American commissioners the ones that it may consider favorable to our claims, and set aside the others.

420. The *fiscales* are reproducing the principles, maxims, and considerations which the *fiscal* of the royal treasury expressed while he was civil *fiscal*, in a reply of July 25, 1807, in these terms: "According to natural and international law, that which does not belong to anyone becomes the property of the first one who occupies it. It is also accepted among civilized nations that any of them may establish itself and make itself owner of the regions of America which either have not been completely occupied or have been occupied only by wandering tribes of savage Indians who do not have a fixed abode, travel from place to place, and do not remain in any place except so long as it supplies them with game and fish. Therefore, the European nation which may prove that it was the first to discover and occupy any such region with the intention of acquiring it for itself, will be its legitimate owner, even though it may not have made any permanent settlement there, for no law imposes this requirement, but simply that of occupation. Much less should such a requirement be exacted of a nation which already has settlements nearby from which it exercises its rights of dominion over the newly-occupied country. This is the situation in which Spain finds herself with respect to her discoveries in Texas, Louisiana, and New Mexico, of which she was the first discoverer, after she had extensive settlements in this New Spain. From here she has continued to exercise her rights of exploring the new discoveries and improving them, by sending missionaries for the reduction and conversion of the Indians, offering them our friendship and protection, which they have accepted, and by performing other similar acts.

421. If later the French intruded upon us in what is called Louisiana, this was a usurpation which Spain always opposed; of this the *fiscal* has seen authentic proof. That is why our court never has been willing to accede to the requests or reports of this government with regard to fixing the limits

between that province and Texas, believing wisely that by this step it would recognize the possession of France as legitimate. According to some publicists, and especially the celebrated Samuel Cocceji, international law does not recognize prescription no matter how ancient, as a method of acquiring possession, and although others, including Grotius, accept it, it is not by virtue only of prescription or lapse of time, but because of the presumed abandonment of the things that may be assumed on the part of him who sees it in the possession of someone else, and does not oppose it within a certain time. International law being, therefore, the vehicle by which disputes between nations should be settled, and Spain having protested against the usurpation of Louisiana by France, the rights of the former to this entire province are still very strong in spite of our retrocession to France and the sale by the latter to the United States of America. For France, in the cession she made to us, gave us only what she had, that is, a litigious possession, and when we lately receded it to her, we gave her the same that she gave us and nothing more, for that is what retrocession means. Consequently we can continue our ancient right and our claims. And now that Spain reconciles herself to recognizing the dominion of the United States as legitimate, it will be only reasonable that the latter come to an agreement with us on the point of limits, especially at those places concerning which there may be some doubt, such as Bayou Pierre and Cadodachos.

422. The authentic evidence which is mentioned in the transcribed paragraphs of the cited reply of the *fiscal*, is found among other royal orders and cedulas of which Father Pichardo has copies, [and in] a royal cedula that he lacks, which is found in the *cedularios* of the royal audiencia and is dated in Buenretiro on February 7, 1756, providing that the Indians of America who are not cannibals, shall not suffer enslavement, particularly those of New Orleans and other places occupied by the French in that region, in as much as the contrary has never been admitted, nor has the usurpation of this country been assented to. On the contrary it has been vigorously opposed. Your Excellency will be pleased to send an official dispatch to the said royal audiencia in order that it may remit a certified copy in quadruplicate of this sovereign order. One of them may be sent to the father commissioner (his Excellency was pleased to order that a legal copy of this cedula be sent to me and it was precisely the one that has been inserted above, in paragraph 227), who may be informed of the measures of your Excellency with a copy of this reply if they be in accord with it, in order that they may serve to guide him and so that, by an appendix to his work or in whatever manner he may see fit, he may improve it with the new evidence and documents thus obtained. When his commission has been fulfilled, your Excellency will be pleased to send a report, together with his work, to the supreme government of the capital of Spain, commending the merit, zeal, and assiduous diligence of the said father, for the remuneration that it may be pleased to grant. Mexico, March 14, 1811. As the señores *fiscales* request. Venegas. This is a copy. Mexico. April 2, 1811. Velázquez.

423. His Excellency was pleased to order a copy signed by his secretary to be placed in my hands, together with the following official dispatch:

In view of what your reverence stated in a paper of February 8, last, concerning the limits of the province of Texas, the señores *fiscales* have drawn up the recommendation which is shown in the enclosed copy, and since it has merited my approbation, I am informing your reverence of it, sending along a certified copy of the royal cedula mentioned, so that with this new evidence and the others that your reverence's zeal and assiduous diligence may obtain, you may improve your work in the manner that has been proposed. In view of this I shall recommend it to the supreme government of our nation, as is proper. God keep your reverence many years. Mexico, April 2, 1811. Venegas. To the Reverend Father Don José Antonio Pichardo.

424. As a result of this official dispatch of the most excellent señor viceroy, the French kept that part of the Misuri which belongs to them, from the place where D'Anville's line cuts it, which is in the 85th degree of longitude, to its mouth, as we have ascertained in Part III, beginning with paragraph 371.

425. The Very Reverend Father Doctor Fray Melchor Talamantes y Baeza, in drawing his dividing line, fell into the same error into which Señor Martos and the Most Reverend Father Puelles fell when they drew theirs. Father Talamantes describes his line in his second treatise, entitled *Nota Instructiva*, number 30, speaking thus:

Description of the limits of the province of Texas and the other dominions of his Majesty in Spanish North America. It is not beside the question to note here that the differences over the limits of these two provinces have arisen from the fact that since they narrowed too much toward the Gulf of Mexico, the extent of Louisiana toward the south and west was very small, while on the other hand the extent of its territory above the presidios of Adaes and Nachitoches was remarkably broad, and those points not being important for navigation, no dispute has ever arisen over setting the boundaries beyond that latitude. Nevertheless, since the settlement of the French in Louisiana was due in large measure to the generous condescension and tolerance of Spain and to her relations with the French House of Bourbon from which she could not extricate herself, the French always restricted themselves to those limits which Spain herself wished to prescribe for them. However, they [the French] made several attempts to push them [the Spaniards] back on the west either by means of hostilities committed in the province [of Texas] in the year 1719, which were entirely thwarted in 1721, or by the moderate and crafty means to which they resorted thereafter, which proved their timidity and lack of confidence in their own cause.

426. In the meanwhile Spain with the authority, decisiveness, and intrepidity of a legitimate owner, always checked foreign invasions, obstructed with repeated measures the attempts that were made to introduce clandestine trade, to the detriment of national industry, built forts in the most remote parts of the province, ignored as unfounded the complaints that were directed to her by several governors of Louisiana, and remained unmistakably in possession of that whole country to where it touches the line formed by the arc of the meridian that runs from the Gulf of Mexico to the presidio and mission of Los Adaes, crossing the Arroyo Hondo and La Gran Montaña, located between the said presidio and the French fort of Natchitoches.

427. The numerous *expedientes* and documents of all kinds that exist in the archives of New Spain relative to the said presidio and mission of Los Adaes, clearly prove the uninterrupted possession of Spain over that territory, her tenacious opposition to the French penetrating by way of that region, and the fact that the authentic exploration of France never went beyond the said line. If later, in 1773, it was necessary to suppress that presidio, it was due to the fact that after Louisiana had passed into the possession of Spain, it was unnecessary to continue expenditures at a place that was in itself defended and where the mission was absolutely useless because of failure to assemble the Indians. From the beginning there was something of inconsideration and heedlessness in this measure which it is beside the point to discuss. What is more important to know is the substance of the act, of which, as well as of everything that has been stated, there are in these archives the least equivocal proofs that could be desired. And it would not be amiss if, for the greater satisfaction of the United States and in order to show more clearly Spain's honor, frankness, and sincerity, Spain would permit the Congress of that nation to name a commissioner who in company with one commissioned by the superior government of Mexico, might examine the said originals in these archives.

428. Under this plan the first dividing line that should be established is the same one that has been put aside, namely, the one formed by the arc of the meridian that runs from the Gulf of Mexico to La Gran Montaña, located between the two said presidios, crossing the Arroyo Hondo and the Spanish lake of Los Adaes, and leaving the presidio of Nachitoches to the east and both banks of the Río de Sabinas on the west. The length of this line will be about two degrees and forty-five minutes, and the shortest distance from it to the east bank of the same Río de Sabinas or to its mouth in the Gulf about seven common Spanish leagues (A).

429. This first step should not involve any difficulty whatever (B), for any resistance that the Anglo-Americans may offer can be based only on ignorance of our rights, clearly shown in the documents cited and by a peaceful and uninterrupted possession. This is not the case with regard to the dividing line that should run beyond Los Adaes. Here one must confess frankly that everything is doubtful and uncertain, and that since we did not make any settlements on that side, beyond the said latitude, neither can any documents exist in these archives which would prove our claims (C). The French,

on the contrary, availing themselves of our omissions and of the misfortune which befell one of our missionaries (D), founded in 1717 the presidio and mission of Los Caodachos, or Caddodachos, on the south bank of the Río de los Nachitoches, penetrating too far to the west-northwest of Los Adaes, and since there was no pronounced resistance on our part and they consequently remained in possession of that land for a long time, it would be a matter of no little difficulty to deprive the Anglo-Americans of it if, knowing of this occurrence, they should wish to support their claims on the basis of that point.

430. A stream with the name of Bayupier, which empties into the Río de Nachitoches, also flows four leagues north of the lake of Los Adaes, following through a large part of its course a west to east direction. The Anglo-Americans affirm that it has belonged to France. It may be that the basis for this assertion is the fact that in Louisiana there is another stream of the same name which, following a direction of north-northwest and south-southwest, crosses a small lake and empties into the Mississippi from the east side at latitude 31° 58'. This being true, it will be easy to prove that the identity of the name signifies nothing in the present case, for in as much as the said stream is not found on the old maps under that name, it is to be believed that it might have taken it after Louisiana passed under Spanish domination (E).

431. If our reflections on this point result favorably (F) and the Anglo-Americans do not insist on maintaining their rights over the land of the Cadodachos, which begins a short distance from the Arroyo de Bayupier, it seems that the second dividing line should be a continuation of the first, crossing the said stream (G) and the Río de Natchitoches [Red River] along the same meridian, until it ends at the Acansas, which flows a short distance from the latter and parallel to it. But since it is not to be expected that disputants who are so clever may be willing to concede us this advantage, we should insist as a last recourse that the first dividing line terminate at the same Arroyo Bayupier, which would serve as a second dividing line along its entire course, and that the third line shall run from the sourse of the latter, perferably in a curve ending at the confluence of the two branches of the Natchitoches [Red] at latitude 34° 5', enclosing our possessions on its convex side and excluding from them on its concave side the land of the Cadodachos (H).

432. Up to now, nothing will have been achieved if, neglecting the present circumstances, we do not take advantage of them to fix the limits of New Mexico and to determine the extent of our possessions in North America. Since New Mexico is unprotected on the east and north and our limits until now are undetermined, and since we have no settlements of any importance there, we would always be in danger of new disputes. The northwest coast of America, to which the Americans are today directing their schemes, would be at their disposal to the detriment not only of our nation but also of the French, the English, and the Russians, who have settlements in that region. And after the Anglo-Americans had made themselves masters of the fur trade and of the commerce of India, and had allied themselves, moreover, with

the barbarous nations of the north, they would in time become our most dreaded neighbors if indeed they did not declare themselves our formidable enemies.

433. All this can be prevented with three dividing lines: First, the arc of the meridian which runs from the confluence of the two branches of the Nachitoches [Red] to the Río de Acanzas; second, a line drawn along the center of this river throughout its entire course to its source, which is at the foot of the mountains which are north of Santa Fé in New Mexico; and [third] this point being fixed, along the arc of the meridian that extends from there indefinitely toward the north pole (I). This division having been made, on the east side there will remain in the possession of the Americans an extremely vast territory of which they could not be the possessors without breaking the limits fixed by France in the treaty of 1783, and as a result their possessions will be greatly increased by this new agreement.

(Here Father Talamantes places a marginal note which states: "See the Appendix." And, indeed, he did add an appendix to his *Nota Instructiva*, which we give along with it in the same second treatise.) (J).

434. In former times it was thought necessary to resort to the Holy See in order to terminate, by means of a dividing line, the heated disputes between the Spaniards and the Portuguese concerning the limits of their conquests. At the present time, in a case so urgent as that, the agreement of both [contending] nations will suffice. Accordingly, it appears that we ought to make common cause with the Russians, the English, and the French, whom our proposal should interest equally: The first, because of the Alaskan Peninsula, which they possess along with all the Kuriles; the second, because of the territory of Nootka, quite near the [bay of] Etzeta [Hezeta], called by the Anglo-Americans Columbia, where they have penetrated recently on the last navigation made up the Misuri; and the last because of El Puerto Francés [Port des Français] which Monsieur de la Perouse discovered and took possession of in the name of France. Without this measure, which will establish our rights irrevocably, it will be useless in the future for us to cite our expeditions into those northern regions, the apostolic travels of our missionaries, our prior discoveries, the navigations along the Misuri, and even the demarcation of those points. For since we have not made any settlement there up to the present and since therefore those regions must be regarded as abandoned, such arguments cannot have much weight in the balance of critical examination and in view of the present relations among nations.

435. It will not be beside the point for us to recall here, by way of warning and precaution, England's conduct toward France with regard to the limits of Acadia. It is very well known that this matter was never settled in spite of the commissioners who were designated for that purpose; that while the question was being discussed the English made settlements in the French part, greatly harassed the individuals of this nation, and succeeded finally

in the Peace of 1763 in making the king of France, forced by the circumstances in which he found himself, cede to England all his rights to Acadia, Canada, the island of Cape Breton, and all the islands of the gulf and river of Saint Lawrence. Such was the result of that discussion which had its origin in 1713. It is therefore greatly to be feared that the English, who do not know any limits to their ambition and bad faith, also may not wish to know them with regard to their possessions, and that if Spain does not avail herself promptly of the means that are presenting themselves to her, she will find herself in time despoiled of the province of Texas and will open the doors of her most precious dominions to restless and turbulent neighbors who, because of their ambitious schemes, are entirely too formidable.

436. The appendix to which Father Talamantes refers in the marginal note is of the following tenor:

After the present work was finished and presented to the superior government of Mexico, there reached my hands a copy of the report of the Junta de Fortificaciones y Defensa de Indias to the señor generalissimo, the Prince of the Peace, who condescended to approve it, as is shown by the official dispatch which the most excellent señor, Don Frey Francisco Gil y Lemus, sent to the most excellent señor, Don Pedro Ceballos, on April 6, 1804. (This is the confidential royal order of which we have spoken above.) His Majesty directed that this be carried out in the royal order of the 17th of the same month and year.

437. It is provided therein, among other things, that the Anglo-Americans cannot claim the least right to the navigation of the Río Misuri, since it was never connected with Louisiana. This well-founded decision has the additional basis of being a result of what had been agreed upon between France and the United States in the treaty of 1783 with regard to the dividing line that should bound the possessions of the said States on the west, and of being entirely in accord with article four of the treaty of the same States with Spain, of October 27, 1795, in which the limits of that power are fixed in the channel or bed of the Mississippi.

438. The navigation of the Río Misuri, frequently practiced in other times by the French who penetrated by way of it about 1,300 miles (we have already stated that the French made themselves masters of the Misuri and possessed it until the cession of Louisiana), and recently by the Anglo-Americans, has always had as its object their settling on the northwest coast of America in order to make trade with India more easy and lucrative. What the former could not bring about the latter have begun to succeed in, having on the last famous voyage made by way of the Misuri (K), turned away from this river in the vicinity of its source in order to continue by way of the Columbia which empties into the South Sea at about the latitude of 43°, in the bay of the same name.

439. Even if this bay had not been, as in fact it was, discovered and explored by our people, who gave it the name of Eceta [Hezeta], the authentic

declaration of England in the treaty of limits of Nootka is sufficient to prevent the Americans being able to establish the least claim upon it. In this treaty it was agreed that the coast above this point should be open to the settlements that England and the other nations could make, without excluding Spain herself, and the entire lower coast was recognized as belonging to the Spanish dominions.

440. It is therefore evident that any claim of the Anglo-Americans on the Río Misuri and their new designs to establish themselves on the coast of America below Nootka are extravagant not only because the Misuri has never belonged to Louisiana, but also because they exceed considerably the limits previously fixed by Spain and France and because it is a violation of the rights of Spain over this part of the coast, authentically recognized by England. Nevertheless, it is necessary to confess that the Río Misuri is far away from our last settlements and that since it is almost impossible to check the navigation of it, the Anglo-Americans can frequent it whenever they wish without our even knowing it. When the French have penetrated many times by way of the Nachitoches [Red River], very far below that river, when they did the same thing on the Acanzas, the English being no less daring in these undertakings, who will be able to keep the latter from navigating the Misuri, by means of which, because of its proximity to their dominions, incursions are very easy for them, without fear of being observed or taken by surprise?

441. Aside from this security, they have the inducement that the greater part of the numerous barbarian nations that inhabit the banks of the Misuri, attracted by trade and by gifts, maintain a close alliance with them, in which a certain conformity to their customs, which many of the Anglo-Americans do not disdain, is also influential. With such opportunities it will not be strange if they found settlements in the places that they wish, if they erect forts wherever it may be most convenient for them, if also they can do both in the land lying between the Misuri and the Río Acanzas, and if news of all this should reach us very late and when the evil may perhaps be irremediable (L).

442. Our position with regard to the Misuri and the land intervening between this river and the Acanzas is entirely opposite. The great distance at which these points are located, the little or no trade with the barbarians who inhabit them, the alliance which the latter maintain with our rivals, the excellent supply of firearms they have from this source, which they manage skilfully, and the difficulty inherent in the temperament and religion of the Spaniards for adapting themselves to the barbarous customs of those people, will always be strong reasons for our expeditions being most laborious, expensive, and dangerous; our fortifications, after causing enormous expenditures, being indefensible; [and] the settlements we may establish being left at the mercy of the barbarians, without our being able to furnish them the least aid except very belatedly and at the cost of innumerable anxieties and expenditures. Meanwhile, Spanish honor is ridiculed, our nation is incapable

of justly sustaining her rights, and our neighbors are in a better position to violate them (M).

443. Under such circumstances prudence seems to dictate that we should try to obtain the greatest advantage out of the difficulty of our position and that we should be somewhat generous and indulgent (N), before finding ourselves obliged to yield later to necessity and force. What interests us most is to cut off the Anglo-Americans from all communication with the northwest coast of America, which end may be attained by the dividing line proposed in the foregoing plan (that is, in the *Nota Instructiva* or second treatise). This is along the arc of the meridian running from the source of the Río Acanzas to the North Pole, and since by this means the navigation along the Misuri directed to making settlements on the said coast will become useless, they should be less frequent in the future and not at all prejudicial to us (O).

444. The advantage that results from the other two dividing lines proposed in the same plan, one that would run along the middle of the Río Acanzas from its source, and the other described by the arc of the meridian which runs from this river to the confluence of the two branches of the Nachitoches, or Colorado [Red River], is to give our possessions a fixed and known boundary, for lack of which foreigners have at various times taken the liberty of introducing themselves into our lands. The boundary established by those two lines, although somewhat contracted, is capable of defense, for which suitable points may be selected for dominating the rivers and checking any incursion, by means of fortifications distributed in adequate places, such as those that I have already indicated to the commandant-general of the Interior Provinces of this America in my official letter of June 3 of the current year, in order that he might propose them to his Majesty (P). The four points mentioned therein, namely, that of Los Adaes, that of the confluence of the two branches of the Natchitoches, the place on the Río Acanzas at which the arc of the meridian that begins at the preceding point terminates, and the one at the source of the same Río Acanzas, are four commanding sites that can mutually succor each other by water or by short overland journeys, give each other prompt reports, and the last of them can be aided without delay by reinforcements which should always be at Santa Fé in New Mexico (Q).

445. It is not necessary, because of this, that Spain should immediately cede (R) to the United States the extensive area which lies between my last dividing line and the west bank of the Mississippi, and between the banks of the Misuri and Acanzas rivers. Indeed, three articles may be proposed to safeguard the titles of Spain without depriving the United States of all recourse: First, that it be expressly declared that the said territory can never be regarded as belonging to Louisiana; second, that in the settlements that may be made in this area, Spain shall always keep the right of preference; third, that no foreign settlement that may be made in the future on the same territory may be used as a basis for the right of possession if previously the consent of Spain may not have been obtained and she may

not have declared that such a settlement would not prejudice her true interests.

446. It may be that by these means the intentions of his Majesty in the royal order cited, resulting from the wise report of the Junta de Fortificaciones, can be reconciled with the plan of limits proposed in the present work, which has been formed with the sole purpose of contributing in some way to the welfare of the monarchy and the greater service of the king, our lord. But if these ends, so important, can be attained, as is possible, through other means and measures, more judicious and superior to my plans, the small work that I have undertaken will always have the glory of being a testimonial of my fidelity to and love for my sovereign. Mexico, June 28, 1807. Fray Melchor de Talamantes.

NOTES

447. (A). Since not all geographers agree in giving to places the same longitude and latitude, there is a great difference on the maps in the distance from the coast to the Arroyo Hondo. On our map this distance, which Father Talamantes gives as 2° 45', does not exceed 2° 15', because we place Los Adaes, as did D'Anville, at 31° 40' of latitude and 76° of longitude, and the coast at this meridian is found at 29° 27'. Taking the smaller number from the larger, we shall have 2° 13', and thus the Arroyo Hondo at the most is the said 2° 15' from the coast, because it is found very near Los Adaes. The difference of two minutes makes it evident that the point on the coast through which the meridian of the Arroyo Hondo passes, is a little farther north than the preceding one, and that the point on the Arroyo Hondo at which we have ended our measurement is found likewise a little above the parallel of Los Adaes. It may be that Father Talamantes used some map which located Los Adaes at 32 degrees of latitude, a few minutes more or less. As for what he says to the effect that the shortest distance from his line to the entrance of the Río de Sabinas into the Gulf of Mexico will be about seven common Spanish leagues, he is badly mistaken, for the point on the coast where he begins his line is found at 75° 53' of longitude, and the mouth of the Río de Sabinas is seen at 77° 38'. Taking the smaller from the larger number, the remainder is 1° 45'. This consists of much more than seven common Spanish leagues, since they are counted as 26⅗, or at 17½ to the degree.

448. (B). This does indeed occasion some difficulty for Spain, because it takes from her the territory between the beginning of

her line on the coast and the Cabo del Norte, which is no less than 38 minutes; for, by taking the longitude of the Cabo del Norte, which is 75° 15′ from that of 75° 53′ at which the line begins, we find 38 minutes in the remainder. Therefore this line is not admissible since it takes from Spain all the land from it as far as the Cabo del Norte and D'Anville's line.

449. (C). But D'Anville eliminated all these doubts and uncertainties with his line.

450. (D). I do not know to which history he is referring in which this misfortune is discussed. What I do know is that Father Espinosa writes as follows in his *Chrónica*, book 5, chapter 17, page 541:

> In this same year [17]18, the Reverend Father Fray Matías Sans [Sáenz][40] de San Antonio went to Mexico and represented to the señor viceroy in the name of the two colleges the manifest risk that he ran of losing that province because of the proximity of the French, who were continuing to penetrate with new settlements and who had a fortification with many people and arms on the Río de los Cadodachos; and a report had been received that they were proceeding to settle in large numbers on both banks of the Palizada, etc.

451. (E). In my opinion Father Talamantes wrongs the Anglo-Americans greatly by imagining that the Bayupier which flows into the Mississippi from the east side, as seen on the map published by La Fon, gives them an occasion and pretext to claim as theirs the other Bayupier which is located west of the Red River. They do not base their claims on this extremely weak argument but they have others, among them those presented above by Doctor Sibley, in Part III, beginning with paragraph 702. But we attempted to show at the same place that in spite of the arguments of Doctor Sibley, that land belongs to Spain.

452. (C). The señores *fiscales*, Don Ambrosio Sagarzurrieta and Don Francisco Robledo de Alburquerque, as ministers of such great talent and so much wisdom, understood very well the commission which was given to Father Talamantes and to me. For that reason they wrote the following in their reply, copied above in paragraph 417:

> But be this as it may, since Father Pichardo's commission ends with the collection of all available documents and historical and geographical accounts

---

[40]See *Pichardo's Treatise* . . . , Vol. III, p. 497, n. 23.

to prove the dates of our settlements at the various points of the Interior Provinces of New Spain and especially in the province of Texas and along the adjacent coast, and with taking notes of everything of importance with reference to them, this is the thing that should be borne in mind even though the result may not be as favorable as we might wish to the project or plan of limits of the cited royal order.

Therefore, if the commission of Father Talamantes and myself consists solely in collecting all possible documents and historical and geographical reports, etc., and if I cannot trespass or go beyond the limit of collecting documents, etc., then Father Talamantes, who went beyond this limit and set himself up as an arbitral judge between the Spanish and Anglo-American nations, exceeded the purpose of his commission in attempting by his comments to draw his dividing line. In fact, this commissioner religious, forgetful of his duty, in making some notes on the demarcation of limits, taken from authentic documents, constituted himself an arbitral judge between Spain and the Anglo-Americans, and with arguments which seemed to him forceful and worthy of being heard and put into effect, he attempted to persuade the two nations that they could accept the dividing line that he was drawing for them. But, in truth, Spain did not give him any authority to draw a line, but only to show what line could be deduced from authentic documents. As far as I am concerned, I cannot be accused of having drawn a line, for the one that I am proposing is not drawn by me but is presented as an authentic document drawn up by the French themselves, who for that reason must accept it. All the notes that I have taken from the other documents have no other purpose than that of confirming this line and showing by means of each one of the points of which it consists how much the French appropriated.

453. When documents are presented to the opposing party which show them clearly how far their claims should reach, they must necessarily be convinced, and should not be heard no matter how much they may insist with futile arguments that they be given more than is just. Consequently, no matter how much the United States may persist in maintaining their claims over the land of the Cadodachos which begins a short distance from the Arroyo Bayupier, they should not be heard just because of the reflections of Father Talamantes, reflections which can have no good result

because they are misguided and without substance, since they have
no other foundation than that there is a Bayupier east of the
Mississippi, that it belonged indisputably to the French, and that
because of the identity of names and the one located west of the
Red River belongs to them.

454. (G). Father Talamantes, it seems, did not know the location of Bayupier very well. He here believes it to be just north
of the Arroyo Hondo since his first line, which runs through the
Arroyo Hondo, crosses the Bayupier at the same meridian as it
does the Arroyo Hondo. But we have seen in Part III, paragraph
701, and we see even more clearly on La Fon's map, that the
Bayupier falls west not only of the meridian of the Arroyo Hondo,
but even of the meridian of Los Adaes, which is west of the Arroyo
Hondo. Consequently, the first line cannot cross the Bayupier.
With this second line Father Talamantes claimed that the Bayupier should belong to Spain and to the United States, the east
side as cut by the line falling to the latter and the west side to
Spain.

455. (H). Under the false supposition that the Bayupier is north
of the Arroyo Hondo and that the meridian or line which passes
through the latter must cross the Bayupier, he now proposes definitely and as an arbitral judge that the line which passes through
the Arroyo Hondo should end and stop on the south bank of the
Bayupier (as if the Anglo-Americans were so covetous of the waters
of the Bayupier that they would not consent to the dividing line
cutting them and leaving them only a fragment of the small region
which is to the north of it and which would be cut by the line).
Therefore the first line which began on the coast and passed
through the Arroyo Hondo should continue along the same meridian to the south bank of the Bayupier. From this point it should
continue west along the same south bank until it touches the west
bank of the same Bayupier. This is the one which he calls the
second line. And he says that on the said bank another line begins, which is the third, and should be curved and end at the
confluence of the two branches of the Nachitoches [Red River],
that is, at the place where that other river, which comes down
from the north and rises on our map at 36° of latitude and 77°
of longitude, joins the Red River. This place is in 34° 18′ of

latitude (Father Talamantes places it in 34° 5′) and 75° 21′ of longitude. Hence at this same confluence Father Talamantes' line cuts the line of Señor Martos, because the two meet there. We remember this river which comes down from the north, in the route of Hernando de Soto. See Part II, paragraph 1564, where we said the following:

> On Michel's map we see a river coming down from the north (where it rises at about 36° of latitude and 95° of longitude west of London . . .) which joins the Red River. For this reason some might believe that it is the Red itself, from its source, and although it is not named on this map, it is given an inscription that says *Salinas.* . . .

456. (I). Here the said father commissioner proposes three other lines. The first begins at the said confluence of the river which comes down from the north with the Red, which is, as we have noted, where his line cuts that of Señor Martos; and it continues along the same meridian as far as the middle of· the Río Acanzas, whence it no longer continues north but turns (and becomes the second line) from this point west, continuing along the center of the said river to its source, where it ends. In this manner the Río Acanzas is divided into two parts. All the southern part would belong to Spain and all the northern to the United States. At the source of the Río Acanzas begins the third line, which continues along the meridian of this source to the pole. By these lines the lands of the United States, which are those that fall toward the east, are separated from those of Spain, which fall toward the west. The result of all this is that Father Talamantes' line is composed of six parts. We have tried to picture it just as he describes it in the cases where it has been possible for us to do so, for in one case it has been entirely impossible for us. This is the section of the line which, coming from the Arroyo Hondo, should end in the Bayupier and from here continue west along the southern bank, for, as we have said, since the Bayupier is not in the same meridian as the Arroyo Hondo, it cannot be drawn as Father Talamantes desires. Our Bayupier falls northwest of the Arroyo Hondo. Therefore the line that passes through this stream would turn northwest until encountering the Bayupier.

457. (J). Here we have Father Talamantes as arbitral judge making new commitments and greatly increasing the possessions

of the United States. Did Spain perchance give him the authority
to alienate her lands and to give them to the United States? If
France did not cede these very extensive lands to Spain, why should
she have to recede them for the benefit of the United States?

458. (K). We have spoken of this famous expedition, which is
that of Monsieur Meriwether Lewis, in Part III, beginning with
paragraph 632, and we have even given an account of it.

459. (L). But if Spain should build two presidios, one on the
Río Acanzas and the other on the Misuri, at the places where
D'Anville's line cuts them, or if some landmarks should be placed
there, what Father Talamantes here fears will be avoided, taking
for granted the good faith of the United States. And if this is lacking, and they have there greater forces than Spain, what Spanish
possessions will be secure? Also Spain, if she has forces there,
will be able to recover what may have been taken from her. The
commission of Father Talamantes was to designate how much Spain
had possessed, not to despoil this nation of the lands of which
she certainly was in possession, because of the risks and fears that
some day they would be taken away from her.

460. (M). It was not within Father Talamantes' province to
make all these observations directed toward despoiling Spain of her
lands. Our government is well advised and will certainly make its
own observations and in view of them will determine what seems
best to it, with undoubted benefit to the nation. Let us suppose
for a moment, for instance, that Spain, realizing that she could
not settle or defend those lands, should try to sell them to the
United States or should give them to her in exchange for others
that she could defend more easily, as for example the island of
New Orleans with all the lands in the vicinity of the Mississippi
and of this island, or for others that she might consider proper.
Would not such an agreement be better in this case than to give
them for nothing to the United States?

461. (N). Here we have an arbitral judge who wants the Spanish nation to be generous and indulgent and to give its lands to
the United States without any other reason than the considerations which he presents.

462. (O). If Father Talamantes had known all the harm he
was going to cause to Spain with his line, he would immediately

have thrown his *Nota Instructiva* together with its appendix into the fire. By attempting to be the author of a dividing line and by not following in the footsteps of Señor Martos, he took away from Spain the lands which the latter gave to her with his line. Señor Martos ran his line along the meridian from the source of the river which comes down from the north and enters the Red, until it encounters the Misuri, as we have stated above, in paragraph 307. And he continued by running his line along its outside bank, which faces the dominions of Spain, as far as its source. Although this line had the disadvantage of taking many lands from Spain, it had at the same time the advantage of being a line as well known as is the Misuri throughout its course. On the other hand, this last line of Father Talamantes was only an imaginary one and aside from this had the most criminal defect of taking from Spain a greater quantity of lands and of leaving her exposed to losing others more useful and already populated. We have seen that the source of the Río Acansas is found in the Sierra de las Grullas at a place located in 40° of latitude and 92° 30′ of longitude, and since the villa of Santa Fé in New Mexico is in 36° 46′ of latitude and 91° of longitude, it necessarily follows that the said source is northwest of this villa. Father Talamantes, by continuing his line to the pole, might perhaps follow a meridian that is found west of the source of the Misuri. Consequently he will take from Spain all the immense quantity of land lying west of the line of Señor Martos in its entire extent. If perchance this line may cut this river, the intersection can only be far to the north and in lands that probably never will be useful to Spain because of their excessive distance from us and their proximity to the Russians. It is not yet known exactly where the Misuri rises nor how far west it extends from the point at which we end it on our map, which is exactly where Perrin Du Lac terminates it. Because of this we cannot even conjecture whether Father Talamantes' line would cut it. But we do affirm that in case it cuts it, it must be at a point which is very close to the pole.

463. If our map is examined, it will be seen that from the place where the Río Misuri ends to Father Talamantes' line there are no fewer than four leagues. Consequently, all the land that lies within these four degrees he takes away from Spain on the west, and

perhaps in these four degrees is located the place in which the 'Misuri rises, far to the north of the said parallel. Therefore, the conjecture that Father Talamantes' line runs west of the source of this river and that it progressively continues taking lands away from Spain is not unfounded.

464. But although this is such a notable injury, that which can come to Spain from this line is infinitely greater. If we subtract the parallel of Santa Fé from the one in which the Río Acanzas rises, that is, the parallel of 36° 46′ from that of 40°, there will remain 3° 14′. But since the Río Acanzas does not flow along the same parallel in which it rises, but turns toward the southeast, there will be fewer degrees from Santa Fé to Father Talamantes' line, and in fact on our map it is seen that there are only 3° 29′. And what shall we say concerning the pueblo of San Gerónimo de los Taos, which is only 1° 40′ from this line, or the equivalent of 43 map leagues? Or, even though this distance may be greater, for our map may not be very exact in this part, it cannot be much greater. Now, then, if the Anglo-Americans take a fancy to build forts and settlements north of San Gerónimo de los Taos or of Santa Fé or at the source of the Río Acanzas, will not the Spaniards of the northern part of New Mexico be imprisoned, so to speak, without being able to extend in this direction, and shut off from the trade of the Cumanches? (Concerning this trade see paragraph 387 and many others of Part III.) If the Anglo-Americans attempt to work the mines which it is said are in the Sierra de la Plata and in the nearby sierras, will they restrict themselves to their fort at the source of the Río Acanzas and not go out in search of them? And will they not perhaps, before beginning the work, try to take these sierras from Spain? And will the pueblo of Taos, and the villa of Santa Fé, and the other settlements of New Mexico be always secure from the hostilities of these enemies? Will it not be necessary for them to be constantly prepared not only against the Indians but also against the Anglo-Americans? There will be new and extremely heavy exenditures for Spain in suppying herself with sufficient arms and troops to oppose and resist these new enemies. And why all this? Because Father Talamantes wanted us to be generous and indulgent toward them at the time of the demarcation of limits.

465. But on what did Father Talamantes base his belief that with his line, run to the source of the Río Acanzas and from there to the pole, the navigation of the Misuri would be useless to them for the purpose of establishing themselves on the coast of the Pacific Ocean, and that in the future such navigation would be less frequent and not at all prejudicial to Spain? Perhaps his line, which is only an imaginary one, constitutes a wall similar to the one the Chinese constructed to check the Tartars who were making incursions into their lands? Is it of bronze or of some other more solid material or metal that would be entirely impenetrable and so high that it cannot be crossed even by the most ingenious machines? The certain thing and the one about which there can be no doubt is that with his line Father Talamantes brought the Anglo-Americans extremely near the Pacific Ocean. From the meridian of the source of the Río Acanzas, which is found in 92° 30′, to the entrance of the Río Columbia into the sea, there are only 14½ degrees. From the Misuri and Señor Martos' line there are 18½ degrees, and from D'Anville's line, 22 degrees. Then Spain with D'Anville's line loses less territory—as much less as there is between 22 and 14½ degrees.

466. It is true that D'Anville's entire line has the same defect as this last one of Father Talamantes in that it is not a river or some other thing that the material eye can see. But if it is based, as I firmly believe it to be, on the rule of Señor Marca,[41] it becomes perceptible to the eyes of even the most stupid. For by only noting the divergence of the rain waters and following the line where it goes, from the Cabo del Norte to the place where he ended it, at 41° of latitude and 85° of longitude, it is recognized that the waters which, coming down from the crests of the mountains, flow toward the east, designate the lands of the French, and on the other hand those which flow toward the west are traversing the lands of Spain. And while D'Anville, as we have stated in Part III, paragraph 352, did not venture to continue his line from the 41st degree of latitude to the pole, because it was not exactly clear to him whether his nation had established itself above this degree at any place located to the west of the 85th degree of longitude, it should nevertheless ascend from this parallel to the pole

---

[41]See *Pichardo's Treatise* . . . , Vol. I, p. 26.

by reason of the large river which issues from the Lago de los Arboles [Lake of the Woods]—see Part III, paragraph 354—even though Señor Marca's rule cannot be deduced from it, that is, the rule concerning the divergence of the waters from the crests of the mountains toward the east. For this divergence may be found to vary greatly, so that in places it will be found west of the said 85th degree of longitude and in places east of it, and perhaps there may be some plains so extensive that this divergence cannot be ascertained on them.

467. Father Talamantes' line, running north from the Bayupier, cuts D'Anville's line at 32° 52' of latitude and 76° 43' of longitude, and thence, after reaching the middle of the Río Acanzas, it continues along it toward the west until it again cuts D'Anville's line at the place where the latter cuts the same Río Acanzas. Consequently all the land from D'Anville's line at the two intersections, to Father Talamantes' line, is a territory which D'Anville's line takes away from Spain and which Father Talamantes' lines gives to her. But Father Talamantes' line should not be preferred for this reason, because this territory is very small in comparison with that which he takes away from her. For, in fact, the territory is much greater which begins at the intersection of 36° 3' of latitude and 82° 37' of longitude and continues north and northwest between the two lines of D'Anville and Father Talamantes, as may be perceived very clearly by all who glance at our map. Therefore Father Talamantes' line should not be accepted, since it is arbitrary and very harmful to Spain.

468. (P). The official letter which he cites here and which is addressed to the señor commandant-general, is of the following tenor:

The royal order of May 20, 1805, which has given rise to the commission which the most excellent señor viceroy, Don José de Iturrigaray, has conferred upon me to collect all the historical and geographical accounts that may exist relating to the province of Texas and the others adjacent to it, directs that copies of all the documents collected be sent to your lordship. And although final compliance with this order rests directly with the said most excellent señor, I, nevertheless, not attempting to usurp his superior faculties nor to anticipate his wise decisions, but from motives peculiar to me individually, have thought it proper to address to your lordship a copy of the memorandum which, in order to do all I can for the fulfillment of the said royal order, I have already placed in the hands of the señor viceroy so that it could be sent promptly to the Ministry of State. I present therein a detailed account of many valuable documents, old and new, which exist in the court, in order that he may obtain information on the said province. In view of it, and after your lordship shall have received the copy that will have to be sent to you by this superior government, you may request the documents that you consider necessary, of which copies must be made in the Secretaría de Cámara, unless your lordship will be kind enough to wait a short while for those which I shall furnish you through the same most excellent señor, which will certainly be the ones best suited to the purpose.

The most important thing in the said memorandum is the plan of limits which accompanies it, a matter worthy of immediate examination by your lordship, who has under your command all this vast territory. If your lordship will consider it attentively and compare it with the maps of the interior of the kingdom, you will note its accuracy. Since the dividing lines which I suggest are the most suitable means for preventing all dispute and for obstructing the enterprises of the Anglo-Americans on the northwest coast of America, your lordship will also note in observing the said plan that, his Majesty having decided to select the most suitable points in the interior for establishing forts with which to defend our frontiers, the ones which become most important in view of this plan are, first, that of Los Adaes, which should be re-established with its original force; second, the one at the confluence of the two branches of the Colorado, or Nachitoches [Red] River; third, that on the Río Acansas at the point at which the arc of the meridian established by the dividing line should end; and, fourth, that at the source of this same river, north of Santa Fé in New Mexico.

470. The last dividing line that I am proposing, which should run indefinitely from the source of the said Río Acanzas to the North Pole, aside from having a precedent in times gone by, has served to fix the limits of the English settlement at Nootka, and from the agreement signed at that time between the two nations it is clear that the English recognized as Spanish territory all that region on the northwest coast which extends from Nootka south— information that should be borne in mind to refute the claims which the Anglo-Americans may advance to the Columbia.

471. Because of all this, which I state briefly to your lordship, I hope that you will have the kindness to support with your representations all the other propositions which you will see in the same plan, before our sovereign, on whose mind your lordship's opinion on the matter will no doubt make the greatest impression, and [I hope] that in recommending my work you will not forget to give some value and credit to my person. May God keep your lordship many years. Mexico, June 3, 1807. Fray Melchor Talamantes. To the Señor Commandant-General Brigadier Don Nemecio Salcedo.

472. Under separate cover he sent him also the following letter which I found among his rough drafts:

Señor Commandant-General Brigadier Don Nemecio Salcedo. My dear and most respected señor: Not thinking it proper that your lordship should add this letter to the governmental correspondence, I am sending it under separate cover. My first object is to assure your lordship how greatly obligated I am for the confidence that you have placed in me by sending me the three maps which I have received successively, especially the last one of the interior of the kingdom (since Father Talamantes sent these maps [back] and no other copies have been made available, I have not been able to see them or to make use of them), which I realize cannot be furnished easily, and I certainly would have exercised the greatest prudence with a paper of such importance. I do not doubt that it will be well received and acclaimed in the court, where they need very accurate information on all these points, but in order that the approbation may be greater, it might be well to indicate the northwest coast with greater accuracy by using the demarcations not only of Cook, La Perouse, and Wancowe [Vancouver?], but also of our mariners, who in some places give it a different shape and extend it farther out.

473. This slight defect has not prevented me from viewing the map with infinite appreciation, not only for the knowledge that it has given me but also because it confirms excellently my ideas and the plan that I have worked out with regard to the limits of Texas and the other Spanish possessions. In fact, in order to hasten [the execution of] my commission, to work in the future without any confusion, and to communicate promptly the information which is needed at the court, I have drawn up a memorandum which I have already placed in the hands of the most excellent señor viceroy in order that he may send it promptly to the Secretariat of State. In it, after indicating all the resources that are available there for obtaining complete information on the province of Texas, its extent and limits, and even on the other interior provinces of the kingdom, I have presented my opinion on the limits which should be established in time, in order to prevent all disputes in the future and to obstruct the enterprises of the Anglo-Americans on the northwest coast. In drawing up this plan, I had to examine many old and modern maps, without losing sight of the most valuable foreign ones, and your lordship will be able to realize the pleasure that I would feel in seeing my manner of thinking confirmed on your last map, without disagreement on a single point.

474. Therefore, since no one will be more interested than your lordship in taking notice of the said memorandum, and since your lordship with your repeated favors has led me to place the greatest confidence in your support, I am sending it to you at this time under separate cover for the reasons that I state therein, hoping that in sending it on to the court, if you are so kind as to support it, you may also be so kind as to recommend my person. It would also be well, in case the said memorandum is not sent to you promptly by this government, that you keep it confidential, although without prejudice to the measures that the government itself may take before the Secretariat of State. . . . Your lordship may be sure of my deepest gratitude, of the sincere affection that I profess for you, of my high esteem for your com-

mendable talents, and of the fact that as your servant and chaplain, who kisses your hand, I wish you the greatest success. Fray Melchor Talamantes.

475. The señor commandant-general answered him in the letter that follows:

With your reverence's official dispatch of June 3, last, I have received a copy of the memorandum which you have drawn up in fulfillment of the commission which the most excellent señor viceroy conferred upon you for the collection of historical and geographical accounts relating to the province of Texas and the other adjacent provinces. This document contains the plan which your reverence has drawn up of the limits of the same provinces with that of Louisiana, belonging at the present time to the United States of America.

476. When the Brigadier Marquis of Casa Calvo was appointed by the king for the demarcation of the same limits, he thought it opportune to receive my opinion, and having given an account to his Majesty, along with my report, he obtained his royal approval following an opinion from the Junta de Fortificación Y Defensa de América and from the señor generalissimo.

477. My opinion regarding this serious matter was different from your reverence's, and therefore, because of the foundations on which it rests as well as because of other recent information from experts, I would not wish the indicated plan of your reverence to fall into the hands of any person who might give an idea of its contents to any individual of the said [United] States. However, even before I received it, there came into my posesssion official papers of persons close to that government in which is denied General Wilkinson's authority for having placed in *status quo* the lands that have always belonged to his Majesty as a part of the provinces under my charge, which measure seems to have been the best to take during the disputes of the end of last year, pending the supreme decision, and especially when the same government tried with armed force to make effective their ambitious claims, which will be interminable as long as the slightest excuse is found on which to base them.

478. I do not doubt your reverence's zeal or the laboriousness and difficulty of your commission. These qualities, together with the others which are combined in your reverence, I shall never hesitate to recommend whenever an opportune occasion may present itself to do so. May God keep your reverence many years. Chihuahua, July 7, 1807. Nemecio Salcedo. To the Very Reverend Father Fray Melchor Talamantes y Baeza.

479. Father Talamantes replied to this as follows:

Through your lordship's official dispatch of the 7th of last July, I am informed that your lordship has received the memorandum which I enclosed in my official dispatch of the third of the preceding June and that you have directed your attention to the plan of limits which the said work contains. After I had finished it, I learned of his Majesty's decision concerning the plan presented by your lordship, of which I have a copy in my possession, and as much for this reason as because of the just arguments which your lordship presents to me, I agree to keep the said plan secret in order to avoid, as your lordship justly fears, its falling into the hands of the Anglo-Americans and giving a motive for new disputes. In the meantime I assure your lordship of my gratitude for your kind disposition to favor me, and I confidently expect from your good will that as soon as an opportune occasion presents itself, you will make the recommendation which you promise me. My present illness, which according to the doctors will prevent me from reading and writing, and the unexpected lack of a clerk, have delayed this answer much longer than was permissible. May God keep your lordship many years. Mexico, August 19, 1807. Fray Melchor Talamantes. To the señor commandant-general, Brigadier Don Nemecio Salcedo.

480. (Q). Here we see new expenditures originating for Spain with these additional reinforcements which she ought to have in Santa Fé.

481. (R). Here Father Talamantes, entirely forgetful of his commission, which was that of seeking documents and taking notes from them, meddles in politics by saying that his line should be disregarded. Why did he draw it if he is advising Spain not to cede all the land between it, the Mississippi, and the Acanzas? Everything he writes in this paragraph, it seems to me, is what is commonly called singing out of tune with the choir. Our government knows very well what it is doing. The only thing that was asked of him was to find out how far the Spanish possessions reached, not to dictate political procedure to it [the government].

482. Having concluded his *Nota Instructiva*, the Very Reverend Father Talamantes sent it to the most excellent señor viceroy with the following official dispatch:

Most excellent señor: Ever since your Excellency had the kindness to entrust to me the difficult commission of investigating the true former limits of the province of Texas, it has been my purpose to examine this subject in all its aspects in order to discharge it with the accuracy, circumspection, and brevity which its importance demanded. For this reason I have from time to time indicated to your Excellency all the instruments that I have thought could throw light on the matter. These have been supplied to me through your generous measures, and I have availed myself at the same time of various private sources no less advantageous.

483. While my mind was running over the different resources that might serve my purpose and was arranging in order the multitude of ideas with which I was successively occupied, I worked out a plan by which the provisions of the royal order of May 20, 1805, could be promptly carried out,

so that after his Majesty had been duly informed of his true rights to the said province, the limits which might belong to it could be fixed by his royal orders.

484. Motivated by this idea, I noticed that the said royal order demands a compilation of historical and geographical documents concerning this province, and of the orders given by his Majesty or by this superior government with regard to its true extent, and that copies should be made of the said documents, which were to be sent to the first Secretariat of State, to the señor commandant-general of the Interior Provinces, and to the Señor Marquis of Casa Calvo. The compilation of historical and geographical documents and of the cedulas, royal orders, and other measures directed in the matter, whether it be made of extracts, as his Majesty permits, or by faithful and exact copies, as seems best for greater authenticity, is by its nature a slow and dilatory work, and pending the occasion for presenting it, which I shall do in due time, it would be necessary to suspend decision in a matter highly important to the peace and safety of the kingdom.

485. In order to avoid, therefore, as far as I am able, the prejudices that could result from such a delay, and in order that your Excellency may obtain the satisfaction of having complied insofar as possible with the said royal order, I have taken the liberty of selecting from among the multitude of papers which I have examined and of which I have knowledge, four or five which are very valuable because of their formality and antiquity, and which I shall place in your Excellency's hands as soon as copies of them are finished, so that they may be used for the purpose for which his Majesty intends them, postponing until that time speaking to your Excellency in more detail with regard to their merit.

486. And in order to make provision for sending the said proofs or documents to the Secretariat of State, as I have prescribed, I have drawn up the memorandum which I am enclosing at the present time in triplicate form, with the respective documents, by means of which it is shown that in the Secretaría de Gracia y Justicia or in the other places which I indicate therein, there should exist large numbers of old and recent documents relating to the history and topography of Texas, which can be easily sought and examined in the same court. In view of this, I judge it convenient that your Excellency, if you should consider it proper, order the said memorandum sent on the first occasion to the Secretariat of State, so that the necessary information and proofs may no longer be lacking there.

487. It is not my intention to exaggerate to your Excellency the labor performed in drawing up this slight work. It is sufficient to tell you that since I was convinced from the very beginning of my commission that the information which was being sought could be found in the court, and since I did not find promptly the documents that might prove my suspicions, I have proceeded on my investigations for a long time as if groping in the dark, until I had to undertake a lengthy examination of the volumes of royal orders and of the correspondence of this viceroyalty with the court. It has been necessary to examine the whole of its thirty-two volumes, from which I have had to take

the entire work as remitted, which I cite in my memorandum, without setting aside other important investigations, and keeping in mind the other matters with which I am charged.

488. This memorandum being drawn up, my spirit was not satisfied until I contributed such reflections as might occur to me for the better welfare of the monarchy, and being imbued with this high purpose, I have formed, in view of the maps of the kingdom, old and new, native and foreign, a plan of limits, well-founded, brief, and compact, which in my opinion is adapted to the present critical conditions and which supplements the said memorandum. I am not unaware that at first sight it presents some small difficulties, but since these will be overcome by the great benefits that should result, I have not hesitated to present it to your Excellency, and I beg you to send it with the same memorandum to the first Secretariat of State in order that his Majesty, after having heard your Excellency's valuable opinion, may decide as to its merits. May God keep your Excellency many years. Mexico, June 20, 1807. Most excellent señor. Fray Melchor Talamantes y Baeza. To the most excellent señor viceroy, Don José Iturrigaray.

489. His Excellency was pleased to order it sent, together with the said official letter, to the señor *fiscal*, Don Ambrosio Sagarzurrieta, who gave him the following reply on it.

Most excellent señor: The civil *fiscal* states that from the *expediente* collected by virtue of your Excellency's superior decree of the 8th of the current month, furnished in conformance with the reply of the *fiscal* of the same day, it seems that by another superior decree of January 27, your Excellency had ordered that everything should be done as was requested by the present writer in his reply of December 31, last; had named as the principal commissioner the Reverend Father Doctor Fray Melchor Talamantes of the military order of La Merced; and had named as his assistant for making the proper drawings and charts, Don Gonzalo López de Haro, lieutenant-of-frigate and adjutant of the corps of pilots of the royal navy. As a result of this, after the proper official dispatches had been issued and the certified copies had been made in triplicate in order to report to his Majesty, the said Father Talamantes sent to your Excellency the preceding official dispatch of June 20, last. He states therein that since the compilation of historical and geographical documents and of cedulas, royal orders, and other measures ordered with regard to the limits of our province of Texas and of Louisiana, is by its nature slow and dilatory, pending its accomplishment in due time, he has taken the liberty of selecting from among the multitude of papers which he says he has examined and of which he has information, four or five very valuable because of their formality and antiquity, which he will place in your Excellency's hands as soon as the copies are finished, in order that they may be sent to the señores commandants-general of the Interior Provinces and to the Señor Marquis of Casa Calvo, as his Majesty orders. He is waiting until that time to speak to your Excellency regarding their merit. And in order

to take care of the remittance of the said proofs or documents that must
also be made to the first Secretariat of State, as prescribed, he sends along
a memorandum in quadruplicate form, by which is shown that in the Secretaría de Gracia y Justicia or in the other places which he indicates therein,
there should exist large numbers of old and recent documents relating to the
history and topography of Texas, which can easily be sought and examined
in the same court.

490. The father commissioner's zeal not being satisfied with this, and since
he wishes to contribute with his reflections to the greater welfare of the
monarchy, he has drawn up a plan of limits, brief and compact (with which
he supplements the said memorandum) which in his opinion is adapted to
the present critical conditions, and which he begs your Excellency to send
with it to the first Secretariat of State in order that his Majesty, after having
heard your Excellency's valuable opinion, may determine its merit.

491. The *fiscal* has examined with great care both the said memorandum
and the plan of limits, and he believes that both works are the result of
Father Talamantes' commendable zeal, and that although they are brief, they
must have cost him no little labor. In the first place we owe to his diligence
the discovery and rescue from the dust of oblivion of the extremely important
Colección de Memorias de Nueva España, arranged in thirty-two folio volumes
under this title by Father Fray Manuel Vega, a Franciscan religious, under
the direction and patronage of his provincial, the Reverend Father Fray
Francisco García de Figueroa. Three copies were made of it. One is in the
Secretaría de Cámara of this viceroyalty, another was sent to the Secretaría
de Gracia y Justicia on December 31, 1792, and probably the same thing was
done with the third in the next maritime mail.

492. The said work, according to the explanation of Father Talamantes,
contains the history of Texas from 1688 to 1779; almost all the diaries of the
first expeditions made to this province, not only of the captains who led them
but also of the missionaries; a résumé of all the measures taken to secure
Spanish domination in Texas, drawn up by the *asesor general* of the viceroyalty,
Doctor Velasco, at the order of the viceroy, the Marquis of Valero, in 1716;
the report of the señor *oidor* and *auditor general de guerra*, the Marquis of
Altamira, presented at the king's order on the same matter in 1744, which,
although part of it is missing, treats somewhat of the eastern limits of the
province; maps and charts of the same province and of those bordering upon
it; and other records and reports relating to the subject. With the aid of
these materials the present question of limits with Louisiana, as Father
Talamantes states, can be promptly and definitely settled. It therefore seems
very proper to the *fiscal* that, as the said father commissioner suggests, his
memorandum and plan of limits be sent immediately to his Majesty in
triplicate, and that the fourth copy be kept in the *expediente*.

493. But, since it may be convenient, as the said father commissioner
also suggests, that he [the king] be informed by your Excellency concerning
the merit of the said plan of limits, the *fiscal* in presenting his opinion will
go into detail with regard to this plan and its fundamental bases.

494. Father Talamantes begins immediately by asserting that the differences over limits of the provinces of Louisiana and Texas have arisen from the fact that since they narrowed too much toward the Gulf of Mexico, the extent of Louisiana toward the south and west was very small, while on the other hand the extent of both territories above the presidios of Adaes and Natchitoches was remarkably broad, and those points not being important for navigation, no dispute has ever arisen (indeed it did arise) over setting the boundaries beyond that latitude. [Father Talamantes also asserts] that, nevertheless, since the settlement of the French in Louisiana was due in large measure to the generous condescension and tolerance of Spain and to her relations with the French House of Bourbon from which she could not extricate herself (she never agreed to this usurpation and indeed always opposed it), the French always restricted themselves to those limits which Spain herself wished to prescribe for them. Although they made several attempts in the west, either by means of hostilities committed in the province [of Texas] in the year 1719, which were entirely thwarted in 1721 by the expedition of the Señor Marquis of San Miguel de Aguayo, or by the moderate and crafty means to which they resorted thereafter, which proved their timidity and lack of confidence in their cause, Spain, with the authority, decisiveness, and intrepidity of a legitimate owner, always checked the foreign invasions, obstructed with repeated measures the attempts that were made to introduce clandestine trade, to the detriment of national industry, built forts in the most remote parts of the province, ignored as unfounded the complaints that were directed to her by several governors of Louisiana, and maintained unmistakably the possession of that whole country to where it touches the line formed by the arc of the meridian that runs from the Gulf of Mexico to the presidio and mission of Los Adaes, crossing the Arroyo Hondo and La Gran Montaña, located between the said presidio and the French fort of Natchitoches. [He states] that this is the first dividing line that should be established, and that this step cannot be difficult by virtue of the uninterrupted possession of Spain over that territory, her tenacious opposition to the French penetrating by way of that region, and the fact that the authentic exploration of France never went beyond the said line, as is clear from the numerous *expedientes* and documents of all kinds that exist in the archives of this New Spain.

495. [Father Talamantes also states] that this is the case with regard to the dividing line which should run beyond Los Adaes, because in this region everything is doubtful and uncertain, and that since we did not make any settlements whatever beyond the said latitude, neither can any documents exist in these archives which would prove our claims. On the other hand, the French, taking advantage of the misfortune which befell one of our missionaries, founded in 1717 (it was in 1716) the presidio and mission of Los Coadachos, or Cadodachos, on the south bank of the Río Nachitoches, penetrating too far west-northwest of Los Adaes. And [he states] that since there was no pronounced resistance on our part and they consequently remained in possession of that land for a long time, it would be a matter of no little difficulty to deprive the Anglo-Americans of it if, knowing of this

occurrence, they should wish to support their claims on the basis of that point. [He states also] that the land of the Cadodachos begins a short distance from a stream called Bayou Pierre, where the Anglo-Americans affirm [torn] has belonged to France. It flows four leagues north of the Laguna de los Adaes and, following for the greater part of its course a west to east direction, it empties into the Nachitoches [Red River]. But [he states] that since on the old maps the said stream is not found under that name, it is to be believed that it took the name after Louisiana passed under Spanish dominion. In Louisiana is found another stream of the same name which, following the direction of north-northwest and south-southwest, crosses a small lake and empties into the Mississippi from the east side at latitude 31° 58'. [He states] that if the United States should not insist on maintaining their rights over the land of the Cadodachos, the second dividing line could be a continuation of the first, crossing the Arroyo Bayou Pierre and the Río Nachitoches [Red River] along the same meridian, until it ends at the Acanzas, which flows a short distance from the latter and is parallel to it; but that if they persist in maintaining their claims, as is probable, we should insist as a last recourse that the first dividing line terminate at the same Arroyo Bayou Pierre, which would serve as a second dividing line along its entire course, and that the third line shall run from the source of the latter, preferably in a curve ending at the confluence of the two branches of the Nachitoches [Red], at latitude 34° 5', enclosing our possessions on its convex side and excluding from them on its concave side the land of the Cadodachos.

496. After this Father Talamantes adds that up to now nothing would have been achieved if, neglecting the present circumstances, we do not take advantage of them to fix the limits of New Mexico and determine the extent of our possessions in North America. For, since New Mexico is as unprotected as it is on the east and north, and our limits up to the present are undetermined, and since we have no settlements of any importance there, we should always be in danger of new disputes. Also, it would be useless for us to cite our expeditions into those northern regions, the apostolic travels of our missionaries, our prior discoveries, the navigations along the Misuri, and even the demarcation of those points, for, since we have not made any settlement there up to the present, and since therefore those regions must be regarded as abandoned, such arguments cannot have much weight in the balance of critical examination and in view of the present relations among nations. [He declares also] that the northwest coast of America, to which the Anglo-Americans are today directing their schemes, would be at their disposal to the detriment not only of our nation but also of the Russians because of the Alaskan Peninsula, which they possess, along with all the Kuriles; of the English because of the territory of Nootka, quite near the [bay of] Eceta [Hezeta], called by the Anglo-Americans the Columbia, where they have penetrated recently on the last navigation which they made along the Misuri; and of the French because of El Puerto Francés [Port des Français], which Monsieur de la Perouse discovered and of which he took possession. In this event, when the Anglo-Americans have made themselves masters of the fur

trade and of the commerce of India, if they should in addition ally themselves with the barbarous nations of the north, they would in time become our most dreaded neighbors, if indeed they did not declare themselves our formidable enemies. And [he states] that all this will be prevented by the three dividing lines: First, the arc of the meridian which runs from the confluence of the two branches of the Nachitoches [Red] to the Río Acanzas; second, a line drawn along the center of this river throughout its course to its source, which is at the foot of the mountains which are north of Santa Fé in New Mexico; third, the arc of the meridian that extends from there indefinitely toward the pole. By these means a vast territory would remain in the possession of the Americans on the east side, of which they could not be the owners without breaking the limits fixed by France in the treaty of 1783, and as a result their possessions would be greatly increased by this new agreement. For this reason also Father Talamantes wants us to make common cause with the French, the English, and the Russians.

497. The *fiscal* agrees with Father Talamantes that there can be no difficulty regarding the first dividing line formed by the meridian which runs from the Gulf of Mexico to the presidio and mission of Los Adaes and crosses the Arroyo Hondo and La Gran Montaña, located between the said presidio and the French fort of Nachitoches, in view of the indisputable titles which we have and the peaceful possession which we have enjoyed as far as that place. The *fiscal* also agrees that it is most important to protect our province of New Mexico with fixed limits on the east and north, and it seems that we should feel very well satisfied if we could secure an agreement from the United States to adopt throughout its extent the demarcation conceived by Father Talamantes. But this event the *fiscal* considers improbable and hopeless, particularly if, in order to obtain it, we do not abandon some of the data and principles set forth by the said father commissioner. For if the French founded and moreover maintained the presidio and mission of Los Cadodachos while they were owners of Louisiana, and on the other hand we did not have and do not have any settlement above Los Adaes, and if, since we did not have it, those regions should be regarded as abandoned; and the arguments taken from our expeditions to the said regions, the apostolic journeys of our missionaries, our first discoveries, navigation along the Misuri, and even the demarcation of those points, as Father Talamantes states, being of little weight in the balance of critical examination and in view of the present policy among nations, where is, or on what does he base, the hope of being able to induce the Anglo-Americans, successors to the rights of the French in Louisiana, to accept a demarcation which confines them and prevents their aspiring to any point on the northwest coast of America, which is their favorite object? Shall we perhaps flatter ourselves that we- will win success by telling them that through this agreement they will be masters of an extremely vast territory of which they could not be the owners without breaking the limits prescribed by France in the treaty of 1783? Unless they are bewildered or deceived to the point of stupidity, they will know and will answer that at the present time their limits are not those of the year 1783, they having acquired

thereafter the province of Louisiana. And arguing with us with our own principles, they will add that therefore that land should be regarded as abandoned in view of the fact that we do not have and have not had any settlement whatever on it. We will not have anything to reply to them, or it will be so little that it cannot act as a counterweight against what they will lose by being deprived of the means of extending their communications to the northwest coast.

498. Even though we might think of making common cause with the French, English, and Russians, which at the present time would be too difficult because of the war and the unfriendly relations among those four powers, the *fiscal* does not see that this means would further the purpose of establishing the proposed line of demarcation throughout its extent. For, even though it is to the interest of the said nations, although not as much as to ours, to turn the Anglo-Americans away from the northwest coast, it still is immaterial to them whether our boundary line with them is straight or curved, whether it runs along the Río Acansas or along the Nachitoches [Red], Sabinas, or any other river farther west, as long as the Anglo-Americans do not approach within a certain distance of the said coast.

499. Moreover, such an alliance of powers could be very harmful to us, if in entering upon an examination of our claims and differences with the United States, they should decide in favor of the latter.

500. Finally, the northwest coast being immense and there being no other settlements on it from ours in the Californias to the North Pole, except that of the English at Nootka, those of the Russians in Alaska and the Kuriles, and a French port (if they happen to have settled and garrisoned it), with what right would we attempt to keep the Anglo-Americans from crossing over from their possessions and establishing themselves at some unoccupied point on the northwest coast, and especially if it is very far from those occupied by the four said nations, provided the principle is once established that no legitimate right is acquired over a country except by permanent settlement? The *fiscal* believes that it does not suit our interests to adopt such principles.

501. According to natural and international law, that which does not belong to anyone becomes the property of the first one who occupies it. It is also accepted among civilized nations that any one of them may establish itself and make itself owner of the regions of America which either have not been completely occupied or have been occupied only by wandering tribes of savage Indians who do not have a fixed abode, travel from place to place, and do not remain in any place except so long as it supplies them with game or fish. Therefore, the Euorpean nation which may prove that it was the first to discover and occupy any such region with the intention of acquiring it for itself, will be its legitimate owner, even though it may not have made any permanent settlement there, for no law imposes this requirement, but simply that of occupation. Much less should such a requirement be exacted of a nation which already has settlements nearby from which it exercises its rights of dominion over the newly-occupied country. This is the situation in

which Spain finds herself with respect to her discoveries in Texas, Louisiana, and New Mexico, of which she was the first discoverer, after she had extensive settlements in this New Spain. From here she has continued to exercise her rights by exploring the new discoveries and improving them, by sending missionaries for the reduction and conversion of the Indians, offering them our friendship and protection, which they have accepted; and by performing other similar acts.

502. If later the French intruded upon us in what is called Louisiana, this act was a usurpation which Spain always opposed. Of this the *fiscal* has seen authentic proof. That is why our court has never been willing to accede to the requests or reports of this government with regard to fixing limits between that province and Texas, believing wisely that by this step it would recognize the possession of France as legitimate.

503. According to some publicists, and especially the celebrated Samuel Cocceji, international law does not recognize prescription, no matter how ancient, as a method of acquiring possession, and although others, including Grotius, accept it, it is not by virtue only of prescription or lapse of time but of the presumed abandonment of the thing that may be assumed on the part of him who sees it in the possession of someone else and does not oppose it within a certain time.

504. International law being, therefore, the vehicle by which disputes between nations should be settled, and Spain having protested against the usurpation of Louisiana by France, the rights of the former to this entire province are still very strong in spite of our retrocession to France and the sale by the latter to the United States of America. For France, in the cession she made to us, gave us only what she had, that is, a litigious possession, and when we lately receded it to her, we gave her the same that she gave us and nothing more, for that is what retrocession means. Consequently, we can continue our ancient rights and our claims. And now that Spain reconciles herself to recognizing the dominion of the United States as legitimate, it will be only reasonable that the latter come to an agreement with us on the point of limits, especially at those places concerning which there may be doubt, such as Bayou Pierre and Cadodachos.

505. These are the principles, maxims, and considerations which the *fiscal* believes we should observe in order to obtain an advantageous position in the present dispute. On the basis of them, your Excellency may be pleased to make a report to his Majesty in support of the plan of limits proposed by Father Talamantes; to recommend the labors and merits of this religious, without prejudice to doing it [again] when his commission shall be completed and his final tasks performed in like manner; and to give him [the king] an account in triplicate that certified copies of this reply and the decision upon it, together with the corrected copies of the memorandum, the plan of limits, and the official dispatch which the said Father Talamantes has sent for this purpose. Mexico, July 25, [1807]. Sagarzurrieta.

Royal Congregation of the Oratory of [torn], 1812.
José Antonio Pichardo (rubric).

BIBLIOGRAPHY

Acosta, Joseph de. See the Bibliography, Vol. II, p. 531.

Aguayo, Marquis of San Miguel de.

Letter to the king, Coahuila, June 13, 1722. Ms., in Arch. de Santa Cruz de Querétaro, K. Legajo 4, n. 10. A Spanish transcript is in The University of Texas Library.

Letter to the viceroy, Nuestra Señora de Guadalupe, August 19, 1721. Ms., in A. G. I., Aud. de Mex., 61–2–2. A Spanish transcript is in The University of Texas Library.

Alcedo y Bexarano, Antonio de. See the Bibliography, Vol. I, p. 545.

Alvárez, Francisco.

Noticia del establecimiento y poblacion de las colonias inglesas en la America Septentrional; religion, orden de gobierno, leyes y costumbres de sus naturales y habitantes; calidades de su clima, terreno, frutos, plantas y animales; y estado de su industria, artes, comercio y navegacion: sacada de varios autores por Don Francisco Alvárez. . . . Madrid, A. Fernández, 1778.

Arricivita, Juan Domingo. See the Bibliography, Vol. I, p. 546.

Atlas Moderne ou Collection de Cartes sur toutes les parties du Globe Terrestre. Par Plusieurs Auteurs. Paris, 1762.

Barcia, Don Andreas González [Don Gabriel de Cárdenas Z Cano]. See the Bibliography, Vol. I, p. 546.

Benavides, Alonso. See the Bibliography, Vol. I, p. 547; Vol. II, p. 533.

Bolton, Herbert E. See the Bibliography, Vol. I, pp. 547–548; Vol. II, pp. 533–534; and Vol. III, p. 556.

Bolton, Herbert E., and Marshall, T. M. See the Bibliography, Vol. I, p. 548.

Bonilla, Antonio. See the Bibliography, Vol. I, p. 548.

Boyer, Abel.

Dictionnaire royal, françois-anglois et anglois-françois. . . . Amsterdam et Leipzig, Arkstée et Merkus, 1752.

Cabeza de Vaca. See Núñez Cabeza de Vaca.

Cárdenas, Don Gabriel de. See Barcia.

Castañeda, Carlos E. (trans. and ed.).

History of Texas, 1673–1779, by Fray Juan Agustín Morfi, Part I (*Quivira Society Publications,* Vol. VI), Albuquerque, 1935. See also the Bibliography, Vol. II, p. 535, and Vol. III, p. 556.

Catholic Encyclopedia, The. See the Bibliography, Vol. II, p. 535 and Vol. III, p. 557.

Caughey, John Walton. See the Bibliography, Vol. III, p. 557.

Chapman, Charles Edward.

A History of California: The Spanish Period. New York, 1930. See also the Bibliography, Vol. I, p. 549.

478   PICHARDO: LIMITS OF LOUISIANA AND TEXAS

Cicero, Marcus Tullius.
De divinatione; De fato; Timaeus; Ottonis Plasberg schedis usus recognovit W. Ax. N.p., n.d.
Clavius, Christophorus.
Christophori Clavii Bambergensis e Societate Iesv Opervm mathematicorvm tomvs primvs-qvintvs . . . Magvntiae, symptibus. A. Hierat, 1611–12. N.p.
Colección de infinitas poesías. N.p., n.d.
Copia de los Capitulos 17, 19, 20, y 25 del dictamen que el Exmo. Sor. Marquez de Rubí dió sobre la mejor situación de los Presidios internos.
Danet, Guillermo (publisher).
La America Meridional y Septentrional levantada sobre los Nuebos descubrimientos y ultimas relaciones de los mejores navegantes de este tiempo conformes á las observaciones astronomicas. Printed in Paris by Depvoix, 1751.
Davenport, Frances Gardiner, and Paullin, Charles Oscar.
European Treaties Bearing on the History of the United States and its Dependencies. Vol. IV. Washington, 1937.
Demonstración de la lealtad española: Colección de proclamas, bandos, órdenes, discursos, estados del ejército y relaciones de batallas publicadas por las juntas de gobierno, o por algunos particulares en las actuales circumstancias. 6 vols. Madrid and Cádiz, 1808–1809.
Diccionario Enciclopédico Hispano-Americano. . . . See the Bibliography, Vol. I, p. 550.
Diccionario de la Lengua Castellana. See the Bibliography, Vol. II, p. 537.
Diogenes Laertius.
. . . De vitis, dogmatibus et apohthegmatibus clarorum philosophorum libri x. graece et latine. . . . Amstelaedami, Apud H. Wetstenium, 1692.
Du Pratz. See Le Page du Pratz.
Encyclopedia Britannica, The. [Fourteenth Edition] 24 volumes. London and New York, 1929.
Espinosa, Isidro Felix de. See the Bibliography, Vol. I, p. 550; Vol. II, p. 538; and Vol. III, p. 558.
Fernández de Medrano, Sebástian.
L'ingenieur pratique; ou, L'architecture militaire et moderne, contenant la fortification reguliere & irreguliere, avec une nouvelle methode de l'auteur, la fabrique des ramparts & des murailles, des quartiers, magazines, etc. . . . . . . Par le Medrano. . . . A. Brusselles, Chez Lambert Marchant MDCXCVI.
Fernández Duro, Cesáreo. See the Bibliography, Vol. I, p. 551.
Fortier, Alcée. See the Bibliography, Vol. I, p. 551.
Focher, Joannes.
Itinerarivm catholicvm profiscentium, ad infidelis couertendos. N.p., 1574.
Gacetas de Mexico. See the Bibliography, Vol. I, p. 552.
Garcilaso de la Vega, el Inca. See the Bibliography, Vol. I, p. 552 and Vol. II, p. 539.
Gayarré, C. See the Bibliography, Vol. I, p. 552.

Gómara, Francisco López de. See the Bibliography, Vol. I, p. 552.

Hackett, C. W.
Revolt of the Pueblo Indians of New Mexico and Otermín's Attempted Reconquest, 1680–1682. 2 vols. (*Coronado Cuarto Centennial Publications, 1540–1940,* Vols. VIII–IX), Albuquerque, 1942.
See also the Bibliography, Vol. I, p. 553; Vol. II, p. 540; and Vol. III, p. 559.

Haring, C. H.
The Buccaneers in the West Indies in the XVII Century. London, 1910.

Harris, John.
Lexicon Technicum; or, an universal English dictionary of arts and sciences. London, 1704.

Hayes, C. H. See the Bibliography, Vol. I, p. 553.

Hennepin, Louis. See the Bibliography, Vol. II, p. 540.

Herrera y Tordesillas, Antonio de. See the Bibliography, Vol. I, p. 554.

Higby, Chester Penn.
History of Europe, 1492–1815. New York, 1927.

Horatius Flaccus, Quintus.
El Arte Poetica . . . traducida en verso castillano, por D. T. de Yriarte . . . Con un discurso preliminar, y algunas notas y observaciones, etc. Madrid, 1777.

Lángara, Don Juan de. See the Bibliography, Vol. I, p. 555.

Langior.
Polyanthea Novicima. N.p., n.d.

Le Clercq, Chrétien. See the Bibliography, Vol. I, p. 555.

Leonard, Irving A.
Spanish Approach to Pensacola, 1689–1693 (*Quivira Society Publications,* Vol. IX), Albuquerque, 1939.
See also the Bibliography, Vol. III, p. 560.

Le Page du Pratz. See the Bibliography, Vol. I, p. 556.

Le Rouge, George Louis. See the Bibliography, Vol. I, p. 556.

"Limits and Extent of Louisiana: A treatise taken from some Manuscript Notes on Louisiana, made by a Military Gentleman who has Resided in Mississippi since the Spring of the year 1803," in *The Mississippi Messenger,* No. 121, Vol. III, December 23, 1806.

López de Vargas Machuca, Tomás. See the Bibliography, Vol. III, p. 560.

Malloy, W. M. (compiler). See the Bibliography, Vol. I, p. 557.

Michel. See Mitchell, John.

Mississippi Messenger, The. See the Bibliography, Vol. II, p. 544.

Mitchell, John. See the Bibliography, Vol. II, p. 544.

Moréri, Louis. See the Bibliography, Vol. I, p. 559, and Vol. II, p. 544.

Morfi, Fray Juan Agustín de.
History of Texas, 1673–1779 (Castañeda translation; *Quivira Society Publications,* Vol. VI, Parts I and II). Albuquerque, 1935.
See also the Bibliography, Vol. I, p. 559; Vol. II, p. 544; and Vol. III, p. 561.

New Spain and the Anglo-American West. . . . See the Bibliography, Vol. II, p. 544.

Núñez Cabeza de Vaca, Alvar. See the Bibliography, Vol. I, p. 560 and Vol. II, p. 545.

Peña, Juan Antonio. See the Bibliography, Vol. I, p. 560.

Perrin du Lac, François Marie. See the Bibliography, Vol. I, p. 560.

Pichardo, José Antonio. See the Bibliography, Vol. I, p. 561.

Prevost, Antoine François.

Manuel Lexique, ou dictionnaire portatif des mots françois dont la signification n'est pas familiere a tout le monde. Nouv. éd. considerablement augm. 2 vols. Paris, Didot, 1755.
See also the Bibliography, Vol. I, p. 561.

Priestley, Herbert Ingram. See the Bibliography, Vol. I, p. 561 and Vol. III, p. 562.

Raynal, Guillaume Thomas François. See the Bibliography, Vol. I, p. 561.

Reglamento e instrucción para los presidios, etc. See the Bibliography, Vol. I, p. 562.

Relacion De la Sorprecha (sic) hecha por los Franceses de la Movila en el Castillo de San Carlos y Punta de Siguenza; y su Restauracion por las Armas de su Magestad (que Dios guarda) el dia 7 de agosto deste Año de 1719. Mexico, 1719.

Robert de Vaugondy, Gilles, and Robert de Vaugondy, Didier. See the Bibliography, Vol. I, p. 562 and Vol. II, pp. 547–548.

Shelby, Charmion C. See the Bibliography, Vol. I, p. 563 and Vol. III, p. 563.

Sibley, John. See the Bibliography, Vol. I, p. 564.

Sigüenza y Góngora, Carlos de. See the Bibliography, Vol. I, p. 564 and Vol. III, p. 564.

Suidas.

Suidae lexicon. L. Kuster edition. 3 vols. Cambridge, 1705.

Talamantes, Melchor de.

Nota Instructiva. N.p., n.d.
Opúsculo. N.p., n.d.
See also the Bibliography, Vol. I, p. 564 and Vol. II, p. 549.

Terracina, Miguel. See the Bibliography, Vol. I, p. 564.

Thomas, A. B. See the Bibliography, Vol. III, p. 564.

Thwaites, R. G. See the Bibliography, Vol. I, p. 565 and Vol. III, p. 564.

Torquemada, Juan de. See the Bibliography, Vol. I, p. 565.

Tratado definitivo de Paz concluido entre el Rey N.S. y su Mag. Critisnisima por una parte y S.M. Britanica por otra en Paris á 10. de Febrero de 1763 con sus articulos Preliminares y la accesion de su Mag. fidelisima á ellos y al mismo Tratado como tambien las Ratificaciones Plenipotencias y demas actos de las Potencias interesadas De orden de S.M. En Madrid: En La Ymprenta Real de la Gaceta. Año de 1763.

Ulloa, Antonio de.

See the Bibliography, Vol. III, p. 564.

The universal library: or, Compleat summary of science. Containing above sixty select treatises. 2 vols. London, printed for G. Sawbridge, 1712.

Valdes, Manuel Antonio.

Apuntes de algunas de las gloriosas acciones del Exmo. Señor D. Bernardo de Galvez, Conde de Galvez, Virey, Gobernador y Capitan General que fué de esta Nueva España, &c. Hacialos en un romance heroico Don Manuel Antonio Valdes, Autor de la Gazeta Mexicana. Mexico, 1787.

Vaugondy. See Robert de Vaugondy.

Vega, Manuel de. See the Bibliography, Vol. II, p. 550.

Vegas, Antonio. See the Bibliography, Vol. II, p. 550.

Vetancourt, Agustín de. See the Bibliography, Vol. II, p. 551.

Villagrá, Gaspar de. See the Bibliography, Vol. 1, p. 566.

Villa-Señor y Sánchez, José Antonio de. See the Bibliography, Vol. I, p. 566.

Wintherbotham, W. See the Bibliography, Vol. I, p. 567.

INDEX

Bibliographical references are to the main body of the text only. For complete data see the bibliography.

Brazos River [Río de los Brazos de Dios, Río Colorado]: exploration of, 319; French traders on, 197, 224, 308; Indians on, 320, 331, 334, 349, 376; location, 206; Los Adaes settlers reach, 196, 197; named by Spaniards, 328, 433.

Brest: Iberville's fleet at, 269, note.

Breve Compendio, of Bonilla: quoted, 185; cited, 426.

Brevel, Monsieur: his reports to Dr. Sibley, 394.

Briseño y Zúñiga, Don Juan José, *juez de residencia* for Sandoval: proceedings of, 121, 412–413.

British: incite slave revolt in Havana, 97. See *English*.

Bucareli, pueblo of [Nuevo Bucareli, Nuestra Señora del Pilar de Bucareli]: founded, 198, note, 199, 201, 213; French traders near, 205; Indians near, 208; location and description, 206ff, 208–209; militia company for, 199; reports on, 151, 204–209; suppressed, 209, 210–211, 213; trade of, 202, 203, 204.

Bucareli y Ursua, Fray Don Antonio María, viceroy: letters and reports to, 199–209; orders Texas missions abandoned, 193–194.

Buckskins: traded by Indians, 71.

Buffaloes: habitat of, 161, 208, 306; trade in wool and hides of, 273–274.

Bustillo y Ceballos [Zevallos], Don Juan Antonio, governor of Texas: aids French against Indians, 94.

Cabello, Don Domingo, governor of Texas: his statements on French and Indians, 212, 407, 408.

Cabo dèl Norte [Punta de Venados]: at beginning of Louisiana - Texas boundary, 214, 215, 218, 244, 360, 373, 375, 383, 391, 422, 456, 463; location, 218, 373; named by Spaniards, 328.

Cadi [*Caddi*], Indian official: mentioned, 57.

Cadillac, Antoine de la Mothe [La Motte, Mota], governor of Louisiana: sends St. Denis to Mexico, 305ff, 310, 311, 318; settlements made by in Louisiana, 314.

Cádiz: mentioned, 257, 373; supplies from for Vera Cruz, 116.

Cadodachos [Caudadachos, Caudachos, Caddoques, Cadojodachos, Cadoda-quis, Cadós, Cadoos, Coadachos], nation and province of: allies of Asinai, 138, 307; Anglo-Americans expelled from, 432; French among, 16, 44, 125, 126, 127, 322, 325, 338, 343, 371, 398, 411, 420, 432, 439–440, 443, 444, 472; Indians near, 245, 246, 399; location and description, 52, 125, 126, 246, 335, 337, 343, 420, 432, 451; Spanish interest in, 23, 138, 335, 337; United States claims to, 447, 450, 457, 473.

Cadodachos [Caudadachos, Caudachos, Caodachos, Caddodachos], post and settlement of: communications of with Natchitoches, 23, 44; conflicting claims to, 23, 476; founded and maintained by France, 135, 146, 370, 429, 450, 474; location, 176; reinforcements for, 8, 10, 15, 16, 33, 35, 105, 153, 173; trade of with Spaniards, 243; troops from attack Texas, 323.

Cadodachos, Río de los [Río de Caudacho]: course of, 186, 236, 265, 345, 398; French post on, 325, 345, 414, 456; French travel by way of, 179; Indians on, 152–153; presidio on, 185, 186.

Calahorra y Sáenz, Fray José: certification of, 61–62, 64, 67, 72–73, 74, 90, 156–157, 333; letter of, 330; threatened by Indians, 9–10, 14–15, 105; visits Tehuacanas, 330–333; warns of Indian plot, 60.

Calcasieu River [Río Carcasiu, Carcasiut, Carcaciut, Calcasiu, Calcasus, Caricut, Quelqueshoe]: at boundary line, 415, 419, 431, 439; course of, 246, 437; identity and location, 228, 246–247; Indians on, 246–247; in Spanish territory, 422; settlements to west of, 419, 423, 434.

California: location, 427–428; map of, 428; mountains above, 381; Spaniards settle in, 475.

California, Gulf of [Red Sea]: Colorado River enters, 347.

Campbell, General John: captured by Spaniards at Pensacola, 292.

Canada: ceded to England, 289, note, 452; communication from to Gulf of Mexico, 259; French from in Louisiana, 147, 273; French settlements in, 286, 362; Iberville in, 271; La Salle's explorations from, 259, note, 269, 303, 304, 338; Louisiana

Margil de Jesús, Fray Antonio: his
missionary labors in Texas, 131, 133ff,
142, 144, 320, 324, 418, 421; letters
of, 131–133, 134–136; life of by
Espinosa, cited, 136, 418, 430–431;
retreats before French invasion, 323,
324.
Marín: Iberville's ship, 269, note.
Marín y Porras, Don Primo Feliciano,
bishop of Nuevo León: visits Texas,
418, 430.
Marine Archives, France: documents
in, 337.
Marquette, Father: explorations of, 261.
Martínez, Esteban José: expedition of
the northwest coast, 403, note.
Martínez Pacheco, Don Rafael: arrest
and trial of, 242–243; his quarrel
with Martos Navarrete, 240ff.
Martos y Navarrete, Don Ángel, governor of Texas: aggressions of French
during his administration, xi, 216,
217, 223ff, 240ff, 244, 355, 374, 423;
correspondence of, 232, 330ff, 429;
his dispute with Macarty, 349, 368,
444; his quarrel with Pacheco, 240ff;
illicit trade of, 235, 241, 243ff; proposes boundary line, xii, 231ff, 397ff,
401, 434, 459, 461, 463; removed as
governor of Texas, 242; report and
statements of on boundaries, 216, 415,
416–417; rivers mentioned by, 225–
226.
Masacra [Massacre, Dauphine] Island:
Indians near, 320; named and occupied by French, 260, 271; Spanish
expedition against, 268, 279. See
Dauphine Island.
Massanet, Fray Damián: letters of,
159, 161, 321–322, 410–411; missionary labors of, 159, 160, 164, 262,
304, 335, 337, 339.
Massé, Monsieur: settles in Spanish
territory, 216, 223, 225ff, 230, 231,
232, 235, 243, 244, 348, 349, 355, 368.
Mata, Don Nicolás de la: offers to
build chapel in Bucareli, 207.
Matagorda Bay: identified with San
Bernardo Bay, 190, note; La Salle
on, 259, note.
Matamoras de Isla, Don Juan Pedro,
governor of Pensacola: surrenders
to French, 277.
Maurepas, Lake: on Louisiana boundary, 287ff.
Meat: traded by Spaniards to French,
4, 104.

Mederos, Antonio de, regidor of villa
of San Fernando: report of, 4–5.
Media Villa y Azcona, Melchor de,
governor of Texas: orders to, 141–
142, 143, 151.
Medina, Don Roque: delivers letters,
195, 198.
Medina River: San Antonio River
joins, 177.
Membré, Fray Zenobio: memoirs of
used by La Clercq, 327.
Memorias para la Historia de Texas,
of Morfi: quoted, 143, 144–152, 170,
171, 177–178, 211–213, 226–227, 319–
320, 323–324; cited, 262.
Mendocino, Cape: mentioned, 378.
Mendoza, Don Gaspar Domingo de,
governor of New Mexico: reports on
French traders, 362.
Menéndez de Avilés, Don Pedro: in
Florida, 266, 405, note.
Mermentou River [Río Mermentao,
Bayuco Mermentao]: as boundary,
415, 419, 431, 434, 439; in Spanish
territory, 422; mouth of, 434, 435;
stream to east of, 228.
Mexican Indians: legendary origins of,
427.
Mexican Mountains: as boundary, 341,
375, 377, 378, 379, 383, 391; French
claims to region of, 296, 357, 359,
360; identity, location and description of, 298ff, 361, 375, 377, 384, 392;
rivers rising in, 297.
Mexicano, Río: as boundary, 225;
identity and location, 215, note, 225.
See Sabine River.
Mexico, City of: French traders sent
to, 101, 117, 225, 305ff, 312–313, 362–
363; Gil Ybarbo visits, 198, 213;
junta general held in, 352; Pacheco's
trial in, 242; Rivera arrives in, 145;
works published in, 257, 258.
Mexico, evangelical province of: archives of its custodia, 419.
Mexico, Gulf of: French exploration,
settlement and claims on, 137, 256,
258, 274, 295, 329, 369ff; French-
Spanish boundary on, 120, 416, 472,
474; mountains near, 392; rivers entering, 137, 218, 305, 308, 422, 437,
455; southern boundary of Louisiana,
375, 376, 383, 395, 472; Spanish
possessions on coast of, 190–191, 268,
295, 373, 418.
Mexico [New Spain], kingdom and
viceroyalty of: founding of, 382;

French desire to communicate with, 369; location, 374; mountains in, 392–393; survivors of Narváez expedition reach, 420, 431. See *New Spain*.

Michilimakinac, Island of [San Miguel Michilimakinac]: Luis del Fierro at, 423, 425.

Michoacán: mountains of, 393.

Military coats: given by French to Indian captains, 108.

Military Gentleman: boundary claims of, 294, 340–341; errors of, 325, 327ff, 352ff, 379, 388ff; treatise of on boundaries, quoted, 154ff, 285–286, 293, 296–297, 302, 329, 340–341, 360, 366–367, 373, 375–376, 382, 383, 384–385, 392, 394; cited, 222, 264, 266, 283, 295, 307, 346, 350, 362.

Mines: reports of, 309, 393, 394, 462.

Ministry of State, Spain: report to, 237.

Miró, Don Estevan, governor of Louisiana: requests extension of western limits, 431, 434.

Mirrors: traded to Indians, 16.

Missions: of Texas, 59, 127ff, 137ff, 140–141, 142, 150, 159–160, 162ff.

Mississippi Messenger [*Mensagero del Misisipi*]: paper published in, on Louisiana boundaries, xi–xii, 253ff, 265, 302, 350, 366, 394.

Mississippi River [Río de la Palisada, Mercharripi, Meschasipi, Misisipi, Colbert, Chucagua, Empalisada, Malbouchia, San Luis, Río Grande]: as boundary, 4, 6, 22, 24, 25, 28, 34, 39, 40, 84, 85, 87, 104, 228ff, 286ff, 293, 295, 366, 375, 383, 397, 398, 416, 452; course of, 227, 380, 381, 382, 391, 419; discovery of, 249, 254, 255, 256, 394; English on, 272, 273, 292, 314; French claims and explorations to west of, x, 214, 296ff, 329, 331, 357, 360, 382, 437, 444; French possession, exploration and settlement of, ix–x, 4, 21, 23, 29, 104, 119, 120, 135, 137, 214, 220, 228, 256, 259, note, 260, 264–265, 268, 269, 271ff, 297, 298, 302, 306, 311, 317, 327, 337, 339, 370, 371, 380, 382, 409ff, 422, 425–426, 431, 456; Indians on, 123, 221, 230, 232, 248, 311, 320, 381, 398; Indians to west of, 215, note, 219, 232; islands in, 423, 424–425; map of its mouth, 374; names given to, 120,

263–264, 271, 306, 328; navigation of, 264, 288, 314, 437, 438; streams entering, 126, 226, 229, 232, 296, 297, 302, 331, 356–357, 358, 439, 450, 456, 458, 473; United States possessions on, 437, 438, 454.

Missouri [Misouri] nation: location, 439.

Missouri River [Río Misuri, Nasatha, Río de San Felipe]: as boundary, xii, 383, 398, 399–400, 416, 419, 431, 434, 435, 439, 461; French exploration, occupation and claims on, 120, 137, 260, 265, 296–297, 302, 345, 357, 380, 382, 399, 415, 417, 419, 425–426, 431, 436, 439ff, 448, 451; frontier defenses of Louisiana on, 426; Indians in vicinity of, 358, 384; Indians on, 334, 341, 399, 400, 439, 453; location of its source, 297, 301ff, 345, 461, 462; Spanish exploration and claims on, 193, 302, 357, 358, 382, 419, 427, 460, 473, 474; streams entering, 297, 302; United States explorations and claims on, 416, 424, 437, 438, 451, 452, 453, 454, 463, 473.

Mitchell [Michel], John: map of, 236, 283, 284, 302, 459.

Mobile [La Movila], settlement of: attacked by Spaniards, 267, 268, 279, 292, 293, 371, note; ceded by France to England, 288, 345; communication from to Pensacola, 282; French from attack Pensacola, 276, 323; French forces sent from, 147, 179; location, 137, 267, 283, 309, 407; not ceded to Spain, 290; St. Denis expedition sent from, 127–128, 305, 306, 308, 309, 317, 318; settled and fortified by France, 137, 275, 370, 408, 418, 430, 431; Spanish explorers at site of, 406, 407. See *Louis, Fort (Louisiana)*.

Mobile River [Río Mobila, Maubila, Movila]: French settlement on, 255, 256, 261, 267, 271, 273; named by Spaniards, 327.

Monarquia Indiana, of Torquemada: quoted, 372–373.

Monclova, Santiago de la, villa of: capital of Coahuila, 125; on frontier defense line, 188, note.

Monte Grande, El, forest of: location and description, 376–377.

Montenegro, *Illustrísimo*: writings, cited, 141.

504   PICHARDO: LIMITS OF LOUISIANA AND TEXAS

Paducas [Padoucas] nation: location,
346, 399, 440, 443.
Palacios, Don Lucas Fernando, governor of Florida: killed by Indians,
287.
Palmas, Río de las: explorations from,
405.
Panamá: defenses of, 150; mountains
of, 393.
Pananas nation: attacks Spaniards, 181,
358, 359; French among, 182, 358.
Paniasas nation: location, 346.
Panipiques nation: French alliance
with, 362. See *Jumanos*.
Panis nation: enemies of, 399; French
among, 44, 126, 440, 443; location,
44, note, 440; Spaniards plan presidio among, 63, 73, 157.
Pánuco, province of: Garay explores
coast to, 295; mountains in, 393.
Pánuco, Río: boundary of Spanish
Florida, 266.
Pardo, Juan: explorations of, 405–406.
Parma, Duchy of: ceded by Spain to
France, 257; desired by Spain, 276,
note.
Parral, El: defense of, 351, 352; French
goods sent to, 243.
Parras: troops from for Aguayo expedition, 137.
Parrilla, Don Diego Ortiz: expedition
of, 146, 332, 410, 411, 420–421, 429,
432; reconnoiters Texas coast region, 190–191.
Pascagoulas, Río de los: Iberville on,
271.
Pascagoulas nation: French fort near,
272; Indians near, 248; location and
description, 247, 306.
Paso de Tomás: Bucareli pueblo established at, 200; French traders at,
197, 224.
Paul V, Pope: orders *Roman Ritual*
published, 45.
Paula Caro, Fray Francisco de: certification of, 333.
Peace of Versailles, 1762: terms of,
286.
Pearl fishing: on Gulf of Mexico, 273–
274.
Pelones nation: location and description, 58, 71, 109.
Peltries: from Atacapas, 220.
Peña, Bachiller Juan Antonio de la:
his diary of Aguayo expedition, 47,
124, 184, 324.
Peñalosa Briceño y Berdugo, Don

Diego Dionisio, governor of New
Mexico: career of, 261, 369.
Penicaut: companion of St. Denis, 312.
Pennsylvania: Louisiana borders upon,
346.
Pensacola [Panzacola, Punta de Sigüenza, Santa María de Galve, Island of Santa Rosa], presidio of:
Boluxas Indians emigrants from, 245;
captured by French, 133, 134, 137,
275ff, 323, 371; captured by Spaniards, 292; French propose to garrison, 275–276; fortification of, 268,
281–282, 320; founded by Spain, 267,
268, 269ff, 274, 295, 407; Iberville
expedition at, 270, 273; recaptured
by Spaniards, 280; reports of governor, 117, 317, 320; restored to
Spain, 280–283, 296; river near, 384;
visited by Charlevoix, 283.
Perdido, Río: on boundary, 267, 283,
284, 290, 293, 375, 383, 384; Frenchman settled on, 284–285.
Peredo, Father Dr. Don José: papers
prepared by, 262–263.
Peregrino Septentrionale Atlante. . . ,
of Espinosa: cited, 422.
Perrin du Lac, François: map of, 381;
work of, quoted, 219–220, 387, 425;
cited, 461.
Peru: mountains of, 393; orders to
viceroy of, 364, 365.
Pez, Don Andrés de: recommends fortification of Pensacola, 268.
Philip [Felipe] V, king of Spain:
French policy toward, 276, note; his
policy toward France, 367, 369, 370,
371; succeeds Charles II, 372, note.
Piacenza, Duchy of: desired by Spain,
276, note.
Pichardo, Father José Antonio: commission of, 444, 456–457; his conclusions on Texas-Louisiana boundary, ix, x, xi, xii–xiii, 457; dispatches to, 443, 445, 448; map of,
166, 168, 218, note, 219, 228, 434–
435, 441, 461, 462; papers, reports
and documents of, 262–263, 436–443,
444, 445, 447; plan of his work, xiii,
442.
Piernas, Don José: given permission to
settle on Calcasieu River, 419.
Pierre, Monsieur: settled west of Red
River, 46, 82, 121.
Pike, Zebulon: explorations of, 424.
Pinckney, Thomas: negotiates treaty,
294, note.

510 PICHARDO: LIMITS OF LOUISIANA AND TEXAS

on, 181, 276; French traders in, 424;
location of, 384, 385, 386, 387, 391,
428, 461, 462; mines reported near,
393, 394; mountains in vicinity of,
299, 300, 386, 392, 399; Pike expedition taken to, 424; Rubí's recommendation on, 191; source of Arkansas River to north of, 298, 451,
465, 474.
Santa María de Galve, bay of: reconnaissance of, 268; Spanish fort on,
269. See *Pensacola.*
Santa María de Galve [Panzacola],
presidio of: French settle near, 137.
See *Pensacola.*
Santa María de las Charcas, mining
camp of: on route to Texas, 128.
Santa María y Mendoza, Fray Pedro
de: at Nacogdoches mission, 130,
164.
Santander, port of: location, 190.
Santa Rosa, island of [Punta de Si-
güenza]: fortification on, 282; French
trade with, 4; presidial captain of
reports on French, 23, 35, 84, 91,
104, 111, 284. See *Pensacola.*
Santa Rosa, presidio of: on frontier
defense line, 188, note.
Santa Rosa, valley of: Los Adaes settlers at, 195, 198.
Santiago, Cristóbal de: declaration of,
52.
Santo Domingo: audiencia of, 115, 363,
364, 365; Ayllón *oidor* of, 404; exploration of Florida from, 404; French
in, 370, 371; Iberville's fleet at, 269,
note.
Santo Tomé, ravines of: site of Pensacola presidio, 269.
San Vicente, presidio of: on Río
Grande, 213.
San Xavier, missions and presidio of:
captain of ransoms Apache captives,
101, 115; founding and location of,
1; French traders approach, 197, 224;
garrison of, 2, 3, 21; reports from
captain of, 65; road to, 190, 197,
224.
San Xavier, Río de: missions on, 3.
Sauvole, Monsieur: with Iberville in
Louisiana, 271, 272; death of, 274.
Secretaría de Cámara, of New Spain:
documents in, 471.
Secretaría de Gracia y Justicia, Spain:
documents in, 469, 471.
Secretariat of State, Spain: documents
sent to, 469, 470, 471.

Segnelay, Marquis of: river named for,
264.
Seno Mexicano: French lands to north
of, 245; Louisiana-Texas boundary in
region of 232, 398, 399; settlement
of, 269; Spanish advance along, 230,
231. See *Gulf Coast.*
Serigny, Monsieur: captures Pensacola, 280.
Seven Years' War: treaty ending, 289,
note.
Sevillano de Paredes, Fray Miguel: his
requests regarding Texas missions
and presidios, 144–145, 151.
Sheep: at Bucareli, 208.
Shepherd, Mrs. Minnie Lee: translations by, 377, 378, 382, 386, 414, 415.
Shining Mountains: see *Rocky Mountains.*
Shot: for Bucareli settlers, 201; traded
to Indians, 9, 11, 15, 16, 54, 55, 58,
64, 70, 71, 74, 105, 108.
Sibley, Dr. John: *Historical Sketches*
of, quoted, 245ff, 394, 433; cited,
126, 321, 456.
Sierra, Don Pedro [Felipe?]: deposition of, 12, 49, 50.
Sierra Blanca: French visit, 298, 301;
identity, location and description, 299,
300, 381, 386; Indians in, 299, 300;
known to Spaniards, 393; woodlands
near, 377.
Sierra de la Plata: mines reported in,
462.
Sierra de las Grullas: Arkansas River
rises in, 298, 300, 345, 385–386, 461;
identity, 361, 377, 385, 386; mountains near, 299.
Sierra de los Faraones [Capirote]: Indians in, 299; location, 299, 347;
mentioned, 428.
Sierra de los Pecos: location, 298–299.
Sierra de los Taos: location, 298, 345;
mountains near, 300; rivers rising in,
303, 345.
Sierra del Almagre: location, 300.
Sierra del Capirote: see *Sierra de los
Faraones.*
Sierra Madre: Pike's exploration in,
424.
Sierra [Cordillera] Nevada: described,
381; known to Spaniards, 393.
Sigüenza y Góngora, Don Carlos de:
work of, 264, 339–340.
Silver: brought into France through
trade, 260; in New Mexico, 320; in
South American mountains, 393; re-

Trinity River [Río de la Santísima Trinidad]: discovered and named by Spaniards, 161, 328, 402, note; French traders on, 223, 364; Indians on, 92, 111, 155, 175, 230, 232, 331, 334, 349, 398; location and course of, 170, 177, 308; Spanish settlement on, 198, 199, 201, 203, 209, 213.

Trofeo de la Justicia Española, of Sigüenza: quoted, 264, 339–340.

Tronontes nation: location, 346.

Tunica [Tonica] nation: French mission among, 306; location, 123, 247; St. Denis among, 311.

Turkeys: found in Texas, 306.

Tusas nation: friendly to the Texas, 109; location, 58, 71.

Tuscany, Duchy of: desired by Spain, 276, note.

Ugarte, Captain Don Joaquín: maps of, 402, 403.

Ulloa, Don Antonio de: frontier defenses erected by, 193, 426; made governor of Louisiana, xi, 216–217, 236, 237, 348, 423; *Noticias Americanas* of, 381; orders reconnaissance of Texas coast, 190; settlement established by, 237–238.

United States: acquires Louisiana, 257, 447, 467, 476; claims of on northwest coast, 450, 451; letter to ministers accredited to, 438; Louisiana boundary claims and negotiations of, 183, 184, 217, 244, 257, 294, 328, 329, 355, 356, 418, 420, 430, 432, 440, 441, 442, 446, 449, 450, 454, 457, 460, 467, 472–473, 474, 475; measures against aggressions of, 183; treaty of with Spain, 415–416.

Unzaga y Amézaga, Don Luis de, governor of Louisiana: names Clouet lieutenant-governor, 240; places posts at Atacapas and Opelusas, 238.

Upper Louisiana: extent of, 425, 431.

Uribarri [Ulibarri], Don Juan de: explorations of, 300, 357, 358, 386.

Urrutia, Captain: Texas Indians request return of, 308.

Ute [Yutas] nation: Anza makes peace with, 358, note; location, 299.

Valcárcel, Don Domingo, *auditor de guerras:* reports and recommendations of, 32, 46, 102, 120–121, 124, 153–155, 158, 175, 176, 178–179.

Valdés, Don Manuel Antonio: poem of, 291.

Valdivia, presidio of: captured French traders to be sent to, 364.

Valero, Marquis of (Baltazar de Zúñiga Guzmán Sotomayor y Mendoza), viceroy: cedulas addressed to, 185, 186, 280–283; letters and reports to, 131–133, 134–136, 321, 324; orders of, 276, 279, 358, 471.

Vallejo [Ballejo], Fray Francisco, president of Texas missions: activities of in Texas, 7, note, 14, 20, 43, 49, 59, 60–61, 107, 121.

Valverde y Cosío, Don Antonio, governor of New Mexico: on Arkansas River, 358; sends expedition to Pananas, 358; statements of on Indians, 299, 300.

Vancouver Island: Russian settlements near, 403, note.

Vanhorn: Dutch buccaneer, 270, note.

Vaudreuil [Baudrevil], Marquis of, governor of Louisiana: letters of, 73; made governor of Canada, 65, 74; protests founding of Spanish presidios, 63, 157; questions powers of viceroy of New Spain, 64.

Vaugondy, Robert de: see *Robert de Vaugondy.*

Vedoya y Osorio, Pedro, *fiscal:* report of, 27, 38, 103.

Vega, Fray Manuel: his *Colección,* cited, 471.

Vegas, Don Antonio: work of, quoted, 287.

Vegetables: grown at Bucareli, 208.

Velasco, Dr., *asesor:* report of on Texas, 312, 321, 322, 471.

Vélez Escalante, Fray Silvestre: expedition of, 427.

Venegas, Don Francisco Xavier, viceroy: *consulta* addressed to, 436–443, 444–447; dispatch of, 443, 448.

Vera Cruz: base for operations against French, 278, 279; expeditions from, 268, 270, 340; garrison and defenses of, 34, 37–38, 81, 94, 95, 110, 113, 150, 174; French ships reported sent against, 134; French traders sent to for deportation, 117; piratical attacks on, 270; Spanish settlement of, 382.

Vergara, Fray Gabriel de: his missionary activities in Texas, 139, 142, 167.